Unacceptable Harm

A History of How the
Treaty to Ban Cluster Munitions Was Won

John Borrie

UNIDIR
United Nations Institute for Disarmament Research
Geneva, Switzerland

UNITED NATIONS

New York and Geneva, 2009

About the cover

F.1 France, from ANTIPERSONNEL © 2004 Raphaël Dallaporta. Image courtesy of Raphaël Dallaporta.

F.1 "Ogre" submunition, France. l: 40mm h: 90mm W: 244g

An "Ogre" F.1 155mm shell contains 63 dual-purpose improved conventional submunitions with self-destruct, each weighing 244g. Each shell leaves a footprint of 10,000–18,000m^2, depending on range. The F.1 used to be manufactured by Versailles-based Giat Industries (now Nexter). In connection with the signing of the 2008 Convention on Cluster Munitions, France withdrew the F.1 from operational service and said it would destroy its stockpile of the weapon.

NOTE

The designations employed and the presentation of the material in this publication do not imply the expression of any opinion whatsoever on the part of the Secretariat of the United Nations concerning the legal status of any country, territory, city or area, or of its authorities, or concerning the delimitation of its frontiers or boundaries.

* * *

The views expressed in this publication are the sole responsibility of the author. They do not necessarily reflect the views or opinions of the United Nations, UNIDIR, its staff members or sponsors.

UNIDIR/2009/8

UNITED NATIONS PUBLICATIONS

Sales No. GV.E.09.0.8

ISBN 978-92-9045-196-9

The United Nations Institute for Disarmament Research (UNIDIR)—an autonomous institute within the United Nations—conducts research on disarmament and security. UNIDIR is based in Geneva, Switzerland, the centre for bilateral and multilateral disarmament and non-proliferation negotiations, and home of the Conference on Disarmament. The Institute explores current issues pertaining to the variety of existing and future armaments, as well as global diplomacy and local tensions and conflicts. Working with researchers, diplomats, government officials, NGOs and other institutions since 1980, UNIDIR acts as a bridge between the research community and governments. UNIDIR's activities are funded by contributions from governments and donor foundations. The Institute's web site can be found at:

www.unidir.org

CONTENTS

ACKNOWLEDGEMENTS

The 2008 Convention on Cluster Munitions was hard won and most people involved in its creation and implementation rightfully cherish the achievement of this important new international legal treaty. Not only are most of those people involved in achieving (or even opposing) the creation of a treaty banning cluster munitions still alive, many are curious—vigilant, even—about how their actions and motivations may be interpreted and reflected, even if the passage of time means they recall these less clearly. Writing a history like this one has felt like a big responsibility.

As I see it, the historian's responsibility under these circumstances is to listen to and try to learn from as many points-of-view as possible. In this case, because of my own access as a relative insider to a decade of Convention on Certain Conventional Weapons talks and throughout the Oslo process, I have also had to do my best to put aside my own preconceived notions built up over the years. Sometimes, working on pulling together the threads of a history of events so complex and recent has felt faintly shamanic. At other times, I've felt more like an archaeologist trying to unearth and gently dust off nuggets of insight to be polished and arranged. This book is absolutely not a memoir, but researching and writing it I occasionally even felt a bit like the Hollywood movie character Forrest Gump, the simple and often-unwitting participant–observer to events we can see were significant in a wide-screen perspective, which I did not without further reflection.

This book is an attempt to construct a narrative of what happened to bring about the cluster munition ban treaty, one that I hope is decipherable for a more general audience than multilateral practitioners or academics. It is not a legal commentary, although some of its contents may contribute to informing such commentary, which is in the works. And while I do believe it vindicates some of the ideas various colleagues and I put forward in a previous project on Disarmament as Humanitarian Action: Making Multilateral Negotiations Work, it is not specifically a work of international relations theory either.

Nor is this book an official history, signed-off on by any government or United Nations functionary. Funding for it came from the Government of Norway, but my experience during the course of research and writing this history has confirmed the impression I formed during previous encounters with Norway as a financial contributor to UNIDIR work—that their representatives are resolute in a fair-minded belief that the best research findings are those independently arrived at. This was also an important ingredient in the Oslo process as a whole as the resources Norway and other governments were willing to provide for independent research on cluster munitions were important to the collective reframing of the cluster munition discourse at the international level, as the reader will see in the course of this history.

My hope is that *Unacceptable Harm* will constitute one platform for further research into a fascinating international process that, I am convinced, has lessons for people of all kinds who are concerned about how to achieve collective security objectives in the twenty-first century. The Oslo process also showed that positive change *is* possible, despite the world's many problems. And, by telling the story of how the cluster munition ban was won in a coherent if inevitably selective way, it should form a structure for others to examine aspects of this story in more detail.

Preparing the book you hold in your hand involved a lot of triangulation between different perspectives. Beside the field and documentary research involved in the project, more than 90 recorded research interviews were carried out with people such as victims of cluster munitions and members of their families, others living with the hazards of unexploded submunitions in their villages, orchards and farms, battle area clearance and explosive ordnance personnel, humanitarian workers, civil society advocates for a cluster munition treaty, academic and policy researchers, journalists, diplomats, military personnel, politicians, UN and Red Cross personnel, as well as many other individuals more difficult to categorize. All of these people have particular views, and perhaps some will be disappointed about the way or the extent to which their perspective is taken up (or not) in the pages that follow. Don't take it lying down! The more people who write about how and why cluster munitions touched upon their lives, the better the picture we will have to inspire others to act on further humanitarian or other imperatives for the global good.

Because this book was completed on a feverish schedule, it is possible (in fact, almost certain) that it contains factual errors or assertions that certain people involved in international efforts dealing with the humanitarian impacts of cluster munitions might take issue with. The responsibility—

and the blame, if it is to be apportioned—is entirely mine. All I can say in my defence is that these were my considered judgements about what happened. It is based on the evidence I had available to me, including, in some cases, my own perspective as an eyewitness. The nature of scholarship being what it is, I trust those finding any errors will mercilessly expose or confront me with my mistakes in the fullness of time.

Nevertheless, I want to take this opportunity to acknowledge the generous advice, insights and time given by so many people, not all of whom can be mentioned here for personal or professional reasons. They include Annette Abelsen, Werner Anderson, Ahmad Arafa, Torfinn Rislaa Arntsen, David Atwood, Simon Bagshaw, Stan "the man" Brabant, Annette Bjørseth, Vera Bohle, Silvie Brigot, Kerry Brinkert, Lt. Col. Jim Burke, Ambassador Dáithí O'Ceallaigh, Tim Caughley, Laura Cheeseman, Simon Conway, Robin Coupland, Kathleen Cravero, Natalie Curtis, Charlotte Darlow, Katarzyna "Kasia" Derlicka, Bonnie Docherty, Ambassador John Duncan, "evil scientist" Ove Dullum, Paul Eavis, Ambassador Susan Eckey, Espen Barth Eide, Mette Sofie Eliseussen, John Flanagan, Tamar Gabelnick, Father Antoine Abi Ghanem, Steve Goose, Paul Hannon, Ambassador Bente Angell-Hanson, Katherine "Katie" Harrison, Susan Hensel, Peter Herby, Mark Hiznay, Tim Horner, Emil Jeremić, Colin King, Peter Kolarov, Ambassador Steffen Kongstad, Gustavo Laurie, ("The") Col. Stein Erik Lauglo, John MacBride, Anna Macdonald, Ambassador Don MacKay, Lou Maresca, Thomas Markram, Richard Moyes, Robert Mtonga, Thomas Nash, Per Nergaard, Bantan Nugroho, Gro Nystuen, Serena Olgiati, Davide Orifici, Grethe Østern, Titus Peachey, Chris Penny, Ambassador Wolfgang Petritsch, Guy Pollard, Eric Prokosch, Brian Rappert, Markus Reiterer, Samantha Rennie, Hans Risser, John Rodsted, Professor Paul Rogers, Jean-Christophe Le Roux, Christian Ruge, Professor Ken Rutherford, Melissa Sabatier, Ambassador Christine Schraner Burgener, Sara Sekkenes, James C. O'Shea, Hilde Janne Skorpen, Declan Smyth, Portia Stratton, Jonas Gahr Støre, Jon Erik Strømø, Erik Tollefsen, Earl Turcotte, Ingunn Vatne, Paul Vermeulen, Susan B. Walker, Mary Wareham, Julian P.G. Wathen, Virgil Wiebe, Professor Jody Williams, Albrecht von Wittke and Reto Wollenmann.

In October 2008 I travelled, along with another researcher, to Southern Lebanon to learn more about the realities in the field for those living with cluster munitions, and to talk with battle area clearance personnel. I am very grateful to the staff of the (then) UN Mine Action Coordination Centre—Southern Lebanon based in Tyre, in particular to Chris Clark,

Tekimiti Gilbert, Allen Kelly, Kerei Ruru, Mary Sack, Rana Elias, Hassan Al Ali, Sleiman Mehri, Ali Fakhouri and Mohamad Baydoun. Our thanks also to Knut Furunes of Norwegian People's Aid, Johan "H" Den Haan and his colleagues at BacTec International Ltd, David Horrocks and Christina L. Bennike of Mines Advisory Group, Mark Holroyd of Handicap International, and Lene Rasmussen of Danish Church Aid, as well as everyone else who took care of us and answered our many, many questions.

Along with examining how states interacted in international efforts to ban cluster munitions, this history looks critically at some of the challenges the Cluster Munition Coalition faced as a campaign, and I hope this is taken in the constructive spirit it is intended. I would also like to thank, in particular, all of the Handicap International Ban Advocates for their leadership and inspirational example in the campaign to outlaw cluster munitions. I first encountered Serbian cluster munition survivor Sladan Vučković at the Belgrade Conference in 2007. Later, he and his father Hrista allowed me to interview them about their experiences. I am indebted both to them and their interpreter Svetlana Bogdanovic for such generosity and patience. I am also very grateful to the many grassroots campaigners of the Cluster Munition Coalition who engaged with me individually and allowed me to be a fly on the wall in their campaigning discussions before and during the Oslo process, from which I learned a huge amount—not least a massive respect for their dedication to ending the use of cluster munitions, and the long hours and huge effort they put in to achieving that objective.

At UNIDIR, Christiane Agboton-Johnson, Anita Blétry, Nicolas Gérard, Theresa Hitchens, Patricia Lewis, Jason Powers, Isabelle Roger and Kerstin Vignard were unfailingly helpful throughout the preparation of this book. And developing this history would have been a much more daunting prospect without the tremendous support and input of Maya Brehm, the project's assistant researcher and international law specialist. Most of all, in this case particular credit is due to the support and encouragement of my partner, Shelley Bulling. Even at the darkest times when a ban treaty—and later, a finished manuscript—seemed too far down the tunnel, her support was invaluable, and is deeply appreciated.

John Borrie, 29 May 2009

ABOUT THE AUTHOR

John Borrie led UNIDIR's project entitled The Road from Oslo: Analysis of Negotiations to Address the Humanitarian Effects of Cluster Munitions as well as a related project, Disarmament as Humanitarian Action: Making Multilateral Negotiations Work (DHA). In late 2006, as part of this work, John co-founded the Disarmament Insight initiative to engage multilateral disarmament practitioners with new perspectives in order to help them make their work more effective (see <www.disarmamentinsight.blogspot.com>).

John's research and working experiences have covered many aspects of arms control and disarmament including the Oslo process, the Convention on Conventional Weapons and the Mine Ban Treaty. As well as editing and contributing to the four published volumes of the DHA project's work, John wrote *A Global Survey of Explosive Remnants of War* for Landmine Action UK in 2003, which fed into international negotiations on a protocol on explosive remnants of war, as well as many other articles and papers published on disarmament-related topics.

Prior to joining UNIDIR, John worked with the Mines-Arms Unit of the International Committee of the Red Cross and was Deputy Head of Mission for Disarmament in Geneva with the New Zealand Government between 1999 and 2002.

For many of those involved in the anti-war protests of the 1960s, the revelation of the existence and use of cluster bombs represented another step in a crescendo of atrocities being perpetrated in Viet Nam. On top of the deforestation, the burning of villages, the napalm, the torture, here was a new weapon designed for the mass destruction of people.

The horror of the revelation is well captured in a description by the US pacifist David Dellinger of what he saw on a visit in late 1966 to the "enemy" territory of North Viet Nam, under sustained bombardment since early 1965:

> Even apart from the widespread destruction of villages, cities and towns, I see no way to explain away the universal use of fragmentation bombs. Fragmentation bombs are useless against bridges and buildings of any kind but are deadly against people. In fact another name of them is antipersonnel bombs. I saw these bombs everywhere I went in North Vietnam.
>
> There are different types of fragmentation bombs, but they all start with a "mother" bomb. ... The mother bomb explodes in the air over the target area, releasing 300 smaller bombs, typically the size of either a grapefruit or a pineapple. Each of the smaller bombs then ejects a spray of 150 tiny pellets of steel, which are so small that they bounce uselessly off concrete or steel, though they are very effective when they hit a human eye or heart. ... From personal observation, I learned that the fragmentation bombs are equipped with timing devices so that they do not all eject their murderous barrage right away. When relief workers are trying to rescue the wounded, or later when the planes have departed and the all-clear has been sounded, hundreds of fragmentation bombs may explode, wounding or killing the innocent.[1]

The "success" of the new cluster bombs induced the US armed forces, heavily engaged in the war, to embark on a frenetic effort for the mass production of cluster bombs, the creation of new versions, and the development of other types of cluster munitions: cluster mines, cluster shells, cluster warheads for guided missiles. In one of many examples, a special army munitions programme was told in spring 1968 to develop, test, produce and deliver "an emergency 'crash' quantity" of cluster shells for the giant 16-inch guns of the battleship New Jersey. The shells were ready in a bare six months, at the beginning of September, enabling the New Jersey to supplement the massive aerial bombardment of North Viet Nam from offshore.[2]

The protests against cluster munitions during the Viet Nam war never reached the scale of the protests against napalm. Anyone can intuitively understand what it is to be burned by napalm; the complexities of cluster munitions design are harder to grasp. But the protests were significant, and they persisted to the end of the war and beyond.

Critics of the war accused the United States of war crimes, and the use of cluster bombs was cited in that context.[3] But the connection to the laws of war took on a new dimension in 1974 with the proposal by Sweden and six other countries to ban the use of anti-personnel fragmentation cluster munitions.[4] There was little support from other states, and the antiwar protest movement had died down with the impending end of the Viet Nam war. The proposal failed, and the issue lay dormant for the next decades. In the meantime, the technologies spread to other countries.

The adoption of the Convention on Cluster Munitions in 2008 was like a wild dream come true. How this came about is the subject of John Borrie's valuable and fascinating book. In this book we see the factors that made the Convention possible—factors that were not present at the time of the Swedish proposal more than 30 years before. Prominent among them was the growing appreciation of the "unacceptable harm" caused by unexploded submunitions left on the ground after an attack. The book also shows the importance of action by civil society in the face of the horrors of war.

Had the Swedish proposal been adopted back then, how many lives would have been saved! We cannot rewrite history. Now we have an excellent Convention, far more comprehensive than the 1974 proposal, and supported by many states. The tasks ahead are to secure the universal ratification of the Convention, to ensure that its terms are respected, to prevent further cluster munition attacks anywhere in the world, to clear the vast amounts of explosive debris, to destroy the stockpiles, to aid the victims and ensure respect for their human rights—and to confront the many other issues in relation to armed conflict where there may be some chance of reducing the dreadful harm caused, both to civilians and to soldiers.

John Borrie's book will help to show the way.

Eric Prokosch

PREFACE

This book is entitled *Unacceptable Harm* for two reasons. First, on 23 February 2007, 46 states made a historic declaration at a conference in the snow-covered hills above Oslo in Norway to complete an international treaty by the end of 2008 to "prohibit the use, production, transfer and stockpiling of cluster munitions that cause unacceptable harm to civilians" and to "establish a framework for cooperation and assistance that ensures adequate provision of care and rehabilitation to survivors and their communities, clearance of contaminated areas, risk education and destruction of stockpiles of prohibited cluster munitions".[1] As we shall see, no agreed international understanding existed at that time on how to define a cluster munition, especially what such a definition should include. The quest to determine the characteristics of cluster munitions "that cause unacceptable harm to civilians"—and, hence, which would be banned—proved to be a key challenge for those representatives of states, international organizations and civil society involved in what would immediately become referred to as the "Oslo process". Defining cluster munitions would be crucial to the eventual achievement of the Convention on Cluster Munitions (CCM) agreed by 107 states on 30 May 2008 in Dublin, Ireland.

The second reason why this book is called *Unacceptable Harm* is because the most controversial issue emerging in the negotiation of the CCM, apart from defining cluster munitions, was that of so-called military "interoperability". At root, the interoperability issue concerned how some of the prospective cluster munition ban treaty's members would square their new legal obligations with their military alliance commitments with the United States, in particular. In public, and in concerns it transmitted to NATO member states and to policymakers in the capitals of other military partners such as Australia, Canada and Japan, the Bush administration claimed, in effect, that an Oslo treaty would cause unacceptable harm to the ability of US military forces to operate with those of their allies. In view of the considerable political and public momentum toward a cluster munition treaty among many of these countries, however, this would not prove to be a showstopper. The real challenge would boil down to developing an arrangement in a cluster munition ban treaty that—if certainly not very welcome in Washington DC—would at least be workable at the legal and operational levels for military joint operations and bases. The evolution of the interoperability issue, the controversy surrounding it, and how interoperability claimed centre stage during the last act of the Oslo process is an important part of the CCM story.

The Oslo process and the CCM, however, are about far more than how cluster munitions were defined or the interoperability issue, even if these were consistently the most controversial elements of the Dublin negotiation. The CCM is a humanitarian treaty, and its aim is to reduce civilian suffering from cluster munitions. The treaty package as it was formally adopted is a stunning achievement: as well as setting a new international legal norm prohibiting the use, development, production, acquisition, stockpiling, retention or transfer of cluster munitions it enshrines measures to clear contaminated land and help victims, with provisions on international cooperation and assistance. These core elements of the CCM should not be obscured, nor should be the way in which they were achieved, which in many cases was through close cooperation between government representatives such as diplomats and NGO experts, including clearance personnel as well as survivors of cluster munitions. Indeed, survivors participating in the Oslo process as Handicap International "Ban Advocates" had an especially powerful effect on even the most hardened and cynical delegates in the Oslo process. As Branislav Kapetanović, a Serbian survivor and Ban Advocate, later observed, "The experience of the survivors points out the suffering of the injured, our families, societies and the state affected. Our presence and sometimes our sheer appearance, the sight of a human being whose body parts were taken away by this weapon, has made an impact".[2]

This history necessarily focuses on developments such as defining cluster munitions and interoperability without treating other provisions of the CCM like clearance and victim assistance in the same depth. But it should not be taken to mean that these provisions of the eventual treaty were any less meaningful or substantial:

> In fact, it is the most extensive weapons-prohibition treaty that includes legal obligations for ensuring the rights and dignity of the victims. It takes victim assistance into the 21st century by making sure that the victims of cluster munitions are able to reclaim their lives. … The victim assistance provisions in the CCM articulate with greater clarity what states must do to ensure that cluster munition survivors can enjoy their rights and be productive members of their communities.[3]

A FEW REMARKS ABOUT METHOD

The Oslo process was a remarkable phenomenon and contained its share of conflict, intrigue and excitement. As a relative insider privileged to see how some of the initiative unfolded, my hope is that this history conveys some of that atmosphere while, of course, remaining sober in its analysis. And the Oslo process certainly featured an ensemble cast: if the reader reaches any conclusions after reading *Unacceptable Harm*, one of those should surely be that the contributions of many, many people counted, only a tiny fraction of whom are featured in this book. In no particular order these people included (but were certainly not limited to) politicians, diplomats, cluster munition and landmine survivors and their families, military personnel, grassroots campaigners and the media. Indeed, one of the striking features of processes like the international cluster munition and landmine campaigns is that while they continued to involve traditional elites such as diplomats and military officers and arms control experts found in orthodox international security fora, they incorporated a wider range of perspectives. Such perspective diversity was not just "nice" in the sense of being arguably more representative: it was, as I have argued elsewhere, an important ingredient of success in the Oslo process and had practical benefits, even if it sometimes generated more scrutiny and confrontation than some diplomats were used to.[4]

It is thus fitting that, in addition to the considerable amount of documentary evidence on cluster munitions generated over the last few years, this book is based in large part on approximately 90 research interviews with a wide range of participants in the Oslo process and the Convention on Certain Conventional Weapons (CCW), as well as others in some way relevant to or affected by cluster munitions. A lot of the book is, moreover, based on my own notes or audio recordings of the events described. Ultimately, these amount to hundreds of hours of audio recordings, and provided a massive bank of insights to sift through.

It was impossible to use all of that material. I was inevitably confronted with the task of creating a narrative out of many different perspectives—a narrative that must be compelling and internally consistent enough to hold the attention of the reader, while trying to be satisfactorily truthful. Everyone has a point-of-view, and the perspectives of those I talked to naturally differed and were occasionally contradictory. And, of course, the people I interviewed provide only a subset of the perspectives immediately relevant to the CCM story. Therefore, as a researcher, I had to make choices about what to represent and how to represent it, especially in view of the reality that some of my respondents were less free to talk "on the record" than others, but nevertheless offered important—and sometimes even startling—perspectives. My general policy in the text was to refer to sources as specifically as possible. But, in certain cases, the identities of certain sources have been kept confidential, and certain quotations are not accompanied by references for that reason. This is less than ideal from a scholarly point-of-view, but I feel it is the ethical thing to do under the circumstances. No doubt corroborating (or corrective) pieces of historical evidence will be added to the public record in coming years that are more attributable, particularly from currently restricted diplomatic and other governmental and inter-governmental correspondence.

My task in researching *Unacceptable Harm* was made at times easier and on other occasions trickier by my own acquaintance with many of the people mentioned in this book, and by my own involvement in some of the events described. Academics call this "participatory observation". But I found that, while my experiences were good for establishing and recalling context, I was often shocked in my research to discover how skewed or just plain wrong certain of my own unverified recollections had been. As psychologist Cordelia Fine wrote in *A Mind of Its Own: How Your Brain Distorts and Deceives*:

> Your unscrupulous brain is entirely undeserving of your confidence. It has some shifty habits that leave the truth distorted and disguised. Your brain is vainglorious. It deludes you. It is emotional, pigheaded and secretive. Oh, and it's also a bigot. This is more than minor inconvenience. That fleshy walnut inside your skull is all you have in order to know yourself and to know the world. Yet thanks to the masquerading of an untrustworthy brain with a mind of its own, much of what you think you know is not quite as it seems.[5]

My research respondents were very helpful here in giving their accounts, answering my questions, and at times correcting my misunderstandings. Also, the transcripts of these interviews subsequently enabled me to compare multiple perspectives in aggregate, along with my records of events such as international meetings and documentary evidence where it could be found. What really happened at certain junctures, like on interoperability in the endgame of the Dublin negotiation in a private meeting of the Irish Chair of the conference, Ambassador Dáithí O'Ceallaigh, with the Cluster

Munition Coalition (CMC), Canada and the United Kingdom, I think can be settled with a fair degree of confidence. In other instances they cannot, and I have flagged in the text certain topics I think particularly deserve further investigation.

The upshot is that, while aspiring to portray the reality of what happened "objectively", I am only too conscious that any account of an endeavour as complex and multidimensional as international efforts to address the impacts of cluster munitions on civilians will fall short in some respect. Rather, what this volume is intended to do is to form a basic narrative and analytical platform for future work on developing insights and drawing lessons from international efforts to address the humanitarian impacts of cluster munitions.

Under the auspices of our joint Disarmament Insight initiative, UNIDIR and the Geneva Forum convened a two-day residential seminar in Glion, Switzerland in November 2008 with about 35 invited diplomats, international civil servants, civil society representatives, humanitarian field personnel and researchers. The title of the symposium was "Learn, Adapt, Succeed: Potential lessons from the Ottawa and Oslo processes for other disarmament and arms control challenges".[6] It brought together some of those who had been central in the Oslo process with people working in other issue areas of relevance like the CCW, work on curbing the illicit trade in small arms, the Arms Trade Treaty initiative, the Geneva Declaration on Armed Violence and Development, and efforts to examine issues around the use of explosive weapons in populated areas. The symposium encouraged these people to compare perspectives with a view to which of their experiences (if any) were transferable or adaptable to other contexts, before memories of the cluster munition ban campaign fade or become mythologized, and people have moved on to other things. In addition, the Glion symposium served to enable some of the Oslo process's participants to learn more about what some others in different positions had been thinking during some of its tougher moments. It is my hope that this book will also help—being not just a record of what happened, but as one contribution to reflecting on how we might do better in responding to other pressing humanitarian and disarmament imperatives.

A final methodological note: research for this book underlined some of the challenges in gathering primary documentary evidence at a time in which written correspondence is increasingly electronically based. On the plus side, it is possible to find many resources on the World Wide Web in a few seconds that previously might have taken a lot of archival research to track down. And some respondents helpfully provided me with e-mail threads from times past of interest to my research that required minimal effort on their part but offered me valuable insights into the evolution of their thinking. It points to a considerable downside, however, and it is that many of the most illuminating forms of correspondence such as e-mails, web pages and even mobile phone text messages are ephemeral, and many are already probably lost to historians forever. Even in diplomatic work like the CCW and in the Oslo process some documents are more equal than others: "unofficial" proposals by delegations and background papers may not have full status and for that reason were not systematically preserved, even if historically significant. Whether unofficial or electronic or both, such sources can also be tricky to verify. In the notes to this history I have been at pains to source materials as comprehensively as possible, even if (and, indeed, because) they are not easily available because without knowledge that these sources exist, future scholarship in this domain will be more difficult. But the World Wide Web continually changes and URL links eventually expire: the references provided to online resources in the notes to *Unacceptable Harm* are therefore on a best endeavour basis.

STRUCTURE

This book is structured in the following way. Following a brief introduction, **chapter 1** looks at what cluster munitions are, how they were used historically and why this weapon technology came to be of humanitarian concern. To begin to put the later Oslo process into context, the earliest attempts to consider cluster munitions at the international level are explored, including the conferences of the 1970s and the origins of the CCW. This chapter also lends consideration to the Ottawa process and the resulting Mine Ban Treaty achieved in 1997 because of their relevance to what eventually followed on cluster munitions.

No progress on addressing the humanitarian impacts of cluster munitions was made for more than 20 years after agreement on the CCW framework treaty in 1980. Yet conflicts like those in Kosovo in 1999, in which both NATO and Serb forces used cluster munitions, led to greater concern about the post-conflict effects, both of this weapon and explosive remnants of war (ERW) more generally—that is, munitions that have failed to function as intended, or which have been abandoned. The International Committee of the Red Cross (ICRC) and NGOs such as Human Rights Watch played significant roles in documenting the problems that unexploded submunitions caused in Kosovo, and added momentum toward the CCW deciding to undertake work on ERW at its second five-yearly review conference in late 2001. **Chapter 2** explores what happened during this period in the CCW, and the origins of the CMC, which was launched in November 2003. The CMC would become a crucial actor in the Oslo process, but it would take some time for it to develop. Meanwhile, Belgium, the first state to ban anti-personnel mines in March 1995, again led the way on prohibiting cluster munitions at a national level 11 years later. The chapter also examines Belgium's unexpected national decision to ban cluster munitions in early 2006, despite protests from its arms industry.

Norway was a key state in the Ottawa process and a major international aid donor for mine action and clearance of unexploded ordnance, and it would eventually emerge as the instigator of the Oslo process. This international leadership role stemmed from the Norwegian government's concerns about the effects of cluster munitions on civilians. In November 2006 the Norwegian Foreign Minister, Jonas Gahr Støre, announced that his government would host a conference on cluster munitions in Oslo the following February. Later, in his invitation letter, Gahr Støre said he hoped the Oslo Conference would be an opportunity to "explore ways to address this pressing humanitarian issue in a determined and an effective manner and [we] are prepared to develop a new legally binding international instrument on cluster munitions".[7] **Chapter 3** examines the domestic and international evolution of Norwegian policy on cluster munitions from 2001 until 2006. How did a state that possessed modern cluster munitions as part of its national military arsenal become the prime mover for a treaty to ban the weapon, even in the face of nervousness and even disapproval from some of its NATO allies?

2006 was a critical year for international efforts to address the humanitarian impacts of cluster munitions in terms broader than the Belgian and Norwegian situations. In mid-July, armed conflict broke out between Israel and Hizbullah in Southern Lebanon. During the 34-day conflict both sides used cluster munitions: Israel's defence forces deployed ground-launched systems on a massive scale in the last few days of the conflict that carpeted Southern Lebanese villages, orchards and fields with submunitions, and Hizbullah attempted to launch cluster munitions among the nearly 4,000 rockets it fired at Israel during this period. The use of cluster munitions and their humanitarian consequences in Southern Lebanon sharply underlined the issues the use of these weapons raise under international law. As of writing, humanitarian operations to clear up unexploded submunitions continue there. In view of the 2006 conflict's importance as a catalyst for international concern about cluster munitions, **chapter 4** provides a brief account of what happened there and its aftermath as told from a battle area clearance perspective. This chapter identifies some lessons to be learned from Southern Lebanon's post-conflict experience with submunitions.

One consequence of the conflict in Southern Lebanon was that, at a diplomatic level, it increased pressure in the CCW to confront the evidence of problems created by cluster munition use at its upcoming review conference in late 2006. Formidable obstacles to negotiation of a cluster munition protocol with real teeth existed in the CCW, however, namely the opposition of some cluster munition possessors such as Brazil, China, India, Israel, Pakistan, Russia and the United States. **Chapter 5** analyses what happened during this period in the CCW, and at the Oslo Conference in February 2007. The latter heralded the formal commencement of parallel international efforts (with caveats by some countries) to those of the CCW on seeking to address the humanitarian effects of cluster munitions. As already mentioned, the Oslo Conference emerged with a joint declaration by 46 states indicating a collective desire for a new treaty significantly more far-reaching that the mandate agreed by consensus in the CCW to discuss cluster munitions further in 2007. At the same time, the Oslo Declaration was masterfully ambiguous.

Chapter 6 examines the period between the February 2007 Oslo Conference and the penultimate international meeting of the Oslo process a year later in Wellington, New Zealand. Because the CCW and Oslo process were intertwined in many ways, these are considered further in the same chapter, along with the development of the civil society campaign, especially the CMC's central call. Another important development in this period was the emergence of the so-called "Like-minded" group, an evolving collection of states loosely united by their concerns about how the Oslo process was being managed by the Core Group and, to a lesser extent, on issues such as interoperability and whether a treaty to be negotiated should contain transition periods allowing further use of cluster munitions. The Like-minded were particularly active following the Vienna Conference in December 2007, which had been a shock for them in a number of respects. For one thing, a report—by Norwegian government scientists, the NGO Norwegian People's Aid and the an independent explosive ordnance consultant and former British army officer, Colin King—on the Israeli-made M-85 submunition and its real-world performance in Southern Lebanon undercut arguments for the acceptability of recent-generation submunitions. The report won support among many countries for the prohibition of cluster munitions, especially among governments from the developing world. Such "Tee-total" countries, as they became known among the Oslo Core Group, would to some extent form a counter-balance to the Like-minded.

The Wellington conference (**chapter 7**) was in many ways the most difficult meeting of the Oslo process. The Like-minded pushed hard for their proposals to be taken up in the draft Convention text. Supported by the rest of the Core Group, the Conference's Chairman, Ambassador Don MacKay of New Zealand, resisted on the grounds that the Dublin negotiation the following May was the appropriate place for specific textual drafting to take place. Arguably, the Wellington conference is where the Oslo process came closest to irreparable damage as relations between the Like-minded and Core Group states reached its lowest ebb, and on the Conference floor debate between the Like-minded and Tee-total delegations polarized. The CMC was also encountering internal differences, and aspects of its campaigning activities and those associated with it around the Wellington conference were controversial for their criticism of some of the Like-minded. This chapter also looks at US policy concerning the Oslo process.

Chapter 8 briefly outlines the evolution of the policies of the ICRC and the United Nations, which were each significant to the CCW and Oslo processes. These entities were not participants in international negotiations, but were sometimes highly influential observers, or facilitators of progress. Although aspects of the contributions of both organizations are covered in other parts of *Unacceptable Harm*, this chapter takes a broader look in order to learn about their roles and the trajectories of their positions in relation to one another. The ICRC, which had long been an active player in the CCW on issues related to cluster munitions, eventually called for the prohibition of cluster munitions that are inaccurate and unreliable, a different call from that of the Oslo Declaration's goal of a prohibition on such weapons that cause unacceptable harm. Meanwhile, many parts of the United Nations played active roles in international efforts on cluster munitions as part of what became known as its Mine Action Team, as well as individually. An abiding issue for both the ICRC and the United Nations concerned how to balance their commitment to the CCW, a UN-administered process encountering persistent obstacles because of the positions of its members, with the free-standing Oslo initiative more likely to achieve the humanitarian goals they supported based on their organizations' field experiences.

Chapters 9 and 10 contain my account of the Dublin negotiations themselves. **Chapter 9** looks first at the state-of-play in the Oslo process at Dublin's commencement, and briefly examines the evolving contributions of the United Nations and the ICRC, as well as extensive Irish and CMC preparations for the diplomatic conference. It also looks at the evolution of the UK's position in the lead-up to and first week of the conference: Britain's difficulties are illustrative of the types of challenge facing the political and military establishments of other countries in the negotiations such as France, Germany and Japan. The bulk of the chapter then analyses the evolution of the CCM text during the first several working days of negotiation there, focusing on work on defining cluster munitions. While differing in their points of view in many other respects, a striking sense shared by all participants in the Dublin conference with whom I spoke was their strong feeling that everyone there wanted success—something certainly not always the case in international conference diplomacy. Not that turning good vibes in Dublin into an agreed cluster munition ban treaty was easy: **Chapter 10** examines the difficult interoperability negotiations, and what happened in the endgame of the Dublin negotiation in the first half of its second week, which culminated in the adoption of the CCM.

Chapter 11 concludes this history of international efforts to address the humanitarian impact of cluster munitions, although those efforts go on. The chapter consists of three parts. The first section looks at features of the cluster munition ban treaty's achievement. The second part outlines some of the likely challenges to the CCM's implementation and the broadening of its membership in view of the fact that several major cluster munition-possessing countries, which shunned the Oslo process, look unlikely to join it soon. Finally, the wider significance of a disarmament–humanitarian discourse in which the notion of "unacceptable harm" has emerged is considered. The broader challenge is to ameliorate the effects of explosive weapons on civilians. Humanitarian law holds that civilians should not be attacked, but this imperative is a sliding rule in practice once military necessity and other considerations are factored in. The Oslo process permitted a collective reframing of cluster munitions' acceptability, eventually bypassing a traditional military utility-centred discourse that favoured permissiveness about the use of weapons without systematic or sincere thought to their humanitarian effects. As such, it could provide the foundations of a discourse for the international community to consider the effects on civilians of explosive weapons as a category, and look at ways in which the protection of civilians in armed conflict can be enhanced.

Meanwhile, multilateral diplomacy is an alphabet soup of acronyms and obscure or arcane terms. Work on cluster munitions was—and continues to be—no exception. A glossary is provided at the back of this volume to help with this shock. The texts of the February 2007 Oslo Declaration, February 2008 Wellington Declaration and the final text of the May 2008 Convention on Cluster Munitions are also included for reference.

INTRODUCTION

"WHAT IS HAPPENING IN MY YARD COULD HAPPEN IN YOURS"

On an overcast day in September 2008 in Geneva, as part of research for this book, I interviewed a Serbian man named Slađan Vučković, his father Hrista and their friend and interpreter, Svetlana Bogdanovic. We met in the Serpentine Lounge, a hang-out for diplomatic conference delegates at the Palais des Nations, the United Nations's majestic European headquarters, which overlooks the lake and faces Mont Blanc and the other peaks of the French Alps. Next door, in a cavernous conference chamber, diplomats and military experts representing the UN Convention on Certain Conventional Weapons (CCW) member states were holding talks on cluster munitions.

We shook hands—my flesh against Vučković's cream-coloured prosthetic limb. He is a survivor of an encounter with a US-made BLU-97 submunition, often known in the humanitarian community as the "yellow killer" for its bright colour and particular hazard to explosive ordnance disposal personnel. In 1999, the year NATO waged an air campaign over the Federal Republic of Yugoslavia, Vučković worked as an army deminer in Serbia. He was experienced at dealing with unexploded ordnance including cluster munitions, and even trained other clearance personnel. On 25 April, Vučković was clearing submunitions that NATO aircraft had dropped in Kopaonik National Park:

> A bomblet exploded; it was a BLU-97, the yellow one. It was the 107th bomblet I had cleared that day. It was the last one. Normally I had assistants to help me, but I did that one alone, since all the others wanted to go home. I approached the bomblet and it exploded. I never touched it. It probably exploded from the vibrations of my steps.[1]

Vučković was taken to a health clinic, and then a hospital, but the ambulance he was carried in was involved in a road accident on the way. Losing blood and consciousness, he was transferred to the back of a police car and driven to a hospital near his hometown of Niš. (Because NATO was bombing Niš,

1

Vučković could not be taken to a hospital there for another two days.) He suffered multiple injuries from the blast and fragmentation, and doctors removed his ruined arms in order to save his life. Vučković's leg was also injured, and he had received multiple injuries to his abdomen. But a rock close to the submunition had shielded him from some of the blast when the bomblet exploded. And a gun he wore, along with a necklace from his wife Dušica and their young children, prevented some of the fragments from penetrating vital organs.

Vučković's experience was a terrible trauma that changed his life, and created new circumstances for his family. At the same time, it is clear from his snowy haired father, Hrista, that they are very proud of him, who eventually became involved in international efforts to try to address the humanitarian impacts of cluster munitions based on the conviction that others should not suffer as he and his family had.

Vučković did not find it an easy decision, however, to become involved in international campaigning to eliminate these weapons. When I first encountered him in Belgrade in 2007 at a conference for cluster munition-affected states organized by the Serbian government and the United Nations Development Programme, I had the sense that Vučković was reluctant to dare to hope that halting the use of the weapon that maimed him might be possible. But, encouraged by how seriously others in this so-called "Oslo process" were considering the problems cluster munitions caused, Vučković—along with other cluster munition survivors from around the world—became a Handicap International Ban Advocate to lend his weight to the enterprise.

Halting the use of cluster munitions is still a goal rather than a reality, but it seems well on the way to being realized based on the progress of the last few years. Ban Advocates like Vučković are proud of the impact they had on the achievement of the Convention on Cluster Munitions (CCM), which was adopted by 107 states after diplomatic negotiations in Dublin in May 2008. This multilateral initiative, instigated by Norway and supported by many other states, international organizations and hundreds of NGOs within the rubric of the Cluster Munition Coalition, grew out of frustration that years of talks in Geneva, next door to where Bogdanovic, the Vučkovićs and I sat, had made so little progress in the face of an urgent humanitarian imperative.

The Oslo process was a calculated risk, but one that those at the centre of this effort thought was achievable if it had a focus on the human impact, had a suitably diverse and inclusive international partnership, used the growing evidence base about the cluster munition problem effectively, and had a clear goal. In 15 months the international initiative delivered a treaty categorically banning cluster munitions, which provides for cluster munition clearance, stockpile destruction and assistance to victims. Vučković told me he was less pleased with other aspects, like exclusion from the treaty's prohibitions of certain advanced weapons sometimes described as cluster munitions, or the CCM's provision for military joint operations between treaty members and other states not party to it. "The Convention is good", he said. "Personally I am not satisfied with the definition of the cluster munition as from the very beginning I was engaged for the total and immediate ban of all types of cluster munitions. But as I am a reasonable person and I try to be as objective as possible, I know that it is maybe the best that we could get".[2]

Few people understand the consequences of cluster munitions more intimately than Ban Advocates like Slađan Vučković, and their perspectives were important to a collective reframing of the acceptability of cluster munitions over the course of the Oslo process. Vučković, for his part, worked with maintaining cluster munitions while in the military, then became a clearer of unexploded submunitions, and now lives with the human consequences of the weapon every day of his life. Yet, surprisingly, for most of the span of intermittent international talks about cluster munitions since the early 1970s, government experts have not sought out the perspectives of those affected by these weapons. In fact, some cluster munition user and possessor states in forums like the CCW have strongly resisted the implications of mounting humanitarian evidence—and still do—that would contradict their insistence that the weapon is legitimate and indispensable. But the legitimacy or acceptability of a weapon can only be properly assessed if the claims made about it by manufacturers and possessors are measured against evidence like its impact on civilians. On cluster munitions, the humanitarian evidence from the field, including the personal testimonies of cluster munition survivors, points to very different conclusions from those of the cosy, circular and un-testable arguments about military utility and legitimacy often heard among cluster munition user and possessor governments.

And that is why Bogdanovic and the Vučkovićs were in Geneva. The Cluster Munition Coalition (CMC), a consortium of 300 civil society organizations, asked Slađan Vučković to try to remind those inside the conference chamber that their deliberations and negotiations have real world implications, and to encourage them to adopt a humanitarian standard on cluster munitions that will have a meaningful impact. The best outcome from the CMC's point-of-view would be if all, rather than just some, of those states present would agree to join the CCM. This is not likely to happen—at least not soon. Nevertheless, if the Ban Advocates helped to ensure a focus on the human impact and lift the humanitarian bar in the Oslo process, it could make a difference in the CCW too. As Vučković pointed out, "We have quite different ways of expression. It's very boring to listen to diplomats. While on the other side, we Ban Advocates have a language that really reinforces our experiences and which is able to reach everyone—everyone can really understand what we are talking about".

Nevertheless, it is not easy. Because Vučković does not speak one of the UN official languages, his statements cannot be interpreted and heard in the CCW conference chamber. But he speaks, with Bogdanovic's help, to a packed lunchtime meeting in a side room on cluster munition victim assistance issues. And, as it was in the Oslo process, diplomats and military people are often very friendly at these meetings and diplomatic cocktail receptions and tell Vučković privately that they share his views, even if they say different things in the official sessions. This, he told me, is why the ongoing work of the Ban Advocates in trying to bring greater focus on the human impact of cluster munitions is important:

> We have to find a way to attract these people, to bring it home to them. Because even these people—these diplomats and military people—are normal people with families, with children. And no one among them would like to be someone who is a victim of cluster munitions … what is happening in my yard could happen in yours. You never know what can happen to you.[4]

Efforts to reframe old issues in more productive ways are at the heart of why the Oslo process achieved a humanitarian treaty on cluster munitions when other attempts failed. This book tells the story of how and why the minds of many people—and the positions of their governments—changed about the acceptability of cluster munitions.

CHAPTER 1

THE TECHNOLOGY OF KILLING

A wide variety of weapons are based on fragmentation effects. Many of these weapons have been so constructed and so used that no questions have been raised as to their legality. Modern developments, however, have brought into production some fragmentation weapons which are apt to be indiscriminate in their effects and/or to cause unnecessary suffering. It would certainly be desirable to introduce a broad prohibition or restriction of use of fragmentation weapons which typically are employed against a very large area, with the substantial risk for indiscriminate effects that such use entails. The formulation of such a broad rule raises great difficulties.

A specific ban on use is less difficult to devise in regard to one type of fragmentation weapons, namely, those which are constructed in the form of a cluster of bomblets and which are primarily suited for use against personnel. These anti-personnel fragmentation weapons tend to have both indiscriminate effects and to cause unnecessary suffering. At detonation a vast number of small fragments or pellets are dispersed, evenly covering a large area. The effects of such a detonation on unprotected persons—military or civilian—in the comparatively large target area is almost certain to be severe with multiple injuries caused by many tiny fragments. Multiple injuries considerably raise the level of pain and suffering. They often call for prolonged and difficult medical treatment and the cumulative effect of the many injuries increases the mortality risk. It is queried whether the military value of these weapons is so great as to justify the suffering they cause.[1]

These words are from a working paper by Egypt, Mexico, Norway, Sudan, Sweden, Switzerland and Yugoslavia. The paper was presented to a grandly titled Diplomatic Conference on the Reaffirmation and Development of International Humanitarian Law Applicable in Armed Conflicts in Geneva, Switzerland, during late February and March 1974. Its contents were prompted by concern that a number of weapons used in the war in Indochina violated two principles of international humanitarian law: against causing unnecessary suffering, and the prohibition on indiscriminate attack.[2]

5

Among the proposals within the working paper was a call for a new international legal rule: "Cluster warheads with bomblets which act through the ejection of a great number of small calibred fragments or pellets are prohibited for use".[3] Thus, more than 30 years before the emergence of successful international efforts to ban cluster munitions—through the Oslo process, and the achievement of the 2008 Convention on Cluster Munitions (CCM)—these kinds of weapon were already causing alarm among governments, and there were calls for a cluster munition prohibition. Why, then, did it take so long for the international community to act to outlaw cluster munitions?

As we shall see, the path toward addressing the humanitarian impacts of cluster munitions would be a long one and full of twists and obstacles. It would entail arriving at a commonly held notion of what a cluster munition is, and why it is of humanitarian concern. And, it would require shifting the burden of proof from the shoulders of those calling for cluster munitions to be outlawed to those defending the weapon's continued use. This would be no mean feat in view of the attachment of many governments to retaining certain cluster munitions in their arsenals, including some of those participating in the Oslo process. And, doing so would necessitate partnership between medium- and small-sized governments, international organizations like the United Nations and the International Committee of the Red Cross (ICRC), and a wide range of civil society actors, including advocacy organizations like the Cluster Munition Coalition (CMC), survivors of incidents with cluster munitions and their families, explosive ordnance and submunition clearance experts, researchers and the media. It would not be a smooth road.

The frenzy of media coverage that the Oslo process generated, particularly during its final stages in 2008, could convey the impression that international concerns about cluster munitions are only a recent phenomenon. Indeed, viewed from afar these concerns might have seemed only to date from the 2006 conflict in Southern Lebanon leading to a general declaration of intent sketching out some basic principles in February 2007 that kicked off the Oslo process, to the completed text of a treaty by the end of May the following year banning cluster munitions. But this would be misleading, and it is certainly not the whole story. The Oslo process needs to be seen in a broader historical context to understand its significance.

As an early step, it is also necessary to set out what we mean when we talk about cluster munitions or consider their effects. As we shall see, these understandings changed over time as the perceived roles of cluster munitions altered, and more information came to light about the post-conflict consequences of submunition contamination, in particular. This evolution in perceptions would be important to the eventual achievement of an international ban on cluster munitions. Correspondingly, this chapter provides an overview of what cluster munitions are, a rough timeline of their development and use, and the concerns such use initially raised. Attempts during the last third of the twentieth century to tackle the humanitarian impacts of cluster munitions at the international level are briefly examined including the ICRC-sponsored conferences in Switzerland of the 1970s and the origins of the 1980 UN Convention on Certain Conventional Weapons (CCW).

Of course, concerns about cluster munitions did not arise purely in isolation, but in parallel to those about other weapons. The Swedish-led 1974 working paper mentioned above, for example, also contained proposals pertaining to incendiary weapons, flechette weapons and anti-personnel mines, among others. In the longer run, dissatisfaction with the ineffectiveness of attempts to ban anti-personnel mines in the CCW would lead to the so-called "Ottawa process" resulting in the 1997 Mine Ban Treaty. The Mine Ban Treaty's achievement is highly relevant to the international campaign against cluster munitions this century, and so is briefly outlined toward the end of this chapter.

CLUSTER WEAPONS

From the early days of multilateral talks about anti-personnel weapons in the 1970s, government experts had a specific idea about what they referred to when they talked about cluster weapons or cluster munitions. In that context, they were discussing weapons with explosive fragmentation submunitions (not simply blast or shaped-charge munitions) and even then, only to those producing "small calibred" fragments.[4] In the field of military ordnance, however, cluster munitions traditionally constituted a broad category, and from their early development encompassed types deploying submunitions other than conventional high explosive:

As with the World War II bomb clusters, there were many types of payload for the cluster bombs produced or under development during the Vietnam War: high explosive, incendiary, chemical, biological, smoke-producing and a fuel-air explosive producing an aerosol of small particles or vapour droplets which spreads over a target and is then detonated. Different models had different payloads and were intended for different purposes.[5]

Overall, defining what is meant by the term "cluster munition" for the purposes of humanitarian regulation or prohibition is therefore not as straightforward as it might seem. In the Oslo process it would be highly contentious because whatever was ultimately defined as a cluster munition would be banned. Linked to this, the process by which to arrive at a cluster munition definition was also controversial—whether such a definition should hinge primarily on the technical characteristics of a munition in sorting "good" from "bad" (an approach to weapons regulation that is customary in the CCW), or based on its effects (as in the Oslo process).

At its most basic, a cluster weapon or munition can be described as a container or dispenser from which explosive submunitions (sometimes called bomblets) are scattered. These submunitions are generally the dangerous parts of a cluster munition because they are designed to explode on impact or after a time-delay and cause damage through blast and fragmentation. (Unless a cluster munition container actually falls from the sky and lands on someone, it is explosive submunitions that should be regarded as the dangerous components of a cluster munition.) Explosive submunitions can be delivered in cluster munitions dropped, dispensed or launched from aircraft or, as has increasingly been the case in recent years, be surface-launched: besides artillery shells containing submunitions, systems are also used that deploy submunitions from rockets or mortar shells.[6]

Although they have been couched in different ways, broadly speaking there are three basic concerns about cluster munitions. First, there are the problems at time of use as cluster munitions are intended to saturate an area with explosive submunitions, which cannot be individually targeted at military objectives. This raises issues under the principle of distinction between combatants and civilians, a principle that is fundamental in international humanitarian law.[7] Second, because of cluster munitions' area effect, it follows that failed submunitions may disperse over a significant area, remaining in streets, ditches, bombed buildings or agricultural lands. Because massive numbers of these inaccurate and unreliable weapons can be fired in a very short time, it is easy to see why concerns have escalated about the potential humanitarian consequences of cluster munition proliferation. Sometimes, cluster munitions can fail to dispense their cargo of submunitions, which poses a different kind of hazard.[8] Both scenarios occurred in the conflict in Southern Lebanon in 2006, in which Israel's military and Hizbullah each used cluster munitions (described in more detail in chapter 4). Both Israel's and Hizbullah's acquisition of cluster munitions are examples of the proliferation of this kinds of weapon—the third basic concern. Moreover, Hizbullah's attempts to fire Yugoslav-designed, Chinese-made cluster munitions into Israel also underline that this proliferation extends to non-state armed groups.

Explosive cluster weapons initially emerged in the course of the Second World War, in 1943. It is unclear whether they were first used by the Soviets against the German army on the Eastern Front, or by the German *Luftwaffe* in its bombing of harbours on the east coast of England, but both the Soviet and German types were air delivered.[9] Cluster munitions as used by the *Luftwaffe* against targets in England caused considerable risk to civilians almost from the very outset. For example, during the night of 13–14 June 1943, the *Luftwaffe* dropped SD-2 submunitions—often referred to as butterfly bombs—on the port of Grimsby.[10] The butterfly bomb was around the size of a fist and was stabilized and braked in the air by a four-winged device that was the origin of its name.[11] Only around one quarter of the approximately 1,000 submunitions dropped on Grimsby exploded on impact or within half an hour. These killed 14 people and ignited numerous fires. The rest of the bomblets lay unexploded, including on roads and roofs and caught in trees and hedges. After the air raid "all clear" signal was given, another 31 people were killed and many more injured as they interacted with these unexploded bomblets. Despite immediate action by the authorities, it took more than 18 days to clear the submunitions and reopen the port, a fact the British took great pains to conceal from the Germans. Decades later, in citing the effects of the Grimsby raid on civilians, the ICRC concluded that it was:

> a self-contained miniaturized illustration of the potential effects of submunitions. The most important point is that the majority of fatalities (47 out of 61) occurred after, not during, the attack. Although a rapid awareness campaign and large-scale clean-up operation compressed the time scale of their effect, this is an indication of the unexploded submunition's capacity to inflict post-conflict damage long after its use.[12]

Despite these consequences, the cluster bomb was seen as a weapon with considerable potential by militaries. The US later copied the *Luftwaffe's* butterfly bomblet, and nestled their replicas in a mother bomb named the M-28.[13] US forces deployed the M-28 in the Korean War in the early 1950s, and later from the skies above Indochina in the 1960s.[14] For their part, the Soviets kept their Second World War air-delivered cluster munition system, the OKT 1.5, in service until recently.[15]

In essence, the development of cluster munitions after the Second World War reflected a broad trend that, as war was waged on a scale that was ever larger and more industrialized, militaries wanted weapons that could kill more efficiently and over a larger area. In his book *The Technology of Killing: a Military and Political History of Anti-Personnel Weapons*, Eric Prokosch traced the development of wound ballistics science and weapons design in the post-war period in the United States. Prokosch showed that the Korean War led to the US military leadership becoming very concerned about the prospect that existing advantages in technology, equipment and training might be nullified and its forces overwhelmed by "human wave" attacks by Chinese and North Korean troops. Research and development efforts into a range of new anti-personnel weapons were redoubled, from mines, incendiary weapons such as napalm, and remote-detonated Claymore devices to improved assault rifles, grenades and what would eventually be known as cluster munitions:

> Superior technology must defeat superior manpower. The search for better nonnuclear means of attacking enemy soldiers was to inspire munitions designers for the next decade. World War II studies of wounding had pointed the way to a solution: the massive deployment of small, high velocity wounding missiles. The key to this was fragmentation.[16]

Traditional fragmentation bombs that exploded on impact would naturally create a number of fragments radiating outward at high speed, damaging obstacles (like people) in their path. But, closely scoring or grooving the case of a munition would generate many smaller fragments of roughly similar size.[17]

Out of these research and development efforts would emerge a new generation of US anti-personnel weapons in time to see their widespread use in conflict in Indochina in the 1960s and 1970s, with devastating consequences for civilians in Viet Nam, Cambodia and Laos. In early 1965, for example, the United States began systematically bombing North Viet Nam in Operation Rolling Thunder, and by the end of the following year word had begun to filter out of the tightly controlled country from visitors like pacifist David Dellinger of the US bombing of urban centres using munitions such as cluster bombs.[18] By now, the US arsenal of fragmentation bombs included munitions such as the CBU-24, comprised of a SUU-30 clamshell-shaped dispenser deploying between 640 and 670 guava-shaped BLU-26 explosive submunitions, each weighing 435g. Each bomblet in turn contained 85g of explosive, an impact fuze and had 300 ball bearings embedded in its casing.[19] Thus, the use of just one CBU-24 could see up to 200,000 steel balls saturating a wide area at high velocity.[20]

> The CBU-24, like the child burned by napalm, became a symbol of the Indochina war. Anti-war protest was focused on the bomb as a means of exposing the nature of the war, accusing the producers of the bomb of complicity in war crimes, and putting pressure on the American Government to stop the war. Honeywell Inc., a leading producer of the CBU-24, was a target of demonstrations, stockholder resolutions, consumer boycotts and other forms of protest in the United States and other countries.[21]

But on the whole, concern among peace groups about the effects of cluster bombs were either studiously ignored or vigorously shrugged off by the US government. Writing in 1974, Michael Krepon observed:

> It is a fair conclusion that military officers in the Pentagon downplayed the question of CBUs to deflect political channels from making an issue of their use, as they had done with napalm. CBUs were categorized and explained as a standard weapon, to be taken off the shelf— "conventional ironmongery".[22]

Reflecting on this in the mid-1990s, Prokosch concluded that a "major increase in antipersonnel battlefield lethality had been accomplished with no public debate and relatively little subsequent protest". He added that "The 'success' of the CBU-24 would lead to a proliferation of cluster technologies to other countries".[23]

THE ICRC CONFERENCES

The CBU-24, however, was just the tip of the iceberg. By the end of the 1960s, the US and its allies had access to an array of new anti-personnel weapons including a variety of cluster bombs and bomblet dispensers to disperse many explosive submunition models. At the time, although these weapons went by various names, including "anti-personnel bombs"[24] and "pellet bombs",[25] the notion of "cluster bombs" appeared to be widely understood—though detailed information about their characteristics and effects was usually hard to come by from those governments possessing them.[26]

Meanwhile, international momentum grew in the early 1970s for the reaffirmation and further development of the humanitarian rules applicable to armed conflict. The rise of non-international armed conflicts and increasing resort to guerrilla warfare as in Viet Nam also raised many challenges for application of these rules, not least for the protection of civilians. In 1969, the Twenty-first International Conference of the Red Cross held in Istanbul passed a resolution[27] asking the ICRC to propose new international humanitarian law rules and to invite government experts to consider them. The initiative was followed up in UN General Assembly resolutions on the topic[28] that set in motion international diplomatic work to this end.[29]

Anti-personnel weapons were subsequently discussed in a series of international conferences during the 1970s. There was, from 1974, the Diplomatic Conference on the Reaffirmation and Development of International Humanitarian Law Applicable in Armed Conflicts convened in Geneva by the Swiss government, and mandated by the United Nations. The Diplomatic Conference's primary task was not weapon-specific at all, but instead was to consider two draft protocols relating respectively to the protection of victims of international armed conflicts (Additional Protocol I) and non-international armed conflicts (Additional Protocol II), and intended to supplement the four 1949 Geneva Conventions.[30] These Additional Protocols would eventually be agreed in 1977. As part of work during the four sessions of this Diplomatic Conference between 1974 and 1977, an Ad Hoc Committee on Conventional Weapons also met to look at specific weapons-related restrictions or prohibitions.

One of the proposals in the working paper by Sweden and others was to ban "Cluster warheads with bomblets" in view of their fragmentation effects. It had been prompted by work among a group of military and medical experts that the Swedish government had convened domestically early in the 1970s.[31] The expert group was doubtless prompted by concerns about the conduct of the war in Viet Nam during that period, which were very strong among the public in Sweden (and in many countries).[32] Sweden and other governments proposed that its expert group's work and proposals be discussed (among other proposals offered by governments) by an ICRC-convened group of international experts. "Confronted with this massive support for the idea, the ICRC thereupon expressed its readiness to act upon the recommendation".[33] This ICRC expert group included representatives from 19 governments but not the US—the main user of cluster munitions—which refused to participate. The expert group produced a report in 1973 on "weapons that may cause unnecessary suffering or have indiscriminate effects".[34] The report reviewed existing legal prohibitions or limitations regarding the use of specific weapons, and framed some categories of weapons in terms of their level of indiscriminateness and degrees of suffering or injury caused. Alongside small-calibre projectiles, time-delay weapons, incendiary weapons and potential new weapons such as lasers, the report considered blast and fragmentation weapons—a category that, although not referring specifically to cluster munitions like the CBU-24, captured them within its ambit. Couched in cautious language, the ICRC expert report stressed that its purpose was not to "present proposals for the prohibition or restriction of the use of any of the weapons or weapon systems discussed". Nevertheless, it concluded that:

> several categories of weapon tend to cause excessive suffering and particularly severe injuries or may, either by their nature or because of the way in which they are commonly used, strike civilians and combatants indiscriminately. ... It is obvious that the trend towards weapons which fragment into vast numbers of small fragments, and are susceptible of covering large areas, increases the risk of multiple injuries and the possibility that civilians will be affected.[35]

From late September to October 1974, the ICRC held a three-week government expert conference in Lucerne, Switzerland, where the expert group report could be discussed. Nevertheless, many of those attending the Lucerne expert meeting were delegates from the Diplomatic Conference, which had encouraged the ICRC to hold a meeting in the first place to help remedy its own deficit in technical expertise—expert was in some cases a loose term.[36] Contemporary analysts also noted the significance of the ICRC meetings in that "they were the first time that the humanitarian issues raised by certain specific weapons, other than nuclear, chemical or biological weapons, had been discussed at an international level since the 1930s".[37] This time the US participated, among delegations from

49 states and national liberation movements as well as experts from the Stockholm International Peace Research Institute (SIPRI) and the World Health Organization.[38] Reactions as expressed at the Lucerne conference were mixed, both to the ICRC report itself, and to proposals like those of Sweden and its co-sponsors on banning or restricting weapons like "cluster warheads with bomblets which act through the ejection of a great number of small calibred fragments or pellets" or flechettes. Instead, aspects of the Swedish-led proposal were rounded upon by the US and a number of European states, to the extent that the Lucerne conference's report cited one participating expert's observation that "the Conference seemed to be divided into two camps, with certain experts describing effects of weapons and proposing the prohibition or limitation of their use, while other experts contested these descriptions and even the utility thereof".[39] The Conference President's closing statement seemed to recognize this:

> Since the newly presented facts need to be digested and further study and research is needed, it was doubted that the [Diplomatic Conference's] Ad Hoc Committee would, at its next session, be ready to adopt new treaty rules concerning the prohibition or restriction on the use of any conventional weapons.[40]

The Conference President also expressed his hope that the ICRC would convene another expert meeting. However, in early 1976 that second ICRC-sponsored expert conference, this time held in Lugano, made little further progress toward a meeting of minds among government experts on banning or restricting fragmentation weapons. If anything, the polarization apparent in Lucerne intensified.[41] Moreover, Prokosch, who attended both the Lucerne and Lugano conferences, noted that although the proposal by Sweden and others remained on the table, the Swedes appeared to have lost interest in it.[42] Indeed, discussion of the proposal was relatively brief.[43] Instead, support had begun to coalesce around other topics. Firstly, Mexico and Switzerland had proposed a ban on weapons the main effect of which was to injure by means of fragments that are undetectable by medical methods such as X-rays. A second idea (put forward by France, the Netherlands and the United Kingdom) proposed obligations for recording the location of minefields and imposing restrictions on remotely delivered or scatterable mines. The third proposal was for a prohibition on attacks on civilian areas using incendiary weapons, and on military objectives within these areas, that is unless "feasible precautions" were taken.[44]

The ICRC expert meetings' discussions were duly transmitted to the Geneva Diplomatic Conference's Ad Hoc Committee, but the latter could not agree on measures to restrict or prohibit specific conventional weapons by the time the Conference's work concluded in 1977.[45] But the Diplomatic Conference did recommend holding a separate, subsequent UN conference to carry the torch on the weapon-specific issues and, if possible, to try to achieve agreements on regulation. This UN Conference was held in two sessions, in September 1979 and around a year later in 1980. It succeeded in negotiating the CCW, a treaty with a tortuous title reflecting its difficult conception, gestation and birth—the *Convention on Prohibitions or Restrictions on the Use of Certain Conventional Weapons Which May be Deemed to be Excessively Injurious or Have Indiscriminate Effect*. Beside a framework treaty containing the CCW's general provisions, three protocols on specific weapons deriving from it were agreed, the lineage of each traceable back to the Lugano conference—on non-detectable fragments (Protocol I), landmines (Protocol II) and incendiary weapons (Protocol III). To become a member of the CCW, however, it was not necessary for a state to adopt all of the CCW's protocols—two were enough, a rule that still stands today, although the CCW now has five protocols.

As in so many instances in the multilateral arms control environment since, delegates involved in the Diplomatic Conference's work and ICRC conferences seem to have been faced with a choice: go with emerging forward momentum on courses of action that were considered more likely to be achieved—even if less ambitious—or strive for more on issues that seemed unpromising for general agreement, but at greater perceived risk of failure. Pragmatism appears to have prevailed. Specific rules on other weapons of concern as raised at the ICRC meetings and by states in the earlier Diplomatic Conference process, including fragmentation cluster warheads, flechettes and fuel–air explosives, were not addressed in the new CCW and its protocols. Conversely, undetectable fragments dealt with in CCW Protocol I had not even been mentioned in the 1974 Swedish working paper, and some felt even prior to the CCW's agreement that this protocol dealt with a:

> weapon myth—the so-called "plastic pellet bomb" ... . The myth concerns the actual wounding effect of a type of bomb and arose during the Vietnam War. Certain US anti-personnel bombs during the war contained steel balls embedded in plastic. Persons wounded by them were later found to have in their bodies plastic fragments not detectable by X-ray.[46]

Yet Protocol I did not even deal with these: its full text amounts to one sentence: "It is prohibited to use any weapon the primary effect of which is to injure by fragments which in the human body escape detection by X-rays". Because plastic pellets were not the primary wounding agent in the alleged culprit weapon, the US Mk-118 Rockeye cluster submunition, CCW Protocol I did not prohibit them.

In less than a decade, the deep humanitarian concern and good intentions of the Swedes and others about the effects of anti-personnel fragmentation weapons like cluster munitions had been swept aside. Cluster munitions would remain off the multilateral negotiating table for the next 27 years.

INDOCHINA

The 1974 Swedish-led proposal and subsequent debates among governments about cluster warheads were predominantly concerned about two of their features: their indiscriminate effects, and the risk of superfluous injury or unnecessary suffering to *combatants* from many small bomblet fragments. In diplomatic work in the 1970s, comparatively little attention was given to the post-conflict hazards created by the dispersal of massive quantities of explosive submunitions. In contrast, in both the CCW and Oslo processes of the twenty-first century the post-conflict effects of submunitions on civilians would also become a driving motivation for specific rules on cluster munitions. The accumulated evidence of post-conflict impact would be crucial pieces of the jigsaw puzzle in international campaigning against cluster munitions.

Post-conflict communities in places like Viet Nam and Laos would serve as some of the gruesome laboratories in which this evidence would eventually be collected. While diplomatic and other government experts were meeting during the mid-1970s in pleasant Swiss cities and resort towns to discuss the relative characteristics of weapons many of them had never seen first hand, the human cost and evidence of the hazards of cluster munitions to civilians was mounting. An American, Earl Martin, who had been working on refugee assistance programmes in Indochina during the Viet Nam war, was one of the earliest to publicly raise the alarm in the West about unexploded submunitions. In a *Washington Post* editorial published in July 1973—before either the Lucerne or the Lugano conferences had taken place—Martin highlighted the post-conflict hazards to rural people:

One type of weapon which Vietnamese farmers will likely be encountering for generations is the "anti-personnel" bomb. This type of bomb, designed not to destroy buildings but to kill or injure people, was used extensively. It consists of a large "mother bomb" which bursts in mid-air dispersing as many as 500 baseball-sized bomblets. A delayed action fuse detonates the bomblets each of which spew out several hundred steel pellets in all directions. The thousands of these small bombs, which failed to explode are among the many lethal weapons which make resettlement of the countryside difficult in many areas of Indochina.[47]

Further research by Martin and others would lead him to conclude that between 1965 and 1973 the US expended at least 14.3 million tonnes of munitions in Indochina—almost twice as much as it had expended in all theatres during the Second World War—and that significant quantities had failed to explode as intended.[48]

In Viet Nam, the hazards from unexploded ordnance were severe, and due to all kinds of explosive munitions. The same was true in neighbouring Laos, in which the US government had begun a covert campaign of massive aerial bombing in 1964. But Martin and others noted the particular dangers to civilians there posed by unexploded bomblets. The US bombing sought to weaken the Pathet Lao forces and interdict supplies and people moving along the "Ho Chi Minh Trail" from North to South Viet Nam via south-eastern Laos. In practice, it meant bombing broad areas in order to destroy local social and economic infrastructure, a task for which cluster munitions were seen as appropriate.[49] (Nevertheless, US airpower never managed to cut the flow of equipment and supplies into Viet Nam, which actually increased over the bombing period.[50]) The United States also lent political and economic support to the Royal Laos Government, and sponsored a secret war in which the US Central Intelligence Agency (CIA) organized and supported a private army that included ethnic Hmong fighters and Thai volunteers.[51] As an element of US airpower, cluster munitions were widely used in massive quantities to provide support to royalist forces in order to compensate for lack of artillery, numerical superiority and logistic support. As a result, Laos is the most heavily bombed nation in the world per capita: according to one estimate, more than 500,000 US bombing missions dropped more than two million tons of ordnance between 1964 and 1973, including in excess of 260 million cluster submunitions,[52] which Laotians call "bombies".

These are staggering quantities of lethal ordnance, and the US bombing had terrible effects on the people of Laos. Fred Branfman compiled many harrowing eye-witness accounts of the bombing and how it disrupted and in some cases completely destroyed life in Laotian villages in one of the worst-bombed provinces, Xieng Khouang, in his 1972 book, *Voices From the Plain of Jars: Life Under an Air War*. Branfman noted at the time that "To this day, the vast majority of people both in the United States and abroad do not have the slightest inkling of what occurred on the Plain of Jars between 1964 and 1969"[53] because the air war was conducted by the US government in secret. Nor are the consequences of the bombing well known in the United States and elsewhere even four decades later.

The civilian population in Laos is still living with the consequences of that bombing more than a generation ago. The Lao National Unexploded Ordnance Programme believes that, even under ideal conditions, with an estimated 30% of the more than 270 million submunitions dropped on the country during the Indo-China war failing to function as intended, this left some 78 million bombies to pose hazard to people going about their daily lives.[54] Fifteen of Laos' 17 provinces were left affected by cluster munitions and other unexploded ordnance, and today 10 provinces are still severely contaminated—with an estimated 300 people injured or killed per year.[55] In 1997, the NGO Handicap International set about conducting a national survey in Laos of the socio-economic impact of unexploded ordnance, and discovered that 25% of the country's roughly 10,000 villages were blighted by the presence of explosive remnants of war—in rice fields, school yards, hillsides, rivers, roads, paths and even town centres.[56] It is not possible to disaggregate from other types of ordnance the numbers of civilian casualties from incidents involving submunitions, but in view of the quantities that were dropped and failed to function as intended, along with the bombies' small sizes, a considerable proportion of these casualties must be due to submunitions. As of mid-2008 the government of Laos and the UN Development Programme reported that, overall, more than 22,000 Laotian people had been casualties of unexploded ordnance (UXO) since the war—11,500 injured and the remainder killed—in a poor, largely rural country in which medical care is limited, and surgical and rehabilitation resources are scarce.[57]

In 1974, the American Friends Service Committee (AFSC), a Quaker service organization, opened a small office in Vientiane, Laos's capital city, to help with refugee issues, and a year later the US Mennonite Central Committee

(MCC) followed. When the communist Pathet Lao movement overthrew the royalist government in 1975, the pacifist Quakers and Mennonites were the only Western NGOs to maintain offices there. Soon AFSC and MCC representatives began to receive reports of injuries and deaths from unexploded ordnance in the Xieng Khouang province, and in 1977 they travelled to the area to see for themselves. Thus began Mennonite and Quaker efforts over subsequent decades to inform the world beyond the reclusive South-East Asian country about the extent of the UXO threat in Laos, and to try to alleviate the humanitarian suffering and developmental problems the war had caused. Some Mennonite and Quaker UXO-focused efforts were rudimentary, but quite effective. For example, they imported shovels and garden forks to distribute among farmers in the worst affected areas of Laos, in the hope that they would be less likely to detonate buried bombies than the traditional Laotian hoe, which is swung over the head and so hits the ground with a heavy impact. This programme continued until 1991, but other initiatives were short-lived. In 1979, for instance, the Laotian government gave the MCC approval to ship into Laos a specially modified tractor with demining attachments such as chain flails. But such machinery proved expensive, it did not work reliably in detonating bomblets, and was soon judged to be dangerous to operators and bystanders.

Mennonite and Quaker shovels and experimentation aside, and the presence of a dozen Soviet demining trainers for 18 months during 1979 and 1980, the worst-affected areas of Laos like Xieng Khouang were largely left to their own resources to clear unexploded submunitions and other ordnance. In documenting MCC efforts in Laos, Bruce Shoemaker's account, *Legacy of the Secret War*, noted:

> In the immediate post-war period most governmental/military efforts went into defusing large bombs and resettling internally displaced refugees. Local farmers needing to clear land to grow food have had to clear the cluster bomblets themselves. This has been a painstaking and dangerous task. Farmers have had to learn how to handle live ordnance by trial and error—with the penalties for errors including serious injury, amputation and death.[58]

Considerable knowledge was built up among some locals in dealing with unexploded ordnance. Nevertheless, in poor, rural communities in Laos, the presence of UXO has also become a risky temptation for the extraction of scrap metal, or explosive content for blasting or fishing. In countries affected by the Indo-China war such as Laos, Cambodia and Viet Nam, it is an unregulated industry that thrives today, and which often depends on children and the poor, to locate and gather these hazardous remnants of war, with sometimes tragic consequences.[59]

In 1981, Titus Peachey and his wife Linda travelled to Laos to join the MCC office there.[60] Around villages in northern Laos they frequently met villagers who had been injured or who had lost family members to cluster bombs. And everywhere they went, the Peacheys heard stories about the bombing and its effects:

> We also saw a lot of cluster bombs and a lot of cluster bomb containers. One of the particular things that grabbed onto us as US citizens was that many of the US containers still had the tags on them that indicated who the manufacturer was and where they were located. And so that had a special significance for us as US citizens, and so when we met with villagers [and] talked to families, the whole question of responsibility was hanging in the air. It wasn't often stated very explicitly, but we felt it very deeply in a personal way that these things were representing us—and it was horrible.[61]

When Titus and Linda eventually returned to live in the US in late 1985, they created a slide show about what they had experienced in Laos, and began travelling and speaking on the issue with anyone who would listen—to churches, peace activists and, periodically, government officials in Washington DC, as the Quakers had also begun doing in 1982. The AFSC had also succeeded in engaging NGOs such as Operation Handicap International (France) to become involved in Laos, which set up rehabilitation centres for UXO casualties, and later the MCC would persuade the Mines Advisory Group (MAG) to begin UXO clearance work in the country.

The Peacheys, like others with humanitarian field experience in South-East Asia, were also concerned about the ongoing production of cluster munitions:

> So I was following up references to cluster bombs, articles about cluster bombs, and I found one in Aviation Weekly/Space Technology and I was turning the pages looking for the article, and there was a picture of a cluster bomb. Underneath the inscription was "this is a new type of cluster bomb produced by ISC Technologies, Lancaster, Pennsylvania". I about fell off my chair, because Lancaster's the home of MCC, my wife's family lived there, and we were just about to move there. So that just hooked me at a very deep level and I was concerned about

shutting the valve off at the top where the production happens and at the political, economic issues to try to get it stopped.[62]

The Mennonites and Quakers tried to create an upswing of interest in the problems caused by cluster munitions. And they were not completely alone, as other civil society groups, most linked to opposition to the Indo-China war such as the Honeywell Project (a peace group in Minnesota that protested against the locally headquartered Honeywell Corporation's production of BLU-26 cluster submunitions and other weapon systems) had also been active.[63] However, overall their successes were modest.

The Viet Nam war was now well over and, as far as many people were concerned, best forgotten. Official US interest in South-East Asian countries it had formerly bombed revolved not around expensive clearance of unexploded ordnance, but in recovering military personnel missing in action during the conflict. A renewed Cold War chill had descended, and in both NATO and Warsaw Pact nations, a new generation of cluster munitions had already begun to move from drawing board to production line, and then into arsenals—so-called "combined-effects submunitions".

"IMPROVED" CLUSTER MUNITIONS

The US had been among the first states to see the need for combined-effects submunitions that could destroy armoured vehicles as well as kill people within an area. During the Viet Nam war, US forces fielded a cluster bomb called Rockeye, comprising submunitions containing a shaped charge to penetrate armour. A later, dual-purpose version of the submunition was enclosed in a metal casing designed to produce anti-personnel fragments on explosion.[64]

The problem was that by the middle of the Cold War, developments in tank armour meant that Rockeye was less than adequate to face the threat of the Warsaw Pact armies just as the strategic planners of both adversaries and their allies were putting greater weight on conventional forces for a possible war in Europe. More emphasis was given to developing weapons that could defeat concentrations of infantry, soft-skinned vehicles and tanks, along with other targets such as military command posts, logistic nodes and artillery. In addition to existing air-delivered systems, the development of new ground-launched cluster munitions that could be fired from artillery or rocket launchers was increased. Also, Dual-Purpose Improved Conventional Munitions (DPICM) began to enter service. DPICM were intended to be more potent versions of submunitions like Rockeye.[65]

Despite differences in manufacture, DPICM submunitions tend to look similar, and all contain a similar flaw in practical usage, as an ICRC report noted in 2000, each being:

> a highly compact design with both anti-armour and anti-personnel effects. A ribbon streamer serves to both stabilize, and through rotation in the airstream, arm the simple fuse. Should the ribbon be caught (by vegetation, for example) or the body strike the ground at an angle, there is a significant chance that the fuse will not function. When armed but unexploded, DPICM are among the most sensitive types of UXO, requiring substantially less force to operate [i.e., detonate] than most mines.[66]

Since the emergence of DPICM submunitions in the 1970s, their manufacture has proliferated to many countries beyond those NATO and Warsaw Pact member states, from Israel (producer of the M-85 bomblet) to Yugoslavia (the KB-1) and China (the MZD-2, which appears to be a KB-1 variant)— along with earlier cluster munition types. A 1995 University of Essex report noted that only five models of cluster bomb were in production or under development outside the US in 1978 as reported by SIPRI (as opposed to 32 US models); in contrast, in 1994 *Jane's Air-Launched Weapons* listed 64 types in 14 countries, only nine of which were US models.[67]

In their proposal to the Swiss conferences in the middle of the 1970s, Sweden and other governments had observed that achieving agreement to ban or restrict "use of fragmentation weapons which typically are employed against a very large area, with the substantial risk for indiscriminate effects that such use entails" would raise "great difficulties".[68] So, they had focused their call for a ban on anti-personnel weapons that contain a "cluster of bomblets" as "less difficult".[69] At that time, they clearly felt that a distinction could be made between anti-personnel and anti-materiel weapons, at least in terms of primary effect. But the new submunitions beginning to enter service during the 1970s made such a distinction moot. DPICMs were avowedly "dual-purpose", binding together into a single explosive device the anti-personnel area effect of cluster weapons considered potentially indiscriminate by some, with an anti-armour capability all militaries agreed on as legitimate and essential.

Of course, governments could simply recategorize their new cluster munitions in ways that emphasized their use against armour while their anti-personnel role remained a core part of the mission. The British had their new combined-effects cluster munition, the BL-755. The virtues of this new munition were even touted at the Lucerne conference in order to counter humanitarian concerns in the ICRC's 1973 expert report, which in a British delegate's view:

> seemed to be inclined to treat cluster bombs as one entity, without differentiating between various classes of cluster bombs designed for entirely different purposes. He thought that such differentiation was necessary. In order to clarify the position as he knew it, he gave a detailed description of the BL-755 cluster bomb. This bomb of about 250kg is designed to replace high-explosive bombs on such targets as armoured and soft-skinned vehicles, parked aircraft, anti-aircraft batteries, radar installations, small ships and headquarters or maintenance areas. It dispenses a number of dual-purpose sub-munitions, distributing them evenly over an area of less than 1 hectare on the ground, an area necessary to take into account movement of the target and errors in delivery. He noted that a far higher degree of high-explosive must be delivered into the target area when using conventional bombs. ... He also pointed out that the fusing of the bomblets is such that detonation on impact is assured regardless of the angle at which the bomblet strikes the target or ground, and the incidence of in-flight bomblet detonation is extremely small, so that the effects of the weapon are contained within the designated area and at the attack time.[70]

The message this sent was sharp yet soothing—these new submunitions were not like those that had gone before. They were better militarily, and they did not pose the same risks of indiscriminacy as the "cluster of bomblets ... primarily suited for use against personnel"[71] the Swedes and others were worried about. Instead, the BL-755's bomblets would be distributed over an area of less than a hectare and were aimed at destroying vehicles and other materiel. Yet, according to Prokosch's account of the Lucerne conference, the phrase "troop concentrations" had been crossed out by hand in the list of intended targets in the original British statement, which suggested these claims were certainly made with a keen eye to the audience.[72] Moreover, the BL-755's bomblets were said to be reliable since "detonation on impact is assured". And, in a refrain that would become very familiar subsequently in both the CCW and Oslo processes decades later, it was opined that cluster munitions were even *necessary*, in humanitarian terms, because otherwise a worse alternative would have to be used.

Time would tell that many of the claims made for the BL-755's submunitions (and, for DPICM generally) were not true. Operational use of weapons like the BL-755 showed both wishful thinking based on arms manufacturers' claims about the accuracy or reliability of their submunitions (tested under ideal rather than realistic conditions) and that they were still clearly intended for an anti-personnel role.[73] In 1982, for example, the UK used BL-755s in combat against Argentine positions in the Falklands/Malvinas. The British NGO Landmine Action later observed that the British government claimed failure rates for BL-755 bomblets of between 5% and 7%, and Landmine Action's own estimate suggested an even higher minimum failure rate of 9.6%.[74] Detonation on impact, then, was certainly not assured.[75] Moreover, British explosive ordnance troops engaged in early attempts at clearance on the islands following the conflict viewed unexploded BL-755 submunitions as highly dangerous: Colin King, author of an ICRC report on explosive remnants of war and himself a former British Army officer with explosive ordnance disposal (EOD) experience in the Falklands/Malvinas during that period, wrote that:

> After early accidents, a mythology has grown up around the BL-755, and British EOD procedures instruct operators to avoid casting a shadow across an unexploded bomblet. From a technical perspective this is quite absurd, but it illustrates the level of distrust with which these, and other unexploded submunitions, are sometimes regarded.[76]

Eventually, in 2007, Britain would unilaterally decide to take the BL-755 out of service on humanitarian grounds.[77]

However, regardless of the weakness of arguments for the continued retention and use of cluster munitions, they prevailed. The results were that both the development of these weapons and their incorporation into military doctrines continued, while the risks they posed at time of use or post-conflict were given little emphasis. In 1991, cluster munitions were used extensively in the Gulf War by US-led Coalition forces. According to one estimate, the US alone dropped more than 61,000 cluster bombs containing approximately 20 million submunitions in Kuwait and Iraq.[78] This total included some modern designs, but others such as the Mk-118 Rockeye dated back as far as the early 1960s. As well as air-delivered systems of various kinds, extensive use was also made of the fearsome Multiple Launch Rocket System (MLRS), a twelve-tube launcher firing a volley of rockets, each containing 644 M-77 DPICM explosive submunitions. In one volley, the MLRS could distribute more than 7,200 submunitions over an area of 200,000m². Estimates for the number of submunitions used in the Gulf War vary, but they run to at least as many as 13 million, and failure rates were high.[79] Colin King noted, for instance, that inspection of former Iraqi military positions after the war indicated Rockeye failure rates on the order of 20–40% in some cases, possibly because of low drop height or impact on soft sand.[80] And, while cluster munitions were judged by Coalition militaries to be effective weapons in destroying Iraqi war equipment, denying access to supplies and lowering Iraqi troop morale, they also had an adverse effect on US troop movements: a US General Accounting Office memorandum in 1993 reported that "in some instances, ground movement came to a halt because units were afraid of encountering unexploded ordnance".[81] The Gulf War also underlined the especially high failure rate and post-conflict hazard of another type of US submunition, the BLU-97—subsequently used in Serbia, Afghanistan and again in Iraq in 2003 by US and NATO forces. The BLU-97 had a yellow case and an extremely sensitive back-up fuze, making it highly unpredictable in its failed state,[82] and for this reason was later dubbed the "yellow killer".[83]

By late 2006, Human Rights Watch researchers estimated that cluster munitions had been used in at least 21 states, by at least 13 states.[84] All instances of their use raised questions under international humanitarian law, in the view of the ICRC.[85] There is not space in this book to give a detailed account of all of these incidents, although annex D provides a basic timeline. Globally, 33 countries were known by 2006 to have produced more than 210 different types of cluster munitions (see annex E for some examples). More than 70 countries were thought to stockpile cluster munitions of varying ages and types, and in various conditions.[86] For its part, a pioneer in cluster munition development, the United States, is thought to have held a total submunition stockpile of nearly *one billion* as of 1994.[87]

Cluster munitions have, from the early days of their use, posed a threat to civilians both at the time of use and after conflict because of their area effect, and the inaccuracy and unreliability of explosive submunitions. This was compounded by the dispensing of submunitions, in truly massive numbers in some cases. This meant that very large areas would be saturated with explosive force. Cluster munition use has raised concerns under international humanitarian law under the principle of distinction, the rule against indiscriminate attacks, the principle of proportionality and the rule obligating military forces to take all feasible precautions to spare civilian populations.[88] And post-conflict it meant that, even if failure rates were low, large numbers of dangerous unexploded submunitions would remain to endanger people. If they were high, then the humanitarian and development consequences could be catastrophic, which is what occurred in Laos. And, in every instance in which submunition reliability rates were independently examined, actual failure rates were always significantly greater than the claims of militaries or submunition manufacturers, as shall be seen in the course of this book.

THE OTTAWA PROCESS AND THE MINE BAN TREATY

This section explores efforts to achieve an international treaty banning anti-personnel mines in view of its relevance to later efforts to ban cluster munitions, which were similar in some respects. Among the weapons of concern for Sweden and other countries from early in the 1970s, along with cluster warheads, flechettes and other weapons, the use of anti-personnel mines in certain circumstances had been raised. Years later, states negotiating the 1980 CCW would also adopt the Protocol on Prohibitions or Restrictions on the Use of Mines, Booby-Traps and Other Devices (Protocol II). But, as legal commentators observed, reaction to the new CCW and its protocols "was subdued and few States chose to adhere to them. Most of the attention concentrated on the continuing, if restricted, legality of the use of incendiary weapons, or the need to address the use of fuel–air explosives"; moreover, Protocol II's effect was "miniscule" in practice as the limits it placed on landmines were modest, and it did not apply to non-international conflicts in which such weapons were often used.[89]

During the period from 1980 until the early 1990s little of note happened in the CCW while, globally, the humanitarian effects of landmines, and anti-personnel mines in particular, worsened. Anti-personnel mines were cheap, usually low-tech and easy to produce in large numbers, and were attractive and expedient weapons for governments and armed non-state groups alike. However, as "victim-actuated" devices, anti-personnel mines were incapable of discriminating between combatants and civilians, with people in war-torn states such as Afghanistan, Angola and Cambodia among the worst affected—and casualties in dozens of other countries around the world. And the persistence of mines in the ground after conflicts ended (and frequently after belligerents had lost track of where the mines were that their forces had sown) posed both a deadly risk to people going about their daily lives and created challenges to reconstruction and development. Rural communities were particularly vulnerable to anti-personnel mines, which hindered both agriculture and safe movement.

In late 1991, NGOs concerned about the effects of landmines began to coordinate, and a few months later six of them—Handicap International, Human Rights Watch, Medico International, MAG, Physicians for Human Rights, and the Vietnam Veterans of America Foundation—began to plan a coordinated campaign against the weapon. These efforts would grow into the International Campaign to Ban Landmines (ICBL), which still exists today and continues to play an important role in monitoring implementation of the treaty banning anti-personnel mines it helped to achieve in 1997. Moreover, Handicap International and Human Rights Watch would later play important roles in the cluster munition campaign, eventually joined by the ICBL itself.

In 1992, however, a treaty banning anti-personnel mines still seemed like a distant—and perhaps impossible—objective to most people. But in 1993 France asked the UN Secretary-General to convene a conference to review the operation of the CCW.[90] The French government wanted to strengthen measures for states' compliance with the CCW. But its initiative also created an opportunity for the international landmine campaign to exploit, as France's request set in motion a sequence of UN expert preparatory work, which would draw attention to several other issues for the CCW to consider as priorities, including strengthening restrictions on the use of anti-personnel mines and, in particular, those without neutralizing and self-destruction mechanisms.[91]

Around this time the ICRC also became much more active at a policy level on anti-personnel mines, largely as a result of prompting from its Medical Division. An important individual in this respect was a young British surgeon, Robin Coupland, who operated for the ICRC in the field from the later 1980s. Coupland was both challenged and appalled by the injuries sustained by victims of anti-personnel mines on the border between Afghanistan and Pakistan, and Thailand's border with Cambodia.[92] Coupland began to analyse and classify the wounds. He established that people injured by anti-personnel mines required a longer hospital stay, more medical operations, more blood for transfusion and were left with more severe disabilities as compared with other conventional weapon injuries. This evidence of the true nature and severity of such wounds was published in medical journals.[93]

This and other medical evidence helped to provide an empirical basis to back up growing international concern and momentum toward addressing the humanitarian effects of anti-personnel mines.[94] And, as it had done earlier in the 1970s in parallel with the Diplomatic Conference, the ICRC set about holding expert meetings, this time focused on anti-personnel mines. But the concerns of field personnel like Coupland and his hospital colleagues had yet to permeate the higher echelons of the ICRC, a courageous but also frequently cautious humanitarian organization. Until 1994, the ICRC's position fell well short of any call for a prohibition, calling only for the incorporation of self-destruct mechanisms in anti-personnel mines so that they did not persist after conflict had ended, and thus endanger civilians. Eventually the ICRC would catch up with NGOs, who were already calling for a total ban on the weapon: in February 1994, the ICRC's President, Cornelio Sommaruga, announced that "from a humanitarian point of view", a "worldwide ban on anti-personnel mines" was "the only truly effective solution"[95]—but only after much internal debate within the organization.[96] Eventually, in June 1994, the ICRC would employ someone full-time on CCW and landmine policy issues in its Legal Division—Peter Herby, a former staff member from the Quaker United Nations Office in Geneva. Herby's experience from the landmine campaign would later be brought to bear on cluster munitions.

Support for a ban on landmines could also increasingly be seen from parts of the United Nations, including from the Secretary-General himself.[97] And the attitudes of many governments were changing too, in part reframed by the attention to the issue from international organizations and civil society actors: a UN General Assembly resolution in December 1994 called for the eventual elimination of landmines, and was passed without a vote.[98] Moreover, in March 1995 Belgium led the world in banning anti-personnel mines through a national law. Whatever the purported (and increasingly contested) military utility of anti-personnel mines for military commanders, it was becoming increasingly understood that the indiscriminate nature of the weapon made it unacceptable in at least some, if not all, circumstances.[99] A year later, an ICRC-commissioned study was published about the military utility of landmines. The study examined the actual use and effectiveness of anti-personnel mines in 26 conflicts since the Second World War and concluded that military benefits from anti-personnel mines were "far outweighed by the appalling humanitarian consequences of their use in actual conflicts".[100] The former soldiers comprising the anti-personnel mine expert group added, "On this basis their prohibition and elimination should be pursued as a matter of utmost urgency by governments and the entire international community".[101]

It was difficult to translate such awareness into momentum in the consensus-driven CCW, however, which had struck various difficulties in its Review Conference preparation process. This Review Conference would ultimately meet in more than one session—in Vienna in September and October 1995, and in Geneva the following January and then from 22 April to 3 May 1996. In addition to a new protocol on blinding lasers, the Review Conference would produce a new "amended" Protocol II on mines and booby-traps and other devices. Characteristic of multilateral disarmament and arms control negotiations, the CCW Review Conference:

> was almost exclusively interstate (although NGOs had already become well engaged with the issue). The negotiations were "top-down" as the negotiations reflected the international power structure with the US, Russia and China leading the negotiations. State sovereignty reigned as decision-making was made on the basis of consensus. This allowed states to prevent the emergence of substantive changes to the status quo, which hamstrung those states that pushed for tangible reforms to the anaemic regulation of landmines in the 1980 Convention.[102]

Amended Protocol II fell short of the expectations of many. The ICRC, for its part, described the new protocol as "woefully inadequate".[103] Despite the evidence of increasing harm to civilians due to the global landmine epidemic, despite the auspicious circumstances and opportunities the end of the Cold War arms race had brought for multilateral disarmament and arms control, and despite a growing chorus of calls to ban a weapon by now widely seen as inherently indiscriminate, the CCW did not produce the ban on anti-personnel mines the UN Secretary-General, the ICRC and ICBL, and governments like Belgium had hoped for. Instead:

> The Protocol banned the use (and transfer) of "undetectable" anti-personnel mines, and remotely delivered anti-personnel mines that did not self-destruct and self-deactivate to a stated standard, but allowed States to opt for a nine-year period of deferral from its entry into force to fully comply with each of the two prohibitions on use. It further required that anti-personnel mines not equipped with self-destruction

and self-deactivation features be laid in marked and protected areas, but included an exception to that requirement (not to the requirement applied to remotely delivered anti-personnel mines) for certain situations, including where direct enemy military action made it impossible to comply, and again allowed for a nine-year period of deferral as long as the use of non-compliant mines was "to the extent feasible" minimized and such mines at least self-deactivated within 120 days.[104]

To the person on the street, such an outcome had the air of legalistic gobbledygook. And ordinary people all over the world *were* becoming more concerned as effective public communication and campaigning by the ICBL and ICRC, including testimony from landmine survivors and images of their injuries, increasingly hit home.[105]

By May 1996, more than 40 states, many of them party to the CCW, had expressed their support for a total international ban on anti-personnel mines. A small number of states began to associate together in support of achieving such a ban, and this became a "core group" comprised of Austria, Belgium, Canada, Germany, Ireland, Mexico, Netherlands, Norway, the Philippines, South Africa and Switzerland (and would later expand to include others) just as, more than a decade later, another core group would arise to drive the Oslo process on cluster munitions. Throughout 1996, members of delegations from these states met with NGOs in the back rooms of Geneva to discuss how to move forward. The problem was that no obvious forum existed for achieving a ban on anti-personnel mines once the CCW had produced its outcome. In principle there was the 61-member Conference on Disarmament (CD) in Geneva, but there were fears that the requirement for consensus in that body would also make achievement of any landmine ban impossible and the CD had (and still has, after more than a decade of deadlock from 1998 to 2009) a long list of other priorities for negotiation.[106]

Canada's decision to change its position on landmines and join in discussions with other pro-ban states and NGOs to find a humanitarian solution to the landmine crisis was especially significant. Together with counterparts from Norway and South Africa, Canadian diplomats would be a major force within the Ottawa core group. In October 1996 Canada hosted an international conference in Ottawa entitled "Towards a Global Ban on AP Mines", which brought together 50 states pledging their support for a total ban on anti-personnel mines, along with 24 observer states. At this conference, Canada's foreign minister, Lloyd Axworthy, challenged participating states to negotiate a ban treaty within a year. Axworthy also offered, on behalf of the Canadian government, to host the signing ceremony for the prospective new treaty—yet to be negotiated—in Ottawa in December 1997—"with this bold pronouncement, the Ottawa Process and the multilateral treaty negotiations were set in motion".[107]

Although the Ottawa process would involve the United Nations, and especially its field agencies, negotiation of the international treaty banning anti-personnel mines would occur outside the CCW and CD, the traditional UN frameworks for weapons regulation. Beside this, and the core group of predominantly medium- and small-sized states propelling it, several other interrelated factors would be distinctive about the Ottawa process:

- As mentioned above, empirical evidence of the hazards created by anti-personnel mines had begun to be gathered, and this helped to swing debate away from traditional inter-governmental debates focused on the military utility of landmines.

- A strong civil society campaign in the form of the ICBL used this evidence to raise public attention to the humanitarian problems created by the weapon and to stigmatize its use. Many of the organizations involved in the ICBL "had years of field experience with the treatment and rehabilitation of mine victims. They were able to provide first-hand knowledge of the impact of such weapons, while few, if any, states were in a position to provide detailed information about the problem on a worldwide or even regional scale".[108] Moreover, NGOs enabled mine survivors themselves to play roles. Although the public involvement of Diana, Princess of Wales, from January 1997 was to bring particular media attention to the international landmine campaign, NGOs setting the agenda, framing solutions, building networks and coalitions, and employing tactics of persuasion and pressure on governments to change their positions and practices had begun long before.[109]

- The Ottawa process's objective was straightforward, ambitious, and couched in humanitarian and not arms control terms—ban anti-personnel mines because of the indiscriminate harm and superfluous injury and suffering they caused. The importance of reframing an arms control issue in humanitarian terms cannot be underestimated. Such a call stood in stark contrast to the patchwork outcome of CCW Amended Protocol II, which had reflected the determination of many states to retain mines in their arsenals while, if possible, restricting the ability of potential adversaries, rather than concerns about vulnerable human beings being maimed or killed. This call resonated with politicians and their electorates in many countries.

- There was also a certain degree of providence in the Ottawa process. For example, changes of government in France and in the United Kingdom in early 1997 resulted in policy changes that were helpful as bureaucrats' entrenched positions were overruled by politicians in the final treaty negotiations.[110]

Although there would also be important differences, all of these ingredients would later feature in some form in the Oslo process on cluster munitions.

After a frenetic period of conferences, regional meetings, lobbying and intense diplomacy in Africa, Asia, Europe and the Americas for almost a year from the October 1996 Ottawa conference, delegations from 85 states gathered on 1 September 1997 in the Norwegian capital, Oslo, to negotiate a humanitarian treaty on anti-personnel mines. Work there proceeded on the basis of a 10-page text that had been husbanded by Austria. Ambassador Jacob Selebi, South Africa's Permanent Representative in Geneva, was designated to preside over the Oslo Diplomatic Conference. Some major users of anti-personnel mines such as China, India, Israel, Pakistan and Russia stayed away. But the US, which throughout the first part of 2007 had sought to have the issue taken up in the CD instead of joining the Ottawa process, announced on 18 August that it had decided to participate in the Oslo negotiations.

The involvement of the US was a coup for its close neighbour Canada, in particular, and undoubtedly a comfort to many of its allies participating in the Oslo negotiations. But it was also a risk: unlike almost all other delegations participating in Oslo, the US had not joined the June 1997 Brussels Declaration, which had committed the 97 states subscribing to it to agree on:

A comprehensive ban on the use, stockpiling, production and transfer of anti-personnel landmines,

The destruction of stockpiled and removed anti-personnel landmines, [and]

International cooperation and assistance in the field of mine clearance in affected countries.[111]

Crucially, the US delegation did not want a comprehensive prohibition on anti-personnel mines—it pursued exceptions in order to retain its minefields along the boundary between the Democratic People's Republic of Korea and the Republic of Korea, and to permit the explosive "anti-handling devices" attached to some US anti-tank mines that, in effect, functioned as anti-personnel mines. And the US used a range of means at its disposal to have its way, among them a request for extension of the Oslo conference by a day (which was granted), during which there was intense bilateral lobbying of many states by senior US politicians and diplomats to back its proposals. Nevertheless, these proposals found little support in a changed international environment in which international opinion now saw anti-personnel mines as repugnant, and which many of those delegates participating in Oslo thought would detract from the Ottawa process's objective to comprehensively ban anti-personnel mines. On 18 September, "the US delegation announced to the plenary that it was withdrawing its proposals as it had been unable to garner the necessary support for them. ... [T]he Convention was formally adopted to a round of enthusiastic applause from States and NGOs alike".[112]

Although the US made it clear it would not join the new treaty, many important US military allies did adopt the Convention on the Prohibition of the Use, Stockpiling, Production, Transfer of Anti-Personnel Mines and on Their Destruction—among them Australia, Canada (despite some late wobbliness under bilateral pressure from Washington to weaken the treaty text in Oslo), France, Germany, Japan and the United Kingdom. Tragically, Diana, Princess of Wales—the public figure who had come to personify the international landmine campaign—was killed in a car accident in Paris in late August, the weekend before the Oslo Diplomatic Conference commenced. According to one account, behind the scenes in Oslo and in London throughout the Oslo conference, "British officials would grumble that they were forced to negotiate with one hand tied behind their backs for fear of being savaged by the press for scuppering 'Diana's treaty'".[113] Nearly 11 years later, the United Kingdom would also heed a broader political imperative to join the Convention on Cluster Munitions in Dublin in May 2008, but for quite different (and less tragic) reasons. Significantly, the CCM's achievement with major cluster munition possessors like the United Kingdom onboard would belie the contention sometimes heard among

Geneva-based diplomats in the intervening period that 1997's Mine Ban Treaty was a one-off humanitarian disarmament outcome resulting from Diana's death—impossible to repeat, and foolish to try.

The Mine Ban Treaty identified and prohibited a wide range of activities related to anti-personnel mines.[114] It banned the development, production, stockpiling, transfer and use of the weapon under any circumstances, and it was prohibited "to assist, encourage or induce, in any way, anyone to engage in any activity prohibited to a State Party under this Convention" (article 1, paragraph 1). It contained provisions for mine clearance within deadlines. The commitment in the Mine Ban Treaty to assisting victims of anti-personnel mines was a novel and significant element in terms of international legal rules on weapons,[115] and the treaty also provided for international assistance and cooperation. Moreover, the Mine Ban Treaty's definition of an anti-personnel mine was significantly clearer and stronger than that found in CCW Amended Protocol II, which talked about "a mine *primarily* designed to be exploded by the presence, proximity or contact of a person and that will incapacitate, injure or kill one or more persons".[116] The Mine Ban Treaty did away with the word "primarily", thus removing any ambiguity.

ELOQUENT BUT GRIM TESTIMONY

Banning anti-personnel mines through the Ottawa process would rightly be held up as a major international achievement. The ICBL and its assiduous coordinator, Jody Williams, would receive the 1997 Nobel Peace Prize. The Mine Ban Treaty's achievement held out hope for other disarmament priorities to be tackled, if necessary by reframing them as humanitarian action. At that time, however, the humanitarian impacts of cluster munitions received little attention among either governments or interested civil society actors—apart from a few Mennonite activists and others—as the challenges of bringing the new Mine Ban Treaty into legal force and practical implementation loomed. If there was a conventional weapons issue moving to share centre stage with anti-personnel mines it was the curbing of the illicit trade in small arms and light weapons. Cold War-era surplus weapons were sloshing from conflict to conflict and being used to kill and maim hundreds of thousands of civilians globally each year. It was increasingly apparent to the international community that small arms violence was a problem of major dimensions in many communities around the globe, especially in the developing world.[117]

The 1990s were relatively productive for arms control: there were the CCW's products, of course, and the ending of the Cold War had removed obstacles to successful negotiation of a number of multilateral accords including the 1990 Conventional Forces in Europe Treaty. The Chemical Weapons Convention was completed in the CD in 1993, and it was followed in 1996 by the achievement of the Comprehensive Nuclear-Test-Ban Treaty. The 1969 Nuclear Non-Proliferation Treaty, which was originally of 25-years duration, was extended indefinitely in 1995. But in the decade following the Mine Ban Treaty's entry into force in 1999, the business of producing new multilateral disarmament accords would all but dry up despite pressing security imperatives. Setting aside the implementation of the Mine Ban Treaty, the brave twenty-first century world of new humanitarian-oriented diplomacy that many hoped the treaty heralded instead began to look more and more like the stymied old one of previous decades.

In view of the landmine epidemic, the Ottawa process came not a moment too soon. And, eventually, the process to ban cluster munitions would invite comparisons with the humanitarian disarmament diplomacy of the Mine Ban Treaty process. Nevertheless, if there is a lesson from these belated efforts it must surely be one Prokosch identified in his history of anti-personnel weapons published earlier in the 1990s, that "The problem of unexploded mines is an eloquent testimony to the failure of the efforts in the 1970s to adopt new bans on especially injurious and indiscriminate weapons".[118] Had the Swedish proposals been adopted then—and respected—the humanitarian problems created by mines and cluster munitions would be much less today.

CHAPTER 2

FROM LITTLE THINGS BIG THINGS WILL GROW

On 24 March 1999, NATO began an air bombing campaign targeting the armed forces of the Federal Republic of Yugoslavia. Internal conflict between the Kosovo Liberation Army (KLA) and the Yugoslav state (dominated by Serbia) had been brewing for some time in the province, and reports emanated of reprisals and ethnic cleansing. But diplomatic talks at Rambouillet in France in early 1999 failed to bring the parties to agreement. This failure precipitated NATO's air campaign, entitled Operation Allied Force—intended to force Yugoslav forces out of Kosovo, allow international peacekeepers in, and permit refugees from the province to return to their homes.[1]

There was a widespread belief that NATO air strike operations would be sharp, but short and surgical in the harm they inflicted. Western airpower had dominated the 1991 Gulf War, and the advent of technologically sophisticated targeting systems and precision munitions had received a high public profile. Besides, according to NATO alliance leaders, this was a war of humanitarian intervention, with the protection of civilians its overriding aim. Early in the war, for instance, NATO's supreme military commander in Europe, US General Wesley Clark, told journalists, "This is not an attack against the Serb people. Every effort is being made to avoid harm to innocent civilians and to avoid collateral property damages".[2]

The moral high ground had been claimed. As always, however, reality confounded initial expectations. Although it was thought that the Yugoslavs' relatively sophisticated air-defence system would pose a substantial threat to NATO strike aircraft, only two manned planes were shot down, and no NATO lives were lost in fighting the campaign. But Operation Allied Force did not prevent large-scale ethnic cleansing operations continuing against Kosovar Albanians. And expectations about a swift end to air operations after precision air strikes with minimum deaths among civilians proved wide of the mark. Thick clouds during the first weeks of the air war meant that even the most sophisticated European NATO aircraft were sometimes unable to attack because their targets were obscured, or aircrew lost control of their weapons after they were launched.[3] And erroneous predictions about a rapid Yugoslav surrender or withdrawal prompted NATO to steeply increase the number of aircraft and missions it launched: instead of the alliance's air campaign concluding victoriously in 48 hours, it ran for 78 days and only ended on 10 June.

NATO aircraft from the US, UK and the Netherlands dropped substantial numbers of cluster bombs of three types that crop up throughout this book as major culprits for harm to civilians. There was the US-made CBU-87, which contained 202 of the infamous, yellow BLU-97 submunitions with the so-called "all-ways acting" fuze. Also dropped in substantial numbers was a revised version of the UK's BL-755—the wonderful cluster bomb pitched to the Lugano and Lucerne conferences of the 1970s—called the RBL-755. Both the BLU-97 and RBL-755 submunitions used a detonator technology that made them extremely sensitive (and thus hazardous) if encountered in an unexploded state after failing to function.[4] And, in lesser numbers, the Viet Nam war-era Mk-118 Rockeye was deployed, a weapon known since at least as early as the Gulf War to have a high failure rate[5] and by now probably ineffective against the Yugoslav army's tanks. In total, an estimated 1,765 cluster bombs, containing about 295,000 submunitions, were dropped in Kosovo, Serbia and Montenegro.[6]

Disturbing incidents involving cluster munitions soon emerged in the course of the conflict. The airport at Niš, Serbia's third largest city, was repeatedly targeted in NATO air strikes with an array of weapons including cluster bombs. Shortly before midday on 7 May, a NATO air strike the alliance said was directed at Niš airport dispersed large numbers of BLU-97 submunitions around the city hospital and a residential suburb, killing 14 civilians and seriously injuring 27.[7] Javier Solana, NATO's Secretary General, confirmed the next day that NATO cluster munitions were responsible, and said the alliance regretted "the loss of life and injuries inflicted",[8] although cluster bombs again fell in civilian areas of Niš that day (with no casualties reported) and, less than a week later, on 12 May during local rush hour. According to Norwegian People's Aid, which later undertook a study of the humanitarian impacts of cluster munition strikes in Serbia, three people were seriously injured and 10 others wounded in the 12 May attack.[9]

In view of the NATO campaign's humanitarian mission, the consequences of the alliance's bombing using cluster munitions were galling at the time, even if in some cases it would require careful research subsequent to the conflict to reveal the precise extent of these consequences for civilians. Human Rights Watch (HRW) documented more than 75 civilian deaths and injuries attributable to incidents involving cluster munitions during the air campaign,[10] and argued that NATO's use of cluster munitions raised "serious concerns" under the international humanitarian law (IHL) rule against indiscriminate attack. This was because of a combination of errors in targeting, inaccuracy of delivery and the area effect of the munitions.[11] The Kosovo conflict would also, in the course of time, underline the post-conflict hazards of unexploded submunitions, especially as a dedicated UN-led Mine Action Coordination Centre was soon established in Kosovo that enabled the systematic collection and comparison of clearance and casualty data.[12] (This Centre, directed by a New Zealand army combat engineer, Maj. John Flanagan, would also act as a laboratory and training ground[13] for many of those involved in the UN's post-conflict clearance operations in Southern Lebanon in 2006.) In 2000, the International Committee of the Red Cross (ICRC) reported that, along with anti-personnel mines, cluster submunitions were "the leading cause of mine/UXO-related injury or death" in Kosovo—together accounting for 73% of incidents individually recorded by the ICRC between June 1999 and the end of May 2000.[14] Landmine Action's 2007 analysis of post-conflict casualties in Kosovo concluded that at least 152 casualties had been caused due to air-dropped submunitions that had failed to function as intended, and confirmed that submunitions posed as great a hazard there as the presence of anti-personnel mines.[15]

The casualties in Kosovo from cluster bombs were inflicted on a population that NATO had come to save, and in other parts of Yugoslavia among civilians that NATO said it was not attacking. As a result, although launched for ostensibly humanitarian reasons, the NATO intervention pushed the effects of cluster munitions back into the public eye and attracted intense criticism. Such outrage died away "all too quickly" as one NGO representative observed,[16] just as public interest had faded following the Gulf War. However, because the situation in Kosovo following the conflict enabled the collection and analysis of data in a systematic manner for the first time about the humanitarian effects of cluster munition use, it would enable the United Nations, the ICRC and NGOs to eventually spell out the problems with cluster munitions in empirical terms. This accumulating evidence would indicate that even when deployed in the Balkans by modern, professional military forces well acquainted with IHL rules and applying them scrupulously, cluster munitions were highly problematic weapons.[17] Moreover, it would eventually contribute to calling into question the military utility of cluster munitions, especially as it transpired that "More NATO troops were killed by unexploded NATO submunitions after the conflict than were killed by Serb forces during the war".[18]

The multilateral forum that in 1999 seemed the natural place for remedying those problems was the Convention on Certain Conventional Weapons (CCW), which was beginning to prepare for its Second Review Conference to be held in late 2001. But in 1999 there was no international campaign against cluster munitions, and only the ICRC and a handful of NGOs were devoting resources to the issue. In part prompted by the use of cluster munitions in the Kosovo conflict, an international civil society campaign would eventually emerge that sought to compel governments to address the consequences of the weapon in a comprehensive way. This civil society campaign would be a critical ingredient of the later Oslo process.

FIRST STEPS

For long-time advocates of banning cluster bombs like Titus Peachey from the Mennonite Central Committee (MCC), the late 1990s was a pretty bleak period. The MCC, like many other NGOs, had been involved in the International Campaign to Ban Landmines (ICBL) during the Ottawa process in 1996 and 1997—in MCC's case primarily because of its experience in Laos with cluster submunitions and other unexploded ordnance. Peachey and a young post-graduate law student and fellow Mennonite, Virgil Wiebe, hoped that efforts to achieve a treaty prohibiting anti-personnel mines might also encompass restrictions or a ban on cluster munitions. But their views were distinctly in the minority. Those in the inner circle of the ICBL's core leadership with an established interest in cluster munitions, like Stephen "Steve" Goose, Director of HRW's Arms Division, were dubious about the viability of a call to ban cluster weapons at that time. Wiebe later noted, "The ICBL and its allies among friendly governments, many of them mid-power states, shared concerns about cluster munitions, but saw the issue as too difficult to address under the same rubric as landmines".[19] At a roundtable meeting in Washington DC on 7 March 1997 that Peachey attended, along with Eric Prokosch and others from North American NGOs with a particular interest in cluster munitions, HRW representatives argued that a landmine treaty needed to be achieved first, and warned that pushing a ban on cluster munitions could risk jeopardizing that.[20] In his notes from the meeting, Peachey wrote to himself:

It's hard to know how the general climate among agencies supporting a ban on landmines will change if/once a ban is achieved. Now, all the available energy and resources are focused on landmines. Even though these agencies/groups would be natural allies in any effort to ban cluster weapons, there is no time/energy available for this now.[21]

Like all NGOs, those involved in the landmine campaign possessed limited financial resources, time and personnel. Yet these were the most likely civil society constituency to take up the issue of cluster munitions because of their familiarity with unexploded ordnance hazards. Thus, an ongoing tension until 2003—and indeed for much of the international campaign against cluster munitions that would follow—would be in managing the competing demands of implementing work on anti-personnel mines with achieving a new norm on cluster munitions. And some NGOs at the time, such as Landmine Action and the Italian Campaign to Ban Landmines, were keen to make anti-vehicle mines the priority for international campaigning among those organizations that had led the way on banning anti-personnel mines.[22]

Human Rights Watch had followed the cluster munition issue since the 1991 Gulf War, and was one of the better-resourced NGOs concerned about the weapon. During the Kosovo conflict, HRW condemned the use of cluster bombs in Operation Allied Force, and called on NATO to stop the weapon's use on the basis of its indiscriminate effects.[23] And, in mid-December 1999, HRW distributed a memorandum to delegations at the CCW calling for a global moratorium on cluster bomb use until humanitarian concerns were "adequately addressed":

> It is clear that at the present time, the use of even the most sophisticated cluster bombs poses grave and unacceptable dangers to civilian populations. There should be no further use until governments can establish either that a technical solution is possible or that new restrictions and requirements regarding use can be effective.[24]

The Mennonites (who sought an outright ban) aside, this was the strongest call from an NGO for international action on cluster munitions, although HRW's report the following February concerning the NATO air campaign in general was toned down in comparison. That report argued that UK and US cluster bomb use in Kosovo indicated "the need for universal, not national, norms regarding cluster bomb use" but in terms of specific recommendations avoided words like prohibition or restriction.[25] At that time, HRW saw potential for trying to engage the US and other governments to find ways to reduce the submunition failure rate, and, as shown by their February 2000 report on NATO bombing in Kosovo, considered that better implementation of existing international humanitarian rules could minimize the risk to civilians at time of use. Those in HRW's Arms Division felt these efforts needed to run their course both in the CCW and in dialogue in Washington.[26] Also, as the post-conflict UXO contamination picture in Kosovo developed from late 1999, a space was opening up for problems associated with cluster munitions to be raised in the CCW process. In view of their experience with Amended Protocol II negotiations, HRW representatives were not especially hopeful about their chances in the CCW, but awareness among governments could be raised and they would be in a position to exploit any opportunities emerging for progress there.

Other NGOs were also taking a greater interest in the work of the CCW in the wake of NATO's use of submunitions in Kosovo and the unexploded ordnance problem generated there by the use of various kinds of munitions. These included Mines Action Canada (MAC): a March 2001 MAC internal paper examined the idea of a campaign against cluster bombs, and recommended that "Mines Action Canada [take] a strong, public position in favour of a moratorium on production, sale, transfer and use of cluster bombs *as soon as possible*" and support work to address the weapon's humanitarian effects through the CCW.[27] There was also the UK Working Group on Landmines, which in late 2000 would change its name to Landmine Action. An extensive picture of the global landmine problem was already emerging, especially as part of civil society monitoring of the Mine Ban Treaty through projects such as *Landmine Monitor*.[28] Landmine Action's director, Richard Lloyd, and his colleague Rosy Cave, and those in other NGOs with experience in the Ottawa process and attending the CCW's meetings, could see that the so-called "experts of governments" in the CCW often knew very little about the field realities of dealing—or living—with mines and unexploded ordnance, and that these problems were greater in scale and more widespread than generally understood there.[29]

Meanwhile, although the Mennonites were always strapped for cash to send representatives to Switzerland, Peachey and Wiebe began to attend CCW meetings between them to the extent they could. These conferences were held in the grand Palais des Nations complex in Geneva, the headquarters of the former League of Nations and now the European headquarters of the

United Nations. It felt far removed both from the Mennonites' heartland in the midwest of the United States, or submunition-affected post-conflict communities like those in Laos that Peachey had lived and worked in. Peacocks roamed the Palais' splendid grounds and dapperly suited diplomats wandered its marble hallways with fancy brief cases. The CCW meetings themselves were formal affairs held in a large, windowless chamber, with each delegate wearing a grey surgical plastic, wired earpiece into which simultaneous interpretation in each of the six UN official languages could be piped. Representatives of international organizations and NGOs sat at the back of the room, and were permitted to speak when asked directly, or at the end of the discussion after government representatives had spoken.

On occasion, Peachey and Wiebe gave lunchtime briefings in side rooms to interested delegates on MCC research reports like *Drop Today, Kill Tomorrow: Cluster Munitions as Inhumane and Indiscriminate Weapons* or *Clusters of Death*—titles that left no doubt as to their authors' views on the weapon.[30] Their reception by CCW government delegates was often not especially warm. At one MCC lunchtime event on the margins of the CCW in November 2000, which around 60 delegates attended and for whom Peachey and Wiebe presented their findings on the impact of cluster munitions on civilians in Laos, Peachey recalled:

> This Pentagon man afterwards … raised his hand and said, "Okay, if cluster bombs are so terrible, and if we're not supposed to use cluster bombs anymore, what kind of bombs are we supposed to use? Tell us, what kind of bombs do you suggest that we use?" which was a rather awkward question for a pacifist to answer!

> I was baffled for a bit at how to respond to his question because it was so far out of the parameters within which I was used to thinking. So there was some real learning that I had to do in those situations realizing that in that context—in those rooms—the parameters of the discussion were presupposing a set of assumptions, which I myself for conscience reasons opposed. But yet I felt like I needed to be in the room to raise questions and to get people to think about the implications of the cluster bombs and how similar they were to landmines and see if it wouldn't be possible to develop some kind of momentum, some kind of tool or language that might eventually result in a treaty. But in those early years it just didn't feel very hopeful.[31]

Nevertheless, the direct messaging of the Mennonites and the more nuanced positions of other NGOs like Human Rights Watch were not falling entirely on deaf ears. If Kosovo was a wake-up call, reports of the effects of cluster munitions elsewhere during this period, such as in Chechnya by the Russians, raised further concern.[32] Cluster bombs were also dropped in the war between Eritrea and Ethiopia: in one incident on 9 May 2000 the Ethiopian air force cluster bombed the Korokon refugee camp in Western Eritrea with British-manufactured BL-755s. The attack led to extensive contamination, which was documented and cleared a short time later by the HALO Trust, a demining NGO.[33] This accumulating evidence, and the experience of the Mine Ban Treaty, energized a number of diplomats in Geneva and in capitals to begin thinking about how the CCW could be turned to humanitarian goals in the unexploded ordnance field, and to see it recover from what they perceived as a loss in its credibility following the Amended Protocol II process. From 1999, lunch meetings involving diplomats from countries such as Austria, Belgium, Canada, Ireland, Mexico, the Netherlands, New Zealand, Norway, Peru, South Africa, Sweden and Switzerland (sometimes along with the ICRC) began turning over issues related to how, in particular, explosive remnants of war (ERW) and "mines other than anti-personnel mines" could be framed effectively in the CCW setting.[34] Important figures in this group included Ambassador Steffen Kongstad from Norway, who had played a major role in the Ottawa process, New Zealand's disarmament ambassador Clive Pearson, and a recent arrival in Geneva, Dutch ambassador Chris Sanders.

EXPLOSIVE REMNANTS OF WAR

A key event occurred in September 2000, when the ICRC hosted a Meeting of Experts on Explosive Remnants of War in Nyon, a lakeside town 20km north of Geneva. The Nyon meeting served to elevate the post-conflict impacts of ERW from a like-minded concern to that of a CCW priority in a discourse that—importantly—included submunitions. The ICRC had done its homework carefully: it gathered a group of representatives from invited governments, humanitarian organizations and NGOs, and it had prepared two reports to help serve as a basis for informed discussion. The first ICRC report, written and introduced by Colin King, a former British Army explosive ordnance disposal expert, set out the basic issues and characteristics of ERW with a particular focus on submunitions.[35] The other report, written by a former ICRC lawyer turned consultant, Stuart Maslen, examined the problems created by mines and unexploded ordnance in the Kosovo conflict the preceding year.[36] Within the ICRC, the Kosovo report had been controversial, since its findings were stark about the consequences of cluster munition use in the 1999 conflict—outcomes unlikely to endear the humanitarian organization to the weapon's users. For other participants in the Nyon workshop, and later in the CCW, it was a reminder of the effects of cluster munitions on civilians more than a year after NATO's air campaign had ended.

Among the proposals the ICRC put to participants in the meeting, it asked the CCW's members to work to ban the use of submunitions against military objectives within concentrations of civilians. Had such a prohibition been in force, it might have prevented NATO from attacking the airport in Niš the preceding year. The ICRC also argued that, "in order to reduce the risk to civilians in future conflicts, cluster bomblets and other submunitions should be fitted with mechanisms which will ensure their self-destruction immediately after the device fails to explode upon impact as designed".[37]

NGOs at the meeting went further. In presenting his report on cluster bombs published by the UK Working Group on Landmines,[38] Rae McGrath called for a moratorium on the use of cluster munitions "until ways were found to reduce their post-conflict impact".[39] The reception from some major cluster munition stockpiling states present was not favourable, and the ICRC's published summary of the meeting reported that "Many participants felt that a moratorium would be difficult to achieve in light of the fact that cluster bomb submunitions had a clear military utility. However, explosive remnants of war served no military purpose and action should be taken to deal with this problem".[40] The discussion confirmed to some in the room that, in the same way that anti-personnel mines had been approached in the CCW, a weapon's alleged military utility would continue to trump humanitarian concerns about it in that setting, no matter how serious those impacts were shown to be. Participants like the Nobel co-laureate and former ICBL Coordinator, Jody Williams (and not someone to mince her words with diplomats), had already been around this CCW mulberry bush in the negotiations on Amended Protocol II, and remarked upon this in a withering broadside at the government representatives present.[41]

Nyon crystallized the major issues concerning both the post-conflict impacts of ERW as a whole, and submunitions in particular. One participant in the September 2000 expert meeting on ERW, the CCW and the later Oslo process felt that "the Oslo process grew out of the CCW, and the CCW work on this really grew out of the Nyon meeting. ... [E]ven in that meeting, we were talking about clusters".[42] It also confirmed that when debate strayed from post-conflict ERW impacts that everyone agreed were problems of munitions failing to function as intended—as it did in Nyon—to deeper questions about the acceptability of cluster munitions, it made cluster munition user states palpably uncomfortable.

Looking at the participants' list of the Nyon meeting almost a decade later, it is remarkable how many of the entities represented and individuals present there would later play significant roles in achieving a treaty to ban cluster munitions, including the ICRC itself. One person of significance to these eventual efforts not present at the Nyon meeting, however, would shortly arrive in Geneva in late 2000. Recruited by the New Zealand Ministry of Foreign Affairs and Trade to join their Disarmament Mission in Geneva as a local staff member, 21-year-old Thomas Nash had no inkling he would eventually emerge at the centre of an international campaign to address cluster munitions—or even that such a campaign would emerge.

Nash joined the New Zealand Disarmament Mission at a busy time for Geneva diplomats. Multilateral arms control work in 2000 had been dominated by a review of the 1968 Nuclear Non-Proliferation Treaty, the cornerstone of the international non-proliferation regime, and intensifying negotiations on a protocol to the 1972 Biological and Toxin Weapons Convention, the latter held in the Palais: it was widely anticipated that this process would culminate in a new agreement in 2001 (in the end, it did not). Separately, there was a multilateral process involving many Geneva diplomats on a Programme of Action to curb the illicit trade in small arms and light weapons. Meanwhile, although deadlocked since 1998, the Conference on Disarmament continued to meet weekly in the Palais des Nations, and preparations were also underway for the CCW's Review Conference in November. Nash consequently found himself thrown in at the deep end in supporting the Mission's two diplomatic negotiators, Ambassador Clive Pearson and myself. Initially employed primarily because of his fluency in French, the Mission began giving Nash a role in attending and reporting Mine Ban Treaty implementation meetings and, as the CCW process intensified, as part of its CCW delegation. Nash, like others, was struck by the contrast between the "can do" atmosphere of Mine Ban Treaty implementation meetings, and the more overt *realpolitik* of the CCW talks.

Nevertheless, momentum was building in the CCW. Capitalizing on its Nyon expert meeting, the ICRC presented a detailed report to the CCW in December 2000 proposing an ERW protocol with a number of elements—including their call for a prohibition on the use of submunitions in concentrations of civilians, and submunition self-destruct.[43] The Swiss also circulated a working paper that December, which called for fuzing mechanisms in submunitions that would ensure self-deactivation and self-destruction to a standard of at least 98%.[44] To one observer, "While a positive step in the sense of 'getting the ball rolling', the 98% solution also had a self-serving air—Swiss military experts claimed informally that Swiss submunitions had a dud rate of no higher than 2%".[45] In this sense, the discourse on cluster munitions as it was emerging in the CCW hinged upon distinctions between supposed "good" and "bad" submunitions, distinctions based on asserted but unproven technical criteria like self-destruct or self-neutralization features. This "good versus bad" mindset would dominate the way cluster munitions were viewed by most governments in the CCW and, indeed, in the ICRC and among some NGOs, until much later in the decade.

Meanwhile, the Dutch had taken an active interest in guiding work toward an agreement on ERW.[46] In December 2000, the Netherlands circulated a paper in the CCW co-sponsored by 26 states, which called for further discussions of ERW in 2001 in the lead-up to the Review Conference.[47] The goal was to achieve agreement to negotiate an ERW protocol there. To try to develop support among CCW states to this end, the Dutch followed this up with an informal meeting of governments and the ICRC in The Hague in late March 2001. NGOs were not invited, and some speculated that their exclusion was due to the unhappiness of certain large states with the results of international work on anti-personnel mines, which had slipped from their control in the consensus-based environment of the CCW and resulted in the Mine Ban Treaty.[48] What *was* clear was that the Dutch wanted buy-in from the large military states in the CCW, who after all were the major producers of ERW of many conflict situations.

The Dutch and others got their wish. In December 2001, the CCW Review Conference agreed on a mandate for work in the ensuing five-year period that included ERW, among other issues such as reducing the humanitarian impact of "mines other than anti-personnel mines" and trying to improve treaty compliance.[49] Sanders, the Dutch Disarmament Ambassador, was appointed as the CCW's ERW Coordinator to chair the work of a new

Group of Governmental Experts (GGE)—a natural step, as he had been responsible for facilitating consultations on the ERW mandate during preparations for the Review Conference. The GGE was told in the mandate to "discuss ways and means to address the issue of Explosive Remnants of War (ERW). In this context the Group shall consider all factors, appropriate measures and proposals", which included the following:

1. factors and types of munitions that could cause humanitarian problems after a conflict;

2. technical improvements and other measures for relevant types of munitions, *including sub-munitions*, which could reduce the risk of such munitions becoming ERW;

3. the adequacy of existing International Humanitarian Law in minimising post-conflict risks of ERW, both to civilians and to the military;

4. warning to the civilian population, in or close to, ERW-affected areas, clearance of ERW, the rapid provision of information to facilitate early and safe clearance of ERW, and associated issues and responsibilities;

5. assistance and co-operation.[50]

As such, the ERW mandate represented a compromise. It was plain to see that while the mandate was much better than nothing in terms of relevance to the problems caused by cluster munitions, within the ambit of ERW it would likely only tackle the post-conflict impacts of submunitions—and not concerns about the particular hazards to civilians cluster munitions posed at time of use. Nor would negotiations on ERW be likely to place specific restrictions on cluster munitions.

The ERW mandate reflected the fact that a growing number of states were concerned about the effects of cluster munitions on civilians, but set against the reluctance of the users and largest possessors of cluster munition for weapon-specific work of any kind. And all of this was in an environment in which the consensus practice ruled. At this time there was virtually no talk among states of outlawing cluster munitions as the CCW's objective—it was simply not regarded as realistic. Nor was a comprehensive ban a call heard from most NGOs, their emphasis instead being on "things to lessen the danger to civilians" such as technical improvements to submunition reliability and a prohibition on cluster munition use in populated areas as positive steps for governments to take.[51] In its proposal for an ERW protocol distributed to delegates on the margins of the CCW's preparatory meetings in September 2001, for instance, the NGO Vietnam Veterans of America, which had played a significant role as part of the ICBL in banning anti-personnel mines, said there was no case that banning submunitions would reduce civilian casualties, and would just increase demand for and thus production of unitary explosive warheads.[52]

Despite the limitations of the ERW mandate, its sole reference to submunitions would be of use over the next five-year period to those trying to sustain and build up momentum to address the humanitarian impacts of cluster munitions in more ambitious terms. Chaired by the Netherlands—a state that on the whole welcomed greater civil society participation in the CCW's work—the ERW negotiations would enable NGOs and international organizations such as the ICRC and UN Mine Action Service to keep feeding information about the humanitarian effects of cluster munitions into the CCW.[53]

AFGHANISTAN, IRAQ AND THE BIRTH OF THE CLUSTER MUNITION COALITION

As negotiations toward a protocol on explosive remnants of war progressed in the CCW in 2002 and 2003, there was growing support among all members of the CCW for the development of generic rules on clearance of ERW, information sharing to facilitate clearance and risk education, and warnings to civilian populations. But this work confirmed the impression gathered in Nyon that agreement among all of the CCW's members on weapon-specific measures would not be forthcoming. Those delegations opposed to such measures wielded various arguments. China, Pakistan and others in the developing world objected to the potential cost of technical improvements in order to improve submunition reliability. And many governments including Russia and the US said that better implementation of existing IHL rules, rather than new rules, was needed.[54]

Although the CCW's consensus practice gave these states the upper hand, the credibility of their arguments against weapon-specific restrictions on cluster munitions was being undermined by events. In late 2001, following the attacks on the World Trade Center in New York and the Pentagon in Washington DC, the US launched a military campaign to oust the Taliban regime in Afghanistan, which had lent support to Al-Qaida. The US depended heavily on its airpower to support Afghan Northern Alliance forces on the ground. Combined, these forces were able to force out the Taliban after some fierce fighting. US use of cluster bombs contributed further to Afghanistan's already extensive unexploded ordnance and mine problem left over from the earlier Soviet occupation, which had also entailed the use of many cluster munitions. Human Rights Watch researchers working in Afghanistan after the 2001 conflict reported that between October 2001 and March 2002, US forces dropped about 1,228 cluster bombs (about 5% of the 26,000 US bombs dropped during that time period) containing 248,056 submunitions. These were mainly BLU-97s delivered from the CBU-87, and the new "wind corrected" CBU-103.[55] In 232 cluster strikes, the United States hit targets across Afghanistan, including military bases, frontlines, villages where Taliban and Al-Qaida troops were hiding, and cave complexes. "Human Rights Watch found ample evidence that cluster bombs caused civilian harm" and that at least 25 civilians died and many more were injured during cluster strikes in or near populated areas—illuminating "common and recurrent problems with these weapons" and "fundamental flaws that require additional changes and new international regulation".[56] And submunition failure rates again appeared to be significant—leaving lethal, unexploded submunitions for civilians to encounter.

It was a similar story in March and April 2003 when UK and US forces invaded Iraq to oust Saddam Hussein, although this conflict differed from Afghanistan in that advancing forces fired a lot of ground-launched cluster munitions rather than dropping cluster bombs from aircraft. In particular, the US made extensive use of their Multiple Launch Rocket System (MLRS), which could rapidly deliver volleys of rockets delivering thousands of explosive submunitions onto a given location from over the horizon. And, in southern Iraq, the British fired artillery projectiles containing Israeli-manufactured M-85 submunitions.

Another difference was that, this time, NGOs explicitly warned the international community ahead of the invasion of the problems cluster munition use would cause. Human Rights Watch stated in March 2003 that "The use of cluster munitions in Iraq will result in grave dangers to civilians and friendly combatants. Based on experiences in the Persian Gulf War in 1991, Yugoslavia/Kosovo in 1999, and Afghanistan in 2001 and 2002, these dangers are both foreseeable and preventable".[57]

The 2003 Iraq conflict would also eventually confirm suspicions among NGOs that submunition failure rates in operational use were significantly higher than the failure rates claimed by cluster munition manufacturers and the militaries deploying them.[58] Moreover, HRW researchers subsequently found that US and UK forces repeatedly used cluster munitions in attacks on Iraqi positions in residential neighbourhoods, often as part of unobserved counter-battery fire. Human Rights Watch concluded, "Since Iraqi forces often occupied populated areas on the edges of towns, the attacks left thousands of duds in urban neighbourhoods and villages near the major cities of Iraq".[59] Richard Downes, a journalist from RTÉ, Ireland's national television and radio broadcaster, personally attested to such cluster munition attacks on Iraqi populated areas during the 2003 invasion. At a conference on development challenges posed by ERW, held in Dublin Castle in late April 2003, Downes told of surviving a near miss from an incoming MLRS cluster munition barrage on the outskirts of Baghdad in the invasion's last days. Organized by the NGO Pax Christi Ireland and the Irish Department of Foreign Affairs, the Dublin Castle conference brought together invited governments, international organizations and civil society[60] and featured presentations from Sanders, as Coordinator of the CCW protocol negotiations, and Landmine Action outlining the scope of the ERW global threat based on a survey report I wrote for them, which was circulated in the CCW the following June.[61] Although the Dublin Castle conference was ostensibly ERW-focused and intended to give the CCW ERW negotiations a boost toward completion, the real attention of many of those present in Dublin had turned toward what to do about cluster munitions in view of their effects in Afghanistan and Iraq,[62] something Downes's disturbing personal account underlined.

In a meeting on the margins of the Dublin Castle conference chaired by Landmine Action, a group of NGO representatives gathered to discuss how to take ERW and cluster munition issues further.[63] The reason, one participant later recalled, was because:

> it had become very evident that NGOs were operating mainly in emergency response mode on cluster munitions, sounding alarm bells whenever they were used in major conflicts, but that biannual outrage would not suffice. The time had come—with Kosovo, Afghanistan, Iraq, and CCW deliberations having raised the stakes and the possibilities—to establish expanded, sustained, proactive, and coordinated NGO work on cluster munitions.[64]

The ICBL was one obvious institutional platform for the cluster munition issue, but those involved in the steering of the landmine campaign, including

Goose representing Human Rights Watch and Paul Hannon, director of Mines Action Canada, felt that the cluster munition issue would be too much for the landmine campaign to take on. Their fear was that cluster munition campaigning would split the ICBL's attention and resources during a crucial period for implementing the Mine Ban Treaty and civil society advocacy to try to broaden its membership.[65] Thus, the decision was taken among roughly 10 NGOs to work together to launch a new NGO initiative on cluster munitions *and* ERW.

The name that eventually emerged for this initiative in the course of preparations during the summer of 2003 was the Cluster Munition Coalition (CMC). "Coalition" was chosen rather than "campaign" because "Campaign implies that we've got lots of organizations very active on it on a daily basis"—and the CMC was clearly going to depend for the foreseeable future on the willingness of member NGOs to put in time and resources.[66] Beside HRW and MAC, these initial volunteer organizations were Austrian Aid for Mine Victims, the Belgian and French wings of Handicap International, International Physicians for the Prevention of Nuclear War (Russia), Landmine Action, the Nepalese Campaign to Ban Landmines, Pax Christi Netherlands, the Landmine Struggle Unit (an Egypt-based NGO, later known as Protection) and the Mennonite Central Committee. Among those NGOs in the forefront were HRW, Landmine Action, MAC (which was funded to work on ERW research) and Pax Christi Netherlands. Coordination meetings took place in Geneva and later in Bangkok on the margins of the Mine Ban Treaty's annual meeting.

The CMC was formally launched on 13 November 2003 in The Hague, at a meeting opened by the Dutch Foreign Minister, Jaap de Hoop Scheffer (who would, the following year, become NATO's Secretary General, a post he would hold until 2009). Despite having given a €100,000 grant to Pax Christi Netherlands to help launch the CMC, Scheffer left no doubt as to the Dutch position on cluster munitions, however, and it fell well short of any kind of prohibition:

> My government would support legally binding measures on technical specifications for cluster munitions. Horrible as it may sound, the world needs better cluster bombs. ... Quite possibly some of you would have hoped for a more ambitious Dutch approach to prevention. You might like to see us support a moratorium on the use, production and trade of cluster munitions. Although I understand and sympathise with the moral basis of such a vision, I believe this is not currently attainable. As

I said, even a provision on technical specifications is too far-reaching in the eyes of some other countries at this point in time.[67]

Top priority for the Netherlands was successful completion of the ERW negotiations in Geneva. And, two weeks later on 28 November, CCW members indeed agreed on a new ERW protocol.[68] Protocol V, as the new legal instrument was known, contained a package of useful generic post-conflict measures to reduce the humanitarian impact on civilians of unexploded ordnance of all kinds. But the new treaty did not contain any specific measures on cluster munitions despite their particular post-conflict hazard, nor did it contain any provisions to deal with the problems created by cluster munitions at time of use, like issues associated with targeting. Nor is Protocol V, which eventually entered into force three years later in November 2006, necessarily retroactive in application: its provisions on areas already affected by unexploded submunitions and other ERW prior to that time are only voluntary.[69]

Moreover, in 2004 and 2005 it would become increasingly apparent that the post-conflict impacts of ERW as encapsulated in Protocol V were the low-hanging fruit in the 2001 CCW Review Conference's mandate for work. Subsequent efforts on mines other than anti-personnel mines would founder in the face of Russian and other opposition. And Pakistan, Russia and the United States, in particular, still saw no need for legally binding rules to result from the remaining ERW track Sanders had separated from his post-conflict ERW work in order to facilitate agreement on the eventual Protocol V. This continuing track related to specific preventive measures to stop ERW from occurring and IHL rules applicable to specific weapons such as submunitions.

Meanwhile, Protocol V "engendered little enthusiasm from the NGO community, even among those like Human Rights Watch that had put a great deal of work into it. The instrument had been put through the CCW grinder, and too little emerged on the other side".[70] The fortnight-old Cluster Munition Coalition made its debut statement at the November 2003 CCW meeting, noting its members' disappointment that the new ERW protocol "does not deal with cluster submunitions and other preventive measures".[71] The CMC's call echoed HRW's urging for states to agree a global moratorium on the use, production and trade of all cluster munitions until their humanitarian problems were successfully addressed.[72] Hannon from Mines Action Canada read the statement because, at this time, although the CMC had a name, a logo and some member NGOs, it had little else—such as a coordinator or full-time staff. Nor did the CMC yet have a detailed campaigning strategy (although it did have a general workplan[73]).

THE CLUSTER MUNITION COALITION

Nash left the employ of the New Zealand Disarmament Mission in December 2002 to follow his fiancée to Ottawa. In the middle of 2003, after a spell in the Canadian Foreign Ministry's Mine Ban Treaty implementation unit, he began working part-time as a consultant to MAC. Initially, Nash's role was to work as part of a multi-NGO team on a follow-up report to the 2003 Landmine Action *Explosive Remnants of War: A Global Survey*; this one to be both larger-scale and more comprehensive than its predecessor, and also covering the issue of anti-vehicle mines. By March 2004, the job had become full-time and, in addition to the ERW report work, Nash became the keeper of MAC's brief on cluster munitions. It was at this time and through the work on the report that Nash began a long-standing collaboration with Landmine Action's Richard Moyes, the lead research coordinator on that project.

That same month, Nash attended an NGO conference in Copenhagen, Denmark, organized by an NGO, DanChurchAid, and a Member of that country's Parliament, Morten Helveg Petersen. This event, entitled "Cluster bombs: Effective Weapon or Humanitarian Foe?" was intended to enable the new CMC's members to develop a campaigning strategy, as well as to create some domestic pressure on the Danish government (which possessed a stock of cluster munitions) to take a more proactive humanitarian role on the weapon in the CCW. This conference covered many different issues about campaigning on cluster munitions, but of particular interest for the purposes of this study were its discussions about the CMC's campaigning call. Participating in the conference's workshops, Nash gathered the impression that while discussions like this were useful in a general sense, not a huge amount of concrete progress was being achieved with so many disparate views being voiced on objectives and strategy.[74] On the one hand there were those participants who sought a comprehensive prohibition on cluster munitions. On the other there were those NGOs with some of the most experience participating in the CCW like HRW, Landmine Action and MAC, which were not prepared to support a ban call. HRW argued, in effect, that it was difficult to argue for more IHL rules when existing IHL had not been implemented properly by any of the users of cluster munitions, including the US, UK and the Netherlands.[75] These NGOs still hewed to a moratorium position.

Yet the CMC's three-part call, which had been declared only the preceding November, was already beginning to look anachronistic. One part called for increased resources for assistance to communities and individuals affected by unexploded cluster munitions and all other explosive remnants of war. A second element called for users of cluster munitions and other munitions that can produce ERW to accept special responsibility for clearance, warnings, risk education, provision of information and victim assistance. In effect, these calls had been largely taken care of by the agreement of CCW Protocol V a short time afterward. Those steering the CMC's development were all aware this would likely be the case; nevertheless, one rationale was that support in the future by governments for the relatively uncontroversial objectives of the ERW protocol (as the Dutch government was already doing) might also serve to supplement CMC resources for work on cluster munitions. More importantly, as they became increasingly used to the CMC's contribution as a civil society voice on ERW-related issues, this would provide it some additional credibility with governments on tackling cluster munitions. And the third, primary element of the Coalition's call— "No use, production or trade of cluster munitions until their humanitarian problems have been resolved"[76]—was far from being achieved. The formulation of the call papered over some fundamental questions about what the humanitarian problems were precisely, and (more challengingly for the cohesion of the CMC's membership) to what extent these problems really could be addressed through technical fixes to try to ensure lower submunition failure rates or selective legal measures like a prohibition on use of cluster munitions in concentrations of civilians.

Landmine Action was a strong contender to act as interim point-of-contact to coordinate the CMC as it had launched its "Clear-up! Campaign" on ERW and submunitions in early 2003.[77] But Landmine Action lacked the funds to continue such campaigning after Copenhagen in March 2004. Instead, because MAC had the financial resources and the willingness to do so, over the months following the Copenhagen meeting Nash assumed an increasing number of the day-to-day responsibilities as interim point-of-contact for the CMC's activities from his base in Ottawa.[78] At this time, for some of those individuals prominent in steering the CMC, the ambiguity of its call was seen as useful in engaging governments reluctant to take a lead on cluster munitions as a specific issue.[79] To Nash, in contrast, the equivocal nature of the CMC's cluster munition-specific call was a growing obstacle, since it was not self-evident what it meant at a time when the CMC was trying to attract NGOs to its banner and begin to build relationships with governments, especially those states in the CCW that might be persuaded to pursue complementary objectives. To be effective, those the CMC was trying to influence needed to know what the coalition stood for achieving. And those within the CMC needed a clearer sense of the game plan (whatever that was to be) and their roles within it.

VOICES IN THE WILDERNESS

Given the lack of progress in the CCW, the lack of government leadership and the lack of funding to work on cluster munitions, 2004 and 2005 were wilderness years for the CMC. Moreover, more experienced hands in the CMC's Steering Committee such as Goose and Hannon were often preoccupied with issues of Mine Ban Treaty implementation. Notably, such work included the annual *Landmine Monitor* report, which was time consuming and resource intensive. But Nash did find a kindred spirit in Richard Moyes, an Englishman from Cumbria who had begun working for Landmine Action in 2004 as a policy researcher following work in Cambodia, Sri Lanka and elsewhere for the Mines Advisory Group (MAG), a demining NGO. As Moyes and Nash got to know each other by telephone and e-mail while completing the ERW global survey, they began to feed off each other's ideas. Gradually the two men began to shape some of the intellectual framework behind what they thought the CMC could and should be doing during a period in 2004 and 2005 when the CMC was not receiving much intellectual or strategic direction from its Steering Committee (which was loosely organized at that stage) and the CCW was drifting on the cluster munition issue. They were helped in their thinking by others such as Brian Rappert, a US academic working in Britain interested in the ethical issues surrounding weapon technologies.[80]

One of Moyes's early contributions was to persuade his boss, Richard Lloyd, to reconsider Landmine Action's reluctance to go beyond a position endorsing a moratorium and technical improvements to submunition reliability. As shall be seen in the next chapter, Moyes would eventually articulate and forcefully argue that the low failure rates claimed for their submunitions by cluster munition manufacturers and user governments could not be trusted and would not stand up to scrutiny—an impression gathered from the information compiled and compared on conflicts like Iraq in the context of the ERW survey that Moyes and Nash helped to coordinate during this period.[81]

Moyes and Nash were not alone in this view. Rae McGrath, another Cumbrian and the founder of MAG, had helped set up and lead the international campaign against landmines in the 1990s as mentioned earlier, and had written and presented one of the reports on cluster munitions at the September 2000 ICRC Nyon expert meeting. McGrath was regarded as a clear communicator and someone who relished confrontation. So in 2004 Nash asked McGrath if he would present the case to governments for specific work in the CCW on cluster munitions in a side event at the CCW to be held in November. As part of his preparatory thinking, McGrath circulated a discussion paper to others within the campaign in October 2004 that cogently argued against the CMC continuing down the road of "technical fixes" like submunition reliability:

> It should not be overlooked that the major military powers have used cluster bombs in unimaginable quantities for years without ever taking any steps to reduce failure rates—their attitude was clear and could be paraphrased as *"so ten per cent fail, we'll drop ten per cent more"*. Meanwhile, the same governments consistently, as a matter of policy, denied that failure rates were unacceptably high—many still do. The reason that some countries are now considering addressing this long recognised problem is that they recognise that the legality of cluster munitions is being widely questioned and, with the Ottawa Treaty and international campaigners, and their perceived ability to motivate civil society in mind, it seems like a smart move to go some way to show good faith. This indicates that the campaign is part of the way along the road to meaningfully addressing cluster munitions already—there is no reason to give this *quick fix* solution for cluster munitions any more credibility than was given to the *"smart mines"* argument of the mid-nineties.
>
> If some nations feel that they can make their cluster weapons less prone to killing non-combatants by using self-destruct mechanisms then they should do so, but there is no reason for the coalition to endorse or even comment on such a decision since we have no way of knowing whether such mechanisms will actually achieve their aim while we **do** know that

they are not designed to address the indiscriminate properties of cluster weapons.

There is no evidence that self-destruct and similar mechanisms would substantially reduce the persistent impact of failed submunitions.[82]

In 11 pages, McGrath set out the essentials of a civil society strategy whose elements—amassing and disseminating reliable and up-to-date evidence; developing strong and accurate arguments based on this; educating the public and engaging the media; and encouraging public debate encompassing governments, the military and cluster munition manufacturers—were all eventual hallmarks of the CMC, as they had been of the ICBL in the Ottawa process. McGrath's paper articulated the logic of moving away from a "worst culprits" approach on submunitions, which Human Rights Watch,[83] Mines Action Canada and others were articulating at the time, toward banning cluster munitions outright. Indeed the CMC had even established a "technical working group" whose task it was to consider a list of the so-called "worst culprits".[84] McGrath's view, in contrast, was that even if nil post-conflict impact could ever be achieved, cluster munitions were unacceptable on the grounds of their indiscriminate effect.

There is little evidence to indicate that McGrath had much impact on the CMC Steering Committee, which collectively took the approach that it should stay the course on the established campaign call. However, McGrath's presentation to a packed room of CCW delegates in the Palais des Nations on 11 November, entitled "Cluster Munitions—Weapons of Deadly Convenience" had an incendiary effect. Focusing on use of ground-launched cluster munitions by British forces, McGrath dissected his own government's position and the situation in the CCW in direct terms, and concluded:

So here we are, back at the CCW, and if you are particularly optimistic you might hope that a solution could be found through this process. But the CCW is a diplomatic charade—this is the forum which talked endlessly and each year promised progress while landmines devastated communities throughout the world. Let's be honest, with so much invested in cluster munitions systems by the major arms producing nations represented here, what should we expect? ...

We should ask ourselves—since it would seem to be in the interests of the user forces to have weapons which work as designed—why half a century of development and combat testing has not resulted in a reliable cluster munition system? The answer must be that the concept has weaknesses which cannot be overcome and, even if the *perfect* cluster munition with a near-to 0% failure rate was designed, it would still be indiscriminate by design and by effect and, therefore, illegal.

These weapons must go the way of anti-personnel mines—it's time that civil society took the issue out of the hands of the CCW.[85]

McGrath's call to take the cluster munition issue out of the CCW was not a viable one for the time being, especially as few (if any) governments at that time would seriously contemplate following suit. But it served notice on CCW delegates that the CMC's gloves were coming off, and that it would focus on cluster munitions rather than the ERW elements of the CMC's three-part call from now on. It also had an important impact on Nash, who had chaired the briefing, and Moyes, who was in the audience, both of whom now felt they were on the right track in challenging governments more directly to account for their policies on cluster munitions.

Like McGrath, Nash and Moyes had arrived at the conclusion that "we need to push the hard angle, which says cluster munitions violate IHL even if they don't generate ERW—otherwise countries will happily say they are working on better bombs that don't generate ERW and they can say that until the cows come home while still killing civilians".[86] They knew this thinking lent itself logically toward a cluster munition ban, even if the political space available internationally, as widely conceived both by governments and in the CMC's Steering Committee, still did not. In a paper it submitted to the CCW's working group on ERW at the end of November, the CMC noted that "The only 100% reliable way to eliminate the humanitarian impact of these weapons is by removing them from military stockpiles and never using them".[87] And the CMC used the word "ban" in the working paper with regard to submunitions that lacked a self-destruct or self-deactivation mechanism, or possessed an all-ways acting fuze, or had an unreliable fuzing and arming system. But this recommendation was a reformulation of its existing call rather than a change to it, and the paper's other recommendations all related to guidance on proper use of the weapon to achieve conformity with IHL rules. At the end of 2004, there simply seemed no prospect of a comprehensive ban on cluster munitions in an environment in which some states saw no further need for work on cluster munitions at all, even if "more and more were embracing the notion that inaccurate and unreliable submunitions were unacceptable."[88]

At the same November 2004 CCW meeting in which the CMC submitted its working paper, states managed to agree to continue talking about the implementation of existing IHL principles related to ERW into 2005. The CCW also agreed to discuss "possible preventive measures aimed at improving the design of certain specific types of munitions, including submunitions, with a view to minimising the humanitarian risk of these munitions becoming explosive remnants of war".[89] The wording reflected a gradual evolution of the mandate text originally agreed at 2001's Review Conference, which took into account that Protocol V had now been negotiated. The difference for work in 2005 was that now the mandate mentioned the participation of "legal experts". Australia had hatched a plan for a questionnaire on IHL and ERW to be circulated, and the results to be analysed and presented to the CCW by a team led by Timothy McCormack, a professor of law at the University of Melbourne and the Asia Pacific Centre for Military Law.

This proposal for CCW members to complete an IHL questionnaire was put forward in March 2005, and attracted support from a range of Western countries including the US and UK, in consultation with the ICRC.[90] For those co-sponsors of the paper also advocating a specific instrument on submunitions like New Zealand, Norway, Sweden and Switzerland, the questionnaire exercise kept their bid alive for progress on new rules specific to the weapon as it asked respondents about the applicability of relevant IHL principles and their national implementation, with submunitions specifically mentioned.[91] For others such as the US and UK, it kept the cluster munition issue on a satisfactorily low heat, especially as the US delegation was pushing hard for completion of an agreement on mines other than anti-personnel mines by the end of the year in the CCW.

The week before this working paper for an IHL questionnaire was put forward in the CCW, the Dutch Ministry of Foreign Affairs hosted a related meeting—this time a small, informal brainstorming seminar on conventional arms control—in Garderen in the Netherlands. Representatives from the governments of Canada, the Netherlands, New Zealand, Norway, Sweden and Switzerland attended, as did representatives from the UN Mine Action Service, ICRC, HRW, Landmine Action, MAC and Pax Christi Netherlands. The Dutch had hosted such retreats while working on the Protocol V text during the ERW negotiations. At this meeting there was again discussion of Protocol V implementation, but the main item on participants' minds was further work on cluster munitions. There was a prevailing view that while the current ERW mandate was sufficient to discuss cluster munitions, a fresh CCW mandate would be needed if much further progress were to be made—with the CCW's next Review Conference at the end of 2006 being the logical point to try to achieve this.

Thomas Nash was listed as MAC's representative at the Garderen meeting. But he was now formally the CMC's interim coordinator, a decision made by the Coalition's Steering Committee in a meeting on the margins of the CCW the preceding November.[92] This was progress, but the CMC remained immature, and guidance on the strategic direction Nash sought to take was still unclear. In part this state of affairs reflected constraints on the amount of time and effort the lead NGOs in the Coalition were able to contribute in view of their other responsibilities and interests, which continued. It also reflected an ongoing tension among CMC members over the relationship between research and campaigning aspects,[93] with emphasis on analysis and collecting empirical evidence of the effects of cluster munitions being the preference of some Steering Committee heavyweights like HRW and Landmine Action at this time. To provide help in identifying a clearer common strategic direction, one of the Steering Committee's member NGOs, Pax Christi Netherlands, asked Rappert, a participant-observer of the Coalition since its origins, to circulate within the CMC a discussion paper on future campaigning strategies after consultations with CMC member organizations and others outside the Coalition (including myself). Rappert's July 2005 paper to the CMC made no recommendations and it did not marry the disparate views within the Coalition. But it did form a useful basis for future discussions within the CMC on campaigning, and it was helpful to Nash and others in figuring out what was being done at the individual NGO member level, and what needed to be done to build the Coalition further.[94]

OUT OF BALANCE

A second report by Rappert—which was to make another significant contribution to campaigning against cluster munitions—was entitled "Out of Balance", which Moyes edited and Landmine Action published in November 2005.[95] British Ministry of Defence officials had presented a working paper to the CCW in March 2005 on the military utility of cluster munitions—essentially, their response to arguments heard in the CCW that the use of this weapon was unacceptable in humanitarian terms.[96] In defending its continued use of the weapon, the UK said it was "committed to improving the technical aspects of its cluster munitions in order to reduce the likelihood of them becoming explosive remnants of war".[97] The UK also said that it accepted that its "air-dropped cluster bombs have a failure rate that is unacceptably high"—that is, the BL-755 and RBL-755, the two models in British use, and these would be taken out of service "in coming years" so that by 2015 "all UK submunitions will contain a self-destruct mechanism reducing their failure rate to less than 1%".[98] On the face of it, this seemed constructive. But to observers like Rappert and Moyes who were familiar with the long history of changing arguments in support of the use of cluster munitions, the UK's policy seemed riddled with contradictions. Specifically, British government officials continued to claim that an appropriate balance had been struck between military necessity (in terms of when, why and how UK forces used cluster munitions) and humanitarian concerns. This was claimed despite evidence from multiple recent conflicts in which the UK's cluster munitions had created hazards to civilians that were entirely foreseeable.

Rappert suspected that British officials did not know what they were talking about. He was also concerned that NGOs in the CMC, including Landmine Action, were too willing to accept that humanitarian issues around the use of cluster munitions could simply be taken care of by clarifying existing IHL—a concern linked to the IHL questionnaire exercise now underway in the CCW.[99] It led Rappert to carefully comb through years of British government documents and parliamentary statements regarding cluster munitions. In "Out of Balance", he reported that the UK government had undertaken no practical assessments or gathered any information of its own on the humanitarian impact of cluster munitions, and it was selective in citing humanitarian data from others to support its official statements. Rappert also formed the view that the UK had sought to discredit external data that cast it in a bad light (despite having no comparable data of its own)—including for submunition failure rates. And, for all of its confident statements in the CCW, the British government had not provided any substantive evidence for how UK forces evaluated and controlled the impact of cluster munitions during operations. Rappert concluded:

> This analysis suggests that over the last 15 years the UK government has done little or nothing to gauge the humanitarian impact of these weapons. As a result, where government officials have determined that "an appropriate balance has been struck" it would appear that they have been working from a fundamentally inadequate base of

evidence. Without this evidence, half of the "balance" is necessarily and substantially being misevaluated . ... [I]n the absence of evidence, the Government systematically gives preference to the military at the expense of increasing risk to the civilian population.[100]

The report attracted considerable attention in the UK. *The Independent* ran a full front-page story about the report, entitled "UK's deadly legacy: the cluster bomb" which also featured a larger-than-life picture of the Yugoslav KB-1 bomblet.[101] And the story noted that "Out of Balance" was prompting renewed concerns among British parliamentarians—maybe justifiably, since the report's conclusions implied that their inquiries to the Government over many years about the risks of its cluster munitions on civilians and corresponding IHL safeguards had, in effect, been fobbed off. (Some of these parliamentarians would retain an interest in the evolution of British policy on cluster munitions over succeeding years, and be helpful to UK-based NGOs in lobbying the British Government during the Oslo process.) *The Lancet*, a prominent British medical journal, noted its astonishment that "a wilful lack of evidence is considered an acceptable basis [by the British Government] for the strict implementation of international humanitarian law".[102] The upshot was that while the Landmine Action report was met with "stony silence"[103] at the CCW and the UK delegation studiously avoided engagement, Moyes, Nash and Rappert were heartened—they felt they were at last beginning to shift the burden of proof on to cluster munition users and possessors.

At the end of 2005, and after two years of existence, the Cluster Munition Coalition and its constituent NGO members were increasingly turning to the next five-yearly CCW Review Conference to be held in November 2006 as a "make-or-break" point for that process.[104] This proved to be tactically astute—and was an important contribution by the experienced ICBL veterans like Goose in particular, who had counselled against yielding to the urge to try to break the shackles of the CCW earlier. In the meantime the CMC had begun working to persuade governments to recognize that cluster munitions caused humanitarian problems (although there were still states such as China and Russia that did not acknowledge this), and planting seeds of doubt among a growing number of states about whether clarification of existing IHL would really be sufficient in addressing these hazards.

In concrete terms, however, beyond the generic post-conflict measures agreed in Protocol V, nothing further had been achieved in the CCW.

Moreover, because of the CCW's consensus practice an international legal instrument to address the humanitarian impacts of cluster munitions—whether improving submunition reliability or pledging no use in populated areas—might never be achieved as long as even a single state held out against commencing a negotiation. At no time was this prospect as glaringly obvious as at the end of 2005 after a proposal negotiated in the CCW over the two preceding years for a new protocol on mines other than anti-personnel mines was rejected by China and Russia. The CCW did agree to continue its discussions on ERW, which by now largely revolved around the IHL questionnaire exercise. Unless something dramatic changed in 2006 it seemed easily conceivable that the CCW would continue either in a near-perpetual pattern of discussion, or negotiation of a submunition proposal would inevitably be followed by CCW minimalists rejecting any worthwhile measures out of hand.

In fact, changes were already in the wind. Norway elected a new government in the autumn of 2005, and this "Red–Green" coalition committed itself to international efforts to ban cluster bombs (which will be explored in the next chapter). Norway still had to align all of its domestic policies with its international humanitarian ambitions, but by the end of 2006 its government would instigate an international process on cluster munitions outside the CCW. Second, the consequences of the Lebanon conflict in 2006 (discussed in chapter 4) would add to frustration about the pace of work in the CCW and give momentum to an outside process. Although the extent of the conflict's central role as a catalyst is disputed among those involved in the process leading to the Convention on Cluster Munitions, Israel's use of massive quantities of ground-launched cluster munitions, in particular, reinforced the hazards to civilians of these weapons in the eyes of publics and their politicians in many countries. But before either of these things manifested themselves, something else occurred that, like the later Lebanon conflict, took almost everyone in the CCW by surprise: in early 2006 Belgium set an international precedent by passing a national law banning cluster munitions.

BELGIUM'S BAN ON CLUSTER MUNITIONS

More than a decade earlier, Belgium was the first state in the world to pass a national law banning anti-personnel mines on 2 March 1995 after sustained lobbying by NGOs such as Handicap International (HI) Belgium and some skilful manoeuvring in the country's national parliament by two senators, Dardenne and Lallemand. Belgium's military had initially been dead set against such a ban, but had progressively modified its position under pressure and did not try to mobilize an opposing lobby. Actually, the law was not a total ban as it did not prohibit stockpiling of anti-personnel mines and would only cover a five-year period unless extended.[105] But it was a shot in the arm for international campaigning for a treaty to eradicate the use of the weapon, which the Ottawa process eventually achieved more than two years later. And the landmine law, passed for humanitarian reasons, did entail political and diplomatic risks for Belgium as a member of the NATO alliance, in which many partners were determined at that time to retain anti-personnel mines. Memories of their country's leadership in banning anti-personnel mines in 1995 therefore instilled a sense of humanitarian pride in many Belgian parliamentarians, and would be a factor in the later process to pass a law prohibiting cluster munitions.

In 2007, Margarita Petrova published a useful account on how ban legislation on cluster munitions and anti-personnel mines came about in Belgium. Petrova observed, "developments regarding the problem of cluster munitions largely followed the lines of the landmine issue".[106] This did not mean the process was straightforward, however, and two individuals from HI Belgium were key to the eventual outcome although they were not lawmakers themselves. One was a gentle, bespectacled man named Stan Brabant, who had extensive field experience with mine and UXO work in Afghanistan and elsewhere; and the other was a former British combat engineer turned deminer, Kevin Bryant, who was himself a landmine survivor and an articulate proponent of banning submunitions in presentations to Belgian parliamentarians and others. Bryant argued that not only were submunitions hazardous to civilians, they were also especially dangerous to explosive ordnance disposal personnel because of their small size, large numbers and sensitive fuzing.[107]

On 2 February 2005, all Handicap International sections had called for a global ban on cluster munitions. It put HI well out in front of CMC's call for a moratorium on use until humanitarian issues could be addressed. It also reflected some of the frustrations within the CMC about the nature of its moratorium-based call, although the public line was that these calls were not inconsistent with one another, since a ban could be seen as the mechanism to ensure "the humanitarian concerns have been addressed" as per the requirement set out in the CMC call.[108] A month later, HI Belgium appealed to the Belgian Senate to work toward such a ban and a few weeks after that, on 7 April, they held briefings in partnership with HRW and another NGO, Netwerk Vlaanderen, entitled "Cluster Munitions: as Wrong as Landmines—European banks and firms involved in cluster munitions" aimed at financial institutions and the media. The speakers urged governments to get rid of cluster munitions, and banks and private companies to divest themselves from companies involved in their production.[109] The two briefings attracted a lot of media attention in Belgium in newspapers,[110] on radio and on television, and two Belgian arms companies, Forges de Zeebrugge and Mecar, immediately denied involvement in the production of "fragmentation bombs or any other weapon of that kind".[111]

The 7 April briefings led HI Belgium into tense exchanges with Belgium's arms producers. They also piqued the interest of Belgian parliamentarians, and a week later Philippe Mahoux, a leading Socialist senator formerly with the NGO Médecins sans Frontières and possessed of a strong interest in humanitarian issues, tabled draft legislation to ban the production, maintenance, trade, distribution, import and transportation of "fragmentation bombs". The draft bill used the term *bombes à fragmentation*, which was a poor French translation of cluster bombs in wide use in the press at that time. And, to Brabant and his colleagues at HI Belgium who only learned of Mahoux's presentation of a draft bill from a parliamentary press release, the text of the draft bill struck them as vague. With Bryant's technical help, Brabant began a dialogue with Mahoux's office to try to help them in reframing the draft bill text, with a definition of cluster munitions based on the draft International Mine Action Standards (IMAS).

Hearings in the Senate's Defence and Foreign Affairs Commission were held on 28 June. HI Belgium representatives included Bryant, who spoke movingly about his own experiences as a deminer and made the appeal to parliamentarians that "by agreeing to ban cluster munitions we can at least make the peace that follows conflict safer for non-combatants".[112] Ministry of Defence representatives came to the Senate hearings with a big box of different kinds of submunitions, and in essence tried to show that the cluster munition issue was very complicated—and therefore not amenable to a prohibition approach.[113] Instead, they argued for an exclusion from the Mahoux bill for those submunitions with self-destruct or self-neutralization mechanisms because this would make it easier for Belgium to meet its international commitments, especially to NATO.[114] It was not enough to persuade the Senate however, especially as the bill also had the support of one of Mahoux's political rivals in the Senate, Isabelle Durant of Ecolo (a francophone Green party in Belgium), who had also been briefed along with Mahoux's people by HI Belgium on the need to clarify what a cluster munition was in the draft bill, and the reasons for a ban. Durant's support was crucial in the Commission accepting that the term *bombes à fragmentation* should be replaced by *sous-munition* (submunition), defined as "any munition that, to perform its tasks, separates from a parent munition. This definition includes all munitions/explosive ordnance designed to explode at some point in time following dispersal or release from the parent cluster munition".[115]

The Ministry of Defence, temporarily beaten back, tried again a week later to persuade the Commission to adopt a more restrictive definition but these efforts did not succeed. Instead, the Senate unanimously adopted a revised text banning the use, "carrying", production, maintenance, trade, distribution, import and transportation of submunitions two days later on 7 July, and forwarded the bill to the House of Representatives, Belgium's other national legislative chamber.

The same day, the European Parliament adopted a resolution calling for a ban on investments in landmines and cluster munitions, which drew further media and public attention.[116] But Belgium's arms industry was not going to take all of this lying down. On 16 July the head of Forges de Zeebrugge— one of the companies named in the April NGO briefing—was interviewed on state-owned television, asking to be heard in Belgium's Parliament on the cluster munition bill. The interview signalled that the defence industry, which had not even been invited to the Senate's mid-year hearings, was mobilizing. By November, when the House of Representatives' Defence Commission were due to consider the Mahoux bill, Forges de Zeebrugge and other arms companies were lobbying hard against a ban law using the threat of job losses in Wallonia, where most of them were based, as an argument they knew would resonate with parliamentarians.[117] In contrast, the Ministry of Defence stood back from the debate. Thus, the draft bill that had sailed through the Senate comparatively easily was to become a highly controversial showdown between those forces in the House of Representatives arguing that the weapon was unacceptable on humanitarian grounds, and those concerned about the economic impacts of ban legislation for Belgium.

On 23 November 2005 the House of Representatives' Defence Commission decided to hold a hearing on 19 December with the arms industry, Ministry of Foreign Affairs and NGOs. At this hearing, industry lobbied for an exception to the ban bill to exclude cluster munitions containing fewer than 10 submunitions and a failure rate less than 1%. But NGOs, especially HI Belgium (which argued that the industry's proposal would not solve the problem of civilian casualties from submunitions), were well prepared. A media trip to Kosovo that HI Belgium organized shortly before the hearings to show the effects of cluster munitions on the population meant that the controversy in parliament attracted wide media coverage that focused on humanitarian impacts, and strengthened the hand of those calling for the ban. Moreover, a petition against cluster munitions HI launched earlier in the year had by now attracted more than 200,000 signatures (a number that increased to 300,000 by the time the law was eventually passed in February 2006). Joint briefings with foreign NGOs underlined international support and efforts in other European countries to a similar end. The CMC, for its part, mobilized its network of members through a number of action alerts asking them to write to lawmakers in Belgium, ensuring they heard the global nature of the civil society call for action. This "NGO mobilization was highly instrumental in maintaining parliamentary support for the law"[118] and as a result the amendments proposed by the arms industry failed.

Nevertheless, passing the Mahoux bill proved to be a struggle that continued throughout the winter. An attempt to put the draft legislation to a vote in the House of Representatives on 25 January 2006 was prevented by filibustering from the political far right, which had aligned itself with the arms industry's concerns. On 9 February Forges de Zeebrugge workers demonstrated against a ban on cluster munitions (to my knowledge, the only time this has occurred anywhere). And throughout February the arms industry and NGOs supporting a ban sparred with each other in the media. In the end, Belgium's legislators settled the matter by passing not one but two laws on cluster munitions. On 16 February the House of Representatives adopted the Mahoux bill without amendment (112 in favour, 2 against and 22 abstentions), but a week later the leaders of the four major political parties tabled another bill to clarify the first law's scope.[119] This legislation, which was passed on 30 March in the House of Representatives and in the Senate on 3 May, excluded non-explosive submunitions (like those for smoke or electronic counter-measures) and:

systems that contain several munitions only designed to pierce and destroy armoured vehicles, that can only be used to that end without any possibility to indiscriminately saturate combat zones, including by the obligatory control of their trajectory and destination, and that, if applicable, can only explode at the moment of the impact, and in any case cannot explode by the presence, proximity or contact of a person.[120]

Was this really a cluster munition ban? Petrova, in considering this in 2007 as the early stages of the Oslo process unfolded, concluded the following:

the second piece of legislation seemed to satisfy everyone and the government coalition partners from the Socialist and the Liberal Party that were bitterly divided over the first law finally reached consensus with this compromise formulation … . Thus the definition in the second law catered to the interests and demands of a diverse group of stakeholders including NGOs, the arms industry, unions, and the military, but this consensus was obviously built upon its vagueness and the ability of each to interpret it as they saw fit. Despite (or rather because of) this vagueness, the new law made possible the achievement of consensus on the issue of cluster munitions nationally in a way consistent with Belgian domestic political culture. Importantly, it also provided NGOs with the opportunity to project internationally the image of Belgium as a trailblazer in banning cluster munitions, whose example would ineluctably be followed by other states (while obscuring details and nuances in the Belgian legislation).[121]

With the benefit of hindsight, the Belgian experience underlined something else important: because it was relatively straightforward to stigmatize the notion of cluster munitions in view of the growing evidence of their humanitarian impact, defining the weapon for the purposes of restriction or prohibition would be hard fought. In presenting the legislation as a triumph in international fora such as the CCW in the first half of 2006, NGOs such as HI Belgium and the CMC would obviously accentuate the positive rather than draw attention to the definitional exclusions. What shall be seen, and what Petrova could not have known when she wrote the analysis above, was that in defining cluster munitions, participants in the Oslo process would—in the end—reach a formulation not dissimilar to the Belgian law in excluding non-explosive submunitions and so-called "sensor-fuzed" or "advanced" submunitions. A crucial point, however, is that the definition achieved in Dublin in May 2008 would not be at all vague, although it would require some highly unorthodox elements such as a weight criterion to close possible loopholes in the international ban.[122]

THE FUTURE IS NOW

The achievement of Belgian national legislation on anti-personnel mines in 1995 had largely been an indigenous campaign.[123] Although supported by the first large-scale mobilization of the CMC membership, it was to be again on cluster munitions in 2005 and early 2006 and, as such, was a campaign predominantly fought below the diplomatic radar of the CCW. Belgium's national ban on cluster munitions was therefore something of a surprise to most of the CCW's participants when announced there in March 2006. Yet for other CCW members, particularly Belgium's European partners, it was perhaps difficult to know how profound its ban law really was. To be sure, it added strength to calls in the European Parliament and among national parliaments in several countries such as France, Germany and the UK for cluster munitions to be restricted or prohibited. But among CCW diplomats themselves there was something of a sense that, although Belgium was a NATO member and once a cluster munition producer, its ban law was not necessarily such a significant precedent in view of that country's small size, low-key diplomatic profile on this issue, and peculiar domestic politics.

Norway's delegation lost no time in publicly congratulating Belgium for its new national legislation banning cluster munitions.[124] The CMC was also visibly buoyed in its statement to the CCW at that March 2006 session.[125] For their part, Belgian diplomats appeared embarrassed,[126] and were to play little in the way of an international leadership role in either the CCW or Oslo process to eventually follow—Belgium would not even join the Oslo process core group of governments to push an international ban treaty forward. Crucially, though, Belgium's law helped to persuade Norwegian policymakers that they needed to move forward on the promise made in their new coalition government's declaration to "work for the introduction of an international ban on cluster bombs".[127] And it was becoming abundantly clear to them even before the conflict in Southern Lebanon that this ban would have to be pursued outside the CCW if it was to stand a fighting chance of being achieved. How this view emerged in Norway is the subject of the next chapter.

CHAPTER 3

NORWAY AND CLUSTER MUNITIONS

From at least as early as the 1990s in Norway, cluster munitions were increasingly seen as at odds with the country's humanitarian credentials among the public and many parliamentarians. Until 2006, however, Norway's authorities had—like most others in states participating in the Convention on Certain Conventional Weapons (CCW) talks in Geneva—sought to differentiate between "good" and "bad" cluster munitions on the basis of presumptions about their relative accuracy and reliability. And Norway was a cluster munition possessor at the turn of the century, with both air-delivered and ground-launched cluster munitions in its military arsenal. How then did Norway become a major instigator of an international process to ban the weapon?

Norway had long-standing humanitarian concerns about anti-personnel weapons of various kinds, concerns that encompassed cluster munitions. For instance, Norway co-sponsored Sweden's 1974 proposal on anti-personnel weapons to the Diplomatic Conference in Geneva, as discussed in chapter 1. Yet Norway's outlook on the world differed from its more populous neighbour to the east. Sweden had remained neutral during the Second World War, while Norway had been brutally occupied by Nazi Germany for several years from 1940. Sweden was never militarily allied to the West during the Cold War; Norway was a member of NATO. NATO's strategic planning throughout the Cold War anticipated that the Warsaw Pact conventional forces would outnumber those of NATO members in a European conflagration, and Dual-Purpose Improved Conventional Munitions (DPICM) were thus seen as important defensive weapons. In Norway's situation, such weapons seemed especially relevant to its military as the country shared a land border with the Alliance's Soviet adversary. And Norway's fears of Russian incursion into the far north of Norway did not recede entirely after the end of the Cold War. In the event of conflict with Russia, Norway would depend on its NATO allies to come to its aid, and Norwegian policymakers were traditionally concerned that Norway be seen as pulling its weight both militarily and diplomatically in the Alliance.

The Norwegian military's possession of, and presumed willingness to use, cluster munitions were not without critics. Norwegian society had a strong humanitarian tradition with roots in Protestant missionary work and relief. Coupled with a social-democratic orientation to Norwegian politics, it "made the promotion and contribution to developmental assistance and equitable economic development a central feature of Norway's foreign policy during (and after) the Cold War".[1] And Norway's resources as a donor—afforded in large part by its relatively new-found oil wealth—gave it significant clout by the standards of the world's less-populous states. Moreover, NATO's intervention in Kosovo in 1999 against Serbia occurred while Norway's role in banning anti-personnel mines was still fresh in the public consciousness, especially as the Mine Ban Treaty's final negotiations had taken place in Oslo in September 1997. The presence of mines in Kosovo, and the problem of unexploded ordnance there largely created by the use of air-dropped cluster munitions by NATO, served to regenerate public stigma in Norway about the latter weapon's humanitarian acceptability.[2]

In the middle of June 2001, a motion was passed in Norway's national parliament, the *Storting*, for Norway to actively support international efforts that might lead toward a prohibition of cluster bombs—along the lines of the ban on anti-personnel mines Norway had played a leading role in achieving as part of the Ottawa process.[3] In June 2001, "international efforts" meant the CCW in Geneva, where diplomats were preparing for that Convention's Second Review Conference (see chapter 2). Two months later, on 14 August, Norway's Ministry of Foreign Affairs wrote to the *Storting* to report that although there was no proposal for a prohibition of cluster bombs on the table at the CCW, its diplomats were participating actively in discussions toward negotiating a protocol on explosive remnants of war (ERW), and it could not be excluded that a restriction or ban on cluster bombs might be an outcome.[4] Later that year, Norway also decided that its air force contribution in support of the US campaign to topple the Taliban in Afghanistan would not use cluster munitions.[5]

In October 2001, Jens Stoltenberg's Labour government was replaced by a centrist minority government led by Kjell Magne Bondevik, a conservative. Now it was up to the new government to make good on the June 2001 *Storting* motion. However, Bondevik's government did not really appear to have much enthusiasm for leading the international charge on new rules for cluster munitions beyond retaining the *Storting*'s confidence, on which it depended. It is conceivable that controversy about cluster munitions might eventually have receded in Norway. But, in October 2002, the issue returned to prominence because of an incident in Hjerkinn, which was host to a large test firing ground belonging to Norway's military, which it allowed other NATO countries to use. At about 10h30 in the morning on 7 October, two F-16 strike jets—one Dutch plane piloted by a Norwegian, the other a Norwegian plane piloted by a Dutchman—each dropped a cluster bomb in the test firing ground as part of a joint exercise that also included Belgian forces (which were not involved in the bombing). One of the cluster bombs was an US-manufactured CBU-87 containing BLU-97 submunitions; the other was a British BL-755. Each were aimed at a target area of around 400m by 600m. Both of the cluster bombs missed their targets; one roughly 300m short, and the other 400m beyond the target, both outside the designated drop zone—although still within the firing ground's boundaries. Four days later Norway's defence forces informed the press that explosive ordnance disposal teams were commencing the task of surveying and clearing unexploded submunitions resulting from the incident.[6]

There was a strong reaction to the Hjerkinn incident when news of it reached the media and the *Storting*. Had not the Norwegian military stopped using cluster bombs? Why, then, were they being used on Norwegian soil, especially in one of the country's most scenic areas? The conservative government's Defence Minister Kristin Krohn Devold was targeted for criticism as it became apparent that she had not been aware of the exercise involving cluster bombs. Neither she nor Norwegian Defence Headquarters were informed beforehand by its District Command East, which supervised the Hjerkinn exercise.

One result of the Hjerkinn incident was that Defence Headquarters issued a directive on 25 October that any use of cluster bombs on Norwegian soil was prohibited with immediate effect—in future the use of any air-delivered cluster munitions in peacetime training and exercises would need the Defence Ministry's explicit, prior approval.[7] There were also hearings in the *Storting* in January 2003 about the incident, in which military representatives were called upon to present their views, as well as others such the Norwegian Red Cross's Secretary General at the time, Jan Egeland, and Norwegian People's Aid.[8] These hearings generated criticism of the government among opposition parliamentarians and in the media, and also some confusion. Crucially, at this time when defence officials and military people referred to cluster munitions or cluster bombs, what they were talking about was air-delivered cluster weapons, *not* ground-launched systems. Ground-launched "cargo ammunition" was portrayed by the Norwegian military as different from cluster munitions, and its representatives at the hearings made much of the stringency of dud rate testing for newer weapons like these in the Norwegian arsenal. Conversely, older air-delivered cluster munitions such as Rockeye and those containing BLU-97 submunitions were portrayed as "bad stuff",[9] and later that year Norway's own stockpile of old Rockeye air-delivered cluster munitions was to be scrapped. A Norwegian working paper submitted to the CCW in November 2003 explained that this was "because of their low level of precision and high dud rate. ... Furthermore, the [Norwegian government's instructions to the defence forces] state that cluster munitions with high dud rates/without self-destruct mechanisms shall under no circumstances be acquired by the Norwegian armed forces".[10] In the same paper, Norway's government proposed regulations on the use of cluster munitions, as, in its view, existing international humanitarian law rules "do not provide sufficient protection for the civilian population against the humanitarian consequences related to ERW".[11] In sum, while air-delivered cluster munitions were on the way out, it was clear that in 2003 the Norwegian government had no plans to remove their ground-launched cluster munitions from service.

GOOD VERSUS BAD

The CCW's proceedings in Geneva during this period showed that the discourse about "good" versus "bad" cluster munitions was not limited to Norway. As outlined in chapter 2, CCW negotiations during 2002 and 2003 on a protocol on ERW focused on generic measures to reduce the humanitarian consequences of munitions that failed to function as intended, or which were abandoned. However, in the wake of various International Committee of the Red Cross (ICRC) and NGO reports about the post-conflict impacts of unexploded submunitions,[12] it was becoming clearer that submunitions were a particular problem because, for instance, of design and use factors such as their small size and dispersal in very large numbers. Nevertheless, there was little appetite among many CCW member states for inclusion of specific rules on submunitions in the draft ERW protocol, and many governments at the talks thought that the particular post-conflict impacts of submunitions could instead be ameliorated through technical means such as better design, electronic fuzing or self-destruct or self-neutralization features. In other words, there was a prevailing view among

CCW experts that while there might be a case that older, air-delivered submunitions such as the BLU-63 or Rockeye were bad, newer designs did not suffer the same high dud rates and therefore were acceptable and improvable weapons that did not require specific regulation.

Grethe Østern and a few others in Norway were not convinced that the good versus bad submunitions debate was useful. In 1999, Østern had worked at the NATO-led Kosovo Force (KFOR) Headquarters as a press officer with the Norwegian army in the wake of NATO's air campaign. She had seen submunition contamination for herself, particularly of US-made BLU-97s, in the course of travel around the province with Italian explosive ordnance troops, and had learned of fatal accidents in the course of BLU-97 clearance that had killed British Army Gurkhas. On returning to Norway, Østern began working at the Norwegian Red Cross, and was eventually assigned to its International Humanitarian Law (IHL) section, talking with parliamentarians on issues such as cluster munitions. (The ICRC had earlier asked Red Cross national societies to take up the issue of explosive remnants of war, including cluster munitions, and the Norwegian Red Cross had obliged.) Østern could sense the frustration of interested opposition politicians that not enough was being done to fulfil the June 2001 *Storting* motion on cluster munitions and she convinced the Norwegian Red Cross to send her to the CCW's Group of Governmental Expert meetings in Geneva as an observer to try to learn more, and to see what Norway's diplomatic delegates at the talks were doing to make good on the government's promise for international action.[13]

What Østern saw of the CCW certainly did not overwhelm her with optimism. It was increasingly apparent that there would be powerful opposition in the CCW to any prohibition on cluster munitions, even of the oldest systems. And, as yet, no state—Norway included—was championing the cause of addressing the humanitarian impacts of cluster munitions with a clear call for action. In November 2003, the CCW agreed its ERW protocol, but the new instrument contained no measures specific to cluster munitions, despite the particular post-conflict problems that they caused now being common knowledge among governments at the talks. Nor was this increased awareness followed up with specific, dedicated work on regulating the weapon. Instead, further CCW talks in Geneva between 2003 and 2005 were to focus mainly on US-led proposals for restrictions on aspects of the design and use of "mines other than anti-personnel mines" (anti-vehicle mines).[14] To try to keep the issue of cluster munitions alive during 2004 and

2005, those CCW delegations with an interest in the cluster munition issue from a humanitarian perspective such as Austria, Ireland, the Netherlands, New Zealand, Norway, Sweden and Switzerland promoted an exercise in which CCW members states would complete an IHL questionnaire for the purposes of analysis in a report by an international legal expert. It was not much, but it was something.

However, continued low-intensity pressure on the issue in Norway was beginning to have an impact on policy there. Norwegian NGOs, including the Norwegian Red Cross and Norwegian People's Aid, and Cluster Munition Coalition (CMC) and Human Rights Watch (HRW) representatives briefed Norwegian parliamentarians on cluster munitions in June 2005, and this appeared to have an impact on the centrist Agrarian Party's platform for the upcoming elections.[15] Others were paying attention to cluster munitions in the Norwegian system too. Since the early 1990s, the Norwegian state had received substantial revenue from its petroleum industry, some of which was invested in the Government Petroleum Fund—making that fund one of the world's largest public funds investing internationally.[16] In November 2004, the Norwegian government adopted ethical guidelines for the Fund that contained mechanisms for negative screening of companies and ad hoc exclusions from the Fund's portfolio. The guidelines also contained criteria for exclusion of companies that produced weapons, which may through normal use violate humanitarian principles of proportionality and distinction.[17] Importantly, the Fund's Advisory Council on Ethics overseeing implementation of the guidelines did not limit itself to recommendations that the Norwegian government disinvest in companies producing weapons already banned by international treaty, such as anti-personnel mines. Certain weapons *not* clearly prohibited under international law might also be considered to violate fundamental humanitarian principles.

On this basis, the Advisory Council on Ethics for the Government Petroleum Fund recommended on 16 June 2005 that companies producing key components of cluster weapons (such as fuzes, guidance components or canisters) be excluded from the Fund's investment "universe". Among those companies the Council advised should be specifically excluded from the Fund were large arms manufacturers such as General Dynamics Corporation, Raytheon, Lockheed Martin, Alliant Techsystems, the European Aeronautic Defence and Space Company (EADS) and Thales. In explaining its view, the Advisory Council noted in its recommendation that:

the principle of distinction could be violated through use of cluster weapons for the following reasons: *During* an attack, explosive devices are scattered indiscriminately over a large area and it is difficult to avoid civilian casualties. *After* an attack, many types of cluster munitions remain unexploded and therefore continue to constitute a danger to the civilian population.[18]

The Advisory Council also decided that not all cluster weapons fell within its criteria for exclusion. "Advanced munitions"—later referred to in the Oslo process as sensor-fuzed submunitions—that each contained no more than 10 submunitions per unit were exempted from the Council's recommendation. The Council's Chair, Gro Nystuen, later explained why:

As the bomblets are target seeking and made to detonate only when they hit armoured vehicles, they were deemed to be of limited risk to civilians during hostilities. The weapon was therefore not classified as an "area weapon" designed to hit randomly over a large area. Moreover, this weapon type contains better fuse mechanisms resulting in lower failure rates, thereby posing less danger to civilians after hostilities. For these reasons, advanced munitions were not considered to be in violation of fundamental humanitarian principles.[19]

The Norwegian government adopted this recommendation soon afterward and excluded these cluster munition producers from the Fund. It is difficult to assess the material impact of this decision. In all likelihood, the direct effects were not at all great, and had reputational rather than financial consequences for those corporations named in the June 2005 and subsequent cluster munition-related recommendations of the Advisory Council. But the impact of the recommendation was significant in at least two other ways. Firstly, it contributed to the stigmatization of cluster munitions as a nasty, questionable type of weapon, especially as the recommendation by the Advisory Council on Ethics could be cited by others growing increasingly uneasy about their own national policies on production, possession or use of cluster munitions, like in Belgium.[20] Secondly, the recommendation served to expose an emerging gap in the Norwegian government's policies. By the Advisory Council's criteria and description of cluster munitions, the Norwegian military's own stocks of cargo ammunition could raise similar concerns under the IHL principle of distinction as the cluster munitions produced by companies that had been excluded from the Fund.

As far as the principle of distinction was concerned, however, Norway's defence forces argued that cargo ammunition out-performed air-delivered cluster munitions at time of use because artillery shells containing submunitions would go where they were targeted—unlike the cluster bombs that went askew in the Hjerkinn exercise in October 2002. This, of course, failed to address the question of the area effect of the weapon. But, increasingly, the central issue around which changes to Norway's policy on cluster munitions would turn concerned submunition failure rates—how many would remain after an attack "and therefore continue to constitute a danger to the civilian population" (in the words of the Advisory Council on Ethics).[21] Confident in its belief that Norway's stock of cargo ammunition had a "less than 1% failure rate", the Norwegian delegation to the CCW in July 2004 announced that Norway had introduced a national "maximum limit of acceptable dud rate of submunitions to 1 per cent. This limit will apply, regardless of type of munition, regardless actual climatic conditions and regardless the terrain in the target area".[22]

Norway's 1% policy sounded good in theory. However, to some, especially among NGOs with field experience in submunition contamination, such a failure rate claim (which was also coming from other quarters in the CCW, such as the UK[23]) sounded too good to be true. As was to be observed later during the Oslo process:

> there are strong grounds for suspecting that the 1% standard has been made up in an arbitrary manner without any consideration of either how it related to reality of civilian harm (the problem that it purportedly solves) and without consideration of how it would be interrogated. The most probable explanation is that the standard has been set because producers and users have determined that 1% is the lowest failure rate reasonably achievable under test conditions and therefore it sets a sufficiently challenging target for them. This approach would not seem to be consistent with a strong commitment to addressing civilian harm from cluster munitions.[24]

How could such claims of 99% submunition reliability actually be tested in a manner that adequately satisfied concerns about the government's objectivity? And, just as importantly, how could this be squared with calls from opposition politicians and NGOs for cluster munitions to be banned? Eventually, following a change of government and the emergence (or re-emergence, in some cases) of several key individuals in the Norwegian cluster munition policy setting, these questions would be answered.

THE "NORWEGIAN MODEL"

This book underlines numerous examples of an informal network of individuals being significant in the eventual achievement of a treaty banning cluster munitions. It was certainly true in the context of the development of Norway's policies toward the weapon. The nature of Norwegian society is still, as one political scientist examining Norway's domestic policy on landmines and cluster bombs described it, a "consociational democracy" in which consensual policymaking is emphasized. And there are many NGOs, including the influential Norwegian Red Cross, Norwegian Church Aid, Save the Children, Norwegian People's Aid and the Norwegian Refugee Council, which maintain close dialogue with the government and with different arms of the civil service bureaucracy.[25]

Although some had changed roles, several figures important to Norway's active participation in the core group of states driving the Ottawa process toward an anti-personnel mine ban treaty in the 1990s were again to become significant in the context of emerging efforts to deal with cluster munitions. They provided important continuity in the Norwegian bureaucracy, and a bank of experience on which to later draw in the course of the Oslo process. Chief among them was Ambassador Steffen Kongstad, the Ministry of Foreign Affairs' Deputy Secretary General for Humanitarian Affairs. Kongstad had a background in NATO security policy, and had also been posted to Norway's Permanent Mission to the United Nations in Geneva from the mid-1990s—becoming an important figure in the achievement of the Mine Ban Treaty. Norway's Ambassador in Geneva, Wegger Christian Strømmen, had headed the Legal Secretariat of the Oslo negotiations on the Mine Ban Treaty in 1997, and would be eventually cross-posted from Geneva in 2007 to Washington DC; Strømmen would be in significant part responsible for maintaining dialogue with the US during the Oslo process. Another person centrally involved on the Norwegian side during the Ottawa process was Gro Nystuen, a Ministry of Foreign Affairs expert in international law who had drafted the Oslo conference's rules of procedure, among other things. Nystuen subsequently left the ministry to take up a post at the University of Oslo, and she also headed the Government Petroleum Fund's Advisory Council on Ethics.

There was also continuity on the civil society side. An important person in this respect was Per Nergaard, a tall, strapping and utterly bald gentleman with bright blue eyes and an anarchic sense of humour, who headed the Mine Action Unit at Norwegian People's Aid (NPA). In the mid-1980s, as a young Norwegian army officer, Nergaard became involved in mine, submunition and other unexploded ordnance (UXO) clearance in Lebanon, and in 1992 he joined NPA to help start its first humanitarian demining programme in Cambodia. NPA played an important part during the Ottawa process in 1996 and 1997, both in the International Campaign to Ban Landmines and in working with the Norwegian government, and for this work Nergaard recruited a young policy specialist, Christian Ruge, who would go on from NPA to eventually advise the Norwegian Ministry of Foreign Affairs throughout the Oslo process. Ruge's successor at NPA, Sara Sekkenes, would later join the United Nations Development Programme's Bureau of Crisis Prevention and Recovery in January 2006 and spearhead that agency's efforts in support of the Oslo process.

Following Sekkenes's departure, Nergaard was on the lookout for a suitable successor:

> I was in need of a new policy advisor and I had taken notice of this little, Colombo-like lady—Detective Colombo. She reminds [me] a lot of Colombo because of her style, naïve approach—doesn't look dangerous at all—but he, Colombo, solves every mystery and never gives up. I took notice of her when she was working at the IHL department of the Red Cross, because they were alongside NPA trying to push on this issue. And we got into dialogue and I realized that she didn't have the framework in the Red Cross sufficient for her ambitions on this issue. And I knew that in NPA I could easily give her all the bells and whistles and the things she needed to get this started.[26]

"Detective Colombo" was Grethe Østern. In February 2006, she left the Norwegian Red Cross to join the NPA Mine Action Unit.

Both Nergaard and Østern were sure something could be done internationally on cluster munitions, despite the CCW's inertia—if the Norwegian government could be pushed toward a leadership role. For years, NGOs like NPA and the Norwegian Red Cross had told the Norwegian government it was not doing enough to lead efforts to address cluster munitions, and had focused increasingly on informing and lobbying the various opposition parties in the *Storting* as it became clear that Bondevik's government did not share their level of ambition. Now, the outcome of parliamentary elections in mid-September 2005 had provided a real opportunity to both re-examine Norway's domestic position on cluster munitions and prod it into more action on the international stage. A "Red–Green" coalition comprised of the Labour, Socialist Left Party and the Centre (or Agrarian) Party now held a small majority of seats in the *Storting*, and were asked by the King of Norway to form a government. Difficult negotiations ensued during October 2005 at the Soria Moria Hotel in the hills above Oslo between the three parties in order to agree on a common governing platform. The outcome was the Soria Moria Declaration, which among its elements on "Peace, Appeasement, Disarmament and a Strengthened UN" contained a commitment to "work for the introduction of an international ban on cluster bombs".[27]

Beside Norway's consociational political culture, another important aspect of Norwegian political life is "elite circulation"[28]—of people turning up in different roles over time on similar issues. A number of those in the Red–Green coalition that would assume government led by Prime Minister Jens Stoltenberg had backgrounds in issues relevant to cluster munitions. The new Deputy Minister of Defence, Espen Barth Eide, had earlier held senior positions in the Norwegian Institute of International Affairs. The incoming Minister of International Development, Erik Solheim, had been a prominent landmine ban supporter, and had in his youth worked for the NGO Handicap International, which was now active in the Cluster Munition Coalition.[29] And the incoming Foreign Minister, Jonas Gahr Støre, had headed the Norwegian Red Cross in the years prior to the parliamentary election. In that role Støre had been sensitized to the humanitarian impacts of cluster munitions by Østern, and by representatives of the ICRC's Legal Division in Geneva. (Støre's immediate predecessor, Jan Egeland, became UN Undersecretary-General for Humanitarian Affairs and Emergency Relief Coordinator in June 2003, and would be outspoken about the effects of cluster munitions on civilians in the conflict in Southern Lebanon in mid-2006; he had had been Deputy Foreign Minister during the Ottawa process.)

Norway now had its first majority governing coalition since 1985, which contained a number of supporters of international efforts to address the impacts of cluster munitions. The way toward a national ban policy and a role in leading international efforts toward international agreement on a prohibition was not necessarily clear, however. Norway's diplomats were instructed to take the moral high ground in the CCW on the humanitarian effects of cluster munitions and the need to start efforts to tackle them through international restrictions, but at home the 1% failure rate doctrine remained in place. Moreover, it was still not clear in statements from the relevant ministers and senior officials in the new government whether cargo ammunition constituted cluster munitions.

Long before Østern's arrival at NPA, Nergaard's strategy with policymakers was to do what NPA had done in the 1990s in the lead-up to the Ottawa process: develop partnerships with opinion formers within the government and the bureaucracy.[30] He saw dialogue with the Ministry of Foreign Affairs' Humanitarian Affairs Department as a logical place to start, especially as Nergaard had a long history of contacts with that department, and with Kongstad in particular, on landmine and ERW issues. As someone familiar with the ways of Geneva and with multilateral disarmament processes such as the CCW's Amended Protocol II negotiations, Nergaard knew Kongstad harboured doubts about the likelihood of that process ever agreeing robust restrictions or prohibitions on cluster munitions. And other advisors within that department with experience of the CCW's methods, such as Susan Eckey and Annette Abelsen, were of similar mind.[31] A big obstacle, as Kongstad saw it, however, was that unlike in the Ottawa process, a strong international civil society campaign was lacking on cluster munitions. Also, based on his earlier experience with landmines, Kongstad felt that a clearly defined objective for an international cluster munition campaign, as well as adequate financial and other resources, including "the right people", would be essential.[32] And while Kongstad was certain the Norwegian government had effective interlocutors on the NGO side in the form of NPA and others, he was less sure that such partners in civil society and like-minded governments were thick on the ground at the international level.

THE RIGHT POLITICAL CONDITIONS

The outcome of Norwegian elections in September 2005 brought the prospect closer of Norwegian international leadership on a process to address the humanitarian impacts of cluster munitions. But a 1% failure rate standard for cluster munitions was not a compelling call for attracting the political momentum necessary for a successful international campaign— let alone its doubtful efficacy in practical, humanitarian terms. Therefore, in early 2006, both NGOs and officials interested in what the new Red–Green coalition government intended to do on cluster munitions were watching for signals not only about what it practically wanted to achieve, but how international objectives and Norway's domestic stance would be harmonized. Their interest was heightened from February 2006 because Belgium's national parliament surprised the world when, as with anti-personnel mines in March 1995, it became the first country to outlaw cluster munitions by national law. It was an especially bold step as Belgium was home to companies that had produced the weapon in the past. But Belgium showed little inclination to lead international efforts toward specific international rules on cluster munitions, and a recent change of government in Sweden increasingly seemed to rule out that country as a leader on the issue despite its active role in the CCW previously.

That same month, NPA publicly called on the Norwegian government to take the plunge with a full national ban on cluster munitions, including cargo ammunition. Privately, however, NPA told the government it could live with a moratorium (at least for the time being) and, like the CMC's Coordinator Thomas Nash, who along with Østern met with the Ministry of Foreign Affairs State Secretary for Humanitarian Affairs, Kjetil Skogrand, in Oslo in late February, focused on encouraging Norway to lead other states on the cluster munition issue. Foreign Minister Støre and Deputy Minister Raymond Johansen were already strongly in favour of international action on cluster munitions. At the policy level, though, lines within the Ministry of Foreign Affairs, which would have to take the lead in making good on the Soria Moria Declaration's commitment at the international level, were not clearly drawn when they assumed office in late 2005. Responsibility for humanitarian action in the ministry was concentrated in the Humanitarian Assistance Department, which also had responsibility for Mine Ban Treaty-related affairs. These matters took Kongstad and his colleagues frequently to meetings in Geneva, where they rubbed shoulders with the diplomats, humanitarian staff of international organizations and NGOs also grappling with the CCW. But the lead on Norwegian efforts in the CCW fell within the purview of the Global Security Department of the Ministry of Foreign Affairs, which managed disarmament and arms control policy.

The Humanitarian Assistance Department, with its focus on coordinating and resourcing humanitarian emergency and development aid delivery, saw the prohibition of cluster munitions on civilians as a logical aim to be pursued without delay, and the Ottawa process as a good model to adapt to this end. However, some within the Global Security Department and within the wider Norwegian bureaucracy had a more traditionalist outlook. It is important to note that the lines between what can be described as the "humanitarian disarmers" and the Atlanticists were never clearly drawn—at no point did they represent the positions of entire departments or ministries. But there were, from the outset of the Red–Green coalition government's rule, concerns among the Atlanticists in the Ministry of Foreign Affairs and in the defence establishment about what the impact of any prospective international process on cluster munitions outside the CCW would have on Norway's most important alliance relationships, including with the United States.

And policy "turf" within the Foreign Ministry was also a consideration. The government's response was to establish what was, in effect, a special project on cluster munitions in March 2006. Politically, it was led by State Secretary Raymond Johansen, with Støre's firm backing, and directed from within the Ministry of Foreign Affairs by Kongstad, with responsibility for pursuing the government's objectives on introducing an international ban on cluster bombs. Kongstad would have to coordinate policy among the various departments and other relevant parts of the bureaucracy, especially the Ministry of Defence. It was, no doubt, a mixed blessing. The project's establishment signalled that the weight of the politicians was behind the cluster munition issue and that it was a priority, and it provided for the Humanitarian Assistance Department's involvement in the CCW in so far as it concerned cluster munitions. It also created a weight of expectation for progress during a period in which prospects for a negotiating process on a protocol to ban or even meaningfully restrict cluster munitions in the CCW did not look bright. As Kongstad realized, making good on the Red–Green coalition government's commitment to the cluster munition issue could well mean going outside the CCW process. It was not a prospect that concerned him, but it would be diplomatically risky, and would need unwavering political commitment from the government to stand a real chance of success.

Meanwhile, Østern realized from the outset of her work at NPA that unanswered questions about the military's cargo ammunition and the 1% failure rate policy might perhaps be turned to advantage in pushing the government to play a greater leading role on cluster munitions. So, one of her highest priority tasks during early 2006 was to try to shed some light of the nature of the Norwegian weapon stockpile. She found a surprising collaborator—an investigative journalist at the Norwegian Broadcasting Corporation (NRK) named Tormod Strand. He later explained:

my way into this was very accidental. Because I was in Afghanistan doing another story … and as a part of this I wanted to find victims of cluster munitions in Afghanistan. And in research into that story, I came over a list from the Swedish Afghanistan Committee that said Norway has still in stock cluster munitions. And for me that was surprising, because I (as many others) had thought that Norway got rid of their cluster munitions in 2004. And I met a woman, aged around 25, who was just crippled in her arms because she had found a Soviet cluster munition when she was a child. So that was the first time I understood what cluster munitions were. So, I decided that when I came back to Norway that I would try to investigate this.[33]

The first aim of their investigation was to determine whether the cargo ammunition the defence authorities were talking about were cluster munitions or something else, as they maintained. Outside experts confirmed that the two types of cargo ammunition in Norway's arsenal, the DM-642 and DM-662, were cluster munitions. Each carried submunitions equipped with self-destruct devices, which were supposed to detonate the bomblets in all cases. The DM-642 carried a submunition designated as the DM-1383, while the DM-662 carried submunitions designated as DM-1385. These DM-1385s were actually Israeli-made M-85 submunitions, but renamed by the German manufacturer of the artillery shell dispensing the submunitions.[34] Thus, as it turned out, much of Norway's wonderful cargo ammunition was basically identical to the L20A1 shells containing M-85 bomblets that the UK had used in Southern Iraq in March and April 2003.[35] According to a study by Human Rights Watch soon after that invasion, US and UK use of ground launched cluster munitions in Iraq "represented one of the major threats to civilians during the war".[36] NRK duly ran television news reports with this news, and NPA and other NGOs undertook an aggressive campaign in the media ridiculing the government's position.

As of writing, controversy still simmers in Norway about the position of the defence authorities until 2006, which maintained that the military's arsenal of 53,000 "cargo ammunition" artillery projectiles were not cluster munitions.[37] Was it misunderstanding, or deliberate disinformation? Strand considered that it was the latter, and he subsequently pursued this line of inquiry in his investigative reporting for NRK.[38] In contrast, sources I interviewed among the Norwegian defence authorities were adamant that, until 2006, they genuinely considered cargo ammunition to be a distinct weapon by virtue of its form of delivery, other technical characteristics such as the DM-1385's submunition self-destruct system, and their belief that, as a consequence, it had a negligible failure rate. They believed the Norwegian military's press spokespeople had done their position on cargo ammunition no favours. But this was a very different weapon than the "bad" Rockeye, the military had thought.

What cannot be doubted is that the public attention generated by the revelations about the mischaracterization of the Norwegian military's cargo ammunition stocks in the spring of 2006 created the pressure to push the government a bit further toward embracing a major leadership role in seeking an international treaty on cluster munitions. On 13 June, the Norwegian Minister of Defence wrote to the five largest Norwegian NGOs (including NPA) to announce a temporary moratorium on the use of ground-launched cargo ammunition until new tests of its stockpile and a full evaluation could be carried out in late September. In explaining the significance of the new policy to her colleagues in the Cluster Munition Coalition, Østern wrote:

> We would have liked to see the moratorium made permanent already today, but have decided to give up our efforts to achieve that. They [the Norwegian government] are adamant that the new tests have to be made and that this process must take its due time. We will come back strongly in the time before the new tests in September, to ensure that proper attention is given to all aspects which influence failure rates plus the fact that there are several reasons why these cluster munitions are problematic even if they do achieve a less than 1 percent failure rate. We don't believe that they will, though.

> It should have great importance that a country like Norway is now using the word moratorium. Even though the moratorium for the time being is time limited, it does send a clear international signal that the Norwegian government and armed forces are recognizing that there are serious grounds for doubt about whether the Norwegian stockpile of cluster munitions are indeed unacceptable seen from a humanitarian point of view. For NGOs in other countries where the same types of cluster munitions are in stock, it will be very important to be able to refer to this doubt and moratorium in Norway. The doubt about the failure rate of the Norwegian stockpile of cluster munitions should also be a strong signal to countries toying with the idea of an international ban focusing on an acceptable failure rate. It is important that the 1 percent is not mentioned in this letter from the Minister of Defense. Regarding the contents of the international initiative which the government wants to start, we now feel that the Norwegian stockpile is no longer an obstacle

and that they have a more exploratory approach where they are happy to have the NGOs pulling in front.[39]

Both NGOs and the Norwegian officials involved in making good on the Red–Green coalition's promise in the Soria Moria Declaration could feel the political wind changing. There was therefore great interest in what this further testing of Norway's cargo ammunition would turn up.

TESTING CARGO AMMUNITION

In late 2005, the British Army carried out in-service tests of its L20A1 cluster munition artillery shell, a system similar to Norway's cargo ammunition. The L20A1 carried M-85 submunitions, and had been used in Iraq in 2003 by British forces, as mentioned earlier. Despite evidence of a significant submunition failure rate in the Iraq conflict, however, British officials in the CCW in March 2005 claimed that no more than 1% would fail to explode in view of the M-85's self-destruct capability.[40]

In the first part of 2006, rumours began circulating among NGOs involved in the CCW talks that the British military's tests of its artillery-delivered cluster munitions confirmed a failure rate significantly higher than 1%. This was noteworthy, not least because test firing of such munitions is usually conducted under optimum conditions—if a munition could not achieve a 1% failure rate fired onto hard ground on a sunny day in low wind with plenty of preparation time and the gun crews not under stress, then it stood to reason that a 1% failure rate was unrealistically low in actual combat conditions. And because ground-launched submunitions could rapidly be dispersed in such massive numbers, small differences in failure rate could mean large differences in the absolute quantity of unexploded bomblets on the ground. The London-based NGO Landmine Action subsequently sought and received information under the UK's Freedom of Information Act from the British Ministry of Defence that the M-85 submunition failure rate in the L20A1 cluster munition artillery shell according to its tests was 2.3%. Landmine Action published an article noting that this was more than twice the failure rate the UK government had confidently claimed for the weapon only the previous year. And the article pointed out that failure rates for other British cluster munitions such as the Multiple Launch Rocket System (MLRS) and its air-delivered BL-755 cluster bomb was either higher again, or not revealed by the British Ministry of Defence. The article's author, Richard Moyes, argued that it was therefore difficult to accept the claims of countries claiming low submunition failure rates, as there were:

- serious concerns about the viability of "failure rates" as a basis for legally binding controls to enhance the protection afforded to civilians.

- The post-conflict threat is always bound up with the number of munitions deployed, not just the failure rate.

- State practice to date has not been sufficient to create confidence in their assertions about failure rates.[41]

Moyes concluded that any controls based on a failure rate approach would be "insufficient".[42]

Where had the UK tested its L20A1 ground-launched cluster munitions? At the Norwegian military's test firing ground in Hjerkinn, with Norwegian Army assistance. Norway's tests of its own M-85/DM-1385s in 2005 also showed a failure rate in excess of 2%.[43] (The Minister of Defence was not aware of the tests, and actually subsequently argued in Norwegian media that their cargo ammunition had a 1% failure rate.[44]) Norway's defence scientists nevertheless still confidently believed that the army's cargo ammunition was a "good" weapon in humanitarian terms. But they now realized that even to miss the symbolic 1% standard by only a few tenths of a per cent would likely be perceived as a failure in the tests promised in Norway's temporary moratorium policy announced by the Minister of Defence in June 2006. And, for obvious reasons, they knew NGOs like NPA were keen to know as much as possible about the upcoming tests in Hjerkinn from mid-September—and their results.

A humanitarian standard for cluster munitions based on a 1% failure rate struck Østern, Moyes and some others active within the CMC as arbitrary and perhaps even politically irresponsible. The process of testing failure rates was to them ultimately a red herring since testing did not resemble the weapon's use and effects in the real world—and they viewed it (indeed, privately some people within the Norwegian government did too) as a hoop to jump through on the way to a Norwegian ban policy. But it could be a dangerous red herring if governments fixated on the 1% failure rate as a panacea for the humanitarian hazards the weapon caused instead of seeking a ban of some kind. Norway's testing would be a key juncture.

In mid-2006, representatives of Norway's Ministry of Defence, the Army General Staff, and government scientists from the Norwegian Defence Research Establishment (FFI)—those who conducted weapons tests for the military—briefed interested NGO representatives in Oslo on the upcoming tests. The NGO side consisted of Østern and Colin King, NPA's technical consultant; King was a former British Army explosive ordnance disposal expert who was a consultant editor to the highly respected Jane's Information Group, and the author of an ICRC report on explosive remnants of war. They were introduced to Dr Ove Dullum, a white-haired and softly spoken FFI physicist given to thoughtful beard-stroking silences. It was the beginning of what was to become a very productive partnership, according to Østern. "NPA's dialogue with the Army, little by little, grew very constructive and we learned a lot from each other. This knowledge eventually became instrumental in ensuring a comprehensive ban internationally. In particular, our dialogue with FFI and Dullum was very good".[45]

King later recalled that Dullum and his colleagues discussed concerns about the 1% failure rate standard the government had set for the tests, and asked the NGOs for their views:

> to their huge credit they wanted some kind of independent thought on this. So the first meeting I ever had was with representatives from their research group FFI and from the government [Ministry of Defence] control and the NPA who brought me in on this. I think it was mainly that NPA wanted some kind of independent technical opinion there, but the others could have easily vetoed it if they had really wanted, so they could have stopped me. For a start they didn't have to speak in English. ... they were talking about how they would configure the tests and I raised a number of points and concerns about how they were doing things, whether it was going to be representative of the real world. And they were unbelievably fair-minded.[46]

Moyes also attended the meeting, and communicated his concerns in direct terms about the upcoming submunition tests. He also circulated them in writing—including with the bureaucratic project on cluster munitions led by the Ministry of Foreign Affairs. Moyes feared, based on his prior examination of the UK's testing policy, that the results of the upcoming Norwegian testing could, in effect, be rigged or the results massaged:

> With respect to the proposed tests in Norway, significant political failings can be identified which mean both the government policy target of 1%

failure rate and the number likely to be produced by the testing process cannot be anchored in reality. Without this anchoring, which needs to come from a political explanation of the assumptions underpinning the policy, the approach is effectively an assertion of random numbers in response to a humanitarian problem.

This arbitrary nature of the approach could be well brought out through the following public questions to government:

- Why 1% not 2%?

- What analysis did you do to decide upon 1% as being an effective figure?

- There has been criticism internationally that failure rates in actual conflict have been very different from in tests—what analysis have you done of that and how do we know that our tests provide an accurate basis for predicting the outcomes of future use?

- Which government official is responsible for setting the policy and setting the terms of reference for the tests that will interrogate that policy?

- If the terms of reference for the tests were not set from "above" how do we know we are doing the right kind of tests?[47]

Moyes' written comments arrived in the e-mail inboxes of his Norwegian contacts soon after the conflict in Southern Lebanon had ended in a ceasefire. During this conflict, Israel used massive quantities of artillery-delivered submunitions—including the M-85 with self-destruct—in the final days of fighting. Although reports from Southern Lebanon were initially confused, even early indications of UXO contamination there indicated that this submunition had a much higher failure rate in actual use than testing results indicated should be the case. In view of its relevance to Norway, NPA decided quickly that it would do everything it could to document the results of the M-85's use in Lebanon.[48]

A rising tide of evidence about the effects of ground-launched cluster munition use in Southern Lebanon would serve to fatally undermine Norwegian confidence in the 1% failure rate, even as its careful tests were being carried out in Hjerkinn from 18 September. These tests were the most comprehensive ever carried out in Norway on cluster munitions, with 192 DM-662 artillery projectiles containing 9,408 DM-1385 bomblets tested. These were fired from 17–21km away onto a specifically designed sand and gravel testing field, and an advanced system using acoustical and optical sensors recorded the time and position of every detonation for analysis. Conditions were perfect, and the munitions were in an excellent state. Nevertheless, there were 104 submunition duds, which gave an average failure rate of 1.11%—just above the Norway's self-imposed maximum failure rate.[49]

The results left Dullum and his FFI colleagues puzzled by the disparity between the Norwegian cargo ammunition testing results and the claims emerging from Southern Lebanon of high M-85 failure rates. And so, with the results of the latest Hjerkinn tests not yet public knowledge, Dullum decided to accept an invitation from NPA to go to see for himself the submunitions that had contaminated Southern Lebanon. In late October, and with others including Østern and Nergaard,[50] Dullum did just that, and he and Østern met with Chris Clark, the head of the UN's Mine Action Coordination Centre, based in Tyre:

> It was hard to accept it initially. I had an argument with Chris Clark down there on the first day when we arrived . … I said we had done very thorough tests and we found that it [the failure rate] was just 1 per cent. But he still said that it was much more than that. And we went out and looked and I had to admit that Chris was right. It was much more than 1 per cent or 1.5 per cent.[51]

After carrying out various checks, Dullum formed the impression that the average failure rate for M-85s with self-destruct devices as used in Southern Lebanon was in the region of 5–10%, and as he and NPA examined data from the best documented cluster munition strike sites there they found the failure rate tended to be at this estimate's upper range. At this time, the M-85 was generally seen, in terms of the quality of its design and construction and because of its self-destruct feature, as the best of the best; and, although the Israeli M-85 lots fired were marginally older, this was the same submunition that had been tested in Norway.

There could be only one logical conclusion: reliability testing could not be depended upon, because as Moyes had earlier described it, it was evidently not "anchored in reality". If the actual rate of submunitions left unexploded in combat was of an order of magnitude greater than in testing, which was what the evidence Dullum could see indeed showed, then Norwegian use of cargo ammunition in combat would also result in many hazardous, unexploded duds despite the M-85's vaunted self-destruct mechanism.

Cluster munitions would always pose a significant post-use risk because of this high actual dud rate and violate the IHL principle of distinction. Norway's cargo ammunition could not be used.

A NEW HOPE

The conflict in Southern Lebanon and its aftermath, in which hundreds of thousands of submunitions of various kinds remained unexploded for returning civilians to encounter, accelerated a process already underway in Norway toward political conditions in which it would instigate international efforts to ban cluster munitions through a humanitarian treaty. The conflict again placed the effects of cluster munitions—essentially identical to weapons in Norway's own stockpile—squarely in the public eye and served to short-circuit debate about the results of the late September tests exceeding the government's target by a few tenths of a per cent. Those results, along with accumulating evidence, including NPA's and Dullum's careful examination of submunitions in Southern Lebanon, now merely confirmed what the Stoltenberg Government had already decided, which was revealed at least as early as 24 October in an answer to a written question in the *Storting* by Foreign Minister Støre:

> the case of Lebanon clearly demonstrates that there is a real need to strengthen humanitarian law in this area. In the Government's view, the human suffering caused by the use of cluster munitions is unacceptable. This is why Norway will take the lead—together with other like-minded countries and international humanitarian actors—to put in place an international prohibition against cluster munitions.[52]

Ten days later, on 3 November, as Dullum and Østern spent their last day in the field in Southern Lebanon, Foreign Minister Støre and Defence Minister Anne Grethe Strøme Erichsen held a joint press conference in Oslo. The English-language media release from this press conference does not mention Norway's cargo ammunition testing, although it was apparently noted there that the Hjerkinn tests had shown the DM-662 to have a dud rate just above 1%, and the shorter range DM-642 as meeting that standard.[53] Instead, the focus was on Norway's new national policy—to extend the temporary moratorium on use of the nation's cluster munitions until an international ban on cluster munitions could be achieved. It was explained that "The Norwegian moratorium is important in itself, but it is also important in terms of giving Norway the necessary international credibility now that the

Government has decided to work for a ban on cluster munitions that cause great humanitarian suffering".[54]

Lebanon and previous conflicts in the Balkans, the Norwegian Ministers said, had demonstrated the unacceptable consequences associated with the use of cluster munitions:

> "Norway is prepared to take a leading role in order to speed up the efforts to achieve an international ban on cluster munitions. Now we must pursue our efforts along another track. We have noted that UN agencies, Norwegian and international humanitarian organisations and other interested countries expect Norway to take the lead in this," said Foreign Minister Jonas Gahr Støre.

> "We mustn't have any illusions about the path to an international ban being an easy one, but we can't let this keep us from doing our part," he said.

> The aim is an international ban against the types of cluster munitions that cause unacceptable humanitarian harm. This is important both for humanitarian reasons and in order to facilitate reconstruction and development. The use of this type of munitions must be stopped before it becomes even more extensive, with all the unforeseeable consequences this could have.[55]

The transformation of Norwegian national policy was now largely complete. Norway's air-delivered cluster munitions had been scrapped. The Norwegian military's ground-launched cluster munitions—which it had insisted, until challenged, did not even fall into the same weapon category—would now be effectively withdrawn from service. And Norway's government had staked out that it would undertake what the NGOs and parliamentarians had been pushing it to do since the middle of 2001: take the lead on an international ban campaign, with the diplomatic and political risks that this held in store. Moreover, Norway had clearly signalled that the path to a cluster munition ban might not be by means of the CCW, which the following week would commence its five-yearly Review Conference in Geneva. In political terms, this was the genesis of the Oslo process.

As important as the 3 November announcement by the Norwegian government was, it was not a mass conversion of the Atlanticists in Norway's civil bureaucracy to the prospect of another Ottawa-style process. Some would continue to express scepticism to the relevant political decisionmakers right up to and during the Dublin negotiations, despite the cluster munition project's backing from the Red–Green coalition. Interoperability and the disapproval of key allies such as the United States were the favoured sticks with which to try to beat the Oslo initiative, which Kongstad and his cross-departmental team drawn from humanitarian affairs, global security and legal affairs within the Foreign Ministry and the defence establishment would have to fend off over the next 17 months.

Quite aside from concerns about relations with Norway's allies, there were other caveats on the new consensus for a ban treaty on cluster munitions within the Norwegian bureaucratic system. Dullum and his FFI colleagues, for instance, and later the artillery specialists in the defence forces, grounded their support for a ban on the dud rate in practice of cluster munitions. Like many others they considered this dud rate to be unacceptable both in humanitarian and military terms—now irrefutable thanks to the evidence from conflicts like Southern Lebanon. But the defence forces did not necessarily share the view expounded by other countries, the ICRC and NGOs that all cluster munitions were inaccurate, for example, or unacceptable because of their area effect at time of attack (and therefore, it was argued, indiscriminate). This foreshadowed that agreement on how to define the characteristics and the effects of cluster munitions would be key for an international campaign on cluster munitions to succeed. Eventually Norway—and Dullum in particular—would play a part in solving that by means of adding a weight criterion he had thought up almost a year earlier to the Dublin draft Convention, after long discussions with Østern on what a potential ban could look like. However, this was yet a long way off. In November 2006, Norway's new policy to achieve a humanitarian treaty on cluster munitions was not accompanied by a viable multilateral process. Within a few months, this would have to change, or the initiative would founder.

CHAPTER 4

LEBANON

In July 2006, armed conflict broke out between Israel and Hizbullah, the latter a non-state armed group operating from Southern Lebanon, whose political wing was represented in Lebanon's parliament and in its governing cabinet. During the 34-day conflict, in which the Israel Defence Forces (IDF) bombed throughout Lebanon and made forays over the UN-monitored "Blue Line" into the south of the country, both the IDF and Hizbullah used cluster munitions. Israel's military forces deployed cluster munitions on a large scale in the last three days of the conflict, in particular, and Hizbullah fired cluster munitions, some carrying MZD-2 submunitions[1] among the 3,970 rockets it targeted at Israel during the conflict, 901 of them into urban areas.[2]

The use of cluster munitions and their humanitarian consequences in Southern Lebanon sharply underlined the issues that use of these weapons raises under international law. Hizbullah deliberately targeted civilians in its rocket attacks.[3] The IDF blanketed Southern Lebanon with massive numbers of submunitions, some of which failed to function as intended and were thus of great hazard to returning civilians. This led a UN Human Rights Council Commission of Inquiry to later report among its findings concerning IDF cluster munition use that "in view of the foreseeable high dud rate, their use amounted to a de facto scattering of anti-personnel mines across wide tracts of Lebanese land".[4] The use of cluster munitions in the conflict added weight to the arguments of those, including some states, the International Committee of the Red Cross (ICRC) as well as the Cluster Munition Coalition (CMC) and its constituent organizations, that action was needed to address these hazards, both at time of use and post-conflict, through an international treaty restricting or banning cluster munitions. Moreover, the 2006 conflict indicated the likely shape of things to come if proliferation of cluster munitions continued—increasing access to and use by non-state armed groups in ways that violate international humanitarian law.

The United Nations became even more concerned about cluster munitions from humanitarian and development perspectives during the course of the 2006 conflict. In effect, it was a firm reminder that issues surrounding cluster munitions were not only of concern to those parts of the UN specialized in arms control or disarmament processes. It led the UN Emergency Relief Coordinator, Jan Egeland, to take the unprecedented step of using his position to publicly call for a global freeze on cluster munition use until "the international community puts in place effective legal instruments to address urgent humanitarian concerns about their use".[5] And, from Southern Lebanon itself, the UN Mine Action Coordination Centre (UN MACC SL, or MACC) based in Tyre would play a significant role in showing fora such as the Convention on Certain Conventional Weapons (CCW) the real humanitarian consequences of cluster munition use by relaying what its staff saw and experienced in the field.

Not all of those involved in what would later become the Oslo process agree over the degree to which the Southern Lebanon conflict was crucial to that international initiative's emergence. For instance, one commentator of international efforts on cluster munitions, the US legal academic Virgil Wiebe, described the conflict as "necessary but not sufficient"[6] in this regard. Nevertheless, it is difficult to understand the concerns animating subsequent international efforts either in the Oslo process or the CCW without a grasp of what happened in 2006 in Southern Lebanon, and how its consequences were to reverberate around the world.

There are also salient lessons to be learned from the 2006 conflict and its aftermath for the future implementation of the Convention on Cluster Munitions. As of writing, almost three years after the conflict, large-scale efforts to clear up unexploded submunitions in local villages, fields and orchards in Southern Lebanon continue. UN clearance experts suspect that as many as 50,000 unexploded submunitions[7] remain on or in the ground in high- and medium-priority areas for clearance at a time when the international community's memory of the humanitarian consequences of the 2006 conflict in Lebanon is fading, and resources for post-conflict assistance are diminishing.[8] Lessons learned from Southern Lebanon's post-conflict experience with submunitions, sometimes at the cost of the lives and livelihoods of both local civilians and clearance personnel, could— and should—be factored into how the Convention on Cluster Munition's substantive obligations are carried out. For the reasons above, this chapter is primarily concerned with briefly telling the story of the 2006 conflict through the eyes of UN personnel in the field, and explores some wider lessons about cluster munitions based on these realities.

THE 2006 CONFLICT

There is not space here to comprehensively describe the origins and causes of the 2006 conflict, especially in view of Lebanon's complex history and the intricacies of both its politics and those of the broader region. Nevertheless, from the perspective of international efforts to address the humanitarian impacts of cluster munitions, Lebanon is a small country with a lot of contamination from mines and unexploded ordnance, much of it originating from before the 2006 conflict. One of the regions of the country most affected by explosive remnants of war is south of the Litani River, which flows into the Eastern Mediterranean Sea less than an hour's drive south along the coast from Beirut. With Israel to its immediate south and east, and the contested Shebaa Farms and Golan Heights as well as Syria to the northeast, the region south of the Litani—Southern Lebanon—has in recent decades been one of the most fought-in places in the Middle East. Submunition contamination stemmed mainly from US-made air-delivered cluster bombs dropped by Israel such as the CBU-58, which the US Air Force had deployed in large numbers during the 1960s and early 1970s in South-East Asia.[9] The CBU-58 typically contains 650 tennis-ball-shaped BLU-63 submunitions, each of which is packed with high explosive and is prone to failure at time of use.[10] Yet the unexploded ordnance problem created by decades of conflict in Southern Lebanon consisted of not only cluster munitions and, as large numbers of mines were also laid, unexploded submunitions were not widely recognized as a particular problem.

The main focus of Hizbullah raids in the first half of this decade was on the Shebaa Farms, an area at the northeast tip of Southern Lebanon around 50km inland from the Mediterranean Sea occupied by Israel since 1967. Also, like the Palestinian Liberation Organization before it, Hizbullah periodically fired relatively inaccurate ground-launched rockets from improvised sites within Southern Lebanon at Northern Israel. The IDF would often retaliate with airstrikes or artillery fire against these launch sites, but escalation was on the whole contained. The sudden lurch into armed conflict in mid-July 2006 therefore came as a surprise to many.

On 12 July 2006, Hizbullah fired two rockets from Southern Lebanon into the Israeli town of Shlomi. That same morning, Hizbullah guerrillas ambushed an IDF patrol across the Blue Line in one of the few sections of the mined and fenced Israeli frontier not under heavy surveillance, about 7km from the Mediterranean coast close to the Blue Line's southern extremity, and roughly opposite a Lebanese hamlet called Alkawzah. Hizbullah forces managed to kidnap two Israeli soldiers, and three others were killed in the attack. An immediate pursuit operation by the IDF suffered further losses, including another five soldiers and a Merkava tank. Sheik Hassan Nasrallah, Hizbullah's leader, claimed that Hizbullah was acting in solidarity with Palestinians in Gaza, where Israeli forces were fighting in order to secure the release of one of their soldiers, taken hostage by Palestinian militants in a raid into Israel on 25 June.[11]

That same day found a former British soldier and head of MACC, Chris Clark, en route to Lebanon following a meeting with his UN colleagues in Geneva. Clark was returning to MACC's headquarters in Tyre (Sur), a town of about 140,000 inhabitants on the Lebanese coast less than 20km north of the Blue Line. While transferring between flights in Istanbul around lunchtime, Clark turned on his mobile phone and heard from his colleagues in Southern Lebanon about that morning's events. In view of the pattern of previous border incidents between Hizbullah and the Israelis, at first he thought, "So what? No big deal".[12]

When Clark landed in Beirut at about 13h00, though, it was clear that things were not business as usual. Israel had launched major air operations against targets in Lebanon and was also commencing a sea blockade of its coast. IDF strike aircraft cratered the runways of Beirut's international airport soon after Clark disembarked the commercial flight he had flown in on. Hizbullah's headquarters were also bombed, and roads and bridges leading into Southern Lebanon from the north and east were being systematically destroyed by the Israeli Air Force.

Tekimiti Gilbert, Clark's deputy, met him at the airport. A former New Zealand Army combat engineer, Gilbert—or "Gilly" as he is universally known in Southern Lebanon—was the MACC's operations chief. He was in Beirut that day to take his eight-year-old daughter to a dentist's appointment, and had offered to pick up Clark in his four-wheel-drive vehicle on the way back. As the morning progressed, the radio room at the MACC in Tyre kept Gilly informed of the deteriorating security situation. So, after meeting at the airport, Clark and Gilly found a café in which they could see satellite television coverage and try to assess whether it would be safe enough to travel back to Tyre from Beirut, along with Gilly's young daughter. They concluded it would be better to try to get to Tyre and back to the MACC while the key roads and bridges remained intact—otherwise they might be stuck in Beirut for days or even weeks, separated from their staff. But would any routes still be passable, especially across the Litani River? "So we made some phone calls", Gilly said. "We determined that there was one bridge that hadn't been bombed, that was left standing. So we made the call: we said, 'let's go'. If we are gonna go, let's go now".

The one bridge still standing across the Litani was roughly 10km inland. Gilly recalled:

> The roads were fairly open, empty as you'd expect. People were afraid. [We] got to the bridge, saw that it was still standing, saw that there was a big hole in the middle of it. We looked up above our heads to see if we could see the [Israeli Air Force] aircraft flying overhead, and saw nothing. So we just shot across it as fast as we could, got across to the other side and made it back to here [to Tyre].

An Israeli bomb had hit the bridge but not completely destroyed it. Passing over the damaged structure, Clark and Gilly could see another 500lbs bomb beneath: the munition had punched through the bridge's decking and failed to explode.

Back once again in Tyre, a new challenge presented itself to the MACC's leadership: accounting for the rest of the Centre's staff, a mixture of about 25 locals and expatriates. The Israeli strikes had commenced suddenly that day, and bombs and artillery fire were being directed at targets throughout the area, presumably attacking known Hizbullah strongholds, but the bombardment had also caught MACC staff out and about. Before the Israeli military strikes had begun that morning, a team from the MACC led by its Planning Officer, another former Kiwi army combat engineer, Allen Kelly, had driven south from Tyre to a United Nations Interim Force in Lebanon (UNIFIL) base near Naqoura, a Lebanese coastal town close to the Blue Line, to run a training course for Chinese military deminers assigned to the UN force. Trapped in the camp by the Israeli bombing of surrounding areas, Kelly and his colleagues joined the UNIFIL contingent in their bunkers for the day, until in the late afternoon they were able to get back to Tyre.

The next day the conflict escalated further. Hizbullah launched a rocket at Israel's third largest city, Haifa. On 14 July, Hizbullah demonstrated an unexpected military capability: it struck an Israeli naval corvette participating in the coastal blockade of Lebanon with an Iranian-supplied Chinese-manufactured C-802 cruise missile. In fact, by 18 July, Hizbullah had fired more than 700 rockets into Israel according to the International Institute for Strategic Studies—"a massive escalation from the previous random harassing fire against border settlements and military posts"—while the Israeli Air Force was flying more than 200 strike missions each day over Lebanon.[13]

People in Tyre largely remained in their homes in these first days, although some expatriates had begun migrating to the Tyre Rest House—a hotel compound on the southern shore of Tyre, which was also designated by the UN as an assembly point. For the United Nations an important question revolved around whether there should be a full-scale evacuation: related to this was the fact that some UNIFIL and other UN staff had members of their families present. Would the conflagration between Hizbullah and the Israelis quickly burn itself out, or would the conflict continue? In other words, was it less dangerous to stay put and wait out the bombing, or leave shelter in an effort to evacuate? It was a conundrum that was soon solved, tragically. On 16 July, an apartment block in Tyre was bombarded by the IDF and collapsed, killing more than 20 people. The following day a UNIFIL staff member and his spouse were killed when a building in Housh, near Tyre, was hit.[14] Gilly recalled:

> And basically it was us as well as thousands of Lebanese people that had evacuated from their homes and villages—had come to the Rest House. So you can imagine, there were only so many rooms and all the rooms were full. So what we were doing was getting the sun chairs from the beach and bringing them [to] a large room below the swimming pool. There is quite a large room there, which has got AC [air-conditioning] in it, and everyone just hauled these beds in there and basically just slept side by side on those sun chairs.

A UN-chartered ship arrived offshore on 18 July to evacuate "non-essential" UN personnel and family dependents to Cyprus, of which there were roughly 300, including Allen Kelly, his wife and young son, and they took with them Gilly's young daughter.[15] With a capacity of a thousand passengers, the ship also accepted hundreds of Lebanese with foreign passports eager to depart, many of whom had come to Southern Lebanon on their holidays and were now caught in the crossfire.

Clark and Gilly, both designated as "essential" personnel by the UN, stayed behind in Tyre while most other UNIFIL essential staff went to compounds around Naqoura to the south. Gilly moved into Clark's apartment for the duration of the conflict because his own apartment building had an Al-Manar (Hizbullah television) antenna on the roof, which could make it an Israeli strike target. The 20 or so local Lebanese staff at the MACC were asked to go home or evacuate to the north if possible, although a couple of them stayed on to ensure the MACC compound kept functioning. Meanwhile, in these first few days of the conflict, many tens of thousands of civilians streamed northward out of Southern Lebanon as best they could, most using improvised crossings across the Litani in private vehicles, the river at that time being low because of the summer weather.[16]

Until the last few days of the conflict those at the MACC—Clark, Gilly, their remaining local staff and a small detachment of Lebanese Army soldiers there to keep the compound secure—had many prosaic issues to manage. Tyre had back-up electricity generation capacity, so the power remained on most of the time, and communications were generally good. But the Centre's staff encountered the same problem as the rest of the Southern Lebanese civilian population: there had not been enough warning before hostilities commenced to stockpile food, fuel and water at the MACC, and supplies soon ran low. Locating food around Tyre and making runs out to the homes of local staff and their families who had not been able to flee Southern Lebanon became a priority. Meanwhile, UN headquarters in New York had to be kept informed of developments around Tyre, especially since the international media's reporting was sometimes wildly inaccurate. In particular, Clark was in daily contact with his boss, John Flanagan at the UN Mine Action Service, an arm of the UN's Department of Peacekeeping Operations in New York, which in turn helped to keep the Security Council informed.[17] There also were many Lebanese nationals with foreign passports still to be evacuated and, as the remaining UN staff in Tyre, it fell to those at the MACC to help them make their arrangements.

These were long, hot summer days, confined to a largely empty town while the condensation trails of IDF strike planes and unmanned aerial drones made circles in the sky. Clark and Gilly worked in the bowels of MACC headquarters near the harbour side to try to gather a picture of what kind of post-conflict effort would be needed for mine and unexploded ordnance (UXO) clearance. It was difficult to assess the damage to civil infrastructure or the nature and extent of contamination from unexploded ordnance in Southern Lebanon, especially as the movements of those remaining at the MACC—and those of UNIFIL forces—were highly restricted by the conflict. There was obviously the damage to key roads and bridges Clark and Gilly had seen during their drive south from Beirut on 12 July, and the damage to Tyre and its immediate environs they could also see with their own eyes. But it was unclear during the first few weeks of the conflict to what extent cluster munitions, as opposed to unitary warhead weapons such as free-fall bombs or high-explosive artillery shells, were being used. And, at that time, the MACC had no inkling that Hizbullah possessed stockpiles of ground-launched rockets containing MZD-2 submunitions:

> at that time we were basing it all on a large UXO clean-up and possibly a mine-clearance project, although we didn't know, we had no information with regards to mines, but we had three technical survey teams [included in the MACC's post-conflict planning] as part of the mix in order to conduct any survey required of new mining.[18]

This seemed a reasonable assumption in view of the nature of Southern Lebanon's pre-2006 mine and UXO problem, and what the MACC had learned in terms of coordinating the response to it. Clark, for example, had arrived in Lebanon in June 2003, and managed a large landmine clearance project funded by the United Arab Emirates called Operation Emirate Solidarity. In the course of this clearance of mines, old cluster bomb strikes were also sometimes encountered, all from prior to the mid-1980s—mostly the BLU-63s mentioned earlier. These unexploded submunitions had been in the ground for more than 20 years, and many were buried down to a metre in depth. Dealing with these required different methods than for landmine clearance (for example, the submunitions had to be destroyed *in situ* as there was no safe way to move them) but when compared with the extent of the landmine problem, their numbers were considered insignificant. The MACC figured submunitions would be among the unexploded ordnance they would need to plan for dealing with when a ceasefire eventually emerged from the 2006 conflict, but—like everyone else—they were not to realize the massive extent of that submunition contamination until later.

CEASEFIRE

Far away in New York, after weeks of blockage in the Security Council, diplomatic efforts intensified from 6 August to try to achieve a ceasefire in Southern Lebanon, based on an initial draft of a resolution prepared by France and the United States. As negotiations on the Security Council resolution progressed that week, far from leading to a lull in military operations between Hizbullah and the IDF, the fighting became more intense. Israel's Security Cabinet approved an expanded military offensive on 9 August, in which Israeli troops were authorized to push as far north as the Litani River.[19] Two days later, on 11 August, UN Security Council resolution 1701 was finally agreed, which among other things called "for a full cessation of hostilities based upon, in particular, the immediate cessation by Hizbollah of all attacks and the immediate cessation by Israel of all offensive military operations".[20] Lebanon's cabinet voted unanimously to accept its terms the next day, and Hizbullah said, "We will not be an obstacle to any decision taken by the Lebanese government".[21] However, while Israel accepted the resolution on 13 August, its offensive operations continued until the ceasefire deadline at 8h00 local time the following morning.[22] These last few days of the conflict saw intensive Israeli bombing and shelling of Southern Lebanon and the widespread use of cluster munitions, especially from 155mm artillery shells and ground-launched rocket systems.

Meanwhile, Hizbullah's rocket attacks continued unabated—on 13 August, it launched 250 rockets into Northern Israel, its most intensive bombardment since the conflict began. From Clark's apartment balcony in Tyre, he and Gilly could watch the Katyusha rockets being fired from the citrus, tobacco and banana plantations south of the city. Since Israeli drones circled continually overhead, keeping Tyre and the surrounding area under surveillance, almost invariably Israeli counter-battery fire would be directed at the launch sites in retaliation. In the last days of the conflict this duelling intensified, until the last 24 hours before the ceasefire was, in Gilly's words, "just off the scale ... continual noise"[23]—a crescendo of shelling, rockets and aircraft flying overhead.

The firing stopped at 8h00 on the morning of 14 August. By that time, a number of UN emergency agencies had managed to send small advance parties down from Beirut to Tyre to prepare for humanitarian operations after the ceasefire and some of these, such as the World Food Programme (WFP) and the Office of the UN High Commissioner for Refugees (UNHCR), had based themselves at the MACC's headquarters. A large WFP–UNHCR relief convoy waited just north of the Litani in the coastal town of Saida, loaded with food, medical supplies and other essential items. Somehow, that convoy had to be brought across the river to Tyre and go onwards to a town called Rumaysh on the border between Lebanon and Israel. Many civilians—some of them people who were too old or infirm to flee the conflict—had been stranded in Rumaysh by the fighting for at least a fortnight. With no information on precisely what the state of the roads, remaining bridges and crossings of Southern Lebanon would be, the immediate task for the MACC staff in Tyre would be to survey a route for the food and medicine trucks to get through to their destination.

Clark headed up the coastal road from Tyre to Qasimiyah shortly after the ceasefire commenced. In normal circumstances the trip is about a 15-minute drive, but that day it took much longer for the UN four-wheel-drive to negotiate the route in view of the disruption caused by the bombardment. When he reached the south bank of the Litani at the Qasmiyah crossing Clark found what he expected: Israeli bombs had destroyed the bridge. So he headed further inland in search of a crossing point that might be passable.

> What I found up there was that the local people (because obviously they knew their families were coming back) had basically got out their bulldozers and excavators, and there was at a certain place about 10km inland from the main crossing at Qasimiyah, where there was a huge [amount] of local activity … . [Locals] were basically dumping concrete culverts into the river and filling over the top of it with soil from the banks, making an improvised crossing.

> There were civilian cars coming across, but it wasn't suitable for the big trucks to come down, so I spoke to them a bit to explain this situation and they very rapidly agreed to grade the bank so that the approach to the crossing and out wasn't [too steep] and was good enough for heavy trucks.[24]

The UN's relief convoy was now in business, at least as far as Tyre.

While Clark was scouting out the route from Tyre to the north, Gilly and a Lebanese driver from the MACC, Bilal Najdi, set out in another of the MACC's four-wheel drive vehicles to survey a route from Tyre to the southeast through to Rumaysh. There are two major routes from Tyre to

Rumaysh: one road leads into the hilly interior of Southern Lebanon to the southeast of the city and winds through hilltop villages and wadis that were until that morning the scene of furious fighting between Hizbullah militiamen and Israeli military forces. The other route, the one Gilly and Bilal took, ran due south from Tyre to Naqoura and past the plantations Gilly and Clark had watched the Hizbullah Katyushas being fired from. Driving cautiously down that coast road, Gilly and his colleague passed the UNIFIL compound Allen Kelly had been trapped in on the first day of the war, before turning inland to travel roughly east along Echo Road. That route would not be without risk: the road runs just to the north and in parallel to the Blue Line and its minefields, and had been breached in places by the IDF as part of its offensive operations. Gilly and Bilal did not know what they would find, and just hoped that the vehicle's UN markings would be enough to protect them from any incidents with jumpy and trigger-happy combatants.

Unexploded mortar and aircraft bombs lay at random intervals on either side of Echo Road. The extent of the devastation Gilly saw amazed him: "that was the first time I'd been out in a month, out of Tyre. And then to see all of the destruction, and bombs ... the roads were cratered and bridges were blown. That was a very interesting day, that day".[25] Although Gilly saw few civilians, he did see plenty of Hizbullah fighters—some living and some dead, the latter being transported in the backs of pick-up trucks. He also observed that a Fox News Team vehicle had begun following them, perhaps hoping the MACC would lead them to a story. Damage to the road meant that the MACC vehicle was often forced to leave the tarmac and manoeuvre cautiously around large shell or bomb craters, the Fox News vehicle doing its best to keep up. The amount of unexploded ordnance of many kinds and copper filaments from wire-guided anti-tank missiles criss-crossing the ground that Gilly saw increased as they travelled eastward.

At one point a goat-herder flagged down the vehicle to ask them for food. Gilly explained that a convoy would come through in the next day or so, and the UN vehicle moved on. It was the same story when he eventually reached Rumaysh: "the people there were just overjoyed to see someone from the UN, crowded around, immediately wanted food. I said, 'Look, you know, I'm only here to prepare the way for the trucks which will becoming tomorrow, and the trucks will be bringing all the food'".[26] Looking around the town, he was surprised at how lightly Rumaysh was damaged compared with the devastation he had seen in the villages on his way there. The Israelis did not appear to have considered Rumaysh a base for Hizbullah militia operations, and largely spared it bombardment. Gilly and Bilal continued westward, toward a junction at the larger town of Bint Jubayl, at which point they hoped to be able to turn back westward to Tyre by the interior route. Bint Jubayl was regarded as a main Hizbullah stronghold—the IDF had mounted a major ground attack against it late in the war—and they found the town heavily bombarded and in parts flattened.

Surreal incidents punctuated the devastation the two MACC staff members saw among the hilltops and wadis that day. At one point they found the road blocked by air-dropped IDF food pallets with parachutes still lying nearby. When they began to inspect the pallets, Gilly and Bilal were waved on at gunpoint by Israeli troops emerging from a nearby building. Further on, they encountered an abandoned Israeli armoured bulldozer, stuck precariously balanced on a low stone wall. Sensing unfriendly eyes watching, the two men retreated to their vehicle.

Meanwhile, by around 14h00, the crossing point on the Litani had been established to the north. Consequently, as Gilly and Bilal neared Tyre after traversing ruined villages and towns of Southern Lebanon's scorched interior, they began to encounter large numbers of civilians driving back to their homes in the south, despite Israeli military warnings not to return yet. When they reached the MACC's compound in Tyre they found Clark along with a 20-strong lorry convoy, which had parked around the outside of the compound and by the harbour side, as well as a throng of relief workers settling in until the next day when the trucks could continue to Rumaysh.

On the day of the ceasefire both Clark and Gilly had seen large amounts of unexploded ordnance resulting from the conflict. Focused on the job of scouting a route for the UN relief convoy, however, they had been struck with the extent of the damage from the bombardment rather than the risk from small, unexploded submunitions being a particular problem, which were in any case hard to see from moving vehicles. But disturbing reports now began to come in to the MACC. A Mines Advisory Group (MAG) demining team returning to its local headquarters in Nabatiyah as part of a civilian convoy on the day of the ceasefire found unexploded submunitions on the road in front of them resulting from an Israeli cluster munition strike. This was not an isolated incident. Later research by the MACC would reveal that there were 15 confirmed civilian casualties from submunitions in the first few days after the ceasefire commenced.[27] Returning civilians on the whole had no idea what the little toy-like submunitions were that littered their streets, gardens or which had penetrated into their houses—or that they could be so dangerous. Clark recalled:

> The next day, which was the 15th, we got a call [because of] multiple casualties in a place called [Tibnan] from cluster bombs. So I drove out to [Tibnan] … Tibnan is the major town in the centre and there were just cluster bombs everywhere—just everywhere. It was like a carpet across the centre of the town. While I was there (because it's also got the main hospital) there was a civilian casualty being brought into the hospital, but they couldn't get in because there were cluster [bomblets] all over the road. So we did some impromptu clearance there, just to get the entrance to the hospital open.[28]

Although the Israelis used air-dropped BLU-63s during the 2006 conflict (some manufactured in the early 1970s, and intended for use before the middle of that decade, let alone the next century),[29] the submunitions littering Tibnan were of a newer generation. These so-called Dual Purpose Improved Conventional Munitions (DPICMs) were smaller and lighter than the older BLU-63s and, rather than resembling iron tennis balls, looked like miniature spray-paint cans, each with a stabilizing ribbon emerging from the top. With simple but error-prone stab detonators, a range of factors could prevent these newer generation submunitions from detonating on impact, such as being damaged in mid-air or getting caught in vegetation that prevented the hard impact from detonating the armed submunition. And despite their innocuous appearance, these M-42s, M-46s, M-77s and M-85s packed a double wallop: each contained a copper cone-shaped charge for penetrating armoured vehicles, while their metal casings were etched for maximum anti-personnel fragmentation effect.

On the 300m stretch of road outside the hospital in Tibnan, which was the centre of a cluster munition strike, there were large numbers of unexploded M-85 submunitions—the M-85 being an Israeli manufactured design considered by its users to be the state-of-the-art in that it contained a self-destruct mechanism in case it failed to function as intended. The Israeli M-85s were basically identical to the DM-1385 submunitions possessed by Norway and the UK's M-85s (discussed in chapter 3). Clearly, the self-destruct feature had not worked properly here. Gilly observed that:

> there shouldn't have been any of them left behind [yet] it must have been in excess of 150, 200 that I could see on the streets and (if you

walked through peoples' gardens) just in that general vicinity. Even at the entrance into the hospital itself, there were cluster bombs at the entrance … By that time people had got back and the word started getting out of this large contamination.[30]

The problem was that the MACC had access to very few resources for clearance as the 2006 conflict halted. There were the four returning MAG teams, which had been demining before the conflict, but they were not specifically trained for battle area clearance or explosive ordnance disposal, which use different techniques and basic methodologies. The UN Mine Action Service had a ready-response plan to supply the necessary financial, managerial and other resources for post-conflict clearance work—a plan that could be reconfigured to take into account the greater scale of the submunition problem—but realistically it would take several weeks for initial surveys to be done and for specialists to be brought into the country to train and lead the personnel necessary to begin submunition clearance. UNIFIL had its own explosive ordnance disposal resources, but these were not available to the MACC, and the Lebanese Army was operating separately of UN coordination. Yet it was nearing harvest time, a driving factor behind the return of many thousands of civilians so soon after the firing stopped, and with roads, fields and orchards infested with submunitions there now seemed the prospect of a humanitarian disaster in the making from unexploded submunitions.

AFTERMATH

For those at the MACC, the dawning realization of the extent of the submunition contamination challenge meant that August and September 2006 was a period of frantic and around-the-clock effort. Gilly recalled that:

by that time, all of our staff had come back. And so we got everyone together—you can imagine, the MACC was full of people, UNHCR, [Office for the Coordination of Humanitarian Affairs], WFP, [Department of Safety and Security], everyone—and then our people came back. So then we needed to get a feeling for the scope of the problem. We got all of our guys, put them into small teams: "Okay, you guys go to this area, you to this area, this area. Take a GPS [global positioning system device]. Whenever you see a cluster bomb, get the coordinates—get as much information as you can. Bring it back here and then we'll enter

it [into the MACC's computer-based geographic information system].
So we were working crazy hours during those first three weeks, just
worked every day ...[31]

Under the direction of Rana Elias (a Lebanese national, and MACC officer
in charge of the information system) a shift also worked overnight at the
Centre to enter into the system the information gathered during the day
and begin to analyse it. What Clark, Gilly and Allen Kelly knew from direct
experience in Kosovo in 1999—as did John Flanagan at UN Mine Action
Service in New York, who had directed submunition clearance there in
the aftermath of that conflict—was that quickly building up a sufficiently
accurate picture of the characteristics of the submunition contamination,
especially the location of strikes, types and numbers used, would be crucial
in the longer term to ensuring that clearance efforts were effective. Dealing
with submunition strikes is quite different from clearing anti-personnel
mines, in which a technical survey is done, an area marked and fenced off,
and mines systematically detected and dealt with in that area according
to well-established international standards. Rather, what is required with
submunitions is to detect roughly where the centre of the strike has occurred,
walk into it, and then scan the area around it for unexploded submunitions
radiating outward to a fade-out zone of around 50m from last evidence of
the presence of submunitions.[32] Most of the submunitions should be on
the surface, but others might become buried: without an accurate surface
picture it is very difficult to know whether sub-surface clearance will be
required, and thus the total area in the region that needs to be cleared,
the clearance resources needed and the most efficient manner in which to
deploy them.

This methodology, which was developed in the aftermath of NATO's
operations in Kosovo in 1999, worked well in an environment in which
roughly a little more than 18,000 unexploded submunitions were eventually
cleared.[33] But the number of cluster strikes in the 2006 Southern Lebanon
conflict was much greater than in Kosovo; it soon became apparent to
the United Nations that the numbers of unexploded submunitions present
were in the hundreds of thousands and, it was initially thought, might be as
high as a million[34]—in a relatively densely populated region at harvest time
to which tens of thousands of civilians were impatient to return.

The density of the submunition contamination from Israeli rockets and
shelling in many places in Southern Lebanon also meant that the elliptical

footprints of individual cluster munition strikes overlapped, which complicated assessment of where the centre of strikes were and obscured clues about where these strike zones faded out. Moreover, clues at the scene that might help assessment were being removed or disrupted in the immediate post-conflict period because of a lot of "informal" clearance of unexploded submunitions, as well as of other forms of ordnance. Usually such informal clearance—the movement or attempted destruction of unexploded munitions by people with no proper training or methodology—was no more sophisticated than picking up a submunition by its body or ribbon and carrying it to an area considered of less risk to surrounding civilians, or adding it to a pile of other unexploded munitions. Anecdotal evidence is that Hizbullah carried out such activities on a wide scale, and some villagers and civilian returnees also moved submunitions they found, for instance scattered in and around their houses and gardens. As the extent of the contamination of agricultural land became apparent to local farmers, some even began paying Palestinian labourers to find and remove any unexploded submunitions,[35] again with no records being kept of clearance.

Often, such submunitions could be seen at the side of the road simply stacked in piles or in fruit boxes. Indeed, Gilly was often shocked in the days and weeks following the ceasefire at the level of nonchalance with which these deadly objects were regarded by some locals, some even gathering up submunitions and offering the lethal objects to MACC staff in the vicinity: "I just used to keep away from them, and just say, 'Mate, this is dangerous, you know?'. And they'd just pick them [the submunitions] up and put them in a box and take them away".

Moving unexploded submunitions is akin to Russian roulette, and we will never know how many people were killed or injured in the course of these informal clearance activities—despite warnings not to do so by Gilly and others from the MACC.[36] And it removed evidence that would help to coordinate systematic submunition clearance of high priority areas in the coming weeks and months. But the (obviously incomplete) picture the MACC was able to piece together showed clearly that post-conflict incidents from submunitions were at their highest in the months immediately after the ceasefire, with 57 people killed or injured in the first month from the end of the conflict on 14 August 2006, falling to the high teens per month for the rest of the year from October.[37]

Clearance of submunitions in Southern Lebanon following the 2006 conflict fell into three main phases. The initial emergency post-conflict phase during the period between the mid-August ceasefire and October 2006 concentrated available MAG, UNIFIL and Lebanese Armed Forces (LAF) clearance resources on the visible hazards, particularly of submunitions, in order to allow the safe return of civilians, as well as risk education efforts aimed at warning the local population about the dangers of unexploded ordnance. It was a period of around-the-clock effort and exhaustion for those involved in battle area clearance and explosive ordnance disposal. Lebanese Army units, in particular, were immediately active in carrying out explosive ordnance disposal in various places around Southern Lebanon. But immediately after the war the LAF's operations and those of the MACC were not closely coordinated and the LAF did not keep detailed records of what it cleared and where.

Systematic clearance efforts largely began from the end of October 2006 in a second phase that lasted until late 2007. This phase consisted predominantly of surface clearance of UXO, augmented by a stream of clearance assets as money and expertise flowed into Lebanon from the international community, and more clearance teams could be trained and certified. The number of these battle area clearance (BAC) teams was to peak at 60 in October 2007 and consisted of a mixture of commercial outfits like BacTec International and not-for-profits such as MAG, DanChurchAid, Handicap International and Norwegian People's Aid,[38] with UNIFIL contributing clearance capacity and countries such as New Zealand and Iceland offering national BAC teams on short-term deployments. With the help of its sophisticated geographic information system, the MACC's staff, in coordination with the Lebanese government and local communities, focused resources on designated high- and medium-priority clearance tasks in highly populated areas such as villages, main roads and around housing. The MACC assessed that unexploded submunitions contaminated more than 35km^2 of land, and by the middle of April 2007 more than 144,000 of these deadly objects were located and destroyed.[39] During this period the MACC and the LAF also worked to improve their coordination structures.

LONGER-TERM CLEARANCE AND
IMPACTS OF UNEXPLODED SUBMUNITIONS

2008 marked the beginning of the third submunition clearance phase in Southern Lebanon. Systematic clearance efforts continued, but with an increasing focus on subsurface clearance. To discover what subsurface clearance actually meant, my colleague Maya Brehm and I travelled to Southern Lebanon in late 2008.

I find myself standing in a wheat field designated as zone CBU-614 near the village of Safeed Al Battikh, which is in Area 3—one of the eight clearance zones Southern Lebanon is carved into. Two Norwegian People's Aid BAC teams are carrying out subsurface survey and clearance here. Two feet away from me an unexploded M-42 DPICM submunition peeks out from the rocky soil. It is armed, and therefore dangerous, and (naturally) I feel slightly nervous about that. Looking carefully at it, Kerei Ruru, the MACC's Operations Officer, along with the leader of the BAC team clearing this zone, are keen to point out the features of the tiny M-42's arming mechanism to Maya and me. I sense that in Maya outward politeness is warring with a similar nervousness to mine when they motion us even closer to the deadly object. I am surprised by how small the submunition is, and how closely its dull, dusty surface blends in with the ground: I could easily have missed seeing it without the wooden stakes joined with red and white plastic hazard tape the BAC team have erected around it. Seen close up, the partially uncovered M-42's arming mechanism looks a bit like the top of a miniature spray-paint can. Its nylon ribbon is invisible, either still buried or rotted away.

Although it is mid-October and this morning is overcast, the temperature here is at least 20°C. In summer the heat climbs into the high 30s and the sun bakes the ground until it sets like concrete and the fields shimmer. Kerei and I both hail from near the alluvial Canterbury Plains in the South Island of New Zealand, so we are relatively familiar with what we consider to be stony soils. But these fields near the village of Safeed Al Battikh are quarry-like by comparison. Even now in autumn the ground is still firm, and the myriad rocks not only radiate heat back from the ground, they can interfere with the hand-held metal detectors the BAC searchers use to locate submunitions and other unexploded ordnance. Norwegian People's Aid BAC personnel nearby in bulky clearance gear—local Lebanese men—smile wanly, and wave to us as we make our way into the field. Perversely, because of its large scale, battle area clearance of submunitions is a big employer of local people, and a relatively well-paid and thus sought-after job. But it is hard work, and I can barely imagine what toiling in the fields in mid-summer wearing a protective vest (which resembles a thick flak jacket) and perspex faceplate must be like. I am told that clearance shifts in such conditions last as little as 20 minutes in view of the risk of heat exhaustion.

As marginal as this land seems to me, the submunition we are examining has been found because a local farmer recently ploughed his field to plant wheat. For economic reasons farming must go on, even though it is a known Israeli cluster strike zone and not yet free of unexploded bomblets. Facing roughly south, the hillside field was on the receiving end of cluster munition strike from Israeli 155mm artillery during the 2006 conflict—overlapping elliptical patterns of submunitions falling roughly longitudinally upon it. The action of rain and plough submerged this submunition in the ground and now ploughing has brought it closer to the surface.

The presence of this submunition in a field that, we are told, has been ploughed a dozen times or more since the conflict underlines that these are not *de facto* anti-personnel mines as they have sometimes been described in the media and in the Human Rights Council's Commission of Inquiry mentioned earlier.[40] An anti-personnel mine is a simple device designed for a purpose: to lie in wait until something or someone comes into contact with it at which point it explodes. In other words, it is designed for a purpose and, although utterly indiscriminate, anti-personnel mines perform their task reliably. Rather, this submunition is here because it has *failed* to function as designed: it signally lacks the predictability or reliability of an anti-personnel mine. Leaning over the hazard tape and peering at the M-42, Kerei points out the submunition's stab detonator mechanism: this dud might be ploughed over repeatedly without exploding, each time being disturbed and probably moved slightly. At some point, though, a plough blade will hit the submunition at an angle that will activate the detonator, or someone will inadvertently step on it with the same effect, and the submunition may finally explode. But the submunition was not designed with a view to blowing off a person's limbs like an anti-personnel mine; it is a weapon designed to punch through several centimetres of steel plate to kill an armoured vehicle's occupants. Farmers driving tractors, shepherds on foot and livestock do not stand a chance.

Later, we are introduced to the local *Muktar* in a nearby village (a Muktar, we are told, is a sort of equivalent to a notary or Justice of the Peace). He seats us at a table in his garden and his family offer us strong coffee. Pointing up from our interview at the table he gestures to distinctive shrapnel patterns on the exterior wall of his house where submunitions struck it during the 2006 conflict. By that time he and his family had fled to the north after neighbours were killed by Israeli bombardment, the Muktar said. He returned to the village immediately after the ceasefire while his relatives remained north of the Litani and waited for an all-clear message from him, and he described to us how he found submunitions littered everywhere in the village. We asked the Muktar whether submunitions on the roads impeded his return. No, he said, Hizbullah cleared the roads as soon as the ceasefire took effect. Inwardly we note that the presence of Hizbullah fighters would, indeed, likely have made objects in the area military targets. (Later, driving out of the village, we see the distinctive yellow Hizbullah billboards that are common in Southern Lebanon—our driver tells us this one portrays the martyrdom of the Muktar's son in the 2006 conflict, who is pictured in military fatigues.)

The Muktar introduces us to his son-in-law, Hussein, a small-time farmer who we are told was injured by a submunition while working in his fields. Hussein shows us scars on his arm from the incident, a wound he says continues to be painful and prevents the limb's full use. An elderly neighbour harvesting olives a few yards away is called over, and he describes how lucky he was when an unexploded submunition he encountered in his grove somehow only lightly wounded him in the head. Of the 261 civilian casualties recorded from unexploded ordnance in Southern Lebanon from the ceasefire until the end of September 2008, 215 were due to submunitions. Twenty of these people were killed, and the rest injured, many grievously, so Yousef (and even Hussein) has reason to count himself lucky.

Casualty figures fail to tell the full story, of course, because they do not take into account the other socio-economic costs of inaccessibility of land, and loss of income and opportunity brought about by submunition contamination on such a massive scale. A 2008 report produced by the British NGO Landmine Action with support from the United Nations Development Programme looked at the cost of lost agricultural production in Southern Lebanon specifically caused by cluster munition contamination, the cost of the response through internationally assisted clearance and risk reduction operations and the economic cost of deaths and injuries directly resulting from it. The report came up with a cost estimate of between US$ 153.8 million and 233.2 million. Also:

> Considering only the costs of lost agricultural production, and estimating based on the size of average land holdings in affected areas, post-conflict cluster munition contamination would have cost some 3,105 individual landowners an average of around US$ 8,000 each—this in a country where the 2006 per capita GDP was US$ 5,300. In the area hardest hit by contamination the primary economic activities are agricultural, further exacerbating the impact.[41]

There were costs for the international community too. While noting that without it the socio-economic costs of cluster munition contamination would have been much greater, Landmine Action's report estimated that clearance and risk reduction activities in Southern Lebanon cost humanitarian donors around US$ 120 million in the period between the ceasefire and May 2008: substantially higher than the US$ 30 million Landmine Action estimated as the cost of the 1999–2005 response to NATO's use of cluster munitions in Kosovo in 1999.[42] And, there have been inevitable accidents involving clearance personnel—inevitable because, despite strict rules, training, and regular quality assurance by the MACC of all clearance teams working under their authority, conditions are difficult, human beings make errors and, most of all, submunitions are highly dangerous and unpredictable. Fourteen clearance personnel were killed and 41 were injured in Southern Lebanon between mid-August 2006 and the end of September 2008.[43] Experience in Southern Lebanon supports the view that submunitions are particularly risky for humanitarian clearance.

LESSONS TO BE LEARNED FROM SOUTHERN LEBANON

As I interviewed MACC staff, personnel from various demining organizations working in Southern Lebanon and talked with the Lebanese themselves, it struck me that the consequences of the cluster munition contamination resulting from the Southern Lebanon conflict hold a number of lessons of particular importance for the Cluster Munition Convention's successful implementation.

The first lesson is that acquisition of strike data as soon as possible after a conflict such as the number, types and locations of munitions fired makes a big difference in reducing the hazards to returning civilians. MACC staff spent a lot of time in the 2006 conflict's aftermath just trying to get an overall sense of the extent and geographical focus of the contamination. While they were familiar with older submunitions such as the BLU-63s they had been clearing for years (and which were used again in 2006 by Israeli forces, despite the weapon's age, many—again—failing to function) a number of the submunitions explosive ordnance disposal personnel found took them some time to identify.[44] Many DPICMs such as the M-42, M-77 and M-85 look much like another, and are often damaged or partially obscured in some way when explosive ordnance disposal personnel first encounter them. Experts were puzzled for some time by Hizbullah's Chinese-made MZD-2 bomblet—itself a copy of the Yugoslav KB-1, in turn an effort to reproduce Western DPICM submunitions.[45] (Many MZD-2s were found in contaminated zones intermingled with unexploded Israeli submunitions, as in some cases Israeli bombardment had destroyed Hizbullah weapons caches or rocket firing platforms and, in the ensuing explosions, scattered the munitions.)

Not knowing *where* to focus limited survey and clearance resources was the biggest problem, however, for the MACC and the Lebanese Army as the hours and days after ceasefire ticked away and large numbers of civilians returned to salvage their homes and livelihoods and tend the harvest. Strike data from the IDF would have helped immensely in reducing civilian casualties from UXO, which spiked in the day following the ceasefire, and would slow to a steady, bloody trickle long afterwards. Indeed, Protocol V to the CCW on explosive remnants of war contains provisions encouraging the timely exchange of this kind of information precisely because it saves lives.[46] Despite repeated pleas by states in the UN Security Council and at the bilateral level, Israel did not provide information about where it targeted its cluster munitions, or how many and what types it used until more than two years after the end of the 2006 conflict.[47] When I visited Southern Lebanon in late 2008, MACC staff showed me the sole fruit of their requests to the IDF, stuck to the wall of their operations briefing room in Tyre: a single hand-sketched map in Hebrew on graph paper with firing angles identifiable but little else. As a result, the MACC and other authorities had to build a picture of contamination from scratch in August 2006, and civilians and clearance teams in Southern Lebanon kept encountering new and unexpected areas of contamination. In mid-May 2009, Israel belatedly handed over some technical data and related maps to UNIFIL.[48]

The second lesson is that a surge in capacity to survey and clear submunitions and to provide warnings to civilians post-conflict makes a major difference in reducing immediate humanitarian harm. This is particularly crucial where use of cluster munitions is concerned as failed submunitions tend to be generated in large numbers, and because they are small it means they are hard for civilians to see (and so avoid) and get caught in trees, shrubs, house roofs and the like. Nevertheless, the harm to civilians caused in Southern Lebanon by massive quantities of unexploded Israeli submunitions fired in the final days of the war was less than it might have been: the area's pre-existing mine and UXO problem meant that expertise and coordination mechanisms such as the MACC were already in place and swung into action very quickly. Efforts by the United Nations and the broader humanitarian community to raise resources to begin post-conflict clearance activities in Southern Lebanon had begun during the conflict itself. Of course, during the fighting, nobody in the UN had any idea of the extent of the submunition contamination that would be caused in the final three days of the conflict, and the amount of resources needed had to be repeatedly revised upwards as the picture became clearer. When the conflict ended, there were only a few MAG demining teams, UNIFIL's explosive ordnance disposal resources and the Lebanese Army's capacity—all of which saved civilian lives by intervening in contaminated areas. But at least there was a capacity there, which could be expanded. The lesson is plain: more teams on the ground quickly means more civilians are saved. And where coordination capacities to handle survey, clearance and other tasks to reduce the hazards of cluster munitions do not exist post-conflict, they must be established with haste, and with the cooperation of national and local authorities in the country they operate in.

The third lesson is that submunition clearance is not the same as mine clearance in terms of its methodology, as described earlier in this chapter. This might seem obvious, but it is not always so in the mine action sector, which is well established in terms of its standards and methodologies and has mature "standard operating procedures" (SOPs)—for clearing mines, that is, not submunitions. The aftermath of the 1999 Kosovo NATO air campaign was a wake-up call in this respect, and served as a laboratory for a number of people who would later be significant in terms of tackling the problems caused by submunitions post-conflict in Southern Lebanon. These included many in the MACC, for instance, including Clark, Gilly and Ruru as well as the Chief of Operations of the UN Mine Action Service in New York, John Flanagan, who had directed the Kosovo UN clearance operation. They understood the differences in methodology between mines and submunitions (since they, in effect, developed some of the latter as they went along) and what needed to be done. So too did some of the NGO demining organizations such as Norwegian People's Aid.[49] But in other areas of the mine action community, awareness of differing methodologies lagged (and still lags) behind, for instance among some newly arriving field staff (the majority of whom have military backgrounds trained in mine clearance) but also among some of those developing related policy at the international level, and among funders. Related to this is the controversy around area reduction. Pioneered in the context of mine clearance, the idea of area reduction was initially bitterly resisted by many in the mine action community as potentially unsafe because it released land back to civilian use after determining through cross-checked information, including interviews with locals, that some areas were free of mines, rather than through painstaking and time-consuming manual clearance. (There was concern that safeguards on the accuracy of cross-checked information might be insufficient to ensure the safety of civilians.)

The fourth lesson of Southern Lebanon is that it shows that area reduction is crucial to reducing the risks of submunitions, since not every square inch of ground can be turned over in the search for them. Kerei Ruru, the MACC's Operations Chief who showed me around submunition-contaminated areas of Southern Lebanon, knows this better than most, as he went from site to site for several years overseeing the BAC teams at work there. He confirmed:

> Mindset is a big issue. [Cluster munitions] pose special risk to clearance personnel. Fourteen have been killed so far in Southern Lebanon—that's quite a lot, and it can become demoralizing. But it's not just that BAC and [explosive ordnance disposal] personnel at the local level may have a mine clearance mentality. It's also conceivably a big point for international efforts—you need awareness that it's a good idea to have SOPs, but you have to be flexible.

He added, "Of course, area reduction can save a lot of time and money. But it has to be based on solid data, and with technical survey assets in order to check".[50] To be effective in releasing land back to civilian use, both clearance and area reduction activities have to be understood by the locals, and have to engender confidence. Moreover, "You've got to have a system for post-clearance review", Ruru said.

It's important to go back to the communities you've worked in a year after clearance to ask the local people if they're actually using the land. If they are, then what are they using it for? If they're not using the land, then why not? Is it because they lack the confidence that the land is safe? Or is it for some other reason like lacking the money to replant the trees in their orchards?[51]

The fifth lesson of Southern Lebanon was one heeded in the Oslo process. For years, discussions both in the CCW and at the national level in many countries such as Norway had assumed that technical fixes were possible to take care of the post-conflict hazards that cluster munitions cause. Specifically, the technical "improvement" most often mentioned was reducing the failure rate of submunitions so that less would be left on the ground in a dangerous state. Self-destruct mechanisms were seen as a key means of achieving this, and the British (as discussed in chapter 2) had pointed to this feature of their Israeli-made M-85 submunitions as a solution, a view shared by the military in Norway and other states that possessed variants of the M-85 with self-destruct. Yet the lesson as communicated from August 2006 by the MACC's Director, Chris Clark, to anyone who would listen in the CCW or the international community more generally, was that self-destruct clearly did not work to a satisfactory standard. Large numbers of dud M-85 bomblets with self-destruct—unexploded submunitions that should not have existed—were nevertheless being found in Southern Lebanon, and were just as dangerous to dispose of as other unexploded submunitions.[52] And the massive quantities fired by the IDF in the war's closing stages had shown the central weakness of any reliability improvement argument—that even low failure rates could still create significant numbers of hazardous duds.

Self-destruct and other technologies in submunitions could, at best, be only part of the solution in reducing the risks to civilians of cluster munitions. The same was true of the other line of discussion in the CCW—to improve the implementation of existing international humanitarian law rules rather than creating new, weapon-specific law for cluster munitions. International humanitarian law prohibits indiscriminate attacks; that is, "those which are not directed at a specific military objective" or "which employ a method or means of combat which cannot be directed at a specific military objective".[53] Yet, egregiously, Hizbullah launched rockets at Israel throughout the conflict (at least a few containing submunitions)[54] too inaccurate to distinguish between military and civilian targets—and there seems precious little evidence Hizbullah made any attempt to observe such a distinction.[55]

Combined with the high risk that cluster munitions can pose to civilians, the 2006 conflict underlined the need for concrete international rules to keep such weapons out of the hands of those inclined to use weapons without regard for humanitarian law.

Israel's use of cluster munitions also underlined the problems associated with the weapon. Israeli warplanes bombed targets in Lebanon during the war with cluster munitions containing very old BLU-63s with ensuing high failures—casings from some of the US-manufactured CBU-58 containers showed their warranties expired in the mid-1970s. And yet there was no international rule to prevent Israel from using ancient stocks of such unreliable munitions again. Then there was the IDF's firing of massive quantities of ground-launched cluster munitions in the final days of the conflict, perhaps intended to interdict Hizbullah forces pulling back. The dispersal of massive numbers of submunitions, combined with their higher operational failure rate than other kinds of explosive munitions like unitary warhead artillery projectiles, mortar rounds and the like, left large numbers of deadly unexploded duds on the ground or hanging from vegetation.

Cluster munition use by Hizbullah and Israel in 2006 underlined that debates on the technical characteristics of weapons and their supposed effects can be a very long way from the effects as seen on the ground. Outrage about cluster munition use in Southern Lebanon would help to commence the Oslo process, to be discussed in the next chapter. The lesson of the Southern Lebanon conflict that alleged technical "fixes" like self-destruct mechanisms were not sufficient in themselves to address the humanitarian problems cluster munitions create took longer to sink in. But in that respect, the lessons gathered in Lebanon during 2007 concerning the M-85 submunition would play a direct role within the Oslo initiative.

CHAPTER 5

THE COMMENCEMENT OF THE OSLO PROCESS

On 23 February 2007, 46 states made a historic declaration at a conference in the snow-covered hills above the Norwegian capital, Oslo. The Oslo Declaration contained commitments to complete an international treaty by the end of 2008 to "prohibit the use, production, transfer and stockpiling of cluster munitions that cause unacceptable harm to civilians" and to "establish a framework for cooperation and assistance that ensures adequate provision of care and rehabilitation to survivors and their communities, clearance of contaminated areas, risk education and destruction of stockpiles of prohibited cluster munitions".[1]

Few people were as surprised as Titus Peachey, who after returning from his years in Laos working with the Mennonite Central Committee had campaigned to raise awareness among about the effects of cluster munitions (see chapter 1), and had even read a speech on behalf of a handful of NGOs at the Convention on Certain Conventional Weapons (CCW) Review Conference in 2001 calling for a moratorium on the production, use and transfer of cluster munitions.[2] (The moratorium call fell short of the Mennonite Central Committee's desire for a ban on the weapon, but was the best that seemed possible at the time under the circumstances.) When Peachey heard news that the Oslo conference would be held, he later recalled:

> it was quite a shock to realize that there was now a collection of governments who were really going to move with this. And immediately the Ottawa process came to mind: perhaps this is going to be a repeat of that in terms of process, with governments and NGOs working together to move toward a treaty that will result in a ban on cluster bombs. Yeah, I was very excited, but also trying not to get my hopes up too high because I had been to the CCW often enough to realize that things move very slowly and that there would be lots of obstacles and rabbit trails and twists and turns along the way.[3]

Only a year earlier, such resolve from so many states—some of them cluster munition possessors—to address the humanitarian impacts of the weapon through an international treaty was hard to envisage. Of course, as told at the end of chapter 2, Belgium's parliament, conscious of the leadership it had shown in banning anti-personnel mines more than a decade earlier, passed a national law prohibiting cluster munitions in February 2006 (and, a short time later, another piece of legislation to clarify what it meant). Norway's new Red–Green coalition of Labour, Socialist and Agrarian party politicians had assumed power in late 2005 and committed itself in its governing manifesto to international action on cluster munitions, as discussed in chapter 3. However, although some states and civil society were in dialogue on strategy by early 2006, it was not clear yet how such aspirations would manifest themselves in real outcomes at the global level. The CCW was the only multilateral forum talking about cluster munitions at that time, and no undertakings had been made there for any negotiations concerning this weapon since it adopted generic post-conflict measures in a protocol on explosive remnants of war in November 2003. Discussions continued in the CCW in which concerns about cluster munitions were raised, but as an adjunct to other topics such as the adequacy of international humanitarian law (IHL) rules in broader terms, or technical discussions about "good" and "bad" cluster munitions, and especially submunition failure rate claims that, as discussed earlier, were not able to be practically tested in that forum. Most of all, despite the growing empirical evidence of harm caused by the use of various kinds of submunitions, a number of states in the CCW such as China, India, Pakistan and Russia still saw no need for new IHL or technical standards related to cluster munitions, and seemed unlikely to permit emergence of a consensus for negotiations on any restrictions there.

This chapter examines what happened concerning international efforts on cluster munitions during the period between Belgium adopting its national legislation in February–March 2006, through the CCW Review Conference in late 2006, and up to and including the Oslo conference in February 2007. During this pivotal period, unpromising multilateral prospects for addressing the humanitarian impacts of cluster munitions were transformed and an international treaty process in parallel to the CCW emerged. Belgium's ban legislation was one factor in this transformation, not only as a national action establishing a precedent but because it provided an important spur to the Norwegian government to move out into the lead on the cluster munition issue,[4] a reorientation well underway before the 34-day Southern Lebanon conflict that broke out in mid-July 2006. Nevertheless, that conflict attracted massive media attention and generated great—if fleeting—international public concern about the use of cluster munitions. In underlining in a clear way the hazards that cluster munitions pose to civilians both at time of use and post-conflict, the Southern Lebanon conflict provided additional impetus for many governments represented in the CCW to show that they were treating the weapon's hazards to civilians seriously, and doing something about it.

An additional and perhaps under-rated point is that UN agencies, the International Committee of the Red Cross (ICRC) and NGOs had, by now, been developing their humanitarian arguments and evidence base about the effects of cluster munitions on civilians for some years. NGOs had even produced in 2005 a report on the effects of cluster munitions in Southern Lebanon prior to the 2006 summer conflict. Cluster Munition Coalition (CMC) Coordinator Thomas Nash and Landmine Action's Richard Moyes argued in the report that the history of cluster munition use in Lebanon "affirmed the need to develop specific restrictions or prohibitions on these weapons" and, in view of the CCW's failure to tackle the specific problems associated with cluster munitions, coupled with the ineffectiveness of bilateral arrangements between the US and Israel to ensure the latter used the weapons in line with international humanitarian law, it suggested that "a prohibition regime, developed outside the framework of the CCW, would offer the best protection to civilians both during and after conflict".[5] As 2006 began, the CMC remained under-resourced and differences persisted between its members over its call and overall campaigning strategy. But, as their Lebanon report indicated, Nash, Moyes and others both within and advising the Coalition had made important progress in framing the problems cluster munitions caused, and in developing responses to many of the counter-arguments they had now become used to hearing from states in the CCW context.

The CCW, moreover, provided CMC members with a forum in which they could raise awareness of the problems cluster munitions caused, and do their best to create pressure on government delegations to take the aim of weapon-specific rules forward. And, by the beginning of 2006, a loose, informal network of individuals concerned about cluster munitions existed that comprised people from many governments and international organizations as well as those associated with the CMC. This network had its origins in the high levels of trust built up among some of those key to the

Ottawa process a decade before, and new partnerships cultivated during the subsequent implementation of the Mine Ban Treaty. But a question mark hung over the potential of such partnerships formed in a humanitarian context to create momentum in the arms-control-oriented CCW, especially as these actors did not necessarily agree among themselves on the best way forward on cluster munitions.

WHAT TO DO ABOUT CLUSTER MUNITIONS

At that time I led a project at UNIDIR entitled Disarmament as Humanitarian Action: Making Multilateral Negotiations Work. In view of the direction of our research, the need for an opportunity for certain of our colleagues to exchange views off-the-record was plain. I had colleagues in Geneva deeply interested in the cluster munition issue who felt the same way. They included Rosy Cave, who had left Landmine Action and joined UNIDIR as a researcher. Another was Patrick McCarthy, Coordinator of the Geneva Forum, a project of UNIDIR, the Quaker United Nations Office in Geneva and the Geneva Graduate Institute of International Studies.[6] Under the Geneva Forum's auspices, we organized a one-day "informal brainstorming meeting" on a snowy Sunday near Geneva the day before the CCW's March 2006 Group of Experts (GGE) talks commenced. In their personal capacities, individuals from the governments of Canada, the Netherlands, Norway and Sweden attended, as did individuals from the UN, ICRC and NGOs including CMC, Handicap International, Human Rights Watch, Landmine Action, Mines Action Canada, Norwegian People's Aid and Oxfam GB. The meeting revolved around four questions about cluster munitions: what really is the problem and how serious is it? What are the best responses (if any) at the international level? What is the international situation at present and where is it leading? And what, realistically, can be done?

The Geneva Forum meeting was perhaps the first opportunity for such a crosscutting group to try to collectively absorb the significance of national developments in Belgium and Norway, and what this could mean for prospects for work on cluster munitions in the CCW. An internal Geneva Forum summary from the meeting captured the sense of the discussion:

> Regarding the CCW, it was widely felt that for this Review Conference year, in tandem with continued pushing for Protocol V ratification, the focus should be on trying to build something on [cluster munitions]

within the CCW, such as a negotiating mandate. For some the benefit of this strategy was said to be in building momentum for something outside the CCW should it fail to deliver, as many expect. It was suggested that one way to do this would be to push key states to go for a ban on the most offensive [cluster munitions] and stick to this; if the CCW failed then another forum would present itself, or be developed through national government and public pressure.[7]

"Another forum" remained to be determined, although some of us were aware of what was happening in Norway and were following developments there with interest (see chapter 3). Among NGOs in the CMC, though, the idea was already well entrenched that the Review Conference should be portrayed for tactical reasons as a "clean break". If the CCW should "succeed" (by achieving a negotiation on a legally binding protocol restricting cluster munitions) as government representatives from Canada, the Netherlands and Sweden fervently hoped, so be it. If the Review Conference's outcome fell short of that, the outcome should be regarded as a failure, and a "new process to eliminate cluster munitions" should be started.[8]

Certainly, the CCW appeared to be going nowhere fast in either its discussions among technical experts or its IHL questionnaire exercise. Three days after the Geneva Forum meeting in March 2006, Australian legal expert Timothy McCormack presented the *Report on States Parties' Responses to the Questionnaire* to the CCW, and told delegates:

> [It is our conclusion that] Protocol V to the CCW and the existing rules of IHL are specific and comprehensive enough to deal adequately with the problem of ERW provided that those rules are effectively implemented. That proviso is an important one. It is not adequate for States that want to use cluster munitions, for example, simply to assert that their use of such weapons is consistent with general "principles" of IHL without a genuine commitment to implement the binding legal rules effectively.[9]

McCormack's report outlined five recommendations on further "practical steps" on explosive remnants of war (ERW) including Protocol V ratification, promotion of IHL rules in general, establishment of national processes of legal review of new and modified weapon systems and the introduction of confidence-building reports about destruction of old or outmoded weapons. None of these was controversial. However, the report also recommended that:

> The GGE [Group of Governmental Experts] should consider the development of a set of non-legally binding Guidelines on "best practice" application of relevant rules of International Humanitarian Law to the problem of ERW.

> It is clear from responses to the questionnaire that very few States have thought through how the Rule on Distinction, the Prohibition on Indiscriminate Attacks or the Rule on Proportionality, for example, apply in practical terms to the problem of ERW. The development of non-legally binding Guidelines on "best practice" application of relevant rules of International Humanitarian Law may well make it easier for more States Parties to the CCW to ratify or accede to Protocol V and could also help States give some practical content to the relationship between relevant binding rules of International Humanitarian Law and ERW. *The Guidelines would not argue for a prohibition on cluster munitions but might indicate best practice technical requirements (including minimum reliability rates, self-deactivation and self-destruct mechanisms)* to ensure compliance with relevant rules of IHL for those States arguing for the continued deployment of such munitions.[10]

This recommendation and aspects of the McCormack report's conclusions were criticized by the ICRC, NGOs such as Human Rights Watch, as well as some governments. The ICRC, for example, which had been formally invited by the CCW GGE's Chair to comment on McCormack's report, said it could not support the recommendation, nor understand how the report's authors arrived at the conclusion that existing IHL was adequate either with respect to "the specific characteristics of cluster munitions" or "the extent to which the long-term effects of ERW must be taken into account in judgements concerning the proportionality of an attack".[11] Human Rights Watch put it more bluntly: "it reaches a wrong conclusion— that IHL and Protocol 5 are adequate to deal with cluster munitions—a conclusion that is not supported by the information and analysis in the paper itself. A new instrument is clearly needed"[12] and they circulated their own critique.[13] The debate prompted some countries, such as Denmark, Ireland, Norway, Sweden and Switzerland, to call for negotiations on a legally binding instrument on cluster munitions, and others such as China, Japan, India, Russia and the United States to state that they thought such talk was premature. In reply, McCormack noted the fact that his report's recommendation on "best practice" had been used to support contrasting positions on cluster munitions. He explained that the reason he had proposed such an approach was simply because he thought this would be more achievable than negotiating a new protocol. In view of what he had heard, McCormack said, this might no longer be the case.[14] In any case, he stressed, to justify inaction based on the report's conclusion was not good enough.

Someone else pondering "the case" on cluster munitions was Ambassador Steffen Kongstad, now leading the Norwegian government's special project on cluster munitions. Had Kongstad not been prevented from attending the Geneva Forum meeting by a snowstorm that grounded him in Munich on the way to Geneva, the conclusions of that brainstorming about what lay ahead might have taken a more ambitious turn. In view of the CCW's track record set against the Norwegian government's intent on cluster munitions in the October 2005 Soria Moria Declaration, Kongstad's thoughts were focused on how to get a more effective cluster munition process started than the talks in the CCW. Experience from the Ottawa process had taught him that strong partners among other governments—in a "core-group"—and a civil society campaign capable of exerting political pressure when obstacles were encountered would be essential.[15]

The week following the March CCW session, Kongstad and many of those who had participated in the Geneva Forum's brainstorming met again in London at a meeting organized by Landmine Action and its funding partner, The Diana, Princess of Wales Memorial Fund.[16] At this key meeting near Westminster at the Fund's headquarters, a broader group of government representatives than had participated in the Geneva Forum meeting was invited, including Belgium, Denmark, Ireland, Lithuania, Mexico, the Netherlands, Norway, Sweden and Switzerland.[17] Kongstad and his colleagues Annette Abelsen and Ministry of Defence lawyer Annette Bjørseth watched and listened carefully.

All eyes were on Belgium, in particular. Would Belgium's new national law now mean it would take on a leading role in international efforts to ban cluster munitions? The London meeting served to reinforce the contrary impression—one formed during the CCW's deliberations the preceding week—that Belgian diplomats did not aspire to such a role. And, among representatives of most other countries present (with the conspicuous exception of Norway) there was nervousness even about talk of initiatives outside the CCW framework. I was asked, for instance, by the organizers to be a devil's advocate and offer my views about productive international responses to the humanitarian effects of cluster munitions, and so I argued that:

The CCW certainly has awareness raising and educative value, even if it's not undertaking negotiations on cluster munitions. I'm also conscious of the concern about exhausting every effort to undertake work within the CCW's ambit because of the potential negative impact on its credibility of taking work elsewhere. I foresee three potential scenarios at this year's Review Conference:

• The first—and, frankly, least likely—scenario is that the review meeting will achieve a robust mandate to negotiate effective cluster munition restrictions. (By effective I mean a comprehensive package of measures of the calibre Human Rights Watch has proposed.) Achieving this would be great. It will also lock you into a CCW negotiation process for up to five years, though. During this time you'll need to be vigilant about attempts to dilute your proposals or procedural gambits to delay work or prevent agreement, which we know are only too easy in the CCW.

• A second scenario is that the Review Conference fails to agree to any further work on cluster munitions.

• The third scenario—and by far the worst one in my view—is that you achieve a mandate for further work that's too weak to alleviate the humanitarian problems created by cluster munition use. A discussion mandate, for instance, would be disastrous. It would lock you into a holding pattern in the CCW for years, and probably doom other international initiatives because of inevitable accusations that they imperil CCW "work". Another fear is that a mandate for continuation could be overly prescriptive and thereby make some desirable measures "off limits".[18]

The CCW, I argued, had become akin to Charles Shultz's Peanuts cartoon strips. Every time Charlie Brown took a run up and tried to kick the ball, Lucy moved it at the very last moment. Charlie Brown always ended up missing the ball and achieving nothing:

The joke is funny (at least to Lucy) because Charlie Brown never seems to realize he should go kick footballs with someone else and always falls for it. It's not so funny in the CCW. If you want a robust mandate on cluster munitions I put it to you that you'll be in a stronger position if the Lucys of the CCW know you mean business. Letting them know, for instance, that if you fail to obtain the robust mandate you want at the review conference you'd work outside the CCW on the issue—play football somewhere else—it would strengthen your hand.[19]

The presentation prompted strong reactions from the Irish and Swedish representatives, in particular, each of them highly sensitive to the CCW process being in any way undermined. I found this highly puzzling, as did some others at the meeting: the CCW stewardship and decision-making apparatus was undermining its credibility—the act of pointing that out was not. There was growing evidence of humanitarian problems associated with the weapon that, if not addressed in the CCW, had to be confronted somehow if states were to be politically and morally consistent with their statements of concern in that forum. Therefore, the contingent scenarios had to be aired, even if it was awkward. And, as it happened, the third scenario of a weak mandate to discuss cluster munitions in the CCW was precisely what later came to pass in November 2006 at the Review Conference.

The London meeting gave Norwegian policymakers some useful insights about the positions of others.[20] And, to other government representatives, the meeting successfully conveyed the organizers' message that the cluster munition issue continued to gather civil society momentum. Returning to Oslo, Kongstad felt that while the CMC needed strengthening, and an international campaign against cluster munitions evoking the Ottawa process on anti-personnel mines still needed firm government partners for Norway to work with, the basic elements were present. In particular, he felt he had identified some more individuals who could help push things forward.

LEBANON AND THE CCW

It is likely that some of the sensitivity of delegates from states like Ireland and Sweden about the CCW concerned their inability to agree on the product of negotiations on "mines other than anti-personnel mines" (MOTAPM) the preceding November. The fate of the MOTAPM draft protocol proposal had induced great nervousness among many CCW delegations that the Convention might be headed for failure at its upcoming five-yearly Review Conference to be held in November 2006. And, the CCW had recently lost two of its leading negotiators—who, if not sympathetic to the idea of a protocol on cluster munitions, each had a good eye for crafting deals. Ed Cummings, the likeable head of the US delegation, passed away in early 2006, and "Victor" Fu Zhigang, the Chinese delegation's affable lead negotiator, was killed in a traffic accident in Beijing a few days before the November 2005 CCW meeting. Without the rapport they and some others among the major military powers shared in the CCW, efforts from November 2005 to bring China and Russia onboard the goal of the US and many other countries of a MOTAPM protocol were not realized.

Instead, states and civil society in favour of a cluster munition treaty were able to fill the diplomatic space in the lead-up to the November Review Conference. This could be seen in June 2006 at the next CCW GGE meeting, which was held against a backdrop of preparatory discussions for the Review Conference and continued exchanges on MOTAPM. Many delegations now referred to the humanitarian impacts of cluster munitions in their statements, and a number, such as the Holy See, New Zealand, Norway and Sweden, called for the Review Conference to agree a negotiating mandate on a legally binding instrument on cluster munitions. Norway's views were the most ambitious, reflecting its own national policy shift just that month:

> Like many other countries, Norway holds cluster munitions as part of its defence arsenals. In the process towards an international regulation prohibiting cluster munitions that may have unacceptable humanitarian effects, the Norwegian government has introduced a moratorium on Norwegian cluster munitions until these munitions have been further tested and a decision on their future is made. ... *It is imperative to start working, without further delay, towards an international ban on cluster munitions that cause unacceptable humanitarian problems.*[21]

The June CCW session also underlined the difficulties facing the European Union in developing a common approach. EU member states such as Austria, Ireland and Sweden were keen to push ahead on a negotiating mandate. Belgium's diplomats kept quiet and the Netherlands, which had traditionally been active on ERW-related issues and had played an important role earlier in the decade in fostering dialogue on submunitions, appeared now to be pulling back, although its diplomats continued to be as proactive as their instructions would permit. France was deeply sceptical of cluster munition restrictions but its head of delegation, Ambassador François Rivasseau, President-Designate of the November Review Conference, was not keen to burn any bridges yet. Germany's position was intriguing—in March it presented a proposal for a definition of cluster munitions, and in June announced to the CCW that (based on Germany's own definition) "With immediate effect, the *Bundeswehr* will not procure any new cluster munitions" and would cease using two existing types immediately in view of their "rate of dangerous duds" being higher than 1%. Germany's accompanying "8-Point-Position on Cluster Munitions" put it at the forefront of states taking practical national measures.[22]

The UK, in contrast, emphatically endorsed all of the McCormack report's five recommendations, and especially the report's main conclusion—as the British delegation saw it—that existing IHL was adequate on ERW, which the UK extrapolated to mean adequacy regarding *all* issues around cluster munitions, despite McCormack's remarks quoted earlier. The UK head of delegation, new Geneva-based disarmament ambassador John Duncan, argued that failure to implement existing IHL fully "may drive some States to make a case against themselves that existing IHL falls short and that new law is required. We urge States not to pursue this route as it is both counterproductive and unnecessary as the [McCormack] report has shown".[23] In short, Austria, as EU President and coordinator, found agreement in the bloc limited to encouraging CCW members to "continue to identify which preventive measures would best result in improving the reliability of those munitions, including sub-munitions, whose failure rates present a significant humanitarian hazard".[24] It was weak stuff, reflecting a lot of late-night and early-morning brokering within the EU caucus on the CCW's margins.

The Lebanon conflict, which broke out in mid-July and concluded with a crescendo of cluster munition use in its final few days in August, exacerbated the EU's internal tensions, now presided over by Finland's Geneva disarmament ambassador, Kari Kahiluoto. Such were the difficulties of bridging the different perspectives of EU member states that, at the CCW's two-week session from late August, the EU's customary joint-statement on ERW failed even to mention what had happened in Lebanon.[25] Nor did many other national statements in the CCW, despite the extensive media coverage of cluster munition use in the conflict and impassioned statements from the CMC, Lebanon's ambassador in Geneva[26] and the Holy See's delegation about the dangers submunitions and other unexploded ordnance were posing to Lebanese civilians. (On 30 August, the UN's humanitarian chief, Jan Egeland, would describe the use of cluster munitions in Southern Lebanon as "shocking and completely immoral".[27]) Nor, in the CCW conference chamber at least, were there probing questions to Israeli government representatives about its military's use of cluster munitions, or to the US government, which had supplied many of these weapons to Israel—highlighted by a *New York Times* editorial on 26 August, which noted "the majority of the unexploded bomblets that United Nations teams have found [in Southern Lebanon] so far have been American-made".[28] Commenting on the opening general debate of the CCW session, in which discussion of submunition contamination in Lebanon might reasonably have been expected, the CMC observed:

> With few exceptions, the statements we have heard this morning have failed to recognise the civilian suffering going on right now because of a weapon widely considered by civil society to be the weapon most in need of new international rules. That this forum can be so disconnected from reality seriously undermines the CCW and these deliberations.[29]

This surreal bubble in the CCW expert group was finally punctured by a lunchtime presentation the CMC organized on the cluster munition-related aftermath of the Lebanon conflict. In a side-room packed with CCW government delegates, journalists and NGOs, the UN Mine Action Coordination Centre South Lebanon's Director Chris Clark presented evidence of massive submunition contamination caused by the Israeli bombardment in the last days of the conflict. It left those present in no doubt as to the severity of the post-conflict risks that failed submunitions posed to returning civilians. And, looking at the slides of submunitions littering village centres, hanging from trees and lying unexploded in homes, it was difficult for some present to comprehend how cluster munitions could possibly have been used in a discriminate manner (although, of course, many civilians had evacuated during the bombardment itself). For his part, working around the clock in Tyre with his colleagues, Clark had gone to Geneva very reluctantly after his boss, John Flanagan, telephoned him from New York at the beginning of September to tell him to go:

> My initial response was, "Are you serious? I'm a little bit busy at the moment!" And you couldn't just fly in and out of Lebanon then—the airport [in Beirut] was still partially closed, there was still an Israeli blockade. So it took like two days to get there. I initially resisted and said I've got better things to do than do that. But in the end I went and gave the presentation and I think it's reasonably fair to say that that was the start point, which allowed the Cluster Munition Coalition and associated groups to have enough emphasis to take the process out of CCW and start the Oslo Process.[30]

Lebanon, and the UN's presentation of initial findings about submunitions on the ground there, provided a graphic illustration of the problems with cluster munitions that CCW delegates from the half-dozen or so states calling for negotiation of a protocol had been telling their capitals for some time. Their national authorities still viewed a desirable negotiation outcome as consisting of technical improvements to reliability, and a prohibition on use of the weapon in populated areas. Now this was changing as the UN's findings were reported back to capitals and the implications about the inadequacy of such a legal solution sunk in. And it was apparent that now a political opportunity was in the offing to go from "We need to do something in the CCW" to "We need to support the negotiation of a legally binding instrument in any form", as one New Zealand diplomat told me.

In New Zealand's case, a policy shift on cluster munitions was aided by a reshuffle of ministerial portfolios in 2006 that saw one of the Labour-led coalition government's most senior politicians, Phil Goff, take on both the defence and the disarmament portfolios. This helped to overcome a policy disconnect—one faced in the bureaucracies of many states—between national security and humanitarian disarmament perspectives presented to different ministers, who then faced off against each other to fight for their departmental turf. Goff received briefings about the CCW situation, including Norway's views, from foreign affairs and trade ministry bureaucrats, and reports about the situation in Lebanon from New Zealand explosive ordnance disposal troops sent there to assist in the post-conflict aftermath. To Goff, as the responsible minister of the New Zealand government, the signs pointed in one direction—toward the need to outlaw the sort of weapons that littered the ground in Southern Lebanon.

First, however, with its preparations in motion already, the CCW Review Conference needed a chance to succeed or fail. Although they had no illusions that it would be capable of commanding a consensus in November, at the end of the August–September GGE session, Austria, the Holy See, Ireland, Mexico, New Zealand and Sweden together presented a formal mandate proposal on "a legally-binding instrument that addresses the humanitarian concerns posed by cluster munitions" to the CCW.[31] Norway, for its part, did not co-sponsor what became referred to as the six-nation proposal—its desire for an international ban on cluster munitions that cause unacceptable humanitarian problems was on record, and it did not wish to become locked into a CCW process.

THE CCW REVIEW CONFERENCE

On the first day of the CCW Review Conference on 7 November, UN Secretary-General Kofi Annan referred to the "atrocious, inhumane effects" of cluster munitions in his official message to the meeting, and called for a range of prohibitions and restrictions on aspects of the weapon.[32] However, it was still by no means clear to those countries calling for a protocol—or more, as in the case of Norway—that any form of cluster munition mandate would be possible in the CCW, let alone a negotiation.

Several times in the course of late 2005 and during 2006, Kongstad and his advisors met with certain other CCW delegations in a series of informal "group of interested states" (GIS) lunches in Geneva. Like the London meeting in March, they offered an opportunity for Kongstad and other participants to take soundings about the positions of others and to develop strategic partnerships. Participation in the GIS lunches was not stable, but usually included Austria, Belgium, Ireland, Mexico, New Zealand, Norway, Sweden and Switzerland. Sometimes others like Germany, or an ICRC or CMC representative, were invited to attend. During the CCW Review Conference's first week, a GIS lunch was held at the residence of the New Zealand Ambassador, Don MacKay, to discuss whether the political impetus existed to try to withhold consensus on a Review Conference outcome unless it delivered a cluster munition mandate of some kind. In the abstract, this seemed a reasonable option. On the eve of the CCW Review Conference, British International Development Minister Hilary Benn had written to his cabinet colleagues calling into question British policies on the use and possession of cluster munitions in view of their humanitarian impacts, in a letter that was leaked to the British *Times* newspaper.[33] This news seemed encouraging, since the UK had previously been opposed to a cluster munition CCW protocol negotiation and there now seemed the prospect that British policy might change. Moreover, it was well known that French Ambassador Rivasseau, the Review Conference's Chair, was determined to achieve a successful CCW outcome at all costs. If it were achieved, a more ambitious EU joint approach on cluster munitions and insistence on a cluster munition negotiation would therefore add a lot of political mass to the calls of those states already calling for such a mandate.

While the EU's member states debated internally and major cluster munition possessors in the CCW such as Israel, Russia and the US continued to oppose any cluster munition-specific mandate on the conference floor, momentum nevertheless grew for a treaty during the course of the Review Conference. There was the UN Secretary-General's message to the Review Conference, as mentioned earlier. There was also an even stronger statement in a press release from outgoing UN Emergency Relief Coordinator, Jan Egeland, who was in Lebanon: "Ultimately, as long as there is no effective ban, these weapons will continue to disproportionately affect civilians, maiming and killing women, children and other vulnerable groups".[34] Meanwhile, Sweden was working to attract support from other CCW states for a declaration on cluster munitions—an exercise in parallel to the EU's internal deliberations—that itself also led to tough negotiations among those governments interested in joining. These included, for instance, Mexico, which said it wanted a total ban, and Germany, which had very well-developed views of its own on how cluster munitions should be defined and what restrictions or prohibitions would be entailed. On the conference's final day, Sweden presented its declaration on behalf of at least 25 states:

> We, the Governments of Austria, Belgium, Bosnia-Herzegovina, Croatia, Costa Rica, Czech Republic, Denmark, Germany, Holy See, Hungary, Ireland, Liechtenstein, Lithuania, Luxembourg, Malta, Mexico, New Zealand, Norway, Peru, Portugal, Serbia, Slovakia, Slovenia, Sweden and Switzerland,
>
> *Recognize* that cluster munitions, due to their tendencies of having indiscriminate effects and/or a high risk of becoming explosive remnants of war, are of serious humanitarian concern during and after armed conflict;
>
> *Welcome* the appeal made by United Nations Secretary-General Kofi Annan to take urgent action to address the issue of cluster munitions;
>
> *Recognize* the fundamental contribution by civil society towards this end;
>
> *Understand*, for the purposes of this declaration, cluster munitions as air-carried or ground launched dispensers that contain submunitions, and where each such dispenser is designed to eject submunitions containing explosives designed to detonate on, prior to, or immediately after impact on the identified target;
>
> *Calls for* an agreement that should *inter alia*:

(a) prohibit the use of cluster munitions within concentrations of civilians;

(b) prohibit the development, production, stockpiling, transfer and use of cluster munitions that pose serious humanitarian hazards because they are for example unreliable and/or inaccurate;

(c) assure the destruction of stockpiles of cluster munitions that pose serious humanitarian hazards because they are for example unreliable and/or inaccurate, and in this context establish forms for cooperation and assistance.[35]

A call by less than a quarter of the CCW's members (and small- and medium-sized members at that) was certainly not a dire threat to the major users and possessors of cluster munitions keen to avoid a cluster munition mandate, especially in view of the CCW's consensus practice. But the Norwegians hoped that the Swedish-led declaration in the CCW could be used to draw those states to an outside process once it became clear the relatively high level of ambition the appeal set (by CCW standards) would probably not be reflected in a mandate. Word leaked readily from the European Union's meetings about how difficult negotiations there were in the view of opposition from the UK (despite earlier hopes) and others to a negotiating mandate, and it seemed unlikely that cluster munition possessors such as China, India, Israel, Russia and the US would be more forthcoming. The scene thus seemed set for an outcome that could only be seen as a failure in view of the aspirations of many to address the humanitarian impacts of cluster munitions.

Matters came to a head in the final week of the Review Conference. In a move that seemed to be intended to cap pressure for a negotiating mandate of any kind, the UK's CCW delegation unveiled its own text for a mandate proposal much closer in form to the discussion mandates on ERW since the completion of Protocol V. The proposal was the product of the UK's own negotiations with China, France, India, Israel, Pakistan, Russia and the US, and it called for one further GGE intersessional meeting to:

consider further the application and implementation of existing international humanitarian law to specific weapons systems that may cause explosive remnants of war, with particular focus on cluster munitions, including the factors affecting their reliability, and their technical and design characteristics, with a view to minimising the humanitarian impact and use of these weapons.[36]

Seen in the context of preceding ERW mandates since 2004, if the British mandate were agreed it would be as if Belgium's legislation, the consequences of use of cluster munitions in the Southern Lebanon conflict and the groundswell of support in the CCW for a negotiation had never happened. It certainly contrasted with the mandate proposal of the EU of which the UK was a member, which called for an open-ended GGE "To address the humanitarian impact of cluster munitions, with the purpose of elaborating recommendations for further action in the CCW"[37] put forward in public that same day. No doubt the British would have preferred it if the timeframe for the CCW's mandate deliberations had not been so compressed in that final week: because the two proposals were presented almost concurrently on 15 November, the UK's instigation of and French support for the weaker ERW mandate proposal undercutting the EU's position were visible to all.

Sweden and others in the EU had used their declaration initiative to try to raise the bar on a cluster munition mandate in the EU; fear among major cluster munition users and possessors about momentum developing for a negotiation helped to persuade them that the UK proposal was preferable. Still, this consensus among the major users and possessors about what they wanted (or rather, did not want) was evidently fragile. China said it would need to think about the UK proposal, although this actually represented tacit support for it. The US said it could live with the UK proposal provided it was not changed further—a clear reply to Canada, which intervened during the discussion to try to amend the UK text. The US intervention was also a warning to India, which although privy to the deal could not resist trying to alter the proposal for its own purposes. And, as if explicit dismissal were now needed for the EU draft mandate—by now clearly dead on arrival—Ronald Bettauer, the US head of delegation, also said it was too "vague" and "un-centred". Mexico argued that the UK mandate proposal's emphasis on technical considerations was at the cost of humanitarian considerations, but like Canada its amendment attempts were seen off. Russia opined that the EU mandate could mean that there would be two ERW mandates in the CCW, although it did not bother to ask EU President Finland to clarify this, which was telling in itself. In presenting the EU mandate proposal, Finland's Ambassador Kahiluoto said it differed from the six-nation proposal in that it did not stipulate a negotiation or a legally binding instrument. While this was no doubt a useful clarification, it hammered several additional nails into the EU proposal's coffin. It was obvious now that no state on either the minimalist or maximalist end of the spectrum had a stake in defending the EU mandate proposal.

Instead, the British mandate proposal was the one agreed in the Review Conference's final document.[38] The mandate did, though, lose a paragraph stating that the 2007 GGE would "inter alia consider the results of the meeting of technical experts on cluster munitions held by the ICRC", which the ICRC had earlier announced it was planning (motivated by a concern to keep the cluster munition issue alive after the Review Conference, whatever the CCW's outcome). The ICRC had objected to this, stating pointedly that the expert meeting in Montreux they were planning would be relevant to *any* process, not just the CCW.

While technically a success in that it achieved a Final Document, the 2006 Review Conference left a number of those involved feeling that the CCW process had become threadbare in humanitarian terms as far as confronting the humanitarian impacts of cluster munitions was concerned. Some government representatives congratulated themselves at its closing that the CCW process was preserved, in that it would at least continue to discuss aspects of the weapon in 2007. However, others regarded the Final Document's mandate as a monumental cop-out—Mexico, for example, declared for the record at the end of the Review Conference that it disassociated itself from the outcome on cluster munitions. The CMC's strong criticism of the British-brokered mandate outcome on the final day goaded the UK, and it led to an unfortunate exchange about relative humanitarian credentials. The CMC also said the CCW's new mandate was not adequate, and that further discussions were at best a go-slow response—a "formula for future failure of the CCW".[39]

The CCW Review Conference had resulted in the scenario I had identified in March in London of a weak mandate falling short of actual negotiation on cluster munitions. Lucy had again prevented Charlie Brown from kicking the football, although NGOs did their best to brand the CCW outcome a failure. As one NGO representative later put it: "On cluster munitions, if you are asking, Did this body take effective action on cluster munitions? Have they established a process that's likely to bring about effective action on an urgent basis in the future? It's a failure".[40] In substance, the CCW cluster munitions mandate stated little more than the obvious—that after adoption of Protocol V in late 2003 and the Southern Lebanon conflict in 2006, attention had turned to cluster munitions. And the process leading to the 2007 discussion mandate discouraged hope that states likes Russia and China would be likely to act more constructively on cluster munitions in continued CCW talks, particularly as they did not waver in their opposition at the Review Conference to new rules on MOTAPM. At the same time, it contributed to a view among more and more states that efforts to address the specific effects of cluster munitions on civilians might be strung along perpetually in the CCW without tangible results, and that in view of the weapon's humanitarian effects this was not acceptable.

Such an emerging view was of strategic importance to the Norwegians, who by now were ready to activate their very un-secret plan for an outside international process on cluster munitions. To anyone paying attention to Norway's statements in the CCW during 2006, talking with its diplomats, or following the development of its national policy, this announcement was no surprise. In November 2006, for instance, UNIDIR published an issue of its journal *Disarmament Forum* that presented articles on cluster munitions from various experts and was circulated to delegates at the opening of the CCW. In a Special Comment to the issue, Norwegian Foreign Minister Støre wrote:

> Current international efforts to regulate the use of cluster munitions have not achieved much. Little progress has been made since the issue was first put on the international agenda some years ago. ... We must not allow the lack of interest in some quarters to prevent small and medium-sized countries from initiating a process to fulfil our humanitarian obligations. We will therefore continue to work toward an international prohibition against unacceptable types of cluster munitions. The time is ripe to intensify our efforts.[41]

On the second-to-last day of the CCW Review Conference, the Norwegians lit the fuse to launch their initiative. Støre announced in Oslo that the Norwegian Government:

> will organise an international conference in Oslo to start a process towards an international ban on cluster munitions that have unacceptable humanitarian consequences .... We must take advantage of the political will now evident in many countries to prohibit cluster munitions that cause unacceptable humanitarian harm. The time is ripe to establish broad co-operation on a concerted effort to achieve a ban ... .[42]

In case anyone in the CCW missed it, Kongstad repeated the announcement at the Review Conference's final session, adding:

> We are well aware of the complexities of the issue, but we do think that acting in good faith we together can find solutions that combine the humanitarian needs with what is militarily acceptable and politically possible. In this spirit we want to establish a partnership with other countries and organisations that can yield concrete results that will prevent future human suffering [from cluster munitions].[43]

The Oslo initiative had begun, but it was by no means universally welcomed. Bettauer, the US delegation head, told the CCW that Washington was "disappointed" with Norway and claimed that the "effort to go outside this framework is not healthy for the CCW" and would "weaken the international humanitarian law effort".[44] The UK CCW delegation was also not pleased, as they had acted on their instructions from London to seize the lead on cluster munitions, and felt now that any fruits to follow in CCW work may have been pre-empted. The British head of delegation later explained:

> We were very annoyed that having done so much heavy lifting in such a short space of time—we'd essentially put together a coalition [to support a CCW cluster munition mandate] in less than five days on something which had been immovable for a long, long time—and then to have the rug pulled from beneath us ... .[45]

It was true that the British had done "heavy lifting" to cobble together a CCW deal. But it was efforts over years by civil society, the ICRC and an increasing number of states concerned about the humanitarian impacts of cluster munitions that had put the topic on the agenda in a way the CCW could no longer ignore.

THE ROAD TO THE OSLO CONFERENCE

Even for a country with Norway's resources, organizing an international conference from scratch would be a major undertaking. A big issue on the minds of Kongstad's team was the diplomatic management of the meeting itself, and he solicited for help representatives of several other states active in calls for a cluster munition negotiation in the CCW and who had participated in the GIS lunch process in Geneva. Ambassadors Pablo Macedo of Mexico and Don MacKay of New Zealand—both experienced diplomatic operators and conference chairpersons, with capable (if small) supporting teams of their own—were key individuals in this respect. These diplomats, along with representatives of Austria, Ireland and Sweden, were to form a first proto-"core group", coalescing around Norway. Other interested states included Belgium, the Holy See, Lebanon and Peru.

The Swedish-led 25-state declaration at the November 2006 CCW Review Conference provided the basis for an initial list of (hopefully) like-minded governments to invite to the Oslo conference, to be held on 22 and 23 February 2007. But it left the question of which other governments should be invited—and which would be prepared to come—since the intent of the conference was not to involve every state at this stage, but instead to gather critical mass to start the process rolling. Many countries affected by the post-conflict effects of cluster munitions were not members of the CCW, and the support of, and buy-in from, such states would be important in establishing the legitimacy of any humanitarian treaty resulting from the initiative. And, what about the US's negative statement made in November about Norway's initiative? On the whole, most other Western states were more positive about the Oslo conference although many regarded it as a leap in the dark. For many, including even the UK, it made sense to be inside the conference room in Oslo because it certainly looked better to the outside world to be involved, and offered the prospect of influence, if not outright control, over the outcome. The Norwegians were well aware of this, but British participation was needed, they felt. Besides, in view of the close military relationship between the UK and US, British involvement in the conference would make other European NATO states more comfortable about participating, they thought. As Norway's Foreign Minister put it, "having the UK on the inside makes it harder [for others] to say you are doing something anti-NATO and anti-allies, let's be frank about it".[46]

On 23 January, British Foreign Minister Margaret Beckett accepted Norwegian Foreign Minister Støre's invitation to the UK. Beckett's written reply offered both a foretaste of some of the challenges ahead for the Oslo process and a glimpse of the political contortionism Whitehall was attempting in order to rationalize its participation and so retain the potential diplomatic matchmaking role Britain's diplomats traditionally sought in multilateral conference diplomacy (and had capitalized upon in the CCW Review Conference). Beckett's letter reminded her Norwegian counterpart that the UK saw the CCW's work as per the newly agreed ERW mandate as:

an essential preliminary step to any international agreements in this area. ... We also welcome the opportunity to participate in your meeting and the ICRC's in April. I am pleased that your initiative does not distance itself from the CCW framework and hope that your meeting and the ICRC's will complement the work of the GGE. I should emphasise, however, that we would not want to create a parallel track of the ongoing, valuable and essential activity within the CCW.[47]

In ink, Beckett had underlined "not" and "parallel" in the final sentence, although she and her advisors must surely have known otherwise. Norway's letter inviting participants made it clear the Oslo conference's ambition was to "come together to outline the objective and develop an action plan for a process leading to a new international instrument of international humanitarian law" on cluster munitions, even if it tipped its hat to the CCW by noting its initiative "does not exclude a continued discussion within the framework of the CCW".[48] Oslo's initiative was nothing if not running in parallel to an exercise in the CCW that Norwegian policymakers had come to view as substantially irrelevant.

Civil society was also busily preparing for the Oslo conference. The Cluster Munition Coalition held its first global campaign meeting since Copenhagen in 2004 in Geneva in November 2006 before the CCW Review Conference. It was clear at this meeting that exciting developments at the national level were afoot. For instance, inspired by Belgium's legislation, parliamentary initiatives were underway in other European countries such as Austria (which would pass national legislation banning cluster munitions in early 2008) and France, stoked by ongoing interest in the issue in the European Parliament. Also, most of the NGOs active in the CMC were also active on Mine Ban Treaty issues (and members of the International Campaign to Ban Landmines), and it was apparent that the prospect of a possible cluster munition ban process outside the CCW led by Norway, which was a major player in the Mine Ban Treaty's implementation, had piqued the interest of many landmine campaigners working at the national level. As one of them put it, a lot of campaigners "were anxious at this point to take on new challenges and saw this as something that they really wanted to do".[49]

Meanwhile, the CMC's leadership recognized that a free-standing international initiative on cluster munitions would mean the Coalition would have to transform itself in order to contribute to the Oslo initiative, and thus to have a say in any outcome. As one prominent campaigner observed, "The CMC has always been a very top-heavy Coalition ... In Washington terms we would call it an 'inside the Beltway' coalition. You know, you are talking to leaders and you are not doing a lot of grassroots mobilizing".[50] Some of those in the CMC's leadership active in the landmine campaign perceived the CMC's relative lack of grassroots national campaigns as its greatest weakness. A decade or more previously, and coordinated by a small team of organizers at the international level, the International Campaign to Ban Landmines (ICBL) had constituted national campaigns that were built up in dozens of countries over several years. But on cluster munitions the scope of the problem was much more limited and not always seen as distinct from the landmine problem in the minds of the public and media. Besides, there might not be time for a mass public mobilization campaign in view of the pace the Norwegians had told the CMC's leadership they wanted to move at—to complete a treaty process by the end of 2008.

There was also awareness within the CMC's leadership that there were important contrasts with the ICBL's formative period in the 1990s. Certainly the international political landscape was radically altered by the attacks of 11 September 2001 and other international shocks that countered the sense of optimism and possibility of the 1990s after the fall of the Berlin Wall. In February 2003, over one million people surged through the streets of London in protest against a war in Iraq, yet a month later, the invasion went ahead. The failure of this protest led many UK NGOs (and the foundations that support them) to reassess the value of mass mobilization in changing government policy.[51] In this new environment and with an issue that did not have the same global appeal as landmines, a more targeted form of political mobilization that drew on the media and public relations techniques of successful political and commercial campaigns might be more appropriate. This was not to abandon grass roots mobilization and a civil society campaign driven from the bottom up by its members, but rather to recognize that the power of those members could be amplified through the strategic use of the media and public events targeted at specific individual decision-makers and around particular events. This campaigning approach also reflected the growing trend of the "professionalization" of many NGOs.[52]

Within the landmine ban movement, there were also numerous campaigners who were willing and able to become members of the new Cluster Munition Coalition and start work on mobilizing their own governments on this issue. While sharing many strategic leaders from among their member NGOs, the activities of the CMC and ICBL had usually been very separate at the working level, and this in part reflected their different situations. The ICBL had a mainstream diplomatic process to contribute to through the Mine Ban Treaty whereas the CMC was seeking to create a new diplomatic process, the objectives of which were not yet entirely clear to all. The arrangement decided in 2003, when NGOs decided not to add the cluster munition issue to the ICBL's plate but instead to set up the CMC (see chapter 2), now began to change. In December 2006, after a decision by the ICBL's leadership, the ICBL added cluster munitions to its mandate and, having secured dedicated funding from the Norwegian government, in early 2007 hired Katarzyna "Kasia" Derlicka to focus on cluster munition advocacy. This was not uncontroversial within the ICBL's membership, but those working to propel the CMC forward welcomed the additional staff time focused on mobilizing campaigners on cluster munitions. The ICBL's objective was to support the CMC and to work as a member within it—a "coalition within a coalition". During the Oslo process, the CMC would be able to draw on the expertise and experience of some of the leaders of the landmine ban movement both from NGO figures such as Brabant, Goose, Hannon, McGrath and Mary Wareham, and those from friendly governments like Norway. The relationship between a new generation of central figures within the CMC and the veteran leaders of the ICBL, who emerged during the 1990s, would not always be without tension as they sometimes had differing ideas about best approaches for strategy and advocacy.[53]

The CMC would develop in a different manner during the Oslo process from the way the ICBL had in the Ottawa process period: while the Ottawa-period ICBL team had largely been comprised of those campaigners its individual member campaigns could spare, in contrast the CMC would emulate the model the ICBL later evolved toward of adding staff dedicated to the international campaign and the Coalition itself, rather than being representatives at the same time of one of its member organizations. The first of these individuals, an Italian–Swiss operations specialist named Serena Olgiati, had already started at the CMC in September 2006 to help organize the Coalition's contribution to the Second Review Conference of the CCW. Others would follow in 2007, including Laura Cheeseman as campaigning officer who, from May, would bring her background and experience from another campaign coalition, the International Action Network on Small Arms (IANSA), to play on cluster munitions.[54]

The CMC's Steering Committee members met at Kentwell Hall in the English county of Suffolk from 5 to 7 January 2007 to plan their strategy. CMC goals as set out in the "Kentwell Plan" were to be focused on:

1. Success of Norwegian initiative as only viable international process on cluster munitions

   a. Establishment of government core group

   b. Cluster munition treaty text developed, negotiating process established, and negotiations concluded in 2 years or less

2. National steps taken on cluster munitions

3. Public awareness raised on cluster munitions.[55]

Detailed measures were set out for coordinating CMC members' activities, support to national campaigning and for provision of advocacy materials. This was all worthy stuff, but the Steering Committee also needed to sort itself out and the way it directed the Coalition. 2004 and 2005 had been years of CMC education and raising external awareness, and in 2006 its advocacy had focused on the CCW and the Review Conference as a break point. Major decisions and management issues were not generally urgent from day to day, and the CMC's Coordinator, Thomas Nash, was usually left to get on with whatever was thrown at him and to report back periodically. The Steering Committee was loose, comprised of between 6 to 10 NGOs, and with rotational Chairs it was sometimes difficult for Nash to get it to focus consistently on issues on which he wanted guidance. So, at Kentwell, the Steering Committee appointed co-chairs. As senior people committed to ongoing leadership responsibility,[56] Simon Conway, Landmine Action's Director, and Goose were sound choices for these roles. Since the CMC was based in Landmine Action's London offices (and Nash had relocated to the UK from Peru in August of 2006) Conway played a role in overseeing the practical aspects of the CMC's running anyway, and Goose had long provided a distinctive strategic vision of his own to the Coalition's development. They were joined by a third co-chair shortly after Kentwell—Grethe Østern of Norwegian People's Aid, whose NGO work in Norway had already been so effective, and who had both relevant practical experience and an excellent working relationship with the Norwegian government. As shown in chapter 3, Østern was also methodical and forensic in her approach and, like her co-chairs, media savvy. Nash, in particular, appreciated the guidance she was able to offer to the CMC executive team.[57]

There remained the issue of the CMC's call for action on cluster munitions. Although, in practice, CMC representatives like Nash talked of banning the weapon in getting the Coalition's aims across to policymakers, the CMC call remained the one agreed in November 2003. In view of the events of the previous year, in particular, pressure was growing from member NGOs such as Handicap International Belgium and France, Norwegian People's Aid and Landmine Action for the call to be updated with an unequivocal call for a ban on cluster munitions. Human Rights Watch and Mines Action Canada resisted however, preferring a formulation calling for a ban on inaccurate and unreliable cluster munitions. These organizations thought the latter formulation was the more persuasive campaigning call in terms of attracting support from states for action on prohibiting cluster munitions. The contest was between two contrasting views of how to address the humanitarian impacts of cluster munitions, a challenge that would soon strike at the heart of the Oslo process—on the one hand there was a "define and ban" approach, and on the other was a "split cluster munitions into categories" approach. Moyes, Nash and some others felt strongly that pursuing the latter course, which in effect was what the technical discussions in the CCW had been about for years, would lead to failure, and would be difficult to campaign on.[58] The compromise was that the Coalition's call would be expressed as follows:

> The CMC is committed to protecting civilians from the effects of cluster munitions
>
> The CMC calls for *a prohibition on cluster munitions that cause unacceptable harm to civilians*
>
> The CMC continues to call for:
>
> 1. No use, production or trade of cluster munitions until their humanitarian problems have been resolved.
>
> 2. Increased resources for assistance to communities and individuals affected by unexploded cluster munitions and all other explosive remnants of war.
>
> 3. Special responsibility for users of cluster munitions and other munitions that become ERW.[59]

The Kentwell meeting's report claimed that this call "binds together the nuances present within Steering Committee members' positions" and noted that "CMC members will maintain full flexibility to campaign on the basis of a total prohibition of cluster munitions".[60] But no one present in Kentwell seems to have liked the updated call particularly, and it would be revisited after the Oslo conference.

In November 2006, Foreign Minister Støre had made it clear in his announcement about the Oslo conference that he saw partnership with international organizations and civil society as important ingredients, and now the Norwegians invited these actors to work with them in several ways. In late January, representatives of NGOs, the ICRC and UNIDIR travelled to Oslo to discuss preparations for the Oslo conference with the Norwegians, and a representative from the Irish Foreign Ministry, Declan Smyth, was also present.[61] UNIDIR, for its part, was asked to prepare informally a draft background paper on cluster munitions for participants at the Oslo conference, a paper developed further and later issued by Norway in its capacity as conference chair.[62] Discussions began on what the Oslo conference should produce in terms of an output.

The Norwegians felt three things were needed from the Oslo conference. First, it needed to result in a clear political commitment from governments. Second, the commitment and the humanitarian difference a humanitarian treaty would make needed to be communicated in media-friendly terms. And, third, the conference needed to agree on what would happen next.[63] Kongstad, in particular, was keen to emphasize that the Oslo conference was just the beginning of a process, and that further milestones would need to be marked out and agreed by governments at that meeting.[64] This would mean persuading other governments to host further conferences, which in turn meant a timetable toward achievement of a treaty on cluster munitions—and its specific aims—would be required. Ireland was an obvious candidate to hold the next meeting, but the Irish did not think that they could pull off such a conference with only a few months warning. Very few other states had yet begun thinking about how to make a free-standing international process actually work, and Oslo would have to focus minds.[65] The logical means was a conference declaration. So, work began. Early drafts of an "Oslo Action Plan on Cluster Munitions" emulated UN General Assembly resolutions, but over the course of February the declaration became plainer in language and briefer as it was informally circulated among the January group and interested governments, and honed by Kongstad and his Mexican colleague Macedo to the point to which they hoped "it would be impossible for many countries *not* to support it".[66] The formulation of the eventual declaration would be key to the Oslo conference's success.

THE OSLO CONFERENCE

It takes special dedication to travel to Oslo in February, when the temperature there can fall to -20°C, and the sun glows only meagrely through the grey clouds for a few hours each day. Nevertheless, a civil society forum on cluster munitions organized by the CMC and Norwegian People's Aid at the Nobel Peace Centre near central Oslo's harbour side the day before commencement of the Oslo conference had an atmosphere that mixed elements of party political rally with Baptist revival.[67] Master of ceremonies was NPA's hulking Per Nergaard, wearing a microphone head-set on his hairless pate and working the assembled throng of NGOs, media and invited government dignitaries with the skill of a stand-up comedian. The meeting nevertheless had a serious purpose—"to raise awareness of the urgent need for states to address the problems caused by cluster munitions"; that is, create a sense for governments participating in the ensuing official conference that the world was watching them expectantly. Nobel Laureate Jody Williams spoke in impassioned terms about the need to take action, as did Norway's Minister for Development, Erik Solheim. Various speakers representing organizations including the CMC, Human Rights Watch, the Lebanese Landmine Resource Centre, Handicap International, along with the ICRC and the United Nations Children's Fund, outlined aspects of the cluster munition problem, and Handicap International's Director General Jean-Baptiste Richardier also presented a petition to ban cluster munitions. Nash presented the cluster munition forum's appeal, which called on "committed governments to act decisively and show their leadership in bringing about a new norm rejecting this 'unjust weapon'" and for an "urgent prohibition on their use, production, trade and stockpiling".[68]

Perhaps the most extraordinary voice of the forum, however, was Branislav Kapetanović's. He was one of two Serbian survivors of cluster munitions present, and spoke of his personal experience and his hopes for the Oslo initiative. Survivors had played important roles in the landmine ban process, and in subsequent implementation of the Mine Ban Treaty, not least in bringing home the human ramifications to government diplomats, politicians and other policymakers of their decisions, and encouraging them to live up to their undertakings. Yet, to date, cluster munition survivors were almost entirely absent from the CCW's talks, and they had not played prominent roles in the formation of the CMC. In part, this was because of the nature of incidents with cluster munitions: if victims were not killed, then multiple injuries from submunitions made the logistics of travel to a place like Geneva, London or Oslo from an affected community in a poor and distant country particularly expensive and difficult.

Serbia was not a rich country, but it was not poor by the standards of Afghanistan or Laos either, and it was less than three hours flying time to Oslo by plane. Kapetanović's presence meant that, speaking through an interpreter, he was able to relate his painful story. In 2000, as a Serbian army deminer he had been clearing unexploded US-made BLU-97 submunitions from a civilian area after a 1999 NATO airstrike. One of the submunitions exploded and Kapetanović suffered multiple injuries: his hands and feet were amputated to save his life, the explosion permanently deafened him in one ear (and blinded him for several months), and his head and lungs were damaged. Kapetanović was confined to a wheelchair.[69] In some senses, as a Serbian, he was lucky—in a country without such effective health care, the multiple operations necessary to keep him alive would not have been available. As it was, his remarks had a stirring effect on the audience.

Norwegian government officials had initially been concerned that the Oslo conference would be under-subscribed in terms of participation by states. However, such fears proved unfounded by the time the Oslo conference began. Instead of meeting the target of roughly 30 governments that Kongstad, Abelsen and others hoped would attend, representatives of 49 governments sought to participate.[70] Some of these governments had not been original invitees in view on their national postures on cluster munitions expressed in the CCW (Japan and Poland, for instance, had each repeatedly stressed the importance and legitimacy of their stocks of cluster munitions) but were there because they strenuously insisted on taking part. The US was nowhere to be seen, but the Norwegians had expected that, to the point that it does not appear that a formal invitation was sent to Washington. Like Brazil, China, India, Israel, Pakistan and Russia—all major possessors of cluster munitions—would shun the Oslo process throughout its course.

Foreign Minister Støre's deputy, Raymond Johansen, and Kongstad headed up the team preparing and running the conference, but Støre lobbied other governments when necessary. Some lobbying activities were easier than others. New Zealand Minister Phil Goff had visited Oslo in January and met with Støre, and cluster munitions were one of a number of issues discussed. Støre had returned the week before from a trip to Afghanistan, a country with which Goff was very familiar, and is an environment heavily affected by the presence of mines and unexploded ordnance including submunitions. As one official present at the meeting put it, "He and Støre sat down together and it could have been the same person talking". Although not a large country, New Zealand would come to play an important role in the Oslo process, and Goff's support for the initiative resulted in time in New Zealand agreeing to host a major Oslo process conference in Wellington to be held a year later.

The Oslo conference was held at the Soria Moria hotel complex in the hills above the Norwegian capital. Although the meeting venue's significance was lost on most participants, it was here that Norway's Red–Green coalition had negotiated its governing agreement in October 2005 including the pledge to take international action on cluster munitions—the political wellspring of the Oslo conference. The Soria Moria was comfortable and large enough to accommodate all of the more than 200 government delegates (although most of the NGO campaigners would have to trek back to central Oslo each night).[71] The blizzard-like conditions and distance from the capital's centre contributed to a secluded diplomatic atmosphere in which civil society nevertheless had a strong presence. All of this was conducive to the sense of urgency and enthusiasm Kongstad and his team wanted conference participants to feel.[72] This was because the work of the conference and agreement of a declaration establishing the road map for the achievement of a treaty needed to be achieved within a day and a half. This would be a challenge in the face of the reality that a significant proportion of those present, especially among Norway's NATO allies, were at the conference rather reluctantly. These governments were uncertain and uncomfortable about how the Oslo initiative sat with their traditional commitment to the CCW, despite that forum's shortcomings.

Governments such as Austria, the Holy See, Ireland, Mexico and New Zealand had, in practical terms, already committed themselves to supporting the Oslo initiative—although Norway, for now, carried the vast share of political risk. Positive signals could reasonably be expected to a greater or lesser degree from a second group of governments such as Afghanistan, Angola, Belgium, Bosnia and Herzegovina, Chile, Colombia, Croatia,

Costa Rica, Guatemala, Iceland, Lebanon, Lithuania, Luxembourg, Malta, Mozambique, Peru, Portugal, Serbia and Slovenia. This left a large group that was harder to predict. It included many of Norway's NATO allies, and others such as Argentina, Japan, Jordan, Indonesia and South Africa. France, Germany and the UK would be especially important and collectively could perhaps tip over the conference if they rejected its outcome because many others would then be likely to follow their lead. Moreover, while Belgium, Sweden and Switzerland had been helpful to Norway in the lead-up to the conference, there were signs that, for various reasons, they would find being part of an Oslo "core group" difficult. While nationally Norway had moved beyond believing in reliability rates as a basis for demonstrating the acceptability of cluster munitions, both the Swedish and Swiss governments appeared set on ensuring that their own cluster munition arsenals were retained at the end of any process—on the basis of their submunitions' minimal alleged failure rates.[73] And, a general election in Sweden in September 2006 saw Prime Minister Göran Persson's Social Democrat-led government fall, and be replaced by a centre–right coalition of four parties less sympathetic to Sweden taking a leading role on international efforts on cluster munitions.

Støre opened the Oslo conference on the morning of Thursday, 22 February, in a session open to the media. The Norwegian Foreign Minister delivered a carefully nuanced speech to delegates sprinkled with buzz phrases diplomats liked to hear, such as "the right dose of realism and pragmatism". While talking about bringing to an end "unacceptable human suffering" from cluster munitions, and halting or no longer using such weapons "that cause such indiscriminate suffering", nowhere did Støre explicitly mention a prohibition or a ban on which opposition to the Oslo initiative might latch. Instead, he said, "Here is our objective: To reach agreement on a plan for developing and implementing a new instrument of international humanitarian law that addresses all the unacceptable consequences of cluster munitions by 2008".[74]

Then the conference's work got underway, organized around sessions on various themes, always with Norway (usually Kongstad) as one co-chair and New Zealand, Ireland or Mexico as the other. Having capable colleagues like Macedo, MacKay or Smyth on the podium was useful from the Norwegians' point of view, but competent diplomats were also needed to help guide the discussion from the floor, especially when it headed toward sticky subjects such as how the Oslo initiative would sit with the CCW, or calls for a definition of cluster munitions to be settled right away. And there was a lot of coordination within the proto-"core group" to this end with some, such as Austria's ambassador Wolfgang Petritsch, very active in helping the co-chairs from the floor in pushing the conference agenda forward.

Norway had cast the net widely in terms of kick-off presentations on topics such as realities about cluster munitions in different field contexts, the sort of cooperation and assistance framework that would likely be needed as part of a humanitarian treaty, and how to translate all of this into political action. One presentation featured Østern on behalf of Norwegian People's Aid. She had travelled to Southern Lebanon late in 2006 to learn about the consequences of the use of cluster munitions there, and her presentation included a three-and-a-half minute film made by the Australian photographer and activist John Rodsted, which she showed on a big screen to all of the delegates in the hall. To show that self-destruct mechanisms were not effective, Rodsted had taken a hand-held video camera and walked through a field in Southern Lebanon pausing to film various unexploded—that is, failed—DPICM submunitions in extreme close-up. Against the sounds of the wind and his footsteps through the contaminated area, Rodsted's film included his impromptu voiceover:

> I won't fool around in this place for terribly long because I admit to feeling quite uncomfortable being here. But I'll just try to give you a bit of an overview as to what this site is like. You can see the road—the large rock on the left hand side [is where] we found our first clusters … in this view you can see one, two, three, four, five, six, seven [unexploded submunitions] all in a line. There are many more around, but we're going to leave that task for the battle area clearance team to sort out. But it does leave us with some very, very irrefutable facts—that M-85s with self-destruct mechanisms simply do not work.[75]

The NPA presentation had a powerful effect in sweeping away a lot of familiar rhetoric inherited from the CCW environment. It added to an atmosphere in the Soria Moria conference in which humanitarian concerns about cluster munitions, rather than the perceived military utility of the weapon, were the central focus, something that had never been possible in the CCW.

Notably, the UN and the ICRC threw their considerable moral authority behind the Oslo initiative's humanitarian aims. The ICRC argued that the conference's participants "should avoid divisive debates about the forum in which those results could best be achieved".[76] It reflected the feeling within the ICRC that Oslo represented greater hope for meaningful restrictions or prohibitions on cluster munitions than the CCW's endless talks in Geneva, despite the ICRC's special role there as the generally recognized "guardian of international humanitarian law". Moreover, drawing on UNIDIR's research both on the humanitarian impacts of cluster munitions and from its Disarmament as Humanitarian Action project, UNIDIR Director Patricia Lewis argued that:

> The debate over research about the humanitarian impact of cluster munitions is similar in many respects to a number of other scientific debates over predicting long-term impact. For example, avian flu and global climate change. The evidence isn't yet all in, and there are gnawing gaps in knowledge to be filled as well as aspects of the phenomena we still don't fathom. But we know enough from the data that if we fail to act in response to problems that loom large now—responses that will demand changes in our behaviour and that may have costs in the shorter term that we are reluctant to bear—we face the likelihood of worse consequences down the line. ...

> We are all here because we have recognized that the impacts of cluster munitions on civilians need to be dealt with effectively and we agree that it is a problem that will require collective action as well as national-level action. Recognition and agreement are crucial first steps in deciding what to do about cluster munitions.[77]

And the United Nations Development Programme (UNDP) spoke, linking efforts to address the impacts of cluster munitions on civilians with the UN's Millennium Development Goals and recalling the UN Secretary-General's November 2006 statement on cluster munitions. Shrewdly, the UNDP statement pushed the parameters of Annan's message, however, stating that "UNDP and other UN agencies strongly feel that it is time for the international community to urgently agree on effective legal instruments to *prohibit cluster munitions that cause unacceptable harm to civilians*".[78] This could be seen as consistent with the Secretary General's message to the CCW Review Conference calling for a freeze on cluster munition use until certain aspects of the weapon were addressed in humanitarian terms. But the formulation also offered wriggle-room that could extend to support by UN agencies for a broad cluster munition ban, if that was the way later work in defining these weapons pointed.

The "unacceptable harm" formulation in the declaration was, meanwhile, the subject of negotiation on the margins on the conference. Negotiating communiqués, declarations and other official documents are the life-blood of conference diplomacy, and the Oslo conference was no exception for the government functionaries there. The biggest issue was: what did it mean to "prohibit the use, production, transfer and stockpiling of cluster munitions that cause unacceptable harm to civilians" in the sense of which weapons it covered? Germany, for instance, would like to have seen a definition of cluster munitions included in the text based, of course, on its own national formulation, put forward earlier in the CCW.[79] Germany had already signalled its intent to move away from weapons traditionally characterized as submunitions toward more advanced munitions targeting points within an area. Would these sensor-equipped munitions be considered cluster munitions that cause unacceptable harm? What about DPICM submunitions, which many states including a number within NATO possessed, with or without self-destruct or self-neutralization functions, as did others like Japan and South Africa? Given the chance, many would have liked to establish exclusions for some or all of these well before any future negotiation. Conversely, for other states participating in the Oslo conference, many of which did not have cluster munitions in their national arsenals, a complete ban on anything that resembled a cluster munition was desirable. The trick for Kongstad and his colleagues in order to successfully tread this fine line would be to convince the spectrum of states interested in the content of the Oslo declaration that the ambiguity about the objective of banning "cluster munitions that cause unacceptable harm to civilians" was a constructive one, to be settled in the course of the subsequent process to develop a treaty, and not substantially improvable before the end of the Oslo conference.

Concern among some of the European states such as the UK was heightened because there was a difference in the language of Foreign Minister Støre's conference invitation letter—it talked about "those" cluster munitions that cause unacceptable harm—and the draft declaration, which dropped the word "those" and thus created the possibility that *all* cluster munitions might be prohibited.[80] The Oslo conference co-chairs therefore had to try to satisfy nervousness about this, in addition to the Oslo initiative's existence in parallel to the CCW. The other issue was the timetable for completion of the initiative's work toward its objective of completing a legally binding international instrument by 2008. Unlike the definitional issue, or for that matter how the Oslo initiative and the CCW were represented in relation to one another, the roadmap needed to be a clear one, and to contain specific undertakings and waypoints. Kongstad felt the declaration draft was good as it stood, and held as firm as he could on changes proposed from various quarters. Consequently, Goose observed, "There was a good measure of drama and uncertainty over the course of the conference as no one was sure on the final day how many of the governments present would endorse the Oslo Declaration, and how many would bail out; some were clearly getting last-minute instructions".[81] Goose and others feared the declaration exercise would lose Canada, Denmark, France, Germany, Italy, South Africa and the UK.

By late on Friday morning, delegates from many of the NATO countries could be seen in the corridors—or shivering with cigarette in hand outside the Soria Moria lobby doors—"running around, making phone calls, forming groups then dispersing rapidly, talking nervously, waving papers, throwing arms, shaking heads", as observed by one campaigner.[82] In London, for instance, last-minute consultations were underway between the three leading departments on cluster munition-related issues—the Foreign Office, Ministry of Defence and its Department for International Development (DFID)—with DFID's Minister Hilary Benn working hard to persuade his counterparts from the other two agencies that the UK should join the declaration.

The final issue was about being seen to move in good company. It is not clear which of the major European NATO states decided first to endorse the declaration, and it may have been simultaneous. But it was instead Canada's head of delegation, Earl Turcotte, who spoke from the floor first to announce his state's support, followed by Italy, Lebanon, Finland and the UK. One by one representatives of 46 countries representing most regions of the world raised their nameplates to announce they would join the Oslo Declaration.

To mounting collective incredulity and broadening smiles on the faces of campaigners and many diplomats alike, by the end, even Egypt and Finland, two countries widely considered unlikely to join the Oslo Declaration, had done so. Those present included Peachey (quoted at the beginning of this chapter) who, expressing "wonderment and surprise" on hearing of the announcement that the Oslo conference would be held, had decided he had to be there to see for himself what would transpire.[83] Only three states had stood aside from joining the Declaration—Japan, Poland and Romania.

Japanese officials explained to the media at the end of the conference, "We cannot take a step to support it at this stage. We need more extensive debate over the issue, including the CCW".[84] (Japan would decide to continue to participate in the Oslo process, in significant part because of rising pressure from Japanese media organizations such as Mainichi Newspapers, Kyodo News, Asahi Shimbun and NHK television, which eventually broadcast a documentary about Kongstad in Japan.)

The Oslo Declaration, as finalized, stated:

A group of States, United Nations Organisations, the International Committee of the Red Cross, the Cluster Munitions Coalition and other humanitarian organisations met in Oslo on 22–23 February 2007 to discuss how to effectively address the humanitarian problems caused by cluster munitions.

Recognising the grave consequences caused by the use of cluster munitions and the need for immediate action, states commit themselves to:

1. Conclude by 2008 a legally binding international instrument that will:

(i) prohibit the use, production, transfer and stockpiling of cluster munitions that cause unacceptable harm to civilians, and

(ii) establish a framework for cooperation and assistance that ensures adequate provision of care and rehabilitation to survivors and their communities, clearance of contaminated areas, risk education and destruction of stockpiles of prohibited cluster munitions.

2. Consider taking steps at the national level to address these problems.

3. Continue to address the humanitarian challenges posed by cluster munitions within the framework of international humanitarian law and in all relevant fora.

4. Meet again to continue their work, including in Lima in May/June and Vienna in November/December 2007, and in Dublin in early 2008, and welcome the announcement of Belgium to organise a regional meeting.[85]

Some governments explained their support for the Oslo Declaration with carefully stated provisos. Many Western states referred to the importance of "all relevant fora" mentioned in the Declaration, which, of course, was code for the CCW. Unsurprisingly, most NATO states referred to the need to determine what were "cluster munitions that cause unacceptable harm". And, in a foretaste of another issue that would be highly contentious in the Oslo process, the UK opined that "a transition period will be required in the final instrument itself"[86] during which cluster munition possessors could hold on to their banned weapons until they had arranged for alternatives. But for the time being, as the departing delegates headed for the line of chartered buses for Oslo airport a short time later, none of this mattered.

What mattered was that the Oslo process was a live birth, and not still born, and explicit international efforts to address the humanitarian impacts of cluster munitions through a legally binding instrument had begun. Importantly for efforts to follow in the Oslo process, the concerns leading to the February 2007 conference in Norway had translated into a clear objective ("to effectively address the humanitarian concerns caused by cluster munitions") by means of the Declaration. Moreover, it did not try to pre-negotiate key understandings crucial to achieving this such as defining the cluster munitions deemed to cause unacceptable harm. The deferral was a smart move by the Norwegians and their advisers among the emerging Core Group, international organizations and civil society and had required patient and inspired diplomacy to achieve. But the challenge of defining those cluster munitions would, henceforth, become increasingly prominent as debate intensified in further international meetings—the next one scheduled for Lima, Peru, in late May. And, after the Oslo conference, Belgium, Sweden and Switzerland gravitated away from the emerging Core Group, which settled around seven governments—Austria, Ireland, the Holy See, Mexico, New Zealand, Norway and Peru.

CHAPTER 6

AFTER OSLO—SHIFTING THE BURDEN OF PROOF

The Oslo conference in February 2007 was a greater success than even the Norwegians had anticipated in terms of the number of states that committed to completing a humanitarian treaty to ban cluster munitions that "cause unacceptable harm to civilians".[1] The Oslo Declaration's clear humanitarian character and objective had made it very hard for participating governments to resist, and an important feature was that its timetable was not necessarily contingent on Convention on Certain Conventional Weapons (CCW) meetings and consensus decision-making. Comprised initially of multilateral conferences in Lima (late May), Vienna (early December), and then Dublin (in "early 2008"), as well as mentioning a European regional meeting to be held in Belgium, the Declaration timetable envisaged the legally binding instrument's completion by the end of 2008 at the latest. In the course of the Oslo process, there would also be regional meetings, an important conference of states affected by cluster munitions held in Belgrade in October 2007, and an additional international conference convened in Wellington in February 2008 to set the stage for the Dublin negotiations, a key juncture in the initiative discussed in the next chapter.

Even if this timetable for what soon became generally known as the Oslo process was not contingent upon the CCW, it did not mean that states had completely broken free from Geneva. In late February, the new UN Secretary-General, Ban Ki-moon, described the CCW's meetings and the fledgling process emerging from the Norwegian-sponsored Oslo conference as "complementary and mutually reinforcing".[2] The phrase served as a convenient mantra for many, and was subsequently widely echoed in various national statements in Oslo process and CCW meetings. In truth, however, while the CCW's expert work on explosive remnants of war over the course of the decade had helpfully raised awareness about cluster munitions, the benefits of two international processes to address the weapon's humanitarian impacts would flow largely from the Oslo process to the CCW in 2007. That is because while the CCW's mandate for cluster munitions in 2007 extended merely to discussions, the emergence of the Oslo process served to spur on efforts over the course of that year toward achievement of a CCW negotiating mandate for 2008. There were now signs of greater flexibility over work on cluster munitions from several major producers and users of the weapons including China, Israel, Russia and the US, which had made it clear they would shun the Oslo process.[3] Miraculously, they were now prepared to give a little on the prospect of legally binding measures on cluster munitions provided they were developed in the CCW's consensus-dominated environment. Moreover, some of those associated with the Oslo Declaration, especially the European NATO states and others such as Australia, Canada, Japan and Switzerland, were at the vanguard of efforts to use the Oslo initiative's political impetus to jumpstart CCW negotiations on cluster munitions.

This was quite a different situation than the one facing those states steering the Ottawa process to ban anti-personnel mines more than a decade before. The Ottawa process had *followed* the CCW's disappointing agreement on anti-personnel mines, Amended Protocol II, in negotiations concluded in 1996. But, this time around, the free-standing process comprising a coalition of the willing would be working in parallel to (although without meetings actually coinciding with) the CCW. This would complicate matters in diplomatic terms, as well as lay the Oslo process open to an unjustified but persistent criticism that its emergence somehow undermined the international humanitarian law regime and especially the CCW.

Conversely, the CCW was now inevitably compared—usually unfavourably— to the Oslo process, particularly by NGOs and increasingly in the media, which had begun to take a greater interest in both tracks following the Oslo conference. In truth, by the end of 2007 the majority of the CCW's members were involved in the Oslo process even while participating in the CCW's much less ambitious work. It meant that, although differing in terms of their political dynamics and composition of states, information flowed freely between the two processes because so many diplomats and other government experts operated in both environments. And, for NGO campaigners, the CCW was still a useful place to congregate and discuss strategy among themselves, as well as to talk to governments.[4]

If there was an easy distinction to be made between the two processes it was that the CCW contained all of the largest cluster munition possessors and producers; the Oslo process, in contrast, would attract many states, particularly in the developing world, which were not members of the CCW, and some of them living with the post-conflict effects of cluster munition use. However, this generalization obscures the fact that the Oslo process did include at least one of the largest users of cluster munitions—the UK, which deployed them in Kosovo in 1999 and Iraq in 2003—and many states stockpiling the weapon. Taking some, let alone all, of these stockpiles out of circulation would be of major and immediate humanitarian benefit in that they would never be used, and so never pose a risk to civilians.

Overall, for all of the helpful talk of "mutual reinforcement" between the CCW and the Oslo processes, in diplomatic and political terms they were entangled. As February ended, it remained to be seen how constraining this entanglement would be for the development of the Oslo process—or how far the CCW would be pulled along in its direction. Many states at the Oslo conference had continued to talk about, for instance, achieving "a proper balance between military and humanitarian interests, as has always been the case with previous instruments in the area of international humanitarian law".[5] It was a piece of sophistry long used in the CCW: what this balance would be was in the eye of the beholder, of course. And, based on the balance of participation in the Oslo conference in which Western industrialized states predominated, those states seemed to expect it would entail them banning some cluster munitions, but retaining newer cluster munition models with features to try to ensure reliability such as a self-destruct, self-deactivating or self-neutralizing mechanism. The UK had even invented a term—"dumb cluster munitions"[6]—for those it envisaged being phased out, rather than its newer M-85 submunitions with self-destruct, or so-called "direct-fire" submunitions such as the CRV-7 or Hydra weapons fired from attack helicopters.[7] In short, the West European NATO states, in particular, assumed they would be able to steer the Oslo process toward an outcome that would not bite substantially into the stocks of newer DPICM-type submunitions in their military arsenals, while being able to publicly claim the humanitarian high ground.[8]

It was not to be. In the year following the Oslo conference, the pendulum of the "burden of proof" for demonstrating the acceptability or otherwise of cluster munitions swung decisively within the Oslo process against states trying to retain some of these weapons. This chapter explores what happened during this crucial period in this reframing of the discourse in the remainder of 2007. Not coincidentally, it was also a period of rapid expansion in the number of governments invested in the Oslo process. Crucially, many of them were states from the developing world more concerned about the impacts of cluster munitions on civilians than on the weapon's military utility. This affected the Oslo process's political dynamics to the point that broad groupings would develop within it—like the so-called "like-minded" and "teetotallers"—that would, by the end of the year, threaten to polarize it and so threaten the initiative's prospects for success.

Non-state actors involved in the Oslo process were facing challenges of their own too. The Cluster Munition Coalition (CMC) was rapidly developing into a full-scale advocacy and campaigning machine, but, coming out of the Oslo conference, the CMC still had unfinished business to resolve internally in terms of its campaigning call. This chapter focuses some attention on these processes and how they fed into international efforts against cluster munitions.

OSLO'S AFTERMATH

Following the Oslo conference, the Core Group of states steering the development of the emergent process now settled down into a configuration comprising Austria, Ireland, Mexico, New Zealand, Norway and Peru. The Holy See would also gravitate into the Core Group and eventually became regarded as a full member in the period leading up to the Lima conference. Privately, there was initial scepticism among some individuals in other Core Group delegations about the efficacy of the Holy See's involvement. In time this view would reverse itself, not least in view of the Vatican's tremendous lobbying powers and strong diplomatic network, especially in the developing world.

The group of diplomats from the Core Group delegations had now come through a baptism of fire together, diplomatically speaking, and a significant degree of trust had been built between them. They would, moreover, see a great deal more of each other over coming months in the lead-up to the Lima meeting in order to prepare the way for next steps. The Core Group would never present (or seek to present) a united front on matters of substance such as the content of definitions or on the issue of interoperability in a humanitarian treaty, and in time the differences of view of its partner governments would become more apparent. Instead, the Core Group acted as a bureau in which member states supported each other to propel the Oslo process, and fend off challenges to its humanitarian objectives, on which they were all agreed.

The Norwegian side continued to be led by Ambassador Steffen Kongstad, as head of the Norwegian government's special project on cluster munitions. His main helpers were Annette Abelsen (who earlier had also worked under his supervision while they were both posted to Geneva), Lars Løken from the Foreign Ministry's Security Policy Department, Annette Bjørseth, a lawyer from the Ministry of Defence, and Christian Ruge, who by now was working almost full time as an external consultant to the government on cluster munitions. Staff from the Norwegian Permanent Mission in Geneva, especially Ingunn Vatne, supported them. An important veteran of the Ottawa process, Gro Nystuen, also contributed in addition to her ongoing roles at the University of Oslo and the Council on Ethics for the Norwegian Government's Pension Fund–Global.

Geneva-based diplomats represented the majority of the rest of the Core Group. There was Austria's disarmament ambassador in Geneva, Wolfgang Petritsch, and his counsellors, Markus Reiterer, who had a particular interest in victim assistance issues and, on the military side, Cornelia Kratochvil. (The Austrians also had a strong team in the Austrian Foreign Ministry in Vienna, led by Alexander Marschik.) Father Antoine Abi Ghanem, the Holy See's working-level representative on disarmament issues in Geneva, a Lebanese Catholic priest and a teacher of political philosophy, was a very able mediator, providing a sympathetic ear to many in the Oslo process as it developed and helping to ensure the Core Group was never blindsided. A young diplomat, James C. O'Shea, was Ireland's point man on cluster munitions in Geneva; on the Dublin side, the Irish foreign affairs team was led by Alison Kelly, with the support of Nicholas Twist and Declan Smyth, a lawyer with extensive experience in international humanitarian law who had recently returned from a disarmament posting in Geneva. Lt Col Jim Burke, an Irish soldier and veteran of CCW work, rounded out the Irish team and was their main technical expert. Ambassador Pablo Macedo directed Mexico's position from capital (he had been Geneva-based until the end of 2006) supported by diplomats in Geneva including Mabel Gómez Oliver and Claudia García Guiza. A young diplomat, Charlotte Darlow, assisted New Zealand's Permanent Representative in Geneva, Ambassador Don MacKay. Peru was a mildly unknown quantity: a young Peruvian diplomat, Diego Belevan Tamayo had been active in the CCW setting until around the time of the Oslo conference, and Peru had agreed to host the next conference in May 2007. But he was returning to capital, and Foreign Service personnel from Lima, including Ambassador Antonio García Revilla and Liliam Ballón de Amézaga, would mainly fill the role of coordinating with the Core Group.

There were others who, while not members of the Core Group or privy to all of its discussions, were nevertheless asked for their views frequently or from time to time. The CMC was consulted, of course— primarily Nash, its coordinator, and its new Steering Committee Co-chairs Conway, Goose and Østern, although it remained to be seen exactly what the dynamic would be between civil society and the Core Group over the longer term. On the International Committee of the Red Cross (ICRC) side, Peter Herby and Louis Maresca were long known and trusted by all for their experience and legal judgment, and were frequently consulted by the Core Group, as they were by many states both within and outside the Oslo process on issues related to international humanitarian law.

And then there was the United Nations. The most important part of the UN to the Oslo process was the United Nations Development Programme (UNDP): its logistical capacity to organize events around the globe, to help to support participation from developing—and particularly cluster munition-affected—countries in the process and to help in promoting a focus on the *effects* of cluster munitions post-conflict would be very important, and in Oslo UNDP had committed itself to this end. The locus of activity within UNDP would be its Bureau of Crisis Prevention and Recovery, and several key individuals including Peter Batchelor, Paul Eavis, Melissa Sabatier, Hans Risser and staff from various UNDP offices around the world, such as Tim Horner from its UXO programme in Laos, all contributed. The Bureau's Director and overall UNDP Assistant Administrator Kathleen Cravero would, at times, intervene at critical points in the UN's internal policymaking process. Cravero was a strong supporter of the Oslo process's humanitarian aims as she saw a treaty on cluster munitions as sitting squarely within the UNDP's crisis recovery remit.[9] The lynchpin in this highly effective team was none other than Sara Sekkenes, formerly of Norwegian People's Aid. Several people in the UN Mine Action Service were also supportive, such as John Flanagan, Chris Clark and Gustavo Laurie, as well as individuals from UNIDIR like myself and occasionally staff from the UN Office for Disarmament Affairs who interacted with the Core Group and also acted as sounding boards from time to time during the development of the Oslo process.

Two immediate issues faced the Core Group. The first was to grow the initiative beyond the 46 states of the Oslo Declaration. As mentioned, there was a bias among these states toward the industrialized West, and a goal for the initiative would be to build support in all regions of the world. The voices of affected countries were perceived as especially important in lending legitimacy to the Oslo process with its humanitarian imperative. Clearly, civil society's network of campaigners, UNDP's offices around the world and the ICRC and national societies within the Red Cross and Red Crescent Movement could lend momentum to this, alongside the Core Group states' diplomatic efforts. The other issue concerned elaborating a strategy for the Oslo process. Strategic issues had been discussed among states supportive of the Norwegian-initiated process well before the Oslo conference, but now the states of the Core Group began turning their minds (with input from others) to developing ideas about how an eventual treaty might look, and how to prepare states in the Oslo process for migrating toward that. It was evident that everything would hinge upon the general scope of the treaty's obligations and how these were packaged—and in particular, how cluster munitions were defined. Cluster munitions were not like anti-personnel mines, and so this would be new territory.

Those involved in the CMC's Steering Committee knew the difficulties of characterizing what should be banned only too well. Prohibiting "cluster munitions that cause unacceptable harm" had been taken up as a formulation by the CMC at its Kentwell strategy retreat in January 2007 (see chapter 5), and subsequently found its way into the Oslo Declaration. The exact provenance and origin of the "unacceptable harm" formulation is unclear, however. Goose had used the phrase as early as 8 November 2006 in a Human Rights Watch statement at the CCW Review Conference,[10] but as we saw in the preceding chapter, the Norwegians were using variations of the phrase in CCW statements in June 2006. The advantage of prohibiting cluster munitions that cause unacceptable harm to civilians as a political objective was that it was imprecise enough to harbour a broad range of viewpoints. But the formulation's ambiguity could eventually backfire. Preoccupation with dividing cluster munitions into "acceptable" and "unacceptable" categories could paralyse the Oslo process. And was not *all* harm to civilians unacceptable, in principle?

For the CMC, there was also the thorny question of how the Oslo Declaration equated precisely with the CMC's own call for action on cluster munitions. During the weekend following the Oslo conference, the CMC's Steering Committee met in Oslo to chew over the issue of the Coalition's call once again.[11] The Kentwell call stated, "The CMC calls for a prohibition on cluster munitions that cause unacceptable harm to civilians". The upshot of the Oslo Declaration was that now, on paper at least, so too did 46 states. The Kentwell discussions in January withstanding, Nash and many on the Steering Committee, including Handicap International France's Jean-Baptiste Richardier, Norwegian People's Aid's Østern, as well as Conway and Moyes from Landmine Action, felt the CMC should now position itself to create a discourse in the Oslo process in which it was increasingly accepted that *all* cluster munitions as commonly characterized caused unacceptable harm and as such should be banned. There should also be a change of emphasis in the CMC's call, away from urging measures such as national moratoria on cluster munition use, and instead toward the achievement of the prospective new "Oslo Treaty". Other members of the Steering Committee, namely Goose and Hannon, did not agree: they felt that the Kentwell call was still sufficiently flexible to allow individual CMC members to advocate as they saw fit on cluster munitions, and feared the unveiling of a new CMC message would undermine its credibility—by seeming to shift the Coalition's objective as soon as states had caught up.

With the benefit of hindsight, it would be easy to judge the reluctance of some in the Steering Committee to make the CMC's call for a ban more explicit as overly cautious. What is striking to me about the personal correspondence between individuals on the Steering Committee during this period over the CMC's call is that it showed they agreed on the call's substance—the real difference was over how they framed the issue. Those wanting to make the prohibition in the CMC's call more explicit seem to have linked it (consciously or otherwise) to issues about the Coalition's central identity. The CMC's "soul" was what it stood for; that is, its call on states. Certainly, as veterans of the Ottawa process, Goose and Hannon were well aware that clear goals and campaign messaging were important factors in mobilizing support and media interest. This was not unrelated to their awareness that a civil society campaign's currency in government-dominated processes, whether in the CCW or in the context of the Oslo initiative, depended on its credibility; hence their concerns about the call's consistency. It pointed Goose toward a particular tactical question concerning further changes to the CMC call: how different would it really be from the one agreed in Kentwell? No different, in Goose's view. So it would be better not to change the CMC call and risk confusion and criticism from those whose behaviour the Coalition was trying to influence.

This was an argument that had prevailed in the past, but would not suffice much longer. The end result of internal CMC negotiations within the Steering Committee over about five weeks following Oslo was a careful compromise crafted by Richardier and Nash to reflect the respective viewpoints within the group. The decision, communicated to CMC members in a message for general distribution from Nash on the Coalition's e-mail list server, read as follows:

> The Cluster Munition Coalition calls for the conclusion of an international treaty banning cluster munitions by 2008. Cluster munitions are understood to be unreliable and inaccurate weapons that are prone to indiscriminate use and that pose severe and lasting risks to civilians from unexploded submunitions. Therefore the CMC urges all States to:
>
> - join the international process launched in Oslo in February 2007 toward an effective and comprehensive treaty;
>
> - take immediate national steps to stop the use, production and transfer of cluster munitions;
>
> - commit resources and capacities to assist communities and individuals affected by cluster munitions.[12]

The deal done within the Steering Committee was that this language would be regarded as an "update" and not a new call, consistent with the views of Human Rights Watch and Mines Action Canada representatives. This development could be viewed as slightly Orwellian, but Nash's message to the CMC duly noted, "The Steering Committee emphasised that this updated call does not represent a change in the CMC's position, but was a consistent updating of the call in the post-Oslo environment". It was welcomed by the CMC's wider membership, many of whom were already calling for a ban themselves and thought that the CMC was too.

To some extent it was true that the precise phraseology of the campaign call did not really matter in terms of the substance of what the Coalition's members believed or advocated to others: this had not changed. On the other hand, the CMC's call "update" would have tactical benefits for the Oslo Core Group and the CMC. The CMC's call contributed to the impression that the Oslo Declaration was positioned in the political middle ground as a response to the impacts on civilians of cluster munitions, with the CMC as demandeur. Moreover, civil society lobbying for banning "unreliable and inaccurate weapons that are prone to indiscriminate use and that pose severe and lasting risks to civilians from unexploded submunitions" could help to counterbalance the attempts many expected to come from Lima onward to split the cluster munition category along the lines of unproven technical "improvements" such as self-destruct. In its preparations for the Lima meeting, the CMC subsequently developed "19 Principles" concerning what any treaty on cluster munitions must include, and this included a basic understanding of cluster munitions that did not exclude from its scope submunitions with self-destruct or a claimed reliability standard. The CMC's first treaty principle called for "a prohibition on the use, production, transfer and stockpiling of cluster munitions, as defined"[13]—a manifestation of the "define, ban, then exclude" approach rather than a "split-the-category" approach to cluster munitions.

THE ICRC'S MEETING OF EXPERTS

The first real opportunity to collectively wrestle with substantive issues related to the content of new international humanitarian law rules on cluster munitions in the post-Oslo conference environment occurred at an ICRC expert meeting held in April 2007. On the eve of the CCW Review Conference in November 2006 and, in a move pre-dating Norway's announcement of a conference in Oslo (which the ICRC had been aware was imminent due to its participation in "interested state" lunches that year with the Norwegians and others), the ICRC had publicly offered to host an international meeting of experts in 2007 to discuss future rules of international humanitarian law that would better protect civilians from the effects of cluster munitions.[14] Earlier ICRC expert meetings—on blinding lasers and anti-personnel mines during the 1990s, as well as explosive remnants of war in 2000 (see chapter 2)—had helped to catalyse international negotiations on those issues.

One selling point of an ICRC-hosted meeting on cluster munitions was that, as the humanitarian organization's representatives had been at pains to make clear in the 2006 CCW Review Conference, it was not specific to any one process and would involve a full spectrum of states with differing positions on cluster munitions. At the same time, the ICRC's own position was well known, which called for an agreement:

- to immediately end the use of inaccurate and unreliable cluster munitions;

- to prohibit the targeting of cluster munitions against any military objective located in a populated area;

- to eliminate stocks of inaccurate and unreliable cluster munitions and pending their destruction, not to transfer such weapons to other countries.[15]

This was clearly far out in front of what many of the states in the CCW were prepared to support. Nevertheless, the ICRC's proposal for an expert meeting was enthusiastically taken up at the CCW review meeting, and even mentioned in the decision on its work programme for 2007, since it was widely perceived that the ICRC's meeting would permit engagement without prejudice to states' differing formal positions in the CCW.[16]

A major difference between the ICRC meeting of experts in Montreux and previous ICRC expert meetings on other weapons was its timing: the success of the Oslo conference in February meant that an international negotiating process to address the humanitarian problems created by cluster munitions was already underway. From the perspective of the Oslo process, the argument could be made that events had overtaken the need for yet more deliberative discussions, which might even act as a drag against international action, and none were more sensitive to this than the ICRC itself.[17] As it turned out, however, the ICRC's meeting was an unrivalled opportunity to evaluate the logic of the various positions on whether and how to address the humanitarian, military and legal challenges of cluster munitions—including as it did many military powers with cluster munitions as well as practitioners from the humanitarian community and representatives from the Oslo Core Group of states.[18] Participating cluster munition possessors outside the Oslo process included Brazil, China, Israel, Russia and the US.

The expert meeting was convened in beautiful surroundings in the Swiss town of Montreux at the grand hotel Eden Palace au Lac in glorious spring weather. Such was the interest in the meeting that it was heavily over-subscribed: a gathering originally intended for 60 experts eventually encompassed about 90 people in what was thus a packed and stuffy meeting room.[19] While not exactly informal, the expert meeting emphasized substantive exchange on technical, legal and policy issues surrounding cluster munitions, and it was difficult for representatives of large cluster munition possessors and user states to avoid direct questioning.

And under questioning, the dissonance between their technical presentations, statements and submunition reliability claims with the actual experience of cluster munitions in recent conflicts such as Southern Lebanon became obvious. In one presentation, Ove Dullum (the Norwegian Defence Research Establishment scientist from chapter 3) briefed participants on the results of Norway's cluster munition testing the previous year, as well as preliminary results of Israeli M-85 submunition failure rates that he and others were examining in Southern Lebanon. He concluded, "it seems quite probable that the dud rate of the M-85 bomblets used by Israeli forces in Lebanon is more than 5%, which is clearly in conflict with what we observe at the Norwegian tests".[20] The clear implication was that even the best tests did not dependably reflect operational conditions in the real world. When Dullum was asked why testing of submunitions could not be conducted under more realistic conditions, he paused for a moment and then replied that if Norway were to regularly test submunitions in such an environment it would create a big unexploded ordnance problem!

Combined with Chris Clark's presentation on the aftermath of the Southern Lebanon conflict, Dullum's presentation at the Montreux meeting underlined serious problems with the line still maintained by major stockpiling states that submunition testing could be a reasonable basis for assessing the reliability of cluster munitions. And they had no comeback except to flatly deny it—without much in the way of supporting argument—something duly exploited in the discussions by NGOs, Oslo Core Group state representatives and humanitarian field personnel like Clark. For example, cross-examined by government and NGO experts about how Switzerland could be so confident in the low failure rate of its Israeli-manufactured M-85 submunitions with self-destruct, a representative from Armasuisse was eventually reduced to admitting Switzerland's confidence was based on the fact that the munitions were assembled in Switzerland.

Despite the word "expert" in the title of the ICRC meeting, many of the diplomats at Montreux were by no means knowledgeable about cluster munitions when it commenced. It was now glaringly apparent to a growing number of them that technical solutions were not sufficient to deal with all aspects of the humanitarian problems that cluster munitions create. One Montreux participant was New Zealand ambassador Don MacKay, who would coordinate the definition issue throughout all of the Oslo process's later conferences. At a meeting the following day that UNIDIR and the Geneva Forum organized to debrief some of the Montreux expert meeting's participants,[21] he remarked that, from his perspective, dealing with cluster munitions had just become "a whole lot harder".[22] And MacKay was by no means alone in this sobering realization.

But the scope of measures needed to credibly address the humanitarian impacts of cluster munitions was not just a challenge for the Oslo process. The growing realization about the inadequacy of technical fixes cast those clinging to the CCW as *the* negotiating forum in a new, more negative, light—a reversal for those states, like the US, who remained unwilling to negotiate new international rules while now acknowledging that cluster munitions caused humanitarian problems. Moreover, Chinese and US positions were further exposed as mutually contradictory. China said at Montreux that it opposed any technical solutions for improving submunitions—further underlining the bleak prospects for effective action in the CCW's consensus-based decision-making environment. In sum, the most prominent cluster munition-stockpiling states arguing for continued retention and use of this weapon came off second best in discussions at Montreux, in the face of opposing perspectives from other governments, humanitarian deminers and NGOs such as the CMC, Handicap International, Human Rights Watch, Landmine Action and Norwegian People's Aid.

THE GERMAN PROPOSAL, AND THE EMERGENCE OF THE "LIKE-MINDED"

Another significant development at Montreux was the unveiling of a non-paper by Germany, later submitted as a working paper for the June CCW expert meeting in Geneva, which contained a draft text for a new CCW protocol on cluster munitions.[23] This proposal had been foreshadowed by Germany's announcement of its national "8-Point-Position on Cluster Munitions" in 2006.[24] The ensuing German CCW protocol proposal was long and very detailed. An NGO analyst encapsulated it as follows:

> "unreliable" or "inaccurate" cluster munitions should be prohibited, but [the proposal] contains a provision allowing for "reliable" and "accurate" cluster munitions to be used for a period of 10 years. So-called "reliable" cluster munitions are defined based on a failure rate of one percent. "Unreliable" cluster munitions are those with failure rates higher than one percent. "Accurate" cluster munitions are those which are "effective only within a pre-defined target area." Target areas are not defined.[25]

The draft protocol was consistent with Germany's declared intent to phase out cluster munitions intended to saturate an area with explosive submunitions and replace them with advanced alternative weapons it described as Sensor Fuzed Area Munitions, designed to home in on point targets *within* an area. (Like cluster munitions, some sensor-fuzed weapons have submunitions that separate from a parent munition, like an artillery shell, but are different in that these submunitions have sophisticated sensor systems to actively seek out and engage point targets, such as tanks, rather than saturating an area with high explosive and fragments.[26]) However the German draft protocol proposal's inclusion of transition periods, which Germany also insisted upon in the Oslo process, would become very contentious.

If Germany had introduced this proposal for a protocol only two years earlier into the CCW, it likely would have been enthusiastically hailed by those states and some of the NGOs calling for cluster munition measures. Now, however, expectations had drastically risen due to the Oslo Declaration. It meant that although welcomed as a further signal of Germany's political commitment to the issue, the proposal for a CCW protocol drew sharp criticism from NGOs and some states for its perceived lack of ambition and clarity on key issues, such as scope, and its faith in an unverifiable percentage failure rate.[27] For other states in the CCW, this technology-based approach was unpalatable as they did not necessarily have access to such new weapon technologies, nor would they necessarily be able to afford them.[28] The German proposal and reactions to it just served to underline the significant differences in approach even among states subscribing to the Oslo Declaration, and warned of the difficulties ahead in achieving convergence in either the Oslo process or CCW.

Many of those governments subscribing to the Oslo Declaration at the February conference (or subsequently), and especially Australia, Canada, Japan and most European NATO allies, all faced an uncomfortable prospect. Somehow they would have to balance public concern about cluster munitions and their commitment to the aspirations of the Oslo Declaration with the operational concerns of their military forces and the disapproval of the United States. Many did not want a comprehensive ban on cluster munitions—therefore they (like the Core Group and NGOs) recognized that defining a cluster munition that causes unacceptable harm to civilians would lie at the heart of the matter in the Oslo process. But some appeared to hope (as Germany did, for instance) that their involvement in both processes would help to keep the Oslo process's ambitions within acceptable bounds for them, and create pressure for agreement on lesser measures in the CCW in 2008—the forum they still preferred—that would stand a chance of attracting those major users and producers of cluster munitions remaining outside the Oslo process.[29]

Over the course of 2007, a loose group of roughly 15 so-called "like-minded" states would emerge, mainly consisting of military allies of the US, with Denmark, France, Germany, Japan, the Netherlands and the UK especially active.[30] At one end of the spectrum among the Like-minded were states like Finland and Japan, which appeared deeply attached to retaining many, if not all, of their existing cluster munition arsenals. At the other end were states such as Australia and Canada, which neither stockpile nor use cluster munitions. Overlapping concerns motivated the Like-minded. Their first major concern was that an eventual ban on cluster munitions causing unacceptable harm would encapsulate weapons they employed (or would like to employ) which use sensor-fuzing technologies. And many of the Like-minded shared a worry that a new cluster munition norm which, for political reasons, would probably be difficult for them to resist joining, would create legal and operational headaches in terms of interoperability with major allies not party to the treaty—a concern the US allegedly encouraged,[31] and which would become a major issue by the time of the Dublin negotiations in May 2008. The biggest concern to unite them, however, was frustration about their collective inability to steer the Oslo process, an issue that would come to a head in February 2008 in Wellington, as shall be discussed in the next chapter.

THE LIMA CONFERENCE

The appearance of Germany's proposal for a draft CCW protocol persuaded Oslo Core Group states to circulate their own discussion text. As mentioned, drafting work had already been going on for some time among interested individuals, loosely shepherded by Nystuen. Building on this, in late March Norway shared with its Oslo Core Group partners its initial stab at a text, which in many ways resembled the Mine Ban Treaty. These governments further debated and revised the language. Ten days or so before the three-day-long Lima conference was scheduled to begin on 23 May, Peru's government, in its capacity as that meeting's Chair, circulated an adapted text to all participants as a discussion paper.[32]

Peru also circulated an agenda for the Lima conference just before it commenced.[33] This agenda was structured around thematic discussion instead of the textual negotiation the earlier discussion paper had implied would take place. Moreover, no time was scheduled to discuss definitions until the conference's final day, with issues like victim assistance, clearance of unexploded cluster munitions, storage and stockpile destruction, as well as transparency reporting, national implementation and compliance, all to be discussed first. The Core Group clearly intended this agenda to emphasize the Oslo process's humanitarian priorities, especially to states now participating in the Oslo process, including many Asian, African and Latin American states, that had not attended Oslo.

Nevertheless, others did wish to focus on defining cluster munitions in view of its priority for them. On the Lima meeting's first day, France challenged the agenda from the conference floor, proposing to move definitions to the top of the agenda, and others echoed this, such as Argentina, Australia, Egypt, Germany, the Netherlands and the UK. While these were logical concerns from the perspective of those supporting France, it may have unintentionally conveyed the impression that they did not share others' emphasis on humanitarian priorities—a perspective not popular with developing countries and those affected by cluster munitions.[34] However, Austria proposed a winning compromise: swap definitions from the last morning to the afternoon of the middle day. Crisis was averted.

Once the agenda issue was resolved, thematic discussions in Lima proved constructive and largely uncontroversial. NGOs, well-prepared and fired up after a civil society forum the day before the formal meeting, made a strong showing, with many proposals based on a comprehensive CMC commentary on the text.[35] There were thoughtful discussions on the necessary elements of a humanitarian legal instrument, including cautions that such a treaty should not just carry over elements of the Mine Ban Convention, but should improve on them in areas like victim assistance. These discussions helped to lay the foundation for the relevant provisions of the eventual draft Convention discussed in Wellington nine months later in February 2008.[36]

Just as important as the substantive issues it canvassed, the Lima conference avoided a damaging and highly public split among states in the Oslo Process on an issue—definitions—that could not realistically be settled until the endgame of eventual negotiations on a cluster munition treaty.

In part it was achieved because of the emphasis on thematic discussion rather than textual drafting, maintained through skilled chairing. It also reflected the evolving composition of the Oslo process: in Oslo in February the great majority of the 49 participating states were developed, Western countries. Sixty-eight states were represented at the Lima conference, many of which were developing countries from Latin America, Asia and Africa and generally more concerned with the effects of cluster munitions rather than their military utility.[37] Moreover, good intentions were gradually being matched with evidence of changing national practice. Hungary, for instance, declared during the meeting a national moratorium on the use of cluster munitions, and Peru announced an initiative to try to create the world's first cluster munition-free zone in Latin America.[38]

"PING-PONG" IN THE CCW

If humanitarian imperatives had captured the attention of new states joining the Oslo process, it was not the case in the CCW, in which the military aspects of cluster munitions continued to receive the bulk of attention. In June, and in line with the Review Conference mandate agreed the preceding November, a Group of Governmental Experts (GGE) met in Geneva, chaired by Latvia. This one-week meeting covered much of the same ground as the ICRC Montreux expert meeting, although in less depth. While representing a step forward for discussions in the CCW, the views expressed in these talks by major users and producers of cluster munitions further highlighted the difficulty of developing enough momentum there to address the humanitarian impact of this weapon through a comprehensive legal instrument.

Nevertheless, there was a subtle shift underway. In CCW informal consultations in Geneva in between the Montreux expert meeting and its June GGE session, major cluster munitions users and producers such as the US and Russia began to soften their statements and even made approving (though non-specific) noises about the prospect of a CCW mandate for work of some kind on cluster munitions.[39] (The US delegation held a press conference during the June session, and subsequently undertook an unprecedented amount of media outreach.) In early June, after lengthy negotiations, European Union members submitted for consideration at the CCW GGE a new joint proposal for a negotiating mandate for a treaty by the end of 2008 to prohibit cluster munitions "that cause unacceptable harm to civilians and [which] includes provisions on cooperation and assistance", which echoed aspects of the Oslo Declaration.[40] And the day before the commencement of the June GGE, the US delegation told journalists that it now supported launching negotiations in the CCW on a global treaty to reduce civilian casualties from cluster bombs, but did not back a ban on the weapons.[41]

During the ensuing CCW meeting, Richard Kidd, Director of the US State Department's Office of Weapons Removal and Abatement, outlined some "practical steps" that "merit examination". However, he limited these to post-conflict effects and argued that the threat cluster munitions pose to civilians "is episodic, manageable within current response mechanisms and, on a global scale, less harmful than threat[s] posed by other types of unexploded munitions".[42] He omitted any reference to hazards to civilians which cluster munitions pose at time of use, or the likely humanitarian consequences of their further proliferation. And, ominously, while the US said it supported *initiation* of a negotiation, it was careful to clarify that it had "taken no position as to the outcome of the negotiations".[43] To some, the apparent change to the US position looked like the time-honoured "ping-pong" diplomatic tactic intended to prevent mass defections to an "Oslo Treaty" in the awareness that it would be politically impossible for Oslo process supporters not to support a CCW negotiating mandate on cluster munitions—after all, the CCW's prior failure to negotiate was the rationale for their efforts.[44]

Despite movement by the US and others, the June expert meeting's recommendation to its Meeting of States Parties to be held in November could not wholly paper over the differences still apparent in the CCW. It recommended that the November meeting make some sort of decision about whether and how the CCW would address the humanitarian impacts of cluster munitions, but its heavily qualified language did not offer a clear pointer about what that decision should be. It amounted to a shrug and a good luck handshake for further work in a process in which states remained divided over whether there should even be a negotiation, let alone its scope.[45]

FATAL FOOTPRINTS

In the course of the Belgian cluster munition ban legislation process in late 2005 and early 2006 (see chapter 2), Stan Brabant of Handicap International (HI) Belgium realized that although some useful research existed about the global socio-economic impacts of cluster munitions, it was in the context of other work, for instance on landmines or explosive remnants of war. He concluded that research showing a global picture of the scale and specific types of effects of cluster munitions on civilians would have been very useful in making the case for a ban in Belgium, and would be in other contexts as well. So, Brabant and HI Belgium's victim assistance coordinator, Katleen Maes, developed an idea for a survey of these socio-economic effects and, on the margins of the London meeting in March 2006, Brabant proposed the project to Norwegian government representatives.[46] Norway's government—also seeing the potential of the research—agreed to contribute funding to it.[47]

The HI Belgium-led research followed in the path of other global survey reports like Landmine Monitor's annual compendium and the Landmine Action-coordinated reports on explosive remnants of war in 2003 and on explosive remnants of war and mines other than anti-personnel mines in 2005 (mentioned in chapter 2). There were by now also a number of country- or conflict-specific reports (some mentioned in earlier chapters) about problems with cluster munitions at time of use and post-conflict, many produced by Human Rights Watch and Landmine Action. But the special contribution of HI's research was that it focused on improving understanding of the impact of cluster munitions in greater depth by "documenting short-, mid- and long-term casualties, cumulative effects of disability, mortality and resource denial on families and communities. It also provides insight into the items and activities posing the greatest threats in affected areas".[48]

And, as it turned out, the HI-led research was in position when the Lebanon conflict occurred during July and August of that year. Post-conflict data collected from Southern Lebanon was included in its preliminary report, *Fatal Footprint*, launched on 2 November in order to try to create pressure on the CCW Review Conference to take action on cluster munitions, and it received a lot of media attention.[49] *Fatal Footprint* was followed six months later by a more comprehensive report, entitled *Circle of Impact*, launched shortly before the Lima conference in May 2007.[50] The latter report reconfirmed the astounding conclusion that:

> civilians are almost the sole victims of cluster munitions at almost 98 percent of casualties. The vast majority of cluster submunitions casualties confirmed by this report were among the poor in their country, area or region, and often among the poorest. This report has gathered extensive information from numerous sources from both previously and newly reported data. Statistical evidence of at least *13,306* recorded and confirmed cluster munitions casualties was compiled. This does not include extrapolations or estimates. A conservative estimate indicates that there are at least 55,000 cluster submunitions casualties but this figure could be as high as 100,000 cluster submunitions casualties.[51]

Even the upper estimate paled in magnitude with the likely total number of victims of anti-personnel mines (although precise figures for mines and unexploded ordnance will never be known, for various reasons). But this proportion of civilian casualties was clearly of special concern. The research supported the conclusions reached in reports like the 2003 Landmine Action survey that submunitions were especially hazardous forms of unexploded ordnance in the limited number of places they had been used. As such, it underlined the importance of curbing the proliferation of cluster munitions to prevent a repeat of a global humanitarian problem on the scale of the landmine epidemic of the 1980s and 1990s.

Growing awareness of the likely preventive benefit of a cluster munition treaty due to research like Handicap International's reports gave impetus to many states previously not engaged in the cluster munition issue to become interested in the Oslo process. And, as a humanitarian initiative trying to distinguish itself from the technocratically-inclined CCW, there was a strong desire among Oslo Core Group states and their non-governmental partners to bring more attention to the humanitarian and developmental dimensions of the consequences of cluster munition use too. An attendant concern for the Core Group was the long-perceived gap between the Lima conference and its next meeting in Vienna, to be hosted by the Austrian government in December 2007. There were fears that political momentum in the Oslo process might stagnate or—worse yet—dissipate over those months. And there was a growing realization based on the Lima talks and ongoing internal Oslo Core Group meetings about just how much work needed to be done to arrive at a robust treaty within the timeframe called for by the Oslo Declaration.

Several events helped to fill this perceived gap. The first was that, in September 2007, the Norwegian government organized a number of high-profile public events in Oslo to commemorate the tenth anniversary of the agreement of the Mine Ban Treaty, which had been negotiated there.[52] Although the ostensible focus was—rightly—on the Mine Ban Treaty's achievements so far and challenges ahead for its implementation, the Norwegians also used the occasion to make the connection between the Ottawa process and the Oslo process as complementary forms of disarmament as humanitarian action. Norway had invited many governments, NGOs and individuals involved in the Ottawa process to Oslo, and Norwegian politicians, diplomats and NGO representatives engaged with them energetically and at every available opportunity in order to enlist their support for the Oslo process. For example, in a keynote speech about the Mine Ban Treaty, Norwegian Foreign Minister Støre noted its more than 150 states parties to date, and argued, "I see no reason why the very same states that adopted the Landmine Convention shouldn't join us in our effort to reach agreement on a realistic ban on those cluster munitions that cause unacceptable humanitarian consequences. Now we are 80 states—can we grow to more than 150?"[53]

It was a shrewd gambit. Many senior government representatives, particularly from mine-affected countries not hitherto involved in the CCW or the Oslo process work on cluster munitions, were exposed to the arguments for a humanitarian treaty on the weapon for the first time. Couched in humanitarian terms, their support for the Oslo process by attending the upcoming Vienna conference in December made perfect sense. A meeting of Latin American states held in Costa Rica that same month built support for the Oslo process in the region, building a sense of Latin American solidarity and with the effect of isolating Brazil.[54] And, in November at the Mine Ban Treaty's eighth annual meeting of states parties held on the shores of the Dead Sea in Jordan, the CMC lobbied member governments to affirm the aims of the Oslo Declaration and participate in Vienna.

BELGRADE AND THE VOICES OF THE CLUSTER MUNITION-AFFECTED

Another event during the autumn of 2007 was the Belgrade Conference of States Affected by Cluster Munitions, held on 3–4 October. Although a smaller scale international meeting, the Belgrade gathering was probably as significant as any of the international conferences of the Oslo process named in the Oslo Declaration. Organized by the Serbian government and UNDP with support from Norway and the CMC (represented by the Norwegian People's Aid office in Belgrade led by Emil Jeremić), the conference's objective was to ensure that perspectives from those affected by cluster munitions were heard.[55] During the one-and-a-half day meeting, participants discussed victim assistance, cluster munitions clearance, international cooperation and assistance, stockpile destruction and proliferation issues. Thirty-seven governments attended, including 22 countries affected by cluster munitions, as well as various entities of the United Nations, the ICRC and a strong NGO presence coordinated by the CMC, which played a major role.[56]

The Belgrade conference was especially important for the opportunity it gave to survivors of cluster munitions to make their voices heard. Serbian cluster munition survivor Branislav Kapetanović, was again vocal, joined by a number of others from various countries including Albania, Lebanon and Tajikistan. Another Serbian deminer injured by a US BLU-97 submunition, Slađan Vučković, spoke movingly to the conference on its last day: he said he had been reluctant to participate because he felt the Oslo process's failure would be too disappointing for him to handle—but listening to the proceedings he had taken heart that a humanitarian treaty worth the paper it was written on would be possible.[57]

Together, these survivor-speakers were the first formal Ban Advocates, a new Handicap International initiative. Following the Lima conference, Brabant and his HI colleagues had begun pulling together the elements of a support system for survivors to participate in the meetings of the Oslo process, and to enable them to articulate the goals of the cluster munition campaign rather than only the able-bodied and predominantly white, Western faces of the CMC's leadership—who might be easier to dismiss by those reluctant to commit to support for a cluster munition ban. The practical problems of enabling the participation of these Ban Advocates in far-flung activities around the world were considerable in view of the practical requirements of people lacking limbs or with damaged senses, on crutches and in wheelchairs, and needing ongoing psychosocial and medical support. And, it had to be done very, very sensitively. There were those within the Cluster Munition Coalition who voiced fears that the exercise could be seen as exploitative of cluster munition victims. Brabant and his colleagues involved in the Ban Advocates project shared these concerns, and consequently went to great lengths to ensure the dignity and full participation of the survivors in the CMC's work as a whole including decision-making about their roles.[58]

Personally, like others involved in international efforts on cluster munitions, I sometimes found the stories told by these submunition-mangled people to be highly affecting. It made me feel very conflicted: the professional, analytical part of my brain hated what their accounts of what had happened to them did to me; the involuntary lump at the back of the throat, the tears blinked back from the corners of my eyes. At the same time I was appalled, and the longer I heard these stories in the course of the Oslo process, and the higher the stakes got closer to Dublin, the more the unfairness of what had happened to them got under my skin. Most were not combatants, and had been blamelessly going about their daily business (or, in Kapetanović and Vučković's cases, were involved in clearance in order to protect civilians). Some had been children when the incident occurred. Now the effects of submunitions had forever blighted their lives—something the users of these faulty weapons had never taken responsibility for.

Yet the involvement of the Ban Advocates also made me pensive. What if, in the end, the Oslo process let these people down? And what would happen to them afterwards? Overall, it was difficult to maintain one's dispassion, and perhaps that was why no concerted efforts had ever been made in the CCW to invite these people to share what they had to say. The few who did ever go to the meetings in Geneva attended with the CMC at its behest, like Kapetanović, and later Vučković, an Afghan man Firoz Ali Alizada[59] and Lynn Bradach, the mother of a US marine killed by a US submunition. On those occasions they sat at the back of the chamber with the other NGO representatives, occasionally speaking at the end of the session on behalf of the Coalition to the embarrassed silence of many of the diplomats and military experts.[60] It seemed to me that the survivors' views were tolerated in the CCW but by no means encouraged, despite their experiences being just as visceral as those of the military men and the weapon designers—if not more so.

In addition to giving much needed attention (including media attention) to the voices of those suffering the effects of cluster munitions such as survivors and their families, the Belgrade conference cemented the humanitarian credentials of the Oslo process. Belgrade's outcome was, in effect, an endorsement by affected states (many of them not members of the CCW) of the Oslo initiative's legitimacy in tackling such concerns and of their support for a comprehensive ban on cluster munitions. This sense of legitimacy was subsequently strengthened by a one-day European regional conference in Brussels on cluster munition victim assistance and stockpile destruction on 30 October.

THE CCW: OLD ARGUMENTS, A NEW MANDATE

Alongside the increasing profile of humanitarian concerns about the consequences of cluster munition use, efforts to achieve a work mandate in the CCW also intensified. In November 2007, the CCW's annual Meeting of States Parties achieved consensus on a mandate to "negotiate a proposal to address urgently the humanitarian impact of cluster munitions, while striking a balance between military and humanitarian considerations".[61] The mandate authorized seven weeks of CCW expert meetings scheduled in Geneva throughout 2008. This was especially important to the Like-minded states: the CCW's 2008 mandate would ensure the continued engagement of major users and producers outside the Oslo process on cluster munition-specific measures, especially the US—at least as long as the Oslo process lasted. It would also help to turn aside accusations that the Oslo process undermined the CCW, to which the Like-minded were sensitive. And, it would keep the CCW in play as an alternative should the Oslo process's final ambitions on scope of a cluster munition prohibition prove too rich for individual Like-minded states to stomach.

The US delegation, for its part, hailed the 2008 CCW cluster munition mandate as a success. In its view, the CCW's achievement of its cluster munition work mandate "means an issue considered important by most states and their publics will be addressed in the appropriate framework".[62] On the face of it, however, the new mandate did seem a change of heart for the CCW. After all, agreement to negotiate on cluster munitions had been resisted in the CCW for more than a quarter of a century. When set alongside the Oslo Declaration, though, the CCW mandate was weaker in almost every way, for example agreeing to "negotiate a proposal" rather than a legally binding international legal instrument. It was also clear that states like Russia and China went along with the commencement of work very reluctantly. Russia, for example, told the November 2007 CCW meeting:

> Frankly speaking, we are not sure that a practical basis for negotiation on cluster munitions has ripen[ed]. We fail so far to agree upon [an] eventual subject for future negotiations, that is on a definition of cluster munitions. Other aspects remain as well, on which there is no agreement amongst us, including also on objectives of possible negotiations.[63]

Russia's position was that while it was prepared to consider proposals to "clarify" existing principles and rules of international humanitarian law with respect to cluster munitions, it did not accept the need for new rules or restrictions on use, any prohibitions on cluster munition types, or the need for technical improvements.[64] Over the following months in CCW expert work, it would become clear that others, such as China, India, Pakistan and even the Republic of Korea, still shared similar views. The CCW's agreement on a mandate to negotiate a proposal, therefore, did not mark a shift in substance of the views of the CCW's membership as a whole on the need to negotiate a treaty to ban cluster munitions that cause unacceptable harm, as the Oslo process sought to do. But a continued CCW process did make sense from a wide range of tactical and political perspectives—even for states opposed to any new measures to protect civilians from cluster munitions.

A DEFINING PERIOD

The issue of defining cluster munitions for the purposes of prohibition was to take centre stage in Vienna. In the lead-up to February's Oslo conference, representatives of the CMC and organizations on its Steering Committee had worked closely with the Norwegians and the emergent Core Group to develop ideas that led to the agenda of the conference and the Oslo Declaration. But it was not the case in Lima and afterward. Nash, Moyes and others in the CMC's leadership circle concerned with definitions became increasingly worried as the Vienna conference approached that the Core Group was keeping the CMC in the dark about how the meeting's definitions discussions would be handled, as these talks would be critical in setting the parameters for eventual negotiations in Dublin.

In particular, Nash and Moyes were worried that the Oslo process would end up adopting a "split-the-category" approach in Vienna that departed from the approach for defining cluster munitions taken in Lima. The Lima text had presented an extremely broad definition, which essentially only excluded certain types of weapons with sophisticated submunitions using sensor-fuzing technology.[65] Despite criticism from some in the Like-minded, this approach remained as viable as ever after Lima, the CMC felt. In addition, the "define, ban, then exclude" approach was consistent with the proposed definition of a cluster munition the CMC itself developed in internal meetings in Belgrade following the October Serbia–UNDP conference.[66]

The CMC's fear was that the Core Group would buckle under pressure from the Like-minded and, in effect, revert to a "good" versus "bad" cluster munition approach in the revised discussion text it was preparing for Vienna. So Nash and Moyes took it upon themselves to energetically lobby the Core Group in the lead-up to the Vienna conference in order to ensure that it stuck with what they saw as the right approach. As part of this, in an e-mail message to the individual members of the seven-government Core Group on 26 October that called for that group to consult with the CMC, Nash made the case for the "define, ban then exclude" approach:

> we have discussed among ourselves whether there could now be political reasons for some states to advocate another approach for the Vienna text so as to build support and inclusion within the Oslo Process of states that are working for weapons (such as the M-85) to be acceptable in the new treaty. We strongly believe that while such political reasons may exist, they lead directly to a position that would dramatically weaken the prospects for a treaty that would be both meaningful from a humanitarian perspective and gain wide support from key countries and civil society.

> We hope then that any revised text will stick to the approach set out in Oslo and Lima and not to take an approach that would split the category of cluster munitions. Taking such an approach would not only communicate the possibility of such broad exclusions such as the M-85 but would also strengthen the negotiating position of those states arguing for such exceptions by confirming their perception that cluster munitions can have good and bad variants. There is simply no evidence we are aware of to support that sort of distinction. The Oslo and Lima approach—the approach we advocate—would make it less likely for those states to secure such broad exceptions because they would be required to provide a higher level of evidence to justify their claims.[67]

Nash and his CMC colleagues in the Steering Committee were aware also that several attempts had been made within the Core Group during 2007 to settle on how to conceptualize cluster munitions in text—without a result. It all posed practical difficulties for New Zealand disarmament ambassador

Don MacKay, who was responsible for managing the Vienna discussions. Referring to the Lima formulation, he told me, "One of the problems about defining this, obviously, is how do you structure the discussion? If you don't have a structured discussion you're lost".[68]

MacKay, too, eventually concluded, "the easier way of structuring the discussion is to structure it in terms of what's out and what's in".[69] To understand what this meant for Vienna, it is necessary to consider for a moment the Vienna text, which, like the Lima discussion paper before it, adopted the format of a preamble section followed by specific operative articles. This is pretty standard stuff in multilateral talks: negotiators want to work on the basis of a specific text, and it makes sense to structure work in a way that reflects the general manner in which the final product of eventual negotiations will be presented, that is, in treaty form. Article 1 of the draft Lima and Vienna discussion paper texts each contained the general obligations and scope of the exercise—what the eventual treaty is supposed to ban or otherwise do. Article 2 defined what the treaty was talking about. In Lima, the approach taken was to say in article 1, in effect, "because of their unacceptable harm, we're going to ban what's defined as a 'prohibited cluster munition' below in article 2". Thus, the Like-minded interpreted the Lima text to mean the Oslo process would eventually agree a treaty banning a *subset* of cluster munitions.

The Vienna text distributed on behalf of the Core Group by the Austrian government three weeks before the Vienna conference commenced on 5 December took a different tack. Its version of article 1 dropped the "unacceptable harm" touchstone language from the Oslo Declaration (itself a formulation differing from Norway's Oslo conference invitation letter discussed in chapter 5). The Vienna text instead simply stated a general obligation "never under any circumstances" to use or possess cluster munitions. And in article 2, the definition of a cluster munition said this:

> For the purposes of this Convention, "Cluster munition" means a munition that is designed to disperse or release explosive sub-munitions, and includes those explosive sub-munitions. It does not mean the following:
>
> (a) …
>
> (b) …
>
> (c) …[70]

The new discussion text's article 1 and 2 provisions generated a wave of concern among the Like-minded. All of a sudden, the illusion of a safety net had vanished from beneath the Oslo process for those seeking to hold on to cluster munitions like the M-85 in their arsenals, or even the more advanced submunitions with sensor-fuzed technology some saw as eventual replacements. The discussion in Vienna would proceed from the starting point that all weapons with submunitions, as broadly sketched, would be banned unless those pursuing exceptions could persuasively make their case to fill in the "dot, dot, dots", as they were referred to by many delegations. The CMC, in contrast, was very happy with the article 2 discussion text language, arguing "This definition is a vast improvement over the Lima text. It adopts the correct approach in beginning with a general prohibition and then calling for an explicit delineation of any potential weapons that do not fall under the definition".[71]

THE VIENNA CONFERENCE

The Vienna conference's Chair, Ambassador Wolfgang Petritsch (Austria's Permanent Representative in Geneva), had three aims going into the meeting. One aim was to advance substantive discussions in all areas, and the second was to definitively characterize the process as a humanitarian, rather than an arms control, endeavour. The third was to try to ensure that the greatest possible number of states participated.[72] On this score, any concerns that the CCW's 2008 mandate on cluster munitions might have undermined international momentum behind the Oslo process were dispelled when 138 states registered with the Austrian government to participate in Vienna. This was almost double the number attending the Lima conference six months earlier.

Delegations from a majority of these states—many from the developing world, and some coming up to speed on the specifics of cluster munitions— did not see why all cluster munitions should not be banned as a matter of principle, as anti-personnel mines were. Moreover, Austria's national parliament passed domestic legislation outlawing cluster munitions (as it defined them nationally) the same week,[73] which added further momentum to this "tee-total" view, as those in the Core Group described it among themselves.[74] Meanwhile, as the sheer number of delegations attending the Vienna conference dawned on the 15 or so states of the Like-minded, they began to fear simply being swept aside by a large number of states that, to their minds, neither possessed cluster munitions nor had a real understanding of them, and therefore lacked legitimate negotiating "equity".

General obligations, scope of application and definitions were allocated a half-day for discussion on the Vienna conference's second day in discussions facilitated by MacKay of New Zealand. Some of the states affiliated with the Like-minded went on the offensive in these definitions talks, which in view of their importance were permitted to run over time.[75] France, Switzerland, the Netherlands and the UK were particularly forceful in reiterating their view that not all cluster munitions have unacceptable consequences for civilians, arguing that concepts of accuracy and reliability should be benchmarks for what is deemed acceptable or not—citing ICRC formulations concerning inaccurate and unreliable submunitions. This was an error, as it drew a sharp response from the ICRC delegation to the talks. The ICRC told the conference that the terms it had used in its institutional position—"inaccurate" and "unreliable"—were *descriptions of the unacceptable characteristics* of cluster munitions, not criteria for creating exceptions for certain cluster munitions. These characteristics, the ICRC said, applied to the vast majority of existing cluster munitions, and virtually all used to date, and which in its view should be banned on humanitarian grounds.

This was really not what those trying to use the prestigious ICRC's position to shore up their own arguments for cluster munition retention had anticipated. However, it was widely noted among other delegations, and Vienna marked the point in the Oslo process at which a spectrum of "tee-total" states, with delegates from Costa Rica, Indonesia, Lebanon and Zambia at the forefront, began to cohere and evolve in opposition to the Like-minded.[76] This would have important consequences down the line for the dynamics of both the Wellington and Dublin conferences. In addition, more than 50 African states participated in Vienna, and they were particularly vocal, with encouragement from a persuasive Zambian CMC campaigner, Robert Mtonga.[77]

Despite the disagreements over articles 1 and 2, the Vienna conference did make useful progress in clarifying aspects of the definition debate, and article 2 exclusion discussions avoided meltdown. This was largely because MacKay spent the bulk of his time on the podium as Friend of the Chair in facilitating an emerging collective view on less problematic exclusions such as mines (already covered by other treaties), flare, smoke and chaff munitions, and submunitions that are inert post impact. Discussion of various proposals for other exemptions for explosive submunitions based on reliability, low number per container or sensor-fuzing technologies (most of them put forward by states among the Like-minded) did not command wide agreement, but were disagreements able to be set aside for the time being. Nevertheless, it led to unhappiness among the Like-minded. They vowed in a meeting amongst themselves at the conclusion of the Vienna conference to force negotiation in Wellington of the issues that mattered to them such as definitions, military interoperability and transition periods, even though there was no unanimity among them on these specific topics.

Vienna is chiefly remembered by many of its participants, however, for the presentation of a report on the reliability of the Israeli M-85 submunition. The report, produced by Norwegian People's Aid, the independent explosive ordnance disposal consultant Colin King, and the Norwegian Defence Research Establishment, perhaps had more immediate impact than any other single study before or after in the Oslo process. *M-85—An Analysis of Reliability* effectively won the burden of proof battle and cemented the Oslo process approach on definitions as it was, rather than in terms of "good versus bad" submunitions. Like-minded states such as Slovakia, Switzerland, and the UK would continue to argue for the acceptability of submunitions with mechanical-style self-destruct features in Wellington, but it was increasingly apparent to most in the Oslo process from Vienna onward that such arguments were untenable.

Grethe Østern first had the idea for the M-85 report and was the driving force behind it. It grew out of the trust she developed with Norwegian defence personnel and Colin King (see chapter 3). E-mail exchanges between Østern and colleagues including King, as well as Conway and Moyes from Landmine Action (who edited the eventual report), show that she had been mulling over undertaking a study to debunk the myth of percentage rate reliability as a basis for a submunition's acceptability in humanitarian terms since at least mid-May 2006. Coming on top of the Norwegian cargo ammunition debate (see chapter 3), the Southern Lebanon conflict soon afterwards offered an extraordinary opportunity, she decided. And what better submunition to study than the type held up by countries like Norway and the UK at that time as the gold standard—the M-85 with self-destruct? By late 2006, Norwegian People's Aid had a battle area clearance programme already underway in Southern Lebanon, and Chris Clark, the Director of the UN Mine Action Coordination Centre there agreed to their request to allocate it sites to be cleared in which quantities of unexploded M-85s with self-destruct were known to be present.[78]

This was the research that Dullum, the careful Norwegian defence scientist, had alluded to at the Montreux ICRC expert meeting. The report was based on evidence carefully collected and analysed of failure rates of M-85 submunitions with self-destruct fired by Israel into Southern Lebanon in real operational conditions, and drew on Norwegian government data from its tests in Hjerkinn. Its findings suggested a consistent dud rate not of 1%, but of *ten times* that. Dullum, King and Østern concluded that:

> Despite the incorporation of a high-quality [self-destruct]-mechanism, M-85 bomblet reliability in combat is substantially worse than has been indicated by tests. It produces post-conflict contamination at a level that, according to the policies of many countries, must be considered unacceptable.

> The specific example of the M-85 demonstrates that while [self-destruct] mechanisms in general may help to lower failure rates, they are not capable of ensuring against post-conflict contamination at an unacceptable level.[79]

The M-85 report systematically debunked the notion put forward by some possessors of cluster munitions with such features that a distinction could be made between hazardous (i.e. "bad") and non-hazardous (i.e. "good") submunition duds. It also showed the inherent flaws of a failure rate approach. Rather, the report's authors argued that the M-85 study demonstrated, based on real world experience, that "All duds are inherently hazardous both to deminers and to the post-conflict civilian populations that are left to deal with them".[80] Overall, the report and its clear and concise presentation, along with King's explanation of how cluster munitions work and how submunitions can fail, made a strong impression on many of those represented in the Vienna conference hall—especially from developing countries—and complemented the ICRC's points mentioned earlier.

The M-85 report and its palpable impact showed how active and well-organized civil society was, coordinated by the CMC, at the Vienna conference. The excitement of campaigners from many countries about the aims of the Oslo Declaration, financial support from Norway, Austria and Ireland and the appointment during 2007 of new CMC staff members like Laura Cheeseman as campaign officer (see chapter 5), as well as media specialists such as Samantha Bolton, made a big difference to what the CMC and its members could do. Individual NGOs, such as the CMC's Austrian Section, Austrian Aid for Mine Victims led by Judith Majlath, did a huge amount of work in supporting aspects of the conference—including many civil society events that generated media and public interest—and as well were instrumental in lobbying for the very strong national legislation banning cluster munitions announced at the Vienna conference. And, in addition to definitions, NGOs were engaging on every element of the discussion text tabled by Austria and the other Core Group states at the Vienna conference. Moreover, those conference discussions resulted in clear signals of collective support for strong victim assistance and assistance and cooperation provisions in the text, for instance, on which CMC member NGOs such as Handicap International and the Landmine Survivors Network (now known as Survivor Corps) had a significant influence. Such provisions had been very hard fought in the Ottawa process a decade before. Now, in talks coordinated by Markus Reiterer of Austria, almost all participating states readily agreed such provisions were important and should be strengthened.[81]

FINAL THOUGHTS

The Vienna conference had, it would seem, largely achieved the Austrians' aims. Two thirds of the world's states had taken part in the talks, in fact making it much better attended than the CCW.[82] The legitimacy of the Oslo process in humanitarian terms was now beyond serious challenge, thanks at least as much to earlier activities such as the Belgrade conference of affected states, although the governments of the Like-minded—and some others—still saw banning cluster munitions through a disarmament or arms control lens, and not as a humanitarian undertaking. Substantive discussions on the text, particularly on victim assistance and cooperation, had been advanced. But the Vienna conference also underlined that there was much further work to be done on the most contentious issues in a prospective humanitarian treaty—over how to define cluster munitions that cause unacceptable harm to civilians, and on the emerging issue of military interoperability and joint military operations with states not party to a future treaty. A related issue concerned whether that treaty should also include "transition periods" for continued use, transfer and other aspects of cluster munitions, as some of the Like-minded wanted and many others among the Tee-total states opposed. The Like-minded had not had their views swept aside, as some of them had feared, especially as the Vienna conference was intended to ventilate views on the big issues in a prospective legally binding instrument and not to negotiate. Following the close of the conference on a grey and chilly Friday afternoon, however, the Like-minded could be seen looking intent and concerned as they met in a huddled circle of cafeteria chairs on a mezzanine. France was the ostensible coordinator of the Like-minded, but the Germans seemed to be doing much of the talking: from their body language they reminded me of a trailing football team in the dressing room at half time.

At the end of 2007, both the Oslo process and the CCW were poised for new phases of activity. After years of talk and dismissal of negotiations on new legal rules dealing specifically with reducing the humanitarian effects of cluster munitions, the CCW had found consensus on a work mandate for 2008—spurred on by the Oslo process's emergence. Meanwhile the Oslo process, still less than a year old, faced the challenge of imminent transition from oral discussions about substantive aspects of a treaty based on papers prepared by members of the Oslo Core Group, to nitty-gritty negotiations on the exact provisions of an international legal instrument. Between the Vienna and Wellington conferences, the Oslo Core Group would change the name of the Vienna discussion text into a "draft Cluster Munitions Convention" in order to tip expectations toward a final eventual outcome they hoped would culminate in formal negotiations in Dublin in May 2008—and not before.[83] But experiences from the Lima and Vienna Conferences during 2007 taught the Like-minded countries to tighten their coordination. In Wellington, they would pursue their negotiating objectives even more aggressively, all the while complaining that they were being manipulated procedurally by the Oslo Core Group. The US, for its part watching the Oslo process gather momentum, would step up its consultations with friends and allies regarding its concerns about a cluster munition treaty. Matters were approaching a crunch point.

CHAPTER 7

CRUNCH POINT

2007 would pass off successfully for the Oslo process in terms of progress toward fulfilling the Oslo Declaration. The Vienna conference was, in the words of its Chair, Ambassador Wolfgang Petritsch, able to "build on quite a solid base".[1] Just as importantly, it had passed off without major adverse incident. But the members of the Core Group and others like the members of the Steering Committee of the Cluster Munition Coalition were acutely aware of imminent challenges. It was clear that the Like-minded were becoming increasingly frustrated with process aspects of the Oslo initiative that they felt thwarted their ability to shape the discussion text. It was also apparent to the Core Group's members that certain of the Like-minded such as Germany and the UK would like to play more central roles in steering the Oslo process.

Moreover, few in the Core Group believed that the next conference in the Oslo process, to be held in New Zealand's capital city, Wellington, on 18–22 February 2008, would attract the participation of as many governments as the 138 attending the Vienna meeting. The distance, travel time and expense involved in flying there began to dawn on many potential participants toward the end of 2007 as they made their travel bookings. It led to a litany of grumbling, especially among the European diplomats—to the bemusement of those of us from that part of the world.[2]

On a more serious note, the entanglement of the Convention on Certain Conventional Weapons (CCW) and the Oslo process was now approaching a most complicated phase. In November 2007 the CCW's Meeting of States Parties had agreed on a mandate committing it to:

> negotiate a proposal to address urgently the humanitarian impact of cluster munitions, while striking a balance between military and humanitarian considerations.

> The GGE [Group of Governmental Experts] should make every effort to negotiate this proposal as rapidly as possible and report on the progress made to the next Meeting of the High Contracting Parties in November 2008.
>
> The work of the GGE will be supported by military and technical experts. The GGE will meet in 2008 not less than three times for a total of up to seven weeks … .[3]

This meant that during the most intense period of efforts in the Oslo process to achieve a cluster munition treaty in the first half of 2008, parallel negotiations in the CCW would be underway; a process galvanized by the existence of the Oslo process, but with less ambitious objectives that might peel support away from the latter. It also raised other issues. For sound reasons, for instance, most states would want to use the same concepts and terminology agreed in one negotiation for the other since enacting domestic legislation to implement any eventual new international rules on cluster munitions would be complicated with two different definitions of the weapon in use. If the CCW could steal a march on the Oslo process on defining such terms, those not participating in the latter could nevertheless have a direct impact on the content of the draft treaty text negotiated in Dublin. In view of the CCW's history and membership, the likely effect of this would be a downward pull on the high humanitarian standards civil society and many states hoped that the work in Dublin would achieve.

Once the rhetoric about the CCW's legitimacy and inclusiveness of major users and possessors of cluster munitions was stripped away, the CCW's work to "negotiate a proposal" amounted to useful leverage to achieve better terms for the Like-minded in the Oslo process—or so some of them thought. Some of their proposals for sections of the Vienna discussion text on topics such as defining cluster munitions and submunitions, transition periods, retention of submunitions for testing and training purposes, and interoperability had rebounded, as was seen in the preceding chapter. Concern among the Like-minded correspondingly heightened; they would try to utilize the CCW's first 2008 session in January to their full advantage, as well as sharpen their spears for confrontation they would be seeking—and expect to win—in Wellington the following month to have their proposals taken up into the basis for work in Dublin.

Dealing with the Like-minded was all the more problematic for the Core Group because the February meeting was the point at which the Oslo process would have to pivot from a series of discussions with a view to an eventual negotiation to the negotiation itself. Emulating the Brussels Declaration in the Ottawa process,[4] Wellington's product was intended to be a document to which governments would have to subscribe if they wished to take part in the subsequent Dublin negotiations on the treaty in May. The prospective "Wellington Declaration" would indicate that those subscribing to it accepted some basic ground rules for Dublin, such as rules of procedure for the negotiations and which text would be the basis for work. And, the Wellington Declaration would be an important tool with which campaigners could persuade governments to commit to taking part in Dublin.

The Wellington Declaration and draft treaty text also presented vulnerabilities if the Like-minded, for instance, threatened to withhold their support at this crucial juncture. What reaction that would engender among the Tee-total countries opposed to many of the proposals of the Like-minded also remained to be seen, and there were fears in the Core Group that excessive polarization between these groups could rip the Oslo process apart. As the Wellington conference approached, it was not apparent that this was sufficiently appreciated by those among the Like-minded: they had focused on the Core Group's perceived control over the Oslo process as the problem. They did not appear to have given much thought to the possibility that the manner in which they presented their concerns in Lima and Vienna was contributing to the emergence of the Tee-total group directly opposed to their positions on definitions, transition periods and interoperability— stances perceived as arrogant by some other delegations.

As noted earlier, rather than opposing the proposals of members of the Like-minded per se, the Core Group did not even agree among themselves on all important issues of substance. In Wellington, Core Group members such as Austria, the Holy See and Norway would, in their dialogue with others, instead refer to the Core Group as a "steering group". What united this group was its determination to retain control over process to ensure the conditions created for an eventual cluster munition negotiation met the aims of the Oslo Declaration. It amounted to this: in Wellington, the outcome would hinge on the pressure that the Core Group (and especially New Zealand, as conference chair) could absorb from the Like-minded without buckling. In other words, the Wellington conference represented the crunch point for the Oslo process. Although views on many specific aspects of the Wellington conference differed among the participants I interviewed as part of my research, it was widely perceived to have been the most bruising of all of the international meetings leading to the Convention on Cluster Munitions.

This chapter explores what happened in Wellington. Before doing so, the development of the US's posture on measures to address the humanitarian impacts of cluster munitions is briefly outlined because of Washington's influence in the CCW, and on some countries in the Oslo process. Next, the January 2008 CCW session's work on definitions and a second highly-significant small-group The Diana, Princess of Wales Memorial Fund meeting in London following it are briefly analysed.

THE US AND CLUSTER MUNITIONS, AND INTEROPERABILITY

Despite not being involved in the Oslo process, the US would have a significant influence on many states participating in the initiative, and at least one of the major concerns of the Like-minded—interoperability—largely resulted from US pressure.

Despite its refusal to participate in the Oslo process and traditional opposition to international legally binding measures of any kind on cluster munitions, US policymakers were certainly not ignorant of the risks cluster munitions pose to civilians. As we have seen in the course of this book, the US is historically the largest user of cluster munitions, in military actions in Cambodia, Laos and Viet Nam, Grenada in 1983, Lebanon in 1983, Iraq, Kuwait and Saudi Arabia in the first Gulf War in 1991, Serbia, Montenegro and Kosovo in 1999, Afghanistan in 2001 and 2002, and Iraq in 2003. Precise estimates of the number of cluster munitions the US possesses today are hard to come by, but NGOs believe the military's total stockpile contains between 700 million and one billion submunitions.[5]

The US was one of the first countries to undertake practical measures to try to reduce the impacts of cluster munitions on civilians. After Kosovo and criticism about US cluster bomb use in air operations, the US Air Force tried to avoid using cluster bombs against targets in or near populated areas in Afghanistan and Iraq.[6] By far the most submunitions are in the inventories of US ground forces, however, with the Army possessing around 88%, and the Marines 7% of US submunitions.[7] A Defense Department report to Congress in October 2004 noted, "Cannon and rocket artillery cluster munitions comprise over 80% of Army fire support capability"[8] and these ground-launched systems were used extensively in the 2003 Iraq invasion.

For both military and humanitarian reasons, the US government also sought to improve the accuracy and reliability of its cluster munitions by technical means.[9] More accurate weapons that detonate as intended are, after all, more effective weapons in achieving military objectives. And unexploded submunitions posed a risk to US military forces, as well as civilians—something noted by the US General Accounting Office as early as the aftermath of the 1991 Gulf War.[10] In 2001, Secretary of Defense William Cohen issued a policy that all submunitions fit for combat use from the 2005 fiscal year must have a failure rate of less than 1%.[11] This appeared to be difficult for US manufacturers of the weapons to achieve, and cluster munition production essentially ceased from 2005 apart from two types. One of these types, the Sensor Fuzed Weapon (discussed in the next chapter), reportedly met the Cohen standard and, as of writing, had only been used in combat in very small numbers. Dual-Purpose Improved Conventional Munitions (DPICMs) for the M-30 Guided Multiple Launch Rocket System were the other type remaining in production, apparently the recipient of a Pentagon waiver from the Cohen policy. The waiver allowed a dud rate of 2% between the weapon's optimal range of 20 to 60km, and 4% at ranges of less than 20km and more than 60km.[12] Each M-30 rocket carries 404 M-101 DPICM submunitions,[13] and therefore up to 16 dud submunitions per rocket was considered acceptable; that is, more than 190 unexploded submunitions remaining from a 12-rocket volley. The weapon could not meet the standard, and so the standard was lowered, it seemed.

Nevertheless, technical improvements to cluster munitions remained the solution in which the US government preferred to put its faith, rather than new international rules or regulations on the weapon. As has been seen in previous chapters, the US delegation to the CCW opposed discussion of possible use restrictions on cluster munitions or any prohibition of specific weapons until 2007. While outcry about the Southern Lebanon conflict in 2006 led many governments in the CCW to favour the idea of a cluster munition protocol, the US insisted that a solution to the hazards to civilians that cluster munitions posed was simply a matter of more rigorous implementation of existing humanitarian law rules applicable to all weapons, and said it did not even see the need for further discussion in the Group of Governmental Experts on explosive remnants of war format that followed the agreement of Protocol V in late 2003. And, when the Oslo initiative emerged, the US was deeply critical of it.

But the success of the February 2007 Oslo conference, and the rapid increase of an international initiative aimed at a treaty banning cluster munitions, saw the US delegation in the CCW start to change its tune. While still opposed to the Oslo process and a ban treaty, by June the US said it was prepared to consider CCW negotiations on the weapon. In November 2007 the US delegation joined consensus on a mandate to "negotiate a proposal" during 2008—all the while continuing to insist that cluster munitions were "legitimate weapons when employed properly and in accordance with existing international humanitarian law" and that "in many instances, cluster munitions result in much less collateral damage than unitary weapons would if used for the same mission".[14]

Domestic pressure may also have had something to do with this newfound flexibility. In September 2006, Senators Dianne Feinstein and Patrick Leahy (both Democrats) proposed amendments to the 2007 fiscal year Defense Appropriations Bill, which would have blocked the export of cluster munitions unless the recipient country agreed not to use them in populated areas. This, the first legislative action in the US on cluster munitions, was voted down, but a:

> prohibition on the export of cluster munitions with a failure rate of greater than 1 percent was later passed as part of the omnibus spending bill in December 2007. Potential importers must also agree to use the weapons only "against clearly defined military targets" and where no civilians are present.[15]

In addition, in February of that year Feinstein and Leahy, along with Representative James McGovern, had introduced a "Cluster Munitions Civilian Protection Act of 2007" to limit the use and transfer of cluster munitions to those with a 99% reliability rate or higher, and to prohibit use in areas where civilians are known to be present.[16] This legislation was not brought to a vote in 2007, but it gathered support in the Senate and House throughout the year. Notably, these initiatives indicate that those involved in the legislative debate in the US still accepted assumptions about the efficacy of purported reliability testing, or decided that tactically this was the only avenue where they could realistically make progress. They do not seem to have seriously enquired into how such testing accurately reflected use in the real world. But it clearly signalled that significant numbers of

US lawmakers were concerned about the humanitarian impacts of cluster munitions and were not reassured by the Bush administration's policies.[17]

While the US government was nonchalantly dismissive in public about the Oslo process, in private consultations with Washington's close friends and allies it appears to have been a different story. Government officials from various countries I interviewed in the course of research for this book told me that Washington maintained diplomatic dialogue about that initiative with their governments in the Oslo process and many others throughout 2007, up to and including the Dublin conference in May 2008. The US, it would seem, was at pains to remind its friends and allies of its concerns, and increasingly these revolved around an issue referred to in shorthand in the Oslo process as "interoperability"—perhaps because of the term's use in a "sensitive but unclassified" paper I was shown entitled "Potential Effects of Criminalizing NATO Interoperability" circulated by US embassies to government officials in at least some NATO countries in late 2007. It noted "The discussion text presented at Lima not only includes restrictions/ bans on use, production, stockpiling and transfer of such munitions, but also criminalizes assisting others in any way regarding these activities (reference Article 1(c) and Article 9 of the Lima discussion text)". Invoking issues the US said arose for NATO states because of the Mine Ban Treaty (but were "tolerable only because Allies do not consider anti-personnel mines central to their ability to fulfill defense and security operations"), the paper argued:

> Imposing these provisions concerning cluster munitions—a weapon more mission critical than anti-personnel landmines—could dramatically impact effectiveness of NATO's combined operations. ... Any Convention that essentially bans cluster munitions and contains provisions along the lines of Article 1(c) and Article 9 *is unacceptable to the United States, and NATO interoperability will be adversely affected* in the following areas should any Allies become States Parties to a treaty containing such language ... .[18]

The paper listed adverse implications for NATO combined planning and joint staff operations, joint training, common procurement and integrated logistics and combined operations in the field.

The upshot was that interoperability would become an increasing preoccupation for most allies of the United States in the Oslo process from the Vienna meeting onward. Many of the Like-minded raised interoperability as a concern in Vienna; Australia, for instance, said it was a national "red line" issue.[19] Though concerned countries were encouraged to put forward specific proposals to address interoperability questions within the Vienna text, members of the Like-minded would not really engage in specifics until Wellington. Norway, for its part as a NATO country, stood apart from the rest as it did not view issues of state responsibility and individual criminal liability asserted by the Like-minded as problematic in this context; instead, the Norwegian delegation's international lawyers would observe in Wellington that issues of interoperability arose in all operations where the states involved were bound by different legal regimes such as Additional Protocol I to the Geneva Conventions or the Mine Ban Treaty (the US is party to neither). Norway argued that while discussion of implications for interoperability was important, it should not be assumed that a cluster munition treaty would pose an obstacle to joint military action. Other NATO countries and allies of the US (especially Australia, Canada, Japan and the UK) did not agree: their military lawyers argued that cluster munitions were more likely to be used by the US than anti-personnel mines, and this exposed their personnel to a risk of prosecution unless there was a clear provision in the treaty permitting military cooperation and operations with states not party to it.[20]

GATHERING FORCES

The CCW

The CCW's states parties convened for a five-day session in mid-January as the first of seven weeks slated for its negotiations on cluster munitions during 2008. There were immediate and unequivocal signs of the newfound US commitment to negotiations on cluster munitions, with two detailed presentations by military experts on why the US believes cluster munitions have military utility, and on the "joint targeting" process used by the military forces with a view to avoiding civilian casualties.[21] (This was the kind of information many would have expected the US to share earlier in making the case for cluster munitions at the International Committee of the Red Cross's Montreux meeting the previous April.) And the new head of the US delegation, Stephen Mathias, even called on the new Chair, Ambassador Bent Wigotski of Denmark, to produce the draft text of a new protocol to the CCW by July.[22] In addition, politically committed to both the CCW and Oslo processes, Australia, Canada, France, Germany and UK were active in keeping discussions going, for instance by reiterating their earlier proposals.[23] But there were lengthy silences in the CCW talks at times, always eventually broken by China, France, Germany, Russia, the UK or the US delegation raising their nameplate to fill up the time with more interventions. The January CCW meeting underlined that a majority of states in the CCW also had a stake in the Oslo process, and seemed content simply to watch with varying degrees of scepticism how this other negotiation unfolded. All told, it was a curious atmosphere.[24]

The main work going on was not in the CCW's plenary, but in its subsidiary consultations of its military and technical experts. Russia had, in its customary way in CCW talks on cluster munitions, focused its opening statement on the obstacles to negotiating a cluster munition proposal, especially the lack of a definition of the weapon.[25] So, from the Chair's podium, Denmark asked the Russians to facilitate immediate discussions of experts to develop one. Russia was reluctant about any work on cluster munitions, but—unable to refuse—now found itself in a higher-profile role than it had envisaged. Nevertheless, Russia found no shortage of delegations among the Oslo process Like-minded states happy to engage in such talks—and eager to see their national preferences for a definition of the weapon in a negotiating text somewhere.

The Vienna conference discussion text language reflected an approach in which there was a generic description of cluster munitions, with exclusions to be added subsequently (see p. 185). Other states such as France, Germany and the UK were keen to have a definition with exceptions for their weapon systems built in centrally, weapons like those with less than 10 submunitions, those with self-destruct mechanisms like the M-85, or direct-fire weapons dispersing submunitions. Both Like-minded and Core Group states could see that coalescence around a definition in the CCW would have implications for the Oslo process definition, for reasons explained at the beginning of this chapter. At first there seemed little chance of such a definition emerging as CCW delegations with widely varying views stuck to their respective guns. But after a Wednesday evening meeting of experts facilitated by the Russians, the situation changed. The risk was not of convergence on the substance of a definition of cluster munitions emerging—there was little likelihood of CCW delegations agreeing on that, and the draft text the Russians developed contained no less that 20 sets of square brackets indicating competing views.[26] Rather, as heavily bracketed as it was, this draft definition of a cluster munition would have sufficient status as a consolidated reflection of views to exert a pull on the direction of the definition work in the Oslo process *away* from a "define, ban, then exclude" approach to a "split-the-category" approach with built-in exceptions the Core Group feared would undermine the Oslo Declaration's objective.

The Irish (who would later become Wigotski's CCW Friend of the Chair on definitions) were sufficiently concerned that they intervened in the Russian-led CCW discussions and put forward a national proposal of their own containing definitions of cluster munitions, explosive submunitions and bomblets.[27] Their views now registered in the draft definition, the Irish also tried to persuade Wigotski to remove reference in the meeting's draft procedural report to the draft definition "as agreed by the Group of Governmental Experts". As nonsensical as the notion was of a draft definition containing dozens of square brackets being in any sense "agreed", the Irish wanted to ensure that the Like-minded or others could not make claims about it being *the* working definition the Oslo process should therefore take up.[28] In the end, the language stayed in the report, but with proviso added that it "provides an appropriate basis for future work. Future work will also take into account other proposals, including proposals presented at this and previous sessions".[29] This formulation was sufficient to blunt any particular impact it might have in Wellington.

THE SECOND LONDON MEETING

The following week, around 30 individuals from some Core Group delegations and other governments, along with selected representatives of NGOs and international organizations, attended a second The Diana, Princess of Wales Memorial Fund meeting in London on cluster munitions.[30] Held in the same room as the discussions in the first of these meetings in March 2006, many of those participants who had attended that gathering were struck by how radically circumstances had altered in 22 months.[31] This time, rather than debating the need for, or extent of, international efforts on cluster munitions, the discussions were mainly tactical—how states could work with civil society to achieve success in Wellington in specific terms, and meet the likely diplomatic and campaigning challenges for the path ahead to Dublin. New Zealand ambassador Don MacKay, in particular, outlined his thinking with a view to how Wellington would be handled.

MacKay, as Chair-designate for the Wellington conference, was a particularly experienced hand at running international meetings. He had presided, for example, over the process leading to the 2006 Convention on the Rights of Persons with Disabilities, and had long experience in multilateral negotiations as diverse as those relating to the Antarctic and the international law of the sea. Because of this, he was well aware of the extent to which multilateral diplomats of all stripes can become process and procedure driven in conferences.[32] MacKay felt he had to prevent discussion of the Wellington Declaration—a document he described as "a purely procedural document to provide the bridge through to the Dublin conference"[33]— becoming an obsession in the Wellington meeting. At the same time he and the Core Group wanted to avoid relinquishing control of that declaration text until the Wellington conference concluded. Instead, the aim was to try to keep delegations' attentions focused on the substantial issues to be ventilated in the draft convention text because Vienna had indicated, in the Core Group's view, that there was a need for further exploration of issues like definitions, interoperability and transition periods in a situation that fell short of a negotiation. On interoperability, for instance, many in the Core Group were still struggling to understand the precise nature of some of the concerns of the Like-minded and how these might be eventually addressed. But the Core Group intended to stick to its position that this should be in a discussion setting—not a negotiation yet.

Most of all, however, MacKay was worried about time. Once the official ceremonies to open the Wellington conference were out of the way there would be less than five days to work through a number of contentious issues. The Core Group's intent was not necessarily to try to bring the Wellington conference's participants to solutions to these issues, but *closer* to convergence. The second aim was to create the requisite sense of reassurance that major concerns could be met once negotiations got underway in Dublin. If these efforts were unsuccessful, then some delegations might not support the Wellington Declaration.

Those at the London meeting all knew that Wellington was the point at which the Oslo process could unravel if the Core Group could not keep a grip on the planned outputs of the conference. It also underlined that although the members of the Core Group were largely agreed on tactical direction (at least, in front of representatives from NGOs and international organizations) there were differences between their respective national positions coming increasingly to the fore such as the content of the definition and interoperability. Norway, for example, did not consider all weapons with submunitions to be cluster munitions and believed certain weapons with sensor-fuzed submunitions should be excluded on the basis of their effects. Austria in contrast was becoming more Tee-total in its approach to any exclusions for submunitions beyond the ones "designed to dispense flares, smoke, pyrotechnics or chaff" or producing "electrical or electronic effects" that arose from the Vienna discussions.[34] The Irish, for their part, were increasingly concerned that a major loophole in the definition might develop that allowed for bomblets (that is, submunitions scattered from aircraft mounted dispensers, rather than parent munitions).

The draft Wellington Declaration, the Core Group's revision of the draft discussion text taking into account December's Vienna conference discussions and their accompanying explanatory notes were made available on the internet in late January 2008.[35] But now the draft discussion text had transformed into a "draft Cluster Munitions Convention". This was an important psychological change necessary, in the Core Group's view, to keep to the Oslo Declaration timetable and prepare for the negotiations on the treaty scheduled for Dublin in May. Although the change of title was widely expected, it strengthened the perception among some of the Like-minded that they were becoming hostage to a multilateral process over which they had no control. It soon became apparent in Wellington that the Like-minded had come to the meeting determined to shape the text straight away and not to wait until Dublin.

THE WELLINGTON CONFERENCE

Nature had turned on its best summer weather for the Wellington conference, in stark contrast to Vienna's chilly winter conditions—perhaps some solace to the Europeans and Africans with body clocks befuddled by the 12-hour time difference. Unsurprisingly, as delegates gathered at the conference venue, the Wellington Town Hall on the capital's waterfront, on Monday 18 February, a lot of tea and coffee cups were in evidence. But the opening ceremony, including a stirring Maori welcome called a *powhiri* by the local Te Atiawa tribe, woke everyone up. One hundred and twenty-two governments had registered for the Wellington conference, and many of the Pacific Island countries were attending an international meeting on cluster munitions for the first time.[36] New Zealand's Disarmament Minister, Phil Goff, exhorted the conference to deal with cluster munitions in a similar manner as anti-personnel mines, "to put the fence at the top of the cliff, and not simply be the ambulance at the bottom. We need to eliminate the use of cluster munitions which have an unacceptable effect on civilian populations. We are getting to the hard end of the Oslo Process".[37]

After only an hour of ceremonies and opening speeches the work of the Wellington conference got underway.[38] As in Vienna, co-chairs from among the Core Group managed discussions on particular aspects of the text in dedicated sessions. Austrian diplomat Markus Reiterer, for instance, took the lead on victim assistance provisions, which by now were becoming well developed. Irish soldier and CCW veteran Jim Burke co-chaired the work on clearance provisions. While there was scope in the discussions in the main hall for engagement on most issues about the text, MacKay also convened open-ended talks (meaning open to any delegation to attend) in a smaller meeting room upstairs. These consultations, some facilitated by MacKay himself, were intended to come to grips with the thorniest issues and discuss them thoroughly.

Like any multilateral process involving lots of different actors with differing perceptions and aims, the Oslo initiative was a process aimed at the collective re-framing of issues so that convergence and agreement is eventually made possible. In this way, although difficult and confrontational compared with the other Oslo process conferences, the Wellington meeting was highly significant. Until now, many of the proposals put forward by the Like-minded on a number of issues of later importance to the Dublin negotiation, such as the scope of the treaty (article 1), the definition of cluster munitions (article 2) and questions concerning interoperability, transition periods and even review of the treaty, tended to bind these issues up together.[39] Comparison of documents over the course of the Oslo process conferences shows that it was not until the discussions in Wellington that these issues really began to be disaggregated. For instance, the UK in a statement on 18 February on general scope of obligations discussed most of these topics in the context of article 1.[40] It had not become clear yet "what would go where" in terms of the issues dealt with in the provisions of the treaty that was the goal of the process. To some extent this was because, as noted previously, the scope of the treaty's prohibitions depended on the definition—a definition that would be located in a different article. And states at this time still saw interoperability as being dealt with in the general scope article (article 1) because that was how it had been done in the Mine Ban Treaty or, alternatively, in article 9 on national implementation measures.[41] At times in Wellington these interconnections made MacKay's upstairs consultations appear intractable to those involved. Gradually, as the issues were teased out things became clearer, especially in view of MacKay's seemingly unhurried and methodical manner of chairing. It ultimately paved the way for issues like the definition of cluster munitions, other definitions and interoperability to be considered separately in differing streams of negotiating work in Dublin.

The consultations also displayed the tighter coordination of the Like-minded compared with Vienna. Both upstairs and in the discussions in the main chamber, Australia, Canada, Finland, France, Germany, Japan and the UK, in particular, pushed very hard for their various proposals to be taken up into the draft convention text. MacKay, as Chair, resisted this in line with the Core Group's wishes: negotiation was for Dublin, he repeatedly stressed. The Cluster Munition Coalition (CMC), meanwhile, made "no changes to the text" its central lobbying message for the Wellington conference. And, in the informal consultations concerning definitions and transition periods, CMC representatives—in particular, its "front bench" comprising Simon Conway, Goose, Moyes, Nash and Østern—were highly effective in cross-examining the proposals put forward by a range of states including those of the Like-minded. In view of their field experience and the research they and their organizations had undertaken into cluster munitions, the CMC's representatives proved at least as well versed as most governments in the various dimensions of the weapon and its effects. So effective were they that, after the Wellington conference, some of the Like-minded appealed to Ireland, the Dublin conference's host, to exclude NGOs from informal consultations there.

DEFINING CLUSTER MUNITIONS

The omnibus nature of some of their written proposals aside, many of the efforts of states among the Like-minded to amend the draft convention text revolved around the content of exclusions from the definition of a cluster munition in article 2, paragraph 2(c). NGOs, in particular, argued that this scope for exclusion was only meant to cater to weapons with submunitions that did not have the effects of cluster munitions. In other words, to justify exclusion of a weapon, a proponent would need to show that it was not really a cluster munition.

However, many proposals in Wellington and Dublin sought to exclude weapons that clearly had the effects of cluster munitions (like those using the M-85) from the definition. The CMC argued that states were trying to use the exclusion slot in 2(c) as a way to carve out what were, in fact, broad exceptions from a cluster munition ban. However this distinction between exclusions (justifiable clarifications for rational reasons consistent with the Oslo Declaration's aims) and exceptions (exclusions sought by key stockpiling countries not consistent with the aims of the Oslo Declaration or with the body of collected empirical evidence) was not well understood: it would later lead to concern in many quarters in Dublin over the definition as it emerged among some Tee-total states and within the CMC's campaigning base. It was also a distinction open to interpretation: whether a proposal merited an exclusion or an exception required comparison against the evidence. Significantly for the Oslo process, this discourse included evidence of humanitarian impact that often showed the shortcomings in practice of ostensibly persuasive arguments for exclusions based on purported technical fixes.

The proposals of the Like-minded on article 2, paragraph 2(c) were various, which just shows that the extent of their like-mindedness was actually rather circumscribed about anything other than dissatisfaction with the running of the Oslo process. Moreover, it became clear that other states, not only the Like-minded, wanted to ensure that certain weapons with sensor-fuzed submunitions like the German SMArt 155 and French-Swedish BONUS systems be excluded from a ban too. A lot of militaries saw these as in fact improving their capacity to target mobile and dispersed armoured vehicles—a capability that had up until then been fulfilled by simply covering an area with explosive force using cluster munitions that saturated areas with submunitions. It could be argued that the trajectory of the Oslo process toward prohibiting cluster munitions forced their hand given that they would have to phase out such area-saturating weapons if a treaty were agreed. The Norwegians shared this concern, and they surprised some among the Tee-total states at the Wellington conference by insisting that Norway had never subscribed to the view that *all* weapons with submunitions necessarily should be banned.[42]

Holed beneath the waterline by the M-85 report in the Vienna conference discussions, the rationale for exclusions from the cluster munition definition based on submunition percentage reliability took on a steepening list in Wellington. The UK and Switzerland, for instance, continued to try to defend submunitions with self-destruct like the M-85—and the CMC's well-prepared experts were highly effective in knocking these arguments back.[43] A presentation by Colin King about the technical aspects of cluster munitions to the conference on its first day had also served to strengthen opinion among many delegations that this was not justifiable as exclusion and in fact would be a broad exception. Hence, it should not be part of the eventual treaty. But the percentage reliability approach was only one of a number of proposals evidently intended to safeguard the continued retention of particular weapon systems. Along with the M-85, for example, the UK was also concerned with protecting its M-73 submunitions, although it cloaked this by formulating an exclusion for so-called "direct fire" munitions. However, in an environment in which the merits of exclusions were being examined on the basis on their humanitarian effects as well as their technical characteristics, the British arguments for exclusion because the Hydra rocket had a flat rather than an arcing trajectory looked weak.[44]

Transition periods

Many in the Like-minded felt that, depending on the outcome of the definition agreed in Dublin, a cluster munition treaty could create problems for their defence procurement. If all cluster munitions were considered unacceptable it could leave perceived military capability gaps—thus the significance of transition periods for a range of states, not only in NATO, but including Japan, Sweden and Switzerland. The fewer the exclusions from a final definition, the more a ban on cluster munitions would bite into their arsenals, therefore the more time would be needed after any treaty was agreed and entered into force internationally for development and procurement of alternative weapons, they thought. And there was an insurance aspect: without knowing what the final definition would look like, those who felt they needed a transition period on use or transfer pushed harder to ensure it was in the text in order to put themselves in the strongest position down the line in Dublin.

Conversely there were many Oslo process delegations who believed transition periods made no sense in political or moral terms. Agreeing to ban cluster munitions because of their unacceptable harm to civilians and then granting a waiver to allow continued use would widely be seen as hypocritical and run counter to the basic aim of the treaty to minimize risk to civilians from the weapon. Many among the Tee-total states adopted the CMC's argument that states with cluster munitions fighting for transition periods should drop the idea, wait until such time as they were in a position to join a treaty with no transition periods and suffer the criticism in the meantime. Continued possessors of cluster munitions could not have their cake and eat it too.

INTEROPERABILITY

The Core Group's "Draft Cluster Munition Explanatory Notes" publicly circulated in January had noted:

> At the Vienna Conference, a number of delegations again expressed the need for detailed work on the issue of military interoperability with States not Party to the Convention with regard to Article 1(c) on assistance. In particular, a need for dedicated consideration of this issue at the Wellington Conference was identified.[45]

The Like-minded delegations came to Wellington with a number of proposals and other papers on the issue of interoperability presented in several rounds of consultations on article 1, chaired by a senior lawyer from the New Zealand Defence Forces, Kevin Riordan. Besides arguing for their proposals to be incorporated into the draft convention text, the Like-minded also tried to persuade others that interoperability provisions should not only concern allies of the US, but any state involved in international operations requiring the militaries of different states to operate alongside each other. These, the Like-minded said, could include UN-led joint operations, or those under the auspices of regional organizations. Article 1(c) as drafted in the Wellington text, the Like-minded contended, could expose armed forces from a wide spectrum of states to criminal liability in cases of joint operations with states not party to the cluster ban treaty.

One useful contribution to these consultations was a discussion paper prepared by Australia's military lawyers and co-sponsored by Canada, the Czech Republic, Denmark, Finland, France, Germany, Italy, the Netherlands, Sweden, Switzerland and the UK. The paper probably did not change the minds of many delegations, but it did set out most of the major interoperability concerns in a clear manner, and identified where solutions might lie in negotiations in Dublin. (The major exception to this was on base hosting, which would become of critical importance in Dublin for states like the UK, but received little attention in the paper or the Wellington discussions.) The paper's authors argued that cluster munitions posed fundamentally different problems for interoperability than anti-personnel mines (APM):

> Many States parties to the Ottawa Convention have accommodated the APM prohibition on assistance, encouragement or inducement by issuing strict guidance limiting involvement in prohibited APM activities. In some cases, States have issued declarations interpreting the scope of the prohibition. In the limited circumstances where embedded officers may be exposed to APMs, these officers can feasibly remove themselves from the decision-making process.
>
> Unfortunately, the same strategies are unlikely to work for cluster munitions.
>
> It is reasonable to expect that cluster munitions are much more likely than APM to be used by States in future operations. Cluster munitions form a critical component in the arsenals of such States. By contrast, APMs are less likely to be used in modern coalition warfare, having reduced military utility where conventional battles are fast-moving or operations are non-conventional or insurgent in nature.
>
> Further, it is much more likely that Oslo-signatories may be inadvertently captured by the prohibition because of the wide variety of planned and unplanned scenarios in which cluster munitions may be used and the short planning lead time involved.
>
> It is not feasible for officers working in coalition headquarters to constantly stand aside from operational planning, or for forces to refrain from calling in air support (in circumstances where it is the effect which is called for, not a particular type of munition), or to refrain from providing general logistical support. The inability to undertake these tasks would undermine significantly the ability of States to operate in coalition and maintain alliance relationships.[46]

Although reordered and using slightly different terminology, the paper by Australia and others raised almost identical points to the four issues in the US paper circulated to its NATO partners the previous autumn—problems for combined planning and joint staff operations, joint training, integrated logistics, and combined operations—with the addition of relaying "intelligence relating to targeting to non-State party personnel". The discussion paper illustrated these problems with scenarios, and it proposed that in the Oslo process:

> the prohibition [on cluster munitions] should not be drafted so as to capture acts of assistance, encouragement or inducement which cannot reasonably be avoided if personnel are to carry out essential inter-operability activities. This would include situations where those personnel may have constructive knowledge that their acts may in some way contribute to the types of activities prohibited under the current discussion text.[47]

The proposals of states to deal with interoperability were various. Japan's idea, for example, was a weaker general prohibition in article 1(c).[48] Baldly stated, while members of the treaty would not be able to assist the US to make its cluster munitions, they could help in ensuring the US could use them. Some of the other Like-minded supported Japan's proposal while proposing their own formulations. France suggested adding a new article to the draft convention stating "nothing in this Convention shall be interpreted as in any way preventing military interoperability between States parties and non-States parties to the Convention".[49] The French article seemed better at capturing the general sentiment of what the Like-minded wanted, rather than specifying what that would mean in practice. Nor were the Germans—usually dependably precise—much more specific.[50] Canada, in a spirit of helpfulness it said, suggested that states be allowed to opt out of the provisions of article 1(c) of the treaty (it did not specify for how long) if they promised to encourage others to join the legal instrument.[51]

In contrast, the Norwegian delegation's spokespeople—Bjørseth, Kongstad, Nystuen and, a new addition from the Foreign Affairs legal department, Torfinn Rislaa Arntsen—professed not to understand why interoperability had to be viewed as such a problem. The Norwegians questioned whether issues of state or individual criminal liability really were so special for cluster munitions:

> we want to underline that although there are a number of issues relating to interoperability, most of these are in fact being solved in practice in ongoing military operations. The challenges resulting from the ban on cluster munitions, require in our view, a practical approach. We are committed to continuing discussions with colleagues and to find solutions to these challenges. Such discussions should be rather specific as to the problems we envisage.[52]

The International Committee of the Red Cross (ICRC) and the CMC supported some of the Norwegian arguments—Conway of the CMC, in particular, contesting the assumption by Australia and others that cluster munitions really did have sufficient military utility to see their continued use despite the humanitarian harm they caused.[53] However strong the substance of the Norwegian case, it was apparent that their posture exasperated other US allies—the words left hovering unspoken throughout the discussion could be paraphrased as "whatever the legal arguments, this is a problem for the US, and therefore for US allies, and therefore we must accommodate an interoperability provision".

"Shock and recover"

As the meetings on Monday and Tuesday unfolded, the Like-minded rhetorically battered away to try to force the Core Group to agree to incorporation of their proposals in the Wellington draft convention text. The lack of tact of some of these efforts left others unimpressed, especially among the many developing and cluster munition-affected countries attending the Wellington conference. These countries were alarmed that the Like-minded could weaken the draft convention text for the Dublin negotiations.[54] Armed with a leaked copy of a paper prepared by the CMC for its campaigners' internal use that set out each state's positions on key issues,[55] a Lebanese delegate, Ahmad Arafa, began pulling together a group of states dubbing themselves "Friends of the Affected". This was a cross-regional sub-group of the very broad Tee-total group, and it included Cambodia, Chile, Costa Rica, Croatia, Indonesia, Laos, Morocco, Sierra Leone and Zambia. The emergence of the Friends of the Affected was directly intended to be a counterweight to the Like-minded[56] and, as such, was welcomed by the Core Group and the CMC.

It seems fair to say that the more heavy-handed among the Like-minded did not see the allergic reaction they were causing among other governments, or else considered it unavoidable diplomatic collateral damage. The British for their part believed they were making every attempt to be constructive, and as a large and politically important state (and one with many interests to defend, including its special relationship with the US) the UK delegation had to ensure its interests were secured. British diplomats saw the UK at risk of being taken hostage in a process in which it had not been able to materially change the text to suit its interests yet, and only had the Core Group's assurances that it would be able to do so at "formal" negotiations later in Dublin:

I think that our concern in Wellington—Wellington was considerably more difficult than Vienna—was that the text should not get any worse than it currently was. There was some bad text coming out of Vienna that did not define what the weapon system was that we were dealing with, had nothing on interoperability, had all sorts of quite difficult legal issues—we had about five "red lines" within the Vienna text. And it would have become unmanageable if that text had become any worse. We would have had great difficulty in signing up to the Dublin process.[57]

Not being able to prenegotiate the text was one thing. Also disturbing for the UK was that, unlike most other processes in the domain of multilateral arms control, it was not at the heart of behind-the-scenes strategic decision-making about the direction of the Oslo process. Thus, inciting an atmosphere of crisis in order to bring home some truths to the recalcitrant was seen as a necessary part of the "diplomatic theatre", a strategy of confrontation in Wellington the British called "shock and recover".[58]

How calculated "shock and recover" was, let alone whether it achieved its intended effect, is a disputed issue among those on the inflicting and receiving ends of the attempts by the Like-minded to have their proposals taken up in the Wellington text. But these efforts certainly did culminate in an ill-tempered exchange between the Australians, British, Danes and Germans on one side and the Core Group on the other in a meeting between Core Group and the Like-minded on Wednesday morning of the conference. France, as nominal coordinator and spokesperson for the Like-minded, had begun the late-morning meeting with a statement in firm but quite measured terms about the Like-minded group's concerns about the meeting process. But then some other Like-minded ambassadors spoke up and MacKay, in particular, became a lightning rod for their criticism. The exchange was, in many respects, a low point in government relations in the Wellington conference and, indeed, the Oslo process. If anything, it made the Core Group more determined not to buckle to pressure (or, conversely, helpfully more focused in the UK's (minority) view).

This determination among the Core Group was combined with their awareness that the atmosphere in the conference was at a potentially dangerous tipping point. Issuing a revised Wellington text could have adverse consequences in view of the polarization occurring between the Like-minded and those of a Tee-total persuasion (especially the Friends of the Affected) on the definition and transition periods. In the lead-up to the Wellington conference, MacKay and his colleagues had certainly been prepared to modify the text in light of the Oslo process discussions in New Zealand, and by mid-week it was already apparent that one benefit of a revised text would be that it could capture useful progress made on the clearance and victim assistance articles.[59] But with the meeting hovering near a "zero-sum game" dynamic, gains for one end of the political spectrum would now be perceived as coming at the expense of the other. Moreover, as the Core Group reminded the Like-minded, the latter still held minority views on transition periods and aspects of exclusions or exceptions from the definition, for instance, despite their strong advocacy, and even if the Like-minded felt they had greater negotiating equity than some of the other states participating in the Oslo process. The Like-minded could protest that the deck was being stacked against them, but this would just alienate others further—and certainly not help them get what they wanted in Dublin.

The Wellington outcome needed to carry *all* of those participating toward Dublin and negotiation of the cluster munition ban treaty, and so how the existing draft convention text was treated was important. MacKay recalled:

> The question was, obviously: if we were going to revise it, how would we revise it? In my view there were two particular areas where we could have given something more to the Like-minded out of the Wellington meeting. Something on interoperability, some language in the Convention, which wouldn't have given them precisely what they wanted, but would have been a holder. And a holder where we expanded 2(c) but did not deal with specific weapon systems—so 2(c) would be expanded in a way that dealt with characteristics generically. We could have, in my view, given them that. And actually we got probably quite close to that point.[60]

As MacKay's conference team and the rest of the Core Group mulled over their options, Thursday brought with it signals of various kinds that helped them to make up their minds that evening. Led by Lebanon, a diplomatic party representing around 30 developing and affected countries—and some of them under pressure from the members of the Like-minded—called on MacKay that afternoon to ask him, as Chair, not to bow to that pressure. In their joint position they expressed "satisfaction with the draft convention on cluster munitions presented to the Wellington Conference and the amendments aiming at strengthening the humanitarian objectives of the text".[61] This was in contrast, they made plain, with some of the proposals of the Like-minded. The Friends of the Affected petitioned the Chair and the Core Group to stand firm on retaining key provisions of the draft convention text as they were: changes now before Dublin would make it look as if the humanitarian objectives of the Oslo Declaration had been abrogated, they said, and would damage the Oslo process.[62] The CMC, for its part, had lobbied at the conference all week with a "don't change the text" message to governments.[63]

In the meantime, in MacKay's lunchtime consultations at a Wellington restaurant that day, certain of the Like-minded privately gave indications of an alternative to revising the Wellington text that they would be able to live with. This alternative was a compendium of national proposals raised in the Core Group's discussions with the Like-minded mid-week, to be distributed by New Zealand with the other documents from the Wellington conference. The Like-minded, it was true, would not get what they wanted in terms of incorporation of their proposals into the draft convention text, but neither would the text be changed in ways that ran counter to their interests, and their proposals would be visible and on-record.

In view of these signals from both the Friends of the Affected and Like-minded, the compendium option seemed like the obvious solution to the Core Group, although on Thursday night it was still by no means certain to MacKay and his colleagues that many of the Like-minded would endorse the Wellington Declaration the following day.[64] Nevertheless, a decision had to be made, and to leave the draft convention text unaltered and go with a compendium was what the Core Group decided. This decision meant that the Austrians and Irish would have to submit the text reflecting progress they had made as conference co-chairs in talks on the preamble and clearance and victim assistance articles as national proposals within the compendium. But this was helpful too. It meant the compendium would not only be made up of the proposals of the Like-minded; it would also send the message that Core Group members were striving to have their perspectives taken up into the draft convention text. Ultimately, textual proposals from 20 countries were included in Addendum 1, as the compendium was formally known.[65] From the Like-minded it would include proposals originating from or co-sponsored by Australia, Canada, the Czech Republic, Denmark, Finland, France, Germany, Italy, Japan, Slovakia, Spain, Sweden, Switzerland and the UK. From Tee-total states there were proposals from Indonesia, Lesotho, Mozambique and Peru. And the ICRC, the UN Mine Action Team and the CMC also submitted suggestions supplementing their comprehensive statements and room papers.

How would the Wellington conference react to the Core Group's strategy? As Friday morning's closing session commenced, there were question marks over Finland, Japan and the UK, in particular—and some in the Core Group even harboured doubts about whether all of the Friends of the Affected would join in view of their annoyance with the Like-minded. Endorsing the Wellington Declaration meant accepting its rules of procedure, which were circulated on the second to last day of the Wellington conference.[66] To no one's surprise, they were very similar to the rules for the Oslo Mine Ban Treaty negotiation in 1997, and each hewing closer to the 1969 Vienna Convention on the Law of Treaties approach[67] than typical disarmament negotiation practice predicated on consensus. Although Rule 36 stipulated that the Dublin conference "shall make its best endeavours to ensure that the work of the Conference is accomplished by general agreement",[68] it was also clear matters could be put to a vote. Meanwhile, with the draft convention text as the "basic proposal"[69] for Dublin (Rule 30 of the Rules of Procedure), one interpretation was that it could take a two-thirds decision to amend it, if other means of agreement could not be achieved. It again raised the spectre for the Like-minded of being outnumbered and outmanoeuvred by procedural means.

The unhappiness of the Like-minded with the way process and procedure were handled was heightened by what they perceived to be aggressive tactics by civil society in the conference—including clapping at certain statements, the direct advocacy by survivors (which certain government delegates privately described as "emotional blackmail") and filming of delegations in the conference hall by NGOs. There were even allegations of heckling.[70] In addition, some delegates were upset at the picketing set up outside the conference centre, which featured some NGO participants who had decided of their own accord to fashion and carry placards targeting Like-minded countries including Australia, Canada, Germany and the UK as they left the building, states which were also "vilified"[71] (as Canada put it) in CMC press interviews and releases.[72] Clearly personally hurt, Canadian chief delegate Earl Turcotte took aim at the tactics of some NGO campaigners on the final day in Canada's closing statement:

> The countries you attack today will be among the strongest supporters [of] a new Convention on cluster munitions, as we are in the Ottawa [Mine Ban] Convention. I urge you not to dismiss our concerns, or to attribute ulterior motives for putting them forward. I urge you to demonstrate the same good faith and respect that you demand of us.[73]

It had all left a slightly sour taste. While the majority of those who spoke in closing praised the Chairman for his leadership and transparency, including the Friends of the Affected, in most of the closing statements of the Like-minded there was dissatisfaction about process or procedure mentioned.

Nevertheless, the spokesperson for the Like-minded, French ambassador Jean-François Dobelle, said that "commitment was intact" and they would do their best to ensure that in Dublin there was a "balance of views".[74] One by one, almost all of the delegations in the Wellington conference made statements to the effect that they would endorse the Wellington Declaration, 82 doing so that day.[75] A total of 111 governments would declare adherence to the Wellington Declaration before the Dublin meeting commenced. This meant that the draft convention text would be forwarded "as the basic proposal for consideration at the Dublin Diplomatic Conference, together with other relevant proposals including those contained in the compendium attached to this Declaration and those which may be put forward there".[76]

Predictably, many of the Like-minded delegations put their own spin on the status of the compendium as compared with the draft convention text described as the basic proposal in the Wellington Declaration. The UK closing statement was a good example:

> As many in the room will know, we were not hopeful that we could support the Declaration at the start of the week. We had, and still have, many concerns about the Draft Convention text and the process itself. At this stage we cannot support the Draft Convention text in its entirety. On process, we would have liked to see more transparency and a consolidated text emerging from these discussions taking into account all relevant positions. This was not to be.

> But through your leadership and flexibility of the Core Group to try to meet our concerns you have produced a compendium that includes all our proposals. This recognition of all parties [sic] concerns is welcome. In our view the Draft Convention text together with the Compendium of proposals can now form a balanced basis for work in Dublin.[77]

There had been hints the previous evening from some of the Like-minded that they would like the Wellington Declaration's text changed to give the compendium equal status with the draft convention text, but the Core Group would have none of it. This was confirmed in a meeting on the Friday morning before the Wellington conference's closing session involving MacKay, French ambassador Dobelle and a new man on the scene, Ambassador Dáithí O'Ceallaigh—Ireland's President-Designate for the Dublin conference. Moreover, both Mackay and O'Ceallaigh conveyed the same message from the podium: the draft cluster munition convention text would be the "basic proposal" under Rule 30, and would be transmitted along with the compendium, the latter considered "other proposals" under Rule 31. O'Ceallaigh subsequently recalled:

> I also told people at Wellington and every time I met them since Wellington that for all effective purposes there was no difference between Article 30 and Article 31 of the Rules of Procedure, that Dublin would be a diplomatic conference, that there was a basic text on the table but that once we got to Dublin the text proposals and so on—they were not the property of the Core Group, they were the property of the Conference.[78]

Such statements about the status of texts were to a great extent for the consumption of Like-minded delegations' officials and capitals. From MacKay's point of view, and as was later proven in the Dublin treaty negotiations, "the status of the compendium is completely irrelevant. Either we'll get a deal in Dublin or we won't, but the compendium is not actually going to affect that".[79] And, it did not change the fact that despite bruising exchanges and increased political polarization, the Wellington conference was successful in achieving its objectives. A highly ambitious draft convention text was now in place for the Dublin diplomatic conference, along with rules for that negotiation and a strong political reaffirmation of the humanitarian goals of the Oslo process. But it was with sighs of relief (and exhaustion) all around that the conference finished its work on a beautiful summery Friday.

CIVIL SOCIETY AT THE WELLINGTON CONFERENCE

The Wellington conference was not only tense for representatives of governments. Both hopes and fears were also running high among civil society representatives attending the meeting from all parts of the globe.

Since the middle of 2006, the Cluster Munition Coalition had undergone a transformation from one full-time staff member—New Zealander Thomas Nash, its coordinator—to a fully-fledged campaigning operation coordinating the burgeoning activities of national campaigns and international events in dozens of countries around the world. Some growing pains were to be expected and, as seen in previous chapters, a major task for the CMC's Steering Committee in 2006 and 2007 was to clarify and agree on the Coalition's central messaging and structure in order to give maximum effort to the emerging Oslo process, which all within the Coalition agreed was the best opportunity for the CMC's call to be fulfilled. With the hectic pace of campaign activity and expansion during the Oslo process's first year, the Wellington conference would, for various reasons, lead the CMC to examine its own role and come to grips with how the civil society campaign should approach the Dublin negotiations.

By the time of the Wellington meeting the CMC had a small and highly competent cadre of full-time staff, mainly based in Landmine Action's London office. It consisted of Nash, its indispensable operations officer Serena Olgiati, Laura Cheeseman as campaigning officer (who brought with her helpful experience of gun control campaigning, and her network of contacts via the International Action Network on Small Arms), Natalie Curtis (who had previously worked at The Diana, Princess of Wales Memorial Fund) as a media and communications officer, and its newest member, Susan Hensel, to be based in Dublin after the Wellington conference in order to prepare the civil society side of the Dublin meeting. Experienced media and communications specialist Samantha Bolton was also an important member brought in to bolster the CMC team at key moments and conferences. The CMC executive team was a small, closely knit group of campaigners, who worked together in a low-key and informal way.

While Nash and his team were youthful, the CMC was able to draw on a reservoir of experience from the landmine campaign in particular. Several members of the CMC Steering Committee like Steve Goose and Paul Hannon had played important roles in the International Campaign to Ban Landmines (ICBL) since its formation, and others like Handicap International's Jean-Baptiste Richardier had also been involved in the landmine campaign of the 1990s. And when the ICBL formally added cluster munitions to its mandate in late 2006, the CMC was also able to tap that campaign's expertise directly, through its staff members, all of whom had relevant expertise and campaigning experience. Moreover, the ICBL committed significant resources of its own to campaigning and advocacy: Kasia Derlicka worked solidly on the issue in 2007 and from the beginning of 2008 Susan B. Walker rejoined the ICBL ranks on a cluster munition treaty: Walker's long experience of building trust with government representatives of all kinds in Geneva and persuading them to get behind the Mine Ban Treaty was a boon to advocacy efforts.

Other veterans of the landmine campaign also had a deep interest in the success of international efforts on cluster munitions. There was Nobel Laureate and former ICBL Coordinator Jody Williams, for example: an NGO she had helped subsequently to establish, the Nobel Womens' Initiative, got in behind the cluster munition campaign and Williams made cluster munitions a focus of her media work. John Rodsted, the Australian photographer and campaigner on landmines and unexploded ordnance, who had created the chilling short film of unexploded submunitions in Southern Lebanon shown at the Oslo conference, was also engaged in the Oslo process, and he and a Norwegian, Mette Sofie Eliseussen, established the Ban Bus initiative, which would travel throughout the world in advance of Dublin raising awareness about cluster munitions. There was also Rae McGrath, the Mines Advisory Group founder and co-founder of the ICBL who had delivered the Nobel lecture on behalf of the ICBL in 1997 and was now Handicap International's spokesperson on cluster munitions.

Perhaps the most important veteran of the landmine campaign with a view to preparing the Wellington conference was a New Zealander, Mary Wareham. Wareham had worked closely with Goose and Williams during the Ottawa process, and as a staff member of Human Rights Watch's Arms Division in Washington DC for several years. In 2006, Wareham returned to Wellington to take up a position as Advocacy Director at Oxfam New Zealand, one of the country's better-resourced NGOs. A protégé of Williams, Wareham was a formidable advocate on both landmines and cluster munitions, and an industrious organizer. She also had a no-nonsense attitude, and over the course of 2007 as the Oslo process unfolded it became clear to her that she should take the lead in making the civil society side of the Wellington conference happen in order to emulate the successful efforts of local campaigners during the first major conference in Oslo in February 2007 and the efforts that were being undertaken for Vienna in December that year. For these meetings, as in Belgrade in October, national campaigners had taken on a great deal of responsibility organizationally while the attentions of Nash and his small team were spread across a range of different challenges internationally.

Wareham and Oxfam New Zealand took on coordination of the Aotearoa New Zealand Cluster Munitions Coalition (ANZCMC) formed of New Zealand NGOs soon after the outset of the Oslo process.[80] Wareham did not attend the Vienna conference, but at a CMC campaigning workshop I sat in on as an observer after that conference ended, her New Zealand colleague Jamilia Homayun was asked to outline what the ANZCMC had in mind for Wellington. Those present were wowed when Homayun laid out what was effectively an entire blueprint for the civil society contingent in Wellington, including a professionally designed and printed campaigning pack, a DVD film and other resources. Civil society advocacy activities around the Wellington conference included media events such as a leaflet drop from a small plane over the capital city in the conference lead-up (this was probably illegal, but proved highly effective), a full-colour daily campaign newsletter during the Wellington meeting, a petition to the New Zealand government calling for a cluster munition ban, and a "stunt" in Civic Square adjacent to the conference venue to attract public attention.[81] Wareham and her team had taken charge of the civil society contingent preparations for the Wellington conference, and it seemed clear to the CMC they were in safe hands.

BLAMING AND SHAMING?

The roles of NGOs in international politics are sometimes described as "naming, framing, blaming and shaming".[82] The CMC had spent much of its early existence since 2003 involved in naming and framing the problems and responses concerning cluster munitions. And when the Oslo process began, the CMC lacked a large number of national campaigns supporting it by actually committing staff time and resources to campaigning as compared with the ICBL when the Ottawa process commenced. This was now changing rapidly, especially with the global network of landmine campaigners in many countries now behind the CMC.

When the Wellington conference commenced, though, the CMC continued to place weight on what it had always done—engage closely with states, work through national campaigners in between conferences to inform and pressure officials and lobby governments on their positions in international meetings and bilateral meetings. Yet, based on their experience of the Ottawa process, some within the civil society contingent present in Wellington felt that the skills and perspectives of some of the NGO representatives were being under-utilized at conference time. The CMC had a delegation seated in the conference hall, but space was limited; it was also participating actively in the Chair's open-ended consultations, but there the Coalition was represented by its front bench of experts drawn predominantly from the Steering Committee. In its sponsorship programme for campaigners, the CMC had also focused on those NGO participants who were effective lobbyists and could engage in detailed discussions with delegates from their regions on the key issues. There was however still a perception among some campaigners that there was not necessarily a lot for some of the NGO representatives to do at the conference itself beyond lobbying those governments they were assigned to work on. And, for a few campaigners, listening to technical debates or hovering around outside the conference was frustrating in view of the great effort involved for them to even get to New Zealand.

Moreover, everyone in the CMC could sense the tension between states at the Wellington conference. Some of the most influential landmine campaign veterans therefore saw more direct forms of advocacy as appropriate; "blaming and shaming" through the media and civil society actions, which could make use of campaigners who wanted to do more than follow discussions and lobby delegates and create additional pressure on the governments they saw as unhelpful to the process (that is, the Like-minded).

The result was the emergence of new tactics that were not part of the CMC's activities and game plan for Wellington harmonized ahead of time by the Steering Committee. So, halfway through the Wellington conference the left hand did not always know what the right hand was doing and the CMC began sending mixed messages. For instance, the CMC front bench was highly professional in the Chair's consultations, whether upstairs in the Wellington Town Hall or at working lunches. But at the same time as those CMC representatives were engaging in the discourse of diplomacy with governments, others, including survivors, were waving placards at delegates emerging from the conference building with messages like "UK, France, Japan, Germany, Denmark: Shame on you!"[83] Perhaps the protests made certain campaigners feel empowered and gave an outlet to the frustration of veteran campaigners wanting a sharper edge to the CMC's lobbying. But it also contributed to making those delegations targeted in such a way feel angry and besieged, as shown by their statements at the conference's closing. And, arguably, it aggravated polarization at a point in the Oslo process when trust-building rather than shame was needed: some in the Like-minded already grumbled that the Core Group and NGOs were joined at the hip, and such actions fed suspicion about a Core Group–civil society conspiracy to stitch them up, as did clapping heard in certain conference hall sessions in response to those statements NGOs approved of.

The general air of fractiousness extended to an internal CMC meeting of Steering Committee members and some others at lunchtime on the Thursday of the conference. Called ostensibly as an initial brainstorm by campaigners on preparations for Dublin, the meeting instead led to a stream of criticism from some prominent landmine campaign veterans. It amounted to public lack of confidence in the CMC executive team. As the CMC's coordinator and co-chairs were at other previously planned events, this criticism was directed at those members of the executive team present, who as less senior were also easier targets. In part this episode probably reflected the anxieties of some campaigners about what the Coalition could usefully do to lend momentum to a positive outcome for the Wellington conference at this stage, which seemingly hung in the balance. But the tone and degree of the criticism nevertheless seemed rather misplaced, especially in a campaign in which there were almost always high levels of professional decorum and collegiality as well as a healthy approach on all sides to providing and acting upon constructive criticism. Mentioned among the criticisms were that the CMC had become too chummy with governments (despite very robust press releases criticizing them on issues like interoperability, and national campaigns in France, Germany and the UK aggressively lobbying and critiquing the positions of their governments), and—unlike the landmine campaign in the Ottawa process—that it was not confrontational enough.

Blaming and shaming has, historically, certainly sometimes been significant in international processes to get governments to change a policy or tactic, including in the Ottawa process. Naming and shaming was also a significant feature of the Oslo process. It is less clear whether confrontational tactics to deliver such messages, like the placard waving outside the venue, had much direct impact in Wellington, apart from adding to an already tense atmosphere. Most of the major recent cluster munition users had shunned the Oslo process, and some of the Like-minded were at pains to point out that they were the good guys, not bad guys—having committed themselves to a ban treaty by means of the Oslo Declaration. Of course, to many in the Oslo process this did not necessarily bear close scrutiny based on the tactics of some of the Like-minded at times, or their alleged "fronting" for the US on issues such as interoperability, or proposals for exclusions from the definition that seemed self-serving rather than humanitarian in nature. But the goal, surely, was to get states to endorse the Wellington Declaration, which would in turn commit them to the negotiations in Dublin, and *then* exert maximum pressure including by blaming and shaming if necessary. And the Like-minded seemed to find the media flak annoying rather than a real hindrance (one or two of the Like-minded ambassadors showed signs, on the contrary, of revelling in the role of being perceived as "bad guys").

That the Wellington conference was a success was largely because the Core Group had held its nerve and made an astute calculation about what the emergent ideological poles in the Oslo process—the Tee-total states (including the Friends of the Affected) versus the Like-minded—could all live with. The Tee-total states had been at least in part motivated and briefed by a geographically diverse group of effective campaigners from the CMC who had spent their week focused on the diplomatic effort and not waving placards. Among the CMC's other contributions, one of the most substantive had been the progress its experts made in chipping away at the various arguments of those states calling for measures such as exclusions from the cluster munition definition and transition periods, and contributing to other important provisions of the treaty such as clearance, stockpile destruction and especially victim assistance. These efforts would all pay off in Dublin.

Tensions dissipated somewhat on the last day of the conference as the Wellington Declaration was widely endorsed, and that evening CMC campaigners began celebrations that lasted until the sun rose the next morning. At a meeting of campaigners that Saturday, representatives of both schools of thought (a crude description might be the "negotiators" and the "confrontationalists") stood by their tactics. It did not matter, as the Wellington conference's successful outcome made it difficult to dispute that the CMC's leadership—both the executive team and the Steering Committee—had delivered on the basis of its strategy. Perhaps criticism had gone too far, certain of the confrontationalists said, and this prompted some reconciliation with several ICBL veterans expressing their support for the CMC staff team publicly.

The difficult Wellington conference taught the CMC's leadership important lessons, which would stand the campaign in good stead for the Dublin negotiations. It underlined the need for an even tighter single coordination structure and detailed game plan for campaigners in Dublin that leveraged their various skills, and did not leave even a single campaigner waiting around for something to happen. Rather than leave such arrangements in the air, Nash, with the help of Conway and other key members of the Steering Committee, began working immediately that Saturday to allocate specific leadership and coordination responsibilities for Dublin in a Steering Committee meeting following that of the campaigners. Conway, a former British army officer and HALO Trust deminer who was Director of Landmine Action, agreed to take responsibility for the logistics and organization of the CMC in Dublin. This was extremely important. Conway's military-inspired approach to organization meant that when the Dublin diplomatic conference began in May, the CMC had in place a strategy that used the hundreds of campaigners there to best effect in lobbying, public demonstrations, media work and other activities—and, indeed, would run many campaigners almost ragged with various activities, in contrast to Wellington.

Conway also had a deep appreciation for how the international media worked, and this was reassuring to the CMC's media team. New Zealand, separated by geography and several time zones from the rest of the world, had been a challenge for attracting sustained international media attention essential to creating pressure on governments. It had led to virtually around-the-clock efforts from lead individuals like Curtis, Bolton and their colleague Daniel Barty from the Australian NGO AustCare to engage journalists overseas. The CMC realized that to exert maximum influence in Dublin—itself not exactly a hub for press agencies and news networks—its media machine would need to be highly sophisticated, and be able to provide services to the media like broadcast footage and satellite feed video, as well as take advantage of "new media" like the internet. The media had changed a lot since the Ottawa process more than a decade before, and so advocacy and communication would be a very different ballgame for the CMC to prepare for.

Before Wellington and confirmation that the Wellington Declaration and draft convention text would be the basis for Dublin, what precisely needed to be done had been hard to envisage clearly. Events in Wellington not only alerted the CMC's lead campaigners that there was a huge amount to do in preparation for Dublin, it also revealed that while basically sound, their internal management systems and strategy should be honed further. Overall, the end of the Wellington conference marked a new phase for the CMC. There were still regional conferences like those in Mexico City and Livingstone—where the CMC could rely on its skilled African and Latin American campaigners to forge even stronger and more effective allies amongst government negotiators from these countries—to take place before Dublin, and a CCW meeting in April which would give campaigners a chance to re-engage with the Like-minded delegates. Psychologically, however, minds were now focusing on the cluster ban treaty's Dublin negotiation, and correspondingly what impact the CMC could have in ensuring that the outcome matched its campaigning call and the Oslo Declaration's aims.

Because of the CMC's rapid expansion and transformation, the Wellington conference also underlined another challenge. At the heart of the CMC was a loose group of expert individuals that roughly (although not exactly) coincided with the Steering Committee's membership, and had a tacit hierarchy with its Steering Committee co-chairs supervising, and being advised by, the Coordinator and his team. Although some NGOs in the CMC had more resources and influence than others, more broadly the CMC was nevertheless a network. This network depended on the goodwill, largely voluntary effort and personal commitment of a host of NGO campaigners from many countries—people with motives, opinions and concerns of their own. Some of these campaigners were not closely involved in the issue of cluster munitions or the CMC before the Oslo process, nor were they close to its decision-making processes. With its increase in tempo and tension, the Wellington conference showed the CMC's leadership that it had to become savvier in understanding and responding to their constituents' expectations if it was to be strong as a campaign in Dublin. It was also clear that these expectations might not necessarily always accord with those in the CMC most closely involved in the government–civil society partnership that was the Oslo process. In the same way as government negotiators dealt with their competing constituents amongst ministries of defence and foreign affairs, as deals began to be struck in the Dublin negotiations in May, keeping campaigners' expectations in sync with CMC's negotiating tactics would not always be easy.

CHAPTER 8

THE EVOLUTION OF CLUSTER MUNITION POLICY IN THE ICRC AND UN

The International Committee of the Red Cross (ICRC) and the United Nations were significant actors in international efforts to address the humanitarian impacts of cluster munitions in both the Oslo and CCW processes. Each organization was a source of field expertise on dealing with the weapon and possessed other knowledge pertinent to developing international legal instruments to tackle cluster munitions' effects. As such, while always consigned to roles as observers in relevant multilateral processes, which included the negotiation of Protocol V as well as later work in the CCW and the Oslo initiative, the ICRC and UN positions influenced other participants' views, including those of many governments. Therefore, any attempt to understand how an international treaty to ban cluster munitions was achieved is incomplete without taking these perspectives into account. To the extent that recent internal policy processes can be discussed openly, they are explored in this chapter.

ICRC POLICY DEVELOPMENT ON CLUSTER MUNITIONS

As seen in chapter 2, by September 2000 the ICRC had arrived at a position on how it thought governments should address the humanitarian problems created by cluster munitions as part of its work to engage them on dealing with explosive remnants of war (ERW). To briefly recap, the ICRC called for national moratoria on the use of cluster munitions until their humanitarian problems could be resolved and a permanent ban on the weapon's use in populated areas put in place. Examined more closely, the ICRC's two reports prepared for the 2000 Nyon expert meeting also showed that the ICRC, like most others at that time involved in the Convention on Certain Conventional Weapons (CCW), operated within the discourse on "good" and "bad" submunitions. The ICRC-commissioned report that Colin King wrote, for instance, recommended, "An appropriate international forum should agree on standards to regulate the manufacture and use of cluster munitions. Such standards could be enshrined through a new protocol" to the CCW.[1] Stuart Maslen's report on Kosovo made six recommendations (three of which would be later taken up in Protocol V as relevant to all munitions that could become ERW), one being to add self-destruct features to bomblets and other submunitions to remedy their post-conflict hazards.[2]

The ICRC's official position on addressing cluster munitions would not change for six years. CCW Protocol V, after all, represented some progress in terms of the weapons-generic measures it contained on ERW. And, in the course of their active participation in the CCW's work,[3] ICRC representatives found themselves under little pressure from others to go further in their call on cluster munitions. The positions of members of the CMC such as Human Rights Watch and Landmine Action were broadly similar to the ICRC's in terms of ambition; positions taken individually or collectively were nevertheless significantly ahead of the curve in terms of the ambitions of most CCW member states during this period. Indeed, following the CCW's inability to agree on a mines other than anti-personnel mines protocol in late 2005 after two years of focused work there seemed scant prospect of *any* agreement forthcoming to negotiate on cluster munitions in the CCW as 2006 began.

Despite the poor apparent prospects for international legally binding measures on cluster munitions, the ICRC's working-level representatives on the issue, Mines-Arms Unit lawyer Louis Maresca, Technical Adviser Dominique Loye, and their boss, Peter Herby, remained well-known faces in CCW meetings. The ICRC fulfils a unique role in multilateral processes like the CCW, as it is perceived by many states as a "guardian of international humanitarian law" (IHL) and an important independent source of expert legal and humanitarian advice. Three clear elements of the ICRC'S mandate, which can be summed up as acting "as a moral authority against the horrors of war; as an operational agent during armed conflict; and as an expert on humanitarian law"[4]—along with the ICRC's long track record in the field—give it a level of credibility with governments that, on the whole, NGOs in the weapons domain cannot match. This meant in the cluster munition context that, as aloof or conservative as its critics might contend the ICRC to be, when it offered its views on the CCW and the eventual Oslo process the ICRC's position mattered, just as it had during the Ottawa process.

On 6 March 2006, the ICRC issued a response to the McCormack report on the IHL questionnaire (see chapter 5).[5] Although its comments were tactful, there was no mistaking the ICRC's continued concern about cluster munitions:

> Indeed the body of the report indicates that cluster munitions raise important issues under the rules of distinction, the prohibition of indiscriminate attacks and proportionality.
>
> In this context it is perhaps also worth noting that the entire CCW regime is based upon a belief in the value of specifying how the general rules of IHL, namely the rules prohibiting indiscriminate weapons and those which cause unnecessary suffering, are to be applied to specific types of weapons. It does not take for granted that the faithful implementation of general rules and principles is adequate. Indeed its development has often been driven precisely by the types of inconsistencies in interpretation or application of general rules that are identified in the report. It is also important to consider in relation to cluster munitions that, as they proliferate, the divergences between users in both the understanding of the law and the capacity or intent to implement it is likely to <u>increase</u> rather than decrease as more actors have access to such systems. *The results could be devastating for civilian populations. It is for these reasons that the ICRC has called for new legally binding rules concerning the targeting of cluster munitions and for the elimination of inaccurate and unreliable models.*[6]

The July–August period brought with it the conflict in Southern Lebanon. Maresca recalled:

> for me, clearly, Lebanon was the perfect storm in a sense and I'm still amazed at the timing of it, the way in which cluster munitions were used. It seems that all of the various aspects of this conflict highlighted every single concern that we or anybody else ever had about cluster munitions. Whether it'd be the use of these weapons by non-state actors or the use of old stuff that doesn't work, to the new stuff, the newer technology failing and not living up to expectations.[7]

Those in the Mines-Arms Unit began to discuss with the Head of the ICRC's Legal Division, Jean-Philippe Lavoyer, and his Director, Philip Spoerri, the prospect of an ICRC-sponsored expert meeting on cluster munitions to be held sometime the following year. Just as the Nyon meeting on ERW in September 2000 had capitalized upon the experience of the Kosovo conflict in 1999, it was hoped that a similar meeting devoted to cluster munitions would engage with experts on a technical level in order to have a facts-based discussion of the real humanitarian, military, technical and legal issues related to cluster munitions since this had proved an elusive goal in the CCW.

Meanwhile, the Southern Lebanon conflict drastically raised the profile of the humanitarian hazards posed by cluster munitions within the wider ICRC hierarchy. The Mines-Arms Unit is a specialized unit of a half-dozen or so people within the ICRC's Legal Division. But the three-hundred-pound gorilla within the ICRC in terms of resources and clout was its Department of Operations. Now, with reports of massive submunition contamination in Southern Lebanon flowing in from ICRC delegates in the field, Operations and the rest of the house woke up to cluster munition hazards that the Mines-Arms Unit had been trying to get the CCW to tackle for years.

On 19 September, the ICRC's Director-General asked the organization's Directorate (its strategic management group) to update its institutional position on cluster munitions in view of their use in Lebanon. The upshot of this process was that it had now become clear to the ICRC leadership that the Red Cross and Red Crescent Movement should be even more active at the international level on cluster munitions. By the middle of October, after meetings involving senior ICRC staff at the Directorate level, the Director-General and its President, Dr Jakob Kellenberger, the ICRC's position on cluster munitions was—to use ICRC parlance—"consolidated" with all of the relevant departments within the organization. The ICRC, it was agreed, would step up its call for governments to address cluster munitions' humanitarian consequences through new international rules, starting with a briefing for Geneva diplomats held at the organization's headquarters on 6 November. The following day, Spoerri presented "key elements of ICRC proposals on cluster munitions [that] the ICRC would introduce to the November Review Conference of States Parties to the CCW".[8] The ICRC's main proposals to states were to:

> immediately end the use of inaccurate and unreliable cluster munitions; to prohibit the targeting of cluster munitions against any military objective located in a populated area; to eliminate stocks of inaccurate and unreliable cluster munitions and, pending their destruction, not to transfer such weapons to other countries.[9]

The banning of cluster munition use in populated areas was a familiar element. However, although foreshadowed by the ICRC's response to the McCormack report, the inaccurate and unreliable formulation was technically new, and itself a formulation pioneered years earlier by Human Rights Watch. (In retrospect there is an irony here: even as the ICRC adopted the inaccurate and unreliable formulation, NGOs in the CMC attached to the language, such as Human Rights Watch and Mines Action Canada, were coming under increasing pressure to agree to move their collective call toward using the word "ban".) Spoerri also confirmed the ICRC's view that it "believes that a new international instrument is needed" and announced the organization would convene an expert meeting early in 2007.[10] Maresca explained the ICRC's reasoning:

> once we started talking about cluster munitions it became very difficult to really be precise [about] what you were talking about, because you had a weapon here which was essentially undefined and encompassed a wide range of weaponry, some of which we were concerned about, because it had humanitarian problems, some of which we weren't concerned about, because it was not a humanitarian problem.

> So, for us … maybe perhaps unlike some of the NGOs, we … weren't focusing on a public communication, we were looking to engage experts at a technical level. We couldn't just walk in and say we wanted to prohibit cluster munitions to technical experts. We had to begin to define what we were talking about. And it was those discussions about how to credibly engage in a dialogue with people on cluster munitions and tell them what we want that the adjectives "inaccurate and unreliable" became part of our position.[11]

Norway's announcement toward the end of the CCW's 2006 Review Conference that it would host the Oslo conference came as no surprise to the ICRC. Those involved in ICRC cluster munition policy were also clear-eyed about what the Norwegian-sponsored conference heralded, including the difficulties a free-standing international process on cluster munitions could pose for the ICRC in view of its guardianship role in the CCW. However, from Herby's perspective:

> the fact that we did support Oslo was never in doubt. I mean, if states are ready to negotiate something which meets some or all of the objectives that the ICRC has called on to address, how could we not support it and be involved in it? What was more sensitive and difficult is: how do we relate to the CCW? I mean, we don't want to do anything, and didn't

want to do anything, to undermine a good faith effort in the CCW framework. But at the same time it was clear that it was going to be very difficult if not impossible for the CCW states, collectively, to take a very ambitious approach to this issue.[12]

This was not only a concern for the ICRC; as shall be seen in this chapter, it was an issue that would exercise the UN's inter-agency process as well.

As discussed in chapter 6, the ICRC's expert meeting held in April 2007 in Montreux underlined the problems with any "split-the-category" approach to defining cluster munitions. In its closing comments in the meeting's published report, the ICRC noted three points that were to go to the heart of the eventual negotiations in Dublin:

- The relative military value of cluster munitions needs to be further examined. This examination needs to be based not only on the doctrine and theory underlying the use of such weapons but also on the actual military effectiveness and consequences of the use of cluster munitions in past conflicts.

- Proposed technical solutions, such as improvements in reliability and accuracy and the integration of self-destruct features, need to be examined not only on the basis of how these technologies are underlined{designed} to function (or function under testing conditions), but also need to take into account how they underlined{will} function under actual conditions of use.

- New norms of international humanitarian law intended to resolve the problems caused by cluster munitions need to integrate legitimate military needs and be clearly stated so they will be effectively implemented by military forces. Clear rules will also facilitate broad adherence to a new instrument.[13]

With two international processes to address the humanitarian consequences of the weapon now underway, in late September the ICRC defined its strategy on cluster munitions carefully, deciding that it should avoid favouring any particular negotiating process. The ICRC would remain engaged in the CCW's discussions on cluster munitions.[14] However, in practice, and as insights from the Montreux expert meeting were absorbed into the organization's outlook, this de facto policy of ICRC interest based on likely results rather than arguments about a process's perceived legitimacy served to bolster its interest in the Oslo process. It was an orientation not lost on many governments looking to the ICRC for a lead in terms of their own priorities and policies: if the ICRC was supportive of the Oslo initiative, it made it easier for some states to justify their participation.

The ICRC's President, Jakob Kellenberger, also became very engaged in the issue of cluster munitions. By various accounts, the President was happy to bring his authority and that of the institution to the Oslo process in view of what had happened in Southern Lebanon, which he had visited in August 2006. In a statement to Geneva diplomatic missions on 25 October 2007, Kellenberger said that Lebanon "vindicated concerns about the proliferation of cluster munitions" and that "To date, the armed forces of the main users of cluster munitions have not, in our view, presented concrete historical evidence that these weapons have achieved specific military results which outweigh their well documented humanitarian problems".[15] It was gutsy stuff by the standards of the usually cautious ICRC.[16] The ICRC called again for a treaty "to prohibit those cluster munitions which have such high costs for civilian populations and to prevent their continued proliferation" and for national moratoria on use and transfer in the meantime. The treaty, Kellenberger said, should:

- Prohibit the use, development, production, stockpiling and transfer of inaccurate and unreliable cluster munitions;

- Require the elimination of current stocks of inaccurate and unreliable cluster munitions;

- Provide for victim assistance, the clearance of cluster munitions and activities to minimize the impact of these weapons on civilian populations.[17]

Three weeks later the CCW agreed its mandate to negotiate a proposal on cluster munitions, but despite this the ICRC's view in-house was that the CCW's mandate was simply not an adequate response to the scale and nature of the cluster munition problem. So, after reiterating the ICRC's new position on cluster munitions in his opening statement to the International Conference of the Red Cross and Red Crescent on 26 November, Kellenberger had this to say:

Unfortunately, the discussions at the annual meeting of the States party to the Convention on Certain Conventional Weapons, which has just ended, did not result in a sufficient basis for achieving this objective in spite of the efforts undertaken. Therefore, as indicated in the Council of Delegates resolution adopted two days ago, the ICRC urges governments that support the Oslo Declaration to continue their efforts to conclude in 2008 a treaty prohibiting the use, production, stockpiling and transfer of cluster munitions that cause unacceptable harm to civilians.[18]

Almost as if an afterthought, the ICRC President added: "The States party to the Convention on Certain Conventional Weapons should continue their efforts and work towards adoption of legally binding rules on cluster munitions".[19] By this time these formulations had become the position of the whole Red Cross and Red Crescent Movement as a result of a resolution of its Council of Delegates, which had convened the preceding week.[20]

At the Vienna conference of the Oslo process in December 2007 the ICRC robustly corrected those among the Like-minded seeking to use its "inaccurate and unreliable" formulation as a cover for trying to retain weapons like the M-85. The ICRC delegation stated that, in its view, virtually all cluster munitions used to date were either inaccurate, unreliable or both.[21] Soon after that, in mid-January 2008, the ICRC Directorate decided to make cluster munitions one of its top three institutional priorities for humanitarian diplomacy (a decision reconfirmed on 6 May, shortly before the Dublin conference began). In late January the ICRC launched an institutional communication effort about addressing the hazards of the weapon to civilians through a new humanitarian treaty that mobilized not only ICRC delegations worldwide but also a large number of national Red Cross and Red Crescent Societies. As well as a multilingual film on DVD, brochures and briefings for delegates, the ICRC held a regional workshop in Bangkok for South-East Asian countries in April, and organized an international media trip to Laos' Xieng Khouang province for print, radio and television journalists. On 9 May, in an editorial published in the *International Herald Tribune*, the ICRC President flagged the upcoming Dublin negotiations and argued, "Participants should agree to a treaty that prohibits inaccurate and unreliable cluster munitions, provides for their clearance and ensures assistance to victims".[22]

The ICRC's call on cluster munitions still remained distinct from that of the Cluster Munition Coalition by the time of the Dublin negotiation. While banning cluster munitions causing "unacceptable harm" would become a widely accepted mantra in the Oslo process following the agreement of the Oslo Declaration, to the ICRC's lawyers it meant inaccuracy, unreliability and use in massive numbers (an element that crept into ICRC statements as the Oslo process advanced). The ICRC's call, having been already agreed by the ICRC's senior hierarchy and later endorsed by the Movement, was what they stuck with. It was not so much a different call to banning cluster munitions that cause unacceptable harm, but the factors that resulted in unacceptable harm to civilians.

CLUSTER MUNITIONS AND THE ORIGINS
OF UNITED NATIONS POLICY

The ICRC was a cautious and often conservative organization, but as a private Swiss entity it was able to act independently of the views of states in a way the United Nations system could not. The UN consisted of 192 states with a range of views on cluster munitions—at least a few of them opposed to any new international rules on the weapon. And just over half of the UN's membership belonged to the CCW, a framework treaty and its protocols all negotiated under UN auspices and serviced by the UN Secretariat's Department for Disarmament Affairs.[23] States shunning the Oslo process like China, Russia and the US might not react well to the UN organization lending wholesale support to this free-standing alternative to the CCW's work on cluster munitions. Meanwhile, views were anything but monolithic among the UN's relevant departments in the Secretariat—like the UN Department of Peacekeeping Operations (DPKO), Disarmament Affairs and the UN Office for the Coordination of Humanitarian Affairs (OCHA), and agencies with field presence such as the United Nations Development Programme (UNDP) and the United Nations Children's Fund (UNICEF)—over how the UN should position itself on cluster munitions. These views made UN inter-agency attempts to develop a collective institutional policy that kept pace with international developments on cluster munitions an ongoing challenge.

Many within the UN concerned with cluster munitions policy also recalled its posture toward the Ottawa process in the 1990s with some regret. To the outside, the UN Secretariat at that time had sometimes appeared dismissive of and occasionally even uncooperative with the emergent international campaign to prohibit anti-personnel mines—efforts that ultimately resulted in the Mine Ban Treaty. The UN, it was widely felt both within and outside the organization, had been left behind on a humanitarian objective—banning anti-personnel mines—that it should have been at the forefront of. The question was: would it be left behind again on cluster munitions?

The issues around the use of cluster munitions were not new for the UN. A 1985 UN Environment Programme publication on mitigating the environmental effects of ERW had highlighted the problems posed by unexploded submunitions for the natural environment.[24] The end of the Cold War and a massive increase in international peacekeeping and humanitarian operations from the late 1980s had resulted in the UN establishing mine action programmes in Afghanistan in 1989 and Cambodia in 1991 to tackle both mines and unexploded ordnance. The UN would eventually become responsible for managing or supporting national demining programmes in more than 40 countries and territories, a development that would inevitably require coordinated UN policies and strategies. Following its establishment in 1997, responsibility for this coordination at the operational level would largely fall to the UN Mine Action Service (UNMAS) within DPKO.[25]

In 1999, the UN set up a mine and unexploded ordnance clearance programme in Kosovo headed by New Zealand soldier John Flanagan. There, for the first time, submunitions posed what was probably a greater threat to civilians than mines in a demining and battle area clearance operation coordinated by the UN. Flanagan had the chance to present some of the lessons he and his UN colleagues learned during the course of the Kosovo operation to the CCW in 2002 and 2003, which he attended at the request of UNMAS's Director, Martin Barber.[26] Flanagan also wrote CCW discussion papers on ERW and mines other than anti-personnel mines.[27] Soon afterward, in August 2003, he became chief of UNMAS field operations. Thus, on the operational side at least, UNMAS possessed some senior staff like Barber and Flanagan who understood the post-conflict humanitarian problems of cluster munitions very well, and throughout succeeding years UNMAS would contribute usefully to technical and practical discussions on cluster munitions in the CCW and eventually the Oslo processes.

Later in 2003, the UN's Assistant Emergency Relief Coordinator delivered a statement to the CCW Meeting of States Parties entitled "A call for a freeze on the use of cluster munitions" on behalf of an Inter-Agency Standing Committee (IASC), a forum for humanitarian action led by OCHA.[28] The IASC statement was significant in several ways. It flagged for the first time in the CCW's ERW work the specific concerns about cluster munitions of the UN's field agencies. Second, it linked the IASC's views directly to those of the ICRC in the version as delivered to the CCW—the ICRC having reiterated its call for new cluster munition rules earlier that day and a freeze on use until humanitarian concerns were addressed. Third, the IASC statement talked about the "unacceptable effects that these weapons have on civilians both during and after conflict"[29]—a formulation remarkably similar to the one settled upon more than three years later in the Oslo Declaration.

And then, for a year, there were few further policy developments within the UN on cluster munitions although the weapon became a regular item on the UN Inter-Agency Coordination Group for Mine Action's (IACG-MA) agenda.[30] Bringing the new CCW Protocol V on ERW agreed in November 2003 into force internationally, ongoing work in the CCW on mines other than anti-personnel mines and the upcoming Review Conference of the Mine Ban Treaty in Nairobi in late 2004 were greater policy priorities. But in January 2005 the IACG-MA—a different entity from the IASC and made up of 14 UN agencies—established a working group on cluster munitions.[31] The group's job was to consider the development of a UN position on cluster munitions to be endorsed at the agency Principals' (that is, directorial) level. It was established against a background of growing awareness and concern about cluster munitions' humanitarian problems, especially given the efforts of the CMC and ICRC, which had also encouraged greater engagement among individuals from different parts of the UN such as UNDP and UNICEF. At a bureaucratic level there was also awareness in UNMAS that another body, the UN Executive Committee for Peace and Security had begun discussing cluster munitions in a series of meetings in the first half of 2005, initially led by Disarmament Affairs.

UNMAS chaired the new IACG-MA working group on cluster munitions, which included more than a dozen UN departments and agencies plus observers such as the ICRC and eventually UNIDIR.[32] Within the UN's inter-agency process, there was general agreement that cluster munitions were problematic weapons in humanitarian terms and that international action should be encouraged toward measures to reduce their hazards. The persistent problem in developing the UN's position throughout the next three-and-a-half years, however, would be over *how* this should be achieved in view of the differing priorities of the IACG-MA working group's members. These differences of approach extended to what the UN should or should not say in public in view of the fears in of some parts of the UN about the potential reactions of powerful Member States, and reluctance to adopt a position more ambitious than what the ICRC and NGOs such as Human Rights Watch were calling for at that time.

Two of the most articulate entities in the working level inter-agency process were Disarmament Affairs and UNDP. UNDP and most of the working group's members encountered cluster munitions at the operational level in the course of fulfilling their various programmes in the field. They viewed the cluster munition issue through humanitarian and developmental lenses, and saw a UN position oriented toward seeking elimination of the weapon as logical without necessarily knowing a lot about the CCW and the nature of the issues in that process. Disarmament Affairs, in contrast, while not a field agency, was the part of the UN responsible for the CCW and felt it best understood the international politics around the weapon. It did not want the UN to "exceed its mandate by suggesting a specific negotiating position on the matter of arms control and disarmament … certain Member States may not welcome the UN Secretariat meddling in the delicate negotiating matters [of the CCW] and trying to take a driver's seat" as one senior UN disarmament bureaucrat put it in a memorandum soon after the inter-agency working group began meeting. Some in Disarmament Affairs were concerned that by calling for ambitious CCW measures on cluster munitions that the process was, for political reasons, not currently capable of, the UN could hurt the CCW treaty regime. In turn, this could have broader negative consequences in what was an already challenging environment for multilateral disarmament. In other words, Disarmament Affairs' general message was: let's develop a common position by all means, but not one that rocks the boat too much.

Almost immediately, these views came into conflict in the new inter-agency process. Barber, UNMAS's Director, hoped the IACG-MA working group would be able to agree on the text of a common statement for the CCW's March 2005 meeting in Geneva. It was not to be. Barber read a joint statement on 7 March to the CCW on behalf of UNMAS, UNDP and UNICEF, but Disarmament Affairs was not a part of it. Ostensibly, this state of affairs was because Principals of the relevant parts of the UN in New York had not had an opportunity to meet to discuss it, but it also reflected the working group's differences. Even so, the joint statement was hardly overwhelmingly ambitious on cluster munitions compared with the IASC statement two years before: it merely called for "a strengthening of the international humanitarian law that currently governs their use. An additional legal instrument within the CCW framework could achieve this aim".[33] At the same meeting, UNMAS, UNDP and UNICEF proposed working definitions of cluster munitions and submunitions to try to foster progress among CCW member states, based on work they had been doing on international mine action standards terminology.[34]

Following the March CCW meeting, UNMAS began to develop a paper on *Options for a UN position on cluster munitions* intended to be a basis for further work in the lead-up to the meetings of Principals in the IACG-MA and the Executive Committee for Peace and Security in May and June 2005. The paper essentially outlined three options: the inter-agency process could adopt one of the positions of the UN agencies (such as UNMAS, UNDP and UNICEF) that had already offered a public view; second, it could call for regulations on the use, stockpiling and transfer of cluster munitions; or, third, the UN could advocate a complete ban. The *Options* paper prompted lively discussion, both at the working level and among UN Principals. The upshot at the more senior level was that the Executive Committee for Peace and Security passed the ball back to the IACG-MA and gradually dropped out of further policy debate; the IACG-MA Principals for their part could not agree on a UN policy, and concluded further work was needed at the working level before November's CCW Meeting of High Contracting Parties. The effect of the discussions at the working group level was two-fold: it further underlined the differences of perspective between Disarmament Affairs and the field agencies, and it cemented UNMAS's role in the group as broker between them. One result was that, subsequently, UNMAS would go out of its way to prevent Disarmament Affairs (or any IACG-MA member, for that matter) from becoming isolated within the IACG-MA—sometimes to the frustration of others in the working group.

One person participating in the inter-agency working group on behalf of UNDP's Bureau of Crisis Prevention and Recovery (BCPR) was Earl Turcotte. In late May 2005, Turcotte and his Mine Action Team prepared a paper for his Bureau head, Kathleen Cravero, entitled *A New Legal Instrument Banning Cluster Munitions: Rationale and Recommendations*. In addition to making the case that UNDP should call for a ban on cluster munitions, the paper argued that the UN as a whole was uniquely placed to exercise leadership on the issue and should do so. Cravero was persuaded, and she in turn sent a memo to UNDP's then-Administrator, Mark Malloch Brown, with a "BCPR recommended position" that:

> at an appropriate time, the UN encourage a dialogue among states aimed at developing a new legal instrument that: (i) bans the production, use, and transfer, of cluster munitions (ii) requires states to destroy stockpiles,

clear contaminated areas within a reasonable period of time, and meets the needs of survivors.[35]

Cravero's memo proposed that these ideas be formally introduced at November's CCW meeting, and that consultations beforehand with states and civil society commence from August.

UNDP's view was met with some scepticism among others in the UN's inter-agency process. Flanagan recalled:

> we'd say "What are you banning? You can't ban all cluster bombs. You've got to be a little more precise in what you're saying. A ban on cluster munitions as a general definition is not going to fly, and is not going to get support". So, this is where people like Earl [Turcotte] actually stood up, and UNDP, I take my hat off, they started making statements and drawing a line in the sand ... when UNMAS, we weren't prepared to go that far because we thought that pragmatically, we were not going to get any support for a complete and utter ban.[36]

The UN inter-agency process was able to agree that greater study was needed into the impacts of cluster munitions. Country case studies were commissioned from UNIDIR,[37] and later that year UNMAS and UNDP also conducted a survey of UN Mine Action Programme directors and advisers to try to gauge their perceptions of the relative dangers of different kinds of unexploded munitions including submunitions.[38] The preliminary conclusions of these field experts, presented to the CCW that November, were unequivocal:

> Cluster munitions and sub-munitions seem to pose a particular problem. They are perceived to represent medium-to-high threat to local populations even when found in low or medium quantities. There is also a strong indication of medium-to-high clearance effort or danger to operators. ... Our preliminary conclusions indicate that addressing the risk of cluster munitions—and to some extent of artillery projectiles, aircraft bombs and guided missiles—from becoming ERW seems to be more urgent than other kinds of ammunition.[39]

Nevertheless, the IACG-MA was not able to develop a common UN policy position on cluster munitions by November's CCW meeting. UNMAS delivered a statement on behalf of 11 UN agencies—but not Disarmament Affairs—encouraging the CCW to add cluster munitions to its 2006 agenda,[40] as did UN Secretary-General Kofi Annan in his message to the CCW on 25

November 2005. But the Secretary-General did not adopt the IASC's 2003 call for a freeze on the use of cluster munitions until their humanitarian problems were addressed, merely calling on "all States to respect existing, applicable humanitarian law regarding the use of cluster munitions"[41] until new measures were agreed in the CCW. The Secretary-General was not specific about what these measures could be.

At the end of 2005, Turcotte left UNDP to return to his native Canada (he would later become Canada's head of delegation to the CCW and Oslo process meetings). Turcotte's successor at UNDP, Sara Sekkenes, almost immediately encountered the problems facing her predecessor in taking forward UNDP's policy in the broader UN system. Meanwhile, by March, and along with colleagues at UNMAS such as Flanagan and its liaison officer in Geneva, Gustavo Laurie, Sekkenes was acutely aware that the Norwegian government seemed increasingly ready to launch a major international campaign to call for some sort of ban on cluster munitions. But this did not sway Disarmament Affairs in the IACG-MA, which on 18 April 2006 told a meeting of the working group on cluster munitions that the Department would not support a position recommending a legally binding instrument on the weapon. The IACG-MA working group was a technical body only and should stick to technical statements in the CCW in June, it was told. UNDP and others strongly disagreed. But, for the time being at least, Disarmament Affairs had its way.

Progress on developing a UN policy position on cluster munition issues appeared to have stalled. But then the Southern Lebanon conflict occurred in July–August 2006. This conflict was a "watershed"[42] in the UN's internal policy discussions—in not dissimilar fashion to the change that occurred in the ICRC's operational outlook at about the same time. The conflict brought issues about cluster munitions home to the UN's humanitarian sector and OCHA in particular, and the outspoken statements of its chief, Jan Egeland, gave working-level OCHA policy staff some scope to take greater initiative.[43] OCHA and UNICEF became important partners for UNDP in the IACG-MA's working group. Disarmament Affairs, too, could see which way the wind was blowing on cluster munitions, and with various proposals for a protocol negotiation in the CCW and rumours of a potential Oslo initiative circulating, it was willing to be more flexible.

One result was a more forceful message on 7 November by the outgoing UN Secretary-General to the CCW Review Conference than he had sent the previous year (see chapter 5).[44] But Egeland, also set to finish up as UN Emergency Relief Coordinator before the end of 2006 and on the ground that day in Lebanon, effectively trumped the Secretary-General's message by telling the media that "Ultimately, as long as there is no effective ban, these weapons will continue to disproportionately affect civilians, maiming and killing women, children and other vulnerable groups".[45] Egeland then reiterated the IASC's 2003 call for a freeze on cluster munition use—but without the tagline "until effective legal instruments that resolve humanitarian concerns are in place". This made it seem the same as a ban, especially in view of the media release's title, "End Use of Cluster Munitions". The same day, Max Gaylard, Barber's replacement as UNMAS Director, read a statement on behalf of the IACG-MA (now known as the UN Mine Action Team) calling for the CCW "to devise effective norms that will reduce and ultimately eliminate the horrendous humanitarian and development impact of these weapons".[46] Combined, these statements sent the world the message that the UN was actively concerned about the effects of cluster munitions on civilians, even if close examination revealed differences in what its prescriptions for the problems were.

THE OSLO PROCESS AND THE UN

After the late February 2007 Oslo conference successfully concluded, a spokesman for the new UN Secretary-General, Ban Ki-moon, offered a statement in response to the media using language provided by Disarmament Affairs' Geneva branch. The Secretary-General welcomed *all* progress to "reduce and ultimately eliminate" cluster munitions, the media were told, and he added, "Both processes have the same humanitarian objective. In these circumstances, they should not be seen as in competition with one another but as complementary and mutually reinforcing".[47]

Neither sentence necessarily bore close examination. But it helpfully enlarged the policy space within the UN and signalled that, like the ICRC, the UN was not going to claim one international process on cluster munitions was less legitimate than another if it could achieve humanitarian results. At the Oslo process's Lima conference in May, the UN Mine Action Team delivered common statements on a number of points in the discussion text. And, over the next several months, the Secretary-General's reports and statements would become steadily stronger as they related to cluster munitions: on 4 April, for instance, Ban Ki-moon said, "International outrage has driven a large group of countries to pursue a new international treaty to deal with these weapons, thus complementing and reinforcing other ongoing efforts. I applaud and encourage all endeavours to reduce, *and ultimately eliminate, the impact of cluster munitions on civilians*",[48] something he backed up in his report to the General Assembly on Assistance in Mine Action later in the year.[49] While it was not ban language, it was not too far off. And, on his behalf, OCHA tried to ensure that cluster munitions were featured in the Secretary-General's periodic statements to the national points of contact in the Security Council.

The CCW Review Conference's outcome and the emergence of the Oslo process did, however, raise some tricky prospects for the UN and for Disarmament Affairs, in particular, in view of its role supporting the CCW. What would some major states *not* supportive of restrictions or prohibitions on cluster munitions and shunning the Oslo process think of these statements emanating from the UN? Such questions prompted Disarmament Affairs and certain policymakers within UNMAS to become increasingly concerned about the potential for the UN to be perceived as facing a conflict of interest in view of the UN Secretary-General's formal role as Depositary of the CCW and its protocols.

These views were not shared by OCHA and the UN's field-based agencies on the Mine Action Team. UNDP, moreover, was by this time providing substantial logistical assistance to the Oslo process, as briefly mentioned in chapter 5. UNDP had more autonomy as an agency than the arms of the UN Secretariat, and it also had its own network of country offices around the world often possessing good networks with policymakers in the developing and cluster munition-affected countries where they were based. Sekkenes recalled:

> Since we already had programmes in most of these countries—I think we're in 17 of the 24 affected countries, if we talk about countries *per se*, beside disputed territories in which we may or may not be present with liaison functions—we already had mine action programmes running. On the ground operationally we obviously don't jump over the cluster munitions and only pick [out] landmines [for clearance] because there's a landmine treaty. We clear explosive remnants of war, in which you find anti-personnel mines and [unexploded ordnance] and cluster munitions and whatever. So we already had dialogues with governments, and we had our counterparts in governments and began

to have more targeted discussions with them in terms of their interests in addressing cluster munitions.[50]

At the conclusion of the Oslo conference, which Sekkenes and colleagues from UNDP attended, Peru's delegation approached UNDP for assistance in organizing the Lima conference to be held in May. Hosting an international conference was a daunting task for all but the largest of countries, and UNDP had obvious strengths in capacity-building, information-sharing and in starting up a sponsorship programme to enable delegates from less wealthy countries to be able to participate in the development of the cluster munition treaty it was hoped they would join. UNDP's role in assisting with the Lima conference was to provide a model for the further Oslo process meetings, all of which UNDP played an important role in by providing logistical, financial and sponsorship assistance—in many ways the sorts of services the UN was also accustomed to offering in the CCW context. One obvious difference was that the funds for these meetings were coming largely out of the pockets of Core Group states, rather than being paid for by a compulsory UN assessment. The Core Group, especially Norway, were to contribute millions of dollars in total to UNDP to fund UN sponsorship of delegates in the Oslo process and the hosting of the various conferences.

On 17 September 2007, the IACG-MA Principals met and adopted a new UN inter-agency position on cluster munitions. The ostensible rationale for the new position was to inform the Secretary-General's message to the November 2007 CCW Meeting of States Parties and other statements by UN officials in the coming months. And it reflected a realization that the ICRC's policy evolution on cluster munitions provided good company for the UN to move in the same direction. Like most UN policy adjustments preceding it, the new position was couched in previously used language, but there was no mistaking that it had taken up the call of the Oslo Declaration. Among its elements, the new position called for the conclusion of a "legally binding instrument of international humanitarian law" that "prohibits the use, development, production, stockpiling and transfer of cluster munitions *that cause unacceptable harm to civilians*" as well as stockpile destruction, clearance, risk education, victim assistance and other related activities; it added, "Until such a treaty is adopted, the UN calls on States to take domestic measures to immediately freeze the use and transfer of all cluster munitions".[51] The new position rapidly circulated among the many delegations in Oslo, commemorating the tenth anniversary of the Mine Ban

Treaty negotiations, and was welcomed as a shot in the arm for the Oslo process.

The Secretary-General's concerns about the humanitarian impacts of cluster munitions also found their way into his *Report on the Protection of Civilians in Armed Conflict* prepared by OCHA, in which he said "Concerted efforts are required to end the use of cluster munitions".[52] And, in public, UN agencies were increasingly vocal in communicating to the public the humanitarian problems with the weapon. In early November, UNDP, along with OCHA, UNICEF, the Cluster Munition Coalition and The Diana, Princess of Wales Memorial Fund, launched an international media blitz including a half-page advertisement in the *International Herald Tribune*. The ad featured images of a plastic toy truck, a teddy bear, an M-85 submunition and a plastic toy necklace with the by-line: "Spot the odd one out! Which product has NOT been recalled from the market because it can be fatal to children?" It urged "politicians and governments in all countries to freeze the use and trade of cluster bombs and negotiate an international prohibition on cluster munitions that cause unacceptable harm to civilians". While the campaign sent a powerful public message, Disarmament Affairs and UNMAS were irritated that the campaign had not been undertaken as a UN Mine Action Team exercise.

It was an example of an undercurrent of tension within the UN Mine Action Team that manifested itself in other ways, including how the CCW was characterized in the UN's public communications. Disarmament Affairs had always been concerned that the UN's support for the Oslo process must not denigrate the CCW. Démarches to the Secretary-General's office during the Oslo process from certain UN Member State missions in New York, such as from US Alternate Representative for Special Political Affairs Jackie Wolcott Sanders on 7 December to take issue with recent UN statements on cluster munitions, increased this sensitivity. Nevertheless, there was by now a widespread view within the UN's inter-agency process that the CCW was unlikely to agree on a negotiating mandate on cluster munitions in November. This view was confounded, however, when the CCW agreed on 13 November to "negotiate a proposal" on cluster munitions in 2008.

All of those involved in the UN Mine Action Team were people committed to the cluster munition issue. Most were convinced that the posture of their own particular department or agency was for sound reasons. It meant that with both work in the Oslo and CCW processes intensifying they were reluctant to compromise on a collective approach that might make the UN look less active and constructive in the Oslo process, or less impartial in the CCW. The two priorities were not impossible to reconcile, but it took some effort and made the period from around the Vienna conference until the Wellington conference a very difficult time within the UN Mine Action Team. UN Mine Action Team representatives met daily in Vienna, in what were sometimes tough discussions. UNDP, UNICEF, OCHA and others pushed for more substantive statements from the Team on topics in the Vienna text on which the UN had obvious expertise such as definitions, clearance and victim assistance. Disarmament Affairs remained cautious. UNMAS did its best to accommodate these differing views—efforts that tended to result in stalemate. In the new year, as preparations began for the UN's contribution to the Wellington conference and UNICEF said it would be prepared to send a high-level representative to make a statement on behalf of the UN, Disarmament Affairs, DPKO and UNMAS made it clear they had reservations about such a collective statement.

Matters came to a head in early February 2008. On 21 January the Secretary-General's supreme policymaking body, the Policy Committee, which he chaired and comprised the different heads of the major departments and agencies of the UN, made a significant internal decision on his behalf. In essence, the Policy Committee's decision was that the UN would advocate strengthening the implementation of existing multilateral disarmament and non-proliferation agreements (that is, the CCW) and achieving their universality, while encouraging and supporting regional and international disarmament and humanitarian initiatives—cluster munitions were specifically mentioned—that complement and reinforce such existing agreements. To the field agencies active in the UN Mine Action Team, it meant that now the Secretary-General had endorsed the Oslo process and there should be no question that joint statements of the Team in that process were permitted without further executive-level UN decisions. Saying nothing at Oslo conferences would not be acceptable because there were substantive issues in the draft convention text, such as scope and definitions, on which the UN needed to make its voice heard.

The question for Disarmament Affairs (supported by UNMAS in its role as UN Mine Action Team coordinator) was how this decision would affect the way in which the UN maintained a balance in its public support for the Oslo and CCW cluster munitions processes. Late on the afternoon of 6 February, UNMAS added an item to the agenda of the IACG-MA Principals, who were due to meet the following morning. The item added was to discuss the Policy Committee's decision. Some of the UN Mine Action Team member agencies perceived the late agenda item addition as an attempt to ambush their Principals in order to prevent the UN from playing an active role at the Wellington conference, since revising the meeting agenda at the last moment—with heads of department not necessarily familiar with the detailed aspects of a subject—is a timeless bureaucratic tactic. It can, if successful, enable a well-briefed participant to overcome working-level objections by trading on the ignorance and acquiescence of his or her less comprehensively briefed senior colleagues to slip an advantageous decision through. Whether or not this was the intention of the late agenda addition, staff from UNDP, OCHA, UNICEF and others worked through the night to ensure their senior representatives were fully briefed for the meeting. Moreover, it became clear the next morning as the meeting began that Jean-Marie Guéhenno, the head of DPKO, who was chairing the meeting, shared the views of OCHA and the field-based agencies that the UN could and should play an active role in Wellington and speak with one voice. Disarmament Affairs' preference to have any collective UN statement in Wellington cleared by the Secretary-General's office failed to carry the day. Moreover, the Principals agreed on the text of the draft speech to be delivered by UNICEF's Deputy Executive Director Hilde Frafjord Johnson, rather than kicking it upstairs along the long and circuitous route to the Secretary-General's Office and back again.

Just as the period around the Wellington conference had represented the crunch point for states in the Oslo process, it had also been a most difficult period for the UN's inter-agency process on cluster munitions. In Wellington, the dynamic within the UN Mine Action Team would be markedly improved, helped by Flanagan's greater role in chairing it (he was now acting UNMAS Director) and the high level of trust he and others with operational experience such as Sekkenes shared. After Wellington, the UN inter-agency process would do everything it could to support a successful outcome in Dublin in addition to its continued roles in CCW work, and issues of perceived imbalance involved in supporting two international processes faded away. Although differences in perspective within the Mine Action Team would naturally persist, the members of the Team would work together to achieve the result the Secretary-General had now repeatedly called for—a treaty banning cluster munitions that cause unacceptable harm to civilians.

Within the ranks of both the ICRC and the UN, after the Oslo conference in February 2007 the Oslo process was widely considered more likely to achieve the humanitarian goals they supported on cluster munitions due to their organizations' field experiences. An abiding issue for both international organizations created by the emergence of two multilateral processes on cluster munitions, however, concerned how to balance their commitment to the CCW, a UN-administered process, with the free-standing Oslo initiative. In many respects, this mirrored the dilemma for many governments in considering political ends and means with respect to tackling the weapon. As for the majority of states participating in the Oslo process by Dublin, focus on the human impact, combined with growing awareness of the effects of cluster munitions based on knowledge from the field, were crucial. As the Dublin conference approached, it was soon time to see whether such concerns would be sufficient to deliver a humanitarian treaty.

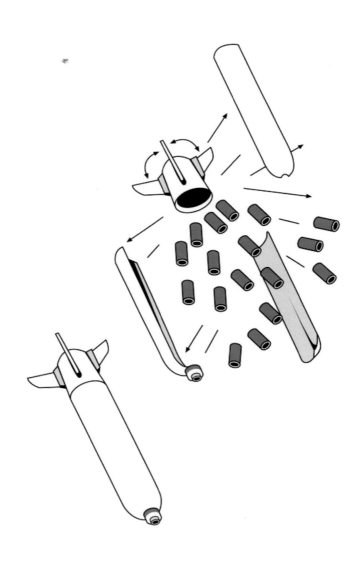

This diagram shows initial release and dispersal of explosive submunitions from an air-delivered cluster munition. (Illustration courtesy of Norwegian People's Aid)

Vietnamese deminers in Gio Linh district of Quang Tri province dig up BLU-63 cluster submunitions in March 2008 that were dropped during the South-East Asia war. A communal theatre and a sports ground were later built on top of where these unexploded submunitions lay. (©www.werneranderson.no)

..over 800 un-exploded sub-munitions in this street.....
(M85 w/o SD and M42/M46)

Entrance to Tibnin Hospital

Total of 10 UX M85 w/o SD's in this circle..same delivery 10/63..15% failure

Slide from a presentation to the ICRC Meeting of Experts in Montreux in April 2007 by the UN Mine Action Coordination Centre South Lebanon's Director, Chris Clark. The slide shows unexploded submunitions on the street in the Southern Lebanese town of Tibnan. (Chris Clark, UN Mine Action Centre South Lebanon)

An unexploded submunition found on concrete in the village of Bayt Yahoun immediately after the end of the 2006 conflict in Southern Lebanon. A pair of sunglasses next to the Israeli submunition gives a sense of scale. (UN Mine Action Centre South Lebanon)

Explosive ordnance personnel found this unexploded M-42 submunition in an olive grove in the Southern Lebanese village of Tulin in early October 2008 and marked it for destruction in situ. This image shows how difficult it can be to see failed submunitions due to their size and colour. (John Borrie)

Close-up of an unexploded M-42 submunition fired by Israeli forces during the July–August 2006 conflict between Israel and Hizbollah. More than two years later, this and other dud M-42s were found in a hillside olive grove in the village of Tulin close to a residential neighbourhood (see also previous image). (John Borrie)

SPOT THE ODD ONE OUT!

Which product has NOT been recalled from the market because it can be fatal to children?

Each of these items has design flaws that could be fatal to children. Three have been recalled from the market. One hasn't — the cluster bomb.

In scores of conflicts over the past 60 years, cluster bombs have failed to function as intended, leaving behind millions of unexploded bomblets that may explode when accidentally disturbed. All too often, it's a child's curious hand that sets off these deadly bomblets. Children are especially at risk of being maimed or

killed by these bomblets as they are easily attracted by their toy-like size and shape. In Kosovo and Cambodia for example the majority of casualties have been children rather than adults.

Despite this, there are no specific international restrictions on the use, production and trade of cluster bombs.

More than 70 countries have cluster bombs containing several billion unreliable bomblets. If their proliferation and use continues, the result will be

tens of millions of unexploded bomblets and a humanitarian crisis even worse than the plague caused by landmines.

We urge politicians and governments in all countries to freeze the use and trade of cluster bombs and negotiate an international prohibition on cluster munitions that cause unacceptable harm to civilians.

The Cluster Munition Coalition (CMC) is a network of around 200 civil society organisations, including NGOs, faith-based groups and professional organisations. It includes among others Handicap International, Human Rights Watch, the International Campaign to Ban Landmines, Landmine Action and Norwegian People's Aid. Join the CMC in campaigning for a ban on cluster bombs. For more information: www.stopclusterbombs.org

In November 2007, civil society organizations and UN agencies joined forces to launch global actions in order to raise awareness about the impacts of cluster munitions on civilians. This advertisement, "Spot the odd one out!", ran in a number of major newspapers including the International Herald Tribune. (Image courtesy of Cluster Munition Coalition and UNDP)

Almost everyone in villages along the Ho Chi Minh Trail in Laos lives completely or partly from the scrap metal trade, some of it scavenged from unexploded ordnance like cluster munitions from US bombing more than 30 years before. Most of the scrap collectors are young boys. Their most important tools are metal detectors. (©www.werneranderson.no, 8 March 2008)

Handicap International Ban Advocates compare notes during their lobbying of negotiators on key issues in the draft treaty text on the margins of the Dublin negotiations in May 2008. (Mary Wareham)

The UN Secretary-General, Ban Ki-moon, addresses the Dublin Diplomatic Conference on Cluster Munitions via a video message on 30 May 2008 welcoming the new treaty. (©www.werneranderson.no)

Grethe Østern (Norwegian People's Aid, and Cluster Munition Coalition Co-Chair) congratulates Irish Foreign Minister Micheál Martin at the closing ceremony of the Dublin Diplomatic Conference on 30 May 2008. (©www.werneranderson.no)

Delegates applaud at the conclusion of the Dublin Diplomatic Conference on 30 May 2008. (©www.werneranderson.no)

Cluster Munition Coalition spokesperson and Ban Advocate Branislav Kapetanović (left) addressed the Convention on Cluster Munitions Signing Ceremony in Oslo on 3 December 2008, as did Thomas Nash, the Coalition's coordinator (right). (John Borrie)

Three of the prime movers within the Norwegian government for a humanitarian treaty on cluster munitions: senior diplomat Steffen Kongstad (left), Foreign Minister Jonas Gahr Store (centre), and State Secretary of Defence Espen Barth Eide (right). (John Borrie)

Norwegian Foreign Minister Jonas Gahr Støre greets Afghan cluster munition survivor and Ban Advocate Soraj Ghulam Habib at the Convention on Cluster Munitions Signing Ceremony in Oslo, Norway, on 3 December 2008. (Federico Visi/Cluster Munition Coalition)

The work to clear submunitions and other unexploded ordnance continues. Pictured are members of a Norwegian People's Aid battle area clearance team taking a brief break from clearing a farmer's field of M-42 submunitions near the village of Safeed Al Battikh in Southern Lebanon in October 2008. (John Borrie)

CHAPTER 9

DUBLIN: DEFINE AND CONQUER

After the travails and ultimate success of the Wellington conference, appetite abated for work on the Convention on Certain Conventional Weapons (CCW) experts' heavily square-bracketed draft working definition in their next meeting in Geneva in mid-April 2008. Perhaps its allure had faded for its proponents after the draft working definition failed to make a significant impact on the work related to article 2 in Wellington, and there were signs of support from certain Core Group countries, especially Norway, for exclusion of weapons like the SMArt 155 and BONUS systems from the definition. The week of CCW talks focused instead on topics such as seeking to clarify existing international humanitarian law provisions on cluster munition use. Moreover, it was now obvious even to the Like-minded that the CCW's prospects for addressing cluster munitions were, at best, uncertain: the positions of China, Russia and others shunning the Oslo process proved no more amenable than they had been earlier toward humanitarian provisions approaching the ambition of those in the Wellington draft convention text. And the United States told the other CCW parties at the April meeting that it needed more time to complete an internal review of its policies on cluster munitions in Washington.[1] Taken together, these factors did not exactly lend momentum to the CCW negotiations, especially as all eyes were on the Oslo process endgame and what that would or would not deliver.

The April CCW expert meeting did prove to be useful additional preparation for the Dublin diplomatic conference. It was generally realized among governments participating in the Oslo process, as well as the Steering Committee of the Cluster Munition Coalition (CMC), that a continuation of the polarized dynamic in Wellington would be unhelpful for Dublin's prospects—it would not help anyone get what they wanted in a negotiated text. Tempers from Wellington having cooled off a bit, the April CCW meeting's margins provided opportunity for some dialogue and attempts at reconciliation. This was helped by the fact that almost as soon as the Wellington conference had finished, Core Group states—especially Ireland—had begun intensive diplomatic efforts to prepare the way for the

Dublin diplomatic conference, and allay any concerns that it would be anything other than a full negotiation, one in which all concerns about the draft convention text would be addressed.

One of the concerns raised by some of the Like-minded about how the Dublin negotiations would be managed concerned the roles civil society would play there. The British, Danes and Germans, in particular, had complained to the Core Group during the Wellington conference that the Oslo process had become an NGO-led circus—a contention the Core Group's members strongly disputed.[2] Knowing full well that the positions they took in Dublin would be subject to intense media scrutiny, the Like-minded were concerned they would be placed in impossible situations if they had to contend with clapping or jeers in the conference chamber, or could not have their views heard and taken up, however unpopular those views might be. At the same time, none among the Like-minded wanted to be seen calling in public for civil society access to be curtailed: it would make them look like they were trying to evade public scrutiny and arguably put them at odds with their commitment to the Oslo Declaration's partnership between governments and civil society.

Dutifully listening to these concerns was the man designated by the Irish government to chair the Dublin negotiations, Ambassador Dáithí O'Ceallaigh. At first glance, O'Ceallaigh might have seemed an odd choice for the role. He was not a multilateral specialist, let alone an arms control or humanitarian diplomat by background. Instead, O'Ceallaigh had spent much of his career working on the peace process in Northern Ireland. He had only recently arrived in Geneva to take up the post as Ireland's Permanent Representative to the United Nations, and had not participated in the Oslo process before the Vienna conference. Nevertheless, if O'Ceallaigh lacked institutional knowledge of the cluster munition issue his status as a relative newcomer also helpfully differentiated him from his senior Core Group colleagues in the Oslo process in the eyes of many of the Like-minded. And because he had deep and extensive contacts in the British establishment due to the peace process and his recent posting to London as ambassador, the Irish felt O'Ceallaigh understood better than most what it would take to bring the British and the other Europeans onboard a treaty in Dublin. His peace process work had certainly shown his skill as a negotiator, and another great strength was, as one of his diplomatic colleagues described it, "he just has a way that makes people like and want to trust the guy".

O'Ceallaigh's talents were to be exercized both in Dublin and in consultations with a wide spectrum of delegations leading up to it, including with the Like-minded. These contacts were both bilateral and, in at least one meeting, between the Irish and the Like-minded, hosted in Geneva by France's disarmament ambassador, Jean-François Dobelle, in which O'Ceallaigh did his best to show that the messages from all of those with whom he was consulting were being understood by the Irish. O'Ceallaigh recalled:

> it was messages like that which were very important to us. We recorded them very carefully and we did a lot of work in Dublin by building a dossier article-by-article about what people's different views were on the different articles. So we had a reasonable view going in about where we were.

> I also think that people like John Duncan, Jean-François Dobelle, I think they realized that we were actually being open and genuine. They negotiated within those parameters, and that's how we got to it [the treaty].[3]

Aspects of France's role over the course of the Oslo process are still to be deciphered, but its contribution to eventual success in Dublin should not be underestimated. As the nominal coordinator and spokesperson for the Like-minded, the sonorously voiced Dobelle often took a firm line in his occasional statements on their behalf, especially in Vienna and Wellington. However, in behind-the-scenes consultations with the Core Group, Dobelle and his delegation were more conciliatory. France's government had recently changed, and Dobelle's incoming Foreign Minister, the humanitarian Bernard Kouchner, had publicly proclaimed France's commitment to the Oslo process.[4] And, many French officials saw the writing on the wall for most cluster munitions. As a country standing apart from NATO in terms of its strategic doctrine and having suffered the effects of unexploded ordnance in two world wars, the French military had never viewed cluster munitions as possessing the versatility that some of the other Europeans felt the weapon had. Senior French officials had asked the defence ministry to conduct an internal review during 2007 on France's stockpile of cluster munitions to ascertain which were really needed. According to a French official I spoke with, this review, apparently completed soon before the Wellington conference, concluded that most of France's arsenal of cluster munitions was of limited use. Substitute capabilities not posing the same humanitarian risks as cluster munitions, such as the BONUS sensor-fuzed system, could at least partly fill the capability gap if cluster munitions were taken out of service, the review concluded. Thus informed, France's diplomats and defence officials would be constructive in building bridges between the Like-minded and the Core Group throughout the first half of 2008.

Moreover, solidarity with the other Like-minded aside, France had further specific interests to secure in Dublin. The French saw an opportunity arising in the Wellington conference, for instance, to begin a bilateral dialogue with the Norwegian government that might help in the context of meeting their concerns on the definition in the draft convention text. The specific catalyst was a presentation at the Wellington conference by Norwegian defence scientist, Ove Dullum, summarizing a report he was writing that examined the military utility of cluster munitions.[5] Due to his M-85 testing-related work, Dullum had for some time been mulling over the idea of the concept of a weight criterion to simplify the draft cluster munition definition and avoid loopholes that would undermine its humanitarian intent, while ensuring weapon systems not causing such humanitarian problems could still be used.[6] Dullum mentioned the idea in his Wellington conference presentation, and it dawned on the French military advisors present that it might help them with the conundrum of how to retain their APACHE runway-attack munition system, which would otherwise have fallen within the definition of a cluster munition shaping up in the Oslo process.[7] And the French knew that, like themselves, the Norwegians were concerned to ensure that munitions with sensor fuzing like the French-Swedish BONUS round were not banned. So, French defence officials began a tentative dialogue with Norwegian experts (including NGOs like Norwegian People's Aid), which would later broaden to include diplomatic and political policymakers, and entail meetings in Paris involving the French and Norwegian governments. It was the sort of back-channel small-group work that contributed enormously to trust.

There was plenty of other activity in support of the Oslo process in the final months leading up to the Dublin conference. Forty African states signed up to the Livingstone Declaration agreed in Zambia on 1 April in support of the Oslo Declaration and a humanitarian treaty banning—on an immediate basis—cluster munitions.[8] Mexico hosted a conference of 22 Latin American and Caribbean states in Mexico City on 16–17 April. On 23–24 April, the International Committee of the Red Cross (ICRC) convened a workshop of around 10 Association of Southeast Asian Nations states in Bangkok to engage them on cluster munition issues, which served to drum up Asian attendance for the Dublin negotiations. And a Global Day of Action on 19 April coordinated by the CMC in more than 50 countries placed the hazards posed to civilians from cluster munitions in the public eye. The Global Day of Action also underlined civil society's herculean advocacy efforts during this period, which included a massive push to get as many states as possible to adhere to the Wellington Declaration and participate in the Dublin negotiations.

States outside the Oslo process were not sitting on their hands either. It was generally known in the CCW and Oslo circles that the United States was talking bilaterally to government authorities in many countries—not only its military allies—about its concerns over a new humanitarian treaty to which it would not be a party. Interoperability was the chief issue. In late April, US State Department official Richard Kidd publicly warned: "cooperation within NATO is in the crosshairs of the Oslo treaty". And, in what seemed a direct attempt to discredit the Oslo process, he claimed, "NGOs were allowed to heckle state delegations in plenary and surrounding venues, using funds provided by one state participant [Norway, presumably] to attack the positions of other state participants. Is this the kind of international system that any administration wants to work in?"[9] Since neither Kidd nor US diplomats had participated in the Wellington conference, it can be assumed that these remarks were based on reports passed to the US from among the Like-minded. At the same time, there were no indications that the Like-minded would shy away from participating in the Dublin conference. Indeed, in the absence of US participation, it was obvious that on issues like interoperability, close allies of Washington would try to ensure that its concerns were met in the final negotiated text.

STATE OF PLAY

Before outlining how the diplomatic conference in Dublin unfolded, it is worth looking at the state of the draft convention text, and the postures of significant groupings within the Oslo process as the negotiations were poised to begin.

THE DRAFT CONVENTION TEXT

The draft convention text introduced after the Vienna conference in December, and which would carry through to the outset of the Dublin negotiations more than six months later, was just over 14 typewritten pages long. The document contained a preamble section and 22 operative articles. The final Convention on Cluster Munitions agreed on 30 May would be four pages longer and contain an additional article, article 21 on "Relations with States not party to this Convention", which constituted the Oslo process's solution to the interoperability problem. However, arriving at the four paragraphs of article 21 was so controversial it would become the focus of the negotiation's endgame, events set out in chapter 10.

Crude comparison between the length and structure of the Wellington text and the treaty agreed in Dublin, of course, does not convey much of substance of the negotiations on the draft convention's content. However, with the ground prepared earlier in Wellington and before, many of the treaty's provisions could likely be agreed relatively easily, the Irish thought. In certain other parts of the draft convention, agreement on inclusion, modification or deletion of provisions would be contingent upon agreement in other parts, thus reflecting the saying in multilateral negotiations that "nothing's agreed until everything's agreed". For instance, the general scope provision (article 1) was associated with the problem of interoperability, and it was not until this was resolved through the new article 21 inserted during the Dublin negotiation (and which served to clarify the nature of the prohibition in article 1) that article 1 could be finalized. Moreover, apart from article 21, most of the later articles of the draft convention text—from article 10 upwards—were standard legal language. However, the number of states inserted into the numerical requirement field for international entry into force of the treaty (ultimately set at 30)[10] in article 17, for instance, could likely only be agreed late after delegations had the opportunity to see the President's proposal for a treaty in the round. Completing the negotiation of the cluster munition treaty would be a puzzle that required not only finding the pieces that fit together, but also ensuring they were put together in the right order.

Starting at the beginning, the draft convention text's preamble was long at nearly two pages, and would become a half page longer in the course of the Dublin meeting. Then, immediately afterward in the text there were the toughest drafting issues for the negotiation. One issue concerned article 1 on general scope, linked as it was to interoperability, and because of the need to ensure the treaty did not leave a loophole for explosive bomblets dispersed from aircraft dispensers. Then there were the definitions in article 2 to be settled, particularly exclusions (or clarifications) for certain weapons with submunitions that might be permitted in paragraph 2(c). Transition periods were another big issue, one to a large extent depending on what the definition of a cluster munition would cover—and what would therefore be banned—and to some extent dependent on how article 1 would finally look.

Interoperability and the cluster munition definition were the issues that would take the most time and effort to solve in Dublin and over which the fate of the negotiation would hinge. But there were several other significant outstanding issues to be settled. The initial foundation for textual work, the Lima discussion text in May 2007, had largely been based on the Mine Ban Treaty. But after a decade of experience in implementation of the latter there were improvements that could be made, and International Campaign to Ban Landmines staff such as Tamar Gabelnick played an important role in identifying and lending thought as to how these could be reflected in a cluster munition treaty. Some other issues familiar to the Mine Ban Treaty also reared their heads: timelines for stockpile destruction (article 3) and clearance (article 4) would have to balance the desires of those wanting the most time possible for practical and financial reasons with the humanitarian imperative of the Oslo Declaration to protect civilians. Some states, especially among the Like-minded, wanted to retain some submunitions they said would be for training explosive ordnance disposal personnel, and for devising counter-measures. While this sounded reasonable in principle, a similar provision in the Mine Ban Treaty had seen some states, like Japan, retain tens of thousands of the banned weapons, which the International Campaign to Ban Landmines and some Mine Ban Treaty states parties argued was against that treaty's spirit, and a situation that should absolutely be avoided on cluster munitions. And there were some experts, like Rae McGrath from Handicap International, who said that it made no sense to retain submunitions for training under any circumstances. Moreover, as we shall see, there were concerns about the strength of the retroactivity of the draft treaty's provisions, particularly for clearance (article 4), which would pit countries such as France, the Netherlands and the UK against affected countries such as Lebanon over particular wording.

Even article 5 on victim assistance, about which so many states fundamentally agreed, would not be trouble-free. Negotiated in light of the 2006 Convention on the Rights of Persons with Disabilities and a decade of Mine Ban Treaty implementation, this draft article contained recognition that victim assistance "is not only about medical treatment or rehabilitation, but is in fact an issue of human rights".[11] However, the Holy See was opposed to mentioning the Disabilities Convention, even in the cluster munition treaty preamble because of its provisions about reproductive rights.[12] And, until Dublin, states that had used cluster munitions such as France, Germany and the UK had liability-related concerns about the breadth of the definition of cluster munition victims because it included affected families and communities in addition to "those persons directly impacted by cluster munitions".[13]

Thanks to Markus Reiterer's steady hand as Friend of the President on article 5, input from member NGOs of the Cluster Munition Coalition such as Survivor Corps and Handicap International, and daily lobbying of hesitant delegations by the CMC, including Ban Advocates, these challenges were to be overcome. Indeed, one of the most memorable sights of the Dublin conference was a formation of cluster munition and landmine survivors in wheelchairs or on crutches energetically rounding up European ambassadors for dialogue on victim assistance and other articles. At the beginning of the Oslo process, there were signs that some government delegations saw meetings with the Ban Advocates as merely tokenistic (or even inappropriate), but the dialogue that developed between them over time eventually had a major impact on a range of issues, especially as survivors like Branislav Kapetanović became integrated into the CMC's negotiating team.[14]

Beyond article 5, there were also some modifications to be negotiated to the articles on international cooperation and assistance (article 6), transparency measures (article 7), facilitations and clarification of compliance (article 8) and national implementation measures (article 9).

LIKE-MINDED GROUPINGS

Managing the Dublin diplomatic conference was to be primarily an Irish show rather than a Core Group one. The Irish drew from among Core Group colleagues for help in coordinating key issues, but the President also turned to the Like-minded and those with Tee-total views for Vice Presidents and Friends of the President. This was logical in view of the need for representativeness, and there appears to have been no resentment or surprise about it among the Core Group, since it had always maintained— even in the face of Like-minded scepticism—that its stewardship of the draft treaty text would end at the Wellington conference's conclusion.

But it also meant that, although it continued on occasion to meet and consult on the margins in Dublin, the Core Group would be less of a force there. Increasingly, Core Group states would fight for their own national prerogatives and some, such as Austria and Mexico, would become important voices among the Tee-total states.

At first sceptical of O'Ceallaigh's reassurances, it was natural for the Like-minded to keep their guard up and to try to orchestrate a genuinely coordinated approach to the treaty negotiations that had always eluded them before. However, as a predominantly reactionary grouping dissatisfied with issues of process and procedure, the raison d'être of the Like-minded began to dissipate in the lead up to Dublin even as the 15 or so delegations continued to meet among themselves. The fact was that not all of the Like-minded had cluster munitions—Australia did not, for instance—and of those which did, these systems varied significantly in age, sophistication and likely acceptability, which meant making common cause was difficult. And while interoperability was of paramount concern to some, it caused less anxiety for states such as Finland, Sweden and Switzerland not part of a military alliance. Solidarity would carry only so far, and as France's bilateral dialogue with Norway mentioned earlier illustrated, those in the Like-minded knew it.

As is clear from the story until now, throughout much of the Oslo process the Like-minded had focused on the Core Group as the main obstacle to its influence over the development of a draft cluster munition ban treaty. Only belatedly did the Like-minded appear to recognize that the biggest counter-weight to their aspirations was actually not a coherent group at all. Instead, it was the Tee-total states. "Tee-total" is a loose description for a very large and amorphous movement within the Oslo process made up mainly of developing and affected countries that instinctively or on principle opposed the views of the Like-minded on exclusions to the definition for any explosive submunitions, transition periods or, by Dublin, even interoperability provisions. Numerically, the African states (with a few exceptions like Egypt and Morocco) were the largest bloc. But among developing countries in general, to be Tee-total was effectively the default position unless a country was a cluster munition possessor: most Latin American, Caribbean states and Pacific Island states, and others among the Asians (notably Laos, the Philippines and Indonesia) and the Middle East were associated with the Tee-total. In Vienna and, most of all, in Wellington, a number of the Tee-total states expanded and refined their rhetoric with the extensive help of the CMC, which provided them briefings, position papers and other materials on which to represent alternative views on the draft convention text aimed at keeping the bar high in humanitarian terms.[15]

Until Wellington, the Like-minded had tended to dismiss those with Tee-total views as lacking expertise or political equity in a treaty negotiation on a weapon that few of the Tee-total had. But many other actors in the Oslo process saw the views of those states as a source of negotiating equity just as important as perceived status as a user or stockpiler of cluster munitions—some of them, like Laos and Lebanon, were living with the effects of the weapon at first hand, after all. Many other states had suffered from the widespread use of landmines and those located in areas prone to conflict, in particular, wanted to prevent such a problem from happening in the future with unexploded submunitions. Who was to say, therefore, that affected countries and their supporters were not legitimate stakeholders? In Wellington, some of the more active among the broad spectrum of states inclined toward Tee-total views had emerged as the Friends of the Affected to counter what they saw as Like-minded attempts to hijack the draft convention text and downgrade their concerns. Though the Friends of the Affected would have liked to meet in order to coordinate positions in the run-up to Dublin, many of their delegations were capital- rather than Geneva-based, and lacked the financial resources to do so. It meant that the Friends of the Affected would be not be a particular force in Dublin, although key members such as Lebanon, Zambia and Costa Rica maintained what one diplomat described as a "friendly ambience"[16] of mutual trust that was useful in supporting each others' positions on the conference floor.

In sum, with the actual textual negotiations on a cluster munition ban treaty approaching, most states engaged in the Oslo process appear to have regarded their work as entering a new phase, with a need for greater focus on securing their national prerogatives in the outcome. The Like-minded and other affiliations did not dissolve completely, but these bonds had loosened considerably by 19 May when the Dublin conference commenced. Whether that loosening was enough to enable the compromise necessary for a negotiating outcome consistent with the Oslo Declaration was a question that remained to be answered. Meanwhile, two blocs with force in Dublin, however, were the Latin American states coordinated by Mexico, and the African states coordinated by Zambia. They had become strongly bound together in the course of the Oslo process and immediately prior to Dublin through the Livingstone and Mexico City regional conferences. In Dublin, they would each hold frequent regional coordination meetings.

The Cluster Munition Coalition in Dublin

As Dublin approached, CMC campaigners in dozens of countries focused on getting governments to endorse the Wellington Declaration and register to participate in the diplomatic conference as well as mastering the arguments on key issues such as victim assistance, definitions, interoperability and transition periods. In particular, the CMC focused on those states it felt it could influence, and which had what were, in its leadership's view, positive positions on key issues in the draft convention text, for instance on definitions or opposition to transition periods. Nash recalled:

> By persuading them to be active and giving them the arguments necessary to win the day in Dublin, we thought we could influence the outcome more than by focusing energy on trying to change positions of problem European states who were only likely to change their positions once in Dublin because of pressure in the negotiations and in the media.[17]

The CMC's central team, meanwhile, continued to build up a sophisticated media campaign in order to try to focus public interest on the Oslo process, and to put banning cluster munitions because of their harm to civilians on the agendas of political decision makers. As part of this, on 19 April, the CMC launched a Global Day of Action to Ban Cluster Bombs,[18] and campaigners lobbied politicians, bureaucrats and faith leaders with the rallying cry, "Support a strong and comprehensive treaty, with NO exceptions, NO delays and NO loopholes".[19] Following the Wellington conference, the CMC also installed a young campaigner, Susan Hensel, in Dublin. Hensel had the daunting task of preparing the ground for the civil society contingent—hundreds of people strong and from all parts of the globe—due to descend on Dublin from the middle of May. Hensel's brief also included working with local NGOs, such as Pax Christi Ireland, an early supporter of international efforts on cluster munitions, to put a strong face on Ireland's cluster munition ban campaign. The CMC's executive team saw this as crucial, as their goal was to have cluster munition-related stories in the Irish press every day of the conference: this would help to engage the international media, and the CMC wanted the conference delegates opening their newspapers over the breakfast table each morning to feel that the public eye was on their efforts.

Natalie Curtis and her team put great effort into thinking through how the CMC could make it as easy and compelling as possible for the international news media to follow the cluster munition treaty negotiations, especially to receive the messages the CMC wanted them to relay. February's Wellington conference, 12 time zones ahead of Europe and at least 18 ahead of North America, had taught the CMC to leave nothing to chance. The media team knew, for instance, that international press interest would peak at the beginning of the conference on 19 May and at its close by 30 May. As Curtis later reported:

> A key challenge was to sustain and create media interest for the two weeks between the start and the end. This was achieved by becoming a regular and credible source of up-to-date information and comment on the negotiations and related issues; by responding quickly to "breaking news" and events; and by creating campaign news stories. The images of the survivors proved invaluable in humanizing and providing a recognizable image to the campaign.[20]

With the help of The Diana, Princess of Wales Memorial Fund, the CMC sought out prominent Irish civil society voices to promote the issue and to help them engage with the media community in Ireland itself, with Amnesty International Ireland director Colm O'Gorman lending weight and advice to the campaign. The CMC also hired an Irish public relations company to help with this work and to advise on a targeted public advertising campaign based on visual art by Ben Branagan.[21] Moreover, the CMC established a satellite link and made arrangements to provide broadcast-quality footage of various kinds for news organizations based in others parts of the globe to use during the conference. Wellington had also taught another useful lesson: that spokespeople for the CMC were needed in a wide range of languages for media interviews, usually at very short notice. The campaign's media team therefore drew up a list of spokespeople and provided them all with mobile phones to ensure they were contactable at any time of the day or night to put the CMC's views across to the media, based on policy papers and lobbying guides the campaign had developed. Preparations even extended to new media, with the CMC posting regular videos on popular websites like YouTube. None of this was cheap, but the CMC's Steering Committee knew that now was do-or-die for civil society to give the biggest possible push toward a cluster munition ban treaty.

Another concern among the CMC's leadership was to ensure that the CMC's many campaigners were used to best effect, and kept busy at all times. If the Wellington conference offered a guide, the Dublin negotiations would be a stressful rollercoaster, and Nash and his Steering Committee co-chairs Conway, Goose and Østern wanted to avoid a dynamic in which anxiety about the conference's outcome among campaigners undermined well-coordinated CMC pressure on governments for a categorical ban on cluster munitions, especially as the Irish informed the CMC that they would only be able to have four speaking representatives in the negotiation room at any one time. As outlined in chapter 7, Landmine Action's Director, Simon Conway, stepped into the role of "team leader" following Wellington, and he approached the organization of the campaign's schedule of activities in Dublin as a military man would—with a carefully outlined hierarchy of responsibilities[22] and a relentless programme of events, public demonstrations, campaigning briefings and meetings from morning to night.[23] The programme proved exhausting for campaigners (which was, in part, the purpose), but more importantly it helped to create the impression among conference delegates that the CMC was a frenetic civil society juggernaut. CMC representatives were ubiquitous in the halls and on the streets, many of them in their distinctive orange and black "cluster bombs can be banned" and "make it happen" T-shirts, jackets and badges.

The CMC's leadership also carefully divided up responsibilities for individual parts of the negotiation. Thematic facilitators were appointed to be "responsible for helping campaigners to identify both problematic and supportive governments on the different issues for regional groups to follow up with in their lobbying work" and, where necessary, to provide "additional information or clarification and helping to find materials to back up our arguments".[24] Goose, for instance, became facilitator on general obligations and scope of the treaty (an issue that encompassed interoperability), Moyes became responsible for definitions, and the US academic Ken Rutherford (himself a landmine survivor) took on victim assistance issues. These were important roles that entailed those people attending as the CMC's representatives in negotiations on the relevant articles in the diplomatic conference. The CMC, as an observer to the negotiation, however, would have little influence unless the arguments it made in the conference room were hooked up to an effective lobbying machine. So regional campaign group facilitator positions for Africa, francophone Africa, the Commonwealth of Independent States, Europe, Latin America and the Caribbean, the Middle East and North Africa, the Pacific, South Asia and South-East Asia were also established. The CMC would convene daily morning briefings to report back on and coordinate its lobbying, as well as evening strategy meetings of all of its facilitators and its global campaign team that included Nash and the co-chairs, in order to "give an overview of the day's negotiations and the campaign's main message for media and campaigning".[25]

CIVIL SOCIETY CAMPAIGNING AND UK POLICY

There were signs too that some states were feeling significant domestic political pressure to promote a successful outcome in Dublin, in good part because of the lobbying efforts of the CMC and its members. The UK, as a prominent past user and current possessor of cluster munitions, a NATO member and close ally of the US, was an important CMC lobbying target. Both the Core Group and the CMC had reached similar conclusions about Britain—that while not necessarily crucial to a successful Dublin outcome, it was an important state to bring on board since that would ease the way for many others, especially among the Like-minded. It is important to note that the UK was by no means the only delegation at the Dublin conference facing difficult decisions about whether it could support the likely outcome of the negotiation, and tensions between its defence and broader political establishments. Japan's policy process, for instance, is a story that hopefully will eventually be told. But for the reasons above, the UK receives special attention in this chapter and in the one that follows.

Over a number of years, the CMC and British NGOs like Landmine Action, Oxfam GB, Amnesty UK, No More Landmines and The Diana, Princess of Wales Memorial Fund had built up a formidable lobbying machine aimed at influencing British government policymakers and the media. The UK government's claims to international leadership in the arms control arena were a powerful point of leverage. Oxfam, for example, had become involved in cluster munitions because of humanitarian concerns about the weapon, but also because it felt the British government's posture in the Oslo process could undermine the UK's credibility as a leader on the Arms Trade Treaty campaign, on which Oxfam, Amnesty International and other British NGOs were working closely with the government.[26] In public, the British government claimed that it was playing "a leading role on the international stage"[27] on cluster munitions, and in November 2007 Prime Minister Gordon Brown said in a major policy speech that the UK's aim was to ban those that cause unacceptable harm to civilians.[28] But the UK's approach in the Oslo process conferences sometimes seemed at odds with the political rhetoric in the view of NGO representatives. Campaigners including Conway, Moyes, Nash, Rappert and Oxfam GB's Anna Macdonald felt the British government should be held accountable for its leadership claims, and be consistent in its approach to the Arms Trade Treaty and the Oslo initiative.[29]

Working together on the cluster munition issue, British NGOs and the CMC cultivated good relationships with British parliamentarians across the political spectrum in both the Houses of Commons and Lords, through the longstanding relationships built up by Landmine Action's Portia Stratton from 2005 onwards. Their friends and allies included Roger Berry, a Labour Member of Parliament and chair of an influential committee, former Minister Lord Rodney Elton (Conservative), well-known and active peer Lord Alfred Dubs (Labour), former general Lord Ramsbotham (Independent), Labour Member of Parliament Frank Cook who had been active on landmines and cluster munitions, and former British Ambassador to the United Nations in New York Lord Hannay. With NGO help, some of these politicians would even turn up at Oslo process conferences to see for themselves what the UK delegation was saying and doing. And, as the Oslo process developed, Landmine Action and Oxfam GB, in particular, entered into frequent dialogue with both working-level policy staff at the Foreign Office, Ministry of Defence and Department for International Development and special political advisors in the offices of the Labour government Ministers of these departments, as well as the Prime Minister's office.

Alongside a group of British parliamentarians,[30] Landmine Action and Oxfam GB representatives got the chance to lobby Ministers personally on 30 January 2008 in a breakfast meeting at Foreign Minister David Miliband's office, which Ministers Des Browne (Defence) and Douglas Alexander (Department for International Development) also attended. Browne, in particular, took a defensive line on the need for the British military to retain the use of its M-85 submunitions. However, it also became obvious over breakfast that the UK government wanted to be part of the eventual cluster munition ban treaty, despite its tough diplomatic rhetoric. The meeting also confirmed the persistence of the UK government concerns about interoperability, as well as on definitions. (Transition periods were also mentioned, and later the question of what to do about US stocks of cluster munitions on British military bases also became a headache for British policymakers.) The meeting encouraged British NGOs to lobby their government hard in the months leading up to Dublin, including by providing their own detailed policy notes to decision makers. However, even by the middle of May 2008, it was not clear what line the UK would take in the Dublin negotiations on its stockpiles of the M-73 and M-85.[31]

Shortly before the Dublin conference, Landmine Action and its NGO partners commissioned an independent opinion poll asking nearly 2,000 British adults around the country about cluster munitions.[32] Among the results, nearly 80% of respondents thought the UK government should support a treaty to ban the use of cluster bombs, and half said that they would be very disappointed if the British government failed to adopt such a treaty.[33] The conclusion to be taken from the poll's findings, the NGOs told their political contacts, was that if the UK walked away from a result in Dublin it would be a public relations disaster for Gordon Brown's government during a period in which, politically, the Brown government had little to feel cheery about. Indeed, in Downing Street foreboding was growing about an imminent 22 May by-election for the Crewe and Nantwich parliamentary constituency. The by-election's result, which made news headlines throughout Britain toward the end of the Dublin conference's first week, saw the Conservative Party sweep to victory—overturning a 7,000-vote majority Labour had won there in the previous General Election.[34]

Conversely, the British government could present the adoption of a cluster munition ban treaty as a humanitarian coup if the Oslo process were successful. It meant that throughout the Dublin conference there would be high-level British political interest in the negotiation's outcome, especially in terms of presenting the UK's role in delivering the humanitarian treaty. Meanwhile, the UK's cluster munition policies and negotiating posture attracted detailed coverage in the British and international media.[35] Moreover, a letter in *The Times* from several senior former British military generals published on 19 May—which coincided with the Dublin's conference's opening—helped to further undermine military arguments for retaining weapons, like the M-85, arguments that the UK government's delegation had proposed during the course of the Oslo process. The idea for the letter had come from Conway at Landmine Action; the support of Lord Ramsbotham (a former top British Army commander) helped to attract other signatories including well-known former senior soldiers like Gen. Sir Michael Rose and Gen. Sir Rupert Smith. These recently retired British field commanders called for "the Government of the United Kingdom to give up its remaining stocks of cluster munitions and agree the strongest possible ban on the weapon in the treaty negotiations in Dublin, starting today. Such a treaty will establish a new benchmark for the responsible projection of force in the modern world".[36] Such views were of significance as British policymakers sought to decide during the first days of the Dublin conference where the UK should stand on supporting the emerging treaty.

THE DUBLIN CONFERENCE COMMENCES

Croke Park, the location for the Dublin diplomatic conference, is a sports stadium complex about a mile from the centre of Dublin and the home of the fiercely Irish sport of Gaelic football.[37] As such, it was an unusual site for a treaty negotiation, although perhaps no more odd than the Lima conference held in a hall that doubled as a casino and from which the gambling machines were temporarily removed, or the Mine Ban Treaty's first meeting of states parties in 1998, held in Maputo, Mozambique, in a giant tent. The Irish had mobilized a large logistical force to cater to the Croke Park negotiations, with dozens of defence personnel, Irish Red Cross volunteers, and university students drafted in to help the Department of Foreign Affairs with the conference services. The running of the conference aside, O'Ceallaigh depended heavily on a small Irish team that had emerged over the course of the Oslo process. It consisted of O'Shea from the Geneva Mission, Burke from the defence forces, and was led on the Dublin side by Alison Kelly, Director of the Irish Department of Foreign Affairs' Disarmament and Non-Proliferation division, supported by her Deputy Nicholas Twist, and one of the Department's leading lawyers, Declan Smyth. Together, they would advise the President throughout the negotiation and script most of his statements.

The conference site itself was a giant U shape, deriving from its location beneath the bleachers of Croke Park. At one end of the complex was a long, thin conference plenary hall with the delegates' desks oriented sideways. The shape was not perfect for face-to-face contact between delegations, but television cameras ensured whoever was speaking during the plenary or Committee of the Whole sessions could be seen on giant projector screens in the conference hall and on flat panel displays in the corridors outside. There were smaller break-out consultation rooms elsewhere of varying sizes. At lunchtime, delegates would be encouraged to march down the side of the U towards large, temporary dining rooms in which meals were served. If they kept walking past the dining rooms, eventually delegates would arrive at the CMC's campaigning headquarters at the opposite end of the U. The sheer distance from the conference's main action made it tough for some of the CMC campaigners: cluster munition survivors with electric wheelchairs like Afghan Ban Advocate Soraj Ghulam Habib became a regular sight in the conference—towing other campaigners in wheelchairs down the long route from one end of the Croke Park complex to the other. Meanwhile, those organizations assigned small rooms as bases nearer the seat of the negotiations, like the United Nations' Mine Action Team, and the CMC's logistic and media teams, discovered they had inherited corporate hospitality boxes overlooking the football pitch. All said it was a very different environment from the Palais des Nations in Geneva.

A definite excitement could be felt in Croke Park as delegates gathered on the morning of Monday, 19 May, for the diplomatic conference's opening session. After all of the challenges involved, the sustained efforts of so many people, all of the political risk, and after all of the years of those calling for the impacts of cluster munitions on civilians to be addressed having been voices in the wilderness, here were 107 governments, the UN, the Red Cross and more than 250 civil society campaigners[38] about to try to achieve a treaty to ban cluster munitions.

And, as the conference commenced, it soon became strikingly apparent that virtually all of the participating states at the Croke Park conference genuinely sought to achieve a treaty. Indeed, strong statements of resolve from Ireland's recently appointed Foreign Minister, Micheál Martin,[39] the UN Secretary General (in a video message), the ICRC's President Jakob Kellenberger,[40] a senior UNDP representative[41] and Branislav Kapetanović on the CMC's behalf[42] were widely welcomed—including by the various Like-minded. For those used to negotiating environments like the CCW, it was a most unusual sense, and one many, including myself, will never forget. It was a feeling of collective intent that would set the tone in what was at times a difficult treaty negotiation, but one in which general commitment would never seriously waver from its achievement, even if it left certain states like the UK and Japan facing very difficult decisions about whether to join.

O'Ceallaigh, for his part, felt this sense too, and it confirmed what he had learned in the course of his pre-Dublin consultations with dozens of governments:

> I think public opinion has a huge amount to do with this. I think the activities of civil society, the activities of the CMC and, let's be honest, they didn't have the advantage that the anti-personnel landmine people had of a Princess Diana. They did it without a Princess Diana. And they

built up a pressure. I think probably the use of these cluster munitions by Israel in Lebanon was something which brought it into the public domain in a very open way. But pressure had built up. I mean I was quite convinced from talking to politicians (as distinct from talking to diplomats) that the politicians wanted to sign up to this if they could.[43]

As President, he left those present in no doubt as to his intentions, telling them:

we will adopt a Convention at the conclusion of this Conference. It's my hope that that Convention will be adopted by consensus, and as I've emphasised throughout my consultations, it's my intention to make every feasible effort to reach general agreement. But I want to underline once again: we *will* adopt a Convention by the end of next week.

After settling procedural matters such as the appointment of conference Vice-Presidents,[44] O'Ceallaigh then began to lead the conference through the draft treaty text in its Committee of the Whole, starting from the beginning, on that first Monday afternoon—spinning off more contentious issues to various Friends of the President as he went. Meanwhile, most unusually (and most welcome) for a diplomatic conference of this size, the plenary wound up its speakers' list of general statements before the end of its first day; delegations had got the message that time was short and to save their breath.

One of the challenges O'Ceallaigh and his team faced in bringing the Oslo process toward a successful conclusion was that of pacing. Although a fortnight in duration, the useful time available to the diplomatic conference was really only around eight or nine working days, since time would be needed to proof the final treaty text (if agreed), give the UN legal services time to pore over it for any problems, and then translate and print it in English, French and Spanish. A concert by Canadian singer Céline Dion at Croke Park scheduled for the evening of Friday, 30 May, meant that the conference would have to be wrapped up by lunchtime that day. Correspondingly, all of the various issues in the draft convention would have to be solved, and brought together into a final text for agreement in a roughly synchronized manner by the middle of the second week. It was a tall order to meet. The Irish needed to ensure that enough time was allocated to settling the major outstanding issues—the top tier being definitions and interoperability, followed by transition periods, and then still-significant differences over the degree of retroactivity of the treaty, deadlines for completion of treaty activities like clearance, and stockpile destruction and the issue of retention of cluster munitions for training and development purposes. There were also other matters on which the Irish wanted to avoid appearing perfunctory, even though they desperately needed all of the time possible for sorting out the most contentious articles. And with so many states involved in the Oslo process negotiations—some for the first time—there was always the possibility that unexpected springs would pop out of the sofa.

The Irish would lean heavily on Friends of the President. These were individuals with no formal office, but on whom consultations would depend for various parts of the draft convention, and they answered directly to O'Ceallaigh. The idea was that they would hand over to him treaty text, based on their consultations, by the end of the first week. They included Don MacKay on the cluster munition definition, Steffen Kongstad on stockpile destruction (article 3), Jim Burke on other article 2 definitions and article 4 on clearance, and (in a move considered controversial by some), the Swiss would coordinate on interoperability. Later, others such as South Africa's head of delegation, Xolisa Mabhongo, and Australian ambassador Caroline Millar would also be drafted in to consulting on parts of the draft convention. If the Friends could not produce text likely to command agreement among all concerned, it would be up to O'Ceallaigh to sort out.

Defining cluster munitions

O'Ceallaigh appointed Ambassador Don MacKay to be Friend on article 2 to continue the task New Zealand had undertaken since the first Oslo conference of finding agreement on the definition of a cluster munition. MacKay, in turn, asked Irish Army Lt Col Jim Burke to take responsibility for negotiations on all of article 2's other definitions with the exception of "cluster munition victim", which was dealt with by Markus Reiterer of Austria, Friend for the victim assistance provisions. MacKay's decision to concentrate his own efforts on the crucial definition of a cluster munition, and those of his colleague and main helper Charlotte Darlow, was a prudent one. Their approach was one of methodical attrition used in Vienna and Wellington: they patiently heard out all of the arguments for and against various proposals for exclusion of submunitions from the definition and cross-examined their proponents about the humanitarian effects, with the input of others in the room.

MacKay worried he would not have enough time to examine the various proposals in play with so many delegations keen to reiterate their established positions. To help him cut through the rhetoric, MacKay often called on former British army explosive ordnance expert Colin King to give his technical assessment, in the latter's capacity as an independent consultant. Inconveniently for some of the Like-minded, and as he had done in Wellington, MacKay insisted on open informal consultations, in which observers such as the ICRC, the UN and NGOs were present and active in the discussions. These observer delegations could not propose formal amendments to text, but the Friends could—and often did—take their comments into account, especially as these tended to attract the support of other delegations.[45] MacKay was adamant that he did not want negotiations to be in a "smoke-filled room" from which some states felt excluded, and in which others inside the small-group negotiation felt freer to maintain unhelpful positions.[46] Shortly before the Dublin diplomatic conference, MacKay had explained the reasoning behind this the approach:

> When I operate in that [facilitating] role I operate interactively. In my view there is no point sitting there as a chairman or facilitator and just saying, "I now give the floor to ...". What you've got to do is probe positions. And you have to probe both sides as well. I guess one of the things about Wellington was that because I started at the lower end of the spectrum, the Like-minded group only saw me probing on their stuff. But when we get to the other end of the spectrum I'll probe on that as well. If people say we shouldn't have any exemptions under (c) then I will say, "We're guided by the Oslo Declaration—the humanitarian concerns—what humanitarian concerns do you identify from a weapon that has these characteristics? Can you point to problems that have arisen from this weapon? Can you point to problems that would arise from this weapon, and what are they?" That's how I'll do it, and some people won't like it.[47]

To structure discussions, MacKay circulated "elements" papers that set out the concepts in the various proposals submitted during the Oslo process for examination.[48] Several proposals remained in play as a basis for the exclusion of certain submunitions in article 2, paragraph 2(c). They included proposed exclusions based on the number of submunitions per weapon, direct fire, self-destruct and self-neutralization capability and sensor fuzing.[49] Many in the room knew that most of these proposals for exclusion failed to stand up to scrutiny in humanitarian terms and were instead fronts for individual delegations' attempts to justify retaining the weapons they had in stockpiles and, as such, were simply straight exceptions from the ban. MacKay's consultations subjected these to cross-examination, a process that exposed shortcomings in some of the arguments of both the Like-minded and the Tee-total states in a very public manner.

Predictably, Like-minded coordination began to fall apart as negotiations advanced on specifics that took care of some delegations' concerns and not others. But a group of around half-a-dozen Tee-total states also very active in the negotiation, including Costa Rica, Kenya, Jamaica, Lebanon, Mexico and Zambia, also had to be handled with particular care. These states felt uncomfortable in MacKay's informal consultations to be negotiating on a provision for exclusions they were in principle opposed to, and he was therefore very careful from time to time to remind those participating in the consultations that:

> "some countries take the position—and we understand the position—that there should be no exclusions, but let's look at what the exclusions might look like in the event that there are exclusions, which these countries don't accept anyway".

> It's a very difficult position for a Tee-totaller because all you can do in that situation is say, "no, we are not going to have any discussion whatsoever". And if we'd reached that point we'd have a problem. But it never reached that point, and so by discussing it as an abstract concept, it gradually assumed form and substance and concretized. And the more you discussed and again kept going back to the Oslo Declaration, to what this was all about, the more the Tee-totallers had to come round to accept that the definition wasn't actually going to be a Tee-totaller definition.[50]

The discomfort of Tee-total delegations about negotiating on exclusions was compounded by linguistic challenges, as interpretation into French and Spanish was not available in informal consultations. Toward the end of the week, at the initiative of a highly efficient UN official, Melissa Sabatier, UNDP organized interpreted lunchtime briefings involving experts such as King and Chris Clark, which helped.

On Wednesday of the first week of the Dublin conference, British Prime Minister Gordon Brown's spokesperson made a public announcement in London, which would serve to have a positive bearing on the definitions work. The spokesperson said:

The Prime Minister had issued instructions to our negotiators in Dublin that we should work intensively to ban cluster bombs that cause unacceptable harm to civilians. We had already gone further than other permanent members of the Security Council by banning two types of cluster bombs, neither of which had a self-destruct or de-activation mechanism. The Prime Minister had asked the Ministry of Defence to assess the remaining munitions to ensure there was no risk to civilians … .[51]

It sent an important signal that the UK supported the Dublin negotiation at the highest political level. And, as it was pretty clear by now that the M-85 did pose risk to civilians, it held out the prospect that the UK would give up the M-85 as part of a treaty outcome. Landmine Action and Oxfam immediately issued a media release saying "Britain has at last come in from the cold", adding, "now we expect the UK to give up the M-85 and M-73".[52]

It is impossible to quantify the effect of the British announcement on the definitions consultations, which were already well advanced. But it did contribute to a collective sense of progress on the article 2 definition of a cluster munition. By the following day MacKay felt that he was ready to transmit negotiated text to the President. To mollify the Tee-total states the paper duly noted "there is also a formal proposal to delete 2(c)".[53] But the proposal MacKay believed stood a chance of agreement was as follows:

> **"Cluster munition"** means a munition that is designed to disperse or release explosive sub-munitions, and includes those explosive sub-munitions. It does not mean the following:
>
> (a) a munition or sub-munition designed to dispense flares, smoke, pyrotechnics or chaff; or air defence systems;
>
> (b) a munition or sub-munition designed to produce electrical or electronic effects;
>
> (c) a munition that has all of the following characteristics which minimise its area effect and the risk of unexploded ordnance contamination from its use;
>
> > a. each munition contains fewer than 10 sub-munitions;

b. each sub-munition is designed to locate and engage a point target within a pre-defined area;

c. each sub-munition is equipped with an electronic self-destruction mechanism;

d. each sub-munition is equipped with an electronic self-deactivating fuse.[54]

Importantly, paragraph 2(c) was *cumulative*, which meant a submunition would have to meet *all* of the characteristics—not just one, like possessing a self-destruct feature. If agreed, it clearly would outlaw weapons including even Britain's M-85 and M-73 submunitions. And the chapeau of paragraph 2(c), which mentioned "area effect and the risk of unexploded ordnance contamination" from cluster munition use was of considerable importance in linking the technical characteristics listed below it to an effects-based determinant. It could be argued on this basis that a weapon meeting all of these criteria could still be banned if it caused such effect, something the CMC's front bench of representatives in the definitions consultations would point out to their campaigning base in the face of criticism of the outcome (see next section).

The text MacKay passed to President O'Ceallaigh nevertheless omitted a key element that the French wanted in order to meet concerns about their runway-attack weapon being caught in the prohibition. France wanted an upper weight criterion in the definition, which would serve as a basis for APACHE's exclusion. A proposal Norway had made in the consultations on 21 May for both upper and lower weight criteria (and which the CMC supported) suited France.[55] But MacKay had not included a weight criterion in his text for the President simply because, although no outright opposition was raised, he felt some delegations in the consultations seemed confused about what it was for and the case had not been made conclusively enough.[56] In fact, it had been the subject of little discussion. This made the French very concerned. The upshot was that Norway was encouraged to reintroduce its proposal, along with an explanatory paper, early in the Dublin conference's second week. The clear explanation it provided eased the inclusion of weight criteria into later versions of the article 2 text.[57]

Another feature of the definition in article 2, paragraph 2(c) was that, on the basis of its cumulative criteria, it excluded some weapons widely referred to as sensor-fuzed submunitions, such as the French-Swedish BONUS and German SMArt 155 artillery rounds each containing two sensor-fuzed submunitions with self-destruct features. However, it did capture within its prohibition the US BLU-108 submunition,[58] developed as part of Textron Systems' Sensor Fuzed Weapon—an air-to-ground strike munition built for the US Air Force. Textron, a US company, had taken a keen interest in both the CCW's work on cluster munitions and the Oslo process and had sent company representatives to make presentations on the CCW's margins and to brief researchers and civil society campaigners. Textron felt the Sensor Fuzed Weapon and its BLU-108 submunitions avoided the humanitarian problems of cluster munitions and should, indeed, not be regarded as such because it attacked point targets within an area and had multiple redundancies built in to make it inert if it failed to function. But because the number of submunitions exceeded the numerical threshold of "fewer than 10" in paragraph 2(c)(i), and each submunition weighed less than the 4kg minimum weight threshold in (ii), the Sensor Fuzed Weapon was captured in the prohibition.

NO EXCEPTIONS, NO DELAYS AND NO LOOPHOLES

The rapidity of the process leading to MacKay's text for the President on article 2, paragraph 2(c) created a difficult situation within the civil society cluster munition campaign. As in Wellington, the CMC fielded a highly competent and experienced team of representatives in the Dublin negotiations. They included Conway, Goose, Moyes, Nash and Østern. Moyes in particular became a force to be reckoned with in MacKay's consultations in peeling away the reasoning behind the proposals of the Like-minded for self-destruct and direct-fire exclusions, in order to expose their rationale as unconvincing in humanitarian terms. Moyes's game plan was to try to steer the negotiations to reject suggested criteria for exclusion such as numbers, self-destruct or direct-fire—as some others in the consultations were also doing—and to argue that the defining characteristic of cluster munitions is that they distribute explosive force across an area. In conceptual terms such a characterization laid the groundwork for excluding weapon systems like the SMArt 155 and similar munitions but captured everything else discussed in the Oslo process.

Moyes and the rest of the CMC's front bench believed that to just sit in the Dublin negotiation's informal consultations and maintain the position that there should simply be no paragraph 2(c) would marginalize them from the negotiation and skew the outcome toward those calling for such exclusions, even if no 2(c) would have been the CMC's preferred outcome.[59] And they hoped, through argument, to pull states they regarded as on the fence such as Australia and Canada away from the Like-minded the CMC regarded as in the "red zone"—something Moyes had explained to campaigners before the start of the week in a presentation given during a detailed orientation session for all those on the CMC delegation.[60] Similar presentations had also been given to states during the regional conferences prior to Dublin and a lot of time and energy was spent seeking to communicate these complex issues.

The CMC team's efforts to chip 2(c) away to a bare minimum through detailed and substantive argument were not necessarily well understood by all of the CMC's campaigners, however. Many NGO representatives were attending an international diplomatic conference for the first time and, because of space limitations, most relied on daily briefings and gossip to gain a picture of what was happening behind the consultation room doors. Surprised at how quickly the parameters of a definition of cluster munitions had come together in the first week, some campaigners became angry that their CMC front-benchers had "given away" too much after receiving a briefing from lead negotiators Goose, Moyes, Nash and Østern at the end of negotiations on Tuesday afternoon about the Norwegian proposal and the support it had garnered from many states, such as Australia and Canada and also France. (These states had previously supported exceptions for the M-85 and other self-destruct weapons.) The Norwegian proposal—which would end up being similar to MacKay's exclusion based on cumulative criteria—that a weapon with less than 10 submunitions, a means to "engage a point target within a pre-defined area", and electronic self-destruction and self de-activating features was not a cluster munition—was portrayed as a major step forward by the negotiating team. But it seemed to some campaigners to be at odds with the CMC's slogan of "NO exceptions, NO delays and NO loopholes", displayed on a huge banner in the CMC campaign headquarters in Croke Park. Why was the CMC not hanging tougher? they challenged.

It was a difficult moment in the campaign, which instead might reasonably have been expected to be one of triumph for the CMC. The truth was that Norway's proposal and the expected text from MacKay were more than the CMC's experts on definitions had dared to hope for—even if they disliked certain aspects of it like the UK's baffling insistence on exclusion of munitions "designed exclusively for an air defence role" added at the last minute to article 2, paragraph 2(a). If agreed, the definition would outlaw practically all of the weapons with submunitions in service of those states possessing them, including M-85-style weapons, direct-fire cluster munition weapons containing the M-73, the Spanish and Swedish cluster munitions with electronic fail-safe mechanisms, and others. Buried in the specifics of the negotiations, themselves euphoric at the implications of MacKay's expected recommendation to the President, and running on adrenaline from two days of negotiations and weeks of intensive preparations, the CMC front-benchers had simply assumed grassroots campaigners would see things as they did.[61] But many of those campaigners had been working tirelessly over many months with the Tee-total states to build up their knowledge and ability to argue for a robust prohibition in the treaty. Now, it seemed, the campaign's opposition to exclusions had simply been overruled by the campaign's front-benchers for expediency's sake. Would it look like a ban on cluster munitions to the Tee-total delegations they had patiently cultivated, which were opposed to any exclusions under article 2, paragraph 2(c)?

Although able to point to the CMC's public, written observations on the draft convention text before the Dublin conference, the CMC's front-benchers recognized that further discussion would probably only inflame matters. In an emerging Oslo process tradition seemingly pioneered by MacKay with the Like-minded diplomats in Wellington, Moyes and Nash met with campaigners the following day to absorb the full force of their criticism—also announcing a day later that there would be a campaign meeting facilitated by Irishman Colm O'Gorman on the coming Saturday to determine coalition-wide positions on the negotiation's endgame and what the CMC could and could not support as an outcome. The two men did their best to demonstrate that the CMC's negotiators *were* listening to their grassroots. Moyes responded to campaigners' questions, while Nash projected onto the big screen for collective editing the draft CMC statement he would read seated next to Moyes later that morning in the definition negotiations.[62] This tough meeting made both Moyes and the CMC's leadership acutely aware of the level of anxiety among campaigners and the many delegations in the negotiations those campaigners were lobbying and gathering information from that the Dublin conference succeed in living up to the aim of a cluster munition ban treaty.[63] And, by taking the heat for the CMC leadership, Moyes also did the campaign a service in helping to maintain its unity at a critical time. It was not, however, an experience he was keen to repeat.

DUBLIN AT THE HALFWAY MARK

By the end of the first week of the Dublin negotiations, O'Ceallaigh and his team could see an outcome taking shape. Monday's proceedings had commenced with strong indications of political support from many quarters, and further political-level announcements followed from states such as France and the UK about their commitment to the aims of the Oslo Declaration and an outcome of the negotiations over the week's course. For example, as well as the statement from Gordon Brown's office, France's Defence Minister announced the decision to unilaterally abolish its stockpile of M-26 cluster munition rockets.[64] Good progress had been made in the Committee of the Whole on less controversial aspects of the draft convention text and, of those issues delegated to Friends of the President, some had been able to return to the President by Friday to offer text they thought could command agreement as part of a wider negotiating package. O'Ceallaigh was in a position to present "Presidency Text" to the conference's plenary that Friday morning on articles 9 through 16, and from articles 20 to 22 along with some preamble language, the cluster munition victim definition and text from article 5 on victim assistance. Meanwhile, article 2 cluster munition definition work under MacKay had made astonishing progress—perhaps too astonishing, as the definition would have to be revisited after the weekend to accommodate the French. The Spanish would also lead a last ditch (but unsuccessful) effort to exclude submunitions with electronic fuzing from the prohibition. And, while of singular importance in terms of directing the scope of what the treaty would ban, the cluster munition definition was only one of more than a dozen definitions, most having been passed to Irish soldier Jim Burke.

Burke found himself to be a very busy man. As well as being one of the President's main helpers on the Irish team, he was responsible for coordinating consultations on clearance in article 4 and somehow finding the time to gather concerned delegations to settle no less than 13 other article 2 definitions. At the end of Dublin's first week these definitions were not ready and, consequently, Burke would call interested delegations to Croke Park during the weekend for consultations.[65] There were a number of issues to be agreed, but the most challenging revolved around "explosive bomblets" and "dispensers". It reflected a long-standing Irish concern that a cluster munition treaty might inadvertently create a loophole that encouraged the development (or redevelopment) of weapon systems deploying vast numbers of explosive devices from a container aboard an aircraft. While Burke did not know if such weapons were currently in service anywhere, bomblet dispensers like the Hayes dispenser were used in the South-East Asia war. According to Prokosch:

> It is a huge boxlike aluminium contraption comprising twenty-four rectangular cells, each of which is loaded with three square boxes or "adapters" containing bomblets. Two dispensers can be fitted in the bomb bay of a B-52 bomber; small versions are available for the B-57 and the C-123 cargo plane. A B-52 with two Hayes dispensers can drop astronomical numbers of small munitions: 10,656 "pineapple" bomblets, 25,488 "guava" bomblets, or 77,040 0.3-lb spherical M-40 fragmentation grenades in a single bombing run.[66]

A weapon that could drop "astronomical numbers" of explosive bomblets was clearly of concern in the Oslo process. But a container like the Hayes contraption might not actually be considered a munition itself, and therefore not fall within article 2's definition of a cluster munition. And if a ban on cluster munitions failed to capture them, Burke thought, such weapons might begin to look attractive again to militaries.[67]

The dispenser issue would be cleared up relatively late in the Dublin negotiation on Tuesday of the second week (see chapter 10). British M-73 submunitions were dispersed from rockets fired from pods fitted to attack helicopters; rockets containing submunitions were only one of the types that could be fired, however, and the British did not want a treaty agreed in Dublin to inadvertently ban the entire CRV-7 system because it was considered a dispenser, with its rockets being considered explosive bomblets. The UK's concerns were cleared up by the inclusion in the "explosive bomblet" definition in article 2, paragraph 13 of the words "which are not self-propelled", thereby excluding rockets.[68] Meanwhile, a new paragraph was added to article 1 of the treaty text on its general scope stating that its ban "applies, *mutatis mutandis*, to explosive bomblets that are specifically designed to be dispersed or released from dispensers affixed to aircraft". (*Mutatis mutandis* means "with the necessary changes made"; in this case to allow for differences in details when comparing weapons that have substantially the same characteristics and effects.)

At least transition periods were now out of the question, the Irish thought. In a Committee of the Whole session that O'Ceallaigh convened with all delegations on Friday morning to work through the draft treaty article by article, he raised the transition period proposals made earlier by Germany,

Slovakia and Switzerland. The Swiss delegation hastily suggested that it might be better to discuss these on Tuesday, when the cluster munition definition was clearer (that is, with a formulation included in O'Ceallaigh's text). Switzerland's call for postponement was immediately supported in interventions from Japan, Denmark, Slovakia and the UK. It was too late. Mexico, a Tee-total state, took the floor to propose that all of the cards be put on the table: other delegations were ready to give their thoughts on transition periods now, the Mexicans said. After a cascade of nearly 60 interventions all opposed to transition periods of any kind, all of those delegates present were left in no doubt that transition periods would never find agreement.[69] As one observer of the negotiations wrote:

> The United Kingdom requested that a Friend of the President be appointed to hold informal consultations on transitions. Venezuela responded that with 80% of the Conference against even contemplating a transition period, no more discussions should be held. (This was met by applause from delegates and for the first time, it was the diplomats, not the campaigners who were reprimanded for being too rowdy.)[70]

In what was perhaps the understatement of the negotiation so far, O'Ceallaigh told those calling for transition periods that they would have to "do more to convince others" and suggested that Germany take the lead in consulting informally on the issue over the weekend with other interested states. (This took the German delegation by surprise, and it accepted with good grace, although that evening O'Ceallaigh would be informed of Germany's concerns in a telephone call from Berlin.) Further consultation and another discussion in the Committee of the Whole on Monday afternoon would make no difference.[71] It was abundantly clear that transition periods were dead in the water (although as shall be seen the Irish considered their inclusion until the very end of their work on a completed convention text).

The transition period episode handed the Tee-total states a psychologically important victory for them at a time when it was becoming certain to the President's team that Tee-total preferences would not prevail in other significant respects of the treaty. The Tee-total majority in the Dublin negotiations would not have their way in expunging any exclusions to the definition under paragraph 2(c)—although they had succeeded in banning the M-85, M-73, Swedish BK-90, Spanish MAT-120 and a host of other cluster munitions that some thought would never be banned. And the suspicion of many Tee-total delegations about interoperability provisions would have to be overcome, as the Like-minded were adamant that such a provision was a vital precondition for their support for a cluster munition ban treaty. Dublin was, after all, a negotiation, and despite the initial postures of the states participating there, they would all have to be prepared to bend.

O'Ceallaigh and his team also knew they were racing against the clock. The President needed a text that he thought stood a shot at agreement by early Tuesday of the second week of negotiations at the latest. Based on that text, the President would then have to gingerly nudge delegations into endgame compromises, probably by means of bilateral meetings in which he would do his best to identify those spaces as well as try to ratchet up pressure for closure, to bring substantive work to completion by Wednesday evening in view of the logistics of physically producing, translating and distributing a draft final document.[72] Yet, several articles, including clearance, stockpile destruction, transparency (a treaty provision which concerns reporting requirements), were still outstanding, along with various definitions. O'Ceallaigh was not too worried about these—for instance, the Norwegian head of delegation, Kongstad, and his main helper on the issue, Christian Ruge, were confident they could craft a deal on article 3 with a bit more time. And O'Ceallaigh had asked an able newcomer to the Oslo process, South African diplomat Xolisa Mahbongo, to lead the consultations on the transparency provision. No, the biggest headache for the endgame would be interoperability. And, although the President and his team were not aware of it yet, the final stretch of the second week would spring another nasty surprise (as well as some good ones).

CHAPTER 10

DUBLIN: ENDGAME

By the second Monday of the two-week Dublin diplomatic conference, the Oslo process negotiations were drawing close to their endgame. The next two-and-a-half days of work would determine whether a Convention on Cluster Munitions could be agreed that could command the support of governments of both Like-minded and Tee-total persuasions. The conference's President, Ambassador Dáithí O'Ceallaigh, and his team now had most of the text of a treaty they thought stood a reasonable chance of achieving agreement among the more than 100 states participating in the Dublin negotiations. Even the central issue of how cluster munitions would be defined—and therefore what would be banned under the treaty—had now been mostly formulated. And O'Ceallaigh felt that the strong collective will to achieve a cluster munition ban treaty evident a week earlier was still intact.[1] However, critical gaps in agreement remained. Now the Irish would have to broker solutions to this handful of issues and the trade-offs between them, and then sell the assemblage of text as a package to the conference.

The preceding chapter outlined how the draft treaty text took detailed shape over the first week of the Dublin negotiations, and it focused in particular on the evolution of the definition provisions. Fifteen months before, it was widely foreseen when the Oslo Declaration was agreed that defining cluster munitions would be a dominant issue in the eventual treaty negotiations. Indeed, many of the more Tee-total in inclination were particularly concerned about the concept of "acceptable" as opposed to "unacceptable" harm: "What is acceptable harm, exactly?" they could be heard to ask. Such reservations were overcome through a consistent emphasis by the Core Group, supported by the United Nations, the Red Cross and Red Crescent Movement and civil society on the Oslo initiative as a predominantly humanitarian rather than arms control process. In this way of thinking, the Oslo process was not framed as a stepping stone to general and complete disarmament, but a means of alleviating the known hazards of cluster munitions on civilians. Correspondingly, the other factor that came to the fore when it got down to the nitty-gritty of article

2 negotiations was the concentration by Don MacKay and his helpers, bolstered by the UN, the International Committee of the Red Cross (ICRC) and the Cluster Munition Coalition (CMC), on demonstrable humanitarian consequences as the basis for definition and ban. Such a discourse taking into account humanitarian evidence boiled away many more political and ideological considerations—be it traditional mantras about disarmament or the North–South divide—just as it evaporated unsupported claims about the acceptability of weapons based on technical characteristics without justification in practice. This reframing of disarmament as humanitarian action was an essential characteristic of development of the Oslo process.

Instead of the definition, interoperability would dominate the cluster munition ban treaty's endgame. The phrase "unacceptable harm" may also be seen as meaningful in the context of interoperability as it neatly paraphrases the concerns being raised by the US in private with many Oslo process states, and especially the Like-minded, of the damage the treaty could do to military cooperation with the US. As the culmination of the Oslo process approached, these warnings became more dire and public. On 21 May, two days after the Dublin conference commenced, Stephen Mull, Acting Assistant Secretary for Political–Military Affairs at the US State Department, held an "On-the-Record Briefing" for journalists in Washington DC to explain why the United States had refused to attend. Mull homed in on military interoperability, claiming:

> for example, if the [cluster munition] convention passes in its current form, any U.S. military ship would be technically not able to get involved in a peacekeeping operation, in providing disaster relief or humanitarian assistance as we're doing right now in the aftermath of the earthquake in China and the typhoon in Burma, and not to mention everything that we did in Southeast Asia after the tsunami in December of 2004. And that's because most U.S. military units have in their inventory these kinds of weapons. So with one stroke, any country that signed the convention as it exists now and ratified it, in effect, would make it impossible for the United States or any of our other allies who rely on these weapons to participate in these humanitarian exercises.[2]

Yet the State Department's press briefings to diplomats were not the only US views being heard. Senators Dianne Feinstein and Patrick Leahy wrote to the Dublin conference's President in a letter timed to coincide with the commencement of the cluster munition ban treaty negotiations, and which was widely distributed there:

As the authors of legislation before the United States Senate that would prohibit the use and export of cluster munitions that cause unacceptable harm to civilians, we offer our support and encouragement to these negotiations. Although the U.S. Government has chosen not to participate in the "Oslo Process", we want you to know that there is support within the United States Congress, and among the American people, for your efforts.

Our legislation has been cosponsored by nearly one-quarter of the members of the Senate, representing tens of millions of Americans. And last year, at our initiative, the President signed into law a prohibition on exports of cluster munitions that have a failure rate of more than 1 percent.

We wish you success in crafting the strongest possible treaty to establish a new global norm governing the use, export and production of cluster munitions.[3]

To the extent that Mull's remarks were noticed by governments participating in the Dublin conference, in all likelihood they contained nothing new beyond what the Bush administration had been telling its friends and allies in private for months. In contrast, with a US presidential election in six months, Leahy and Feinstein's letter was a timely reminder that US policy on cluster munitions was not set in stone, and that there were policymakers in Washington who saw a humanitarian treaty to restrict or prohibit the weapon as an objective to pursue. And Leahy himself briefly visited the negotiations in Dublin as a gesture of his support.

Nevertheless, the Bush administration's range of attempts to influence a treaty negotiation process it publicly shunned were not primarily aimed at affecting which specific weapons a Convention on Cluster Munitions would ban. The Dublin conference's negotiations on interoperability were where its influence was felt. US allies such as Australia, Canada, Denmark, Italy, Japan and the UK would strive to secure an outcome that would not impede US use of cluster munitions, and avoid damage to their defence relationships with Washington. This chapter provides an overview of those interoperability negotiations. Settling interoperability would be a severe test for the UK, in particular, and require political commitment at the highest level in London to achieving a cluster munition ban treaty. Nevertheless, the solution (in the form of article 21) would come under fire from some states as clunky and detracting from the strong provisions of the rest of the Dublin outcome, and be criticized by the CMC as the "only stain on the fine fabric of the treaty text".[4] This chapter also follows the story to its conclusion of how the international cluster munition ban was won—negotiations featuring an unexpected crisis only minutes before the treaty was put before the Dublin conference for agreement.

INTEROPERABILITY

Deciding how the interoperability issue should be handled was tricky for O'Ceallaigh and his team in the lead-up to the Dublin conference. It seemed certain that, like definitions and the other more difficult issues in the draft convention text, a mechanism would be needed for interoperability consultations outside (and, for time reasons, probably working in parallel to) the Committee of the Whole's work. Prior to Dublin, MacKay had chaired most interoperability-related discussions in the Oslo process as part of his responsibilities for article 1 (on general scope) along with article 2 (definitions). But MacKay would have his hands full with the cluster munition definition, and he asked O'Ceallaigh to find someone else to take on his other tasks. O'Ceallaigh could not assume responsibility for interoperability consultations himself, as he needed to be available to chair the Committee of the Whole, and his team were stretched thin enough as it was. So, a Friend of the President on interoperability would be needed.

It was well known among the Core Group that Norway wanted the role. Norway, after all, was a NATO member as well as a state active in international peacekeeping on which the interoperability-related provisions of an eventual Convention on Cluster Munitions would have a bearing. Norway was influential with a broad range of governments involved in the Oslo process, and had very good links among the developing and affected countries, which had only strengthened over the course of the Oslo process in view of its humanitarian leadership. And, of course, the Norwegians had relevant expertise and capacity, with both experienced diplomats like Steffen Kongstad and lawyers from both the Ministries of Defence and Foreign Affairs as part of their Dublin delegation.[5] In this way, the Norwegians saw Kongstad as the logical choice to coordinate on interoperability.

Yet the prospect of Norway coordinating interoperability negotiations was not welcome to those of the Like-minded most concerned with the issue. In Vienna and in Wellington, Norway's views on interoperability had differed from those of the majority of NATO members and others such as

Australia, Canada and Japan. The Norwegian delegation had consistently argued that interoperability in the cluster munition treaty context was nothing special, or anything in particular to worry about (see chapter 7). Yet Norway was in touch with the US just as the Like-minded were, and was receiving similar signals about the importance of the interoperability issue. It was thus a source of frustration to the Like-minded that, despite this, Norway's views did not accord with their own. Moreover, as Norway was instigator of the Oslo process in which some of the Like-minded had felt pushed and cajoled all the way to Dublin, certain of them—like British and Danish diplomats—were highly suspicious of Norway becoming an arbiter on an issue of such vital concern to them. O'Ceallaigh did not have any doubts that Norway was up to the job, but these dynamics would not be helpful to achieving an outcome. There was also representativeness to be considered: the Core Group had insisted throughout the Oslo process that the Dublin negotiations would be a level playing field, and that their role in shepherding the development of the text would end. With individuals from Austria, New Zealand and Ireland playing roles as Friends on issues in the draft convention text, in the interests of balance the President felt he needed to look further afield than the Core Group to fill other key roles.

O'Ceallaigh decided to ask the Swiss to coordinate on interoperability. A week before the Dublin conference commenced, he telephoned Ambassador Christine Schraner Burgener at the Swiss Federal Department of Foreign Affairs in Bern, to ask her to be the Friend. Schraner, pleasant and gently spoken, had headed the Swiss delegation at the Oslo conference and, although she had not been at the Lima, Vienna or Wellington conferences, O'Ceallaigh knew she would lead the Swiss team in Dublin. It was a shrewd choice by the Irish: Switzerland was one of the Like-minded; it possessed the M-85 submunition with self-destruct, and was very concerned about transition periods. Yet because of its military neutrality, Switzerland did not share the strong interoperability concerns of most other Like-minded—although, on the flip side, that could lead to criticism that the Swiss were not in a position to properly understand the ins and outs of interoperability problems. Nevertheless, putting one of the Like-minded in the interoperability hot seat largely eliminated the potential for further accusations from the Like-minded of bias against their interests. And Schraner agreed to take on the Friend role, although she later recalled, "I didn't realize at that moment how difficult it was".[6]

Schraner was to take a different approach to her first-week consultations in Dublin than MacKay did in his open informals on the definition. In part this was due to the nature of the issue: definitions were of relevance to all states in the cluster munition treaty negotiations because those weapons defined as cluster munitions would be what the treaty banned. In contrast, interoperability was arguably of key importance for only a limited number; but these states presented a legally workable solution on interoperability as a prerequisite for them signing and ratifying a cluster munition ban treaty.

The delegations represented in the interoperability negotiations could be described as falling within three concentric circles, or rings. In principle, within the largest, outermost ring fell all countries involved in joint multinational operations, whether United Nations-led, or under the auspices of a regional organization like the African Union or the Economic Community of West African States in which non-states parties to a cluster munition ban treaty might operate alongside member states of the treaty. In practice, although the Like-minded had made the point in Vienna and Wellington that all states should be concerned about impact on multinational operations, interest was rather more circumscribed.

In contrast, within the middle ring was a subset of countries largely consisting of US allies like those in NATO: these governments worried about draft article 1, paragraph 1(c)'s implications for their joint operations with the US, because it stated:

> 1. Each State Party undertakes never under any circumstances to:
>
> (a) Use cluster munitions;
>
> (b) Develop, produce, otherwise acquire, stockpile, retain or transfer to anyone, directly or indirectly, cluster munitions;
>
> (c) *Assist encourage or induce anyone to engage in any activity prohibited to a State Party under this Convention.*[7]

Paragraph 1(c) was very similar to that of the Mine Ban Treaty.[8] As the Australians and other Like-minded had underlined in their discussion paper in Wellington,[9] their overall concern was over what exactly "assist, encourage or induce" would mean for countries dependent, for instance, on US fire support in military operations for a weapon used in very different ways than anti-personnel mines. It meant the middle ring delegations were most active in pushing for interoperability provisions in Schraner's consultations that would create explicit exemptions from state liability, as well as from individual criminal liability for their national personnel.

In the third, innermost ring was a small subset of those countries of the middle ring—the UK, in particular—concerned about the ramifications of the cluster munition ban treaty for the hosting of foreign military bases (especially US ones) on territory under their jurisdiction or control.

Differences in how MacKay and Schraner conducted their respective consultations also reflected their differing tactical approaches. MacKay's definitions meetings in the large room had the potential to become slightly rambunctious, but it played to his approach of covering an exclusion in the discussion, pulling back, and running over it again—each time shaving away at the problem or flattening resistance a little more until an outcome had been achieved (some participants even dubbed this the "lawnmower" approach). If MacKay came at discussing definitions from the perspective of a barrister's cross-examination, Schraner applied her experience as a court mediator of trying to bring a representative group of the parties to mutual agreement in a smaller, more informal setting.[10] So, although Schraner's first interoperability consultation on the Tuesday of the first week in Dublin would be open to all delegations, she would subsequently work in a smaller, and what she hoped was a roughly representative group of 22 or less in a small conference room.[11]

Interoperability issues had briefly been covered in the main hall on the conference's first afternoon. There, the President ran quickly through article 1, at which point he formally appointed Schraner as Friend "to present the proposal that she thought might best balance the interests of States concerned if a consensus proposal did not emerge".[12] All that the Committee of the Whole discussions did was underline how contentious the interoperability question was. So, the following morning in her first consultation, which was open-ended, Schraner circulated a few points to kick-start the discussion that took into account the Monday exchange of views. The first point concerned the need for more information about the alleged problems that article 1, as it stood, would create for joint operations between states parties and non-states parties. In this vein, since article 1 was so similar to the Mine Ban Treaty's general scope provision, was clearer language needed for article 1, paragraph 1(c), or would the existing language work in combination with national declarations of interpretation? Third, did anyone disagree with Schraner's impression that even those happy with the existing wording of article 1, paragraph 1(c) would not have a problem in principle with additional language somewhere in the treaty for the benefit of those who needed it?

Schraner was not trying to find a solution at this stage. Instead, she and her main helper, Reto Wollenmann, were orienting themselves, and working out whom the Friend should invite to smaller room consultations commencing at 16h00—not an easy task as many of the African and Latin American delegations were preoccupied with other issues.[13] Australia, Canada, France, Germany, Ireland, Italy, Jamaica, Japan, Morocco, New Zealand, Nigeria, the Philippines, the UK, Zambia and a late addition—Austria—were the Swiss picks, a group in which the major differing views on interoperability as expressed in the Committee of the Whole were represented along with a number of different regions. (This group later expanded as the Swiss came to the view that it was no longer useful to prefer consultations limited to a smaller set of delegations.) The CMC was also involved: its main representative on the issue was Steve Goose of Human Rights Watch, a veteran of the article 1 negotiations on the Mine Ban Treaty—supported largely by Bonnie Docherty, a Harvard legal academic and researcher—as well as his CMC co-chair, Grethe Østern.

Schraner's decision to embark on smaller group work was not popular in the wider conference among those not involved in the interoperability consultations. However, with parallel work underway during much of the first week in the Committee of the Whole, and on provisions such as definitions, stockpile destruction and victim assistance, many delegations were hard pressed to cover interoperability as well. Schraner, for her part, was certainly not opposed to others joining her consultations, but wanted to cultivate an atmosphere with a focus on the specific legal issues. These discussions were to be dominated by Australia, Canada, Japan and the UK's military lawyers because Schraner wanted to listen first to what language would solve their concerns on interoperability, and then use this as a basis for a more political negotiation.[14]

As the consultations on interoperability continued each day throughout the Dublin conference's first week, some progress was made. For example, discussions about proposals for interoperability provisions to be inserted into article 1 soon led to the general feeling that monkeying around with general scope could create more problems than it solved.[15] The CMC and states in the consultations such as Austria, Jamaica and Zambia fought against any attempts they perceived as weakening the general prohibitions in article 1, and active Like-minded such as Australia, Canada, Germany and the UK did not want to lend the impression they were trying to do that—a lesson learned from Wellington. Thus, a new, general provision on interoperability elsewhere in the treaty would be preferable. By mid-week, Schraner set out a four-paragraph "Article xx (tbc)" in an informal paper with a note that "Article 1 of the Draft Convention would remain unchanged".[16] Subsequent iterations kept this four-paragraph structure until the end of the Dublin negotiation, although it was not until Tuesday night in the second week that O'Ceallaigh and his team decided the draft article on "Relations between States Parties and States not party to this Convention" should be placed near the end of the treaty as draft article 21.

HOSTING

By the end of Schraner's consultations of the first week it was apparent that the outermost ring of states' concerns could be accommodated. Then there was the strong wish of the Like-minded to safeguard their military personnel from liability in joint operations with forces of states not party to the treaty in which cluster munitions were used—the middle ring. By early in the second week, the Like-minded seemed reasonably comfortable with the text of draft article 21 as it pertained to this concern. But there remained the basing problem for the UK, Japan and Italy to some extent. France, meanwhile, had no US bases on its soil, and the terms of Germany's agreements with Washington over bases in its territory were such that Berlin did not exercise legal jurisdiction over them. It seemed that at this stage these states were trying to act in solidarity with the UK on interoperability, rather than possessing serious remaining concerns of their own on hosting— since both would want British cover within NATO for joining a Convention on Cluster Munitions.

Solving British concerns seemed a rather intractable challenge. While US military bases on British territory, which included places like Diego Garcia in the Indian Ocean, as well as on mainland Britain, were in practice controlled by the United States, the British government was legally responsible for them. These controversial arrangements had recently been highlighted over the use of British facilities in the rendition of people deemed by the US government to be terrorist suspects from other parts of the world without due legal process. In the context of interoperability, the concern was that the US would likely have cluster munitions stockpiled in many of these hosted bases, which could put the UK in violation of the Convention on Cluster Munitions if it became a state party. Concerns about the interoperability draft article as regards hosting of foreign bases also affected Italy, Japan and Central and East European members of NATO to varying degrees.

To resolve the hosting problem the UK wanted a provision in the third paragraph of the interoperability article stipulating that a state party to the cluster munition treaty would be able to "host States not party to this Convention which engage in activities described in Article 1"—that draft article being the list of the treaty's prohibitions. It reflected the UK government's view that the US was unlikely to join a cluster munition ban treaty any time soon, and so British Ambassador John Duncan and his delegation were difficult to budge in their insistence on the language that would provide the UK an ironclad assurance it would not be held liable for hosting. The hosting formulation was duly included in Schraner's proposal for the Committee of the Whole at the end of week one,[17] which ran up against opposition from a large number of delegations.[18] Rightly or wrongly, and perhaps because so many of the states participating in the Dublin conference were not directly involved in the Swiss consultations, "hosting" was widely perceived among the Tee-total states as tantamount to a get-out clause from the treaty's prohibitions, and clearly a US-oriented exception. Yet it was a crucial provision for the UK along with Japan and Italy if they were to sign up to the Dublin negotiations' eventual outcome.[19]

The interoperability draft article's third paragraph was contentious from other perspectives too. Throughout interoperability consultations and, indeed, in the final version of the eventual agreement, the draft article's four-paragraph structure had begun with two paragraphs obliging states parties to encourage states not party to the cluster munition treaty "to ratify, accept, approve or accede to this Convention" (paragraph 1) and, in paragraph 2, stating that a state party shall "notify the governments of all States not party to this Convention, referred to in paragraph 3 of this Article, of its obligations under this Convention, shall promote the norms it establishes and shall make its best efforts to discourage States not party to this Convention from using cluster munitions".[20]

Paragraph 4, like these first two paragraphs of the draft article, was also intended to place bounds on paragraph 3 by explicitly stating that nothing in the latter provision authorized a state itself to have cluster munitions, use them or "expressly request the use of cluster munitions in cases where the choice of munitions used is within its exclusive control".[21] All of this caution was because paragraph 3 was considered so sensitive and dangerous by many—to the point where, in a paper on Thursday 22 May, Norway's lawyers proposed a complete redrafting to make it clearer that "This provision is meant to facilitate military cooperation, not modify [a] States Party's [international humanitarian law] obligations".[22] However, this textual proposal failed to gain traction with the Like-minded, which preferred the trajectory of the evolving language in Schraner's various, consecutive proposals.

Nevertheless, Schraner had run out of time by Tuesday of the second week. The hosting problems were not within the power of the legal and diplomatic negotiators in the interoperability consultations or Schraner herself to settle in the interoperability draft article. It would require a political solution. Schraner submitted her final draft text to the President, a proposal that, significantly, did *not* contain reference to hosting.[23] Her text was circulated in the Committee of the Whole meeting that afternoon although O'Ceallaigh told delegations he did not propose to discuss it there at that time,[24] since he knew it would require further negotiation.

THE ENDGAME

Also on Tuesday afternoon, President O'Ceallaigh told his Friends before convening the Committee of the Whole at 15h00 that he would now resume direct responsibility for the draft Convention text. While much of the draft convention text had taken shape, there were still several open issues—notably finalizing definitions and interoperability—to be resolved. The President told the Committee of the Whole that he intended to use the next 24 hours for bilateral consultations, but that delegations should remain at the Croke Park complex as he wished to meet with them collectively at some point that evening to give everyone his "composite text".[25] (The Irish held out some hope that agreement would emerge on a text by the end of the night. The Irish also needed to be able to find the delegations they wished to meet with bilaterally, and having delegations stay at Croke Park made that task easier.) O'Ceallaigh and his team carefully kept their worries about interoperability to themselves: they now felt confident that a treaty would be achieved with or without the British. But they also had many reasons to believe that if the UK were not on board it would make it harder for other Like-minded states with stockpiles of cluster munitions and US alliance commitments to join—and those states were anxious. To lose the British, in other words, would be a blow. But having asked the UK delegation directly for greater flexibility on hosting there was little more the President could do.

At 16h30, the President and his team began their bilateral meetings. With some delegations the Irish took the initiative to arrange meetings one-by-one in the President's upstairs office. Other delegations the President consulted at their request. In all, the Irish team were involved in excess of 30 bilateral meetings over the course of the late afternoon and evening of 27 May. By 21h00 the Presidency had met with delegations including (roughly in order) Zambia, Canada, France, the UK, Norway, Costa Rica, South Africa, Mexico, Germany, Japan, Argentina, the CMC, Indonesia, the ICRC, Australia and Finland. According to O'Ceallaigh, the Irish asked every delegation the same specific questions: could they accept the text on interoperability? Could they accept the proposal on definitions (updated that week by MacKay with the Norwegian weight criterion to address French concerns, and with inclusion of dispensers in article 1 by Burke)? Third, could they accept the outcome on transition periods? Lastly, the Irish asked a general question of all delegations they met with: did they have any problems elsewhere in the text?[26]

By 21h00, hundreds of delegates, including myself, had been waiting in anticipation for nearly five hours under fluorescent lights in a mood tinged with both weariness and great expectation as the sun set over Dublin. Famished delegates had also emptied every accessible vending machine in Croke Park, and many agitated souls had even run out of cigarettes. Meanwhile, O'Ceallaigh now knew there would be no composite text to distribute that night, but he and his team had not given up. The President interrupted his consultations to return to the conference podium and briefly resume the Committee of the Whole: go back to your hotels, he told the assembled delegates. There was a need to consult further on outstanding issues, but the President said he would present a complete draft text of a cluster munition convention at 10h00 the next day.[27]

As delegations filed out of Croke Park, the Irish continued their bilateral consultations in the backrooms, talks that would last until almost midnight. Among those consulted were New Zealand, Austria, Switzerland, Italy (an important meeting, in view of Italy's problems on hosting), Slovakia (which produced a submunition with mechanical self-destruct and was unhappy with article 2, paragraph 2(c)) and Spain.

The Irish were also watching the British delegation closely. Throughout much of the day, the British head of delegation, Ambassador John Duncan, could be seen near the front entrance of Croke Park (its smokers' corner), cigarette in hand and in animated conversation on a mobile phone with his authorities in London. Early on Tuesday evening Duncan hinted to O'Ceallaigh that a major British policy announcement was in the wind, but before that there were a few areas where the UK's expectations needed to be met. The UK implied that it now recognized the game was up for transition periods, but would still not budge from insistence on hosting language in the interoperability draft article. And the British still seemed concerned about wording in article 4 on clearance that related to the article's obligations on retroactive responsibility for cluster munition user states—a bone of contention between the British and some of the states of the Friends of the Affected (Lebanon, in particular) over the duration of the Dublin negotiations.

As Tuesday night grew late, it emerged from the contacts between President O'Ceallaigh's team and the British delegation that the UK would be prepared to drop its unpopular proposal to amend Schraner's interoperability language for the President. This change of heart can be interpreted in different ways. It could be seen at face value—as a late and agonizing British concession. However, when the UK's alleged difficulties with the interoperability language in Schraner's proposal are seen alongside the seeming evaporation of its other major concerns in the negotiation on Tuesday evening, it suggests that privately the UK government had already made up its mind that it would join the treaty. Britain's delegation in Dublin was holding out for the best possible deal, but not at the cost of tipping the negotiation over.

It seems more likely that the crucial political decision time for the UK had occurred in the middle of the first week. A continual stream of stories in the British media in the lead-up to and during the negotiations had been primed and pumped by the CMC, Landmine Action and Oxfam GB, and

British political decision makers sensed an important political opportunity—as the 21 May statement from 10 Downing Street indicated. It was then that the UK effectively stood on the political threshold requiring it to choose between joining a cluster munition ban treaty—in which case it could try to claim a stake in leadership in a humanitarian victory for the British public—or walk away from the negotiations with all of the accusations that would bring. Yet the negotiations seemed to be on an acceptable trajectory. The UK had stuck with the process, very publicly and at Prime Ministerial level, which would make an exit even more difficult and politically costly.

The British announcement, when it came, was a further message of commitment from Prime Minister Gordon Brown. A news story appeared on the website of *The Guardian* late on Tuesday night, to be printed in its newsstand edition the next morning; it reported that the British government "is preparing to scrap Britain's entire arsenal of cluster bombs".[28] (This was confirmed on Wednesday when Prime Minister Brown announced that "In order to secure as strong a Convention as possible in the last hours of negotiation we have issued instructions that we should support a ban on all cluster bombs, including those currently in service by the UK".[29]) According to the Irish, they would only learn what was the content of that high-level British announcement after their bilateral consultations finished that Tuesday night.[30] But they must have strongly suspected.

At midnight, when O'Ceallaigh called his bilateral consultations to an end, he sat with his team for another hour and a half as they compared notes on the night's negotiations. Among the choices they had to make were what the lower weight threshold in article 2, paragraph 2(c)(ii) should be (they decided on 4kg), finalizing the wording of the third paragraph in article 21 on interoperability, and whether the final text should have a transition period (no, was the decision). Finally, they all felt that, after such intensive consultations, this was as close as the conference was ever going to get to a text that could command consensus. There was no sense in prolonging the negotiations further even if more time had been available. As one of the President's team, James C. O'Shea, recalled: "I think we had a fairly good idea at that stage, based on the bilaterals, that it could be very difficult to do anything [to significantly change the Presidency texts]—that if you went to one side or the other there was a serious risk of unravelling everything".[31] But the Irish were still by no means certain that the package they had in mind *would* secure consensus support the next day, even though they had increasing confidence now that the British would join.[32] Other delegations, after all, still potentially had difficulties, and had not necessarily sent the same kinds of positive political signals the UK had.

At about 1h30 on Wednesday morning, O'Ceallaigh walked across the road to the Croke Park Jury's Inn hotel to catch some sleep. He left O'Shea, Smyth and Burke to ready the draft convention text the President had promised that he would deliver to the conference the next morning for its consideration. They could only hope their aim was true.

"How far we all have come"

Dáithí O'Ceallaigh had a sprightly, grandfatherly look about him, and a grandfather was what he was. As the President dressed for the day in his hotel room each morning of the Dublin conference, he told me, he looked at a photograph of his new grandson for a moment and asked the baby in the picture what his grandfather had gotten himself into.[33] Then O'Ceallaigh headed downstairs for his first meeting. By Wednesday of the second week, most of these meetings had fallen into something of a daily routine. O'Ceallaigh and his team of Burke, Kelly, O'Shea, Smyth and Twist ate breakfast together in the hotel restaurant, which was an opportunity to compare notes and gather their thoughts for the day. Soon after, they would each head over to the conference centre and O'Ceallaigh and Kelly might touch base with the conference's Secretary-General, Colm Ó Floinn. (With Kelly acting as coordinator, the logistic and substantive sides of the Dublin conference were run largely separately, an arrangement that allowed O'Ceallaigh to focus on the business of negotiating—but working to a tight conference timetable meant that the practical aspects of the conference such as translation and publication of key documents had to be synchronized with the President's plans as exactly as possible.)

Then, each morning of the Dublin conference at 9h15, the President met with his eight vice presidents (Chile, France, Hungary, Lebanon, Mauritania, Mexico, Norway and Zambia) and the Friends (such as Austria, New Zealand, Switzerland, South Africa, and later Australia) along with his Irish team. Vice presidents are often viewed as merely procedural in many arms control-related negotiations and they play little role, but O'Ceallaigh wanted to be able to actively coordinate with all of these actors in the conference "so that I would be able to tell people what we were planning for the day or what the strategy was for the day or what the tactics might be, but also to learn from them what the problems might be and *where* the difficulties might be".[34] Otherwise, from the splendid isolation of the podium, it would be only too easy for O'Ceallaigh to fall out of touch with a real sense of the mood of different regions and political groupings within the negotiations. This, the Irish felt, could only result in nasty surprises. His daily 9h15 meetings throughout the course of the Dublin negotiations were thus integral. O'Ceallaigh said:

> What I was trying to build up was a sense that the Chair was involved geographically with people in the [negotiating] room, and also that there was a way for, say, the Africans to speak to Zambia and they knew it would get through [to me]. So it was a very good sounding board, a lot of exchange of information and I got a lot of advice from these people every morning. It helped us run the conference in what I think was seen as a fairly open way. I don't think we were in anybody's pocket—we were genuinely trying to find an outcome which would reflect the mood in the room.[35]

As shall be seen, this feedback and coordination mechanism was not faultless. The President's final obstacle in the negotiations that culminating day of the Dublin negotiations was to involve Lebanon—one of his vice presidents.

That morning, O'Ceallaigh talked through his game plan for Wednesday with those assembled in his extended bureau. Then, a little after 10h00, he went down the stairs to the main conference hall. There he called the Committee of the Whole to order to introduce his Presidency Paper containing a consolidated draft of a Convention on Cluster Munitions—finished during the night and printed that morning, to be distributed to delegates following his remarks.[36] O'Ceallaigh remarked that about two thirds of the articles were identical to the various Presidency texts he had already forwarded to the conference's Plenary following discussions in the Committee of the Whole. The rest reflected Committee of the Whole discussions, his Friends' consultations, or consultations O'Ceallaigh or members of his team had undertaken. He said:

> I would ask delegations to consider the text carefully. And I ask everyone to reflect on how far all in this room—how far we all—have come in the last 18 months. The headline definition of a cluster munition in this text will lead to the prohibition of all cluster munitions that cause unacceptable harm to civilians. It will involve the removal of all cluster munitions from national stocks for a large number of states here represented in this room. The provision on relations with states not

party to this Convention will be difficult for some, but for others it is not enough.

The President paused, then continued:

> The provisions on clearance and removal of cluster munitions remnants, victim assistance and international cooperation and assistance will ensure the mobilization of significant resources to eliminate the risk of proliferation, and to eliminate the use of cluster munitions as well as addressing the consequences of past use by providing assistance to victims and ensuring the removal of the threats posed by unexploded submunitions.[37]

O'Ceallaigh then ran through the Presidency Paper, commenting briefly on each article.[38] Concerning article 1 on general scope, he noted a change to the wording on the exclusion of mines from the purview of the Convention on Cluster Munitions, and the addition of the part on aerial dispensers to avoid a loophole (left unspoken was that he now had British agreement to this). On the article 2 definition of a cluster munition, he said, "The main definition, that of a cluster munition, which was already quite demanding, had been added to by the inclusion of criteria regarding weight, which my consultations showed to enjoy broad support".[39] With regard to article 4 on clearance and the recent difficulties between Lebanon and the UK in particular, O'Ceallaigh said of his consultations and those of Burke as the relevant Friend, "While consensus was not achieved among all delegations the text in the draft represents in our view the best compromise available to accommodate the concerns of all interested delegations".[40] Events would prove this assessment not quite accurate. And, noting that almost all delegations concerned with the issue of how many ratifying states should be necessary for international entry into force of a cluster munition ban treaty in article 17 favoured either 20 or 40, O'Ceallaigh said the figure of 30 had been chosen, a point that caused many delegates to chuckle.

Eventually the President came to the new article 21 on interoperability:

> This is a new article intended to address the concerns of a considerable number of participating States, from all regions, regarding their ability to continue to participate in military cooperation and operations, including multi-national peace support operations, with States not party to the Convention. This is an issue which affects a wide range of states of differing sizes and positions in the world both within and without military alliances.

The text of the article is based closely, with only one small addition, on the paper circulated yesterday afternoon by my Friend of the President, Ambassador Schraner of Switzerland, which was regarded by almost all delegations as a very good basis for work. I'm very grateful to my good Friend Ambassador Schraner for her dedicated work on this difficult issue.[41]

The "small addition" the President had mentioned was to add "and operations" alongside military cooperation in paragraph 3.[42] Overall, O'Ceallaigh said, the draft text was an ambitious attempt to address the humanitarian concerns associated with the use of cluster munitions in line with the Oslo Declaration's commitments. After reiterating some of his opening remarks, O'Ceallaigh mentioned—as if in passing—that there were no transition periods in the Presidency Paper. Then he asked all delegations to consider the text carefully, and seek instructions from their capitals on whether they could accept it at the Committee of the Whole in the afternoon. The Presidency Paper would simultaneously be made available on the conference's website so that authorities in capitals could more easily examine it, O'Ceallaigh said.

FINAL ENDGAME

O'Ceallaigh's presentation of the Presidency "composite" text had taken just over 18 minutes. The President and his team had expended what was likely to be their only shot at a Convention on Cluster Munitions. Delegations now went their separate ways to study the convention text. There is the old saying that "it's not over until the fat lady sings" (although thin lady is perhaps more appropriate in the case of the Croke Park negotiations in view of Friday's Céline Dion concert), and O'Ceallaigh now knew he had to go out and do his best to sell the agreement. Many Tee-total states still opposed any paragraph 2(c) exemption in the cluster munition definition on principle. Moreover, some Tee-total delegations still struggled to understand the weight criterion concept reinserted into the definition as part of cumulative criteria for exclusion. At the same time, some delegations would have to come to terms with the fact that paragraph 2(c) would exclude—based on their effects—certain submunitions using sensor-fuzed technologies such as the German SMArt 155 and the French-Swedish BONUS systems from the definition of a cluster munition and hence from a ban. On the other hand, cluster munitions as a category were to be clearly banned, and there were no transition periods, something many of the Like-minded had wanted. And the CMC was very unhappy about the article 21 interoperability provision.

During lunchtime on Wednesday, O'Ceallaigh and his military colleague Jim Burke met with the African group and then the Latin American states to try to sell the Presidency text. They were both, by various accounts, tough meetings in which both O'Ceallaigh and Burke were asked to justify, for instance, certain aspects of the definition. Emerging from these meetings sometime in the middle of the afternoon, the President still felt less than certain that all of these Tee-total states would support the adoption of the Convention.

By now, delegations had begun to gather again, as instructed, in the main conference hall for a resumption of the Committee of the Whole to tell the President whether his treaty package was acceptable. They would have to wait longer, however, as the Spanish language version of the Presidency Paper was still not available, and would not be until 15h30.[43] And, while O'Ceallaigh and Burke had been in the African and Latin American regional meetings, other members of the Irish team had been chatting with delegations in the corridors and trying to gauge reactions to the Presidency Paper. They had detected a problem, and when O'Ceallaigh emerged they escorted him to meet with delegates from the CMC, Canada and the UK in an upstairs consultation room.

The gathering was held at the request of the CMC's representatives. CMC campaigners at the Dublin conference were unhappy about the interoperability formulation in the Presidency Paper. In view of the evident strength of the rest of the paper in humanitarian terms, in private most within the CMC agreed that the campaign should not repudiate it over the precise wording of the interoperability article. But their representatives—Conway, Goose and Nash—thought it might be possible to persuade O'Ceallaigh to make the changes that the CMC believed would improve the article and further specify the prohibition on assistance to prohibited activities by a non-state party in article 1. "It was very important for campaigners to know that we were still fighting right up until the very last minute to strengthen the text in article 21", Nash later said.[44]

Paragraph 3 of article 21 said, "Notwithstanding the provisions of Article 1 of this Convention and in accordance with international law, States Parties, their military personnel or nationals, may engage in military cooperation and operations with States not parties to this Convention that might engage in activities prohibited to a State party".[45]

The CMC wanted to limit the provisions of the paragraph to just one part of Article 1—paragraph 1(c). And they did not like the "Notwithstanding" at paragraph 3's beginning, aiming to replace it with "Without prejudice to",[46] the same formulation the Norwegians had tried (without success) to have included in the interoperability proposal evolving throughout Schraner's consultations the previous week. At root was their concern to make it as clear as possible that the treaty's article 1 prohibitions took precedence over article 21, paragraph 3. Goose and Nash thought that their earlier conversations with Earl Turcotte, Canada's head of delegation, and Ambassador John Duncan of the UK indicated some flexibility in that regard.[47] If the CMC could secure agreement from Canada and the UK, two states that had been among the toughest on interoperability, perhaps the President could be persuaded to amend article 21, paragraph 3. The CMC also noted that interoperability had not been discussed in the Committee of the Whole since the conference's opening day apart from brief statements by O'Ceallaigh and Schraner, which had hinted at later open-ended discussions that never arrived, and which alone might provide procedural grounds for such a revision.

Beside Conway, Goose and Nash from the CMC, in the small room were O'Ceallaigh and the chief lawyer on the Irish team, Declan Smyth, along with Turcotte and Duncan. Nash made the CMC's pitch for its changes, arguing that these could be justified in procedural terms because interoperability had not been comprehensively discussed in the Committee of the Whole.[48] But the CMC's representatives discovered, contrary to their expectations, that the Briton and the Canadian were not prepared to accept further changes to the text the President had already put on the table. Duncan said he felt that although the Presidency text demanded some difficult compromises for the UK, it reflected a package Britain could go along with, and that civil society should be very happy with it all things considered. Turcotte was more direct in his response to the CMC: "This was essentially a red line for Canada. I think I used the word 'red line'. My instructions were expressly clear".[49] In Canada's view, the President's text struck the right balance: one that offered protection to civilians, which would at the same time enable the prospective treaty's member states to continue to engage in combined military operations with non-party states.[50]

O'Ceallaigh now also spoke up to say that no further changes to the Presidency text would be entertained:

> I was convinced at this stage that if I re-opened anything we were in trouble because I'd just come from the Africans and Latin Americans and was not in any way certain that I'd persuaded them that this was by far the best deal they would get, and that it was a deal worth going for. We hadn't left either group [with that group] saying, "We're behind you". So I wasn't anxious—because it wasn't that sort of thing—but I was reasonably certain that if I opened this text we were done for, we just would not get it done in time … I said that to the CMC.[51]

The result was a blow for the CMC, and when I spoke with Goose and Nash later that afternoon both were clearly crestfallen. They had been unhappy with the closed nature of the interoperability consultations throughout the Dublin conference, and could not help but feel misled and a little cheated by the process, which in their view had seemed neither fair nor transparent. Article 21, paragraph 3 was a clumsy solution that had the potential to allow states to evade their obligations to uphold the spirit and purpose of the prohibitions of the Convention on Cluster Munitions, in their view. Goose later told me:

> It was a manipulated process that ended with a bad result. Having said all that, I think ultimately it's going to make no humanitarian difference whatsoever. I don't think that we are ever going to see a state party to the new convention knowingly—intentionally—assist the US or anybody else with the use of cluster munitions. … And in the end, the fact that the prohibition on assistance remained in the earlier main prohibition article and that this [article 21] was tacked on the end was a positive development. The addition of the language about having to inform others of your obligations and to actively discourage them from use—that was a very positive development within the framework of how we were trying to handle the issue. But in the end it's something that was there to create some ambiguity about what it means to assist with a prohibited act.[52]

Strongly encouraged

By now it was nearing 17h00. The conference clock had been stopped and more than a hundred delegations had been waiting for several hours for the Spanish version of the Presidency Paper to become available. Now that this version was in delegates' hands, there was an urgent need for the President to convene the promised Committee of the Whole session.

However, O'Ceallaigh now had another outstanding problem to solve. Throughout the negotiations, his colleague Burke had struggled to bridge the differences between the Like-minded such as France, Germany, Italy and the UK with Lebanon, a state affected by cluster munitions and an active and influential state among the Tee-total on certain aspects of clearance in article 4, paragraph 4. This provision related to:

> cases in which cluster munitions have been used or abandoned by one State Party prior to entry into force of this Convention for that State Party and have become cluster munition remnants, that are located in areas under the jurisdiction or control of another State Party at the time of entry into force of this Convention for the latter.[53]

The issue at hand concerned whether the past user state was obliged to provide assistance to the other state once both joined the treaty. Lebanon felt that if affected states were obliged to take on the treaty's obligations such as clearance, then user states should also bear some aspects of it, and it wanted states joining the cluster munition ban treaty to be "strongly encouraged" to provide assistance. This would not be a mandatory obligation, it was plain, but a small victory that would be perceived to be of great symbolic value by Lebanon and other affected countries. The UK's retroactivity concerns largely taken care of by the word "encouraged", the British nevertheless had opposed "strongly" because they thought it would just be poor drafting—there was, they said, no real difference between the two formulations in practical terms.

The Lebanese delegation approached O'Ceallaigh now to tell him that Lebanon would not agree to the draft Convention unless the word "strongly" was added to the provisions in article 4 to give more weight to calls for assistance from past user states for clearance of cluster munition remnants and risk reduction education. It was a sticky moment in view of Lebanon's prominent role in the Oslo process. Lebanon denouncing the Convention on Cluster Munitions at the hour of its agreement would create a disastrous impression among many participating states and in the international media. Conferring on the spot with the Lebanese and British delegations, O'Ceallaigh asked Duncan if the UK would flex just a tiny bit more. Duncan went to confer by telephone with his authorities in capital. In two minutes, the answer came back from London: yes, we will go along with the change. But how would the President sell this change to the draft Convention text that he had adamantly refused to change moments before in his consultation with Canada, the CMC and the UK on interoperability?

Visibly nervous as he seated himself at the conference podium, O'Ceallaigh called the Committee of the Whole meeting to order. Without further ado, he asked the Deputy Foreign Minister of Zambia, Fashion Phiri, to speak, following protocol about seniority in speaking order. O'Ceallaigh hoped that this influential member of the Africa group would speak in support of the draft Convention text. While talking in generally supportive terms, however, Zambia did not endorse the draft Convention as a final product. So O'Ceallaigh spoke again, and reviewed his modus operandi and the main points of the draft text for the meeting. Noting that agreement was now needed, he reiterated:

> The Presidency Paper before us represents my assessment at this point of where the best balance of interests and compromise consistent with the Oslo Declaration now lies. It is a package of elements that entails concession for all sides but remains nevertheless an extremely ambitious Convention text that meets the objectives we set ourselves in Oslo in February last year.[54]

Zambia took the floor again, this time on behalf of the Africa group, and now made it clear that the Africans could endorse the package, although they remained unhappy with certain elements of the text. After commending Gordon Brown's Wednesday announcement about destroying the UK's cluster munitions stockpile, however, Zambia sternly warned that if others opened up the text the Africans would reconsider. A cascade of endorsements ensued with New Zealand, Canada, Mexico, South Africa, Switzerland, France, the Philippines and Indonesia echoing support for the "ambitious, detailed and balanced text".[55] Spotting his moment, O'Ceallaigh intervened again to alter article 4, paragraph 4(a) to make a "correction"[56] and insert the word "strongly" agreed with the Lebanese and the British. No one objected, and in this discreet manner the Chair was able to take advantage of the momentum to meet Lebanon's concerns.

More than two hours of statements endorsing the Convention on Cluster Munitions followed from states, the United Nations, the ICRC and the CMC. Finally, early that Wednesday evening, O'Ceallaigh ended the Committee of the Whole and reconvened the meeting in a five-minute long Plenary so that negotiators at the Dublin conference could take the decision to return to Croke Park the day after next—on Friday, 30 May 2008—to formally adopt the Convention (see annex C).[57] The indisputable reality was that the world now had a new humanitarian treaty banning cluster munitions.[58]

THE AGREEMENT OF THE CONVENTION ON CLUSTER MUNITIONS

Although difficult decisions awaited certain states about whether to join the new Convention on Cluster Munitions, for most this lay in the future. For the Dublin conference as a whole, the roller coaster of the negotiations had now ended. There would be no more surprises that risked the Oslo process's derailment before Friday's morning's adoption of the Convention on Cluster Munitions. For many of the delegates, Thursday would be a day of recuperation. There was not only the intense negotiating process to recover from, there had also been an impromptu celebration at the Jury's Inn hotel (where many of the delegates were staying) across the road from Croke Park that continued into the wee hours that night as we watched the newsfeeds on a big screen reporting on the new treaty. On Thursday, Norway's Foreign Minister, Jonas Gahr Støre, stopped briefly in Dublin on his way back to Norway from a meeting of government ministers in Greenland to congratulate O'Ceallaigh, Norway's delegation, and some of us from the UN, ICRC and CMC. He found us still elated but very tired. That day, principal members of the Core Group including the President, O'Ceallaigh, and Ambassadors Alexander Marschik (Austria), Don MacKay (New Zealand) and Steffen Kongstad (Norway) also addressed the assembled CMC campaigners about the agreement, congratulating the CMC on its contribution and answering questions.

The period from Wednesday night until 10h00 on Friday morning would be one of frantic work to ready the final documents in the meeting's official languages of English, French and Spanish for the Dublin conference's secretariat. When Friday's Plenary session began, the first order of business was to have the 107 states participating in Dublin[59] adopt the text of the Convention on Cluster Munitions, as delegations had agreed to do on Wednesday evening. In a powerfully emotional moment following formal adoption of the treaty, the several hundred delegates in the packed Croke Park conference room rose to their feet and cheered. Many also turned to applaud the cluster munition and landmine survivors present. The efforts of these Ban Advocates had been key in reminding government delegates of their humanitarian responsibilities throughout the Oslo process, and the joy on the faces of these survivors captured what many in the room were feeling. For some of the people present the achievement of the cluster munition ban treaty represented the achievement of a major goal in their lives—efforts that began in some cases many years or even decades before.

Statements followed the treaty's adoption from dozens of delegations—all welcoming the new Convention on Cluster Munitions.[60] As one observer reported:

> The historic significance of the Convention, with its many groundbreaking provisions, began to sink in as delegation after delegation referred to the Convention as a new chapter in disarmament and a milestone of international law. Many praised the new standards for victim assistance, international cooperation and assistance, clearance of contaminated areas, stockpile destruction, and transparency contained in the Convention, emphasizing the profound effect the Convention will have in making a real difference in affected areas and ensuring the prevention of future tragedies. Others pledged to promote the rapid entry into force of the Convention and its universality.[61]

It would be easy to be cynical about these statements of appreciation and support. Some of the most effusive praise came from delegations that claimed until earlier in the week to harbour almost insuperable reservations about the text of the treaty as it was shaping up. Yet it was, to use the words of one senior diplomat involved in the Dublin negotiations, all part of the "diplomatic theatre". Everyone had haggled hard, and the bargain struck after much metaphorical eyebrow furrowing and shaking of heads was one that most delegations could live with. The emotional atmosphere of the Dublin conference's final day was certainly not an artificial bonhomie; even the most taciturn diplomatic negotiators seemed genuinely affected at the new international legal standard they had played their parts in achieving.

And, behind the rhetoric, there were signals of real intent. Germany said, for instance, that it unilaterally renounced the use of all types of cluster munitions, and would destroy its stocks as quickly as possible—rounding out a week in which other major possessors such as France and the UK had decided to do the same. Thus, regardless of when the new Convention entered into force, these cluster munitions would no longer be in circulation. The new treaty entailed real costs for these and some other possessor states now confronted with having to find substitute military capabilities for cluster munitions. Some states, like many of the Like-minded, had joined the Oslo Declaration without necessarily anticipating that the "good" submunitions they considered they possessed with technical features like self-destruct would be among those eventually captured within the cluster munition treaty's prohibitions. Cluster munitions now prohibited by the Convention constituted significant proportions of national munitions stockpiles in some states. Replacing these capabilities would take time and cost money.

Of course, while the product of the Dublin negotiations had been acclaimed by consensus it did not necessarily imply unanimity among all of the more than one hundred delegations present that their governments would join the treaty. That so many states did announce in their statements that they would accede to the Convention as soon as possible was significant—and showed the sense of humanitarian ownership even the more reluctant had acquired. In this sense, while it did not say it would join, Japan's decision to support the adoption of the text on 30 May was also a step forward as it had previously indicated it might not. Japan had a large stockpile of cluster munitions, especially of older types without features such as self-destruct, and saw the weapons as important in repelling national invasion.[62] Throughout the Oslo process, however, Japan's government came under increasing pressure at home to ban a weapon that, if used on Japan's soil in a defensive conflict, would create hazards to Japanese civilians. Japanese media, such as Mainichi newspapers, NHK Television, Kyodo News and Asahi Shimbun put Japan's policies under public scrutiny. A visit to Japan to lobby Japanese policymakers by Ban Advocate Branislav Kapetanović earlier in 2008 had received widespread attention. Japanese journalists like Katsumi Sawada (Mainichi) and Izumi Aoki (NHK) were tireless in following the cluster munition issue, and by the end of the Dublin negotiations were as knowledgeable as many diplomats about the various dimensions of the Oslo process. The unexpected Japanese decision to join consensus was also an important psychological victory for the CMC campaigners and helped to outweigh any concerns about not having achieved 100% of the desired outcome. Far from receding from its support for the new Convention after its formal adoption on 30 May, Japanese lawmakers would make accession to the treaty a priority. (Japan, along with Germany, was one of the first 15 states to ratify the CCM in the middle of 2009).

It was not all good news. As widely expected, Estonia, Finland and Slovakia said they would have to think carefully before deciding whether or not to join the CCM, although they did join the consensus in adopting the treaty text. Slovakian manufacturers produced a submunition with mechanical self-destruct, and its representatives had seemed genuinely taken aback that these were to be banned. Finland had from the start been a rather reluctant participant in the Oslo process, and was unwilling to abolish its relatively new stockpile of cluster munitions.[63]

This did not detract from the atmosphere, however, especially in view of poignant statements from cluster munition-affected countries such as Lebanon welcoming adoption of the Convention. There were also statements from a broad range of states that article 21 would not be allowed to become a loophole, or be allowed to diminish confidence in the Convention. Kongstad, speaking on Norway's behalf, said the Norwegian government would host the Convention's signing ceremony in Oslo, in early December.[64]

The Dublin conference closed with a brief ceremony. Fittingly, Østern, Sekkenes and Herby—three important individuals in the network that had driven the emergence of the Oslo process—represented the CMC, UN and ICRC respectively on the podium alongside Norwegian Deputy Defence Minister Espen Barth Eide and Irish Foreign Minister Micheál Martin. Sekkenes read a statement on behalf of the UN Secretary-General accepting treaty depositary functions and praising the new Convention.[65] Ireland's Foreign Minister called on those present to focus on the future:

> I suggest that we set ourselves three immediate goals. First, we need to do all that is necessary nationally to allow us to ratify the Convention as soon as possible after signature. …
>
> The second goal must be to ensure the greatest possible number of accessions to the Convention. We want ultimately to see it ratified by all Member States of the United Nations. We should work together to explain and argue for its provisions with those who are not here.
>
> Third, we need to plan to do what is necessary to implement the Convention in full, not least in regard to victim assistance and clearance.[66]

Obstacles to achieving these goals are not trivial. In the next and final chapter, these and other challenges to the Convention on Cluster Munitions are briefly considered. Some final thoughts on how the international treaty to ban cluster munitions was won are also outlined.

CHAPTER 11

THE END OF THE BEGINNING

> I remember two years ago people were still saying this ban couldn't happen. It's taken countless stunts, events, petitions, relentless badgering of journalists and parliamentarians and of course two weeks locked in a Gaelic football stadium, but here we are. The success has come from so many individual contributions adding up to far more than the sum of the parts. It reminds us it is possible to change the status quo and we are all responsible for doing it. It is simply wrong to justify inaction by saying it can't be done.[1]

Thomas Nash spoke these words in Oslo as part of the Cluster Munition Coalition (CMC)'s statement to welcome the signing there of the Convention on Cluster Munitions (CCM) on 3 December 2008. Despite the cold Scandinavian weather, delegations from around one hundred governments, the UN, the International Committee of the Red Cross (ICRC) and hundreds of civil society campaigners had created a warm atmosphere in the cavernous and sombrely beautiful Oslo City Hall.

The bonhomie even permeated a party of Foreign Ministers from NATO countries that included Bernard Kouchner of France, Frank-Walter Steinmeier of Germany and David Miliband from the United Kingdom. The Ministers had arrived together on a plane from Brussels chartered by their NATO and Norwegian counterpart Jonas Gahr Støre to sign the new Convention before flying on to a summit of the Organization for Security and Co-operation in Europe to be held in Helsinki. Each Minister welcomed the cluster munition ban treaty in glowing terms.[2] Kouchner pushed aside his prepared speech to proclaim (in French), "Yes we can! We can, and the US can, sign this treaty, Russia and China can", adding that he would press leaders in these countries to do so.[3] To no one's surprise, however, those governments were absent from the signing ceremony. So were other governments that had shunned the Oslo process such as India, Israel and Pakistan, although Brazil sent an observer to be present at the signing. Far away in Washington, a US State Department spokesperson for the outgoing Bush administration asserted that "the CCM constitutes a ban on most types of cluster munitions: such a general ban on cluster munitions will put the lives of our military men and women, and those of our coalition partners, at risk".[4] This did not seem to be the view of those coalition partners, the majority of which were signing the new ban treaty in Oslo.

Laos, the most heavily affected country on earth from unexploded submunitions, was a prominent and early signer of the CCM at the ceremony. The Deputy Prime Minister, Thongloun Sisloulith, did not hesitate to pinpoint what his government saw at stake:

> Here, in Norway and in other countries of Western Europe, after the Second World War, peoples have been able to fully enjoy peace and devote their efforts and capabilities to the development of their countries, and children can enjoy their basic rights to life and safe environment, in which to develop, learn and play; while in the Lao [People's Democratic Republic], although the war ended more than thirty years ago, the Lao people continue to bear its legacy and the Lao children are denied the basic rights to which they are entitled.

> Against this backdrop, the signing of this Convention is already one step forward to its realization, but at the same time, it is just the beginning of our journey to the ultimate goal of eradicating the scourge of cluster munitions and liberating the people and our children from fear and threat of such silent killer [sic].[5]

With the agreement of the Oslo Declaration in February 2007, efforts to achieve a ban treaty had formally commenced and, just as the outcome of the work in the Soria Moria had marked a significant juncture, the signing ceremony a year and a half later marked another in the story of addressing the humanitarian impacts of cluster munitions. Just because a new treaty had been negotiated did not mean those humanitarian consequences had miraculously taken care of themselves, however. An immediate and visible challenge was that the cluster munition ban treaty now had to be brought into force internationally. Most of all, the CCM would have to be implemented effectively to actually make a positive difference to the lives of people and their communities affected by the weapon those instigating the Oslo process had invoked as the initiative's purpose. Attention would increasingly turn to those challenges: in the Oslo conference's margins, an informal "Friends of the CCM" group of state, international organization and civil society representatives active during the Oslo process met to consider some of the tasks ahead.

Meanwhile, the efforts of the Convention on Certain Conventional Weapons (CCW) to negotiate a proposal on cluster munitions continued, though its lower level of humanitarian ambition was glaringly obvious. Following the Dublin negotiations, some CCW participants began to openly question the need for, or desirability of, a protocol that might implicitly legitimize some of the weapons now banned by the CCM. At the same time, many delegations to the CCW of states also participating in the Oslo process said they saw value in a protocol if it could avoid this conflict and deliver some sort of meaningful humanitarian benefit since the CCW was a forum that included all of the largest users and producers of cluster munitions. It was increasingly clear, though, that the CCW's vaunted membership was also a weakness when it came to delivering such results. The bottom line for many governments (including those of the European Union) that the CCW draft protocol should include some sort of prohibition related to cluster munitions to be credible or attractive could not, for the time being at least, secure support of all of the users and producers. Faced with failure to meet their self-imposed deadline of completion of a proposal for a protocol by the end of 2008, in November the CCW's membership voted for extra time for their efforts during early 2009. Those further negotiating sessions were also unable to achieve consensus on a protocol on cluster munitions, and informal consultations continued in August 2009 without result.

The CCW's negotiations on cluster munitions were galvanized into existence by the emergence of the Oslo process, itself an initiative stemming from frustration with the CCW's inability to collectively tackle the weapon's hazards. The root cause of this inability was not the CCW's consensus practice, although that hardly helped. Instead, one can see from the story told in this book that, for fear it might impinge on their continued ability to use the weapon, some states in the CCW have been reluctant even to recognize the threat cluster munitions pose to civilians and its logical implications, let alone move decisively to address such problems. These troubling implications extend to the cluster munition testing regimes of producers, states' criteria for choice and use of the weapon in combat operations and the weapon's broader acceptability consistent with humanitarian law and the public conscience.

Among the most militarized powers, failure to come to grips with these implications reflects a long thread of confirmation bias running through international discussions related to cluster munitions. Forums like the ICRC conferences in the 1970s and the CCW, historically, tended to be environments in which government experts sought out the information that confirmed their pre-existing positions and beliefs about the legitimacy and utility of cluster munitions.[6] It meant that, for a long time, in the context of international measures on cluster munitions, the importance of humanitarian considerations was praised while simultaneously buried. Perhaps this should not surprise us, as confirmation bias is a problem with expert judgement that social scientists like Philip Tetlock have shown affect many kinds of prediction- and decision-making.[7] For many governments, such utility arguments were simply no longer convincing once the evidence mounted of the problematic nature of cluster munitions—evidence that also served to undermine "good" versus "bad" technically minded debates about the weapon. Yet, regardless, it is exactly the path the CCW Group of Government Experts have gone down in their belated negotiations on cluster munitions; an approach largely divorced from facts on the ground about the inaccuracy and unreliability of cluster munitions in operational conditions. Those representing states participating in the Oslo process and the CCW let this occur, for various reasons. It could be argued that the draft cluster munition protocol process has come to resemble the pursuit of an expedient outcome at the cost of a real solution, a solution that now exists in the form of the CCM for those with the conviction to adopt it.

As of writing, it remains to be seen whether the CCW's efforts to achieve a cluster munition protocol will result in something of humanitarian benefit or not, or whether the process simply will fizzle out in view of other international priorities. Whatever happens, the ultimate outcome of the CCW's efforts on cluster munitions is a curious story of its own that, for practical reasons, lies beyond the scope of this book. Instead, this final chapter briefly considers some of the distinctive features of the Oslo process, features that might help to explain its success. This success—so far—has to be balanced against some significant challenges that may yet qualify or even nullify the CCM's achievement. Lastly, some thoughts are offered about what international efforts to address cluster munitions could offer in terms of future directions for tackling the effects of explosive violence on civilians.

FACTORS IN THE ACHIEVEMENT OF THE CLUSTER MUNITION BAN TREATY

Some people feel the Oslo process reflects a humanitarian disarmament "model" along the lines of the Ottawa process.[8] There can be little doubt that there are many similarities between the Ottawa and Oslo initiatives, just as it is possible to identify some significant contrasts between them. And for some national diplomats—the people their governments task with the details of building and maintaining multilateral regimes—the prospect of free-standing international processes like those leading to the CCM and Mine Ban Treaty always raises tricky questions about the relative value of ends and means.[9] One prominent senior diplomat from among the Like-minded states told me during research for this book, for example, that the abiding lesson from the Oslo process in his view was that it was an example to avoid emulating in the future: "It was a hell of a gamble probably justified because of the problem and urgency to do something about it. But it could easily have gone wrong", he said. Others I talked with would beg to differ. My own view is that there is a place for both standing multilateral processes like the CCW and free-standing international initiatives, provided they have a reasonable chance of improving humanitarian protection for civilians and do not simply become diplomatic soapboxes.[10] In this respect, it is worth recalling that many of those going into the Oslo process did so not with joyous hearts, but because they had become convinced that the standing CCW machinery was incapable of delivering a meaningful response, coupled with a recognition that this did not reduce their moral or political culpability for failing to tackle the hazards cluster munitions pose to civilians. The degree to which the Ottawa and Oslo processes really do represent a formula for international action is a question both multilateral practitioners and scholars will debate for years and even decades to come.

There is also a danger that if we always look at efforts to tackle cluster munitions through the prism of the landmine process—or the CCW, for that matter—we will always tend to see what we want to see. This would be a mistake because the cluster munition ban treaty's importance transcends whether it vindicates or discredits these other approaches. Bearing this in mind, let us consider for a moment some of the distinctive features of the Oslo process. In November 2008, as part of work on research for this book, I was involved in convening an informal symposium with representatives from governments, intergovernmental and civil society organizations and academic institutions in Glion, Switzerland. (Fittingly, the site of the meeting overlooked Montreux, where the ICRC meeting on cluster munitions was held a year and a half before, and the venue's high vantage point offered views over the lake toward a distant Palais des Nations in Geneva). One objective of the Glion symposium *was* to identify and elaborate key lessons that could be drawn from the Ottawa and Oslo processes with a view to seeing how these might be of relevance to other multilateral work. In the course of discussions at that meeting, however, several key characteristics of the Oslo process emerged, some of which were also relevant in the Mine Ban Treaty context.[11] These are now briefly discussed.

FOCUS ON THE HUMAN IMPACT

The nature of humanitarian law-related discussions in the 1970s and later consideration in the CCW (at least until very recently) meant that the emphasis of the discourse on cluster munitions was on the alleged military utility of the weapon category. It perhaps did not help that the CCW is a humanitarian law process administered largely by disarmament diplomats with little direct experience of the effects of cluster munitions. Eventually, as this history shows, attention *was* drawn to the impacts of the weapon on human beings, which served to alter the traditional discourse's weighting. At the conclusion of the Dublin negotiations, Norway's delegation reviewed the factors it saw as important during the Oslo process and argued that "by insisting that it was essential to approach this issue from the humanitarian angle, we were able to take action in an adequate way. In essence, this process, and the new Convention on Cluster Munitions, is disarmament as humanitarian action".[12]

Norway's views are significant in this respect as its government instigated what became known as the Oslo process because of its concerns that the CCW was failing to act in the face of growing evidence of the human impact of cluster munitions. As a country with a strong humanitarian tradition, cluster munitions became a resurgent domestic political issue there from the 1999 Kosovo conflict, and after a 2005 change of government Norway was eventually prepared for the risk of leading on the issue internationally. The Norwegian government's conclusion, based on careful testing of its state-of-the-art cluster munition stockpile, that this weapon should be prohibited was grounded on their foreseeable human impact on civilians if used. Nevertheless, as for policymakers in many other countries during the Oslo process, it was not without controversy, even in Norway. As one Norwegian official noted:

> it's also a division between traditionalists and people who are more open to seeing possibilities, and also applying a broader perspective. The traditionalists will defend whatever [weapon] they've got, whatever it is. They won't necessarily look at it from a broader political perspective, and definitely not from a humanitarian perspective. And that's the good

thing about the humanitarian aspect, or perspective, that you can look at things from a different angle, and see that they can look politically attractive and are morally, politically important. If you see this from a more traditionalist, or trans-Atlantic crowd's perspective, this is just a nuisance. And you would always look for a minimum, like the 1% submunition failure-rate for instance that would make this acceptable, without going deeper into it. What does 1% actually mean? On the ground it doesn't mean anything. It's completely irrational.

CREDIBILITY THROUGH RESEARCH AND PRACTICE

The Oslo process became highly data-driven, even though before the initiative began there was arguably less systematically gathered information available about the impacts of the weapon on civilians than there had been about anti-personnel mine impacts a decade earlier when the Ottawa process commenced. (In part this is a good thing: the hazards of cluster munitions had not yet reached the global proportions of the "landmine epidemic" of the 1990s.) Notably, some of the initial information on the socio-economic impacts of cluster munitions was gathered as a by-product of work by international organizations and NGOs to build a more comprehensive understanding of the landmine and explosive remnants of war (ERW) problems.

The growing awareness of the humanitarian problems cluster munitions caused was important in creating the international conditions for the Oslo process, but the nature of the empirical evidence also played an important role in framing its conceptual parameters. The proposal by Sweden and other states in 1974 had taken account of effects of cluster warheads on civilians, but it was primarily concerned about the impacts *on combatants at time of use,* for which it was not easy to gather evidence because cluster munitions at the time were possessed by relatively few countries. Moreover, although cluster bombs had been dropped in massive quantities on South-East Asia in the 1960s and early 1970s, at that time little information existed in the public domain about their humanitarian effects on civilians beyond accounts from eyewitnesses like David Dellinger and, later, Fred Branfman and the Mennonites and Quakers. These calls of alarm proved easy for governments to dismiss. The effects of cluster munitions on combatants, and particularly problems at time of use, were of consequence for those campaigning in the twenty-first century on cluster munitions too. By now, though, the periodic use of cluster munitions around the world had left a discernible trail of human suffering that served to emphasize the impacts of the weapon *post-conflict and on civilians*. Even in Laos, one of the world's more reclusive states, the tragic consequences of cluster munitions on civilians were eventually documented and published abroad. Taken together, the research showed that in conflicts in which cluster munitions were used, civilians often took the brunt of a class of weapon that failed in large numbers to function as designed—with deadly consequences for them long after conflict ended.

This firm evidence of post-conflict civilian harm gathered subsequent to the 1970s diplomatic conferences would be at the heart of the arguments of those calling for international measures during this decade. The evidence base of post-conflict cluster munition harm to civilians was harder for states in the CCW to argue around, especially as other CCW participants became more sensitized to the issues of deadly duds from explosive weapons in general.

SHIFTING THE BURDEN OF PROOF

Individual states could try to dismiss such research, but the steady accumulation of evidence served to counter statements by governments that the types of cluster munitions they had in stock carried no particular risk of creating humanitarian problems. It also contributed to the growing stigmatization of cluster munitions in view of their effects on civilians. And, although it had started much earlier, a phenomenon discernible by the time of the ICRC's Montreux expert meeting in April 2007 was a shift in who bore the burden of proof about the acceptability of the weapon. Talks at that meeting and in the Oslo process, in particular, were moving away from a situation in which cluster munition users, producers and manufacturers could make any claims they chose without really being called on to justify these assertions, to a discourse in which they were increasingly called upon to demonstrate that their weapons did *not* cause unacceptable harm. It was an important distinction, and Richard Moyes and Brian Rappert later hailed it as a breakthrough application to a weapon system of a precautionary orientation previously seen in health and environmental domains.[13]

The Core Group's resolve (despite wavering in the lead-up to the December 2007 Vienna conference) to maintain an approach to Oslo process work on definitions in which the onus was on those possessing types of cluster weapons to publicly justify their exclusion was therefore significant. It meant that, along with others questioning the acceptability of cluster munitions being proposed for exclusion:

> NGOs within the CMC did not have to make a positive case for what should be banned and could instead criticise the justifications for retention put forward during the Oslo Process by states such as Spain, Japan, Germany, the United Kingdom, Finland, Switzerland, and France. And because the CMC is an alliance of diverse NGOs with varying positions, there was the additional benefit of allowing disagreements to be handled as internal issues. Rather than putting up front where the line of acceptability should be drawn, the CMC could adopt the reactive position of demanding more evidence from certain states to justify proposed exclusions.[14]

Powerful reinforcement was the *M-85: An Analysis of Reliability* report prepared jointly by Norwegian government defence scientist Ove Dullum and NGO co-authors, which was presented at the Vienna conference.[15] The report dealt a fatal blow to the notion that explosive submunitions with self-destruct features and their ilk could be an adequate humanitarian solution to the effects of cluster munitions. A small number of diplomats and military people have grumbled subsequently about specific aspects of the report like its sample size or supposedly unique features of the 2006 Southern Lebanon conflict that they felt should have blunted the report's impact. But (tellingly), they never managed to develop adequate counter-arguments to persuade others of their case based on a transparent examination of evidence.

BROAD PARTNERSHIPS

Although states were in the driving seat in the Dublin negotiations, civil society and international organizations were important partners with governments in the Oslo process. In many cases, civil society and international organizations were where real expertise on aspects of cluster munitions (such as their effects) resided, after all.

Relationships within the Oslo process between its various partners were not without strain. To a profound extent the story of international efforts to ban cluster munitions is one of collective reframing of problems, and among those involved this movement occurred at different rates toward the idea of a categorical ban. The evolution of the CMC's call, for instance, indicates that even among truly like-minded actors such as the NGOs in the

Coalition, the way ahead was not always self-evident—it took work to build agreement. For states it was obviously the case that there were differing views, and so it was also significant that the composition of the Oslo process differed from that of the CCW, with both developing and affected countries not traditionally active in the CCW playing active and prominent roles. The interest of countries such as Afghanistan, Laos, Lebanon and Serbia in a humanitarian outcome and their association with the Tee-total states served as a counter to the "split-the-category" approach to cluster munitions some others would have preferred.

Even among the Core Group there were some differences, but what is striking is that differing preferences were instrumental rather than fundamental; that is, how to achieve the goal, rather than what the goal should be. Perhaps the Core Group's greatest collective achievement in that respect, then, is that it managed to steer the Oslo process to a negotiation using a prohibition on "cluster munitions that cause unacceptable harm" as a uniting goal. The resolve of the Core Group did not allow the Oslo initiative to descend into a fratricidal debate that, for much of the process, would have revealed differing fundamental preferences about what the nature of the prohibition should be until the humanitarian evidence was properly aired, the burden of proof had shifted, and broad political support for humanitarian objectives had gathered behind it.

Urgent action, broad objectives

The Oslo Declaration provided the political framework for the process of moving toward a humanitarian treaty. It followed events such as the 2006 Southern Lebanon conflict that contributed to a sense of international urgency to tackle cluster munitions. But, on its own, awareness of a crisis is not sufficient: potential solutions simple enough to communicate publicly and persuade must be also in the offing—efforts that commenced long before that conflict described by some as a "necessary but not sufficient" catalyst for a ban campaign. Earlier, the CMC, for example, had used Belgium's national legislation banning cluster munitions in 2006 to convey a sense of momentum in stigmatizing cluster munitions. And, as we have seen, key leaders in Norway and the CMC established their broad respective objectives early, even if their specific corporate positions would subsequently evolve in relation to achieving these objectives.

The legitimacy of both the diplomatic process and the CMC came to depend heavily on actors from all regions of the world, including from cluster-munition affected countries and from among individual survivors and their families willing to act as humanitarian advocates. Geographical balance, regional involvement and inclusiveness in the process promoted a shared feeling of ownership, but it was never easily achieved. It was also not the situation when the initiative to hold the Oslo conference was announced in late 2006 by Norway, and steered by a small group of states. As if following the mantra "build it and they will come", the Oslo process gathered strength once it became clear that it was a viable avenue for tackling cluster munitions, which entailed some courage, quite a bit of bluff and astute diplomacy in achieving the Oslo Declaration. Interestingly, the emphasis put on the CCW by the major users and producers of cluster munitions that it was more legitimate, in effect, because it included all of them—coupled with the CCW's lack of swift progress—probably contributed to many states, especially in the developing world (a significant number of them stockpiling the weapon), taking a greater interest in participating in the Oslo process.

The one constant in the many explanations I heard for the success of the Oslo process in the course of preparation of this book was on the importance of a diverse range of individuals, adding to "far more than the sum of its parts" as Nash put it. It is why I have tried to illustrate this history with so many "colourful" stories, albeit about a small fraction of those people. The commitment of individuals is visible all the way back to the 1970s, whether Swedish government officials like Torgil Wulff and Hans Blix trying to give effect to the anti-personnel weapon initiative, researchers and campaigners gathering evidence such as Eric Prokosch (whose book *The Technology of Killing* would be a reference in the 1990s for landmine campaigners and later on cluster munitions) and Stockholm International Peace Research Institute researcher Malvern Lumsden, or the Quakers, Mennonites and others trying to help those affected by ERW in South-East Asia and raise the alarm about cluster munitions back in the US. This decade it extended to politicians in countries like Belgium, Norway and later others, like in Austria, who saw a link between the Mine Ban Treaty and a humanitarian agreement on cluster munitions. Indeed, recall the degree to which the achievement of the CCM benefited from trust networks developed and in some cases sustained by the Mine Ban Treaty implementation process and concurrent talks in the CCW this decade. These processes forged relationships and alliances that continued or were reactivated on cluster munitions—it is striking how many of the same names pop up repeatedly. While appreciating that cluster munitions were different from anti-personnel mines, many of these individuals seemed to regard the Ottawa process as at least providing a rough "road map", one that could be adapted. Central to it, as one senior Norwegian diplomat told me, was the need for "the right people, enough resources, and political backing toward a clear objective".[16] Their (outward) confidence that cluster munitions could be tackled, and history of cooperation with others on issues such as mines and ERW, served to create its own momentum and helped to pull the cluster munition issue from out of the political undergrowth.

Besides the veterans of the Mine Ban Treaty and ERW processes, there were also many new individuals who became involved in the Oslo initiative and grew with it—both on the government and civil society sides—and their energy and insights helped to give it a distinctive character. The impact of survivors was a clear example, as Handicap International concluded after the CCM's adoption:

> we learned how individuals affected by cluster munitions could play a key role in shaping what will now be a new international norm. When we launched the Ban Advocates initiative, we knew that we had a lot to learn from working with individuals whose lives have been dramatically changed because cluster munitions were once used against their community. More than us, cluster munition *victims* know what a cluster munition is and why it should be banned. They know what the needs of their communities are. And beyond the theoretical discussions that often take place in multilateral talks, they can inject a much-needed sense of reality ... In Dublin, the Ban Advocates team concentrated its time and efforts on working together with countries that had reservations about a comprehensive ban on cluster munitions. We rapidly realised that the regular meetings the Ban Advocates had with delegations were having a major impact since we would see the positions and attitudes of those delegations evolving on a daily basis. This tells us something about human beings from different backgrounds connecting with each other and developing new policies for future generations.[17]

The achievement of the CCM was not simply a confluence of factors, but of people involved in a collective reframing of cluster munitions and the humanitarian responses to them.

Above, some of the distinctive features of the Oslo process have been summarized. It is not nearly so difficult to identify distinctive characteristics as it is to reach firm conclusions about the relationships between such elements, to rank them in importance, or to arrange them in definitive cause-and-effect relationships. The Glion symposium and my dozens of research interviews with individuals involved in international efforts on cluster munitions suggest to me that this is highly influenced by vantage point. There are perhaps as many explanations for the achievement of the CCM as there were individual participants in the Oslo process. Those deeply involved in civil society efforts at lobbying governments directly often saw that as key; some diplomats saw their own exploits as central to success; some saw the Southern Lebanon conflict as a key catalyst while others did not, and so on. And, as a participant-observer in international work on cluster munitions in different guises over the years, I am probably not immune to this bias either, despite my best efforts, which is one reason why this history does not claim to be definitive.

Meanwhile, any explanations based on ranking distinctive factors usually fail to deal well with the role that chance has to play. As the British military historian Hew Strachan wrote of efforts to understand recent events in Iraq, "As history is turned into political science, it makes a casualty of contingency".[18] To what extent the Oslo process owed its eventual success in adopting a treaty to contingency will, I suspect, not be a debate cleared up by the version of events put forward in this book. There will remain those who have an interest in minimizing chance's role (such as the overall significance of the Lebanon conflict as a catalyst) or maximizing it (for instance, domestic political circumstances in the UK during the first week of the Dublin negotiations which might have made a successful treaty outcome irresistibly attractive to political decision makers). Those central to efforts to get an initiative underway to negotiate an international humanitarian treaty on cluster munitions in the course of this decade certainly exploited opportunities that came their way, such as the one the Lebanon conflict tragically afforded. But as is clear from the story told in these pages, opportunism would not have been enough without vision, preparation and commitment—all of which existed well before 2006 among various individuals.

CHALLENGES TO THE CONVENTION
ON CLUSTER MUNITIONS

However distinctive the process leading to the CCM, there are some significant challenges ahead that may qualify or even nullify the CCM's achievement. Some are briefly considered below, for at least two reasons. The first is lest the reader gather the impression that this history is simply a paean to the Oslo process that omits or glosses over the outcome's imperfections. The second reason is that while this book has related a narrative of international efforts to address the humanitarian impacts of cluster munitions up to the adoption of the CCM, these efforts continue.

It is one thing to negotiate an ambitious agreement, and quite another to give effect to its provisions through practical action. Poor implementation of the CCM will diminish its achievement, so any attempt to tell the story of the CCM's achievement needs to at least glance toward the horizon. How will the new treaty's accomplishment translate into attempts to make its membership as universal as possible, and give effect to its obligations? For instance, what does the CCM's interoperability article—the stain on the fine fabric of the treaty, in the CMC's parlance—mean in practice? How much of an obstacle to the effectiveness of the new treaty regime is it that some major states possessing large stockpiles of cluster munitions did not take part in the Oslo process, and seem unlikely to sign or ratify the CCM anytime soon? Will the treaty's prohibitions keep up with future advances in military technology? And, with the world in the midst of a serious global recession and with many other arms control and humanitarian challenges to face, what are the prospects—and the stakes—involved in proper implementation of the CCM's substantive provisions in areas such as clearance of unexploded submunitions, stockpile destruction and victim assistance?

BUILDING AND BROADENING THE REGIME

One often repeated criticism of the new CCM (heard especially from Oslo process non-participants in CCW meetings in Geneva) is that it does not include major producers and possessors of cluster munitions, namely Brazil, China, India, Israel, Pakistan, Poland, Russia and the US. This was an issue within the ranks of Oslo states too, and most of the states that would become the Like-minded said at the Oslo conference in February 2007 that they continued to support the CCW's efforts on cluster munitions partly for this reason. Subsequent to the adoption of the CCM in May 2008, they and many other Oslo participants have stuck with the CCW's efforts in the hope of attracting the major users and possessors outside the Oslo process to some kind of higher weapon-specific humanitarian standard than that rump of states adheres to now.

Such criticism is clearly supposed to imply that the cluster munition ban treaty cannot be effective without those states on board. But is that really true? Moreover, what is the benchmark for effectiveness? Obviously, if those states do not join the cluster munition ban treaty then its provisions for activities such as national reporting, stockpile destruction and victim assistance do not apply to them as they would for CCM member states. But the broader question is over whether the existence of the new treaty will reduce the amount of harm to civilians from the weapons that those in the Oslo process defined as cluster munitions and therefore banned. Seen in that light, it does not necessarily matter much what states hostile to joining the CCM say if the stigma it generates against using the weapon positively alters their behaviour. That is because, as I observed elsewhere, by pursuing partnerships among themselves, would-be cooperators—those who see benefit over time of a cooperative strategy like the CCM—affect pay-offs globally, including for defectors (that is, those shunning such cooperation).[19]

A real-world example of this is the Mine Ban Treaty. In the decade or so since its international entry into force, this treaty has attracted 156 member states—a staggering achievement considering that momentum behind it was generated by a Core Group of small- and medium-sized countries similar to that driving the Oslo process, along with the active support of transnational civil society. The emergence of that norm against a weapon on humanitarian grounds faced opposition of supposed key states like those mentioned above too. One important reason for its continuing success is that many states which initially defected for narrow national security reasons have come to see the benefits of belonging to a global ban on anti-personnel mines and so joined the ranks of the cooperators. While it is true that states like China, Russia and the US are still outside the treaty, the significance of the Mine Ban Treaty regime can clearly be seen in the fact that anti-personnel mine production, transfer and use have largely dried up.[20] What this shows is that a cluster of cooperators has been able to stigmatize a weapon system to such a great extent that they have clearly affected the behaviour of defectors, even powerful ones. An added benefit is that while these self-appointed key states stand outside the treaty regime, they have fewer opportunities to suppress the enthusiasm of those driving it—or to undermine their work.

Critics of such a view might point out that cluster munitions are not the same as anti-personnel mines. One of the big assumptions of military lawyers from NATO countries such as Australia, Canada and the UK in interoperability work in the Oslo process, for instance, was that in view of their characteristics cluster munitions were more likely to be used by US forces than anti-personnel mines ever would be. It is not clear, though, to what degree they factored in changing perceptions about the *acceptability* of using cluster munitions by virtue of more than half of the world's states banning the weapon on humanitarian grounds—or indeed the impact of their own compulsory efforts, as states parties, to stop use of the weapon by others in the future.[21] And, if nothing else, the CCW's work on ERW and cluster munitions over the last decade has raised the awareness of its member governments of the unintended consequences of a weapon that tends to be inaccurate and unreliable, and therefore quite likely to be less useful than previously thought. Once this is all factored in—let alone the strong negative reaction that the use of cluster munitions now brings internationally—it may well make states possessing the weapon think twice before using it in future.

Such stigma can be expected to strengthen over time.[22] Admittedly at present the record is a little mixed. Neither Georgia nor Russia participated in the Oslo process. In what seems to have been the only use of cluster munitions since the adoption of the CCM (and the first since the use in the Israel–Hizbullah conflict of 2006), both states deployed them in their conflict over South Ossetia in August 2008. Interestingly the belligerents each denied use (although Georgia later admitted it), which could indicate that they understood the stigma of cluster munition use might undermine their respective claims to the moral and political high ground in the conflict before international public opinion.[23] Human Rights Watch, which conducted a detailed independent investigation, concluded that cluster munitions from both sides landed in populated areas, and that Russian attacks using the weapon were "inherently indiscriminate and thus unlawful"[24] under existing international humanitarian law rules. Georgia's M-85s appear to have malfunctioned—landing short of their targets, and in areas where Georgian civilians were present, which Human Rights Watch argued underscored the unreliability and humanitarian risks of cluster munitions. While continued cluster munition use by anyone is deeply counter-productive, the long-run effect of the August 2008 war may well be to strengthen international stigma since the conflict further confirmed the humanitarian hazards of the weapon for civilians.

International entry into force of the CCM will occur six months after the thirtieth instrument of ratification has been deposited, and will constitute a strong signal of global support for the new legal norm against cluster munitions. In the immediate future, therefore, getting those hundred or so states that have signed the CCM so far to ratify or accede to it is the next step for campaigners. (In the meantime, by virtue of article 18 of the 1969 Vienna Convention on the Law of Treaties, states that have signed are under an obligation to refrain from acts which would defeat the object and purpose of the CCM.) What is also needed is for all states supporting the CCM to take the necessary steps to implement the CCM into their national laws, and make a start on tasks to ensure their compliance with the treaty, including meeting deadlines for reporting, clearance, stockpile destruction and other applicable activities. The CCM regime looks to be making quite rapid progress to this end: at the end of the northern summer in 2009, the international community is more than halfway to the entry-into-force threshold. In view of the legislative, bureaucratic and other national timetables involved, the rate at which states ratify can be expected to accelerate soon. It is possible that the cluster munition ban treaty will hold its first annual meeting of states parties, to be convened in Laos, as early as 2010.

As mentioned above, cooperation is a dynamic phenomenon, and perceived pay-offs evolve over time. Some states ambivalent about, or negative toward, the Ottawa process such as Brazil and Turkey eventually joined the Mine Ban Treaty as their suspicions about the process leading to it faded, and these states began to recognize the norm's real benefits. There is reason to be optimistic that such perceptions will also improve over time with regard to the CCM—provided the treaty delivers the humanitarian benefits it promises.

INTEROPERABILITY

Interoperability, which was eventually handled by means of article 21 in the CCM on "Relations with States not party to this Convention" was a vexed issue during the later stages of the Oslo process. When it was agreed, the provision was criticized by the CMC. Certainly, in an ideal scenario it would be better not to have a provision like paragraph 3 of article 21 in an international treaty, which is clumsily worded and even a "step backward" in the words of one legal analyst.[25] Those with some level of concern to ensure interoperability provisions included some Core Group states such as New Zealand and Norway, not only the Like-minded like Australia, Canada and the UK, which were the most vociferous. And, as an issue, interoperability had some history behind it as it cropped up in the Mine Ban Treaty's implementation. That treaty's implementation process depended on national statements interpreting terms in its article 1 and 2 provisions like "assist", "encourage" and "transfer", but unanimity was never achieved. There was a widespread desire, therefore, for more clarity in the CCM, with article 21 the eventual result.

This means that how the CCM's interoperability provision is implemented is an issue to watch as states indicate their intentions through their national actions on practical issues like transit and foreign stockpiling of cluster munitions on their territories, as well as joint operations. The fact that article 21 is in the CCM, unlike in the Mine Ban Treaty, will at least form some benchmark for monitoring. This is certainly something that the CMC, and member NGOs such as Human Rights Watch and Landmine Action, have recognized, and they can be expected to be active in coming years in calling "for states to develop common understanding on these issues, so that there is consistent implementation of the convention".[26] The interpretation the CMC and its members wish to see accepted is that the CCM's prohibition should be taken by all member states to mean that no intentional assistance is ever allowed with a prohibited act and that there is:

> a ban on the transit of cluster munitions across or through the national territory, airspace, or waters of a State Party. It has also said that it should be seen as banning the stockpiling of cluster munitions by a state not party on the territory of a State Party. Most countries that have weighed in on these issues have agreed, but some have not.[27]

Implementing article 21 will also be something that others involved in the Oslo process may closely watch. The interoperability issue risked accumulating a totemic ideological importance in the negotiations on the CCM as developing and affected countries unsympathetic to the interoperability concerns of states in alliance relationships like NATO regarded any perceived concession to the strict ban on assistance with illegal acts as a potential get-out clause from the CCM's prohibitions. The development of interpretations on interoperability in implementing the treaty that do not take heed that such suspicions exist could damage the considerable good will and willingness to work in partnership built up in the course of the Oslo process.

One person in no doubt as to the positive contribution the CCM could make, and who said so both in Dublin's closing session and in Oslo at the signing ceremony, was cluster munition survivor Branislav Kapetanović. Observing the turn-out of governments, media, international organizations and civil society in Oslo, he said:

> I hope the unity and determination showed here in Oslo today will mark the future of international cooperation, especially for victim assistance and clearance. ... For us here, this is not the end of our road: we still have to make sure the Treaty is implemented, monitored and that funding is available for those in need.[28]

The challenges Kapetanović identified are not trivial. Here the CCM has already learned a lot—and can still learn—from the Mine Ban Treaty's implementation experience. A decade after it entered into force, many of that treaty's deadlines for states to destroy their stockpiles and complete clearance of mines on their territories are falling due. Some states started too late and may miss these deadlines. Thus, one of the messages both governments and civil society campaigners have been trying to emphasize in the context of CCM implementation is that these activities need to be started early by member states if they are to be achieved within reasonable timeframes. Clearance of unexploded submunitions often occurs, of course, in the context of clearance of other forms of ERW and mines, but the scale of the task of submunition-specific clearance in certain countries such as Cambodia, Iraq, Lebanon and particularly Laos and Viet Nam is massive.[29] There is no excuse for states party to the CCM to be complacent either in meeting their own specific obligations, or in helping each other meet these goals.

Stockpile destruction is another issue, as dozens of states possess cluster munitions, often of especially antiquated and unreliable kinds. The adherence of many states possessing such weapons to the CCM means now that they will never be used or transferred to others and then used or abandoned (with attendant humanitarian consequences). This is good news, but it raises a host of practical challenges for countries, especially in the developing world. Meanwhile, in tough economic times for all countries, there are competing financial priorities: the temptation may be strong to put fulfilling stockpile destruction obligations off until later. This temptation must be resisted by continued political focus and firm, friendly pressure via the CCM's implementation process.

A key task will be to monitor the implementation of the new treaty. Treaties like the CCM have official national reporting requirements, of course, but these often require analysis and additional information to be meaningful. As Rappert argued:

> An important element in ensuring this outcome will be the ongoing work of States Parties and civil society to monitor practices by States Parties and states not party alike in relation to the provisions of the treaty. This monitoring and reporting function, both through formal and informal mechanisms, will play an important role in developing the stigma against these weapons.[30]

NGOs have played a major role in the implementation of the Mine Ban Treaty through the International Campaign to Ban Landmines' *Landmine Monitor* project,[31] and already these entities, along with the CMC and some of its more research-focused NGO members, have begun publishing information on government policy and practice on cluster munitions.[32] If the Mine Ban Treaty is any guide, such work fulfils important functions in building confidence in compliance, as well as for general transparency and norm promotion. But despite its generally high quality, it is work done largely by volunteer NGO researchers working long hours for low pay (or no pay, in many cases). Government representatives are always happy to extol the virtues of this research and monitoring, but the pool of donor countries is a small one. Despite the achievement of the new cluster munition ban treaty, the overall amount of money available from donors for both mine and cluster munition monitoring activities is unlikely to increase much (and could decline). But it is an important contribution at a bargain cost for states, and governments need to adequately support such activities financially if they want the CCM to be a viable and healthy regime.

The role of civil society in implementing the CCM is an important question overarching this, and is something the CMC and its constituent NGOs have been reflecting on carefully through an internal process of consultation since the cluster munition ban treaty's adoption. With the ICBL a member of the CMC, and many NGOs belonging to both campaigns, the destiny of the two coalitions is likely to become even more intertwined. A concern throughout the early years of the CMC's existence for landmine process veterans like Steve Goose and Paul Hannon was how the CMC could be grown, while allowing the ICBL to do its job effectively. In a related vein, a looming issue for the future of the CMC and ICBL, whatever form that their collaboration or cohabitation takes, is over how to maximize civil society's impact on both CCM and Mine Ban Treaty implementation, and not allow one to simply subsume the other's identity. NGOs have done a valuable job in the field of efforts against anti-personnel mines and cluster munitions in keeping states focused and honest: there would be no better way to impede effective implementation of the CCM than a lack of scrutiny or an absence of constructive criticism from civil society. To reiterate a point made earlier: in many cases, NGOs are the entities doing the practical humanitarian work in the field to alleviate the humanitarian impact of cluster munitions and have relevant expertise and experience—states need to recognize this, and work in partnership with them wherever possible.

Nowhere is this partnership between the states that join the CCM and non-governmental actors more important than on an issue Kapetanović specifically referred to—that of victim assistance. Experts on victim assistance and state representatives alike hailed the CCM's victim assistance-related provisions, including the way in which it built upon and improved the Mine Ban Treaty's provisions and took into account the subsequent Convention on the Rights of Persons With Disabilities. Compared to the Mine Ban Treaty, the CCM contains mandatory reporting requirements for states about what they are doing to assist victims (article 7) and strengthens the obligation to do so (article 5). Moreover, the CCM "recognises that victim assistance is not simply a medical or rehabilitation issue—it is a human rights issue".[33] While this is splendid in principle, past experience in the Mine Ban Treaty context indicates that this form of assistance is not simply a one-off or short-term contribution for clearance of land or stockpile destruction but may necessitate life-long medical, psychosocial and other support for survivors. And it tends not to receive the attention or resources it needs. Few people possess a better grasp of such issues than Austrian diplomat Markus Reiterer, the Oslo process's Friend of the Chair on victim assistance issues, who also coordinated such work in both the Mine Ban Treaty and CCW. In November 2007, in closing remarks at the Mine Ban Treaty's eighth annual meeting of states parties, he made the following observation, which is equally pertinent to implementation of the CCM:

> One of the key lessons learnt in the victim assistance-related work of the Convention is that if a meaningful difference is going to be made in enhancing the well-being and guaranteeing the rights of landmine victims, victim assistance must no longer be seen as an abstraction but as a concrete set of actions for which specific States Parties hold ultimate responsibility.[34]

Victim assistance is not simply about enough money, although that is obviously important: it also takes time, commitment and willingness to consult in order to build the capacities of assistance providers at the national and local levels, as well as appropriate policies and strategies and infrastructure in which practical services can be delivered. And it needs to involve those it purports to help like cluster munition survivors and their communities, as the negotiation of the CCM did.

THE DISCOURSE OVER THE MILITARY UTILITY OF CLUSTER MUNITIONS

There is an important distinction between arguments to ban cluster munitions on the basis that their use is unacceptable, and arguing that cluster munitions have no military utility. The categorical ban on cluster munitions in the CCM was not adopted because there was consensus among those participating in the Dublin negotiation that the weapon had no usefulness on the battlefield, although the utility of cluster munitions *independent of their humanitarian consequences stemming from their use* was also increasingly being questioned. Rather, cluster munitions were banned because the consequences of the weapon (for civilians), based on field evidence and greater awareness of the likely results of continued use were taken into account. Once they were, the claims of manufacturers and presumptions about the weapon's accuracy and reliability that formed the basis for legitimacy claims were found to be sorely wanting.

In fact, such claims and arguments had always been wanting—it was only now that they were rigorously and transparently tested. Moreover, the upswing in international campaigning against cluster munitions this decade came at a time when a number of governments were waging war on behalf of what they said were humanitarian values, or the spreading of "freedom" and democratic principles to societies in other parts of the world such as Kosovo, Afghanistan and Iraq. The use of cluster munitions that saturate entire areas with explosive force by virtue of their design—and leave many unexploded remnants to pose hazard post-conflict because of failure to work as designed—raises questions of compatibility with such values. Making good on the promise to ban cluster munitions that cause unacceptable harm would thus split the decision-making establishments of many states participating in the Oslo process between humanitarian and broader political interests and those with traditional defence concerns. There was the issue, of course, of national defence establishments facing the prospect of having to give up some or all of their stockpiled cluster munitions and the strategic, operational and financial implications that carried. For some, there were also fears about being at odds with major allies, especially the US. This was a characteristic concern for the "traditionalists" or "Atlanticists" mentioned earlier in the Norwegian case, but by no means limited to that country.

If nothing else, cluster munitions were simply the weapons some militaries had, and defence establishments could reasonably be expected to fight for the right to deploy what they have in their arsenals using whatever policy argument is expedient. Historically, they have certainly done so.[35] In the CCW, for example, military experts were accustomed to explaining the continued necessity of cluster munitions based on scenarios they proposed. One scenario could be that of neutralizing an anti-aircraft weapon mounted on top of a dam above a village:[36] cluster munitions would be the best option to destroy the weapon because a large high-explosive bomb might breach the dam and kill all of the civilians in the village. Such scenarios underline that it is impossible to exclude a hypothetical situation in which the weapon under consideration might be the "right" one, and therefore necessary from a military perspective because it has the most perceived "utility". It is an approach that has a long tradition as remarks like those of the British military officer in Lucerne about the BL-755 cluster bomb more than 30 years before showed (see chapter 1). Without considering elements of the broader humanitarian and political context, however, such deliberations are rhetorically circular: nerve gas, poison-tipped darts and anti-personnel mines are conceivably useful in certain military scenarios, but they are all banned as their use is seen by a large majority of the international community as repugnant because of their broader consequences. In other words, their advantage in very selective circumstances does not make them acceptable weapons.

Another feature of military utility-centred arguments about cluster munitions that scenarios like the hypothetical one above illustrate is that, in effect, "if you don't let us use this weapon, we'll be forced to use something worse". This is a claim heard repeatedly over decades in opposition to restrictions on virtually any weapon system, and seems to overlook the fact that international humanitarian law rules still apply if alternative weapons to cluster munitions are used—rules such as that of distinction, the rule against indiscriminate attack, the rule of proportionality and the rule on feasible precautions.[37] Humanitarian law rules apply to the use of *all* weapons. In contexts like the CCW, governments are, by their own admission, meant to balance military and humanitarian requirements. To pretend that the humanitarian side of the balance does not exist in the choice and use of weapons is actually counter-productive to promoting adherence to these rules.

Arguments from NGOs such as Human Rights Watch and Landmine Action and governments like Norway that cluster munitions are less militarily useful than traditionally thought were important supplements to the collective reframing going on about the weapon and international responses to it over the last few years, and they contributed to the shifting of the burden of proof discussed earlier this chapter. Such arguments went, "Look, in view of their effects you can't use cluster munitions in the war-fighting scenarios you're likely to face in the foreseeable future" rather than "cluster munitions have zero use in any military scenario". Signs were that by the end of the Oslo process such arguments had gained some ground, and perhaps helped to ease the way for a ban solution as it became more obvious that cluster munitions were a category of weapon unlikely to be appropriate to what British General Sir Rupert Smith (one of the signatories of the May 2008 generals' letter to *The Times* calling for a cluster munition ban) called "war among the people".[38] Nevertheless, they remain subsidiary to the central point that cluster munitions, as defined by the CCM, were banned on grounds of lack of acceptability.

Meanwhile, in the wake of exclusion of certain weapons using advanced sensor-fuzed technologies from the definition of a cluster munition in article 2 of the CCM, there was a sense of critics wanting to have their cake and eat it too. The categorical ban created by article 2 excluded, in effect, the German SMArt 155 and French-Swedish BONUS artillery rounds, and some diplomats and others I have spoken with from states shunning the Oslo process claim not to understand this, or imply that it was a measure to favour the industries of the cluster munition producers of states in the Oslo process at the expense of those outside it.[39] The straight answer is that those weapons were excluded because overall the states involved in the Dublin negotiations were satisfied that weapons meeting the strict criteria of the treaty will not cause the particular humanitarian harm of cluster munitions, and can therefore not be regarded as such. Not all states were satisfied with this outcome, and Austria and some other Tee-total states proposed further specific weapons review measures in Dublin, which Ambassador O'Ceallaigh and his team in the end did not include in the composite text.[40] But the provisions of article 2 defining cluster munitions are very robust, to the extent that almost all submunition weapon systems must now be destroyed including variants of the M-85 several NATO states thought they would have in service for many years to come. The challenges this has created for defence establishments in these countries, which include Norway, Switzerland and the UK, are real, and weapons like the SMArt 155 or BONUS are not guaranteed to be complete substitutes if that is what they elect to buy to replace cluster munitions. The CCM's article 2 definition is an implausible way to give Oslo process states an industrial leg up, especially when only France, Sweden and Germany, of the states participating in the Dublin negotiations, had any excluded weapons in production.

Overall, the critical point is that the "define, and then exclude weapons not causing unacceptable harm to civilians" approach is distinct from the technical characteristics approach in the CCW. This can be seen in the cluster munition ban treaty's definition of a cluster munition: in subparagraph (c)—the provision that was the focus of definition negotiation in Dublin—the chapeau is effects-based in that the cumulative technical criteria it sets out below it are "in order to avoid indiscriminate area effects and the risks posed by unexploded submunitions". In promoting adherence to the CCM, the treaty's supporters should, in general, avoid becoming sucked into arguments over the military utility of cluster munitions, which are almost infinitely malleable, without broader consideration of the humanitarian consequences of the weapon to keep them in perspective. The broader humanitarian calculus, after all, anchored international efforts against cluster munitions and ultimately made the CCM a reality. It should not be abandoned now.

FINAL THOUGHTS ON THE MEANING OF "UNACCEPTABLE HARM"

At the opening of the Wellington conference in February 2007, New Zealand's Disarmament Minister Phil Goff described a humanitarian treaty's purpose in reducing the hazards cluster munitions pose as the fence at the top of a cliff in contrast to the ambulance waiting at the bottom.[41] Goff was emphasizing the preventive value of a cluster munition ban treaty alongside its remedial effects. If the metaphor is viewed another way, historically international efforts to address the hazards of cluster munitions spent far longer finding purchase at the bottom of that cliff than climbing it and building the fence. Once underway, completion of the task was quite rapid in the Oslo initiative's case—in the CCW it continues. The CCM's achievement entailed factors such as increased post-conflict evidence, greater focus on the human impact of the weapon, and the right combination of individuals, organizations and governments working in partnership, all of which contributed to a gradual but steady reframing of expectations about what could be achieved. Although some, like the Mennonites, were early converts to the notion of a ban on cluster munitions, it was an idea that just simply did not seem feasible to most informed people until this decade. Even then, it took time for the sense that a humanitarian treaty banning cluster munitions was possible—even among some at the heart of international efforts on the civil society side alongside government representatives—to catch up with new political and diplomatic circumstances. And it should not be forgotten that it took courage for Norwegian policymakers to do what the CMC had been encouraging Norway and others to do, which was to launch an international initiative with a humanitarian objective they were aware some powerful countries would probably criticize and ridicule.

The achievement of an international treaty banning cluster munitions required a massive burst of effort, resources and generation of international attention including from the Core Group, civil society and, indeed, from the ICRC and UN. Such a rapid tempo is difficult to sustain for long, even if in a weapon-specific process like the Oslo initiative it was aided by a broad, clear negotiation objective. A valid question is, therefore, what does the CCM's achievement presage for the future? Other armed violence-related challenges receiving particular attention today, after all, are not necessarily weapon specific like cluster munitions or anti-personnel mines. Discussions at the Glion symposium revealed no consensus among experts about lessons from the Oslo and Ottawa processes to automatically carry over to international work on curbing the illicit small arms and light weapons trade, the Arms Trade Treaty initiative or the Geneva Declaration initiative on armed violence and development, for instance. Meanwhile, for most of those individuals building the Oslo process during its prologue and then steering the initiative for some of its course, the Ottawa process—for all of its apparent similarities—represented an example to learn from, and adapt, rather than follow too closely.

Whatever conclusion one draws about the level of applicability of features of the Oslo initiative, it has raised questions about the humanitarian impact of explosive weapons more broadly. Cluster munitions are highly prone to indiscriminate use, but all explosive weapons are prone to creating effects their users cannot precisely foresee or control. That civilians (and civilian objects) shall not be the object of attack and enjoy general protection against dangers arising from military operations is a fundamental principle of international humanitarian law.[42] From it derives the rule that attacks expected to cause incidental civilian harm disproportionate to the military advantage anticipated are prohibited. Likewise, it is prohibited to use weapons that are indiscriminate, for instance because their effects cannot be limited to a military objective. In practice, application of these rules turns out to be difficult. Although indiscriminate attacks are prohibited and attacks have to be proportionate, civilians often bear the brunt of violence in reality. As such, analysts of the CCM have already noted that "the notion of 'unacceptable harm' to civilians could be used to promote a higher standard for the precautions to be taken in attacks in or near urban or densely populated areas"[43] in the humanitarian law regime.

The need for such a discourse is clear. This decade seems to have seen an upswing in the frequency and lethality of attacks using explosive weapons in areas of civilian population by a widening range of actors. It prompted the UN Secretary-General to single such attacks out for special concern in his report on the protection of civilians in armed conflict he presented to the Security Council in May 2009:

> As demonstrated by this year's hostilities in Sri Lanka and Israel's campaign in Gaza, the use in densely populated environments of explosive weapons, that have so-called "area effect", inevitably has an indiscriminate and severe humanitarian impact. First, in terms of the risk to civilians caught in the blast radius or killed or injured by damaged and collapsed buildings. Second, in terms of damage to infrastructure vital to the well-being of the civilian population such as water and sanitation systems.[44]

States currently find it difficult to engage in a substantive discourse on explosive weapons if corresponding debate in the Security Council context is any guide.[45] Yet explosive violence that kills or injures civilians is one of the defining problems of our age, whether caused by cluster munitions, aerial drones or improvised explosive devices delivered by suicide bombers. It is a messy and complex phenomenon, but responses to the problems created by explosive force in populated areas must be grasped if the international humanitarian law regime is to effectively protect civilians. To do so will entail moving beyond the narrowly weapon-specific.

The basis for a more promising discourse exists. Drawing on experience of international efforts on cluster munitions alongside other research on the use of explosive force around civilians in armed conflict, Landmine Action argues that explosive weapons constitute a coherent category of their own.[46] This category is one that is not *explicitly* recognized in law at the moment, but one that should be recognized based on the pattern of states' own common usage of explosive force (and, increasingly, that of armed non-state groups too). That is, these actors do not generally use explosive weapons against their "own" populations. Governments, for instance, use explosive weapons in the "special circumstances" of armed conflict—occasionally where the state's own territory is in danger of fragmenting through civil conflict, but often against foreigners, in places other than the state's own territory, and even in areas of dense civilian population. As Moyes points out, "Explosive weapons are not used for policing. They kill and wound too many people that you don't want to kill and wound".[47]

This raises a number of questions. Why do governments not seem to consider their actions accountable—or as accountable—when it comes to protecting the lives of civilians from explosive violence in other societies? In a globalizing, urbanizing age of insurgency and "war among the people" it is an important question. Questioning policies underpinning the control of explosive weapons is a logical extension of efforts to protect civilians from the hazards of cluster munitions. The problematic effects of cluster munitions—explosive force across an area at the time of use and a legacy of unexploded ordnance—are shared to different degrees by all explosive weapons. For that matter, such investigation could be seen as a corollary of the CCW's Protocol on ERW, which goes a long way to recognizing explosive weapons as a category in need of special controls and which some of those states which shunned the Oslo process aim to adhere to: why accept special responsibilities regarding the after-effects of explosive weapons but not recognize also the categorical problems with this technology at the time of use? It also raises issues involving non-state armed groups deploying explosive weapons, and the degree to which they comply (or fail to comply) with legal norms, which could influence the attitudes toward and use of explosive force by their adversaries, which are often states.

Landmine Action has suggested that several next steps present themselves.[48] The first is to build the debate—to agree on some basic terms like explosive weapons and populated areas, and to recognize that the use of the former in the latter represents a distinct humanitarian and ethical problem. A second step would be to build transparency around the use of explosive force in populated areas through better data collection and analysis, not only by NGOs and international organizations, but also by states themselves. This was something sometimes conspicuously absent in conflicts in recent years, prompting the creation of independent efforts such as the NGO Iraq Body Count. It is, after all, tendentious for states to argue they are protecting civilians in armed conflict if they make no effort at demonstrating their claims based on facts. Third, accountability could be enhanced if states would publish policy statements regarding when the use of explosive weapons is acceptable, including in populated areas, and whether or how this relates to accountability for such use. Fourth, states should recognize and act on their responsibilities to the victims of explosive weapons, as they have already accepted an obligation to do through treaties such as the CCM, the Mine Ban Treaty and the CCW's ERW protocol.

The notion of our collective responsibility to the victims of weapons brings us back to cluster munition survivors such as Slađan Vučković, Soraj Ghulam Habib and Branislav Kapetanović. These people, and entire communities in places like Laos and Southern Lebanon, have paid a terrible price in terms of what the majority of the international community eventually acknowledged as the unacceptable harm caused by cluster munitions. Awareness of the conditions of people directly affected by cluster munitions demanded consideration of the weapon's consequences—consideration that in the Oslo process would include their contributions. This allowed a collective reframing, eventually bypassing a military utility-centred discourse that favoured permissiveness about the use of weapons without systematic or sincere thought to their humanitarian effects, and perhaps is why the active participation of cluster munitions survivors was never actively sought out in fora like the CCW. Along with the positive difference the CCM's implementation will make on the ground for cluster munition-affected communities, one possible legacy may be its implications for changing the way the world thinks in the long run about the impact of explosive weapons on civilians. More broadly still, the active participation of survivors and the rationale of prohibition based on "unacceptable harm" provides a powerful model for pressing states to consider directly the actual outcomes of armed violence. In that sense, the achievement of the cluster munition ban treaty is not only the end of the beginning for international efforts to address the humanitarian impacts of cluster munitions, it could mark a significant milestone in how we can identify ways to protect civilians in armed conflict more broadly.

NOTES

Foreword

1   David Dellinger, *Vietnam Revisited, From Covert Action to Invasion to Reconstruction*, South End Press, 1986, p. 73.
2   "This all-out drive enabled the battleship to proceed on schedule to her station in Vietnam waters, where her tremendous 16-inch firepower was immediately utilized to disrupt strong enemy drives along the coastline". Project Manager for Selected Ammunition, US Army Picatinny Arsenal, "PMSA Submission for USAMC Tenth Anniversary, 1962–1972: 16-inch Projectile, Mk19", unpublished memo. See also Stockholm International Peace Research Institute, *Anti-Personnel Weapons*, 1978, p. 140, table 5.6.
3   See for example John Duffet (ed.), *Against the Crime of Silence; Proceedings of the Russell International War Crimes Tribunal; Stockholm-Copenhagen*, 1968.
4   *Working Paper submitted by Egypt, Mexico, Norway, Sudan, Sweden, Switzerland and Yugoslavia to the Diplomatic Conference on the reaffirmation and development of international humanitarian law applicable in armed conflicts*, 21 February 1974.

Preface

1   *Declaration of the Oslo Conference on Cluster Munitions* (also referred to as the Oslo Declaration), 23 February 2007, <www.clusterconvention. org/pages/pages_vi/via_oslodeclaration.html>.
2   Statement by Branislav Kapetanović to the Convention on Cluster Munitions Signing Ceremony, Oslo, 3 December 2008, <http://blog. banadvocates.org/index.php?post/2008/12/03/Branislavs-statement-Convention-on-Cluster-Munitions-signing-ceremony-opening-ceremony-Oslo-3-December-2008>.
3   Kenneth Rutherford, Nerina Čevra and Tracey Begley, "Connecting the Dots: The Ottawa Convention and the CCM", *Journal of Mine Action*, vol. 12, no. 2, 2008.
4   See John Borrie and Ashley Thornton, *The Value of Diversity in Multilateral Disarmament Work*, UNIDIR, 2008.

5   Cordelia Fine, *A Mind of Its Own: How Your Brain Distorts and Deceives*, Icon, 2006, p. 2.
6   A summary report of this event is online at <www.unidir.org/pdf/activites/pdf3-act275.pdf>.
7   Letter of invitation from the Norwegian Minister of Foreign Affairs, Jonas Gahr Støre, to UNIDIR, 4 January 2007.

Introduction
"What is happening in my yard could happen in yours"

1   Slađan and Dušica Vučković, "Our story", *Ban Advocates Blog*, 2 November 2007, <http://blog.banadvocates.org/index.php?post/2007/11/02/Slaan-Vukovi2>.
2   Author's interview with Slađan Vučković, 4 September 2008.
3   Idem.
4   Idem.

Chapter 1
The technology of killing

1   *Working Paper submitted by Egypt, Mexico, Norway, Sudan, Sweden, Switzerland and Yugoslavia to the Diplomatic Conference on the reaffirmation and development of international humanitarian law applicable in armed conflicts*, 21 February 1974, p. 8.
2   See Eric Prokosch, "Technology and its Control: Antipersonnel Weapons", *International Social Science Journal*, vol. 28, no. 2, 1976, p. 342.
3   *Working Paper submitted by Egypt, Mexico, Norway, Sudan, Sweden, Switzerland and Yugoslavia to the Diplomatic Conference on the reaffirmation and development of international humanitarian law applicable in armed conflicts*, 21 February 1974, p. 9.
4   Author's interview with Eric Prokosch, 5 February 2009.
5   See Eric Prokosch, "Cluster Weapons", *Papers in the Theory and Practice of Human Rights*, no. 15, Human Rights Centre, University of Essex, 1995, p. 4.
6   For a technical overview see Colin King (ed.), *Jane's Explosive Ordnance Disposal 2008–2009*, Jane's Information Group, 2008, pp. 275–93.

[7]   See, for instance, articles 48 and 51 of 1977 Additional Protocol I to the 1949 Geneva Conventions and paragraph 78 of the International Court of Justice's 1996 Advisory Opinion on nuclear weapons.

[8]   See John Borrie and Rosy Cave, "The humanitarian effects of cluster munitions: Why should we worry?", *Disarmament Forum*, no. 4, 2006, pp. 5–13.

[9]   An ICRC study suggests Soviet use of cluster munitions came first. See International Committee of the Red Cross, *Explosive Remnants of War: Submunitions and Other Unexploded Ordnance—A Study*, 2000, p. 10.

[10]   Ibid.

[11]   Ove Dullum, *Cluster Weapons—Military Utility and Alternatives*, Norwegian Defence Research Establishment (FFI), 2008, p. 11.

[12]   International Committee of the Red Cross, *Explosive Remnants of War: Submunitions and Other Unexploded Ordnance—A Study*, 2000, p. 11.

[13]   Eric Prokosch, "Cluster Weapons", *Papers in the Theory and Practice of Human Rights*, no. 15, Human Rights Centre, University of Essex, 1995, p. 1.

[14]   Ibid.

[15]   Ove Dullum, *Cluster Weapons—Military Utility and Alternatives*, Norwegian Defence Research Establishment (FFI), 2008, p. 11.

[16]   Eric Prokosch, *The Technology of Killing: a Military and Political History of Anti-Personnel Weapons*, Zed Books, 1995, pp. 32–3.

[17]   See Eric Prokosch, "Technology and its Control: Antipersonnel Weapons", *International Social Science Journal*, vol. 28, no. 2, 1976, pp. 345–6.

[18]   See David Dellinger, *Vietnam Revisited: From Covert Action to Invasion to Reconstruction*, South End Press, 1986, pp. 73–4.

[19]   Ove Dullum, *Cluster Weapons—Military Utility and Alternatives*, Norwegian Defence Research Establishment (FFI), 2008, p. 92.

[20]   See Eric Prokosch, *The Technology of Killing: a Military and Political History of Anti-Personnel Weapons*, Zed Books, 1995, pp. 83–5.

[21]   See Eric Prokosch, "Technology and its Control: Antipersonnel Weapons", *International Social Science Journal*, vol. 28, no. 2, 1976, pp. 345–2.

[22]   Michael Krepon, "Weapons Potentially Inhumane: The Case of Cluster Bombs", *Foreign Affairs*, vol. 54, no. 3, 1974, p. 51.

[23]   Eric Prokosch, *The Technology of Killing: a Military and Political History of Anti-Personnel Weapons*, Zed Books, 1995, p. 98.

24   Stockholm International Peace Research Institute, *World Armaments and Disarmament SIPRI Yearbook 1973*, Almqvist and Wiksell/SIPRI, 1973, p. 133.

25   Hans Blix, "Current efforts to prohibit the use of certain conventional weapons", *Instant Research on Peace and Violence*, vol. 4, no. 1, 1974, p. 21.

26   The Stockholm International Peace Research Institute (SIPRI) collected data about many of these cluster munition systems in the 1970s. See Malvern Lumsden, *Anti-Personnel Weapons*, Taylor and Francis/SIPRI, 1978, pp. 147–58.

27   Resolution XIII, *Reaffirmation and Development of the Laws and Customs applicable in Armed Conflicts*.

28   For instance, General Assembly, *Respect for human rights in armed conflict*, UN document A/RES/2597(XXIV), 16 December 1969.

29   For an overview, see Stockholm International Peace Research Institute, *World Armaments and Disarmament SIPRI Yearbook 1973*, Almqvist and Wiksell/SIPRI, 1973, pp. 134–5.

30   The text of these instruments can be found on the ICRC's website at <www.icrc.org/ihl.nsf/CONVPRES>.

31   Torgil Wulff et al., *Conventional Weapons, their Deployment and Effects from a Humanitarian Aspect, Recommendations for the Modernization of International Law,* Swedish Ministry for Foreign Affairs, 1973.

32   See Hans Blix, "Current efforts to prohibit the use of certain conventional weapons", *Instant Research on Peace and Violence*, vol. 4, no. 1, 1974, p. 21.

33   Frits Kalshoven, "The Conference of Government Experts on the Use of Certain Conventional Weapons: Lucerne, 24 September–18 October 1974", *Netherlands Yearbook of International Law 77*, 1975, pp. 77–101.

34   ICRC, *Weapons that May Cause Unnecessary Suffering or Have Indiscriminate Effects: Report on the Work of Experts*, 1973.

35   Ibid., p. 71.

36   Stockholm International Peace Research Institute, *World Armaments and Disarmament SIPRI Yearbook 1975*, MIT Press/SIPRI, 1975, pp. 47–8.

37   Ibid., p. 47

38   SIPRI's main representative, Malvern Lumsden, played a significant role in the Lucerne conference and the later Lugano conference, and was also active in the Diplomatic Conference on the Reaffirmation and Development of International Humanitarian Law Applicable in Armed Conflicts. SIPRI also later published an important independent report

on anti-personnel weapons; see SIPRI, *Anti-Personnel Weapons*, Taylor & Francis, 1978.

[39]   ICRC, *Conference of Government Experts on the Use of Certain Conventional Weapons (Lucerne, 24 September–18 October 1974): Report*, 1975, p. 61, para. 218.

[40]   "Statement by the President at the Conference of Government Experts, Lucerne, 24 September–18 October, 1974", reproduced in SIRRI, *World Armaments and Disarmament SIPRI Yearbook 1975*, MIT Press/SIPRI, 1975, p. 59.

[41]   See ICRC, *Conference of Government Experts on the Use of Certain Conventional Weapons (Second Session—Lugano, 28 January–26 February 1976): Report*, 1976, p. 17, para. 46.

[42]   See Eric Prokosch, *The Technology of Killing: a Military and Political History of Anti-Personnel Weapons*, Zed Books, 1995, pp. 156–60.

[43]   See ICRC, *Conference of Government Experts on the Use of Certain Conventional Weapons (Second Session—Lugano, 28 January–26 February 1976): Report*, 1976, pp. 69–76 and pp. 120–1, paras. 69–72.

[44]   Ibid.

[45]   Adam Roberts and Richard Guelff (eds), *Documents on the Laws of War*, 3rd ed., Oxford University Press, 2000, p. 515.

[46]   SIPRI, *World Armaments and Disarmament SIPRI Yearbook 1980*, Taylor & Francis/SIPRI, 1980, pp. 390–1. Later, according to Simon Conway, Director of the British NGO Landmine Action, the use of plastic tail fins to stabilize the US Mk-118 Rockeye submunition "gave rise at the time to the charge that this was an anti-personnel weapon designed to produce undetectable fragments". See ICRC, *Humanitarian, Military, Technical and Legal Challenges of Cluster Munitions—Expert Meeting Report, Montreux, Switzerland, 18 to 20 April 2007*, 2007, p. 14.

[47]   Earl S. Martin, "Defusing the Rice Paddies", *Washington Post and Times-Herald*, 8 July 1973.

[48]   Earl S. Martin and Murray Hiebert, "Explosive remnants of the Second Indochina War in Viet Nam and Laos", in Arthur H. Westing (ed.), *Explosive Remnants of War: Mitigating the Environmental Effects*, Taylor & Francis/SIPRI/UNEP, 1985, p. 39.

[49]   Bruce Shoemaker, *Legacy of the Secret War*, 1994, <www.mcc.org/clusterbombs/resources/research/legacy>.

[50]   ICRC, *Explosive Remnants of War: Submunitions and Other Unexploded Ordnance—A Study*, 2000, p. 30.

51   Bruce Shoemaker, *Legacy of the Secret War*, 1994, <www.mcc.org/clusterbombs/resources/research/legacy>.

52   Lao National Unexploded Ordnance Programme, *Annual Report 2007*, 2008, p. 1.

53   Fred Branfman, *Voices From the Plain of Jars: Life Under an Air War*, Harper Colophon Books, 1972, p. 6.

54   Lao National Regulatory Authority, Lao National Unexploded Ordnance Programme and UNDP Lao, *Hazardous Ground: Cluster Munitions and UXO in the Lao PDR*, 2008. Of course these numbers are approximate, and we will never know exactly how many submunitions were left unexploded.

55   Lao National Regulatory Authority, Lao National Unexploded Ordnance Programme and UNDP Lao, *Hazardous Ground: Cluster Munitions and UXO in the Lao PDR*, 2008, p. 3.

56   Handicap International, *Living with UXO: Final Report, National Survey on the Socio-Economic Impact of UXO in the Lao PDR*, 1997, p. 6.

57   Lao National Regulatory Authority, Lao National Unexploded Ordnance Programme and UNDP Lao, *Hazardous Ground: Cluster Munitions and UXO in the Lao PDR*, 2008. See section "New Victims of an Old War".

58   Bruce Shoemaker, *Legacy of the Secret War*, 1994, <www.mcc.org/clusterbombs/resources/research/legacy>.

59   See Geneva International Centre for Humanitarian Demining, *A Study of Scrap Metal Collection in Lao PDR*, 2005.

60   Author's personal correspondence with Titus Peachey, 6 August 2009.

61   Author's interview with Titus Peachey, 3 December 2008.

62   Idem.

63   See Eric Prokosch, *The Technology of Killing: a Military and Political History of Anti-Personnel Weapons*, Zed Books, 1995, pp. 126–47.

64   For a technical overview see Colin King (ed.), *Jane's Explosive Ordnance Disposal 2008–2009*, Jane's Information Group, 2008, pp. 282–3.

65   See Ove Dullum, *Cluster Weapons—Military Utility and Alternatives*, Norwegian Defence Research Establishment (FFI), 2008, p. 12.

66   ICRC, *Explosive Remnants of War: Submunitions and Other Unexploded Ordnance—A Study*, 2000, p. 34.

67   Eric Prokosch, "Cluster Weapons", *Papers in the Theory and Practice of Human Rights*, no. 15, Human Rights Centre, University of Essex, 1995, p. 8.

68   *Working Paper submitted by Egypt, Mexico, Norway, Sudan, Sweden, Switzerland and Yugoslavia to the Diplomatic Conference on the*

reaffirmation and development of international humanitarian law applicable in armed conflicts, 21 February 1974, p. 8.

69   Ibid.

70   ICRC, *Conference of Government Experts on the Use of Certain Conventional Weapons (Lucerne, 24 September–18 October 1974): Report*, 1975, pp. 53–4, para. 173.

71   *Working Paper submitted by Egypt, Mexico, Norway, Sudan, Sweden, Switzerland and Yugoslavia to the Diplomatic Conference on the reaffirmation and development of international humanitarian law applicable in armed conflicts*, 21 February 1974, p. 8.

72   See Eric Prokosch, *The Technology of Killing: a Military and Political History of Anti-Personnel Weapons*, Zed Books, 1995, p. 154.

73   ICRC, *Explosive Remnants of War: Submunitions and Other Unexploded Ordnance—A Study*, 2000, p. 14. See also Annex D of that report that reproduces an advertisement by the weapon's manufacturer, Hunting Engineering, of refurbished BL-755s, which describes them as "Anti-armour *General Purpose* Cluster Weapons" for "Air-delivered attack against armoured formations, artillery and vehicle concentrations and *other land* and naval targets". Emphasis added.

74   Rae McGrath, *Cluster Bombs: The Military Effectiveness and Impact on Civilians of Cluster Munitions*, UK Working Group on Landmines, 2000, p. 2

75   ICRC, *Humanitarian, Military, Technical and Legal Challenges of Cluster Munitions—Expert Meeting Report, Montreux, Switzerland, 18 to 20 April 2007*, 2007, p. 15.

76   ICRC, *Explosive Remnants of War: Submunitions and Other Unexploded Ordnance—A Study*, 2000, pp. 15–6.

77   Richard Norton-Taylor, "British forces banned from using 'dumb' cluster bombs", *The Guardian*, 19 March 2007.

78   See Margarita H. Petrova, "Curbing the use of indiscriminate weapons: NGO advocacy in militant democracies", in Matthew Evangelista, Harald Müller and Niklas Schörnig, *Democracy and Security: Preferences, Norms and Policy-Making*, Routledge, 2007, p. 75, table 5.1, compiled from US and UK government data and Human Rights Watch reports.

79   ICRC, *Humanitarian, Military, Technical and Legal Challenges of Cluster Munitions—Expert Meeting Report, Montreux, Switzerland, 18 to 20 April 2007*, 2007, p. 15.

80   ICRC, *Explosive Remnants of War: Submunitions and Other Unexploded Ordnance—A Study*, 2000, p. 17.

81   US General Accounting Office, "Operation Desert Storm: Casualties Caused by Improper Handling of Unexploded U.S. Submunitions", document GAO/NSIAD-93-212, 1993, p. 9.

82   See Ove Dullum, *Cluster Weapons—Military Utility and Alternatives*, Norwegian Defence Research Establishment (FFI), 2008, p. 98.

83   See Norwegian People's Aid, *Yellow Killers: The Impact of Cluster Munitions in Serbia and Montenegro*, 2007.

84   See Mark Hiznay, "Operational and technical aspects of cluster munitions", *Disarmament Forum*, no. 4, 2006, p. 17.

85   "The ICRC's position on cluster munitions and the need for urgent action", statement to Geneva Diplomatic Missions by Dr Jakob Kellenberger, President of the ICRC, 25 October 2007.

86   These being Algeria, Angola, Argentina, Austria, Azerbaijan, Bahrain, Belarus, Belgium, Bosnia and Herzegovina, Brazil, Bulgaria, Canada, Chile, China, Croatia, Cuba, Czech Republic, Democratic People's Republic of Korea, Denmark, Egypt, Eritrea, Ethiopia, Finland, France, Georgia, Germany, Greece, Honduras, Hungary, India, Indonesia, Iran, Iraq, Israel, Italy, Japan, Jordan, Kazakhstan, Kuwait, Libya, Moldova, Mongolia, Morocco, Netherlands, Nigeria, Norway, Oman, Pakistan, Poland, Portugal, Republic of Korea, Romania, Russian Federation, Saudi Arabia, Serbia and Montenegro, Singapore, Slovakia, South Africa, Spain, Sudan, Sweden, Switzerland, Syria, Thailand, Turkey, Turkmenistan, Ukraine, United Arab Emirates, United Kingdom, United States, Uzbekistan, Yemen and Zimbabwe. See Mark Hiznay, "Operational and technical aspects of cluster munitions", *Disarmament Forum*, no. 4, 2006, p.18.

87   Cluster Munition Coalition, Human Rights Watch, International Campaign to Ban Landmines, Landmine Action and Landmine Monitor, *Banning Cluster Munitions: Government Policy and Practice*, 2009, p. 258. This report also observed that a 2004 report to the US Congress by the Department of Defense provided a figure of 5.5 million cluster munitions containing about 728.5 submunitions, but that this did not include additional cluster munitions part of the War Reserve Stocks for Allies. See also US Department of Defense, "Report to Congress: Cluster Munitions", 2004, pp. 2–6, <www.cdi.org/clusters/Report%20 to%20Congress.pdf>.

88   See Louis Maresca, "Cluster munitions: moving toward specific regulation", *Disarmament Forum*, no. 4, 2006, pp. 28–9.

89   Adam Roberts and Richard Guelff (eds), *Documents on the Laws of War*, 3rd ed., Oxford University Press, 2000, p. 645.

90   *Progress report of the Group of Governmental Experts to Prepare the Review Conference of the States Parties to the Convention on Prohibitions or Restrictions on the Use of Certain Conventional Weapons Which May Be Deemed to Be Excessively Injurious or to Have Indiscriminate Effects*, UN document CCW/CONF.I/GE/4, 8 March 1994, para. 3.

91   See Stuart Maslen, *The Convention on the Prohibition of the Use, Stockpiling, Production, and Transfer of Anti-Personnel Mines and on their Destruction*, Commentaries on Arms Control Treaties, vol. 1, Oxford University Press, 2004, p. 19.

92   Author's communication with Dr Robin Coupland, ICRC, 12 February 2009.

93   See R.M. Coupland and A. Korver, "Injuries from antipersonnel mines: the experience of the International Committee of the Red Cross", *British Medical Journal*, vol. 303, no. 6816, 1991, pp. 1509–12. An editorial in the same edition of the British Medical Journal was the first written call for a ban on landmines, R. McGrath and E. Stover, "Injuries from land mines", *British Medical Journal*, vol. 303, no. 6816, 1991, p. 1492.

94   See S. Jeffrey, "Antipersonnel mines: who are the victims?", *Journal of Accident and Emergency Medicine*, vol. 13, no. 5, 1996, pp. 343–6. Data presented in this article was used from 1993 in presentations about the effects of anti-personnel mines.

95   "Statement of Cornelio Sommaruga, President, International Committee of the Red Cross, Geneva, Switzerland, 24 February 1994", in Louis Maresca and Stuart Maslen (eds), *The Banning of Anti-Personnel Landmines: The Legal Contribution of the International Committee of the Red Cross 1955–1999*, Cambridge University Press, 2000, pp. 264–5.

96   Stuart Maslen, *The Convention on the Prohibition of the Use, Stockpiling, Production, and Transfer of Anti-Personnel Mines and on their Destruction*, Commentaries on Arms Control Treaties, vol. 1, Oxford University Press, 2004, p. 20.

97   General Assembly, *Moratorium on the export of anti-personnel landmines, report of the Secretary-General*, UN document A/49/275, 27 July 1994, paras. 25–6.

98   General Assembly, *General and complete disarmament*, UN document A/RES/49/75[D], 15 December 1994.

99   See Robert G. Gard, Jr, "The Military Utility of Anti-Personnel Mines", in Maxwell A. Cameron, Brian W. Tomlin and Robert J. Lawson (eds), *To Walk Without Fear: The Global Movement to Ban Landmines*, Oxford University Press, 1998, pp. 136–57. Gard provided a useful condensation of a range of viewpoints on this question in the later

1990s, and concluded of anti-personnel mines: "It is evident that their military utility is convincingly outweighed by the humanitarian costs of their use" (p. 154). Interestingly, Gard mentioned cluster munition systems such as the M-26 MLRS as alternatives to anti-personnel mines to fulfil battlefield area denial functions.

100 ICRC, *Anti-Personnel Mines: Friend or Foe? A Study of the Military Use and Effectiveness of Anti-Personnel Mines*, 1996, p. 73.

101 Ibid.

102 Michael Dolan and Chris Hunt, "Negotiating in the Ottawa Process: The New Multilateralism", in Maxwell A. Cameron, Brian W. Tomlin and Robert J. Lawson (eds), *To Walk Without Fear: The Global Movement to Ban Landmines*, Oxford University Press, 1998, p. 392.

103 Louis Maresca and Stuart Maslen (eds), *The Banning of Anti-Personnel Landmines: The Legal Contribution of the International Committee of the Red Cross 1955–1999*, Cambridge University Press, 2000, pp. 445–6.

104 Stuart Maslen, *The Convention on the Prohibition of the Use, Stockpiling, Production, and Transfer of Anti-Personnel Mines and on their Destruction*, Commentaries on Arms Control Treaties, vol. 1, Oxford University Press, 2004, p. 22.

105 For instance, see Jean-Philippe Lavoyer and Louis Maresca, "The Role of the ICRC in the Development of International Humanitarian Law", *International Negotiation*, vol. 4, no. 3, 1999, pp. 515–7.

106 As of writing in 2009, the CD has 65 member states.

107 Michael Dolan and Chris Hunt, "Negotiating in the Ottawa Process: The New Multilateralism", in Maxwell A. Cameron, Brian W. Tomlin and Robert J. Lawson (eds), *To Walk Without Fear: The Global Movement to Ban Landmines*, Oxford University Press, 1998, p. 403.

108 Jean-Philippe Lavoyer and Louis Maresca, "The Role of the ICRC in the Development of International Humanitarian Law", *International Negotiation*, vol. 4, no. 3, 1999, p. 521.

109 See Don Hubert, *The Landmine Ban: A Case Study in Humanitarian Advocacy*, Thomas J. Watson Jr. Institute for International Studies, Occasional Paper no. 42, 2000.

110 See Stuart Maslen, *Mine Action After Diana: Progress in the Struggle Against Landmines*, Pluto Press, 2004, p. 2.

111 Declaration of the Brussels Conference on Anti-Personnel Mines, in Stuart Maslen, *The Convention on the Prohibition of the Use, Stockpiling, Production, and Transfer of Anti-Personnel Mines and on their Destruction*, Commentaries on Arms Control Treaties, vol. 1, Oxford University Press, 2004, p. 377.

[112] Stuart Maslen, *The Convention on the Prohibition of the Use, Stockpiling, Production, and Transfer of Anti-Personnel Mines and on their Destruction*, Commentaries on Arms Control Treaties, vol. 1, Oxford University Press, 2004, p. 43.

[113] Stuart Maslen, *Mine Action After Diana: Progress in the Struggle Against Landmines*, Pluto Press, 2004, p. 6.

[114] See ICRC, *Banning Anti-Personnel Mines: The Ottawa Treaty Explained*, 1998.

[115] See Ken Rutherford, "State Legal Obligations to Landmine Victim Assistance", *Journal of International Law and Policy*, vol. 7, no. 1, 2001, p. 42.

[116] See article 2 of the Protocol on Prohibitions or Restrictions on the Use of Mines, Booby-Traps and Other Devices as amended on 3 May 1996. Emphasis added.

[117] See John Borrie, "Small arms and the Geneva Forum: Disarmament as Humanitarian Action?", in John Borrie and Vanessa Martin Randin (eds), *Disarmament as Humanitarian Action: From Perspective to Practice*, UNIDIR, 2006, pp. 139–48.

[118] Eric Prokosch, *The Technology of Killing: a Military and Political History of Anti-Personnel Weapons*, Zed Books, 1995, p. 182.

Chapter 2
From little things big things will grow

[1] "NATO's objectives in relation to the conflict in Kosovo were set out in the Statement issued at the Extraordinary Meeting of the North Atlantic Council held at NATO on 12 April 1999 and were reaffirmed by Heads of State and Government in Washington on 23 April 1999: a verifiable stop to all military action and the immediate ending of violence and repression; the withdrawal from Kosovo of the military, police and paramilitary forces; the stationing in Kosovo of an international military presence; the unconditional and safe return of all refugees and displaced persons and unhindered access to them by humanitarian aid organisations; the establishment of a political framework agreement for Kosovo on the basis of the Rambouillet Accords, in conformity with international law and the Charter of the United Nations". See <www.nato.int/kosovo/history.htm>.

2   "Press Conference by NATO Secretary General, Dr. Javier Solana, and SACEUR, Gen. Wesley Clark", 25 March 1999, <www.nato.int/kosovo/press/p990325a.htm>.

3   See International Institute for Strategic Studies, "Air-power over Kosovo: A Historic Victory?", *Strategic Comments*, vol. 5, no. 7, 1999.

4   ICRC, *Explosive Remnants of War: Cluster Bombs and Landmines in Kosovo*, 2000/revised 2001, p. 7.

5   See Human Rights Watch, *Ticking Time Bombs: NATO's Use of Cluster Munitions in Yugoslavia*, 1999, <www.hrw.org/legacy/reports/1999/nato2/>.

6   Stephen D. Goose, "Cluster Munitions in the Crosshairs: In Pursuit of a Prohibition", in Jody Williams, Stephen D. Goose and Mary Wareham (eds), *Banning Landmines: Disarmament, Citizen Diplomacy and Human Security*, Lanham, Rowman and Littlefield, 2008, p. 221. However, the precise number of cluster munitions used may never be known.

7   Norwegian People's Aid, *Yellow Killers: The Impact of Cluster Munitions in Serbia and Montenegro*, 2007, p. 23.

8   "NATO has confirmed that the damage to the market and clinic was caused by a NATO weapon which missed its target. This strike was directed against the Niš airfield utilising cluster munitions. The attack was aimed at destroying Serbian aircraft which were parked on the airfield, air defence systems and support vehicles, targets to which cluster munitions are appropriately suited. Once again of course civilian casualties were never intended and NATO regrets the loss of life and injuries inflicted". See "Press Conference given by NATO Secretary General, Javier Solana, NATO Spokesman, Jamie Shea and SHAPE Spokesman, Major General Walter Jertz", 8 May 1999, <www.nato.int/kosovo/press/p990508b.htm>.

9   Norwegian People's Aid, *Yellow Killers: The Impact of Cluster Munitions in Serbia and Montenegro*, 2007, pp. 21–5.

10   As acknowledged in Richard Moyes, *Cluster Munitions in Kosovo: Analysis of Use, Contamination and Casualties*, Landmine Action, 2007, p. 3. In its February 2000 report, Human Rights Watch estimated that "Altogether, some ninety to 150 civilians died from cluster bomb use. The first confirmed incident was on April 10 … and the last was on May 13 … ". See Human Rights Watch, *Civilian Deaths in the NATO Air Campaign*, 2000, p. 30.

11   Human Rights Watch, *Ticking Time Bombs: NATO's Use of Cluster Munitions in Yugoslavia*, 1999, <www.hrw.org/legacy/reports/1999/nato2/>.

[12] A point acknowledged in a later report by the Geneva International Centre for Humanitarian Demining (GICHD) circulated in the CCW. See Adrian Wilkinson, *Explosive Remnants of War (ERW): A Threat Analysis*, GICHD, 2002, p. 29.

[13] See, for instance, *Explosive Remnants of War: Experience from Field Operations*, UN document CCW/GGE/II/WP.13, 15 July 2002.

[14] ICRC, *Explosive Remnants of War: Cluster Bombs and Landmines in Kosovo*, 2000/revised 2001, p. 9.

[15] Richard Moyes, *Cluster Munitions in Kosovo: Analysis of Use, Contamination and Casualties*, Landmine Action, 2007; see p. 3 for summary of post-conflict casualties, and pp. 55–7 for the methodology behind Landmine Action's assessment of risk from submunitions. According to Landmine Action, evidence "strongly suggests that quantity of contamination is not the only problem that makes cluster munitions a particular threat to civilian populations".

[16] See Stephen D. Goose, "Cluster Munitions in the Crosshairs: In Pursuit of a Prohibition", in Jody Williams, Stephen D. Goose and Mary Wareham (eds), *Banning Landmines: Disarmament, Citizen Diplomacy and Human Security*, Lanham, Rowman and Littlefield, 2008, p. 221.

[17] For discussion of some of the legal aspects of the NATO bombing of Kosovo, Serbia and Montenegro using cluster munitions, see Thomas Michael McDonnell, "Cluster Bombs Over Kosovo: A Violation of International Law?", *Arizona Law Review*, vol. 44, no. 1, 2002, pp. 31–129.

[18] Richard Moyes, *Cluster Munitions in Kosovo: Analysis of Use, Contamination and Casualties*, Landmine Action, 2007, p. 46.

[19] Virgil Wiebe, "Cluster bombs and explosive remnants of war: Cooperation and conflict between non-governmental organizations and middle power states", in Kenneth R. Rutherford, Stefan Brehm and Richard A. Mathew (eds), *Reframing the Agenda: The Impact of NGO and Middle Power Cooperation in International Security Policy*, Praeger, 2003, p. 97.

[20] Author's personal communication with Titus Peachey, 18 December 2008.

[21] Author's personal communication with Titus Peachey, 21 January 2009.

[22] Author's personal communication with Stephen D. Goose, 7 September 2009.

23   "Summary and Recommendations" in Human Rights Watch, *Ticking Time Bombs: NATO's Use of Cluster Munitions in Yugoslavia*, 1999, <www.hrw.org/legacy/reports/1999/nato2/>.

24   Human Rights Watch, "Cluster Bombs: Memorandum for Convention on Conventional Weapons (CCW) Delegates", 15 December 1999, <www.hrw.org/en/news/1999/12/15/cluster-bombs-memorandum-convention-conventional-weapons-ccw-delegates>.

25   HRW, *Civilian Deaths in the NATO Air Campaign*, 2000, p. 8.

26   Author's interview with Stephen D. Goose, 21 November 2008, and with Mark Hiznay, 9 July 2008. At that time HRW knew that a new US Department of Defense policy on submunition acquisition and failure rates was in the works. Later known as the Cohen doctrine, this 2001 policy is discussed in Chapter 8.

27   Although this report was dated March 2001, its concluding recommendations were dated "revision 6, April 5 2001". Mines Action Canada, "The Campaign Against Cluster Bombs: Key Considerations for Mines Action Canada", 2001, p. 15. Document on file with the author.

28   See Mary Wareham, "The role of *Landmine Monitor* in promoting and monitoring compliance with the 1997 Anti-Personnel Mine Ban Convention", in John Borrie and Vanessa Martin Randin (eds), *Disarmament as Humanitarian Action: From Perspective to Practice*, UNIDIR, 2006, pp. 79–108.

29   See Rosy Cave, "Disarmament as humanitarian action? Comparing negotiations on anti-personnel mines and explosive remnants of war", ibid., p. 57.

30   Virgil Wiebe and Titus Peachey, *Drop Today, Kill Tomorrow: Cluster Munitions as Inhumane and Indiscriminate Weapons*, MCC, 1997/ revised 1999; and Virgil Wiebe and Titus Peachey, *Clusters of Death*, MCC, 2000.

31   Author's interview with Titus Peachey, 3 December 2008.

32   Even today, relatively few details are known about the precise extent of cluster munition use in Chechyna, although this appears to have been considerable. See Virgil Wiebe and Titus Peachey, *Clusters of Death*, MCC, 2000, pp. 59–78.

33   See Richard Moyes, Richard Lloyd and Rae McGrath, *Explosive Remnants of War: Unexploded Ordnance and Post-Conflict Communities*, Landmine Action/Cooperative Bank, 2002, pp. 50–3.

34   The author participated in many of these meetings as a representative of the New Zealand Disarmament Mission in Geneva.

35   ICRC, *Explosive Remnants of War: Submunitions and Other Unexploded Ordnance—A Study*, 2000.

36   ICRC, *Explosive Remnants of War: Cluster Bombs and Landmines in Kosovo*, 2000/revised 2001.

37   For the ICRC's proposals, see ibid., p. 37.

38   Rae McGrath, *Cluster Bombs: The Military Effectiveness and Impact on Civilians of Cluster Munitions*, UK Working Group on Landmines, 2000.

39   ICRC, *Expert Meeting on Explosive Remnants of War, 18–19 September 2000: A Summary Report*, 2000, p. 10.

40   Ibid., p. 15.

41   Author's recollection, confirmed in author's personal communication with Jody Williams, 18 March 2009.

42   Author's interview with Stephen D. Goose, 21 November 2008.

43   *Report of the International Committee of the Red Cross to the First Preparatory Committee for the 2001 Review Conference of the United Nations Convention on Certain Conventional Weapons—Scope of application of the CCW and explosive remnants of war*, UN document CCW/CONF.II/PC.1/WP.1, 11 December 2000.

44   *Regulation on Submunitions*, UN document CCW/CONF.II/PC.1/WP.4, 14 December 2000.

45   Virgil Wiebe, "Cluster bombs and explosive remnants of war: Cooperation and conflict between non-governmental organizations and middle power states", in Kenneth R. Rutherford, Stefan Brehm and Richard A. Mathew (eds), *Reframing the Agenda: The Impact of NGO and Middle Power Cooperation in International Security Policy*, Praeger, 2003, p. 101.

46   Ambassador Chris Sanders later claimed that "Dutch interest in the issue stemmed from both the Netherlands' traditionally active role in the humanitarian field and its direct involvement in the Kosovo campaign". See Chris C. Sanders, "Contending with Explosive Remnants of War", *Arms Control Today*, vol. 34, no. 7, 2004. However, individual interest from Sanders and a highly capable Dutch Ministry of Foreign Affairs desk officer based in The Hague working on mine and UXO issues, Alex Verbeek, also certainly played a part.

47   *Explosive remnants of war*, UN document CCW/CONF.II/PC.1/WP.6, 14 December 2000, presented by the Netherlands and co-sponsored by Argentina, Austria, Belgium, Bulgaria, Canada, Cambodia, Denmark, Finland, France, Germany, Greece, Hungary, Ireland, Israel, Italy,

Luxembourg, New Zealand, Norway, Peru, Portugal, Slovakia, Spain, Sweden, Switzerland, the United Kingdom and the United States.

48   Virgil Wiebe, "Cluster bombs and explosive remnants of war: Cooperation and conflict between non-governmental organizations and middle power states", in Kenneth R. Rutherford, Stefan Brehm and Richard A. Mathew (eds), *Reframing the Agenda: The Impact of NGO and Middle Power Cooperation in International Security Policy*, Praeger, 2003, p. 102. Nevertheless, the ICRC (which had played an important role in the Ottawa process) *was* invited to The Hague. Some NGOs, such as Human Rights Watch, were closely in touch with the Dutch and other governments leading efforts toward and ERW negotiation in the CCW and fed in substantive input, including in the lead-up to meeting in the The Hague; author's personal communication with Stephen D. Goose, 7 September 2009.

49   See Louis Maresca, "Second Review Conference of the Convention on Certain Conventional Weapons", *International Review of the Red Cross*, vol. 84, no. 845, pp. 255–62.

50   *Final Document*, UN document CCW/CONF.II/2, 2001, p. 13. Emphasis added.

51   Author's interview with Stephen D. Goose, 21 November 2008.

52   Vietnam Veterans of America Foundation, *Proposed Protocol to Address Explosive Remnants of War*, 25 September 2001. Document on file with the author.

53   Some NGOs had feared their opportunity to have input would be curtailed. See Virgil Wiebe, "Cluster bombs and explosive remnants of war: Cooperation and conflict between non-governmental organizations and middle power states", in Kenneth R. Rutherford, Stefan Brehm and Richard A. Mathew (eds), *Reframing the Agenda: The Impact of NGO and Middle Power Cooperation in International Security Policy*, Praeger, 2003, pp. 103–4.

54   See Louis Maresca, "A new protocol on explosive remnants of war: The history and negotiation of Protocol V to the 1980 Convention on Certain Conventional Weapons", *International Review of the Red Cross*, vol. 86, no. 856, 2004, p. 821.

55   A small number of US Navy CBU-99s, CBU-100s and JSOW-As were apparently also used.

56   Human Rights Watch, *Fatally Flawed: Cluster Bombs and their use by the United States in Afghanistan*, 2002, pp. 1–3.

57   Human Rights Watch, "Cluster Munitions a Foreseeable Hazard in Iraq", briefing paper, 2003, p. 2.

58   See Mines Action Canada, Actiongroup Landmine.de and Landmine Action, *Explosive Remnants of War and Mines Other Than Anti-Personnel Mines: Global Survey 2003–2004*, Landmine Action, 2005, pp. 86–7.

59   Human Rights Watch, *Off Target: The Conduct of the War and Civilian Casualties in Iraq*, 2003, pp. 104–5.

60   See *Explosive Remnants of War and Development—Voices from the Field: Conference Report*, Pax Christi Ireland, 2003.

61   John Borrie, *Explosive Remnants of War: A Global Survey*, Landmine Action, 2003.

62   One sign of this was a Landmine Action editorial in *New Scientist* that month, which argued that cluster munition use in Iraq underscored the need to "take every step necessary to protect civilians from cluster bombs and the exceptional problems they cause". See Richard Lloyd, "No way to win the peace", *New Scientist*, 12 April 2003, p. 27.

63   The author attended this meeting. According to the meeting's minutes, the other attendees were: Rosy Cave, Richard Lloyd and Anne Quesney (Landmine Action), Pierrot Ngadi (Congolese Irish Partnership), Maine Ni Bheagaoch (PANA), Roman Dolgov (International Physicians for the Prevention of Nuclear War, Russian Campaign to Ban Landmines), Yuri Donskoy (Peacekeepers Association Ukraine), Malcolm Rodgers (Christian Aid UK), Kasia Derlicka (Polish Campaign to Ban Landmines), John Rodsted (Australian Campaign to Ban Landmines), Ayman Sorour (Landmine Struggle Unit), Salyia Edirisinghe (Sri Lankan Campaign to Ban Landmines), Tony West (Handicap International Belgium), Peter Le Sueur (Afghan Technical Consultants), Faiz Muhammad Fayyaz (CMDO Pakistan), Dr Rafaat Misak (Kuwait Landmine Monitor researcher), Raymond Kimika (Humanitarian Action, CEFI), Fuad Giacaman (Arab Educational Institute), Peadar O'Neill (Pax Christi Ireland), Sarah Njeri, Andrew Purkis (The Diana, Princess of Wales Memorial Fund), Tobias Gasser (Swiss Campaign to Ban Landmines), Mohamed Fawz (SLIRI), Stephen D. Goose (Human Rights Watch), Virgil Wiebe (Mennonite Central Committee), Judith Majlath (Austrian Aid For Mine Victims), Christine Lefort (Handicap International France), Purna Shova Chitrakar (Nepalese Campaign to Ban Landmines), Maria-Josep Pares (Movíment per la Pau), Sheila Keetharuth (Landmine Monitor researcher) and Paul Hannon (Mines Action Canada). The minutes are on file with the author.

64   Stephen D. Goose. "Cluster Munitions in the Crosshairs: In pursuit of a prohibition", in Jody Williams, Stephen D. Goose and Mary Wareham

(eds), *Banning Landmines: Disarmament, Citizen Diplomacy and Human Security*, Lanham, Rowman and Littlefield, 2008, p. 223.

65   Author's interview with Stephen D. Goose, 21 November 2008.

66   Idem.

67   Speech by Dutch Minister of Foreign Affairs, Jaap de Hoop Scheffer, in Pax Christi Netherlands, *Conference Report: Cluster Munition Coalition International Launch Conference, 12–13 November 2003, The Hague*, p. 37. Document on file with the author.

68   Protocol on Explosive Remnants of War (Protocol V to the 1980 Convention), 28 November 2003.

69   Protocol V's provisions were also weakened by the presence of caveats sprinkled in the text such as "where feasible" and "where appropriate".

70   Stephen D. Goose, "Cluster Munitions in the Crosshairs: In pursuit of a prohibition", in Jody Williams, Stephen D. Goose and Mary Wareham (eds), *Banning Landmines: Disarmament, Citizen Diplomacy and Human Security*, Lanham, Rowman and Littlefield, 2008, p. 223.

71   "Cluster Munition Coalition Statement to the CCW Meeting of States Parties, 27 November 2003", in Pax Christi Netherlands, *Conference Report: Cluster Munition Coalition International Launch Conference, 12–13 November 2003, The Hague*, pp. 58–9. Document on file with the author.

72   See Stephen D. Goose, "Cluster Munitions in the Crosshairs: In pursuit of a prohibition", in Jody Williams, Stephen D. Goose and Mary Wareham (eds), *Banning Landmines: Disarmament, Citizen Diplomacy and Human Security*, Lanham, Rowman and Littlefield, 2008, p. 236, note 14.

73   Author's personal communication with Stephen D. Goose, 7 September 2009.

74   Author's interview with Thomas Nash, 24 July 2008.

75   See "Humanitarian Consequences and International Response", presentation by Stephen D. Goose, in Human Rights Watch, *Cluster Bombs: Effective Weapon or Humanitarian Foe? Conference Documentation*, 2004, p. 25.

76   See "CMC launch statement", in Pax Christi Netherlands, *Conference Report: Cluster Munition Coalition International Launch Conference, 12–13 November 2003, The Hague*, p. 41. Document on file with the author.

77   Landmine Action launched its international Clear Up! Campaign on ERW in partnership with The Diana, Princess of Wales Memorial Fund

on 28 February 2003. During the CCW's negotiations, it called on governments to tackle the humanitarian post-conflict problems caused by ERW and reiterated the call for a freeze on the use and transfer of cluster munitions until new international law that effectively dealt with their effects was put in place. See Landmine Action, *Landmine Action Campaign*, issue 7, 2003, p. 8.

78 Author's conversation with Thomas Nash, 23 March 2009.

79 Author's personal communication with Stephen D. Goose, 7 September 2009.

80 Author's interview with Thomas Nash, 24 July 2008.

81 It is possible to see their increasing scepticism about a 1%, 2% or 5% failure rate's viability in operational use in passages of the report. See Mines Action Canada, Actiongroup Landmine.de and Landmine Action, *Explosive Remnants of War and Mines Other Than Anti-Personnel Mines: Global Survey 2003–2004*, Landmine Action, 2005, pp. 86–7.

82 Rae McGrath, "Campaigning against Cluster Munitions—Strategic Issues: A Discussion Paper", 2004, p. 10. Document on file with the author.

83 For instance, CCW delegates were told in July 2004 that "Human Rights Watch favours a CCW protocol that regulates, but does not completely prohibit, all cluster munitions. It thus acknowledges that certain models of cluster munitions used in certain circumstances may be legitimate yet takes a strong stand against the humanitarian damage caused by these weapons". See Human Rights Watch, *Memorandum to CCW Delegates—Cluster Munitions and International Humanitarian Law: The Need for Better Compliance and Stronger Rules (Prepared for the Convention on Certain Conventional Weapons (CCW) Group of Governmental Experts on Explosive Remnants of War (ERW) July 5–16, 2004*, 2004, p. 8.

84 See "Minutes of the Meeting of [the] Cluster Munition Coalition", in Human Rights Watch, *Cluster Bombs: Effective Weapon or Humanitarian Foe? Conference Documentation*, 2004.

85 In asking what the world could realistically expect from the CCW, McGrath argued that at most would be agreement to (1) warn civilians (if feasible) ("which may simply be a warning to 'get out of town'"), (2) more funding for clearance ("but never as much as is expended on causing the problem"); or/and (3) improvements to the design of cluster munitions to minimize failure rates ("good contract opportunities for the arms industry, including the same arms companies who have profited from selling the original weapons"). Rae McGrath, "Cluster Munitions—

Weapons of Deadly Convenience? Reviewing the Legality and Utility of Cluster Munitions", Meeting of Humanitarian Experts, Palais des Nations, Geneva, 11 November 2004.

86 E-mail from Thomas Nash to John Rodsted, "Re: Photo and video material for CMC", 30 December 2004.

87 *Dealing with the Impact of Cluster Munitions*, UN document CCW/GGE/IX/WG.1/WP.1, 29 November 2004, p. 4.

88 Stephen D. Goose, "Cluster Munitions in the Crosshairs: In pursuit of a prohibition", in Jody Williams, Stephen D. Goose and Mary Wareham (eds), *Banning Landmines: Disarmament, Citizen Diplomacy and Human Security*, Lanham, Rowman and Littlefield, 2008, p. 224.

89 *Report of the Meeting of the States Parties*, UN document CCW/MSP/2004/2, 13 December 2004, p. 4.

90 *International Humanitarian Law and ERW prepared by* (8 March 2005), UN document CCW/GGE/X/WG.1/WP.2, 8 March 2005. The document reads that it was prepared by Australia, Canada, New Zealand, Norway, Sweden, Switzerland, the UK and the US in consultation with the ICRC.

91 Author's personal communication with Annette Bjørseth, 10 August 2008.

92 According to the minutes, "The CMC decided to appoint Thomas Nash as CMC Coordinator, on a voluntary basis until funding is secured". *Minutes from the CMC Steering Committee meeting*, Geneva, 12 November 2004.

93 Author's interview with Brian Rappert, 23 July 2008.

94 Brian Rappert, "The campaign against cluster weapons: discussing future CMC campaigning strategies", Pax Christi Netherlands, 2005 (CMC internal document).

95 Brian Rappert, "Out of Balance: the UK Government's Efforts to Understand Cluster Munitions and International Humanitarian Law", Landmine Action, 2005.

96 *Military Utility of Cluster Munitions*, UN document CCW/GGE/X/WG.1/WP.1, 21 February 2005.

97 Ibid., p. 3, para. 17.

98 Ibid.

99 Author's interview with Brian Rappert, 23 July 2008.

100 Brian Rappert, "Out of Balance: the UK Government's Efforts to Understand Cluster Munitions and International Humanitarian Law", Landmine Action, 2005, p. 2.

[101] Ben Russell, "UK's deadly legacy: the cluster bomb", *The Independent*, 21 November 2005.

[102] "Cluster bombs: measuring the human cost", *The Lancet*, vol. 366, no. 9501, 2005, p. 1904.

[103] Author's personal communciation with Brian Rappert, 25 March 2009.

[104] Author's interview with Stephen D. Goose, 21 November 2008.

[105] See Margarita H. Petrova, "Small States and New Norms of Warfare", EUI Working Paper, European University Institute, 2007, p. 7. The Mine Ban Treaty, when eventually implemented into Belgian law, superseded the time limit in the earlier law.

[106] Ibid., p. 9.

[107] Bryant later set out his views in an article for UNIDIR. See Kevin Bryant, "Cluster munitions and their submunitions—a personal view", *Disarmament Forum*, no. 4, 2006, pp. 45–9.

[108] Author's conversation with Thomas Nash, 27 March 2009.

[109] One of the invited speakers at this event was Dr Gro Nystuen, Chair of the Norwegian Government Petroleum Fund's Ethics Council, discussing its posture on investment in companies producing cluster munitions. In June 2005, this Ethics Council recommended to the Norwegian government that it end investment in companies producing key components of cluster munitions.

[110] For instance, see Olivier Mouton, "Interdire les armes à sous-munitions", *La Libre*, 8 April 2005.

[111] "Bombes à fragmentation: Forges de Zeebrugge dissent ne pas en produire" [Forges de Zeebrugge say is doesn't produce fragmentation bombs], *Belga*, 19 April 2005. Document on file with the author.

[112] Speech by Stan Brabant, Zak Johnson, Kevin Bryant and Didier Simons (Handicap International), Belgian Senate, Brussels, 28 June 2005, <www.handicapinternational.be/COMMUNIQUES-DE-PRESSE-Presentation-d-Handicap-International-au-Senat-belge-28-juin-2005_a58.html>.

[113] Author's interview with Stan Brabant, 2 September 2008.

[114] See Margarita H. Petrova, "Small States and New Norms of Warfare", EUI Working Paper, European University Institute, 2007, p. 10.

[115] This is the IMAS definition; see <www.gichd.org/mine-action-and-erw-facts/faq/cluster-munitions>.

[116] European Parliament, *A world without landmines: European Parliament resolution on a mine-free world*, EU document P6_TA(2005)0298, 7 July 2005.

117   Margarita H. Petrova, "Small States and New Norms of Warfare", EUI Working Paper, European University Institute, 2007, p. 11.

118   Ibid.

119   These political parties were the Dutch-speaking socialists (Socialistische Partij Anders), the French-speaking socialists (Parti socialiste), the Dutch-speaking "liberal" right-wing (Vlaamse Liberalen en Democraten) and French-speaking "liberal" right-wing (Mouvement réformateur). Author's personal communication with Stan Brabant, 30 March 2009.

120   Quoted in HI Belgium, "The Belgian Campaign to Ban Cluster Munitions: A Brief History", February 2007.

121   Margarita H. Petrova, "Small States and New Norms of Warfare", EUI Working Paper, European University Institute, 2007, p. 12.

122   "Effects-based" language would also be added to tighten it further. See chapters 9 and 11.

123   Author's interview with Stan Brabant, 2 September 2008.

124   Opening statement by Norway at the meeting of the CCW Group of Governmental Experts, March 2006; Norway said: "We have noted with interest the move by the Belgian parliament to unilaterally put a ban on cluster munitions. We congratulate Belgium on taking a strong position in the case of these types of weapons". Norway went on to say: "Norway's point of departure, however, is to focus first on international law in the area of cluster munitions, then implement nationally. We strongly believe in an instrument on cluster munitions, and we are willing to pursue the issue on a wide front". Document on file with the author.

125   Statement by the Cluster Munition Coalition to the CCW GGE, 10 March 2006. Document on file with the author.

126   See, for instance, Belgium's statements to the CCW GGE, 9 March and 20 June 2006. Documents on file with the author.

127   Office of the Norwegian Prime Minister, *The Soria Moria Declaration on International Policy*, 2005, see section "Peace, Appeasement, Disarmament and a Strengthened UN".

Chapter 3
Norway and cluster munitions

1   Margarita H. Petrova, "Small States and New Norms of Warfare", EUI Working Paper, European University Institute, 2007, pp. 16–7.

2   Author's interview with Christian Ruge, 27 August 2008.

3   "Vedtak nr.667", 14 June 2001, in *Stortingsmeldingar 2001–2001*,
     p. 62, <www.regjeringen.no/Rpub/STM/20012002/004/PDFA/
     STM200120020004000DDDPDFA.pdf>.
4   "Utenriksdepartmentet uttaler I brev datert 14. august 2001" [Letter by
     the Ministry of Foreign Affairs], 14 August 2001, in *Stortingsmeldingar
     2001–2001*, p. 63, <www.regjeringen.no/Rpub/STM/20012002/004/
     PDFA/STM200120020004000DDDPDFA.pdf>.
5   Norwegian Ministry of Defence, "Forsvarsministerens redegjørelse om
     bruk av klasebomber i Hjerkinn skytefelt", [Report by the Minister of
     Defence on the use of cluster bombs at the Hjerkinn firing range],
     30 October 2002, <www.regjeringen.no/en/archive/Bondeviks-2nd-
     Government/ministry-of-defence/233255/233551/forsvarsministerens_
     redegjorelse.html?id=233691>. See also Norwegian Ministry of
     Defence, "Brev fra Forsvarsdepartementet v/statsråden til Stortingets
     forsvarskomité, datert 23. desember 2002" [Letter by the Ministry of
     Defence to the Parliament's Defence Committee], 23 December 2002,
     p. 5, <www.stortinget.no/Global/pdf/Innstillinger/Stortinget/2002-
     2003/inns-200203-115.pdf>.
6   Norwegian Ministry of Defence, "Forsvarssjefens rapport—Bruk av
     klasebomber i Hjerkinn skytefelt" [Report by the Chief of Defence
     on the use of cluster bombs at the Hjerkinn firing range], 30 October
     2002, <www.regjeringen.no/nb/dokumentarkiv/Regjeringen-
     Bondevik-II/fd/233255/233551/forsvarssjefens_rapport_-bruk_
     av.html?id=233692>.
7   See *National interpretation and implementation of International
     Humanitarian Law with regard to the risk of Explosive Remnants of
     War*, UN document CCW/GGE/VI/WG.1/WP.3, 24 November 2003,
     pp. 1–2.
8   See for instance "Må møte i høring", *NRK Nyheter*, 31 October
     2002, <www.nrk.no/nyheter/1.507570>. See also "Åpen høring
     om klasebomber", *NRK Nyheter*, 23 January 2003, <www.nrk.no/
     nyheter/1.508561>.
9   Author's interview with Grethe Østern, 26 August 2008.
10   *National interpretation and implementation of International Humanitarian
     Law with regard to the risk of Explosive Remnants of War*, UN document
     CCW/GGE/VI/WG.1/WP.3, 24 November 2003, pp. 1–2.
11   Ibid., p. 3.
12   See for instance, John Borrie, *A Global Survey of Explosive Remnants of
     War*, Landmine Action, 2003.
13   Author's interview with Grethe Østern, 26 August 2008.

14   "Anti-personnel mine" as defined in Article 2 of Protocol II to the CCW as amended on 3 May 1996.

15   See Margarita H. Petrova, "Small States and New Norms of Warfare", EUI Working Paper, European University Institute, 2007, p. 25.

16   In 2006, the Government Petroleum Fund changed its name to the Norwegian Pension Fund–Global.

17   These guidelines are available at <www.regjeringen.no/en/dep/fin/Selected-topics/andre/Ethical-Guidelines-for-the-Government-Pension-Fund---Global-/the-ethical-guidelines.html?id=434894>.

18   The Advisory Council on Ethics for the Norwegian Government Petroleum Fund, *Recommendation on exclusion of cluster weapons from the Government Petroleum Fund*, 16 June 2005, <www.regjeringen.no/pages/1661742/Tilrådning%20klasevåpen%20eng%2015%20juni%202005.pdf>.

19   Gro Nystuen, "Investment policies and arms production—experiences from the Norwegian Pension Fund–Global", in John Borrie and Vanessa Martin Randin (eds), *Thinking Outside the Box in Multilateral Disarmament and Arms Control Negotiations*, UNIDIR, 2006, p. 214.

20   Author's interview with Stan Brabant, 2 September 2008.

21   The Advisory Council on Ethics for the Norwegian Government Petroleum Fund, *Recommendation on exclusion of cluster weapons from the Government Petroleum Fund*, 16 June 2005, <www.regjeringen.no/pages/1661742/Tilrådning%20klasevåpen%20eng%2015%20juni%202005.pdf>.

22   Intervention by Norway to the Meeting of Governmental Experts on Explosive Remnants of War, 12 July 2004, quoted in Colin King, Ove Dullum and Grethe Østern, *M-85—An Analysis of Reliability*, Norwegian People's Aid, 2007, p. 34.

23   See *Military Utility of Cluster Munitions*, UN document CCW/GGE/X/WG.1/WP.1, 21 February 2005, p. 1, para. 5.

24   Comment by Richard Moyes of Landmine Action UK referred to in Colin King, Ove Dullum and Grethe Østern, *M-85—An Analysis of Reliability*, Norwegian People's Aid, 2007, p. 38, note 52.

25   Margarita H. Petrova, "Small States and New Norms of Warfare", EUI Working Paper, European University Institute, 2007, p. 15.

26   Author's interview with Per Nergaard, 4 July 2008.

27   Office of the Norwegian Prime Minister, *The Soria Moria Declaration on International Policy*, 2005.

28   Author's interview with Espen Barth Eide, 26 August 2008.

29   Margarita H. Petrova, "Small States and New Norms of Warfare", EUI Working Paper, European University Institute, 2007, p. 25.

30   Author's interview with Per Nergaard, 4 June 2008.

31   Author's interview with Annette Abelsen, 3 September 2008.

32   Author's interview with Steffen Kongstad, 27 August 2008.

33   Author's interview with Tormod Strand, 28 August 2008.

34   Israel licenses production of some or all parts of its field artillery cluster munition ("cargo ammunition") systems to other countries. For example, the UK produced the 155mm L20A1, Germany the 155mm DM-662, and Romania the 152mm CG-540 and CG-540 ER, all containing Israeli Military Industries M-85 submunitions, although sometimes given different designations by the licensees. See Colin King, Ove Dullum and Grethe Østern, *M-85—An Analysis of Reliability*, Norwegian People's Aid, 2007, p. 11. Norway's DM-1383 submunition, although also equipped with a mechanical/pyrotechnical self-destruct system, was different in design from the M-85/DM-1385, and was produced by Rheinmetall in Germany.

35   See Brian Rappert and Richard Moyes, *Failure to Protect: A Case for the Prohibition of Cluster Munitions*, Landmine Action, 2006, pp. 12–3.

36   Human Rights Watch, *Off Target: The Conduct of the War and Civilian Casualties in Iraq*, Human Rights Watch, 2003, p. 80.

37   Together, the stocks of DM-642 and DM-662 totalled around 40% of Norwegian artillery ammunition. See Colin King, Ove Dullum and Grethe Østern, *M-85—An Analysis of Reliability*, Norwegian People's Aid, 2007, p. 59.

38   Author's interview with Tormod Strand, 28 August 2008.

39   "Norwegian moratorium on cluster munitions", e-mail from Grethe Østern to the CMC list server, 13 June 2006.

40   *Military Utility of Cluster Munitions*, UN document CCW/GGE/X/WG.1/WP.1, 21 February 2005, p. 1, para. 5.

41   Richard Moyes, "Failure rates and the protection of civilians", *Landmine Action Campaign*, issue 12, Landmine Action, 2006, p. 5.

42   Ibid.

43   Colin King, Ove Dullum and Grethe Østern, *M-85—An Analysis of Reliability*, Norwegian People's Aid, 2007, p. 59.

44   Author's personal communication with Grethe Østern, 26 May 2009.

45   Author's personal communication with Grethe Østern, 27 May 2009. Indeed, according to Østern this relationship became "So good that NPA, our technical consultant C. King Associates and FFI ended up writing a report on the M-85 submunition together, where all parties

provided important perspectives. It was a rare kind of cooperation, resulting in a report that had credibility both in the humanitarian world and among military experts" (see Chapter 6).

46   Author's interview with Colin King, 4 September 2008.

47   "Testing of M-85 submunitions: Comments from Richard Moyes", August 2006, p. 1. Document on file with the author.

48   Author's personal communication with Grethe Østern, 26 May 2009.

49   This average failure rate includes testing results of the DM-642 rounds containing DM-1383 submunitions. These met the 1% standard, and so the failure rate for DM-1385 submunitions is actually higher than 1.11%.

50   NPA (among others) moved into Southern Lebanon quickly after the end of the 2006 summer war to set up explosive ordnance clearance operations (see chapter 4).

51   Author's interview with Ove Dullum, 25 August 2008.

52   Reply by the Norwegian Minister of Foreign Affairs to Olav Akselsen's (Labour Party) question regarding the war in Lebanon and the use of cluster munitions, 24 October 2006, <www.regjeringen. no/en/dep/ud/about_mfa/minister-of-foreign-affairs-jonas-gahr-s/ Speeches-and-articles/2006/reply-to-olav-akselsens-question-regardi. html?id=420888>.

53   "Subject: [cmc_international] Moratorium on Cluster munitions continue", e-mail from Christian Ruge to the CMC list server, 3 November 2006.

54   Norwegian Ministry of Foreign Affairs, "Norway to take the lead in efforts to achieve an international ban on cluster munitions", press release no. 142/06, 3 November 2006, <www.dep.no/ud/english/ news/news/032171-070930/dok-bn.html>.

55   Norwegian Ministry of Foreign Affairs, "Norway to take the lead in efforts to achieve an international ban on cluster munitions", press release no. 142/06, 3 November 2006, <www.dep.no/ud/english/ news/news/032171-070930/dok-bn.html>.

Chapter 4
Lebanon

1   See Human Rights Watch, *Civilians Under Assault: Hezbollah's Rocket Attacks on Israel in the 2006 War*, 2007, pp. 46–7, 83–4 and 121.

[2]   According to the International Institute for Strategic Studies (IISS), Hezbollah predominantly used the Zelzal-2 missile (with a range of approximately 200km), Fajir-5 (75km range), Fajir-3 (43km) rockets and the Haseb multi-barrel rocket launcher as its main indirect fire weapons, all supplied by Iran. These weapons could be fired from mobile launchers, including customized trucks. See IISS, *The Military Balance 2007*, 2007, p. 210. Anecdotal evidence from battle area clearance personnel with whom the author spoke indicated that some Hezbollah rockets were fired from basic firing frames, sometimes using timers in view of IDF counter-fire.

[3]   See Human Rights Watch, *Civilians Under Assault: Hezbollah's Rocket Attacks on Israel in the 2006 War*, 2007, p. 9.

[4]   General Assembly, *Report of the Commission of Inquiry on Lebanon pursuant to Human Rights Council resolution S-2/1*, UN document A/HRC/3/2, 23 November 2006, p. 5, para. 24.

[5]   "UN Emergency Relief Coordinator: End use of cluster munitions", 7 November 2006, <www.reliefweb.int/rw/RWB.NSF/db900SID/EVOD-6VBKJK>.

[6]   Author's conversation with Virgil Wiebe, 16 October 2008.

[7]   All such estimates are essentially guesswork in the absence of detailed Israeli strike data. This guess, however, is that of the MACC's Chief of Staff and its Operations Officer, as offered to the author at a briefing on 6 October 2008.

[8]   "Cash crisis hits Lebanon cluster bomb clearance", *Reuters*, 22 August 2008. With sufficient resources, the final 12,000,000m^2 of cluster munition contaminated land (a quarter of total contaminated land) in Southern Lebanon could be largely cleared in 2009. This is farmland people rely on for their livelihoods or which is close to populated areas and a risk to people's safety. The waning funds and interest of the international community has led to important cuts in demining operations, slowing down clearance; see "Lebanon: Funding struggle slowing cluster bomb clearance in south", *Integrated Regional Information Networks*, 5 February 2009. For Mine clearance activities alone, there is a funding shortfall for 2009 of US$ 16,071,786 according to the Electronic Mine Information Network, see <www.mineaction.org/projects_funding.asp?c=16&pillar=2&sh=%2C&aa=>.

[9]   According to the NGO Landmine Action, "The transfer of cluster munitions from the U.S. to Israel was governed by a confidential letter of 1976 that applied restrictions on the circumstances when these specific weapons could be used. The existence of this letter was acknowledged

after concerns were raised in Congress over civilian casualties from the use of cluster munitions in the 1978 and 1982 offensives in Lebanon". See Stuart Maslen and Virgil Wiebe, *Cluster Munitions: A Survey of Legal Responses*, Landmine Action, 2007, p. 23.

10   Ove Dullum, *Cluster Weapons—Military Utility and Alternatives*, Norwegian Defence Research Establishment (FFI), 2008, p. 121.

11   John Kifner and Steven Erlanger, "Truce Allows Thousands of Lebanese to Return Home", *New York Times*, 14 August 2006.

12   Narrative and quotes in this chapter concerning Clark drawn from author's interviews with Chris Clark on 16 July and 10 October 2008, and with Tekimiti Gilbert on 10 October 2008.

13   Andrew Brookes, "Air War Over Lebanon", International Institute for Strategic Studies, 8 August 2006.

14   Security Council, *Report of the Secretary-General on the United Nations Interim Force in Lebanon* UN document S/2006/560, 21 July 2006, para. 10.

15   Allen Kelly would soon return to Lebanon from Cyprus to establish a MACC liaison office in Beirut, along a New Zealand Army officer seconded to UN Mine Action Service, Maj. Todd Hart, and they would participate in the Tyre office's post-conflict planning.

16   United Nations Office for the Coordination of Humanitarian Affairs, *Lebanon response OCHA situation report No. 02*, OCHA document OCHA/NY–2006/0002, 22 July 2006: "There are some 80,000 displaced people in the Aleye Valley. ... Currently there are around 30, 000 IDPs [internally displaced persons] in the Beirut area mostly both from shelled Beirut suburbs and further south. Sixty thousand people have been evacuated from Lebanon to Cyprus so far". UN Development Programme, *Situation Report 15/7/2006 to 21/7/2006*, <www.undp.org.lb/early-recovery/sitreps/sitrep1.cfm>: "The Number of Internally Displaced Population has increased tremendously since the 21 July 2006 and now its more than 84,000 ...".

17   Author's interview with John Flanagan, 4 June 2008.

18   Author's interview with Tekimiti "Gilly" Gilbert, 9 October 2008.

19   See David Fickling, James Sturcke and agencies, "Israel to widen ground offensive", *The Guardian*, 9 August 2008.

20   Security Council, UN document S/RES/1701(2006), 11 August 2006, para. 1.

21   Harvey Morris, Ferry Biedermann and Jonathan Birchall, "Lebanon ceasefire comes into effect", *Financial Times*, 13 August 2006.

22   Ibid.

23 Author's interview with Tekimiti "Gilly" Gilbert, 9 October 2008.

24 Author's interview with Chris Clark, 10 October 2008.

25 Author's interview with Tekimiti "Gilly" Gilbert, 9 October 2008.

26 Idem.

27 For instance, the United Nations Children's Fund reported on 16 August 2006 that "UNMAS has reported a number of incidents relating to unexploded ordnance, including the death of a child in Tyre and eight civilian injuries from cluster munitions". See "UNICEF strengthens support to Lebanese returnees in the South", 16 August 2006, <www.unicef.org/media/media_35351.html>.

28 Author's interview with Chris Clark, 10 October 2008.

29 See Chris Clark, "Speakers Summary: Unexploded cluster bombs and submunitions in South Lebanon: Reliability from a Field Perspective", ICRC, *Humanitarian, Military, Technical and Legal Challenges of Cluster Munitions—Expert Meeting Report, Montreux, Switzerland, 18 to 20 April 2007*, 2007, p. 42.

30 Author's interview with Tekimiti "Gilly" Gilbert, 9 October 2008.

31 Idem.

32 Author's personal communication with Tekimiti "Gilly" Gilbert, 4 February 2009.

33 Landmine Monitor reported: "Clearance data indicates that at least 18,318 cluster submunitions were destroyed between June 1999 and 2005. Submunition duds continue to be cleared". See Landmine Monitor, "Landmine Monitor Factsheet: Cluster Munition Contamination and Clearance", May 2008, p. 3, <www.icbl.org/content/download/30200/477658/version/1/file/LM08_Cluster_Contamination_Clearance.pdf>.

34 Chris Clark, "Speakers Summary: Unexploded cluster bombs and submunitions in South Lebanon: Reliability from a Field Perspective", ICRC, *Humanitarian, Military, Technical and Legal Challenges of Cluster Munitions—Expert Meeting Report, Montreux, Switzerland, 18 to 20 April 2007*, 2007, p. 41.

35 See Rebecca Murray, "Palestinians Brave a Hazardous Profession", *Inter Press Service*, 18 December 2007.

36 MACC, "2006 Legacy, Cluster Bombs in South Lebanon", 2007, p. 6, <www.maccsl.org/publications/Newsletters/Newsletter%20Issue%208.pdf>.

37 Figure taken from MACC, "September 2008 Report of the Mine Action Co-ordination Centre, South Lebanon", 6 October 2008, p. 2, graph

"Civilian Cluster Bombs Victims Graph since 14 August 2006 Up to 30 September 2008".

[38] See Greg Crowther, *Counting the Cost: The Economic Impact of Cluster Munition Contamination in Lebanon*, Landmine Action, 2008, p. 18, note 35. Crowther notes that: "These comprised of one commercial organisation, BACTEC International, and six non-governmental organisations—Handicap International (France), Swedish Rescue Services Association (SRSA), Norwegian Peoples Aid (NPA), DanChurchAid (DCA), Swiss Demining Federation (FSD) and Mines Advisory Group (MAG). Another commercial clearance agency, ArmorGroup, was operational in the period October 2006–December 2007. Several of these organisations had existing activities in Lebanon prior to the 2006 conflict".

[39] See Chris Clark, "Speakers Summary: Unexploded cluster bombs and submunitions in South Lebanon: Reliability from a Field Perspective", ICRC, *Humanitarian, Military, Technical and Legal Challenges of Cluster Munitions—Expert Meeting Report, Montreux, Switzerland, 18 to 20 April 2007*, 2007, pp. 41–4.

[40] General Assembly, *Report of the Commission of Inquiry on Lebanon pursuant to Human Rights Council resolution S-2/1*, UN document A/HRC/3/2, 23 November 2006.

[41] Greg Crowther, *Counting the Cost: The Economic Impact of Cluster Munition Contamination in Lebanon*, Landmine Action, 2008, p. 3. The Landmine Action report does not include direct costs borne by the Lebanese government in funding LAF clearance.

[42] Ibid.

[43] Figure taken from MACC, "September 2008 Report of the Mine Action Co-ordination Centre, South Lebanon", 6 October 2008, p. 3, table "Demining/CBU Accidents". Although these figures also apply to incidents in the course of clearance of mines (which were not used, as far as the MACC is aware, in the 2006 conflict), the vast majority are from incidents involving submunitions.

[44] Eventually, the MACC was to identify at least 10 basic types of cluster munition in Southern Lebanon: the M-42/M-46, M-77, M-85, MZD-2, BLU-63B, BLU-61A, M-43, BLU-18, BLU-26B and Mk-118, not counting various carrier projectiles. See MACC, *War 2006: Threat Factsheet*, ver. 2, 10 April 2008.

[45] Author's interview with Colin King, 4 September 2008, and discussions with MACC SL staff, 5–12 October 2008.

[46]   See article 4 of Protocol V. Although Israel is not yet a party to Protocol V, Amended Protocol II on mines, booby-traps and other devices to which it is party recognizes the importance of providing information on mined areas after the cessation of hostilities; see article 9(2).

[47]   Dalila Mahdawi, "Israel to hand over cluster bomb maps—Israeli media", *The Daily Star*, 6 March 2009.

[48]   UN News Service, "Israel hands over cluster bomb maps to UN force in Lebanon", 13 May 2009.

[49]   Author's interview with Knut Furunes and Per Nergaard, 8 October 2008.

[50]   Author's discussion with Kerei Ruru, 11 October 2008.

[51]   Idem.

[52]   According to the MACC, M-85 submunitions with self-destruct cannot be rendered safe; see MACC, *War 2006: Threat Factsheet*, ver. 2, 10 April 2008, p. 6.

[53]   See for instance article 51(4) of the 1977 Additional Protocol I to the 1949 Geneva Conventions, which is widely considered to reflect customary law in the matter.

[54]   These were 122mm Type 81 rockets containing 35 MZD-2 submunitions. The number launched is unknown. See MACC, *War 2006: Threat Factsheet*, ver. 2, 10 April 2008, p. 9. More information is available at <www.globalsecurity.org/military/world/para/hizballah-rockets.htm>.

[55]   See Human Rights Watch, *Civilians Under Assault: Hezbollah's Rocket Attacks on Israel in the 2006 War*, 2007, p. 3.

Chapter 5
The commencement of the Oslo process

[1]   See annex A for the text of the Oslo Declaration.

[2]   "The Call for a Moratorium on the Production, Use, and Transfer of Cluster Munitions: Statement read by Titus Peachey, Mennonite Central Committee, December 12, 2001". The NGOs subscribing to this call (which pre-dated the Cluster Munition Coalition's formation by almost two years) were the Mennonite Central Committee, the Swiss Campaign to Ban Landmines, Landmine Action UK, the German Initiative to Ban Landmines, the New Zealand Campaign Against Landmines (CALM), Handicap International, Medico International, Engineers for Social Responsibility New Zealand, Mines Action Southern Africa, Swedish

Peace and Arbitration Society, "NGOs in Canada" and the International Committee for the Peace Council. Document on file with the author.

3   Author's interview with Titus Peachey, 3 December 2008.

4   Author's interview with Annette Abelsen, 3 September 2008.

5   Richard Moyes and Thomas Nash, *Cluster munitions in Lebanon*, Landmine Action, 2005, p. 2.

6   More information about the Geneva Forum is available at <www.geneva-forum.org>.

7   Geneva Forum, "Informal Brainstorming Meeting on Cluster Munitions (Sunday 5 March 2006): Internal Report", p. 8. Document on file with the author.

8   Thomas Nash, "Stopping cluster munitions", *Disarmament Forum*, no. 4, 2006, p. 42.

9   *Report on States Parties' Responses to the Questionnaire on International Humanitarian Law & Explosive Remnants of War, CCW/GGE/X/WG.1/WP.2, Dated 8 March 2005*, UN document CCW/GGE/XIII/WG.1/WP.12, 24 March 2006, p. 7.

10   Ibid., p. 8. Emphasis added.

11   *Comments on the "Report on States Parties' Responses to the Questionnaire" on International Humanitarian Law and Explosive Remnants of War, CCW/GGE/X/WG.1/WP.2, Dated 8 March 2005*, UN document CCW/GGE/XIII/WG.1/WP.15, 24 March 2006, p. 4.

12   Human Rights Watch, "Statement to the Convention Conventional Weapons Thirteenth Session of the Group of Governmental Experts", 6 March 2006. Document on file with the author.

13   Human Rights Watch, "Responses to the IHL and ERW Questionnaire and the McCormack Report: Memorandum to CCW Delegates", 6 March 2006.

14   From author's notes of the CCW meeting. In a working paper submitted to the CCW later in 2006, the Asia Pacific Centre for Military Law (i.e., McCormack and his colleagues) wrote, in clarifying criticism of the March report, that: "Some States have indicated their agreement with the general conclusion that applicable rules of IHL are adequate to cover the ERW problem and have used that conclusion to justify their position that nothing should be done. That is a wholly unsatisfactory response that will result in two likely outcomes: (1) the GGE on ERW risks becoming irrelevant and possibly even redundant; and (2) States, international organisations and non-governmental organisations may well become so frustrated with the lack of substantive progress in the context of the CCW process that they will initiate an 'Ottawa' type

alternative track process to negotiate a legally binding instrument on cluster munitions". See *Remarks on Documents CCW/GGE/XIII/WG/1/ WP.12, CCW/GGE/XIII/WG.1/WP.12/Add.1 and CCW/GGE/XIII/WG.1/ WP.12/Add.2,* UN document CCW/GGE/XIV/WG.1/WP.1, 4 May 2006, p. 2, para. 7.

15   Author's interview with Steffen Kongstad, 27 August 2008.

16   Apparently, the seed of the idea for this meeting had come from discussions between Norwegian diplomats and Simon Conway, Director of Landmine Action, on the margins of an annual meeting of the Mine Ban Treaty, held in late 2005 in Zagreb, Croatia.

17   New Zealand's disarmament delegation in Geneva was also invited to participate, but did not attend because of other commitments.

18   John Borrie, "Addressing the humanitarian effects of cluster munitions— reframing the response", Landmine Action/Diana, Princess of Wales Memorial Fund Cluster Munitions Seminar, London, 13–14 March 2006.

19   Ibid.

20   Interview with Annette Abelsen, 3 September 2008.

21   *Norwegian statement on ERW,* 20 June 2006. Emphasis added.

22   *Statement by H.E. Ambassador Bernhard Brasack, Permanent Representative of Germany to the Conference on Disarmament, on "Explosive Remnants of War/Cluster Munitions",* 19 June 2006, <www. streubombe.de/documents/8%20point%20cluster.pdf>.

23   *Statement by H.E. Ambassador John Duncan,* 20 June 2006.

24   *Statement by Mr. Markus Reiterer, Deputy Permanent Representative of Austria on behalf of the European Union on Explosive Remnants of War,* 20 June 2006.

25   *EU Statement on Explosive Remnants of War,* 28 August 2006. This statement reflected the tortuous negotiations within the EU and a slight change: the statement said that "The EU is in favour of continuing the further work on munitions which may become ERW in the CCW beyond the Review Conference, in particular on the implementation of existing IHL and on possible preventive technical measures. Therefore we hope that the States Parties can come to agreement on a mandate to this effect".

26   Lebanon was not (and, as of writing, still is not) a party to the CCW, but participated as an observer.

27   "UN denounces Israel cluster bombs", *BBC,* 30 August 2006.

28   "No Place for Cluster Bombs", *New York Times,* 26 August 2006.

29   *Statement by the Cluster Munition Coalition to the 15th session of the Group of Governmental Experts*, 28 August 2006.

30   Author's interview with Chris Clark, 10 October 2008.

31   *Proposal for a Mandate to Negotiate a Legally-Binding Instrument That Addresses the Humanitarian Concerns Posed by Cluster Munitions*, UN document CCW/CONF.III/WP.1, 25 October 2006.

32   "The Secretary-General: Message to the Third Review Conference of the Convention on Certain Conventional Weapons", 7 November 2006, <www.unog.ch/80256EDD006B8954/(httpAssets)/81D9D5CB D4AC8BC3C1257220002F981A/$file/UNSG+message+re+CCW+T hird+RevCon+(final).doc>.

33   "Benn Slams Cluster Bombs", *Sunday Times*, 5 November 2006. Two days later, the left-wing journalist and current affairs commentator George Monbiot wrote in *The Guardian* that "Benn appears to be alone. The foreign office maintains that 'existing humanitarian law is sufficient for the conduct of military operations, including the use of cluster munitions, and no treaty is required.' The government seems unable to break its habit of killing [civilians at random]". See George Monbiot, "Britain is determined to protect its right to kill civilians at random", *The Guardian*, 7 November 2006.

34   United Nations Office for the Coordination of Humanitarian Affairs, "UN Emergency Relief Coordinator: End Use of Cluster Munitions", press release, 7 November 2006.

35   *Declaration on Cluster Munitions by Austria, Belgium, Bosnia-Herzegovina, Croatia, Costa Rica, Czech Republic, Denmark, Germany, Holy See, Hungary, Ireland, Liechtenstein, Lithuania, Luxembourg, Malta, Mexico, New Zealand, Norway, Peru, Portugal, Serbia, Slovakia, Slovenia, Sweden and Switzerland*, 17 November 2006.

36   *Proposal for a Mandate on Explosive Remnants of War*, room paper, presented 15 November 2006.

37   *Statement by H.E. Ambassador Kari Kahiluoto, Permanent Representative of Finland to the Conference on Disarmament on behalf of the European Union: Cluster Munitions*, 15 November 2006.

38   *Third Review Conference of the High Contracting Parties to the Convention on Prohibitions or Restrictions on the Use of Certain Conventional Weapons which May be Deemed to be Excessively Injurious or to Have Indiscriminate Effects*, UN document CCW/CONF.III/11(Part II), p. 6, decision 1.

39   Cluster Munition Coalition, "NGOs call on states to join Norwegian initiative for a new cluster munitions treaty: Calls for a new treaty come

as Conventional Weapons talks fail to deliver results", press release, 17 November 2006.

40   Author's interview with Stephen D. Goose, 21 November 2008.

41   Jonas Gahr Støre, "Special Comment", *Disarmament Forum*, no. 4, 2006, pp. 3–4.

42   Norwegian Ministry of Foreign Affairs, "Norway takes the initiative for a ban on cluster munitions", press release no. 149/06, 17 November 2006.

43   *Statement by Norway at the Third Review Conference of the CCW by H.E. Steffen Kongstad, Ambassador, Norwegian Ministry of Foreign Affairs*, 17 November 2006.

44   US Mission to the United Nations in Geneva, "Statement by Ronald J. Bettauer Head of the U.S. Delegation to the Closing Plenary Session of the Third Review Conference of the Convention on Certain Conventional Weapons (CCW)", press release, 17 November 2006.

45   Author's interview with John Duncan, 30 June 2008.

46   Author's interview with Jonas Gahr Støre, 29 August 2008.

47   Letter from the British Foreign Secretary Margaret Beckett to Norwegian Foreign Minister Jonas Gahr Støre, 23 January 2007. Document on file with the author.

48   Invitation letter from the Minister of Foreign Affairs of Norway to UNIDIR, 4 January 2007. Document on file with the author. The author's understanding is that this was a generic letter in content sent to all invitees.

49   Author's interview with Stephen D. Goose, 21 November 2008.

50   Idem.

51   Author's personal communication with Samantha Rennie, 16 July 2009.

52   Author's personal communication with Thomas Nash, 6 July 2009.

53   Author's personal communication with Samantha Rennie, 16 July 2009.

54   Author's interview with Laura Cheeseman, 1 September 2008.

55   Thomas Nash, "Draft: Cluster Munition Coalition—'The Kentwell Plan'", January 2007, p. 2. Document on file with the author.

56   Author's personal communication with Stephen D. Goose, 7 September 2009.

57   Author's conversation with Thomas Nash, 16 June 2009.

58   Author's conversation with Thomas Nash, 8 April 2009. Nash also underlined the contribution of Brian Rappert in developing these

conceptualizations of the "define and ban" and "split the categories" approaches and their relative strengths and weaknesses.

59   Thomas Nash, "Draft: Cluster Munition Coalition—'The Kentwell Plan'", January 2007, p. 5. Emphasis added. Document on file with author.

60   Ibid.

61   Participating in this meeting were Thomas Nash (CMC), Stan Brabant (Handicap International Belgium), Stephen D. Goose (Human Rights Watch), Peter Herby (ICRC), Declan Smyth (Irish government), Simon Conway (Landmine Action), Paul Hannon (Mines Action Canada), Grethe Østern and Per Nergaard (Norweigan People's Aid), Rosy Cave (UNIDIR), and attendees from the Norwegian government included Steffen Kongstad, Annette Abelsen and Christian Ruge. Author's personal communcation with Rosy Cave, 30 January 2007.

62   E-mail from Steffen Kongstad to Patricia Lewis (UNIDIR Director), 24 January 2007. Cave and I subsequently drafted this paper, with input from Lewis, and sent it to the Norwegian Ministry of Foreign Affairs in early February. Others, such as CMC, Human Rights Watch and the ICRC then also had input into the version eventually circulated to participants in advance of the conference. Available at <www.regjeringen.no/ upload/UD/Vedlegg/Hum/OsloCCM%20background%20paper%20 1502.pdf>.

63   Author's conversation with Annette Abelsen, 17 April 2009.

64   Author's personal communication with Rosy Cave, 30 January 2007.

65   Author's personal communication with Christian Ruge, 31 January 2007.

66   Author's interview with Steffen Kongstad, 27 August 2008.

67   The author participated in this event as an observer.

68   "Appeal to governments from the Cluster Munition Coalition", 21 February 2007, <www.regjeringen.no/upload/UD/Vedlegg/ Cluster%20Munition%20Coalition.pdf>.

69   Branislav Kapetanović's own account of his experience is available <http://blog.banadvocates.org/index.php?post/2007/11/02/Branislav-Kapetanovick>.

70   There were delegations from Afghanistan, Angola, Argentina, Austria, Belgium, Bosnia and Herzegovina, Canada, Chile, Colombia, Croatia, Costa Rica, Czech Republic, Denmark, Egypt, Finland, France, Germany, Guatemala, Holy See, Hungary, Iceland, Indonesia, Ireland, Italy, Japan, Jordan, Latvia, Lebanon, Liechtenstein, Lithuania, Luxembourg, Malta, Mexico, Mozambique, Netherlands, New Zealand, Norway, Peru, Poland, Portugal, Romania, Serbia, Slovakia, Slovenia, South Africa,

Spain, Sweden, Switzerland and United Kingdom. As well the CMC, ICRC, UN Office for the Coordination of Humanitarian Affairs, UNIDIR, UNDP, UNHCR and UNICEF took part, as well as individual invited participants.

71 CMC was permitted 12 campaigners in the conference room at any one time—a small fraction of those attending the Oslo conference. More than 100 returned to town each night, and during the conference itself were mainly confined to common areas of the Soria Moria complex.

72 Author's interview with Steffen Kongstad, 27 August 2008.

73 Norway's views, as expressed by its Foreign Minister at the Oslo conference, were that "Technical improvements in weapons technology will not be enough to address the complex humanitarian problems caused by cluster munitions. They may improve the reliability rates under controlled conditions. But the actual reliability of an individual submunition depends on the context in which it is used. This includes factors such as age, storage and handling conditions, user competence, and terrain and weather at time of deployment. In practical terms, it is impossible to create a 100% reliable weapon". See opening statement by Jonas Gahr Støre, Oslo Conference on Cluster Munitions, 22–23 February 2007, p. 2, <www.regjeringen.no/upload/UD/Vedlegg/ NorwayOpening%20Statement.pdf>. See also statement by Sweden, Oslo Conference on Cluster Munitions, 22–23 February 2007, p. 2, <www.regjeringen.no/upload/UD/Vedlegg/ClusterSweden.pdf>, which laid down markers about Sweden's policy on its national arsenal of BK-90 cluster muntions: the Swedish armed forces "expect to keep them for the time being. The BK-90 holds a very high quality, a dud rate of 1–2% and is equipped with self-destruction mechanisms **and** self-deactivation. The result is that there are no dangerous duds left in the area". Emphasis in original.

74 See opening statement by Jonas Gahr Støre, Oslo Conference on Cluster Munitions, 22–23 February 2007, <www.regjeringen.no/upload/UD/ Vedlegg/NorwayOpening%20Statement.pdf>.

75 Rodsted's film was later posted on NPA's website, and on the popular internet video-sharing service YouTube where, as of writing, it had received nearly 183,000 viewer hits; <www.youtube.com/watch?v=v_ jsyObTG8k>.

76 Statement of the International Committee of the Red Cross, Oslo Conference on Cluster Munitions, 22–23 February 2007, p. 3, <www. regjeringen.no/upload/UD/Vedlegg/ClusterICRC.pdf>.

77 Statement of Patricia Lewis, UNIDIR, Oslo Conference on Cluster Munitions, 22–23 February 2007, p. 1, <www.regjeringen.no/upload/UD/Vedlegg/ClusterUNIDIR%20Lewis.pdf>.

78 Statement by Peter Batchelor, UNDP, Oslo Conference on Cluster Munitions, 22–23 February 2007, p. 5, <www.regjeringen.no/upload/UD/Vedlegg/ClusterUNDP%20Batchelor.pdf>. Emphasis added.

79 See statement by Heinrich Haupt, Oslo Conference on Cluster Munitions, 22–23 February 2007, <www.regjeringen.no/upload/UD/Vedlegg/ClusterGermany%20Haupt.pdf>.

80 Author's personal communication with John Duncan, 4 August 2009.

81 Stephen D. Goose, "Cluster Munitions in the Crosshairs: In pursuit of a prohibition", in Jody Williams, Stephen D. Goose and Mary Wareham (eds), *Banning Landmines: Disarmament, Citizen Diplomacy and Human Security*, Lanham, Rowman and Littlefield, 2008, pp. 226–7.

82 Kasia Derlicka, "A Campaigner in Oslo Writes From the 'Interpreters' Booths'", *ICBL Newsletter*, April 2007, <www.icbl.org/index.php/icbl/Library/News-Articles/ICBL-News-April-2007>.

83 Author's interview with Titus Peachey, 3 December 2008.

84 "Japan refuses to support Oslo declaration on cluster bomb ban", *Kyodo News*, 26 February 2007.

85 Declaration of the Oslo Conference on Cluster Munitions, 23 February 2007.

86 Statement by Ambassador John Duncan, Oslo Conference on Cluster Munitions, 22–23 February 2007, <http://ukunarmscontrol.fco.gov.uk/resources/en/pdf/pdf1/postgv_statementatosloconference>.

Chapter 6
After Oslo—Shifting the burden of proof

1 Author's interview with Steffen Kongstad, 27 August 2008.

2 "Statement attributable to the Spokesperson for the Secretary-General On Cluster Munitions", 23 February 2007, <www.un.org/apps/sg/sgstats.asp?nid=2456>.

3 See, for instance, "A change of heart or a change of tactic? A grudging response to America's new line on cluster bombs", *The Economist*, 21 June 2007.

4 Author's personal communication with Thomas Nash, 15 July 2009.

5   Statement by Sweden, Oslo Conference on Cluster Munitions, 22–23 February 2007, p. 1, <www.regjeringen.no/upload/UD/Vedlegg/ClusterSweden.pdf>.

6   UK statement on cluster munitions made at the Third CCW Review Conference, Geneva, 13 November 2006, <https://ukunarmscontrol-stage.fco.gov.uk/resources/en/pdf/pdf1/postgv_clustermunitionsstatement>.

7   For a technical description of the Hydra 70 rocket system and CRV-7 warheads see Robert Hewson (ed.), *Jane's Air-Launched Weapons (Issue 53)*, Jane's Information Group, 2009, pp. 610–3.

8   This term—"dumb cluster munitions"—was immediately attacked by NGOs such as Landmine Action. See Landmine Action, "Dumb Cluster Munition Policy: Comments on the UK paper on ERW of 13 November 2006", 14 November 2006, <www.wilpf.int.ch/disarmament/CCW/Statements/LandmineActionNOV14.pdf>.

9   Author's interview with Kathleen Cravero, 11 September 2008.

10   Human Rights Watch, statement during the General Exchange of Views, Third Review Conference of the CCW, 8 November 2006.

11   At this time the CMC Steering Committee consisted of Human Rights Watch, Landmine Action and Norwegian People's Aid as co-chairs, as well as DanChurchAid, Handicap International, International Physicians for the Prevention of Nuclear War Russia, Landmine Resource Centre (Lebanon), Mines Action Canada, Pax Christi and Protection (Egypt). One of the items on the agenda for the Steering Committee meeting in Oslo was to add the International Campaign to Ban Landmines to its membership; author's personal communication with Thomas Nash, 15 July 2009.

12   E-mail from Thomas Nash to CMC list server, "Subject: Message to CMC", 19 April 2007. Document on file with the author.

13   Cluster Munition Coalition room document at the Lima conference. In June, the CMC submitted these principles as a working paper in the CCW's Group of Governmental Experts; *Treaty Principles*, UN document CCW/GGE/2007/WP.7, 19 June 2007, p. 1.

14   ICRC, "Cluster munitions: ICRC calls for urgent action", press release, 6 November 2006.

15   "ICRC statement to the Third Review Conference of the Convention on Certain Conventional Weapons", 7 November 2006, <www.icrc.org/web/eng/siteeng0.nsf/html/conventional-weapons-statement-071106>.

16   *Third Review Conference of the High Contracting Parties to the Convention on Prohibitions or Restrictions on the Use of Certain Conventional Weapons which May be Deemed to be Excessively Injurious or to Have Indiscriminate Effects*, UN document CCW/CONF.III/11(Part II), p. 6, decision 1.

17   In welcoming the Oslo Declaration at the outset of the meeting of around 90 governmental and other invited experts in Montreux, a senior ICRC official expressed the hope that "this expert meeting will deepen insights, identify options and speed up efforts, thus bringing closer the day when the tragic impact of cluster munitions is a thing of the past". See "Statement by Dr Philip Spoerri", ICRC, *Humanitarian, Military, Technical and Legal Challenges of Cluster Munitions—Expert Meeting Report, Montreux, Switzerland, 18 to 20 April 2007*, 2007, p. 8.

18   See ibid.

19   Government experts attended from Afghanistan, Argentina, Australia, Austria, Belgium, Brazil, Canada, China, Denmark, Finland, France, Germany, Greece, India, Ireland, Israel, Japan, Kenya, Latvia, Lebanon, Lithuania, Mexico, Netherlands, New Zealand, Norway, Pakistan, Russia, Serbia, South Africa, Sweden, Switzerland, United Kingdom and the United States of America. NGO and international agency experts from the CMC, Handicap International Belgium, Human Rights Watch, ICRC, Mines Action Canada, Norwegian People's Aid, Norwegian Red Cross, UN Office for Disarmament Affairs, UNDP and UN Mine Action Service participated. The author represented UNIDIR.

20   ICRC, *Humanitarian, Military, Technical and Legal Challenges of Cluster Munitions—Expert Meeting Report, Montreux, Switzerland, 18 to 20 April 2007*, 2007, p. 46.

21   This was a meeting of the Disarmament Insight initiative, organized by UNIDIR's Disarmament as Humanitarian Action project, which the author led, and the Geneva Forum. It was held on 21 April at the Château des Penthes, near Geneva.

22   As recalled by Don MacKay in an interview with the author, 13 May 2008.

23   *Draft CCW Protocol on Cluster Munitions*, UN document CCW/GGE/2007/WP.1, 1 May 2007.

24   See "Statement by H.E. Ambassador Bernhard Brasack, Permanent Representative of Germany to the Conference on Disarmament", 19 June 2006, <www.streubombe.de/documents/8%20point%20cluster.pdf>.

25 Katherine Harrison, *Report from the Lima Conference on Cluster Munitions, 23–25 May 2007*, Women's International League for Peace and Freedom, pp. 14–5.

26 Two examples of such systems are the German SMArt 155 and French-Swedish BONUS systems. For more explanation of sensor-fuzing technologies as they pertain to cluster munitions, see Ove Dullum, *Cluster Weapons—Military Utility and Alternatives*, Norwegian Defence Research Establishment (FFI), 2008.

27 See CMC, "German proposal is not a basis for a new cluster munition treaty", 27 April 2007. Document on file with the author.

28 The end point of Germany's proposal was effectively quite similar to the eventual outcome of the Convention on Cluster Munitions—i.e. a comprehensive ban on cluster munitions, as defined. However, the transition period allowing for use of M-85 style weapons marginalized it as a basis for work within the Oslo process.

29 For instance, Germany told the Lima conference "as our delegation did in Oslo, we would like to reiterate here that the CCW process seems to have, under the present circumstances, the best potential to make a real difference in creating and enforcing humanitarian rules on cluster munitions for the benefit of the civilian population: In particular, only the CCW ensures the full participation of the main holders and users of Cluster Munitions. The immediate priority action, after Lima, should therefore be a joint effort to get the best result out of the upcoming meeting of the CCW Group of Governmental Experts on cluster munitions in Geneva". See *Lima Conference on Cluster Munitions (Lima, 23–25 May 2007): Statement by Mr. Heinrich Haupt, Head of Division/ Conventional Arms Control, Federal Foreign Officer, Berlin*. Document on file with the author.

30 The composition of this group never became fixed, but generally the "like-minded" refers to Australia, Canada, Czech Republic, Denmark, Finland, France, Japan, Germany, Italy, Netherlands, Slovakia, Spain, Sweden, Switzerland and the UK, with observers in the Oslo process such as Poland and Romania sometimes participating in its discussions.

31 Stephen D. Goose, "A Shift in U.S. Policy on Cluster Munitions?", *Arms Control Today*, vol. 38, no. 1, 2008, p. 9.

32 See "Chairs' discussion text for Lima Conference", <www.clusterconvention.org/pages/pages_vi/vib_opdoc_chairslima.html>.

33 "Draft Agenda of the Lima Conference", <www.wilpf.int.ch/disarmament/clustermunitions/LIMA/statements/Draft_Agenda.pdf>.

34   For an alternate point of view, one serving to underline differences between the paramount concerns of some Like-minded states and others, see N. van Woudenberg, "The Long and Winding Road Towards an Instrument on Cluster Munitions", *Journal of Conflict & Security Law*, vol. 12, no. 3, 2008, pp. 479–80.

35   "CMC Observations on the Lima Chair's Draft Discussion Text", <www.wilpf.int.ch/disarmament/clustermunitions/LIMA/statements/CMCchairtext.pdf>. This document was circulated in Lima.

36   The text of this draft Cluster Munition Convention, along with the Wellington Conference Declaration and an additional compendium of proposals, is available online at: <www.mfat.govt.nz/clustermunitionswellington>.

37   According to one report of the Lima conference, 67 states participated fully: 14 from Africa (Angola, Burundi, Chad, Ghana, Guinea-Bissau, Lesotho, Liberia, Mauritania, Mozambique, Nigeria, Senegal, Tanzania, Uganda and Zambia); 14 from the Americas (Argentina, Bolivia, Canada, Chile, Colombia, Costa Rica, Dominican Republic, Ecuador, Guatemala, Mexico, Panama, Paraguay, Peru and Venezuela); 8 from the Asia Pacific (Australia, Bangladesh, Cambodia, Indonesia, Japan, Laos, New Zealand and Thailand); 28 from Europe (Albania, Austria, Belgium, Bosnia and Herzegovina, Croatia, Czech Republic, Denmark, Estonia, Finland, France, Germany, Greece, Holy See, Hungary, Ireland, Italy, Lithuania, Luxembourg, Malta, Netherlands, Norway, Poland, Portugal, Serbia, Slovakia, Spain, Switzerland and the UK), and 3 from the Middle East (Egypt, Lebanon, and Yemen). See Katherine Harrison, *Report from the Lima Conference on Cluster Munitions, 23–25 May 2007*, Women's International League for Peace and Freedom, p. 31.

38   Ibid., p. 17.

39   For instance, at an informal consultation convened by the GGE Chair, Latvia, in the Palais des Nations on 16 May 2007 that the author attended.

40   See *Draft CCW Negotiating Mandate on Cluster Munitions*, UN document CCW/GGE/2007/WP.3, 1 June 2007.

41   "U.S. open to negotiations on cluster bombs but no ban", *Reuters*, 18 June 2007.

42   "U.S. Intervention on Humanitarian Impacts of Cluster Munitions", 20 June 2007, pp. 6–7, <www.wilpf.int.ch/disarmament/CCWGGE2007/Kidd%20CCW%20200607.pdf>.

[43] See "Statement on the Outcome of the CCW Group of Governmental Experts Meeting", 22 June 2007, <http://geneva.usmission.gov/Press2007/0622CCW-GGE.html>.

[44] For a discussion of "ping-pong" and other negotiating tactics, see Rebecca Johnson, "Changing Perceptions and Practice in Multilateral Arms Control Negotiations", in John Borrie and Vanessa Martin Randin (eds), *Thinking Outside the Box in Multilateral Disarmament and Arms Control Negotiations*, UNIDIR, 2006, pp. 55–87.

[45] See *Procedural Report*, UN document CCW/GGE/2007/3, 9 August 2007, annex III.

[46] Author's interview with Stan Brabant, 2 September 2008.

[47] Belgium also contributed, as part of its funding for HI Belgium as a whole, and Germany helped to fund the second report, *Circle of Impact*, according to Brabant.

[48] Handicap International, *Fatal Footprint: The Global Human Impact of Cluster Munitions*, 2006, p.8.

[49] See, for instance, Richard Norton-Taylor, "Civilians main cluster bomb victims", *The Guardian* 3 November 2006. Also, Kim Sengupta, "Study says almost all cluster bomb victims are children", *The Independent*, 3 November 2006.

[50] Handicap International, *Circle of Impact: The Fatal Footprint of Cluster Munitions on People and Communities*, 2007.

[51] Handicap International, *Circle of Impact: The Fatal Footprint of Cluster Munitions on People and Communities*, 2007, p. 136. Emphasis in original.

[52] The author participated in some of these events.

[53] "Norway's commitment to mine action and human security", 17 September 2007, <www.regjeringen.no/nb/dep/ud/dep/utenriksminister_jonas_gahr_store/taler_artikler/2007/mineaction.html?id=481024>.

[54] Author's personal communication with Thomas Nash, 15 July 2009.

[55] H.E. Mr. Vuk Jeremić, Minister of Foreign Affairs of Serbia, in his welcoming remarks to the Belgrade Conference of States Affected by Cluster Munitions, Belgrade, 3 October 2007.

[56] The author participated in this conference on behalf of UNIDIR.

[57] More information about Slađan Vučković's story is available at <http://blog.banadvocates.org/index.php?category/Slaan-Vukovi>.

[58] Author's interview with Stan Brabant, 2 September 2008.

[59] Alizada, a mine victim, spoke at the 2006 CCW Review Conference as a CMC campaigner representing Handicap International Afghanistan.

60   In August 2008 I interviewed Vučković, who had sat outside the CCW for several days (along with his father Hrista and an interpreter) to lobby diplomats on behalf of the CMC to try to strengthen the CCW's draft package on cluster munitions: perhaps understandably, his experience there, and in view of the recent achievement of the Convention on Cluster Munitions in Dublin, had led him to the view that the CCW's cluster munition work was a waste of time. Author's interview with Sladan and Hrista Vučković, 27 August 2008.

61   *Report of the Meeting of the High Contracting Parties to the Convention on Prohibitions or Restrictions on the Use of Certain Conventional Weapons Which May Be Deemed to Be Excessively Injurious or to Have Indiscriminate Effects*, UN document CCW/MSP/2007/5, 3 December 2007, p. 9.

62   "Closing Statement by Ronald J. Bettauer", Meeting of States Parties to the Convention on Certain Conventional Weapons, 13 November 2007, <http://geneva.usmission.gov/Press2007/1211CCW.html>.

63   *Statement by the Delegation of the Russian Federation at the Meeting of the High Contracting Parties to the Convention on Certain Conventional Weapons*, 7 November 2007. Document on file with the author.

64   See *Position Paper on Cluster Munitions*, UN document CCW/GGE/2007/WP.6, 19 June 2007.

65   Article 2 of this text said: "The following weapons systems shall be considered prohibited cluster munitions under this treaty: Air carried dispersal systems or air delivered, surface or sub-surface launched containers, that are designed to disperse explosive sub-munitions intended to detonate following separation from the container or dispenser, unless they are designed to, manually or automatically, aim, detect and engage point targets, or are meant for smoke or flaring, or unless their use is regulated or prohibited under other treaties". See "Chairs' discussion text for Lima Conference", <www.clusterconvention. org/pages/pages_vi/vib_opdoc_chairslima.html>.

66   At this meeting of the CMC's experts (including Colin King), the CMC decided to define a cluster munition in the following way: "A *cluster munition* is a weapon comprising multiple explosive submunitions which are dispensed from a container. An *explosive submunition* is a munition designed to be dispensed in multiple quantities from a container and to detonate prior to, on, or after impact." This definition thus made no exception for submunitions with self-destruct, self-deactivation or self-neutralizing features; submunitions based on a specified reliability rate; so-called "direct fire" submunitions (like the CRV-7 or Hydra); cluster

munitions based solely on a limit on the number of submunitions, or sensor-fuzed submunitions. The definition did exclude non-explosive or inert submunitions, and pyrotechnic submunitions such as smoke, flare or illuminating submunitions. See *Cluster Munition Coalition Definition for the Future Cluster Munition Convention*, October 2007. Document on file with the author.

67 E-mail from Thomas Nash to the Oslo process Core Group, "Subject: Consultations between CMC and the core group", 26 June 2007. Moyes sent a similar note.

68 Author's interview with Don MacKay, 13 May 2008.

69 Idem.

70 See "Chairs' discussion text for Vienna Conference", <www.clusterconvention.org/pages/pages_vi/vib_opdoc_chairsvienna.html>.

71 These views were communicated in at least two ways. The quote above is from a document distributed for the Vienna conference entitled "Observations by the Cluster Munition Coalition on the discussion text for the Vienna Conference on Cluster Munitions, 5–7 December 2007" and much of the content of this paper was read orally into the record. In addition, Human Rights Watch offered its own "Human Rights Watch Observations on the Cluster Munition Convention discussion text circulated in advance of the Vienna Conference on Cluster Munitions, 5–7 December 2007" with virtually identical language concerning cluster munitions. Documents on file with the author.

72 Author's interview with Wolfgang Petritsch, 7 February 2008.

73 Nick Cumming-Bruce, "Austria bans cluster munitions", *International Herald Tribune*, 7 December 2007.

74 Author's interview with Don MacKay, 13 May 2008.

75 Author's interview with Wolfgang Petritsch, 7 February 2008.

76 Note that there is no evidence I am aware of that this Tee-total group ever described itself in this way—it was merely a badge of convenience used by the Core Group. Probably coined by the Irish or the New Zealanders in the Core Group, tee-total was a colloquial reference to historical temperance movements advocating the total prohibition of alcohol, even in moderate (and presumably not unacceptably harmful) types and quantities.

77 This did not necessarily mean that the African states were entirely united, however, as they would later discover at the Livingstone conference in Zambia in the lead-up to the Dublin negotiations in 2008. South Africa was a producer and possessor of cluster munitions, and some of the North African states (especially Egypt) had linked in their minds dealing

with the humanitarian consequences of cluster munitions with issues of general and complete disarmament. For the meantime, however, such problems were in the future.

[78]   Author's interview with Per Nergaard, 4 July 2008.

[79]   Colin King, Ove Dullum and Grethe Østern, *M-85—An Analysis of Reliability*, Norwegian People's Aid, 2007, p. 5.

[80]   Ibid., p. 7.

[81]   See Katherine Harrison, *Report from the Vienna Conference on Cluster Munitions, 5–7 December 2007*, Women's International League for Peace and Freedom, pp. 20–1.

[82]   As of 18 April 2008, the CCW had 105 states parties, although the number of national delegations participating in expert group meetings is typically around half of this total.

[83]   The Vienna discussion text (14 November 2007) and the Draft Cluster Munitions Convention (21 January 2008) are available at <www. clusterconvention.org/pages/pages_vi/vib_osloprocess_documents. html>.

Chapter 7
Crunch point

[1]   Ambassador Wolfgang Petritsch of Austria, at a briefing meeting held in the Palais des Nations in Geneva, Switzerland on 7 February 2008 on the forthcoming Wellington conference.

[2]   At least as diplomats they would travel first or business class, unlike NGO representatives. The response of some European diplomats, was, "Yes, but what about our spouses back in economy class?"

[3]   *Report of the Meeting of the High Contracting Parties to the Convention on Prohibitions or Restrictions on the Use of Certain Conventional Weapons Which May Be Deemed to Be Excessively Injurious or to Have Indiscriminate Effects*, UN document CCW/MSP/2007/5, 3 December 2007, p. 9, para. 37.

[4]   See Stuart Maslen, *The Convention on the Prohibition of the Use, Stockpiling, Production, and Transfer of Anti-Personnel Mines and on their Destruction*, Commentaries on Arms Control Treaties, vol. 1, Oxford University Press, 2004, pp. 36–7. For the text of the Brussels Declaration see Louis Maresca and Stuart Maslen (eds), *The Banning of Anti-Personnel Landmines: The Legal Contribution of the International*

Committee of the Red Cross 1955–1999, Cambridge University Press, 2000, pp. 545–6.

5   Cluster Munition Coalition, Human Rights Watch, International Campaign to Ban Landmines, Landmine Action and Landmine Monitor, *Banning Cluster Munitions: Government Policy and Practice*, 2009, p. 251. See also chapter 1.

6   These efforts were not entirely successful. See, for instance, Human Rights Watch, *Fatally Flawed: Cluster Bombs and Their Use by the United States in Afghanistan*, 2002; and Human Rights Watch, *Off Target: The Conduct of the War and Civilian Casualties in Iraq*, 2003.

7   Cluster Munition Coalition, Human Rights Watch, International Campaign to Ban Landmines, Landmine Action and Landmine Monitor, *Banning Cluster Munitions: Government Policy and Practice*, 2009, p. 258.

8   See US Department of Defense, "Report to Congress: Cluster Munitions", 2004, p. 2, <www.cdi.org/clusters/Report%20to%20Congress.pdf>.

9   See Stephen D. Goose, "A Shift in U.S. Policy on Cluster Munitions?", *Arms Control Today*, vol. 38, no. 1, 2008.

10   US General Accounting Office, "Operation Desert Storm: Casualties Caused by Improper Handling of Unexploded U.S. Submunitions", document GAO/NSIAD-93-212, 1993.

11   Secretary of Defense William Cohen, "Memorandum for the Secretaries of the Military Departments, Subject: DoD Policy on Submunition Reliability (U)", 10 January 2001. Document on file with the author.

12   See Cluster Munition Coalition, Human Rights Watch, International Campaign to Ban Landmines, Landmine Action and Landmine Monitor, *Banning Cluster Munitions: Government Policy and Practice*, 2009, p. 257.

13   Ibid.

14   "Opening Statement by Ronald J. Bettauer", Meeting of States Parties to the Convention on Certain Conventional Weapons, 7 November 2007, <http://geneva.usmission.gov/Press2007/110707CCW.html>.

15   Stephen D. Goose, "A Shift in U.S. Policy on Cluster Munitions?", *Arms Control Today*, vol. 38, no. 1, 2008.

16   *Cluster Munitions Civilian Protection Act of 2007*, Bill S.594, <www.fcnl.org/issues/item.php?item_id=2338&issue_id=138>.

17   See John M. Donnelly, "Ban on Exports of Most Cluster Bombs Becomes Law as Part of Omnibus", *Congressional Quarterly Politics*, 11 March 2009.

18   Emphasis added.

19   See Katherine Harrison, *Report from the Vienna Conference on Cluster Munitions, 5–7 December 2007*, Women's International League for Peace and Freedom, p. 13.

20   Author's notes.

21   These presentations were by Lee Springer, a US Army fuze expert, and the other by Maj. Michael McClung, a US Joint Staff Targeting Procedure expert and Lt Col John Havranek, Legal Advisor to the Joint Chiefs of Staff. See "U.S. Statement by Stephen Mathias", Meeting of the Group of Governmental Experts of the CCW, 14 January 2008, <www.us-mission.ch/CD/updates/0114CCWOpeningStatement.htm>.

22   See "Closing Statement by Stephen Mathias", Meeting of the Group of Governmental Experts of the CCW, 18 January 2008, <www.us-mission.ch/CD/updates/0118ClosingStatement.html>.

23   See Germany's *Draft CCW protocol on cluster munitions*, UN document CCW/GGE/2007/WP.1/Add.1, 3 May 2007, and *Draft CCW protocol on cluster munitions*, UN document CCW/GGE/2007/WP.1/Corr.1, 9 May 2007; the UK's *A possible definition of a cluster munition and a submunition—draft proposals*, UN document CCW/GGE/2007/WP.9, 28 June 2007; and France's *Definitions of cluster weapons*, UN document CCW/GGE/2008-I/WP.1, 16 January 2008.

24   See John Borrie, "Cluster munitions: From Russia with love", *Disarmament Insight*, 16 January 2008, <http://disarmamentinsight. blogspot.com/2008/01/cluster-munitions-from-russia-with-love.html>.

25   *Statement by the Delegation of the Russian Federation at the Meeting of the Group of Governmental Experts of the Convention on Certain Conventional Weapons (CCW)*, 14 January 2008. Document on file with the author.

26   *Procedural report*, UN document CCW/GGE/2008-I/3, 24 January 2008, annex III.

27   *Definitions*, UN document CCW/GGE/2008/-I/WP.2, 17 January 2008.

28   Author's interview with James C. O'Shea, 28 July 2008.

29   *Procedural report*, UN document CCW/GGE/2008-I/3, 24 January 2008, p. 3, para. 18.

30   Government representatives from Norway, Ireland, Austria, New Zealand, Mexico, Peru, Belgium and Zambia attended. Although not Core Group members, Zambia and Belgium were asked to participate by the organizers because of their strong regional roles. Representatives from United Nations Development Programme, UNIDIR, the International Committee of the Red Cross, The Diana, Princess of Wales Memorial Fund, Cluster Munition Coalition staff and Steering Committee members

from Landmine Action, Human Rights Watch, Handicap International, Norwegian People's Aid and International Physicians for the Prevention of Nuclear War Zambia participated.

[31]   Author's notes of that meeting.

[32]   Author's interview with Don Mackay, 13 May 2008.

[33]   Ambassador Don MacKay, "Preparations for the Wellington Conference", presentation at a briefing meeting held in the Palais des Nations, Geneva, Switzerland, 7 February 2008.

[34]   See article 2, paragraph 2(a) and (b) of the Draft Cluster Munitions Convention, <http://www.clusterconvention.org/pages/pages_vi/vib_opdoc_draft.html>. This "Wellington text" released between the Vienna and Wellington conferences incorporated what the Core Group considered to be common understandings achieved at Vienna.

[35]   See <www.mfat.govt.nz/clustermunitionswellington/conference-documents/index.php>.

[36]   Participating were Afghanistan, Albania, Algeria, Angola, Argentina, Australia, Austria, Bahrain, Bangladesh, Belgium, Belize, Benin, Bosnia and Herzegovina, Botswana, Brazil, Brunei Darussalam, Cambodia, Canada, Chile, Cook Islands, Croatia, Cyprus, Czech Republic, Democratic Republic of the Congo, Denmark, Dominican Republic, Ecuador, Egypt, Estonia, Fiji, Finland, former Yugoslav Republic of Macedonia, France, Germany, Ghana, Guatemala, Holy See, Honduras, Hungary, Indonesia, Ireland, Italy, Jamaica, Japan, Kenya, Kuwait, Kyrgyzstan, Laos, Lebanon, Lesotho, Lithuania, Luxembourg, Madagascar, Malawi, Malaysia, Mali, Malta, Marshall Islands, Mauritania, Mexico, Moldova, Montenegro, Morocco, Mozambique, Nauru, Nepal, Netherlands, New Zealand, Nigeria, Niue, Norway, Oman, Palau, Papua New Guinea, Paraguay, Peru, Philippines, Portugal, Qatar, Samoa, Saudi Arabia, Senegal, Sierra Leone, Slovakia, Slovenia, South Africa, Spain, Sudan, Suriname, Sweden, Switzerland, Tajikistan, Thailand, Timor-Leste, Togo, Tonga, Trinidad and Tobago, Turkey, Uganda, Ukraine, United Kingdom, Uruguay, Vanuatu, Vietnam and Zambia.

[37]   Statement by Phil Goff, Wellington Conference on Cluster Munitions, 18 February 2008. <www.mfat.govt.nz/clustermunitionswellington/conference-documents/MDAC-opening-address.pdf>.

[38]   For a comprehensive and useful overview of the Wellington conference proceedings, see Katherine Harrison, *Report from the Wellington Conference on Cluster Munitions, 18–22 February 2008*, Women's International League for Peace and Freedom.

39   For instance, see France's proposal of 19 February for text on scope of application of the treaty, definitions and review clauses; <www.mfat. govt.nz/clustermunitionswellington/conference-documents/France-discussion-paper.pdf>. Likewise, a Swiss proposal offered the same day concerned definitions and scope of application; <www.mfat.govt. nz/clustermunitionswellington/conference-documents/Switzerland-statement-definitions.pdf>.

40   In a statement on 18 February, UK Ambassador John Duncan said "On the text itself: Article 1 will need to be specifically linked to Article 2. The inclusion of 1c renders coalition and multinational operations, including UN chapter VII, NATO, EU operations, difficult or even untenable with those members of the coalition who are not states parties to the convention deploy those types of cluster munition that could be prohibited under this treaty. Mr Chairman, you [also] raised the issue of transition periods. We agree that if transition periods are agreed, Article I is the right place to include them. There is an argument that in the real world of delivering an improvement to those whose communities affected by Cluster Munitions that rather than having no commitment from possessing states at all, it would be better to put in place a structured plan for the removal from service of weapons systems"; available at <www. mfat.govt.nz/clustermunitionswellington/conference-documents/UK-intervention.pdf>.

41   In fact, interoperability would be dealt with in the Convention on Cluster Munitions in a separate, new provision—article 21.

42   On 19 February 2008, Norway stated: "We have never argued that every munition that contains more than one sub-munition should be prohibited regardless of their humanitarian consequences. We think there is a difference between a total ban on every weapon containing more than one sub-munition, and a total ban on cluster munitions as defined in the new convention". "Intervention by Norway on Article 2, Definitions", <www.mfat.govt.nz/clustermunitionswellington/ conference-documents/Norway-Statement%20_Definitions.pdf>.

43   For instance, the CMC had prepared a briefing note setting out arguments for and against the main exclusion proposals such as the presence of a self-destruct mechanism, meeting a failure rate percentage requirement, "dangerous duds", electronic fuzing and self-deactivations, numbers (less than 10), "direct fire", and submunitions with sensor fuzing. One of the paper's key conclusions was "overriding everything else, the critical policy point is that the burden of proof is

on the would be users to <u>demonstrate</u> that these exclusions are really a solid basis for protecting civilians. The burden of proof goes beyond making unsubstantiated assertions". See Richard Moyes, "Briefing note on certain proposed exclusions from the Oslo Process definition of cluster munitions ", Landmine Action, 29 January 2008. Document on file with the author.

44   The UK would not give up on Hydra until late in the negotiations in Dublin, and its Ministry of Defence officials were surprised the UK gave them up.

45   Draft Cluster Munitions Convention Explanatory Notes, 21 January 2008, p. 1, <www.mfat.govt.nz/clustermunitionswellington/conference-documents/draft-cluster-munitions-convention-explanatory-notes. doc>.

46   "Discussion paper—Cluster munitions and inter-operability: The Oslo Process discussion text and implications for international operations", p. 5, <www.mfat.govt.nz/clustermunitionswellington/conference-documents/Discussion-paper-Au-et-al.pdf>.

47   Ibid.

48   "Comments on the Draft Cluster Munitions Convention", <www.mfat. govt.nz/clustermunitionswellington/conference-documents/Japan-article-one-comments.pdf>.

49   See "Compendium of Proposals Submitted by Delegations During the Wellington Conference. Addendum 1", p. 8, <www.mfat.govt. nz/clustermunitionswellington/conference-documents/WCCM-Compendium-v2.pdf>.

50   Germany's proposal as amended at 9h50 on 21 February 2008 for article 1(c) (and supported by Denmark, France, Italy, Spain and the UK) was that each state party would undertake never under any circumstances to "Assist, encourage or induce anyone to engage in any activity prohibited to a State Party under this Convention. This provision does not preclude the mere participation in the planning or the execution of operations, exercises or other military activities by the Armed Forces or by an individual national of a State Party to this Convention conducted in combination with Armed Forces of States not Parties to this Convention which engage in activity prohibited under this Convention". Document on file with the author.

51   Canada's alternative text read: "Notwithstanding any other provision of this Convention, a State, on becoming a party to this Convention, may declare that, for a period of [xx] years after the entry into force of this Convention for the State concerned, it does not accept the

application of Article I(c) with respect to its participation in combined operations and activities with non-party states. A declaration under this article may be withdrawn at any time. During this period in which the declaration under this article remains in force, the State concerned shall take steps to encourage the government of any non-party state participating in such combined operations and activities to ratify this Convention." See "Compendium of Proposals Submitted by Delegations During the Wellington Conference, Addendum 1", p. 8, <www.mfat. govt.nz/clustermunitionswellington/conference-documents/WCCM-Compendium-v2.pdf>.

52   "Statement on general scope and obligations in relation to interoperability", p. 2, <www.mfat.govt.nz/clustermunitionswellington/conference-documents/Norway-interoperability-statement.pdf>.

53   Conway and others first made these arguments in presentations and dialogue at the ICRC Experts Meeting in Montreux in April 2007. Conway said, for instance, that in the Kosovo bombing campaign in 1999, "NATO bombing records indicate that they were a weapon of convenience used against a wide range of static and mobile targets with very little evidence of effectiveness". In contrast, US experts at the Montreux meeting argued that cluster munitions were legitimate weapons with ongoing military utility. See ICRC, *Humanitarian, Military, Technical and Legal Challenges of Cluster Munitions—Expert Meeting Report, Montreux, Switzerland, 18 to 20 April 2007*, 2007, p. 16 and pp. 28–31.

54   Author's interview with Ahmad Arafa, 11 May 2009.

55   This internal paper was generally referred to within the CMC as the "traffic light lobbying paper" as it categorized states participating in the Oslo process on general scope (article 1) and definitions (article 2) in terms of one of three phases: red ("The country is seeking to weaken a strong and comprehensive cluster munition ban treaty"), amber ("The government's position is unknown or their position is unclear") and green ("The country supports a strong and comprehensive prohibition on cluster munitions within the Oslo process"). This document was repeatedly revised over the course of the Wellington conference.

56   Author's conversation with Ahmad Arafa, 8 May 2009.

57   Author's interview with John Duncan, 30 June 2008.

58   Idem.

59   This was discussed at The Diana, Princess of Wales Memorial Fund–Landmine Action meeting the author attended from 21 to 22 January 2009.

60   Author's interview with Don MacKay, 13 May 2008.
61   The text of the joint position reads, "The following affected countries and friends of affected countries gathered in the Wellington Conference raise their common voice to highlight their support for a strong comprehensive and precise legally binding instrument prohibiting cluster munitions. They express their satisfaction with the draft convention on cluster munitions presented to the Wellington Conference and the amendments aimed at strengthening the humanitarian objectives of the text". Document on file with the author.
62   Author's interview with Ahmad Arafa, 11 May 2009.
63   Author's conversation with Thomas Nash, 20 July 2009.
64   Author's interview with Don MacKay, 13 May 2008.
65   "Compendium of Proposals Submitted by Delegations During the Wellington Conference, Addendum 1", <www.mfat.govt. nz/clustermunitionswellington/conference-documents/WCCM-Compendium-v2.pdf>.
66   "Diplomatic Conference for the Adoption of a Cluster Munitions Convention, Dublin, May 2008: Draft Rules of Procedure", <www. mfat.govt.nz/clustermunitionswellington/conference-documents/Draft-RoP-Dublin-21-feb-2008.pdf>.
67   In his remarks to the Wellington conference's closing session, Ambassador Dáithí O'Ceallaigh noted: "Delegations will have seen the draft rules of procedure for the Diplomatic Conference. These are standard rules for the adoption of treaties including important instruments of international humanitarian law. They are based in particular on the rules of procedure for the adoption of the Additional Protocols to the Geneva Conventions, the Rome Statute of the International Criminal Court and the Landmine Ban Convention, and on the general United Nations rules of procedure". See "Arrangements for the Dublin Diplomatic Conference: Remarks by Ambassador Dáithí O'Ceallaigh", <www.mfat. govt.nz/clustermunitionswellington/conference-documents/Statement-Closing-Plenary-Wellington.pdf>.
68   "Diplomatic Conference for the Adoption of a Cluster Munitions Convention, Dublin, May 2008: Draft Rules of Procedure", p. 8, <www. mfat.govt.nz/clustermunitionswellington/conference-documents/Draft-RoP-Dublin-21-feb-2008.pdf>.
69   Ibid., p. 7.
70   The author attended most sessions, and neither saw nor heard such.

71 "Closing Remarks—Canada", p. 2, <www.mfat.govt.nz/ clustermunitionswellington/conference-documents/closing-statements/ Canada-closing-statement.pdf>.

72 For instance, see "Nine Governments Seek to Weaken Draft Treaty to Allow US to Continue Using Cluster Munitions", CMC press release, Wellington, 19 February 2008, <www.icbl.org/index.php/icbl/Library/ News-Articles/The-Treaties/interoperability>.

73 "Closing Remarks—Canada", pp. 2–3, <www.mfat.govt.nz/ clustermunitionswellington/conference-documents/closing-statements/ Canada-closing-statement.pdf>.

74 As quoted via interpretation in the author's notes.

75 Press release from the Office of the Minister for Disarmament and Arms Control, Phil Goff, "Cluster munitions—More than 80 countries sign Declaration", 22 February 2008, <www.beehive.govt.nz/release/more +80+countries+cluster+munitions+conference+have+already+sig ned+wellington+declaration+–+>.

76 From the Declaration of the Wellington Conference on Cluster Munitions, 22 February 2008. See annex B for the text of the Declaration.

77 "Closing Statement for the United Kingdom", p. 1, <www.mfat.govt.nz/ clustermunitionswellington/conference-documents/closing-statements/ UK-closing-statment.pdf>. Emphasis in orginial.

78 Author's interview with Dáithí O'Ceallaigh, 12 June 2008.

79 Author's interview with Don MacKay, 30 July 2008.

80 This Coalition consisted of Amnesty International NZ, Aotearoa Lawyers for Peace, NZ Campaign Against Landmines, Caritas Aotearoa NZ, Christian World Service, Development Resource Centre, Engineers for Social Responsibility NZ, International Physicians for the Prevention of Nuclear War NZ, National Council of Women of New Zealand, National Consultative Committee on Disarmament, Oxfam NZ, Parliamentarians for Nuclear Non-proliferation and Disarmament NZ, Pax Christi Aotearoa-NZ, Peace Foundation NZ, Disarmament and Security Centre, Peace Movement Aotearoa, United Nations Association NZ, United Nations Youth Association of NZ, United Nations Children's Fund NZ and Women's International League for Peace and Freedom, Aotearoa. Wareham discusses the formation of the ANZCMC in a short film online at <www.youtube.com/watch?v=VVdC2TbrG1M>.

81 See "Public Action: Let the Chalk Talk", Cluster Ban News, 21 February 2008, <www.stopclusterbombs.org.nz/wp-content/uploads/2008/02/ thursday-final.pdf>.

82 Shamima Ahmed and David M. Potter, *NGOs in International Politics*, Kumarian Press, 2006, p. 37.

83 ANZCMC, *Report on Activities: Wellington Conference on Cluster Munitions, 18–22 February 2008*, p. 2, photo.

Chapter 8
The evolution of cluster munition policy in the ICRC and UN

1   Colin King, *Explosive Remnants of War: Submunitions and Other Unexploded Ordnance—A Study*, ICRC, 2000, p. 41.

2   The three recommendations taken up in Protocol V were to (1) make users responsible for clearance, (2) oblige them to exchange technical information after hostilities or giving it to a coordinating third party like the UN to aid the clear-up, (3) warn civilians about post-conflict hazards of unexploded munitions. See ICRC, *Explosive Remnants of War: Cluster Bombs and Landmines in Kosovo*, 2000/revised 2001, p. 37.

3   The ICRC, like the United Nations, had Observer status in the CCW, which in practice meant it could attend all of the process's formal meetings and many of its informal meetings as well.

4   Caroline Moorehead, *Dunant's Dream: War, Switzerland and the History of the Red Cross*, Harper Collins, 1998, p. 712.

5   *Report on States Parties' Responses to the Questionnaire on International Humanitarian Law and Explosive Remnants of War, CCW/GGE/X/WG.1/WP.2, Dated 8 March 2005*, UN document CCW/GGE/XIII/WG.1/WP.12, 24 March 2006.

6   *Comments on the "Report on States Parties' Responses to the Questionnaire" on International Humanitarian Law and Explosive Remnants of War, CCW/GGE/X/WG.1/WP.2, Dated 8 March 2005*, UN document CCW/GGE/XIII/WG.1/WP.15, 24 March 2006, p. 4. Underlining in original; emphasis added.

7   Author's interview with Louis Maresca, 5 August 2008.

8   *Key elements of ICRC proposals on cluster munitions to be presented at the November Review Conference of the States Parties to the CCW*, non-paper, 13 October 2006.

9   "ICRC statement to the Third Review Conference of the Convention on Certain Conventional Weapons", 7 November 2006, <www.icrc.org/web/eng/siteeng0.nsf/html/conventional-weapons-statement-071106>.

10 Ibid.

11   Author's interview with Louis Maresca, 5 August 2008.

12   Author's interview with Peter Herby, 12 December 2008.

13   ICRC, *Humanitarian, Military, Technical and Legal Challenges of Cluster Munitions—Expert Meeting Report, Montreux, Switzerland, 18 to 20 April 2007*, 2007, p. 81. Emphasis in original.

14   For instance, on 21 June 2007 the ICRC made a statement to the CCW on cluster munitions; see *Observations on the Legal Issues Related to the Use of Cluster Munitions*, UN document CCW/GGE/2007/WP.8, 25 June 2007.

15   "The ICRC's position on cluster munitions and the need for urgent action", 25 October 2007, <www.icrc.org/web/eng/siteeng0.nsf/html/cluster-munitions-statement-251007>.

16   Kellenberger said: "There is no basis for believing that improving the reliability of cluster munition fuses or adding self-destruct features can be the sole or primary solution to the cluster munitions problem. Such technological approaches may be part of a response, but they cannot be relied upon alone to function correctly under a range of circumstances so as to provide adequate protection for civilian populations". See "The ICRC's position on cluster munitions and the need for urgent action", 25 October 2007, <www.icrc.org/web/eng/siteeng0.nsf/html/cluster-munitions-statement-251007>.

17   Ibid.

18   "Opening statement by ICRC President, Dr. Jakob Kellenberger", 30th International Conference of the Red Cross and Red Crescent, Geneva, 26–30 November 2007, <http://www.icrc.ch/web/eng/siteeng0.nsf/html/30-international-conference-statement-271107>.

19   Ibid.

20   See "Resolution 8: International humanitarian law and cluster munitions", in *30th International Conference of the Red Cross and Red Crescent (Geneva, 26–30 November 2007)/Council of Delegates of the International Red Cross and Red Crescent Movement (Geneva, 23–24 November 2007): Resolutions*, ICRC, 2008, pp. 60–1, <www.icrc.org/Web/Eng/siteeng0.nsf/htmlall/p1108/$File/ICRC_002_1108.PDF>.

21   Author's notes, confirmed by ICRC participants at the Vienna conference in interviews with the author.

22   Jakob Kellenberger, "Banning cluster bombs", *International Herald Tribune*, 9 May 2008.

23   The UN's Department for Disarmament Affairs became the Office for Disarmament Affairs in the middle of 2007.

24 Arthur Westing (ed.), *Explosive Remnants of War: Mitigating the Environmental Effects*, Taylor & Francis, 1985.

25 The UN General Assembly created UNMAS in 1997 to serve as the UN focal point for mine action and to support the UN's vision of "a world free of the threat of landmines and unexploded ordnance, where individuals and communities live in a safe environment conducive to development, and where mine survivors are fully integrated into their societies". For more information see <www.mineaction.org/overview. asp?o=22>.

26 Author's interview with John Flanagan, 4 June 2008. One lesson was that cluster munitions had to be singled out because of their high level of threat to civilians, as shown by casualty rates in Kosovo. A second lesson was that a demining mind-set would not work: new procedures for surveying and dealing with unexploded submunitions were needed that differed from demining techniques. As explored in chapter 4, the international humanitarian demining community did not necessarily realize the importance of these lessons right away.

27 Flanagan's discussion paper prepared for UNMAS for the CCW concluded: "Sub-munitions pose a particular threat and require specific attention as part of post-conflict clearance operations". See *Explosive Remnants of War: Experience from Field Operations*, UN document CCW/GGE/II/WP.13, 15 July 2002, p. 4.

28 "A Call for a Freeze on the Use of Cluster Munitions", 27 November 2003,   <www.mineaction.org/downloads/IASC%20Statement%20 on%20cluster%20munitions.pdf>. "Based on our work in the field, the IASC is convinced that within the overall problem of ERW, cluster munitions pose an exceptional humanitarian threat both during and after conflict ... Although we recognise and appreciate the efforts of States Parties to address the problem of ERW, the IASC is concerned that the issue of cluster munitions has not been adequately addressed. On reflection we believe that those who use cluster munitions are unable to prevent the *unacceptable effects that these weapons have on civilians both during and after conflict*. The IASC members, like the ICRC has said before, therefore would reiterate earlier calls for a freeze on the use of cluster munitions until effective legal instruments that resolve humanitarian concerns are in place." Emphasis added. According to the statement, the IASC was made up of "FAO, OCHA, UNICEF, UNDP, UNFPA, WFP, WHO, UNHCR", with standing invitees: "Interaction, ICRC, IFRC, ICVA, IOM, UNHCR, RSG-IDPs, SCHR, World Bank". The version quoted here is as delivered to the CCW. The IASC statement's

sponsors did not include DPKO, UNMAS or Disarmament Affairs, but UNMAS (and thus DPKO) had considerable input into it (author's personal communication with Gustavo Laurie, 3 September 2009).

29   Ibid.

30   Author's personal communication with Gustavo Laurie, 3 September 2009.

31   Fourteen UN departments, programmes, funds and agencies are involved in mine action to varying degrees, in accordance with their mandates, areas of expertise and comparative advantages, and thus are members of the IACG-MA. These are DPKO, the Food and Agriculture Organization of the United Nations (FAO), OCHA, the Office of Disarmament Affairs (ODA), the Office of the High Commissioner for Human Rights (OHCHR), the Office of the Special Adviser on Gender Issues (OSAGI), UNDP, UNICEF, the United Nations High Commissioner for Refugees (UNHCR), the United Nations Office of Project Services (UNOPS), UNMAS, the World Bank, the World Food Programme (WFP) and the World Health Organization (WHO). The IACG-MA is chaired by the Under-Secretary-General for Peacekeeping Operations at the Principals' level, and by the Director of UNMAS at the working level. All mentioned departments, programmes, funds and agencies are members of the IACG-MA, except for the World Bank, which is an observer, as are other entities such as UNIDIR and the ICRC.

32   These meetings were almost all held in New York, although at least one of the first meetings was convened in Geneva. The Geneva branch of Disarmament Affairs, UNMAS's liaison officer Gustavo Laurie, UNIDIR and sometimes UNDP representatives participated in the meetings via conference call or videoconference link.

33   "Statement to the CCW Group of Governmental Experts", 7 March 2005, <www.mineaction.org/docs/2213_.asp>.

34   *Proposed definitions for cluster munitions and sub-munitions*, UN document CCW/GGE/X/WG.1/WP.3, 8 March 2005.

35   UNDP interoffice memorandum, "Subject: Joint Meeting of the Inter-Agency Coordination Group and Mine Action and Executive Committee on Peace and Security regarding Cluster Munitions (CMs)", 1 June 2005. Document on file with the author.

36   Author's interview with John Flanagan, 4 June 2008.

37   These were eventually published. See Rosy Cave, Anthea Lawson and Andrew Sherriff, *Cluster Munitions in Albania and Lao PDR: The Humanitarian and Socio-Economic Impact*, UNIDIR, 2006.

38 "Humanitarian threat posed by munitions and sub-munitions that have become explosive remnants of war: Assessment by Mine Action Programme Managers and EOD Technical Advisors", September–October 2005. Document on file with the author.

39 "Survey on humanitarian threat posed by munitions and sub-munitions that have become ERW: Assessment based on responses and findings", presentation by UNMAS, 17 November 2005, p. 3. Document on file with the author.

40 *Statement on behalf of DPKO, UNMAS, UNDP, UNICEF, OCHA, FAO, UNOPS, UNHCR, UNHCHR, WHO, WFP, OSAGI read by Gustavo Laurie, UNMAS Liaison Officer, to the 15 November 2005 meeting of the GGE on ERW and IHL.* Document on file with the author.

41 "Disarmament and Arms Control Processes Can Impact Human Security Positively, Secretary-General Tells Parties to Certain Conventional Weapons Convention", UN press release SG/SM/10230 DC/2998, 25 November 2005.

42 Author's interview with Sara Sekkenes, 1 July 2008.

43 There is evidence to suggest that before the 2006 CCW Review Conference, Jean-Marie Guéhenno, head of DPKO, approached OCHA (the IASC's coordinator) to deliver a statement on behalf of the IASC on cluster munitions to that meeting—its first since 2003. In the end, though, the need for this appears to have been overtaken by the Secretary-General's message to the Review Conference.

44 "The Secretary-General: Message to the Third Review Conference of the Convention on Certain Conventional Weapons", 7 November 2006, <www.unog.ch/80256EDD006B8954/(httpAssets)/81D9D5CB D4AC8BC3C1257220002F981A/$file/UNSG+message+re+CCW+T hird+RevCon+(final).doc>.

45 United Nations Office for the Coordination of Humanitarian Affairs, "UN Emergency Relief Coordinator: End Use of Cluster Munitions", press release, 7 November 2006.

46 "Statement of the UN Mine Action Team to the Third Review Conference of States Parties to the CCW Convention", 7 November 2006, <www. unog.ch/80256EDD006B8954/(httpAssets)/35F4F97BD01410D9C125 722000483811/$file/30+UNMAS.pdf>.

47 "Statement attributable to the Spokesperson for the Secretary-General On Cluster Munitions", 23 February 2007, <www.un.org/apps/sg/ sgstats.asp?nid=2456>.

48   "In Message on Mine Awareness Day, Secretary-General Encourages Experts to Eliminate Impact of Cluster Munitions on Civilians", UN press release SG/SM/10933 OBV/617, 4 April 2007. Emphasis added.

49   General Assembly, *Assistance in mine action, Report of the Secretary-General*, UN document A/62/307, 24 August 2007, p. 18.

50   Author's interview with Sara Sekkenes, 1 July 2008.

51   See "The UN Position on Cluster Munitions", <www.undp.org/cpr/whats_new/cluster_munitions_un_position.shtml>. Emphasis added.

52   Security Council, *Report of the Secretary-General on the protection of civilians in armed conflict*, UN document S/2007/643, 28 October 2007, p. 17.

Chapter 9
Dublin: define and conquer

1   The US Secretary of Defense, Robert Gates, would eventually sign-off on a new policy on "cluster munitions and unintended harm to civilians" on 19 June 2008, see <www.defenselink.mil/news/d20080709cmpolicy.pdf>.

2   Author's interview with Don MacKay, 13 May 2008.

3   Author's interview with Dáithí O'Ceallaigh, 12 June 2008.

4   See Bernard Kouchner, "Stop aux bombes à sous-munitions", *Libération*, 22 January 2008.

5   Ove Dullum, *Cluster Weapons—Military Utility and Alternatives*, Norwegian Defence Research Establishment (FFI), 2008.

6   In September 2007, at the Mine Ban Treaty anniversary celebrations in Oslo, Dullum had discussed this initially with Human Rights Watch and Norwegian People's Aid.

7   APACHE (*Arme Propulsée Antipiste à Charges Ejectables*) is a cruise missile system that dispenses anti-runway submunitions. See Robert Hewson (ed.) *Jane's Air-Launched Weapons (Issue 53)*, Jane's Information Group, 2009, pp. 234–9.

8   Livingstone Declaration on Cluster Munitions, 1 April 2008, <www.iss.co.za/dynamic/administration/file_manager/file_links/LIVINGSTONEDECL.PDF.

9   Richard Kidd, "Is There A Strategy for Responsible U.S. Engagement on Cluster Munitions?", "Connect Us Fund" Roundtable Dialogue, Aspen Institute, 28 April 2008, <www.disam.dsca.mil/pubs/Vol%2030_3/Kidd.pdf>.

[10] For detail of these discussions on the number of ratifications required for international entry into force see Diplomatic Conference for the Adoption of a Convention on Cluster Munitions, *Summary Record of Fifth Session of the Committee of the Whole*, document CCM/CW/SR/5, 18 June 2008.

[11] "Connecting the Dots: Victim Assistance and Human Rights", Survivor Corps (formerly Landmine Survivors Network), May 2009, p. 7.

[12] For example, article 23 of the Convention on the Rights of Persons with Disabilities states that, in taking effective and appropriate measures to eliminate discrimination against persons with disabilities in all matters relating to marriage, family, parenthood and relationships, on an equal basis with others, States Parties should ensure: "(b) The rights of persons with disabilities to decide freely and responsibly on the number and spacing of their children and to have access to age-appropriate information, reproductive and family planning education are recognized, and the means necessary to enable them to exercise these rights are provided".

[13] See article 2 of the Convention on Cluster Munitions.

[14] Author's interview with Anna Macdonald, 24 June 2009.

[15] In addition to national campaigners, members of the CMC's Steering Committee, Laura Cheeseman and Susan B. Walker, and its Coordinator, Thomas Nash, were key interlocutors with the Tee-total, as well as Serena Olgiati with the Latin American group of countries.

[16] Author's interview with Ahmad Arafa, 11 May 2009.

[17] Author's conversation with Thomas Nash, 21 July 2009.

[18] The CMC had also held a Global Day of Action on 5 November 2007.

[19] E-mail from Laura Cheeseman, CMC Campaign Officer, to the CMC e-mail list-server, "Subject: The Global Day of Action to Ban Cluster Bombs: 19 April 2008", 26 March 2008. Document on file with the author.

[20] Natalie Curtis, "Cluster Munition Coalition: Dublin Diplomatic Conference on cluster munitions—media report, 19–30 May 2008", p. 2. Document on file with the author.

[21] British graphic artist Ben Branagan had developed visual identities for CMC's other campaigns such as "stop killing civilians; start banning cluster bombs" and he designed the "make it happen" slogan and motif eventually taken up by the Norwegian Foreign Minister in his invitation to states for the Oslo Signing Conference in December 2008.

[22] CMC, "Dublin Diplomatic Conference on Cluster Munitions—Civil Society Team: CORE TEAM roles and responsibilities", internal

document, version dated 13 May 2008. Document on file with the author.

23 See "Cluster Munition Coalition Dublin Diplomatic Conference on Cluster Munitions 2008 Participant Handbook". Document on file with the author.

24 "Cluster Munition Coalition Dublin Lobbying Guide", p. 14. Document on file with the author. Other thematic facilitation topics were clearance of unexploded ordnance (Eva Veble, DanChurchAid), storage and stockpile destruction (Mark Hiznay, Human Rights Watch), international cooperation and assistance (Ayman Sorour, Protection), transparency and compliance (Tamar Gabelnick, International Campaign to Ban Landmines) and national implementation (Paul Hannon, Mines Action Canada).

25 Ibid.

26 Author's interview with Anna Macdonald, 19 June 2008.

27 *Letter from Ministry of Defence to Mr. T.A. Rigg*, 14 May 2008. Document on file with the author.

28 On 12 November 2007, Prime Minister Gordon Brown said: "having led the way by taking two types of cluster munitions out of service, we want to work internationally for a ban on the use, production, transfer and stockpiling of those cluster munitions which cause unacceptable harm to civilians". See "Lord Mayor's Banquet Speech—12 November 2007", <www.number10.gov.uk/Page13736>.

29 View based on author's interviews with Simon Conway, Richard Moyes, Thomas Nash, Brian Rappert and Anna Macdonald.

30 Lord Wallace of Saltaire, Lord Ramsbotham, Lord Jay of Ewelme, Lord Elton, Lord Dubs and Roger Berry. Author's personal communication with Anna Macdonald, 26 June 2009.

31 Author's interview with Anna Macdonald, 23 June 2009. Earlier, in March 2005, the UK had unilaterally removed its RBL-755 cluster bombs and MLRS M-26 submunition stocks from service.

32 NGOs had also commissioned an opinion poll soon after the Oslo conference in 2007.

33 The YouGov company surveyed 1,961 people around the UK between 9 and 12 May 2008. See letter from Amnesty International UK, Oxfam GB and Landmine Action, "Cluster bombs", *The Times*, 27 May 2008.

34 See <www.crewe-nantwich.gov.uk/your_council/elections/by-elections_2008.aspx>.

[35] For instance, see Sangita Myska, "UK seeks cluster bomb exemption", *BBC News*, 19 May 2008; and Julian Borger and Patrick Wintour, "MoD lobbies to keep 'smart' cluster bombs", *The Guardian*, 17 May 2008.

[36] Letter from General Sir Hugh Beach, Field Marshal Lord Bramall, Major-General Patrick Cordingley, Lieutenant-General Sir Roderick Cordy-Simpson, Lieutenant-General Sir Jack Deverell, Major-General the Rev Morgan Llewellyn, General Lord Ramsbotham, General Sir Michael Rose and General Sir Rupert Smith, "Cluster bombs don't work and must be banned", *The Times*, 19 May 2008.

[37] Croke Park was also the site of the notorious Bloody Sunday massacre on 21 November 1920, in which 14 spectators watching Dublin playing Tipperary were shot and killed, and hundreds injured by Black and Tans and auxiliaries. See Tim Pat Coogan, *Ireland in the Twentieth Century*, Arrow, 2003, p. 84.

[38] Author's conversation with Thomas Nash, 21 July 2009.

[39] See the opening statement by Micheál Martin, 19 May 2008, <www.clustermunitionsdublin.ie/documents/general-statements/ireland.pdf>.

[40] See the statement by Jakob Kellenberger, 19 May 2008, <www.clustermunitionsdublin.ie/documents/general-statements/icrc.pdf>.

[41] See the statement by Ad Melkert, 19 May 2008, <www.clustermunitionsdublin.ie/documents/general-statements/undp.pdf>.

[42] See the statement by Branislav Kapetanović, 19 May 2008, <www.clustermunitionsdublin.ie/documents/general-statements/cmc.pdf>.

[43] Author's interview with Dáithí O'Ceallaigh, 12 June 2008.

[44] These eight Vice-Presidents were Chile, France (Dobelle), Hungary, Lebanon, Mauretania, Mexico (Macedo), Norway (Kongstad) and Zambia. All were influential countries in the Oslo process for various reasons.

[45] President O'Ceallaigh reconfirmed this for the benefit of the UK in the Committee of the Whole on Friday, 23 May 2008: "With regard to interventions by observer delegations, only participating States can propose amendments to the text of the Convention. A Friend of the President can take the comments of observer delegations into account in seeking to reach consensus on the text. The comments of the ICRC on Article 3 this afternoon had been favourably supported by a number of participating states". Diplomatic Conference for the Adoption of a Convention on Cluster Munitions, *Summary Record of Eighth Session of the Committee of the Whole*, document CCM/CW/SR/8, 18 June 2008, pp. 4–5.

[46] Author's interview with Don MacKay, 30 July 2008.

47   Author's interview with Don MacKay, 13 May 2008.

48   There were at least two: one first circulated on 19 May and discussed in the course of 20 May ("Friend of the President: Informal consultations on the definition of 'Cluster munition'") and, reflecting the general trend of debate toward a definition containing a cumulative list of criteria necessary for a weapon's exclusion, a paper circulated during the morning of 21 May entitled "Proposals that have been made on cumulative lists of criteria".

49   For a good overview of these different exclusion proposals, see "Compendium of Proposals Submitted by Delegations During the Wellington Conference, Addendum 1", <www.mfat.govt.nz/clustermunitionswellington/conference-documents/WCCM-Compendium-v2.pdf>.

50   Author's interview with Don MacKay, 30 July 2008.

51   "Afternoon press briefing from 21 May 2008", 22 May 2008, <www.number-10.gov.uk/output/Page15599.asp>. According to people the author interviewed, this announcement was originally intended to be in response to a Parliamentary Question to be asked of the government that day in the British House of Commons. Because there was not time, the announcement was instead made on the afternoon of 21 May from 10 Downing Street.

52   Landmine Action/Oxfam GB, "UK comes in from the cold on cluster bomb ban", press release, 21 May 2008.

53   Friend of the Chair's Paper on Definition of a "Cluster Munition", 22 May 2008. Document on file with the author.

54   Ibid. Note that this proposal differs from that finally agreed in the CCM.

55   Norway summarized its 21 May proposal as follows: "More than 20 kilogrammes per submunition—excluded from the scope of the convention; Between 5 and 20 kilogrammes per submunition—excluded under the condition that they meet strict requirements of single target, self destruct and self-deactivation; Less than 5 kilogrammes per submunition—categorically prohibited". See "How to address the humanitarian effects of unacceptable cluster munitions: Explanatory note on the Norwegian informal proposal based on weight criterion to Article 2 on definitions", 21 May 2008. Document on file with the author.

56   Author's interview with Don MacKay, 30 July 2008.

57   See "How to address the humanitarian effects of unacceptable cluster munitions: Explanatory note on the Norwegian informal proposal

based on weight criterion to Article 2 on definitions", 21 May 2008. This paper, although dated 21 May, was not circulated widely until 26 May. It should also be noted that, although Norway proposed 5kg (any submunition weighing less than this being prohibited), the final weight agreed was 4kg. Australia argued for a 3kg threshold, which would then have excluded US manufacturer Textron Systems' Sensor Fuzed Weapon, which deployed BLU-108 submunitions: this was not taken up, however, and the result was that the Sensor Fuzed Weapon fell within the treaty's prohibition. Document on file with the author.

58 See <www.globalsecurity.org/military/systems/munitions/blu-108.htm>.

59 Author's interview with Richard Moyes, 3 July 2008.

60 E-mail to author from Richard Moyes, 16 April 2009. A slide in Moyes' presentation split states active on the article 2 cluster munition definition issue into three categories according to level of concern (green, amber and red). See also Richard Moyes, "Briefing note on certain proposed exclusions from the Oslo Process definition of cluster munitions", Landmine Action, 29 January 2008. Document on file with the author.

61 The CMC's observations on the draft convention text issued before the Dublin negotiations argued that there should be no exceptions for submunitions with self-destruct, self-deactivation or self-neutralizing features, for submunitions with a certain reliability (or failure) rate, or for so-called "'direct fire" submunitions. There should be no exception for munitions based solely on factors such as the capacity to detect, engage and strike point targets within an area; electronic fuzing; "sensor-fuzing" technology or a limited number of submunitions. See *CMC Policy Papers, prepared in advance of the Dublin Diplomatic Conference on Cluster Munitions*, 8 May 2008. Document on file with the author.

62 One of the changes incorporated from campaigners that morning was a line to "fully support" the proposal known to be coming that day from a range of states calling for the deletion of any article 2, paragraph 2(c). Author's conversation with Thomas Nash, 21 July 2009.

63 Author's interview with Richard Moyes, 3 July 2008.

64 "Tricky Dublin talks home in on cluster bomb ban", *Agence France Press*, 23 May 2008.

65 Burke later said: "I proposed resuming consultations on Sunday afternoon in order to inject a sense of urgency into the process and jolt delegates out of their weekend mood. Having got agreement for this it was almost inevitable that I would offer to resume with the 'other definitions' segment. It also gave me more time to complete the

remaining 'fixes'". Author's personal communication with Jim Burke, 9 September 2009.

66 Eric Prokosch, *The Technology of Killing: a Military and Political History of Anti-Personnel Weapons*, Zed Books, 1995, p. 105. Prokosch also noted in an e-mail to the author on 14 June 2009 that other aircraft-mounted dispensers, the SUU-7 and the SUU-14, were widely used in the South-East Asia war.

67 Author's interview with Jim Burke, 25 July 2008.

68 The final definition in article 2, paragraph 13 would be: "'explosive bomblet' means a conventional munition weighing less than 20 kilograms, *which is not self-propelled* and which, in order to perform its task, is dispersed or released by a dispenser, and is designed to function by detonating an explosive charge prior to, on or after impact". Emphasis added

69 For a detailed summary see Diplomatic Conference for the Adoption of a Convention on Cluster Munitions, *Summary Record of Eighth Session of the Committee of the Whole*, document CCM/CW/SR/8, 18 June 2008.

70 Katherine Harrison, "Half Way There", Women's International League for Peace and Freedom, 23 May 2008, <www.wilpf.int.ch/disarmament/clustermunitions/Dublin%202008/Friday23May.html>.

71 See Diplomatic Conference for the Adoption of a Convention on Cluster Munitions, *Summary Record of Eleventh Session of the Committee of the Whole*, document CCM/CW/SR/11, 18 June 2008.

72 Indeed, O'Ceallaigh told the conference this repeatedly, for instance on Monday, 26 May, in the Committee of the Whole. See Diplomatic Conference for the Adoption of a Convention on Cluster Munitions, *Summary Record of Tenth Session of the Committee of the Whole*, document CCM/CW/SR/10, 18 June 2008, p. 1.

Chapter 10
Dublin: endgame

1 Author's interview with Dáithí O'Ceallaigh, 10 July 2008.

2 "Ambassador Mull Briefs on U.S. Cluster Munitions Policy", 21 May 2008, <www.america.gov/st/texttransenglish/2008/May/20080522163101eaifas0.8921015.html>.

3 Letter from US Senators Dianne Feinstein and Patrick Leahy to Ambassador Dáithí O'Ceallaigh, Distinguished Diplomats and

Distinguished Members of Civil Society, 19 May 2008, <http://www.uscbl.org/negotiations/99_letter.pdf>.

4   *Cluster Munition Coalition Statement on the Agreement to Adopt the Cluster Munition Convention*, 28 May 2008. Document on file with the author.

5   The Norwegian Ministry of Defence's primary legal expert was Annette Bjørseth. Torfinn Rislaa Arntsen, Assistant Director General of the Section for International Humanitarian and Criminal Law, participated from the Norwegian Ministry of Foreign Affairs. Prior to Dublin, their legal expertise was supplemented by Dr Gro Nystuen from the University of Oslo, but during the Dublin conference Nystuen was seconded to the conference's Secretariat at the request of the Irish, in view of her experience of the Mine Ban Treaty negotiations in Oslo in 1997.

6   Author's interview with Christine Schraner Burgener, 15 October 2008.

7   Diplomatic Conference for the Adoption of a Convention on Cluster Munitions, *Draft Convention on Cluster Munitions*, document CCM/3, 19 May 2008. Emphasis added.

8   Paragraph 1(c) of article 1 states that each state party undertakes never under any circumstances: "c) To assist, encourage or induce, in any way, anyone to engage in any activity prohibited to a State Party under this Convention". See Convention on the Prohibition of the Use, Stockpiling, Production and Transfer of Antipersonnel Mines and on their Destruction.

9   "Discussion paper—Cluster munitions and inter-operability: The Oslo Process discussion text and implications for international operations", <www.mfat.govt.nz/clustermunitionswellington/conference-documents/Discussion-paper-Au-et-al.pdf>.

10   Author's interview with Christine Schraner Burgener, 15 October 2008.

11   Views differ among participants in the interoperability consultations as to how open-ended they were. For instance, the Swiss said that only their first two small-room meetings were "closed". Others have noted that the Swiss did not advertise the fact that later meetings were, in contrast, open-ended, and that they were still held in a small and often-crowded room. Schraner said that as Friend of the President she invited at an early stage every state to participate and had many bilateral consultations with states, especially with the head representative of the different regions—even inviting them to the President's room for lunch at one stage for "intensive discussions"—but many did not want

to participate in the interoperability consultations because they were occupied with other issues more important to them. Author's personal communication with Christine Schraner Burgener, 8 August 2009.

[12] Diplomatic Conference for the Adoption of a Convention on Cluster Munitions, *Summary Record of First Session of the Committee of the Whole*, document CCM/CW/SR/1, 18 June 2008, p. 3.

[13] Author's personal communication with Reto Wollenmann, 27 May 2009.

[14] Idem.

[15] This understanding was confirmed in the Committee of the Whole's discussions the following Monday. See Diplomatic Conference for the Adoption of a Convention on Cluster Munitions, *Summary Record of Tenth Session of the Committee of the Whole*, document CCM/CW/SR/10, 18 June 2008, p. 6.

[16] *Informal Proposal by the Friend of the President on Interoperability*, 21 May 2008. Document on file with the author.

[17] *Proposal by the Friend of the President on Interoperability for the Committee of the Whole*, 23 May 2008. Document on file with the author.

[18] For instance, see Diplomatic Conference for the Adoption of a Convention on Cluster Munitions, *Summary Record of Tenth Session of the Committee of the Whole*, document CCM/CW/SR/10, 18 June 2008, pp. 7–10.

[19] Author's personal communication with Reto Wollenmann, 27 May 2009.

[20] Paragraphs 1 and 2 quoted from *Informal Proposal by the Friend of the President on Interoperability, revised version*, 22 May 2008. However, the language quoted is basically identical to the final text agreed in the Convention on Cluster Munitions. Document on file with the author.

[21] Article 21, paragraph 4 of the Convention on Cluster Munitions. This formulation—"expressly request the use of"—in paragraph 4 was apparently developed on Friday evening of the first week of the Dublin negotiations (author's personal communication with Reto Wollenmann, 20 May 2009).

[22] "Interoperability (22 May): Relations between States Parties and non-States Parties to this Convention", 22 May 2008. Document on file with the author.

[23] *Final, Final Proposal by the Friend of the President on Interoperability*, 27 May 2008. Paragraph 3 of this Friend's paper (in which hosting language had earlier resided) now said: "Not withstanding the provisions

of Article I of this Convention and in accordance with international law, States Parties, or their military personnel or their nationals, may engage in military cooperation with States not party to this Convention which might engage in activities prohibited to a State party". Apart from minor grammatical changes, this would be the paragraph 3 formulation of the final Convention on Cluster Munitions text. Document on file with the author.

24   See Diplomatic Conference for the Adoption of a Convention on Cluster Munitions, *Summary Record of Thirteenth Session of the Committee of the Whole*, document CCM/CW/SR/13, 18 June 2008, p. 1.

25   Ibid., p. 5.

26   Author's interview with Dáithí O'Ceallaigh, 10 July 2008.

27   See Diplomatic Conference for the Adoption of a Convention on Cluster Munitions, *Summary Record of Fourteenth Session of the Committee of the Whole*, document CCM/CW/SR/14, 18 June 2008.

28   Richard Norton-Taylor, "UK ready to scrap killer cluster bombs", *The Guardian*, 28 May 2008.

29   "Breakthrough on cluster bombs draws closer", 28 May 2008, <www.number10.gov.uk/Page15608>.

30   Sources differ within the President's team over when precisely they first knew of the British Prime Minister's announcement. Certainly, it seems to have been no earlier than the adjournment of the Committee of the Whole at around 21h00, and collectively they may not have discussed it until after consultations concluded around midnight.

31   Author's interview with James C. O'Shea, 28 July 2008.

32   O'Ceallaigh recalled that "pretty much up until late Tuesday I was by no means certain that the British would be able to join the consensus We on the Irish side were resigned to the fact that they might not be able to join". Author's interview with Dáithí O'Ceallaigh, 10 July 2008.

33   Author's interview with Dáithí O'Ceallaigh, 12 June 2008.

34   Idem.

35   Idem.

36   Diplomatic Conference for the Adoption of a Convention on Cluster Munitions, *Draft Convention on Cluster Munitions*, document CCM/PT/15, 28 May 2008.

37   Transcription from President's verbatim remarks to the Committee of the Whole, morning of 28 May 2008.

38   See Diplomatic Conference for the Adoption of a Convention on Cluster Munitions, *Summary Record of Fifteenth Session of the Committee of the Whole*, document CCM/CW/SR/15, 18 June 2008.

39   Transcription from President's verbatim remarks to the Committee of the Whole, morning of 28 May 2008.

40   Ibid.

41   Ibid.

42   In fact, there were a number of small differences between Schraner's proposal to the President on Tuesday and the Presidency "composite" text the next day. For instance, the phrase cluster munitions "as defined in Article 2" was removed from paragraphs 2 and 4(a).

43   The French version was distributed at around lunchtime. Author's interview with James C. O'Shea, 28 July 2008.

44   Author's conversation with Thomas Nash, 21 July 2009.

45   Diplomatic Conference for the Adoption of a Convention on Cluster Munitions, *Draft Convention on Cluster Munitions*, document CCM/PT/15, 28 May 2008, art. 21, para. 3.

46   Author's personal communication with Thomas Nash, 20 May 2009.

47   Author's interview with Stephen D. Goose, 21 November 2008.

48   Author's personal communication with Thomas Nash, 21 July 2009.

49   Author's interview with Earl Turcotte, 25 July 2008.

50   Author's personal communication with Earl Turcotte, 3 August 2009. Turcotte said that he added to this remark, "We believe we have negotiated a solid text that offers real protection to civilians. But we have to be able to continue to engage in combined military operations with non-party states, as do many states participating in these negotiations. This text strikes the right balance. Please, accept it as is".

51   Author's interview with Dáithí O'Ceallaigh, 10 July 2008.

52   Author's interview with Stephen D. Goose, 21 November 2008.

53   Diplomatic Conference for the Adoption of a Convention on Cluster Munitions, *Draft Convention on Cluster Munitions*, document CCM/PT/15, 28 May 2008, art. 4, para. 4.

54   Transcription from President's verbatim remarks to the Committee of the Whole, afternoon of 28 May 2008.

55   Transcription from Switzerland's verbatim remarks to the Committee of the Whole, afternoon of 28 May 2008.

56   Transcription from President's verbatim remarks to the Committee of the Whole, afternoon of 28 May 2008.

57   See Diplomatic Conference for the Adoption of a Convention on Cluster Munitions, *Summary Record of Third Session of the Plenary*, document CCM/SR/3, 18 June 2008.

58   The Conference agreed on Wednesday to adopt the Convention text on Friday. This was the substantive decision; that is, the adoption on

Friday 30 May was formal confirmation of the decision already taken on Wednesday evening. See Diplomatic Conference for the Adoption of a Convention on Cluster Munitions, *Final Document*, document CCM/78, 30 May 2008, para. 16.

[59] The following 107 states participated in the Conference: Albania, Argentina, Australia, Austria, Bahrain, Belgium, Belize, Benin, Bolivia, Bosnia and Herzegovina, Botswana, Brunei Darussalam, Bulgaria, Burkina Faso, Burundi, Cambodia, Cameroon, Canada, Chad, Chile, Comoros, Cook Islands, Costa Rica, Côte d'Ivoire, Croatia, Czech Republic, Democratic Republic of the Congo, Denmark, Dominican Republic, Ecuador, El Salvador, Estonia, Fiji, Finland, France, Germany, Ghana, Guatemala, Guinea, Guinea-Bissau, Holy See, Honduras, Hungary, Iceland, Indonesia, Ireland, Italy, Jamaica, Japan, Kenya, Kyrgyzstan, Laos, Lebanon, Lesotho, Lithuania, Luxembourg, Madagascar, Malawi, Malaysia, Mali, Malta, Mauritania, Mexico, Moldova, Montenegro, Morocco, Mozambique, Netherlands, New Zealand, Nicaragua, Niger, Nigeria, Norway, Palau, Panama, Papua New Guinea, Paraguay, Peru, Philippines, Portugal, Qatar, Republic of the Congo, Samoa, San Marino, São Tomé and Principe, Senegal, Serbia, Seychelles, Sierra Leone, Slovakia, Slovenia, South Africa, Spain, Sudan, Swaziland, Sweden, Switzerland, Tanzania, The former Yugoslav Republic of Macedonia, Timor-Leste, Togo, Uganda, United Kingdom of Great Britain and Northern Ireland, Uruguay, Vanuatu, Venezuela and Zambia. The following 20 states attended the Conference as observers: Colombia, Cyprus, Egypt, Eritrea, Ethiopia, Greece, Iraq, Kazakhstan, Kuwait, Latvia, Libya, Oman, Poland, Romania, Saudi Arabia, Singapore, Thailand, Turkey, Ukraine and Viet Nam. See Diplomatic Conference for the Adoption of a Convention on Cluster Munitions, *Final Document*, document CCM/78, 30 May 2008.

[60] See Diplomatic Conference for the Adoption of a Convention on Cluster Munitions, *Summary Record of Fourth Session of the Plenary*, document CCM/SR/4, 18 June 2008.

[61] Katherine Harrison, "A Gift to the World", Women's International League for Peace and Freedom, 30 May 2008, <www.wilpf.int.ch/disarmament/clustermunitions/Dublin%202008/Friday30May.html>.

[62] See "Japanese taxpayers face heavy burden over cluster bomb ban", *Mainichi Daily News*, 7 June 2008.

[63] See "Why is Finland reluctant to ban cluster bombs", *Mainichi Daily News*, 7 December 2008.

64   "Statement By Ambassador Steffen Kongstad Of Norway, 30 May", 30 May 2008, <www.clustermunitionsdublin.ie/pdf/Norway.pdf>.

65   "Message on the Adoption of the Convention on Cluster Munitions", 30 May 2008, <www.clustermunitionsdublin.ie/pdf/UNSG.pdf>.

66   "Statement by Minister Micheál Martin at Closing Ceremony", 30 May 2008, <www.clustermunitionsdublin.ie/pdf/Ireland.pdf>.

Chapter 11
The end of the beginning

1   "Opening Statement by Thomas Nash, Coordinator, CMC", Convention on Cluster Munitions Signing Conference, Oslo, 3 December 2008, <www.stopclustermunitions.org/wp/wp-content/uploads/2008/12/cmc-opening-statement-thomas-031208.pdf>.

2   See David Miliband and Frank-Walter Steinmeier, "Towards a safer world", *The Guardian*, 3 December 2008.

3   Author's contemporaneous notes.

4   "US stands by refusal to sign cluster bomb ban", *Agence France-Presse*, 2 December 2008.

5   "Remarks by H.E Dr. Thongloun Sisoulith, Deputy Prime Minister, Minister of Foreign Affairs of the Lao PDR at the Signing Ceremony", 3 December 2008, <www.clusterconvention.org/pages/pages_i/documents/LaoPDR.pdf>.

6   See John Borrie and Ashley Thornton, *The Value of Diversity in Multilateral Disarmament Work*, UNIDIR, 2008, pp. 43–4.

7   Philip E. Tetlock, *Expert Political Judgment: How Good Is It? How Can We Know?*, Princeton University Press, 2005.

8   For discussion see Jody Williams and Stephen D. Goose, "Citizen Diplomacy and the Ottawa Process: A Lasting Model?", in Jody Williams, Stephen D. Goose and Mary Wareham (eds), *Banning Landmines: Disarmament, Citizen Diplomacy and Human Security*, Lanham, Rowman and Littlefield, 2008, pp. 181–98.

9   For one examination of these issues see John Borrie, "Cooperation and Defection in the Conference on Disarmament", in John Borrie and Vanessa Martin Randin (eds), *Thinking Outside the Box in Multilateral Disarmament and Arms Control Negotiations*, UNIDIR, 2006, pp. 89–108.

10   For some of the author's views on the subject, see John Borrie, "Tackling Disarmament Challenges", in Jody Williams, Stephen D. Goose and

Mary Wareham (eds), *Banning Landmines: Disarmament, Citizen Diplomacy and Human Security*, Lanham, Rowman and Littlefield, 2008, pp. 263–80.

11   See John Borrie, Maya Brehm, Silvia Cattaneo and David Atwood, "Learn, adapt, succeed: potential lessons from the Ottawa and Oslo processes for other disarmament and arms control challenges", *Disarmament Forum*, no. 2, 2009, pp. 19–25.

12   Statement by Ambassador Steffen Kongstad of Norway, 30 May 2008, p. 1, <www.clustermunitionsdublin.ie/pdf/Norway.pdf>.

13   Brian Rappert and Richard Moyes, "The Prohibition of Cluster Munitions: Setting International Precedents for Defining Inhumanity", *Nonproliferation Review*, vol. 16, no. 2, 2009, pp. 237–56.

14   Ibid., p. 247.

15   Colin King, Ove Dullum and Grethe Østern, *M-85—An Analysis of Reliability*, Norwegian People's Aid, 2007.

16   Author's personal communication with Steffen Kongstad, 27 August 2008.

17   See "Editorial", *Ban Newsletter*, Handicap International, issue 23, September 2008, p. 1.

18   Hew Strachan, "Strategy and the Limitation of War", *Survival*, vol. 50, no. 1, 2008, p. 36.

19   See John Borrie, "Cooperation and Defection in the Conference on Disarmament", in John Borrie and Vanessa Martin Randin (eds), *Thinking Outside the Box in Multilateral Disarmament and Arms Control Negotiations*, UNIDIR, 2006, pp. 89–108.

20   See *Landmine Monitor 2008: Executive Summary*, International Campaign to Ban Landmines, 2008.

21   Article 21, paragraph 2 of the CCW obliges states party to the treaty to "notify the governments of all States not party to this Convention, referred to in paragraph 3 of this Article, of its obligations under the Convention, shall promote the norms it establishes and shall make its best efforts to discourage States not party to this Convention from using cluster munitions".

22   See Brian Rappert, *A Convention Beyond the Convention: Stigma, Humanitarian Standards and the Oslo Process*, Landmine Action, 2008.

23   Indeed, Georgia condemned Russia for using cluster munitions "against civilian population" [sic], quoted in Human Rights Watch, *A Dying Practice: Use of Cluster Munitions by Russia and Georgia in August 2008*, 2009, p. 64. In a colourfully worded letter to a CMC campaigner

dated 18 August 2008, a Russian official wrote, "Do you really suppose that any Russian general could give the order to use one or two cluster munitions to kill 11 people, as you assert, to put his country under international criticism for illegal use of inhuman [sic] weapons? Are you serious?". See letter from Embassy of the Russian Federation in Nepal to Purna Shova Chitrakar. Document on file with the author.

24   Human Rights Watch, *A Dying Practice: Use of Cluster Munitions by Russia and Georgia in August 2008*, 2009, p. 79.

25   Bonnie Docherty, "Cluster munitions convention is an international humanitarian law milestone", *Jurist Online*, 2 June 2008, <http://jurist. law.pitt.edu/hotline/2008/06/cluster-munitions-convention-is.php>.

26   Human Rights Watch, Landmine Action, Landmine Monitor, International Campaign to Ban Landmines and Cluster Munition Coalition, *Banning Cluster Munitions: Government Policy and Practice*, 2009, p. 24.

27   Ibid.

28   "Opening Statement on behalf of Cluster Munition Coalition delivered by Branislav Kapetanovic", Convention on Cluster Munitions Signing Conference, Oslo, 3 December 2008, <www.clusterconvention.org/ pages/pages_i/documents/CMCopeningBK.pdf>.

29   In Laos' case there is no chance that its territory will be cleared within the next decade of all or even most of the tens of millions of submunitions thought to still remain there even if clearance efforts increase. However, there is widespread international recognition that Laos is a special case because of the scale of its submunition contamination from US bombing, but that its membership of the CCM is the best available means to focus greater donor attention and resources to reduce the ERW hazard to civilians there.

30   Brian Rappert, *A Convention Beyond the Convention: Stigma, humanitarian standards and the Oslo Process*, Landmine Action, 2008, p. 4.

31   See Mary Wareham, "The role of *Landmine Monitor* in promoting and monitoring compliance with the 1997 Anti-Personnel Mine Ban Convention", in John Borrie and Vanessa Martin Randin (eds), *Disarmament as Humanitarian Action: From Perspective to Practice*, UNIDIR, 2006, pp. 79–108.

32   See Human Rights Watch, Landmine Action, Landmine Monitor, International Campaign to Ban Landmines and Cluster Munition Coalition, *Banning Cluster Munitions: Government Policy and Practice*, 2009.

[33]   Kenneth Rutherford, Nerina Cevra and Tracey Begley, "Connecting the Dots: The Ottawa Convention and the CCM", *The Journal of ERW and Mine Action*, vol. 12, no. 2, 2009.

[34]   "Closing remarks: Statement by Mr. Markus Reiterer, Austria, Co-Chair of the Standing Committee on Victim Assistance and Socio-Economic Reintegration", Eighth Meeting of the States Parties to the Convention on the Prohibition of the Use, Stockpiling, Production and Transfer of Anti-Personnel Mines and on Their Destruction, Jordan, 18–22 November 2007, p. 4, <www.apminebanconvention.org/fileadmin/pdf/mbc/MSP/8MSP/day4/8MSP-Item11d-21Nov2007-AustriaClosing-en.pdf>.

[35]   The CCW, for instance, saw presentations as recent as June 2007 on the military utility and role of cluster munitions. See Col. Gary S. Kinne, US Army, "The Ongoing Military Utility and Role of Cluster Munitions", presented to the Convention on Certain Conventional Weapons, Geneva, Switzerland, 19 June 2007. Document on file with the author.

[36]   This scenario is illustrative, and is not attributed to Col. Gary S. Kinne.

[37]   See Louis Maresca, "Cluster munitions: moving toward specific regulation", *Disarmament Forum*, no. 4, 2006, pp. 27–34.

[38]   Rupert Smith, *The Utility of Force: The Art of War in the Modern World*, Allen Lane, 2005, p. xiii.

[39]   This was an impression not always helped by media reports. For instance, one newspaper story after the Dublin negotiations concluded reported incorrectly that "Britain, France, Germany and Sweden, which all use or manufacture similar weapons, pushed through amendments to the treaty to exclude them because of their size and ability to self-destruct". See Michael Smith, "Gordon Brown blows a loophole in ban on cluster bombs", *The Times*, 1 June 2008.

[40]   CCM article 12 provides generically for review.

[41]   Goff said, "It is, however, now time to put the fence at the top of the cliff, and not simply be the ambulance at the bottom. We need to eliminate the use of cluster munitions which have an unacceptable effect on civilian populations". See Statement by Phil Goff, Wellington Conference on Cluster Munitions, 18 February 2008. <www.mfat.govt.nz/clustermunitionswellington/conference-documents/MDAC-opening-address.pdf>.

[42]   This is an established principle of customary international law and reflected in articles 48–52 of Additional Protocol I to the Geneva Conventions.

43   Tommaso Di Ruzza, "The Convention on Cluster Munitions: Towards a Balance between Humanitarian and Military Considerations?", *Military Law and the Law of War Review*, vol. 47, no. 3–4, 2008, p. 441.

44   Security Council, *Report of the Secretary-General on the protection of civilians in armed conflict*, UN document S/2009/277, 29 May 2009, p. 9, para. 36.

45   See Security Council, UN document S/PV.6151, 26 June 2009.

46   See Richard Moyes, *Explosive Violence: The Problem of Explosive Weapons*, Landmine Action, 2009.

47   Richard Moyes, "Explosive violence in areas of civilian concentration", presentation at the meeting "'Cities are not targets!' towards a prohibition on the use of explosive force in populated areas", 28 October 2008, p. 2, <www.landmineaction.org/resources/Explosive%20violence%20in%20areas%20of%20civilian%20concentration%20-%20presentation%2028%20Nov%2008.pdf>.

48   These steps, and the issues around the use of explosive weapons in populated areas are comprehensively explored in Richard Moyes, *Explosive Violence: The Problem of Explosive Weapons*, Landmine Action, 2009.

OSLO CONFERENCE ON CLUSTER MUNITIONS, 22–23 FEBRUARY 2007

Declaration

A group of States, United Nations Organisations, the International Committee of the Red Cross, the Cluster Munitions Coalition and other humanitarian organisations met in Oslo on 22 – 23 February 2007 to discuss how to effectively address the humanitarian problems caused by cluster munitions.

Recognising the grave consequences caused by the use of cluster munitions and the need for immediate action, states commit themselves to:

1. Conclude by 2008 a legally binding international instrument that will:

   (i)   prohibit the use, production, transfer and stockpiling of cluster

   munitions that cause unacceptable harm to civilians, and

   (ii)   establish a framework for cooperation and assistance that ensures adequate provision of care and rehabilitation to survivors and their communities, clearance of contaminated areas, risk education and destruction of stockpiles of prohibited cluster munitions.

2. Consider taking steps at the national level to address these problems.

3. Continue to address the humanitarian challenges posed by cluster munitions within the framework of international humanitarian law and in all relevant fora.

4. Meet again to continue their work, including in Lima in May/June and Vienna in November/December 2007, and in Dublin in early 2008, and welcome the announcement of Belgium to organise a regional meeting.

Oslo, 23 February 2007

DECLARATION OF THE
WELLINGTON CONFERENCE ON CLUSTER MUNITIONS

States met in Wellington from February 18 to 22, 2008, to pursue an enduring solution to the grave humanitarian consequences caused by the use of cluster munitions. They are convinced that this solution must include the conclusion in 2008 of a legally binding international instrument prohibiting cluster munitions that cause unacceptable harm to civilians.

In that spirit they affirm that the essential elements of such an instrument should include:

- A prohibition on the use, production, transfer and stockpiling of cluster munitions that cause unacceptable harm to civilians,

- A framework for cooperation and assistance that ensures adequate provision of care and rehabilitation to survivors and their communities, clearance of contaminated areas, risk education, and destruction of stockpiles.

The following States:

encouraged by the work of the Wellington Conference, and previous Conferences in Vienna, Lima and Oslo;

encouraged further by numerous national and regional initiatives, including meetings in Brussels, Belgrade and San José, and measures taken to address the humanitarian impact of cluster munitions;

encouraged by the active support given to this subject by the United Nations, and in other fora;

encouraged, finally, by the active support of the International Committee of the Red Cross, the Cluster Munition Coalition and numerous other Non-Governmental Organisations;

welcome the convening of a Diplomatic Conference by the Government of Ireland in Dublin on 19 May 2008 to negotiate and adopt a legally binding instrument prohibiting cluster munitions that cause unacceptable harm to civilians;

also welcome the important work done by participants engaged in the cluster munitions process on the text of a draft Cluster Munitions Convention, dated 21 January 2008, which contains the essential elements identified above and decide to forward it as the basic proposal for consideration at the Dublin Diplomatic Conference, together with other relevant proposals including those contained in the compendium attached to this Declaration and those which may be put forward there;

affirm their objective of concluding the negotiation of such an instrument prohibiting cluster munitions that cause unacceptable harm to civilians in Dublin in May 2008;

invite all other States to join them in their efforts towards concluding such an instrument.

CONVENTION ON CLUSTER MUNITIONS DUBLIN 19–30 MAY 2008

The States Parties to this Convention,

Deeply concerned that civilian populations and individual civilians continue to bear the brunt of armed conflict,

Determined to put an end for all time to the suffering and casualties caused by cluster munitions at the time of their use, when they fail to function as intended or when they are abandoned,

Concerned that cluster munition remnants kill or maim civilians, including women and children, obstruct economic and social development, including through the loss of livelihood, impede post-conflict rehabilitation and reconstruction, delay or prevent the return of refugees and internally displaced persons, can negatively impact on national and international peace-building and humanitarian assistance efforts, and have other severe consequences that can persist for many years after use,

Deeply concerned also at the dangers presented by the large national stockpiles of cluster munitions retained for operational use and *determined* to ensure their rapid destruction,

Believing it necessary to contribute effectively in an efficient, coordinated manner to resolving the challenge of removing cluster munition remnants located throughout the world, and to ensure their destruction,

Determined also to ensure the full realisation of the rights of all cluster munition victims and *recognising* their inherent dignity,

Resolved to do their utmost in providing assistance to cluster munition victims, including medical care, rehabilitation and psychological support, as well as providing for their social and economic inclusion,

Recognising the need to provide age- and gender-sensitive assistance to cluster munition victims and to address the special needs of vulnerable groups,

Bearing in mind the Convention on the Rights of Persons with Disabilities which, *inter alia*, requires that States Parties to that Convention undertake to ensure and promote the full realisation of all human rights and fundamental freedoms of all persons with disabilities without discrimination of any kind on the basis of disability,

Mindful of the need to coordinate adequately efforts undertaken in various fora to address the rights and needs of victims of various types of weapons, and *resolved* to avoid discrimination among victims of various types of weapons,

Reaffirming that in cases not covered by this Convention or by other international agreements, civilians and combatants remain under the protection and authority of the principles of international law, derived from established custom, from the principles of humanity and from the dictates of public conscience,

Resolved also that armed groups distinct from the armed forces of a State shall not, under any circumstances, be permitted to engage in any activity prohibited to a State Party to this Convention,

Welcoming the very broad international support for the international norm prohibiting anti-personnel mines, enshrined in the 1997 Convention on the Prohibition of the Use, Stockpiling, Production and Transfer of Anti-Personnel Mines and on Their Destruction,

Welcoming also the adoption of the Protocol on Explosive Remnants of War, annexed to the Convention on Prohibitions or Restrictions on the Use of Certain Conventional Weapons Which May be Deemed to be Excessively Injurious or to Have Indiscriminate Effects, and its entry into force on 12 November 2006, and *wishing* to enhance the protection of civilians from the effects of cluster munition remnants in post-conflict environments,

Bearing in mind also United Nations Security Council Resolution 1325 on women, peace and security and United Nations Security Council Resolution 1612 on children in armed conflict,

Welcoming further the steps taken nationally, regionally and globally in recent years aimed at prohibiting, restricting or suspending the use, stockpiling, production and transfer of cluster munitions,

Stressing the role of public conscience in furthering the principles of humanity as evidenced by the global call for an end to civilian suffering caused by cluster munitions and *recognising* the efforts to that end undertaken by the United Nations, the International Committee of the Red Cross, the Cluster Munition Coalition and numerous other non-governmental organisations around the world,

Reaffirming the Declaration of the Oslo Conference on Cluster Munitions, by which, *inter alia*, States recognised the grave consequences caused by the use of cluster munitions and committed themselves to conclude by 2008 a legally binding instrument that would prohibit the use, production, transfer and stockpiling of cluster munitions that cause unacceptable harm to civilians, and would establish a framework for cooperation and assistance that ensures adequate provision of care and rehabilitation for victims, clearance of contaminated areas, risk reduction education and destruction of stockpiles,

Emphasising the desirability of attracting the adherence of all States to this Convention, and *determined* to work strenuously towards the promotion of its universalisation and its full implementation,

Basing themselves on the principles and rules of international humanitarian law, in particular the principle that the right of parties to an armed conflict to choose methods or means of warfare is not unlimited, and the rules that the parties to a conflict shall at all times distinguish between the civilian population and combatants and between civilian objects and military objectives and accordingly direct their operations against military objectives only, that in the conduct of military operations constant care shall be taken to spare the civilian population, civilians and civilian objects and that the civilian population and individual civilians enjoy general protection against dangers arising from military operations,

HAVE AGREED as follows:

Article 1
General obligations and scope of application

1.　Each State Party undertakes never under any circumstances to:
　(a)　Use cluster munitions;
　(b)　Develop, produce, otherwise acquire, stockpile, retain or transfer to anyone, directly or indirectly, cluster munitions;
　(c)　Assist, encourage or induce anyone to engage in any activity prohibited to a State Party under this Convention.

2.   Paragraph 1 of this Article applies, *mutatis mutandis*, to explosive bomblets that are specifically designed to be dispersed or released from dispensers affixed to aircraft.

3.   This Convention does not apply to mines.

Article 2
Definitions

For the purposes of this Convention:

1.   **"Cluster munition victims"** means all persons who have been killed or suffered physical or psychological injury, economic loss, social marginalisation or substantial impairment of the realisation of their rights caused by the use of cluster munitions. They include those persons directly impacted by cluster munitions as well as their affected families and communities;

2.   **"Cluster munition"** means a conventional munition that is designed to disperse or release explosive submunitions each weighing less than 20 kilograms, and includes those explosive submunitions. It does not mean the following:

(a)   A munition or submunition designed to dispense flares, smoke, pyrotechnics or chaff; or a munition designed exclusively for an air defence role;

(b)   A munition or submunition designed to produce electrical or electronic effects;

(c)   A munition that, in order to avoid indiscriminate area effects and the risks posed by unexploded submunitions, has all of the following characteristics:

(i)   Each munition contains fewer than ten explosive submunitions;

(ii)   Each explosive submunition weighs more than four kilograms;

(iii)   Each explosive submunition is designed to detect and engage a single target object;

(iv)   Each explosive submunition is equipped with an electronic self-destruction mechanism;

(v)   Each explosive submunition is equipped with an electronic self-deactivating feature;

3. **"Explosive submunition"** means aconventionalmunition that in order to perform its task is dispersed or released by a cluster munition and is designed to function by detonating an explosive charge prior to, on or after impact;

4. **"Failed cluster munition"** means a cluster munition that has been fired, dropped, launched, projected or otherwise delivered and which should have dispersed or released its explosive submunitions but failed to do so;

5. **"Unexploded submunition"** means an explosive submunition that has been dispersed or released by, or otherwise separated from, a cluster munition and has failed to explode as intended;

6. **"Abandoned cluster munitions"** means cluster munitions or explosive submunitions that have not been used and that have been left behind or dumped, and that are no longer under the control of the party that left them behind or dumped them. They may or may not have been prepared for use;

7. **"Cluster munition remnants"** means failed cluster munitions, abandoned cluster munitions, unexploded submunitions and unexploded bomblets;

8. **"Transfer"** involves, in addition to the physical movement of cluster munitions into or from national territory, the transfer of title to and control over cluster munitions, but does not involve the transfer of territory containing cluster munition remnants;

9. **"Self-destruction mechanism"** means an incorporated automatically-functioning mechanism which is in addition to the primary initiating mechanism of the munition and which secures the destruction of the munition into which it is incorporated;

10. **"Self-deactivating"** means automatically rendering a munition inoperable by means of the irreversible exhaustion of a component, for example a battery, that is essential to the operation of the munition;

11. **"Cluster munition contaminated area"** means an area known or suspected to contain cluster munition remnants;

12. **"Mine"** means a munition designed to be placed under, on or near the ground or other surface area and to be exploded by the presence, proximity or contact of a person or a vehicle;

13. **"Explosive bomblet"** means a conventional munition, weighing less than 20 kilograms, which is not self-propelled and which, in order to perform its task, is dispersed or released by a dispenser, and is designed to function by detonating an explosive charge prior to, on or after impact;

14. **"Dispenser"** means a container that is designed to disperse or release explosive bomblets and which is affixed to an aircraft at the time of dispersal or release;

15. **"Unexploded bomblet"** means an explosive bomblet that has been dispersed, released or otherwise separated from a dispenser and has failed to explode as intended.

Article 3
Storage and stockpile destruction

1. Each State Party shall, in accordance with national regulations, separate all cluster munitions under its jurisdiction and control from munitions retained for operational use and mark them for the purpose of destruction.

2. Each State Party undertakes to destroy or ensure the destruction of all cluster munitions referred to in paragraph 1 of this Article as soon as possible but not later than eight years after the entry into force of this Convention for that State Party. Each State Party undertakes to ensure that destruction methods comply with applicable international standards for protecting public health and the environment.

3. If a State Party believes that it will be unable to destroy or ensure the destruction of all cluster munitions referred to in paragraph 1 of this Article within eight years of entry into force of this Convention for that State Party it may submit a request to a Meeting of States Parties or a Review Conference for an extension of the deadline for completing the destruction of such cluster munitions by a period of up to four years. A State Party may, in exceptional circumstances, request additional extensions of up to four years. The requested extensions shall not exceed the number of

years strictly necessary for that State Party to complete its obligations under paragraph 2 of this Article.

4.   Each request for an extension shall set out:

(a)   The duration of the proposed extension;

(b)   A detailed explanation of the proposed extension, including the financial and technical means available to or required by the State Party for the destruction of all cluster munitions referred to in paragraph 1 of this Article and, where applicable, the exceptional circumstances justifying it;

(c)   A plan for how and when stockpile destruction will be completed;

(d)   The quantity and type of cluster munitions and explosive submunitions held at the entry into force of this Convention for that State Party and any additional cluster munitions or explosive submunitions discovered after such entry into force;

(e)   The quantity and type of cluster munitions and explosive submunitions destroyed during the period referred to in paragraph 2 of this Article; and

(f)   The quantity and type of cluster munitions and explosive submunitions remaining to be destroyed during the proposed extension and the annual destruction rate expected to be achieved.

5.   The Meeting of States Parties or the Review Conference shall, taking into consideration the factors referred to in paragraph 4 of this Article, assess the request and decide by a majority of votes of States Parties present and voting whether to grant the request for an extension. The States Parties may decide to grant a shorter extension than that requested and may propose benchmarks for the extension, as appropriate. A request for an extension shall be submitted a minimum of nine months prior to the Meeting of States Parties or the Review Conference at which it is to be considered.

6.   Notwithstanding the provisions of Article 1 of this Convention, the retention or acquisition of a limited number of cluster munitions and explosive submunitions for the development of and training in cluster munition and explosive submunition detection, clearance or destruction techniques, or for the development of cluster munition counter-measures, is permitted. The amount of explosive submunitions retained or acquired

shall not exceed the minimum number absolutely necessary for these purposes.

7.   Notwithstanding the provisions of Article 1 of this Convention, the transfer of cluster munitions to another State Party for the purpose of destruction, as well as for the purposes described in paragraph 6 of this Article, is permitted.

8.   States Parties retaining, acquiring or transferring cluster munitions or explosive submunitions for the purposes described in paragraphs 6 and 7 of this Article shall submit a detailed report on the planned and actual use of these cluster munitions and explosive submunitions and their type, quantity and lot numbers. If cluster munitions or explosive submunitions are transferred to another State Party for these purposes, the report shall include reference to the receiving party. Such a report shall be prepared for each year during which a State Party retained, acquired or transferred cluster munitions or explosive submunitions and shall be submitted to the Secretary-General of the United Nations no later than 30 April of the following year.

Article 4
*Clearance and destruction of cluster munition remnants
and risk reduction education*

1.   Each State Party undertakes to clear and destroy, or ensure the clearance and destruction of, cluster munition remnants located in cluster munition contaminated areas under its jurisdiction or control, as follows:

(a)   Where cluster munition remnants are located in areas under its jurisdiction or control at the date of entry into force of this Convention for that State Party, such clearance and destruction shall be completed as soon as possible but not later than ten years from that date;

(b)   Where, after entry into force of this Convention for that State Party, cluster munitions have become cluster munition remnants located in areas under its jurisdiction or control, such clearance and destruction must be completed as soon as possible but not later than ten years after the end of the active hostilities during which such cluster munitions became cluster munition remnants; and

(c) Upon fulfilling either of its obligations set out in sub-paragraphs (a) and (b) of this paragraph, that State Party shall make a declaration of compliance to the next Meeting of States Parties.

2. In fulfilling its obligations under paragraph 1 of this Article, each State Party shall take the following measures as soon as possible, taking into consideration the provisions of Article 6 of this Convention regarding international cooperation and assistance:

(a) Survey, assess and record the threat posed by cluster munition remnants, making every effort to identify all cluster munition contaminated areas under its jurisdiction or control;

(b) Assess and prioritise needs in terms of marking, protection of civilians, clearance and destruction, and take steps to mobilise resources and develop a national plan to carry out these activities, building, where appropriate, upon existing structures, experiences and methodologies;

(c) Take all feasible steps to ensure that all cluster munition contaminated areas under its jurisdiction or control are perimeter-marked, monitored and protected by fencing or other means to ensure the effective exclusion of civilians. Warning signs based on methods of marking readily recognisable by the affected community should be utilised in the marking of suspected hazardous areas. Signs and other hazardous area boundary markers should, as far as possible, be visible, legible, durable and resistant to environmental effects and should clearly identify which side of the marked boundary is considered to be within the cluster munition contaminated areas and which side is considered to be safe;

(d) Clear and destroy all cluster munition remnants located in areas under its jurisdiction or control; and

(e) Conduct risk reduction education to ensure awareness among civilians living in or around cluster munition contaminated areas of the risks posed by such remnants.

3. In conducting the activities referred to in paragraph 2 of this Article, each State Party shall take into account international standards, including the International Mine Action Standards (IMAS).

4. This paragraph shall apply in cases in which cluster munitions have been used or abandoned by one State Party prior to entry into force of this Convention for that State Party and have become cluster munition remnants that are located in areas under the jurisdiction or control of another State Party at the time of entry into force of this Convention for the latter.

    (a)   In such cases, upon entry into force of this Convention for both States Parties, the former State Party is strongly encouraged to provide, *inter alia*, technical, financial, material or human resources assistance to the latter State Party, either bilaterally or through a mutually agreed third party, including through the United Nations system or other relevant organisations, to facilitate the marking, clearance and destruction of such cluster munition remnants.

    (b)   Such assistance shall include, where available, information on types and quantities of the cluster munitions used, precise locations of cluster munition strikes and areas in which cluster munition remnants are known to be located.

5. If a State Party believes that it will be unable to clear and destroy or ensure the clearance and destruction of all cluster munition remnants referred to in paragraph 1 of this Article within ten years of the entry into force of this Convention for that State Party, it may submit a request to a Meeting of States Parties or a Review Conference for an extension of the deadline for completing the clearance and destruction of such cluster munition remnants by a period of up to five years. The requested extension shall not exceed the number of years strictly necessary for that State Party to complete its obligations under paragraph 1 of this Article.

6. A request for an extension shall be submitted to a Meeting of States Parties or a Review Conference prior to the expiry of the time period referred to in paragraph 1 of this Article for that State Party. Each request shall be submitted a minimum of nine months prior to the Meeting of States Parties or Review Conference at which it is to be considered. Each request shall set out:

    (a)   The duration of the proposed extension;

    (b)   A detailed explanation of the reasons for the proposed extension, including the financial and technical means available to and required by the State Party for the clearance and destruction of all cluster munition remnants during the proposed extension;

(c)   The preparation of future work and the status of work already conducted under national clearance and demining programmes during the initial ten year period referred to in paragraph 1 of this Article and any subsequent extensions;

(d)   The total area containing cluster munition remnants at the time of entry into force of this Convention for that State Party and any additional areas containing cluster munition remnants discovered after such entry into force;

(e)   The total area containing cluster munition remnants cleared since entry into force of this Convention;

(f)   The total area containing cluster munition remnants remaining to be cleared during the proposed extension;

(g)   The circumstances that have impeded the ability of the State Party to destroy all cluster munition remnants located in areas under its jurisdiction or control during the initial ten year period referred to in paragraph 1 of this Article, and those that may impede this ability during the proposed extension;

(h)   The humanitarian, social, economic and environmental implications of the proposed extension; and

(i)   Any other information relevant to the request for the proposed extension.

7.   The Meeting of States Parties or the Review Conference shall, taking into consideration the factors referred to in paragraph 6 of this Article, including, *inter alia,* the quantities of cluster munition remnants reported, assess the request and decide by a majority of votes of States Parties present and voting whether to grant the request for an extension. The States Parties may decide to grant a shorter extension than that requested and may propose benchmarks for the extension, as appropriate.

8.   Such an extension may be renewed by a period of up to five years upon the submission of a new request, in accordance with paragraphs 5, 6 and 7 of this Article. In requesting a further extension a State Party shall submit relevant additional information on what has been undertaken during the previous extension granted pursuant to this Article.

Article 5
Victim assistance

1.   Each State Party with respect to cluster munition victims in areas under its jurisdiction or control shall, in accordance with applicable international humanitarian and human rights law, adequately provide age- and gender-sensitive assistance, including medical care, rehabilitation and psychological support, as well as provide for their social and economic inclusion. Each State Party shall make every effort to collect reliable relevant data with respect to cluster munition victims.

2.   In fulfilling its obligations under paragraph 1 of this Article each State Party shall:

(a)   Assess the needs of cluster munition victims;

(b)   Develop, implement and enforce any necessary national laws and policies;

(c)   Develop a national plan and budget, including timeframes to carry out these activities, with a view to incorporating them within the existing national disability, development and human rights frameworks and mechanisms, while respecting the specific role and contribution of relevant actors;

(d)   Take steps to mobilise national and international resources;

(e)   Not discriminate against or among cluster munition victims, or between cluster munition victims and those who have suffered injuries or disabilities from other causes; differences in treatment should be based only on medical, rehabilitative, psychological or socio-economic needs;

(f)   Closely consult with and actively involve cluster munition victims and their representative organisations;

(g)   Designate a focal point within the government for coordination of matters relating to the implementation of this Article; and

(h)   Strive to incorporate relevant guidelines and good practices including in the areas of medical care, rehabilitation and psychological support, as well as social and economic inclusion.

Article 6
International cooperation and assistance

1.   In fulfilling its obligations under this Convention each State Party has the right to seek and receive assistance.

2.   Each State Party in a position to do so shall provide technical, material and financial assistance to States Parties affected by cluster munitions, aimed at the implementation of the obligations of this Convention. Such assistance may be provided, *inter alia*, through the United Nations system, international, regional or national organisations or institutions, non-governmental organisations or institutions, or on a bilateral basis.

3.   Each State Party undertakes to facilitate and shall have the right to participate in the fullest possible exchange of equipment and scientific and technological information concerning the implementation of this Convention. The States Parties shall not impose undue restrictions on the provision and receipt of clearance and other such equipment and related technological information for humanitarian purposes.

4.   In addition to any obligations it may have pursuant to paragraph 4 of Article 4 of this Convention, each State Party in a position to do so shall provide assistance for clearance and destruction of cluster munition remnants and information concerning various means and technologies related to clearance of cluster munitions, as well as lists of experts, expert agencies or national points of contact on clearance and destruction of cluster munition remnants and related activities.

5.   Each State Party in a position to do so shall provide assistance for the destruction of stockpiled cluster munitions, and shall also provide assistance to identify, assess and prioritise needs and practical measures in terms of marking, risk reduction education, protection of civilians and clearance and destruction as provided in Article 4 of this Convention.

6.   Where, after entry into force of this Convention, cluster munitions have become cluster munition remnants located in areas under the jurisdiction or control of a State Party, each State Party in a position to do so shall urgently provide emergency assistance to the affected State Party.

7.   Each State Party in a position to do so shall provide assistance for the implementation of the obligations referred to in Article 5 of this Convention to adequately provide age- and gender-sensitive assistance, including medical care, rehabilitation and psychological support, as well as provide for social and economic inclusion of cluster munition victims. Such assistance may be provided, *inter alia*, through the United Nations system, international, regional or national organisations or institutions, the International Committee of the Red Cross, national Red Cross and Red Crescent Societies and their International Federation, non-governmental organisations or on a bilateral basis.

8.   Each State Party in a position to do so shall provide assistance to contribute to the economic and social recovery needed as a result of cluster munition use in affected States Parties.

9.   Each State Party in a position to do so may contribute to relevant trust funds in order to facilitate the provision of assistance under this Article.

10.   Each State Party that seeks and receives assistance shall take all appropriate measures in order to facilitate the timely and effective implementation of this Convention, including facilitation of the entry and exit of personnel, materiel and equipment, in a manner consistent with national laws and regulations, taking into consideration international best practices.

11.   Each State Party may, with the purpose of developing a national action plan, request the United Nations system, regional organisations, other States Parties or other competent intergovernmental or non-governmental institutions to assist its authorities to determine, *inter alia*:

(a)   The nature and extent of cluster munition remnants located in areas under its jurisdiction or control;

(b)   The financial, technological and human resources required for the implementation of the plan;

(c)   The time estimated as necessary to clear and destroy all cluster munition remnants located in areas under its jurisdiction or control;

(d)   Risk reduction education programmes and awareness activities to reduce the incidence of injuries or deaths caused by cluster munition remnants;

(e)   Assistance to cluster munition victims; and

(f)   The coordination relationship between the government of the State Party concerned and the relevant governmental, intergovernmental or non-governmental entities that will work in the implementation of the plan.

12.   States Parties giving and receiving assistance under the provisions of this Article shall cooperate with a view to ensuring the full and prompt implementation of agreed assistance programmes.

Article 7
Transparency measures

1.   Each State Party shall report to the Secretary-General of the United Nations as soon as practicable, and in any event not later than 180 days after the entry into force of this Convention for that State Party, on:

(a)   The national implementation measures referred to in Article 9 of this Convention;

(b)   The total of all cluster munitions, including explosive submunitions, referred to in paragraph 1 of Article 3 of this Convention, to include a breakdown of their type, quantity and, if possible, lot numbers of each type;

(c)   The technical characteristics of each type of cluster munition produced by that State Party prior to entry into force of this Convention for it, to the extent known, and those currently owned or possessed by it, giving, where reasonably possible, such categories of information as may facilitate identification and clearance of cluster munitions; at a minimum, this information shall include the dimensions, fusing, explosive content, metallic content, colour photographs and other information that may facilitate the clearance of cluster munition remnants;

(d)   The status and progress of programmes for the conversion or decommissioning of production facilities for cluster munitions;

(e)   The status and progress of programmes for the destruction, in accordance with Article 3 of this Convention, of cluster munitions, including explosive submunitions, with details of the methods that will be used in destruction, the location of all destruction sites and the applicable safety and environmental standards to be observed;

(f)   The types and quantities of cluster munitions, including explosive submunitions, destroyed in accordance with Article 3 of this Convention, including details of the methods of destruction used, the location of the destruction sites and the applicable safety and environmental standards observed;

(g)   Stockpiles of cluster munitions, including explosive submunitions, discovered after reported completion of the programme referred to in sub-paragraph (e) of this paragraph, and plans for their destruction in accordance with Article 3 of this Convention;

(h)   To the extent possible, the size and location of all cluster munition contaminated areas under its jurisdiction or control, to include as much detail as possible regarding the type and quantity of each type of cluster munition remnant in each such area and when they were used;

(i)   The status and progress of programmes for the clearance and destruction of all types and quantities of cluster munition remnants cleared and destroyed in accordance with Article 4 of this Convention, to include the size and location of the cluster munition contaminated area cleared and a breakdown of the quantity of each type of cluster munition remnant cleared and destroyed;

(j)   The measures taken to provide risk reduction education and, in particular, an immediate and effective warning to civilians living in cluster munition contaminated areas under its jurisdiction or control;

(k)   The status and progress of implementation of its obligations under Article 5 of this Convention to adequately provide age- and gender- sensitive assistance, including medical care, rehabilitation and psychological support, as well as provide for social and economic inclusion of cluster munition victims and to collect reliable relevant data with respect to cluster munition victims;

(l)   The name and contact details of the institutions mandated to provide information and to carry out the measures described in this paragraph;

(m)   The amount of national resources, including financial, material or in kind, allocated to the implementation of Articles 3, 4 and 5 of this Convention; and (n)　　The amounts, types and destinations of international cooperation and assistance provided under Article 6 of this Convention.

2.　　The information provided in accordance with paragraph 1 of this Article shall be updated by the States Parties annually, covering the previous calendar year, and reported to the Secretary-General of the United Nations not later than 30 April of each year.

3.　　The Secretary-General of the United Nations shall transmit all such reports received to the States Parties.

Article 8
Facilitation and clarification of compliance

1.　　The States Parties agree to consult and cooperate with each other regarding the implementation of the provisions of this Convention and to work together in a spirit of cooperation to facilitate compliance by States Parties with their obligations under this Convention.

2.　　If one or more States Parties wish to clarify and seek to resolve questions relating to a matter of compliance with the provisions of this Convention by another State Party, it may submit, through the Secretary-General of the United Nations, a Request for Clarification of that matter to that State Party. Such a request shall be accompanied by all appropriate information. Each State Party shall refrain from unfounded Requests for Clarification, care being taken to avoid abuse. A State Party that receives a Request for Clarification shall provide, through the Secretary-General of the United Nations, within 28 days to the requesting State Party all information that would assist in clarifying the matter.

3.　　If the requesting State Party does not receive a response through the Secretary-General of the United Nations within that time period, or deems the response to the Request for Clarification to be unsatisfactory, it may submit the matter through the Secretary-General of the United Nations to the next Meeting of States Parties. The Secretary-General of the United Nations shall transmit the submission, accompanied by all appropriate information pertaining to the Request for Clarification, to all States Parties. All such information shall be presented to the requested State Party which shall have the right to respond.

4.   Pending the convening of any Meeting of States Parties, any of the States Parties concerned may request the Secretary-General of the United Nations to exercise his or her good offices to facilitate the clarification requested.

5.   Where a matter has been submitted to it pursuant to paragraph 3 of this Article, the Meeting of States Parties shall first determine whether to consider that matter further, taking into account all information submitted by the States Parties concerned. If it does so determine, the Meeting of States Parties may suggest to the States Parties concerned ways and means further to clarify or resolve the matter under consideration, including the initiation of appropriate procedures in conformity with international law. In circumstances where the issue at hand is determined to be due to circumstances beyond the control of the requested State Party, the Meeting of States Parties may recommend appropriate measures, including the use of cooperative measures referred to in Article 6 of this Convention.

6.   In addition to the procedures provided for in paragraphs 2 to 5 of this Article, the Meeting of States Parties may decide to adopt such other general procedures or specific mechanisms for clarification of compliance, including facts, and resolution of instances of non-compliance with the provisions of this Convention as it deems appropriate.

Article 9
National implementation measures

Each State Party shall take all appropriate legal, administrative and other measures to implement this Convention, including the imposition of penal sanctions to prevent and suppress any activity prohibited to a State Party under this Convention undertaken by persons or on territory under its jurisdiction or control.

Article 10
Settlement of disputes

1.   When a dispute arises between two or more States Parties relating to the interpretation or application of this Convention, the States Parties concerned shall consult together with a view to the expeditious settlement of the dispute by negotiation or by other peaceful means of their choice,

including recourse to the Meeting of States Parties and referral to the International Court of Justice in conformity with the Statute of the Court.

2.   The Meeting of States Parties may contribute to the settlement of the dispute by whatever means it deems appropriate, including offering its good offices, calling upon the States Parties concerned to start the settlement procedure of their choice and recommending a time-limit for any agreed procedure.

Article 11
Meetings of States Parties

1.   The States Parties shall meet regularly in order to consider and, where necessary, take decisions in respect of any matter with regard to the application or implementation of this Convention, including:

(a)   The operation and status of this Convention;
(b)   Matters arising from the reports submitted under the provisions of this Convention;
(c)   International cooperation and assistance in accordance with Article 6 of this Convention;
(d)   The development of technologies to clear cluster munition remnants;
(e)   Submissions of States Parties under Articles 8 and 10 of this Convention; and
(f)   Submissions of States Parties as provided for in Articles 3 and 4 of this Convention.

2.   The first Meeting of States Parties shall be convened by the Secretary-General of the United Nations within one year of entry into force of this Convention. The subsequent meetings shall be convened by the Secretary-General of the United Nations annually until the first Review Conference.

3.   States not party to this Convention, as well as the United Nations, other relevant international organisations or institutions, regional organisations, the International Committee of the Red Cross, the International Federation of Red Cross and Red Crescent Societies and relevant non-governmental organisations may be invited to attend these meetings as observers in accordance with the agreed rules of procedure.

Article 12
Review Conferences

1.   A Review Conference shall be convened by the Secretary-General of the United Nations five years after the entry into force of this Convention. Further Review Conferences shall be convened by the Secretary-General of the United Nations if so requested by one or more States Parties, provided that the interval between Review Conferences shall in no case be less than five years. All States Parties to this Convention shall be invited to each Review Conference.

2.   The purpose of the Review Conference shall be:
   (a)   To review the operation and status of this Convention;
   (b)   To consider the need for and the interval between further Meetings of States Parties referred to in paragraph 2 of Article 11 of this Convention; and
   (c)   To take decisions on submissions of States Parties as provided for in Articles 3 and 4 of this Convention.

3.   States not party to this Convention, as well as the United Nations, other relevant international organisations or institutions, regional organisations, the International Committee of the Red Cross, the International Federation of Red Cross and Red Crescent Societies and relevant non-governmental organisations may be invited to attend each Review Conference as observers in accordance with the agreed rules of procedure.

Article 13
Amendments

1.   At any time after its entry into force any State Party may propose amendments to this Convention. Any proposal for an amendment shall be communicated to the Secretary-General of the United Nations, who shall circulate it to all States Parties and shall seek their views on whether an Amendment Conference should be convened to consider the proposal. If a majority of the States Parties notify the Secretary-General of the United Nations no later than 90 days after its circulation that they support further consideration of the proposal, the Secretary-General of the United Nations shall convene an Amendment Conference to which all States Parties shall be invited.

2.   States not party to this Convention, as well as the United Nations, other relevant international organisations or institutions, regional organisations, the International Committee of the Red Cross, the International Federation of Red Cross and Red Crescent Societies and relevant non-governmental organisations may be invited to attend each Amendment Conference as observers in accordance with the agreed rules of procedure.

3.   The Amendment Conference shall be held immediately following a Meeting of States Parties or a Review Conference unless a majority of the States Parties request that it be held earlier.

4.   Any amendment to this Convention shall be adopted by a majority of two-thirds of the States Parties present and voting at the Amendment Conference. The Depositary shall communicate any amendment so adopted to all States.

5.   An amendment to this Convention shall enter into force for States Parties that have accepted the amendment on the date of deposit of acceptances by a majority of the States which were Parties at the date of adoption of the amendment. Thereafter it shall enter into force for any remaining State Party on the date of deposit of its instrument of acceptance.

Article 14
Costs and administrative tasks

1.   The costs of the Meetings of States Parties, the Review Conferences and the Amendment Conferences shall be borne by the States Parties and States not party to this Convention participating therein, in accordance with the United Nations scale of assessment adjusted appropriately.

2.   The costs incurred by the Secretary-General of the United Nations under Articles 7 and 8 of this Convention shall be borne by the States Parties in accordance with the United Nations scale of assessment adjusted appropriately.

3.   The performance by the Secretary-General of the United Nations of administrative tasks assigned to him or her under this Convention is subject to an appropriate United Nations mandate.

Article 15
Signature

This Convention, done at Dublin on 30 May 2008, shall be open for signature at Oslo by all States on 3 December 2008 and thereafter at United Nations Headquarters in New York until its entry into force.

Article 16
Ratification, acceptance, approval or accession

1.   This Convention is subject to ratification, acceptance or approval by the Signatories.

2.   It shall be open for accession by any State that has not signed the Convention.

3.   The instruments of ratification, acceptance, approval or accession shall be deposited with the Depositary.

Article 17
Entry into force

1.   This Convention shall enter into force on the first day of the sixth month after the month in which the thirtieth instrument of ratification, acceptance, approval or accession has been deposited.

2.   For any State that deposits its instrument of ratification, acceptance, approval or accession after the date of the deposit of the thirtieth instrument of ratification, acceptance, approval or accession, this Convention shall enter into force on the first day of the sixth month after the date on which that State has deposited its instrument of ratification, acceptance, approval or accession.

Article 18
Provisional application

Any State may, at the time of its ratification, acceptance, approval or accession, declare that it will apply provisionally Article 1 of this Convention pending its entry into force for that State.

Article 19
Reservations

The Articles of this Convention shall not be subject to reservations.

Article 20
Duration and withdrawal

1.   This Convention shall be of unlimited duration.

2.   Each State Party shall, in exercising its national sovereignty, have the right to withdraw from this Convention. It shall give notice of such withdrawal to all other States Parties, to the Depositary and to the United Nations Security Council. Such instrument of withdrawal shall include a full explanation of the reasons motivating withdrawal.

3.   Such withdrawal shall only take effect six months after the receipt of the instrument of withdrawal by the Depositary. If, however, on the expiry of that six-month period, the withdrawing State Party is engaged in an armed conflict, the withdrawal shall not take effect before the end of the armed conflict.

Article 21
Relations with States not party to this Convention

1.   Each State Party shall encourage States not party to this Convention to ratify, accept, approve or accede to this Convention, with the goal of attracting the adherence of all States to this Convention.

2.   Each State Party shall notify the governments of all States not party to this Convention, referred to in paragraph 3 of this Article, of its obligations under this Convention, shall promote the norms it establishes and shall make its best efforts to discourage States not party to this Convention from using cluster munitions.

3.   Notwithstanding the provisions of Article 1 of this Convention and in accordance with international law, States Parties, their military personnel or nationals, may engage in military cooperation and operations with States not party to this Convention that might engage in activities prohibited to a State Party.

4.   Nothing in paragraph 3 of this Article shall authorise a State Party:

    (a)   To develop, produce or otherwise acquire cluster munitions;

    (b)   To itself stockpile or transfer cluster munitions;

    (c)   To itself use cluster munitions; or

    (d)   To expressly request the use of cluster munitions in cases where the choice of munitions used is within its exclusive control.

Article 22
Depositary

The Secretary-General of the United Nations is hereby designated as the Depositary of this Convention.

Article 23
Authentic texts

The Arabic, Chinese, English, French, Russian and Spanish texts of this Convention shall be equally authentic.

TIMELINE OF CLUSTER MUNITIONS USE

Date	Location(s)	Known details
1943	USSR	Soviet forces used air-dropped cluster munitions against German armour. German forces used SD-1 and SD-2 butterfly bombs against artillery on the Kursk salient.
1943	United Kingdom	German aircraft dropped more than 1,000 SD-2 butterfly bombs on the port of Grimsby.
1965–1975	Cambodia, Laos, Viet Nam	According to an analysis of US bombing data by Handicap International, approximately 80,000 cluster munitions, containing 26 million submunitions, were dropped on Cambodia between 1969 and 1973; over 414,000 cluster bombs, containing at least 260 million submunitions, were dropped on Laos between 1965 and 1973; and over 296,000 cluster munitions, containing nearly 97 million submunitions, were dropped in Viet Nam between 1965 and 1975.
1970s	Zambia	Remnants of cluster munitions, including unexploded submunitions from air-dropped bombs, have been found at Chikumbi and Shang'ombo.
1973	Syria	Israel used air-dropped cluster munitions against non-state armed group training camps near Damascus.
1975–1988	Western Sahara	Moroccan forces used artillery-fired and air-dropped cluster munitions against non-state armed group.
1978	Lebanon	Israel used cluster munitions in Southern Lebanon.

Date	Location(s)	Known details
1979–1989	Afghanistan	Soviet forces used air-dropped and rocket-delivered cluster munitions. Non-state armed group also used rocket-delivered cluster munitions on a smaller scale.
1982	Lebanon	Israel used cluster munitions against Syrian forces and non-state armed group in Lebanon.
1982	Falklands/Malvinas	UK forces dropped 107 BL-755 cluster bombs containing a total of 15,729 submunitions.
1983	Grenada	US Navy aircraft dropped 21 Rockeye bombs during close air support operations.
1983	Lebanon	US Navy aircraft dropped 12 CBU-59 and 28 Rockeye bombs against Syrian air defence units near Beirut in Lebanon.
1986–1987	Chad	French aircraft dropped cluster munitions on a Libyan airfield at Wadi Doum. Libyan forces also used AO-1SCh and PTAB-2.5 submunitions.
1991	Saudi Arabia	Saudi Arabian and US forces used artillery-delivered and air-dropped cluster munitions against Iraqi forces during the battle of Khafji.
1991	Iraq and Kuwait	The US, France and the UK dropped 61,000 cluster bombs containing some 20 million submunitions. The number of cluster munitions delivered by surface-launched artillery and rocket systems is not known, but an estimated 30 million or more DPICM submunitions were used in the conflict.
1992–1994	Angola	PTAB submunitions found in various locations.
1992–1994	Nagorno-Karabakh, Azerbaijan	Submunition contamination has been identified in at least 162 locations in Nagorno-Karabakh. Submunition types cleared by deminers include PTAB-1, ShOAB-0.5 and AO-2.5. There are also reports of contamination in other parts of occupied Azerbaijan, adjacent to Nagorno-Karabakh.

Date	Location(s)	Known details
1992–1995	Bosnia and Herzegovina	Forces of Yugoslavia and non-state armed group used cluster munitions during civil war. NATO aircraft dropped two CBU-87 bombs.
1992–1997	Tajikistan	ShOAB and AO-2.5RT submunitions have been found in the town of Gharm in the Rasht Valley, used by unknown forces in civil war.
1994–1996	Chechnya	Russian forces used cluster munitions against non-state armed group.
1995	Croatia	On 2–3 May 1995, a non-state armed group used Orkan M-87 multiple rocket launchers to conduct attacks in the city of Zagreb. Additionally, the Croatian government claimed that Serb forces used BL-755 bombs in Sisak, Kutina and along the Kupa River.
1996–1999	Sudan	Sudanese government forces used air-dropped cluster munitions in southern Sudan, including Chilean-made PM-1 submunitions.
1997	Sierra Leone	Nigerian Economic Community of West African States Monitoring Group (ECOMOG) peacekeepers used BLG-66 Beluga bombs on the eastern town of Kenema.
1998	Ethiopia and Eritrea	Ethiopia and Eritrea exchanged aerial cluster munition strikes. Ethiopia attacked Asmara airport and Eritrea attacked Mekele airport. Ethiopia also dropped BL-755 bombs in Gash-Barka province in Eritrea.
1998–1999	Albania	Yugoslav forces used rocket-delivered cluster munitions in disputed border areas, and NATO forces carried out six aerial cluster munition strikes.
1998–2003	Democratic Republic of the Congo	BL-755 bombs used by unknown forces in Kasu village in Kabalo territory.
1999	Yugoslavia	The US, UK and the Netherlands dropped 1,765 cluster bombs containing 295,000 submunitions in now Serbia, Montenegro and Kosovo.

Date	Location(s)	Known details
2001–2002	Afghanistan	The US dropped 1,228 cluster bombs containing 248,056 submunitions.
Unknown	Uganda	RBK-250/275 bombs and AO-1SCh submunitions found in the northern district of Gulu.
2003	Iraq	The US and UK used nearly 13,000 cluster munitions, containing an estimated 1.8 to 2 million submunitions, in the three weeks of major combat.
2006	Lebanon	Israeli forces used surface-launched and air-dropped cluster munitions against Hizbullah. The United Nations estimates that Israel used up to 4 million submunitions.
2006	Israel	Hizbullah fired more than 100 Chinese-produced Type-81 122mm cluster munition rockets into northern Israel.
2008	Georgia	Russian and Georgian forces both use cluster munitions during August 2008 conflict. Submunitions found so far by deminers include air-dropped AO-2.5 RTM and rocket-delivered 9N210 and M-85.

Source: Human Rights Watch, February 2009.

TYPES OF CLUSTER MUNITIONS IN GLOBAL STOCKPILES

Type	States Stockpiling * Indicates States that Signed the 2008 Convention on Cluster Munitions	Submunition Photo (illustrative example)
DPICM projectile no self-destruct	Bahrain, Belgium*, Bosnia and Herzegovina*, Canada*, China, Egypt, Germany*, Greece, Honduras*, Israel, Italy*, Japan*, Jordan, Morocco, Netherlands*, Pakistan, Republic of Korea, Russia, Serbia, Slovakia, Turkey, UK*, US	KB-1 DPICM (former Yugoslavia)
DPICM projectile self-destructing	Austria*, Colombia*, Denmark*, Finland, France*, Germany*, Greece, India, Israel, Italy*, Norway*, Pakistan, Poland, Republic of Korea, Romania, Serbia, Singapore, Slovakia, South Africa*, Spain*, Switzerland*, Turkey, UK*, US	OGR DPICM (France)
surface-launched rockets and missiles no self-destruct	Algeria, Bahrain, Belarus, Bosnia and Herzegovina*, Brazil, Bulgaria*, China, Croatia*, Czech Republic*, Democratic People's Republic of Korea, Egypt, France*, Georgia, Germany*, Greece, Guinea*, India, Iran, Iraq, Israel, Italy*, Japan*, Kazakhstan, Kuwait, Moldova*, Netherlands*, Poland, Qatar, Republic of Korea, Russia, Saudi Arabia, Serbia, Slovakia, Sri Lanka, Turkey, Turkmenistan, Ukraine, UK*, US, Uzbekistan, Yemen	9N210 (USSR)

Type	States Stockpiling * Indicates States that Signed the 2008 Convention on Cluster Munitions	Submunition Photo (illustrative example)
air-launched rockets and missiles no self-destruct	France*, Germany*, Japan*, Netherlands*, Pakistan, Republic of Korea, Turkey, UK*, US	M73 Hydra (US)
air-dropped bombs no self-destruct	Angola*, Argentina, Azerbaijan, Belarus, Belgium*, Brazil, Bulgaria*, Canada*, Chile*, China, Colombia*, Croatia*, Cuba, Czech Republic*, Democratic People's Republic of Korea, Egypt, Eritrea, Ethiopia, France*, Georgia, Germany*, Greece, Guinea-Bissau*, Honduras*, Hungary*, India, Indonesia*, Iran, Iraq, Israel, Italy*, Japan*, Jordan, Kazakhstan, Libya, Montenegro*, Morocco, Netherlands*, Nigeria, Norway*, Oman, Pakistan, Peru*, Poland, Portugal*, Republic of Korea, Romania, Russia, Saudi Arabia, Serbia, Slovakia, South Africa*, Spain*, Sri Lanka, Sudan, Switzerland*, Syria, Thailand, Turkey, Uganda*, Ukraine, UAE, UK*, US, Zimbabwe	BL-755 (UK)
dispensers	Algeria, Angola*, Bosnia and Herzegovina*, Croatia*, Cuba, Czech Republic*, Democratic People's Republic of Korea, Georgia, Germany*, Greece, Hungary*, India, Iran, Iraq, Israel, Libya, Mongolia, Poland, Romania, Russia, Slovakia, Sudan, Sweden*, Syria, Ukraine, Yemen	AO-2.5RT (USSR)

Source: Human Rights Watch, February 2009.

GLOSSARY

The information in this glossary is drawn in part from:

Convention on Cluster Munitions, 2008. [CCM]

Convention on the Prohibition of the Use, Stockpiling, Production and Transfer of Anti-Personnel Mines and on Their Destruction, 1997. [MBT]

Cluster Munition Coalition, Human Rights Watch, International Campaign to Ban Landmines, Landmine Action and Landmine Monitor, *Banning Cluster Munitions: Government Policy and Practice*, 2009. [Banning Cluster Munitions]

Ove Dullum, *Cluster Weapons—Military Utility and Alternatives*, Norwegian Defence Research Establishment, 2008. [FFI]

Trevor Dupuy (ed.), *International Military and Defense Encyclopedia*, Brassey's, 1993. [Encyclopedia]

Robert Hewson (ed.), *Jane's Air-Launched Weapons (Issue 53)*, Jane's Information Group, 2009. [Jane's Air-Launched]

"Glossary of mine action terms, definitions and abbreviations", International Mine Action Standards 04.10, 2nd ed., UN Mine Action Service, 2003. [IMAS]

Colin King (ed.), *Jane's Explosive Ordnance Disposal 2008–2009*, Jane's Information Group, 2008.

Mine Action Coordination Centre South Lebanon, *War 2006: Threat Factsheet*, ver. 2, 10 April 2008 [MACC SL]

NATO Standardization Agency, *NATO Glossary of Terms and Definitions (English and French)*, NATO document AAP-6(2008). [NATO]

Eric Prokosch, "Cluster Weapons", *Papers in the Theory and Practice of Human Rights*, no. 15, Human Rights Centre, University of Essex, 1995.

Eric Prokosch, "Technology and its Control: Antipersonnel Weapons", *International Social Science Journal*, vol. 28, no. 2, 1976. [Prokosch 1976]

ReliefWeb, *Glossary of Humanitarian Terms,* 2008, <www.reliefweb.int/glossary/>. [ReliefWeb]

"United Nations Mine Action", Electronic Mine Information Network, <www.mineaction.org/overview.asp?o=21>. [E-mine]

UN Mine Action Service, *Mine Action Programming Handbook,* 2004. [UNMAS]

US Department of Defense, *Dictionary of Military and Associated Terms,* DOD document JP 1-02, 2001 (as amended through 17 March 2009). [US DoD]

Vienna Convention on the Law of Treaties, 1969. [VCLT]

Note: words in **bold face** indicate a separate entry in the glossary.

A

AFSC	American Friends Service Committee. A US faith-based **NGO** active on the **cluster munition** issue since the 1970s. Member of the **ICBL**.
air-delivered	Dropped from aircraft in flight.
anti-personnel mine	"a **mine** designed to be exploded by the presence, proximity or contact of a person and that will incapacitate, injure or kill one or more persons. **Mines** designed to be detonated by the presence, proximity or contact of a vehicle as opposed to a person, that are equipped with anti-handling devices, are not considered anti-personnel **mines** as a result of being so equipped" [MBT, art. 2(1)].
Anti-personnel Mine Ban Convention/Treaty	*See* Mine Ban Treaty.
area reduction	The process through which the initial area indicated as contaminated (during any information gathering activities or surveys)

is reduced to a smaller area. It may involve some limited clearance, such as the opening of access routes and the destruction of **mines** and **ERW**, which represent an immediate and unacceptable risk, but it will mainly be a consequence of collecting more reliable information on the extent of the hazardous area [**IMAS**].

artillery-delivered

Launched from large-calibre land- or ship-based weapons, such as cannons, howitzers, rocket and missile launchers.

B

battle area clearance

The systematic and controlled clearance of hazardous areas where the hazards are known not to include **mines** [**IMAS**].

BK-90

A Swedish **air-delivered cluster munition** system capable of deploying MJ-1 (anti-armour) and MJ-2 (anti-personnel) **submunitions**.

BL-755

A British general-purpose, **air-delivered cluster munition** carrying 147 dual-purpose **submunitions**.

BLU-63

A US-manufactured small, spherical, high-explosive **fragmentation submunition, air-delivered** in a CBU-58 **cluster munition**.

BLU-97

Also referred to as the **"yellow killer"**, this US manufactured combined-effects **submunition** without a **self-destruct** mechanism and with an all-ways acting **fuze** is particularly sensitive and dangerous to clear. Typically delivered in a CBU-87 **cluster munition**.

bomblet

The term as it is used in this book generally refers to an explosive bomblet. An explosive bomblet means "a conventional munition, weighing less than 20 kilograms, which is not self-propelled and which, in order to perform its task, is dispersed or released by a **dispenser**, and is designed to function by detonating an explosive charge prior to, on or after impact" [**CCM**, art. 2(13)].

BONUS

French-Swedish manufactured artillery shell incorporating two **sensor-fuzed submunitions** equipped with sensors for target detection and engagement, and which also incorporated electronic **self-destruct** mechanisms.

butterfly bomb

See SD-2.

C

cargo ammunition

Common name for a **cluster munition** fired from a ground-based platform, such as from artillery.

CBU

Cluster Bomb Unit. Common name for a container carrying explosive **submunitions**, other types of **submunitions**, **anti-personnel mines** or **MOTAPM**.

CCM

Convention on Cluster Munitions. An international treaty adopted on 30 May 2008 as the result of the **Oslo process** on **cluster munitions**. The treaty prohibits the use, production, stockpiling, and transfer of **cluster munitions**.

CCW

The 1980 Convention on Prohibitions and Restrictions on the Use of Certain Conventional Weapons Which May be Deemed to be Excessively Injurious or to Have Indiscriminate Effects as amended on 21 December 2001. Several protocols are annexed to the Convention, three of which are related to **mine action**: 1980 Protocol II on landmines, booby traps and other devices, 1996 Amended Protocol II, and 2003 Protocol V on explosive remnants of war (**ERW**).

cluster bomb

Common name for an **air-delivered cluster munition**.

cluster munition

"A conventional munition that is designed to disperse or release explosive **submunitions** each weighing less than 20 kilograms, and includes those explosive **submunitions**" [**CCM**, art. 2(2)]. A cluster munition consists of a container and **submunitions**. Launched from the ground or air, the container opens and disperses the **submunitions** over a wide area. **Submunitions** are typically designed to pierce armour, kill personnel, or both [Banning Cluster Munitions].

CMC

Cluster Munition Coalition. An international coalition of 300 **NGOs** in more than 80 countries, working to protect civilians from the effects of **cluster munitions** by promoting universal adherence to and full implementation of the **CCM**.

D

demining

Activities which lead to the removal of **mine** and **UXO** hazards, including technical survey, mapping, clearance, marking, post-clearance documentation, community liaison and handover of cleared land.

direct fire

Fire delivered on a target using the target itself as a point of aim for either the weapon or the director [US DoD]. The US Hydra and Canadian CRV-7 are direct-fire weapon systems.

dispenser

"A container that is designed to disperse or release explosive **bomblets** and which is affixed to an aircraft at the time of dispersal or release" [**CCM**, art. 2(14)]. The term is often used to denominate any **cluster munition** container, whether affixed or not.

DPICM

Dual-Purpose Improved Conventional Munition. A generation of **submunitions** that entered service from the 1970s and which are optimized for anti-armour and anti-personnel **fragmentation** effect.

dud

An **explosive ordnance** item that has not functioned as intended. It may or may not be armed [FFI]. All duds are potentially hazardous.

E

ERW

Explosive remnants of war. ERW includes **UXO** and abandoned **explosive ordnance** [**CCW** Protocol V, art. 2(4)].

explosive ordnance

Conventional munitions containing explosives, with the exception of **mines** [**CCW** Protocol V, art. 2(1)].

explosive ordnance disposal

The detection, identification, evaluation, render safe, recovery and disposal of **explosive ordnance** [**IMAS**].

F

flechette

Pointed steel projectile, with a vaned tail for stable flight; can be used in air-dropped **submunitions**, artillery shells or small arms.

footprint	The area over which the **submunitions** from a single **cluster munition** are dispersed. Its dimensions depend on the speed and altitude at which the **submunitions** are released.
fragmentation	"When a high explosive inside a metal case is detonated, the explosive is converted very rapidly into hot gases. Under the pressure of the expanding gases, the case swells momentarily, then ruptures in many places, and the fragments from the case are propelled outwards at high velocity" [Prokosch 1976, p. 345]. Fragmentation is a key characteristic of explosive **submunitions**.
fuze	A device with explosive components (a detonator) designed to initiate a fire train or detonation in an ammunition item at the correct time or under the correct circumstances. This can be done by various means. A **cluster munition** container may be opened to disperse the **submunitions** by a time-delay or proximity fuze. A **submunition** may be detonated on contact with the target or ground by an impact fuze. Some fuzes incorporate **self-destruct** features [Encyclopedia]. *See also* sensor-fuzed.

G

Geneva Conventions and Additional Protocols	The four Geneva Conventions of 12 August 1949 and the two Additional Protocols of 1977 relating to the protection of **victims** in armed conflict are the principal instruments of international humanitarian law (**IHL**). Together, these instruments seek to limit the effects of armed conflict by protecting persons who are not or are no longer participating in the hostilities, and to restrict the means and methods of warfare. These instruments are

monitored principally by the International Committee of the Red Cross (**ICRC**) [ReliefWeb].

H

Handicap International

An international non-religious, non-political and non-profit **NGO** specialized in the field of disability with programmes in about 60 countries. Member of the **ICBL** and of the **CMC** Steering Committee.

Human Rights Watch

A non-profit, human rights **NGO** with headquarters in New York. Its Arms Division, which played active roles in both the **ICBL** and **CMC**, is based in Washington DC. HRW is a member of the **CMC** Steering Committee.

humanitarian action

Assistance, protection and advocacy actions undertaken on an impartial basis in response to human needs resulting from complex political emergencies and natural hazards. Humanitarian action is governed by **IHL**, human rights law and guided by related principles, in particular the principles of humanity, neutrality and impartiality.

I

IACG-MA

See UN Mine Action Team.

ICBL

International Campaign to Ban Landmines. A global network of **NGOs** in over 70 countries working for a world free of **anti-personnel mines** and **cluster munitions**, where landmine and **cluster munition survivors** can lead fulfilling lives. Member of the **CMC** Steering Committee.

ICRC

International Committee of the Red Cross. An independent, neutral Swiss organization based in around 80 countries. The ICRC ensures humanitarian protection and assistance for **victims** of war and other situations of violence. The ICRC is at the origin of both the International Red Cross/Red Crescent Movement and of **IHL**, notably the **Geneva Conventions**.

IHL

International humanitarian law. A body of rules that form part of **international law** and which seek, for humanitarian reasons, to limit the effects of armed conflict. It protects persons who are not or are no longer participating in the hostilities and restricts the means and methods of warfare by prohibiting weapons that make no distinction between combatants and civilians or which cause unnecessary injury, suffering or damage. The four **Geneva Conventions** of 1949 and their two Additional Protocols of 1977 are the principal instruments of IHL [ReliefWeb].

IMAS

International **Mine Action** Standards. Documents developed by the **UN** on behalf of the international community, which aim to improve safety and efficiency in **mine action** by providing guidance, by establishing principles and, in some cases, by defining international requirements and specifications [IMAS].

international law

A body of written and non-written (customary international law) legal rules that primarily govern the relationships among states and international organizations. It includes the legal field of **IHL**.

interoperability

NATO defines military interoperability as "The ability of military forces to train, exercise and operate effectively together in the execution of assigned missions and tasks" [**NATO**]. In relation to the **CCM**, interoperability refers to "military cooperation and operations with States not party to this Convention that might engage in activities prohibited to a State Party" [**CCM**, art. 21(4)].

K

Katyusha

Denominates a range of different artillery rockets (most frequently the 122mm rocket) named after Second World War Soviet rockets. Certain non-state armed groups possess and have used such rockets in the past. Some can be fitted with **cluster munition** warheads that scatter explosive **submunitions**.

KB-1

A Yugoslav-manufactured **DPICM submunition** without **self-destruct**, based on the design of the US **M-42**. Like the Chinese **MZD-2**, the outside of the KB-1's casing is fitted with a matrix of small steel balls set in plastic, which are scattered to enhance the anti-personnel effect.

L

Landmine Action (UK)

A British not-for-profit **NGO** committed to good governance and the development of civil society through the promotion of **IHL**, the relief of poverty and the empowerment of communities marginalized by conflict. Member of the **CMC** Steering Committee and of the **ICBL**.

M

M-42/M-46

US-manufactured cylindrical **DPICM submunitions**. Both have a mechanical impact **fuze** and a nylon stabilizing ribbon. They are dispensed from a 155mm artillery projectile.

One M483A1 projectile, for instance, contains 64 M-42 and 24 M-46 **submunitions**. Used by the IDF, these **submunitions**, along with the M-77, were the most commonly found **unexploded submunition** in the wake of the 2006 conflict in Lebanon [**MACC** SL].

M-85

An Israeli-manufactured **DPICM submunition** (based on the design of the US **M-42**), which can be delivered by a variety of **cluster munitions**. The M-85 exists in two variants, with and without a mechanical **self-destruct** feature. Disturbing an unexploded M-85 with **self-destruct** mechanism may initiate the **self-destruct** delay. They cannot be rendered safe by **battle area clearance** personnel and have to be destroyed in situ [**MACC** SL].

MACC

Mine Action Coordination Centre. A centre established by **UNMAS** in humanitarian emergencies and peacekeeping settings, which carries out **mine** risk education training, conducts reconnaissance of mined areas, collects and centralizes **mine** data and coordinates local **mine action** plans with the activities of other agencies, **mine action** NGOs and local deminers [**UNMAS**].

MAG

Mines Advisory Group. A British neutral and impartial humanitarian **NGO** clearing the remnants of conflict for the benefit of communities worldwide. Member of the **ICBL**.

MCC

Mennonite Central Committee. A faith-based US-Canadian relief, development and peace **NGO** active on the **cluster munition** issue since the 1970s. Member of the **ICBL** and **CMC**.

mine	"A munition designed to be placed under, on or near the ground or other surface areas and to be exploded by the presence, proximity or contact of a person or vehicle" [MBT, art. 2(2)]. **Mines** include **anti-personnel mines** and **MOTAPM**.
mine action	The five pillars of **mine** action are: **mine clearance**, including survey, mapping, and marking and fencing off contaminated areas; **mine** risk education to teach people how to protect themselves from danger in a **mine-** or **UXO**-affected environment; **victim assistance**; helping countries destroy their stockpiled **anti-personnel mines**; advocacy for a world free of landmines and support a total ban on **anti-personnel mines**.
Mine Ban Treaty	Shorthand for the 1997 Convention On The Prohibition Of The Use, Stockpiling, Production And Transfer Of **Anti-Personnel Mines** And On Their Destruction, also known as the **Anti-personnel Mine** Ban Convention/ Treaty.
mine clearance	The clearance of **mines** and **ERW** from a specified area to a predefined standard [**IMAS**].
Mines Action Canada	A coalition of Canadian **NGOs** committed to the goal of eliminating the serious humanitarian, environmental and development consequences of landmines and other **ERW**. Member of the **ICBL** and **CMC** Steering Committee.
Mk-118	*See* Rockeye.
MLRS	Multiple Launch Rocket System. A US vehicle-based multiple rocket launcher capable of

firing salvos of up to 12 artillery rockets in less than 1 minute.

MOTAPM

Mines other than **anti-personnel mines**. A type of **mine** designed to be activated by the presence, proximity or contact of a vehicle, such as a tank. MOTAPM retain their ability to function years after they have been placed and they can be triggered by civilian vehicles. Like **anti-personnel mines**, they present a threat to civilians during and for an indefinite duration after a conflict, but each MOTAPM has the potential to kill large numbers of people. No international treaty presently bans MOTAPM.

MZD-2

A Chinese **DPICM submunition** without a **self-destruct** feature, delivered to the target by 122mm rocket. It is based on the design of the US **M-42** and like the Yugoslav **KB-1**, the outside of the MZD-2's casing is fitted with a matrix of small steel balls set in plastic, which are scattered to enhance the anti-personnel effect.

N

NATO

North Atlantic Treaty Organization. A military alliance of 28 (as of 2009) states from North America and Europe committed to collective defence, crisis management and military partnership with non-NATO states.

NGO

Non-governmental organization. An organized entity that is functionally independent of, and does not represent, a government or state [ReliefWeb].

Norwegian People's Aid

A humanitarian organization rooted in the Norwegian Labour Movement. NPA is one of the leading organizations worldwide in humanitarian **mine action**. Member of the **ICBL** and the **CMC** Steering Committee.

O

OCHA

UN Office for the Coordination of Humanitarian Affairs. OCHA's mission is to mobilize and coordinate effective and principled **humanitarian action** in partnership with national and international actors. OCHA shares information with other organizations about the humanitarian impact of landmines and works with **UNMAS** on resource mobilization for **mine action** [E-mine].

Oslo process

The diplomatic process undertaken from 2006 to 2008 that led to the negotiation, adoption and signing of the 2008 **CCM** [Banning **Cluster Munitions**].

P

Pax Christi

A non-profit, faith-based international peace movement working on a global scale on a variety of issues. Pax Christi International is a co-founding **NGO** of the **CMC** and member organizations such as Pax Christi New Zealand, Pax Christi Ireland and IKV/Pax Christi Netherlands are **CMC** members or on the **CMC** Steering Committee.

R

RBL-755

A BL-755 **cluster munition** that has been upgraded with a radar proximity **fuze** [Jane's Air-Launched].

retroactivity

In accordance with a principle of **international law**, the provisions of a treaty, unless otherwise stated, do not bind a party in relation to events that took place before the entry into force of the treaty with respect to that state [VCLT, art. 28]. **CCW** Protocol V on **ERW**, for instance, is not retroactive in its application. In the context of the negotiations of the **CCM**, the question arose whether users of **cluster munitions** should be under a retroactive legal obligation to assist with the clearance of foreign land contaminated by them.

Rockeye

US-manufactured anti-armour combined effects **submunition, air-delivered** by the Mk-20 Rockeye II **cluster munition**.

S

SD-2

This **air-delivered**, anti-personnel **sub-munition** used by the *Luftwaffe* in the Second World War was delivered by one of the first **cluster munitions** ever used in combat.

self-deactivating/
self-neutralizing

"Self-deactivating means automatically rendering a munition inoperable by means of the irreversible exhaustion of a component, for example a battery, that is essential to the operation of the munition" [**CCM**, art. 2(10)]. Self-deactivation applies to electronic **fuzes** while self-neutralization applies to mechanical ones.

self-destruct

"Self-destruction mechanism means an incorporated automatically-functioning mechanism which is in addition to the primary initiating mechanism of the munition and which secures the destruction of the munition into which it is incorporated" [**CCM**, art. 2(9)].

sensor-fuzed

A munition that has a **fuze** equipped with sensors capable of scanning an area and detecting heat and shape patterns. When the sensors detect a target signature for which they were programmed, the **fuze** initiates detonation.

SMArt 155

German-manufactured artillery shell incorporating two **sensor-fuzed submunitions** equipped with sensors for target detection and engagement and with electronic **self-destruct** mechanisms.

stab detonator

A type of mechanical detonator with a charge that is sensitive to friction or impact. Once the **fuze** functions, the detonator is stabbed by a firing pin, which fires the detonator charge [Encyclopedia].

stockpile destruction

The physical destructive procedure toward continual reduction (and eventual elimination, in the case of **cluster munitions** and **anti-personnel mines**) of national stockpiles of weapons.

submunition

The term as it is used in this book generally refers to an explosive submunition. An explosive submunition means "a conventional munition that in order to perform its task is dispersed or released by a **cluster munition** and is designed to function by detonating an explosive charge prior to, on or after impact" [**CCM**, art. 2(3)]. The term is also used to designate any munition that, to perform its task, separates from a parent munition.

survivor

Persons either individually or collectively who have suffered physical, emotional and psychological injury, economic loss or substantial impairment of their fundamental rights through acts or omissions related to the use of **mines** or the presence of **ERW**. **Mine/**

ERW survivors or **victims** include directly impacted individuals, their families, and communities affected by landmines and **ERW** [**IMAS**].

Survivor Corps
A global network of **survivors** that grew in 2008 from the Landmine **Survivors** Network and which aims at helping all **survivors** of war to overcome war and rebuild their communities. Member of the **CMC** Steering Committee.

U

UN
United Nations. An intergovernmental organization with near-universal membership aimed at facilitating cooperation in **international law**, international security, economic development, social progress, human rights, and in achieving world peace. The role of the UN in **mine action** is primarily one of coordination through the development of guidelines and standards, the collection and dissemination of information, the coordination of operational activities and the mobilization of resources [**UNMAS**]. *See also* UN Mine Action Team.

UNDP
United Nations Development Programme. The **UN**'s global development network. UNDP assists **mine**-affected countries to establish or strengthen national and local **mine action** programmes. Because landmines and **ERW** are an obstacle to sustainable development, UNDP is including **mine action** in the mainstream of its broader development programmes [E-mine].

unexploded submunition
A **submunition** that has failed to explode as intended, becoming **UXO**.

UNICEF	United Nations Children's Fund. A **UN** fund that works with others to build a world where the rights of every child are realized. This includes children in **mine**-affected countries globally. UNICEF supports the development and implementation of **mine** risk education and **victim assistance** projects and advocacy for an end to the use of landmines, **cluster munitions** and other indiscriminate weapons [E-mine].
UN Mine Action Team	Formerly the **UN** Inter-Agency Coordination Group on **Mine Action** (IACG-MA), which brings together 14 **UN** departments, programmes, agencies and funds (including **UNDP**, **UNICEF**, **UNMAS** and the **UN Office of Disarmament Affairs**) involved in **mine action**. They share a vision for a world free of the threat of landmines and **ERW**, where individuals and communities live in a safe environment conducive to development and where the needs of **victims** are met [E-mine].
UNMAS	United Nations **Mine Action** Service. The focal point for **mine action** in the **UN** system. UNMAS is responsible for ensuring an effective, proactive and coordinated **UN** response to landmines and **ERW** through collaboration with the other members of the **UN Mine Action Team**. In peacekeeping and emergency settings, UNMAS establishes and manages **MACCs** in **mine**-affected countries, plans and manages operations, mobilizes resources and sets **mine**-action priorities in the countries and territories it serves [E-mine].
UN Office of Disarmament Affairs	Formerly the **UN** Department of Disarmament Affairs. The Office of Disarmament Affairs, among other things, advises and assists the **UN** Secretary-General in his work related to the

Mine Ban Treaty and the **CCW**. The Office of Disarmament Affairs promotes universal participation in international legal frameworks related to landmines and **ERW** and assists states in complying with their treaty obligations [E-mine].

UXO

Unexploded ordnance. "**Explosive ordnance** that has been primed, **fused**, armed, or otherwise prepared for use and used in an armed conflict. It may have been fired, dropped, launched or projected and should have exploded but failed to do so" [**CCW** Protocol V, art. 2(2)].

V

victim/survivor assistance

Forms part of **mine action** and refers to all aid, relief, comfort and support provided to **victims** (including **survivors**) with the purpose of reducing the immediate and long-term medical and psychological implications of their trauma [**IMAS**].

victim

A person who has suffered harm as a result of a **mine** or **ERW** accident. In the context of the **CCM**, **cluster munition victims** are "all persons who have been killed or suffered physical or psychological injury, economic loss, social marginalisation or substantial impairment of the realisation of their rights caused by the use of **cluster munitions**. They include those persons directly impacted by **cluster munitions** as well as their affected families and communities" [**CCM**, art. 2(1)].

Y

yellow killer

Name given to the US-manufactured **BLU-97 submunition** because of its yellow casing.

This **submunition** was used by **NATO** in its bombing campaign against the Federal Republic of Yugoslavia in 1999.

INDEX

ACRONYMS

AFSC	American Friends Service Committee
BAC	battle area clearance
CCM	Convention on Cluster Munitions
CCW	Convention on Certain Conventional Weapons
CD	Conference on Disarmament
CMC	Cluster Munition Coalition
DHA	Disarmament as Humanitarian Action: Making Multilateral Negotiations Work
DPICM	Dual-Purpose Improved Conventional Munitions
DPKO	UN Department of Peacekeeping Operations
ERW	explosive remnants of war
FFI	Norwegian Defence Research Establishment
GGE	Group of Governmental Experts
GIS	group of interested states
HI	Handicap International
HRW	Human Rights Watch
IACG-MA	UN Inter-Agency Coordination Group for Mine Action
IASC	UN Inter-Agency Standing Committee
ICBL	International Campaign to Ban Landmines
ICRC	International Committee of the Red Cross
IDF	Israel Defence Forces
IHL	international humanitarian law
LAF	Lebanese Armed Forces
MAC	Mines Action Canada
MACC	Mine Action Coordination Centre South Lebanon
MAG	Mines Advisory Group
MCC	Mennonite Central Committee
MLRS	Multiple Launch Rocket System
MOTAPM	mines other than anti-personnel mines
NATO	North Atlantic Treaty Organization
NGO	non-governmental organization
NPA	Norwegian People's Aid
NRK	Norwegian Broadcasting Corporation
OCHA	UN Office for the Coordination of Humanitarian Affairs
SIPRI	Stockholm International Peace Research Institute
UNDP	United Nations Development Programme

,R	Office of the UN High Commissioner for Refugees
EF	United Nations Children's Fund
IDIR	United Nations Institute for Disarmament Research
UNIFIL	United Nations Interim Force in Lebanon
UNMAS	UN Mine Action Service
UXO	unexploded ordnance
WFP	World Food Programme